DEMOCRACY IN AMERICA

Alexis de Tocqueville

Alexis de Tocqueville

DEMOCRACY
IN AMERICA

Edited by Eduardo Nolla

Translated from the French by James T. Schleifer

VOLUME I

LIBERTY FUND

Indianapolis

English translation, translator's note, index, © 2010 by Liberty Fund, Inc.
Foreword to this edition, © 2012 by Liberty Fund, Inc.

The French text on which this translation is based is *De la démocratie en
Amérique,* première édition historico-critique revue et augmentée. Edited by
Eduardo Nolla. Librairie Philosophique J. Vrin; 6, Place de la Sorbonne; Paris, 1990.

Frontispiece: Portrait of Alexis de Tocqueville by Léon Noël,
reproduced with kind permission of the Beinecke Library, Yale University.

Map of the United States appearing in the first edition of
Democracy in America (1835), reproduced with kind permission of
the Special Collections Research Center, University of Chicago Library.

P 10 9 8 7 6 5 4 3 2

Library of Congress Cataloging-in-Publication Data
Tocqueville, Alexis de, 1805–1859
[De la démocratie en Amérique. English]
Democracy in America/Alexis de Tocqueville;
edited by Eduardo Nolla;
translated from the French by James T. Schleifer.—[Student ed.]
p. cm.
Includes bibliographical references and index.
ISBN 978-0-86597-840-9 (set: pbk.: alk. paper)
ISBN 978-0-86597-838-6 (v. 1: pbk.: alk. paper)
ISBN 978-0-86597-839-3 (v. 2: pbk.: alk. paper)
1. United States—Politics and government.   2. United States—Social
conditions—To 1865.   3. Democracy—United States. I. Nolla, Eduardo.
II. Schleifer, James T., 1942–   III. Title.
JK216.T713 2012
320.973—dc23   2011041363

LIBERTY FUND, INC.
8335 Allison Pointe Trail, Suite 300
Indianapolis, Indiana 46250-1684

DEMOCRACY IN AMERICA

Contents

DEMOCRACY IN AMERICA
(1835)

VOLUME I

Part I

Part II

DEMOCRACY IN AMERICA
(1840)

VOLUME II

Foreword   690

Part I: Influence of Democracy on the
Intellectual Movement in the United States

xv

Part II: Influence of Democracy on the Sentiments of the Americans

Part III: Influence of Democracy on
Mores Properly So Called

*Part IV: Of the Influence That Democratic Ideas and
Sentiments Exercise on Political Society*

Translator's Note

This new translation of Tocqueville's *Democracy in America* is intended to be a close, faithful, and straightforward rendering of Tocqueville into contemporary American English. A second key goal is to present a smooth, readable version of Tocqueville's classic work. Part of my challenge has therefore been to maintain the right balance between closeness and felicity, between faithfulness and readability.

The translation scrupulously follows Tocqueville's somewhat idiosyncratic paragraphing and attempts to reflect the varied sentence structure of the original. I have tried, where possible, to follow Tocqueville's sentence structure and word order. But in many cases this effort would be inappropriate and untenable. It would not work for constructing sentences in English and would obscure Tocqueville's meaning. So sometimes I have shifted Tocqueville's word order and rearranged, even totally recast, his sentences. At times, for example, Tocqueville's extraordinarily long sentences, built from accumulated phrases, had to be broken to fit English usage. Nonetheless, the translation tries to reflect Tocqueville's stylistic mix of long, complex sentences with short, emphatic ones. Occasionally Tocqueville's sentence fragments are retained; more often, I have turned them into complete (though still very brief) sentences by inserting a verb.

As part of the effort to achieve a contemporary American English text, I have avoided translating the French *on* as *one;* almost invariably, I have used *you* (sometimes *we* or another pronoun, depending on context), or have changed the sentence from active to passive. And with the goal of closeness in mind, I have also used cognates where they fit and are appropriate.

Another basic principle for this translation has been consistency, especially for key terms. But a rigid or narrow consistency can be a false and dangerous goal, even a trap. Words often have many meanings and therefore need to be translated differently depending on context. There are several good examples. *Objet* can mean object (the object of desire), subject (the subject under consideration), matter (the matter under discussion), or objective (the objective of a plan). *Biens* can mean property or goods, or the opposite of evil(s): good, good things, or even, on a few occasions, advantages. And *désert* can mean wilderness, uninhabited area, or desert. The reader will find other examples of such clusters of possible meanings in the translation. But for the key terms used by Tocqueville, the principle has been to be as consistent as possible. (See Key Terms.)

Finally, the translation follows these more specific principles: (1) words referring specifically to France, to French institutions and history, such as *commune, conseil d'état, parlement,* are usually left in French; (2) quotations presented by Tocqueville from Pascal, Montesquieu, Rousseau, Guizot, and many other French writers have been newly translated; (3) on a few occasions, specific translator's notes have been inserted; (4) the French *De* at the beginning of chapter or section titles has been retained and translated invariably as *Of* (eg. *Of the Point of Departure . . .*). The great exception, of course, is the name of the book itself, *Democracy in America,* a title simply too familiar in English to be altered; and (5) in cases where Tocqueville quotes directly and closely from an English-language source, the original English text has been provided; but in cases where Tocqueville has quoted an English-language source from a French translation, or has only paraphrased or followed an English text very loosely, Tocqueville has been translated.

The Nolla edition, on which this translation is based, presents an enormous amount and variety of materials from the drafts and manuscript variants of Tocqueville's work, as well as excerpts from closely related materials such as travel notes and correspondence, and several chapters or partial chapters never included in the published text.

Within this collection of drafts, variants, and other materials there exists an important, but not always clear, hierarchy of manuscript materials.

These layers largely reflect chronology, the development over time of Tocqueville's thinking from early notes and sketches, through successive draft versions, to final text (still often overlaid with last-minute thoughts, queries, and clarifications). But they also reflect the tangled paths of his musings, including intellectual trials, asides, and dead ends.

And from these diverse materials comes a major challenge for the translator: to reflect the stylistic and chronological shifts from early to late, from informal to formal, from rough to polished versions of Tocqueville's book. In some of the drafts, especially, the translation must try to reproduce Tocqueville's tentativeness and confusion, as reflected in incomplete, broken, or ambiguous sentences. Most important, the many layers of text need to be translated in a way that maintains parallel phrasing, but at the same time reflects key variations in wording as they occur in the unfolding development of Tocqueville's work. The various stages of manuscript variants and the final text need to match, to be harmonious where they are more or less the same, and to differ where Tocqueville has made significant changes in vocabulary or meaning.

The very act of translation teaches a great deal about the author being translated. Tocqueville, like all good writers, had certain stylistic characteristics and idiosyncrasies that a translator must grasp in order to render a faithful translation.

In general, Tocqueville's sentences are much more dense and compact in volume I of *Democracy* than in volume II, where they are more abstract and open. In the first volume, his sentences often seem stuffed with short, qualifying phrases. This difference results from the more abstract and reflective nature of the second volume, but it also arises from the more detailed, concrete, and historical subject matter that takes up much of volume I.

Tocqueville often painted verbal pictures to summarize and to express his ideas in a single image that he hoped would grab and even persuade his readers. To create these images, he repeatedly used certain clusters of related words. Among his favorite word pictures, for example, are images of light and darkness, of eyes and seeing, of shadows and fading light;

images of movement, motion or stirring; dramatic images of rising flood-waters or raging rivers; and such geometric images as the circle, the sphere, and converging beams or roads. I have been careful to reproduce these word pictures as faithfully as possible. Examples occur throughout the *Democracy.*

A key to Tocqueville's writing is his reliance on parallel structures: parallel or matched sentences, phrases, or even words. I have tried to retain such parallels, because they reveal how Tocqueville thought habitually in pairs, especially in contrasting pairs, a feature of his thinking that elsewhere I have called "pairs in tension."

Still another key to Tocqueville's writing is its very deductive, even syllogistic nature. This is one of the defining characteristics of his thought. In the *Democracy,* he frequently offers deductive sets of ideas, expressed in chains of paragraphs or sentences, or even in chains of phrases within a single, long sentence. Many segments of his book are essentially elaborate syllogisms. In an attempt to carry the reader along by the sheer force of logic, Tocqueville often presents his ideas as a tight logical sequence: *since . . . , and since . . . , so;* or *this . . . , moreover this . . . , therefore . . . .* (*Donc* and *ainsi* are two of his favorite words, especially in volume I.) Again, as translator, I have attempted to retain this syllogistic flavor.

Acknowledgments

My work as translator has benefited greatly from the careful readings and suggestions of several individuals: my initial reader, Alison Pedicord Schleifer; my primary reader, Paul Seaton; the other members of the editorial committee, Peter Lawler, Pierre Manent, Catherine Zuckert, Eduardo Nolla, and Christine Henderson, Senior Fellow at Liberty Fund. I would also like to thank Melvin Richter and David Bovenizer, who were involved in the early phases of the project, and Emilio Pacheco, executive vice president of Liberty Fund, who provided constant support throughout the project. I extend my deepest appreciation to all for their insights, attention, support, and good will along the way. This project has made us colleagues and friends.

The resulting translation is mine, and I take full responsibility for any weaknesses or failings.

James T. Schleifer
New Haven 2007

Key Terms

Certain key terms used by Tocqueville present particular translation difficulties. Some, for example, have no precise English equivalent (e.g., *lumières*); others are extremely abstract or have a variety of meanings, depending on context. As translator, my goal was to choose the best alternative and then to be consistent throughout the edition. The following terms should be noted:

· *état social*—translated closely as *social state,* instead of *social condition.*

· *idée mère*—translated as either *generative* or *main idea.* The same principle is used for *pensée mère, passion mère,* etc. But *science mère* is rendered as *mother science.*

· *inquiétude*—usually translated as *restlessness* (and *inquiet* as *restless*), but sometimes it can be *concern* or *worry.* Earlier French dictionaries show that traditionally the word meant primarily an inability to be at rest, or restlessness; the more modern sense of worry or concern was not as important. A closely related word, *agitation,* is almost always rendered as the cognate, *agitation,* except occasionally when it is translated as *constant motion* or *constant movement.*

· *intérêt bien entendu*—translated as *interest well understood* or *well understood interest,* rather than *interest properly understood, self-interest properly/well understood,* or *enlightened self-interest,* all of which are unnecessary glosses on the meaning.

· *liberté d'écrire*—In English, for freedom of written expression, there is no equivalent such as freedom of speech for freedom of spoken expression; freedom of the press is a more specific term. So for *liberté d'écrire,* I have simply used *freedom to write.* Related terms to note include *liberté de penser, freedom of thought,* and *liberté d'esprit, freedom of mind* (in the sense of intellectual freedom).

· *lumières*—usually translated as *enlightenment,* occasionally as *knowledge* or *learning.*

· *mœurs*—translated as *mores,* not an ideal word, but the best available option in English.

· *pouvoir d'un seul*—translated as *power of one man* or, occasionally, *power of one man alone,* rather than *power of a single man,* which is ambiguous.

In addition, the following less crucial, but still important words should be noted:

· *affaires*—almost always translated as *public affairs,* unless clearly otherwise (such as *matters*).

· *empire*—translated as *dominion,* or a few times, as *sway* or *rule.*

· *État*—translated as *State* (upper case) when referring to the nation, the general political body; otherwise, *state* (lower case) when referring to one of the American states.

· *fonctionnaire*—translated as *officer* when related to the American town (town officer); otherwise, *official.*

· *intelligences*—No good English equivalent exists; usually translated as *minds;* sometimes the phrase is altered to use the adjective *intellectual.*

· *la justice*—In certain chapters of Tocqueville's book the word means *justice,* but usually it means the *judicial system* or *court system.*

· *législateur*—translated as *law-maker* when Tocqueville is talking about the maker of fundamental law, the constitution-maker; otherwise, *legislator.*

· *patrie*—translated as *native land* or *country,* rather than *fatherland* or *homeland.*

· *sauvage*—either *savage* or *wild,* depending on the context.

· *solitudes*—closely related to *désert(s)* (see Translator's Note, p. xxii); usually translated as *uninhabited* (or *empty*) *places* (or *areas*), sometimes as *wilderness,* and once or twice as *solitude* or *seclusion.*

Foreword

"In this regard, you will pardon me, I hope, if I express a regret that I believe is general. You have pushed too far a scruple, otherwise very laudable, of not wanting to publish anything that had not absolutely received the final touch of the author. I know well the conscientiousness that caused our friend to present the expression of his thought to the public only after he had brought it to the highest perfection that he felt capable of giving it; but it is one thing to put a piece of writing aside in order to make it more perfect and something else to want it suppressed when fate has decreed that the process of perfecting it cannot take place. Even the rough drafts of a thinker and observer like Tocqueville would be of inestimable value for thinkers to come; and unless he opposed it while alive, it seems to me that there would be no disadvantage in publishing his imperfect manuscripts while presenting them only for what they are and scrupulously retaining all the indications of an intention to go back to some piece and to submit its ideas to a later verification."[1]

In these words, following the publication of the complete works, John Stuart Mill expressed his regret to the editor, Gustave de Beaumont, for not having been able to read the whole body of Tocqueville's unpublished papers.

Within the framework of this edition, I wanted to revisit Beaumont's decision and in part to satisfy Mill's desire. I have resolved not only to offer to the reader the text of *Democracy in America* revised and corrected, but also to give an important place to the notes, drafts, and materials of all kinds that accompanied the period of its writing.

I have therefore chosen to present to the reader at the same time a new

---

1. *The Later Letters of John Stuart Mill, 1849–1873* (Toronto: University of Toronto Press, 1972. *J. S. Mill Collected Works,* XV), p. 719. [Note: Original is in French.]

edition of the *Democracy* and a *different* edition. This new *Democracy* is not only the one that Tocqueville presented to the reader of 1835 and then to the reader of 1840. It is enlarged, amplified by a body of texts that has never existed in the form that I give it today. If the added pages that follow are indeed from Tocqueville's pen, most of them existed only as support, as necessary scaffolding for the construction of the work. As such, they were naturally meant to disappear from the final version.

Drawn out of obscurity, they are going to reappear in the middle of the known text. These fragments, revived by the choice of the editor, appear between brackets in the main text and in notes. They must be treated with caution. Although they have been brought back to life here, it is advisable not to forget that Tocqueville had condemned them to disappearance. If they often lead to some interesting site, they also lead many times to a labyrinth or to an impenetrable wall. Then we will be forced to agree with the judgment that once relegated them to oblivion.

What interest does their presence have then? Above all that of vividly highlighting the extraordinary complexity of the writing of the *Democracy* and aiding in its comprehension by presenting a portion of the erasures and over-writings, the prodigious "layering" of Tocqueville's great work. The reader will discover, for example, how Tocqueville, often hesitant, uncertain about the direction to follow, asks for advice from his family and friends, and how the latter guide his thought when writing some paragraphs and sentences. He will better understand the reasons for certain additions and deletions. He will also be able to note certain changes due to the criticisms made by the first readers of the manuscript. Finally and above all, he will see how Tocqueville proceeded with the elaboration of the main ideas of his book.

Every text is unstable for a long time. When it has acquired a certain coherence and the author judges it complete, it is printed. Every typographic reproduction leads, however, to adulteration, an adulteration as necessary as it is inevitable. The printed book cannot convey either the handwriting or the look of the manuscript. Only a facsimile, a perfect reproduction of the original, made on the same paper, damaged by time and humidity, would manage to show to the reader *Democracy in America* in all its complexity and liveliness. But it would be an illusory *Democracy,* entirely as hard to read and grasp as the original, and one whose intrinsic value would be lost.

If the edition that is being presented today is careful to restore to the *Democracy* part of its difficulties of composition, of its mistaken ideas, and of its faltering efforts, it is not trying to and cannot in any way take the place of the manuscript, any more than it can come close to being a facsimile. A good number of research projects will still have to return to the unique object that the manuscript represents.[2]

The Manuscripts of Tocqueville

The preparation of the first edition of the complete works goes back to 1859, and comes just after the death of Tocqueville. The work of Gustave de Beaumont, who held Tocqueville's manuscripts from his widow, Mary Mottley, was done with the aid of Louis de Kergorlay.

Beaumont knew Tocqueville's obsession to publish nothing that had not been read and reread a hundred times. Since the author was no longer there to ensure the correction of his texts, Beaumont took charge of it. In so doing, he doctored certain passages; he deleted certain others without indication; and finally he destroyed an indeterminate number of documents (perhaps in response to the demands of Tocqueville's wife).

That first edition, which elicited considerable criticism, possesses almost as many good qualities as failings. We know that the editorial practices of the period differed markedly from ours, that mutilations and corrections of all sorts did not as clearly give rise to condemnation. Some of the people cited in the correspondence were still alive at the time of publication. Fi-

---

2. The working manuscript of *Democracy in America* is at the Beinecke Rare Book and Manuscript Library of Yale University. It is divided among four boxes (with the classification CVIa) and follows the order of chapters of the book. Only chapters 1, 18, 19, and 20 of the second part of the 1840 volume are missing. When, for this edition, I refer to the manuscript, it is this text that I mean.

The Yale collection does not have the definitive version of the *Democracy,* the one that Tocqueville had sent to the publisher, Charles Gosselin. This version, which George W. Pierson believed that he had seen in France in 1930, was not found at the time of the purchase of the manuscripts of the *Democracy* in 1954. Everything suggests that this final version did not present perceptible differences from the first edition.

nally, the political situation of the Second Empire weighed on the decision of the editor to make a certain number of modifications.

It is no less true that Beaumont provided an impressive work in a relatively short time. Nine volumes appeared in the space of seven years.

Mary Mottley died in 1865. Since her relations with the Tocqueville family were never good, she bequeathed all of her husband's papers to Gustave de Beaumont. The family of the latter possessed them until 1891. At that time Christian de Tocqueville acquired them.

Not long after the end of the First World War, Paul Lambert White, professor at Yale University, became interested in Tocqueville's manuscripts. He went to France, where he consulted and catalogued all of the manuscripts in the possession of the Tocqueville family. Moreover, he obtained the authorization to have the manuscripts that concerned America copied. M. Bonnel, the schoolteacher at Tocqueville, was charged with this work.[3]

At the death of Paul White, George W. Pierson, then a doctoral student at Yale, went in turn to France with the encouragement of John M. S. Allison. He proceeded to do a new catalogue of the manuscripts[4] and obtained the money necessary for the continuation of the work of copying. In this way Bonnel continued to work and to send copies regularly to the United States.

Several years after World War II, a new inventory revealed the disappearance of most of the manuscripts copied for the American university by Bonnel. Yale found itself from that time on in possession of invaluable documents.

Little by little, the collection grew, augmented over the years by new acquisitions and bequests. One of the most important contributions was the purchase, over a period of about twenty years (from 1953 to 1973), of the quasi-totality of the manuscripts of Gustave de Beaumont. In 1954, Yale acquired the manuscript and the final drafts of *Democracy in America*.

---

3. White also gained permission to have copies made of certain documents in the hands of Antoine Rédier who was then preparing his book, *Comme disait Monsieur de Tocqueville* (Paris: Perrin, 1925). These copies were done by the secretaries of Abel Doysié, responsible for copying for the Library of Congress documents belonging to the French diplomatic archives.

4. Yale owns copies of all of the catalogues of Tocqueville's manuscripts.

At that time, the American university became the sole depository of the vast majority of the texts, notes, and correspondence relating to Tocqueville's principal work.[5]

The collection holds original manuscripts as well as copies of lost originals. In the work of this edition, the drafts and the manuscript called the "working manuscript" of the *Democracy* have received particular attention.

The greater part of the drafts of the second part of the *Democracy*, to which the author gave the name "rubish"[6] and which constitutes perhaps the most interesting portion of the Yale collection, is unfortunately in very bad condition. Insects and moisture have led to its deterioration, the handwriting is particularly hard to read, and the paper is crumbling into pieces. A quantity of minuscule bits of paper remains at the bottom of the two boxes that protect the Rubish.[7]

Other drafts of the second part of the book, and all those belonging to the first part, exist only as copies (that all together number about 1,500 pages divided into sixteen notebooks); they can be relatively trusted.[8]

To all of that, the notes written by Tocqueville during his journey to America[9] must be added, and a group of more than three hundred letters,

5. The other important collection of Tocqueville's manuscripts is at the château de Tocqueville.

6. The English *rubbish* means debris, remnants, trash. Following Tocqueville, we spell the word incorrectly throughout this edition. By the word, we mean either the drafts of each chapter (*rubish*), or the whole body of the drafts of the second part (*Rubish*).

7. Some omissions could be filled in by consulting the microfilm done at the time of the arrival of the manuscript at Yale and a partial copy of the *Rubish* in Bonnel's hand.

8. The comparison of this copy of one part of the *Rubish* with the original shows some differences and omissions, as well as a certain arbitrariness in the placement of the text on the page. Bonnel also resorted, perhaps a bit too rapidly, to the expedient of "illegible word," although this type of abuse is more desirable in a copyist than is an excess of imagination. I have corrected a number of obvious errors.

9. These notes have been published in the fifth volume of the *Œuvres complètes* published by Gallimard. I have nonetheless preferred to refer to the Yale texts, given the presence in that edition, on more than one occasion, of differences and omissions.

some still unpublished. This involves Tocqueville's and Beaumont's correspondence with Americans and the English during and after their visit to the United States, and letters written to their families and to various French correspondents.[10]

Other documents that are of interest for understanding the *Democracy* include bibliographies, lists of questions posed by Tocqueville and Beaumont to the Americans they spoke to, and above all, numerous documents in Beaumont's hand for the writing of his novel, *Marie, ou l'esclavage aux États-Unis,* and for that of his essay on Ireland.

Some Details Concerning the Present Edition

Theodore Sedgwick, a correspondent of Tocqueville, said jokingly that the handwriting of the latter oscillated between hieroglyphics and cuneiform.[11] The condition of notes meant by Tocqueville to be read only by himself can be imagined.

Following a system frequently used at the time, the draft occupies the right side of the folio and leaves the left side free for notes and variants.[12] The text, nonetheless, often extends beyond the right side and successively invades the left side, the margins, and the space between the lines.

Supplementary sheets are added at the end of each chapter, small pieces of paper are glued over the original, and sometimes other papers are even

---

10. The letters sent by Beaumont to his family during the American voyage have been published by André Jardin and George W. Pierson with the title *Lettres d'Amérique* (Paris: PUF, 1973).

11. In a letter of 15 January 1856 (YTC, DIIa).

In a letter of 28 December 1856 to the countess de Grancey (*OCB,* VII, p. 424), Tocqueville makes the Abbé Lesueur responsible for his bad handwriting: "He had the singular idea of making me learn to write before teaching me spelling. Since I did not know how to write my words, I muddled them as well as I could, drowning my errors in my scribbling. As a result, I have never known how to spell perfectly, and I have continued to scribble indefinitely." We know, moreover, that Didot, the first publisher of *L'Ancien Régime et la Révolution,* sent the manuscript back to the author twice in succession because of illegibility.

12. In certain cases, I have reproduced the notes in pencil that are in Tocqueville's hand.

stuck to the first ones. Crosses, *x*'s, ovals, circles, letters, and diacritical signs are multiplied to indicate transfers and additions. It is clear that an exact reproduction of the many minor changes in the text of the manuscript is as unnecessary as it would be boring, and I have not bothered with it.

Notes in the margin testify to Tocqueville's doubts about certain passages, his desire to review them, and sometimes his intention to ask for the opinion of his friends or their criticisms. The fragments that he intended to eliminate are generally circled.

At the point of finishing the composition of *Democracy in America*, Tocqueville wanted his family and certain of his friends to be able to read the manuscript, comment on it, and critique it. With this intention, in 1834, he hired the services of a copyist.[13] This copy of the manuscript, which could have been sent to the publisher once definitively corrected, has been lost except for a few loose sheets that are found with the manuscript. The reading of these pages reveals the difficulties experienced by the copyist; it is probable, from several notes in the manuscript, that Tocqueville himself dictated a good part of the book.[14]

References made elsewhere give an idea[15] of this copy, which contained a certain number of errors, as did, we can assume, the copy that constituted

13. Perhaps Monsieur Parier, cited in note o of p. 384. A letter of Édouard to Alexis de Tocqueville (CIIIb, 2, pp. 65–67, reproduced in note c of pp. 142–43) suggests the idea that the copy was done in notebooks. Two notes in the drafts speak about the price of the copies and the number of pages copied (YTC, CVh, 3, p. 17, and CVh, 2, p. 11).

In a letter to Beaumont of 23 October 1839 (*Correspondance avec Beaumont, OC*, VIII, 1, p. 389), Tocqueville refers to a copy of the second *Democracy*.

14. On the jacket of chapter VII of the fourth part of volume II, we read, for example: twenty minutes. Is this an allusion to the time taken to read the chapter?

15. The commentaries from the Tocqueville family, from Gustave de Beaumont, and from Louis de Kergorlay often reproduce the fragments to which they are referring. Most of the commentaries of the first readers of Tocqueville's book relate to details of writing, style, and the vocabulary used. Of course, I have reproduced at the bottom of the page only those criticisms that seemed of some theoretical interest.

the final version sent to the publisher. The printing process inevitably introduced others.[16]

The editions that followed worked to correct the errors of the first edition, but added new ones. For his part, Tocqueville also made certain deletions and several additions.[17]

At the time of the preparation of this edition, I began by comparing the most important French editions (those of 1835, 1838, 1840, and 1850). I discovered a certain number of differences from one edition to another: corrections by the author, modifications of punctuation, omissions, etc. After recovering the missing passages, I then compared the whole text with the manuscript and identified more than a hundred diverse errors. To those, some errors made by Tocqueville had to be added. For the latter, I have merely pointed out the error; I tried to correct it if possible, but I have not in any way modified the text.

I then incorporated the fragments that I chose into the known text.[18] To do this, a meticulous selection of texts was made among the multiple var-

16. For example, where Tocqueville wanted to say that "aristocratic countries are full of rich and influential individuals who know how to be self-sufficient and who are not easily or secretly oppressed" (II, p. 1267), certain editions assert: "aristocratic countries are full of rich and influential individuals who do *not* know how to be self-sufficient and who are not easily or secretly oppressed" (my emphasis).

In chapter IV of the second part of the first volume (p. 306), the author maintains that in 1831 the proposal of the partisans of the tariff circulated in a few days "due to the power of the printed word," while several editions attribute this fact to "the birth of the printed word." The editions in use contain more than a hundred errors of this type.

17. The reader will find in the notes the reasons that led to certain of these corrections. For instance, the deletion of the allusion to John Quincy Adams (note k for p. 214).

The editors of the new edition of the complete works of Tocqueville, published by Gallimard, preferred to produce the last edition corrected by Tocqueville, the thirteenth, which dates from 1850. That edition nonetheless presents a good number of the errors present in previous editions. It also introduced a certain number of new errors.

18. The writing of the fragments that I cite is not always, as you will see, at the level of the published texts. The sometimes maladroit, sometimes frankly incorrect sentences that are reproduced have clearly not received the attention accorded to the published texts. You will find in particular certain stylistic and grammatical archaisms, as well as certain errors in the use of tenses, moods, and prepositions that I have not tried to modify in any way.

iants and versions present in the manuscript; the selection was made for obvious reasons of interest as well as placement. I have deliberately chosen to concentrate the greatest portion of the additions in the chapters that seem to me to have the most interest, and in particular in the second part of the book. The additions to the main text appear between brackets; they may be preceded and followed by various diacritical signs whose meaning is set forth below.[19]

The notes consist of marginalia, of variants or versions predating the final version, which belong to the drafts, travel notes, fragments of correspondence, and criticisms put forth by friends and family. Their sources have been carefully and systematically indicated. To these notes is added the critical apparatus that I wanted to be useful as well as succinct.

Finally, at the end of the fourth volume, I have included in the form of appendixes six texts of different types.[20] The first two, *Journey to Lake*

---

19. The new fragments that this edition presents are reproduced as they can be read in the manuscript. I have nonetheless made a certain number of corrections and modifications necessary for comprehension:

1. Punctuation and capitalizations have been added in almost all of the new fragments.

2. Spelling errors, particularly those of foreign proper names, such as *Massachusetts* or *Pennsylvania*, written indifferently in a correct or incorrect way, have always been corrected. When the error is systematic, I have included the correct word in brackets.

3. In many cases, the manuscript includes several variants of the same fragment, the same sentence, or the same word. I have chosen to present the version that seemed to me the most appropriate. I have not always presented all the versions that exist in the manuscript if they seemed to have nothing more than a philological interest. Sometimes the gender or the number of the verb in the original agrees with only one of the variants; in this case, I have reestablished the correct form of the verb.

4. I have completed some of the abbreviations used by Tocqueville in the manuscript.

5. All of the italics are Tocqueville's, with the exception of citations in the criticisms by Tocqueville's family and friends, and, sometimes, of titles of books. On this point I have made modifications due to usage.

20. The thirteenth edition included for the first time as an appendix the report of Tocqueville to the *Académie des sciences morales et politiques* on the book by Cherbuliez, *De la démocratie en Suisse,* and Tocqueville's speech of 27 January 1848 to the Chamber, in which he foresaw the February revolution. Tocqueville's intention had been as well

Oneida and *A Fortnight in the Wilderness,* had been written by Tocqueville during his journey in the United States. Everything suggests that they would have constituted appendices to the *Democracy* if Beaumont had not written *Marie.* We know in fact from the latter that Tocqueville had judged the two narratives to be too close to his travel companion's fictional venture to consider publishing them.[21]

The two texts that follow are part of the drafts. Without the polish and the quality of the two preceding ones, they still have a certain documentary interest.

To include a certain number of ideas that will constitute the keystones of Tocqueville's political thought, I have added an unpublished letter from the author, dating from 1830 and addressed to Charles Stoffels.

Finally, I believed it was good to recapitulate in appendixes the foreword to the twelfth edition and all of the works cited by Tocqueville in his book as well as in the drafts, in order to aid in the reconstruction of the "Tocqueville library."

---

to include as an appendix a short work written in October 1847 and published with the title "De la classe moyenne et du people" ["Of the middle class and the people"] (*OC,* III, 2, p. 738–741), which he sent to Pagnerre (letter from Tocqueville to Pagnerre of 13 September 1850, at the National Assembly). Because of length, the present edition does not reproduce the two appendixes of the 1850 edition.

21. See *OCB,* V, p. 27.

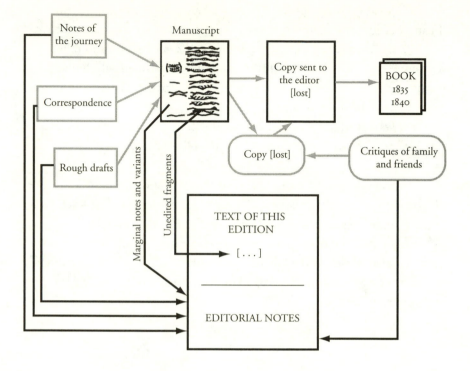

Abbreviations and Symbols Used in This Edition

[. . .]	Text not crossed out in the manuscript.
< . . . >	Text circled or surrounded in pen (this generally concerns fragments that Tocqueville wanted to delete, but the presence of a circle around a word sometimes served solely to draw the author's attention: Is the use pertinent? Does the word conflict phonetically with the one following?).
≠ . . . ≠	Word or text crossed out by one or several vertical or diagonal lines.
{ . . . }	Word or text crossed out horizontally.
/	Sign placed at the end of the sentence to indicate that a horizontal line separates it in the manuscript from the one that follows.
.-.-.-.-	Illegible for physical reasons. Generally due to the very poor condition of the original.
[*]	Note of Tocqueville, present in the manuscript but absent from the published version.
*	Note of Tocqueville, omitted in certain editions.
[. . . (ed.)]	Information given by the editor.
a, b, c, . . .	Notes of the editor.
(A), (B), . . .	Notes of Tocqueville that refer to the end of the volume.
1, 2, 3, . . .	Notes of Tocqueville placed at the bottom of the page.
OC	Edition of complete works published by Gallimard under the direction of J. P. Mayer at first, and François Furet and Jean-Claude Casanova afterward.

Œuvres complètes. Paris: Gallimard, 1951–:
t. I: *De la démocratie en Amérique.* 2 vols. (1951)
t. II: *L'Ancien Régime et la Révolution.* 2 vols. (1952, 1953)
t. III: *Écrits et discours politiques.*
         vol. 1. (1962)
         vol. 2 . (1985)
         vol. 2 . (1990)
t. IV: *Écrits sur le système pénitentiaire en France et à l'étranger.* 2 vols. (1985)
t. V: *Voyages.*
         vol. 1: *En Sicile et aux États-Unis.* (1957)
         vol. 2: *En Angleterre, Irlande, Suisse et Algérie.* (1958)

t. VI: *Correspondances anglaises.*
            vol. 1: *Avec Henry Reeve et John Stuart Mill.* (1954) [cité
            comme *Correspondance anglaise.*]
            vol. 2: *Correspondance et conversations d'Alexis de
            Tocqueville et Nassau William Senior.* (1991)
            vol. 3: *Correspondance anglaise.* (2003)

t. VII: *Correspondance étrangère d'Alexis de Tocqueville.* 1 vol.
            (1986)

t. VIII: *Correspondance d'Alexis de Tocqueville et de Gustave de
            Beaumont.* 3 vols. (1967)

t. IX: *Correspondance d'Alexis de Tocqueville et d'Arthur de
            Gobineau.* 1 vol. (1959)

t. X: *Correspondance et écrits locaux.* (1995)

t. XI: *Correspondance d'Alexis de Tocqueville et de Pierre-Paul
            Royer-Collard. Correspondance d'Alexis de Tocqueville et
            de Jean-Jacques Ampère.* 1 vol. (1970)

t. XII: *Souvenirs.* 1 vol. (1964)

t. XIII: *Correspondance d'Alexis de Tocqueville et de Louis de
            Kergorlay.* 2 vols. (1977)

t. XIV: *Correspondance familiale.* (1998)

t. XV: *Correspondance d'Alexis de Tocqueville et de Francisque de
            Corcelle. Correspondance d'Alexis de Tocqueville et de
            Madame Swetchine.* 2 vols. (1983)

t. XVI: *Mélanges.* (1989)

t. XVII: *Correspondance à divers.* Not yet published.

t. XVIII: *Correspondance d'Alexis de Tocqueville avec Adolphe de
            Circourt et Madame de Circourt.* 1 vol. (1984)

OCB   Edition of complete works directed by Gustave de
            Beaumont.

            Œuvres complètes publiées par Madame de Tocqueville. Paris:
            Michel Lévy Frères, 1864–1878:

            t. I–III: *De la démocratie en Amérique.*
            t. IV: *L'Ancien Régime et la Révolution.*
            t. V: *Correspondance et œuvres posthumes.*
            t. VI: *Correspondance d'Alexis de Tocqueville.*
            t. VII: *Nouvelle correspondance.*
            t. VIII: *Mélanges, fragments historiques et notes sur l'Ancien
                        Régime et la Révolution.*
            t. IX: *Études économiques, politiques et littéraires.*

manuscript In the notes of the editor, the working manuscript of the
            Democracy in America (YTC, CVIa, four boxes).

v: variant

YTC		Yale Tocqueville Collection. Collection of manuscripts of Yale University, belonging to the Beinecke Rare Book and Manuscript Library. Sterling Library owns several supplementary manuscripts.
YTC, BIIb		In this classification: lists of questions meant for American interlocutors.
YTC, CIIc		In this classification: "Sources manuscrites," alphabetic list, drawn up by Tocqueville, of travel notes.
YTC, CVa–CVk		In this classification: drafts of *Democracy.*
	CVa	"Bundle no. 8" "Notes that very probably have no place to be used" (59 pp.)
	CVb	"Bundle no. 13" "Various documents on the system of administration in America from which a note can be done for the chapter titled Of Government and Administration in the United States;" (34 pp.)
	CVc	"Bundle no. 6" "That equality of conditions is an accomplished, irresistible fact, that breaks all those who will want to struggle against it. Consequence of this fact" (9 pp.)
	CVd	"Bundle no. 5" "Ideas and fragments that all relate more or less to the great chapter titled: how the ideas and sentiments that equality suggests influence the political constitution" (53 pp.)
	CVe	"Bundle no. 17" (two copies of 13 and 17 pp.)
	CVf	"Bundle no. 4" "Notes, detached ideas, fragments, criticisms, relative to my two last volumes of the Democracy" (52 pp.)
	CVg	"Bundle no. 9" "Drafts of the chapters of the second part of the Democracy" (partial copy in Bonnel's hand, three notebooks numbering a total of 416 pp. and two boxes with the original manuscript). This is the so-called "Rubish."
	CVh	"Bundle no. 3, 1–5" "Notes, documents, ideas relative to America. Good to consult if I again want to write something on this subject" (five notebooks, 484 pp.)
	CVj	"Bundle no. 2, 1–2" ". . . detached . . . on the philosophic method of the Americans, general ideas, the sources of belief . . . to be put in the . . . and that cannot be placed in the chapter" (two notebooks, 138 pp.)
	CVk	"Bundle no. 7, 1–2" "Fragments, ideas that I cannot place in the work (March 1840) (insignificant collection)" (two notebooks, 148 pp.)

Note on the Manuscripts

In addition to the documents of Yale University, the editor quotes or reproduces, with the kind permission of the libraries mentioned, the following documents:

— Letter of Hervé de Tocqueville, 15 January 1827, Bibliothèque de Versailles.

— List of questions on the situation of Blacks in the United States, library of Haverford College, Pennsylvania (E. W. Smith, no. 955).

— Letter to Edward Everett, 6 February 1833 (Tocqueville, Alexis de. Letter to Edward Everett, 6 February 1833. Edward Everett papers); letter to Edward Everett, 15 February 1850 (Tocqueville, Alexis de. Letter to Edward Everett, 15 February 1850. Edward Everett papers); passages drawn from the journal of Theodore Sedgwick (Sedgwick, Theodore III. Paris journal, volume 3, November 1833–July 1834, pages 80–81, 85. Sedgwick family papers), Massachusetts Historical Society.

— Review project (General Manuscripts, Miscellaneous, TI–TO); letter to Basil Hall, 19 June 1836 (General Manuscripts [MISC] Collection, Manuscripts Division, Department of Rare Books and Special Collections), library of Princeton University.

— Documents relating to the question of the indemnities (Dreer Collection), Historical Society of Pennsylvania.

— Letter to Sainte-Beuve, [8 April 1835]; letter of Sainte-Beuve to Beaumont, 26 November 1865, bibliothèque de l'Institut, Spoelberch de Lovenjoul collection.

— Letter to Richard M. Milnes, 29 May 1844; letter to Richard M. Milnes, 14 April 1845; and letter to Richard M. Milnes, 9 February 1852, Trinity College, Cambridge (Houghton papers, 25/200, 201 and 209).

— Letter to the prefect, 3 December 1851 (Ms. 1070), bibliothèque historique de la ville de Paris.

— Letter to Charles Monnard, 15 October 1856, library of the *canton* and university of Lausanne.

Acknowledgments

I very much want to extend my deep thanks to the Beinecke Rare Book and Manuscript Library of Yale University, which continually put at my disposal the innumerable manuscripts that I was able to consult. My thanks go to the entire staff, and very particularly to two curators, Marjorie G. Wynne and Vincent Giroud. I also thank the Beinecke Library for its kind permission to quote and to reproduce the manuscripts and documents of the Tocqueville collection.

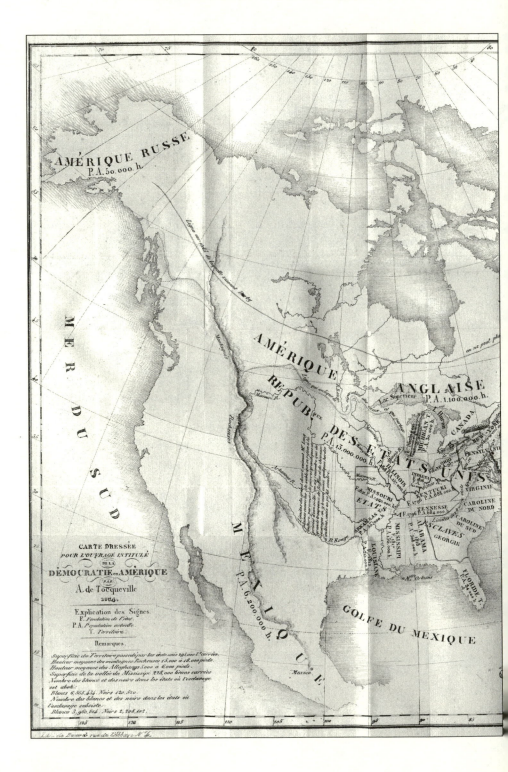

AMÉRIQUE RUSSE
P.A. 50.000 h.

MER DU SUD

AMÉRIQUE
RÉPUBLIQUE DES ÉTATS UNIS
P.A. 15.000.000 h.

ANGLAISE
P.A. 1.100.000 h.

CANADA

Lac Supérieur
MICHIGAN

OHIO
INDIANA
ILLINOIS
F. 1790
KENTUCKI
P.A. 688.000 h.
MISSOURI
F. 1821
P.A. 140.000 h.
ÉTATS
ARKANSAS T.
F. 1796 P.A. 684.000 h.
TENNESSE
VIRGINIE
CAROLINE
DU NORD
R. Rouge
MISSISSIPI
P.A. 136.000 h.
ALABAMA
ESCLAVES
GEORGIE
CAROLINE
DU SUD
LOUISIANE
P.A. 215.000 h.
N. Orleans
FLORIDE T.
P.A. 34.000 h.

MER

MEXIQUE
P.A. 6.200.000 h.

GOLFE DU MEXIQUE

Mexico

CARTE DRESSÉE
POUR L'OUVRAGE INTITULÉ
DE LA
DÉMOCRATIE en AMÉRIQUE
PAR
A. de Tocqueville
1834.

Explication des Signes.
F. Fondation de l'état.
P.A. Population actuelle.
T. Territoire.

Remarques.

Superficie du Territoire possédé par les états-unis 295.000 l. carrées.
Hauteur moyenne des montagnes Rocheuses 15.000 à 18.000 pieds.
Hauteur moyenne des Alleghanys 3.000 à 6.000 pieds.
Superficie de la vallée du Mississipi 228.000 lieues carrées
Nombre des blancs et des noirs dans les états où l'esclavage
est aboli:
Blancs 6.565.434. Noirs 120.520.
Nombre des blancs et des noirs dans les états où
l'esclavage subsiste:
Blancs 3.960.814. Noirs 2.208.102.

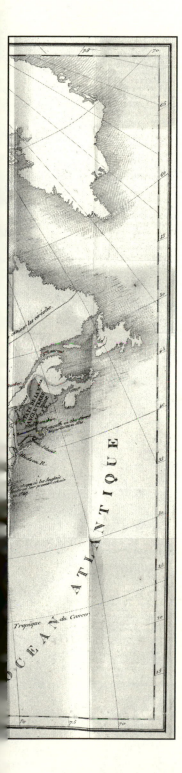

Map of the United States appearing in
the first edition of *Democracy in America* (1835)
(*with kind permission from Special Collections
Research Center, University of Chicago Library*).

Editor's Introduction

"Man obeys first causes of which he is unaware, secondary causes that he cannot foresee, a thousand caprices of his fellows; in the end, he puts himself in chains and binds himself forever to the fragile work of his hands."

—Alexis de Tocqueville

"I have spoken and dreamed a great deal about what I have seen; I believe that if I had the leisure after my return, I would be able to write something passable on the United States. To embrace the whole in its entirety would be foolishness. I am incapable of aiming at a universal exactitude; I have not seen enough for that; but I already know, I think, much more than we have ever been taught in France about it, and certain points of the picture can be of great, even current interest."[22]

Published in two parts, in 1835 and 1840 successively, republished more than one hundred and fifty times and translated into fifteen languages, *Democracy in America* has elicited an enormous interest since its appearance. Elevated to the status of a classic of political philosophy and, as such, probably the last great text of that discipline, Tocqueville's work continues to attract readers, researchers, thinkers, and politicians, thanks to a modernity that few works of the nineteenth century can claim.

Regarding *Democracy*, the question of its *topicality* is often discussed. This is entirely appropriate if by it we mean that this exceptional work still continues to be understood and studied.

22. Letter to Édouard de Tocqueville, Washington, 20 January 1832. This letter belongs to the Yale University collection of manuscripts (Yale Tocqueville Collection—hereafter cited as YTC—classification BIa2). The reader will find in the Foreword a complete list of the abbreviations and symbols used in this edition.

With the perspicacity that was characteristic of him, Tocqueville envisaged the reception of his book in this way: "Some will find that at bottom I do not like democracy and that I am harsh toward it; others will think that I imprudently favor its development. I would be happier if the book were not read, and perhaps that happiness will come."[23]

Readers have not failed to multiply, but they have indeed divided as the author forecast. It could not have been otherwise since this contradictory interpretation coincides precisely with Tocqueville's thinking and its development.

I

Legacies

Alexis de Tocqueville belonged to an old Norman family, Clérel, which took the patronymic *de Tocqueville* in 1661.[24] In the following centuries, the family, Clérel de Tocqueville, left their land from time to time to serve the church or the crown, imitating in this their ancestor, Guillaume Clarel, who had participated in the battle of Hastings.

The Revolution surprised a family firmly established on the Cotentin peninsula, on good terms with its vassals, and honoring its seigniorial duties. When the revolutionary tide reached Normandy, it carried away only

---

23. In a letter of the correspondence with Kergorlay [1835] (*OC*, XIII, 1, p. 374), but probably addressed to someone else.

24. The village of Tocqueville and the château are about fifteen kilometers from Cherbourg. On the origins of the Tocqueville family see G.-A. Simon, *Les Clarel à l'époque de la conquête d'Angleterre et leur descendance dans la famille Clérel de Tocqueville* (Caen: Société d'Impression de Basse Normandie, 1936); and *Histoire généalogique des Clérel, seigneurs de Rampan, Tocqueville, Clouay, Lignerolles, . . .* (Caen: Imprimerie Ozanne et Cie., 1954).

My intention here is to present the principal features of Tocqueville's biography during the years that preceded the *Democracy*. For more details, refer to R.-Pierre Marcel, *Essai politique sur Alexis de Tocqueville* (Paris: Félix Alcan, 1910); Antoine Rédier, *Comme disait Monsieur de Tocqueville* (Paris: Perrin, 1925); J.-P. Mayer, *Prophet of the Mass Age: A Study of Alexis de Tocqueville* (London: J. M. Dent and Sons, 1939); André Jardin, *Alexis de Tocqueville* (Paris: Hachette, 1984); Hugh Brogan, *Alexis de Tocqueville: A Life* (New Haven, Connecticut: Yale University Press, 2007).

the dovecote of the château. It took from the Tocqueville family just the privilege of raising pigeons.

Hervé de Tocqueville welcomed the revolution with a certain sympathy. After a short stay in Brussels, disgust for the life of the *émigré*—the notes of his son on the depravity of a powerless aristocracy are the direct echo of the opinions of the father—led him to return to Paris, where he enlisted in the national guard. On 10 August 1792, Hervé de Tocqueville was part of a section of the national guard that, coming from the *faubourg* Saint-Victor, was preparing to defend the Tuileries. Rallying to the opinion of citizens met along the way, the men who made up the section decided to march against the palace; following this sudden change of opinion Hervé surreptitiously abandoned the section.

After several months in Picardy, Hervé returned to Paris in January 1793. At the end of the month, he went to Malesherbes and, on March 12, married Louise Le Peletier de Rosanbo, granddaughter of the famous Malesherbes.

The refuge at Malesherbes protected its inhabitants until the end of autumn. The defender of Louis XVI was strongly urged to leave France, but he stubbornly remained, intending perhaps to serve as the defender of the Queen. On 17 and 19 December, two members of the revolutionary committee arrested all the inhabitants of the château. Hervé de Tocqueville, his wife, the Peletier d'Aunay family, and the young Louis de Rosanbo owed their lives only to 9 Thermidor. They would see Malesherbes, Madame de Rosanbo, Jean-Baptiste de Chateaubriand, and his wife perish.[25]

The unpublished memoirs of Hervé de Tocqueville speak, not without some melancholy, about moments spent in the company of Malesherbes and other prisoners at Port-Libre (Port-Royal).[26] The months that preceded the trial and inevitable sentence of death for Malesherbes brought forth within Hervé a boundless admiration for the noble old man who with dignity mounted the scaffold following his daughter and granddaughter.

25. Monsieur de Rosanbo was guillotined on 20 April 1794; Malesherbes, Madame de Rosanbo, Jean-Baptiste de Chateaubriand and his wife, the older daughter of the Rosanbos, were guillotined the following day.

26. On the captivity and execution of Malesherbes, Édouard de Tocqueville published one part of the memoirs of his father with the title "Episodes of the Terror," *Le contemporain, revue d'économie chrétienne,* January 1861, republished as a brochure in 1901.

Such events must have been evoked many times in the family, and Alexis always saw in his great-grandfather, Malesherbes, an exemplary figure without peer.[27] At one time he would conceive the project of writing a book on his ancestor. The idea would come to nothing, but the shadow of Malesherbes hovers over many pages of *Democracy*.[28] A bust of the President of the *Cour des Aides,* placed on the worktable of the author, would preside silently over the writing of many works.

Under the Empire, the Tocqueville family lived in Paris in the winter and at Verneuil in the summer, where Hervé[29] accepted the more or less symbolic position of mayor.[30] The education of the children was entrusted to the Abbé Lesueur, who had been Hervé's private tutor and who did not

27. When Tocqueville was looking for a position, his father wrote him a letter of recommendation in which he explained:

> My last son Alexis de Tocqueville intends to pursue a career as a magistrate. He has just completed his law degree with some success, and I beg the support of your excellency in opening this career to him. In his family there are examples that will impose on him the obligation to follow it with zeal. Grandson by his mother of President de Rosanbo and of M. de Malesherbes, if he cannot equal them in talent, he will at least try to approach them in the qualities that distinguish a good magistrate. He would be very happy to begin under your auspices.

Letter of 15 January 1827 to an unspecified recipient, with the kind permission of the Bibliothèque de Versailles.

28. Tocqueville's political career finished with a gesture worthy of President Malesherbes. Arrested with many of his colleagues at the time of the coup of Louis-Napoleon Bonaparte, Tocqueville in prison at Vincennes received an order to be set free. He immediately wrote to the prefect: "I have just received an order setting me free. I had not solicited it and I have authorized no one to solicit it; since it does not include all of my colleagues detained for the same reason and in the same way in the same prison, I have reason to believe that it has been addressed to me by mistake, and in any case, I cannot benefit from it, since my intention is to leave here only with my colleagues." Vincennes, 3 December 1851, with the kind permission of the Bibliothèque historique de la ville de Paris.

29. According to André Jardin, Hervé could have been the secret agent of the Count d'Artois during the Empire (*Alexis de Tocqueville,* p. 16). This book also devotes a chapter to his career as prefect (pp. 18–39).

30. The father of Alexis seems to have fulfilled his duties with a zeal that was particular to him, but not without presenting a certain resistance to the orders of the Emperor. In 1814, for example, he organized the mass marriage of young men about to be conscripted into the army and posted decrees so high that it was impossible to read them. Antoine Rédier, *Comme disait Monsieur de Tocqueville,* p. 34.

hide his partiality for Alexis.[31] Several documents attest to the anti-liberal tendencies of Lesueur as well as to his position as an intransigent Catholic monarchist; in this he seemed in better agreement with the *ultra* sympathies of the Countess de Tocqueville than with the more conciliatory and intelligent position of her husband.[32]

The days of the future author of *Democracy* were occupied by the lessons of the Abbé, reading sessions with the family, composition exercises, and visits by relatives and friends.[33] The private tutor believed in a brilliant future for his pupil.[34] Like his brothers and his intimate

31. Hippolyte, the eldest, was born on 1 October 1797, and began a military career on 1 July 1814. He participated in the Spanish expedition with the rank of captain and left the army on 15 October 1830. Married to Émilie Evrard de Belisle, he would spend most of his time developing his property of Nacqueville, in the Contentin.

Édouard, born in 1800, entered the army in 1816, but had to leave it in 1822 for health reasons. In 1829, he married Alexandrine Ollivier, who owned a large property at Baugy, in Oise. Tocqueville would feel particular affection for their sons, René and Hubert. André Jardin, *Alexis de Tocqueville,* pp. 46–50.

Alexis was born in 1805.

32. In a letter from Lesueur to Édouard, 13 September 1822, we read regarding secret societies:

It is more than time to deal with them. All of Europe is infected by this accursed race. It seems impossible to destroy the germ, but vigorous means must be invented to stop their contagion. There must be a pest house in the Siberian oceans in which the leaders of the plague would be enclosed; there they would be forcibly quarantined not for days, but for years. I am persuaded that not one would return from there. They would poison each other, kill each other, consume each other (YTC, AIV).

33. The catalogue of the library of the Tocqueville château, established in 1818, includes, among other prestigious names, those of Montaigne, La Bruyère, Locke, Bacon, Fontenelle, Pope, Morelly, Montesquieu, Thomas More, Buffon, Corneille, Racine, Molière, Voltaire, Plutarch, Grotius, Hume, and Bossuet. YTC, AIe.

34. At the time of a family celebration in 1822, the Abbé Lesueur addressed to the Countess de Tocqueville the following verse regarding her son:

As wise as a Demosthenes
is the youngest of your sons
going to appear in the arena:
to testify to his victory,
the name of the great Alexis
will be inscribed in the history [of the college].

friend, Louis de Kergorlay,[35] the young Alexis considered a military career.

We perhaps owe the abandonment of Alexis's military plans to the Abbé Lesueur's insistence: "My dear Édouard," wrote the Abbé in 1822, "you must counsel him against becoming a military man. You know the drawbacks better than we, and I am sure that he will rely more on his brothers than on his father. That character, Louis de Kergorlay, put this idea in his head. They are going to meet again, and indeed my plan is to ask M. *Loulou* to leave us alone and to mind his own business."[36]

A distant cousin, from a quite similar family background, Kergorlay had established the bonds of a profound friendship with Tocqueville. They expressed it in an abundant correspondence that deals as much with Tocque-

---

> Let us postpone our homage,
> it is the wisest course,
> and to regain our spirits,
> let us wait until next year.
>   Next year, the Monarchy,
> its foundations reestablished,
> will see the liberals flee;
> and our King on his throne,
> finally master of his kingdom,
> will want to cure all our ills.
> Tune: When the oxen go two by two, the plowing goes better . . . (Letter from
>   Lesueur to Édouard de Tocqueville, 25 August 1822, YTC, AIV).

35. During the weeks that followed the July Revolution, Tocqueville would momentarily regret not having followed his initial impulse, that of entering a military career: "I regret more than ever not having followed the initial ideas of my youth and not entering the army"—he confessed to his friend Charles Stoffels on 26 August 1830.

> Those in the army are also humiliated, but they have a thousand occasions before them to rise up again, and we do not. The thought of striking a saber blow for France, if foreigners wanted to invade her territory for a third time, is the only one that rouses me amid the disgust that surrounds me. Love of independence of our country, of its external grandeur, is the only sentiment that still makes something in my soul vibrate (YTC, AVII).

36. Letter from the Abbé Lesueur to Édouard de Tocqueville, 14 September 1822, YTC, AIV. The same idea is found in a letter dated 16 September: "How sad it would be to smother under a helmet a talent that promises so many distinctions."

ville's works as with books, parliamentary opinions, and the matrimonial plans of Kergorlay; it also includes many commentaries and recommendations of the latter on the writings of his friend.[37] Kergorlay's mark on the pages of *Democracy* is clear and easy enough to spot.

With the Restoration, Hervé began a roving career as a prefect, beginning in 1814 in Maine-et-Loire. Hervé afterward fulfilled the same functions in Oise and in Dijon (1816). In 1817, he accepted the prefecture of Metz, where he remained until 1823. He then moved to Amiens, and in 1826 was finally back in Versailles. His nomination as a peer of France on 4 November 1827 forced him, for reasons of incompatibility of duties, to leave his position in January 1828. The July Revolution would eliminate the peerage and remove him forever from political life.[38]

The Countess Louise de Tocqueville, who seemed never to have been able to recover from her months of detention, followed her husband in his different posts until 1817, the moment that she settled definitively in Paris. The family correspondence shows her prostrate, requiring the constant attention of those around her. Alexis lived with her until 1820.

In April of that year, while his two brothers began their military careers, Alexis rejoined his father in Moselle to complete his studies at the royal college of Metz, which he finished in 1823.[39] He then returned to Paris to begin his studies in law.[40]

37. This correspondence is published in the two tomes of volume XIII of the *Œuvres complètes*.

38. In 1829, Hervé de Tocqueville had published a brochure on the proposed municipal law, entitled *De la charte provinciale*. On this point, the ideas of the son would not be those of the father, but they would partially echo them. In 1847, Hervé de Tocqueville published *Histoire philosophique du règne de Louis XV,* in two volumes, and in 1850, *Coup d'œil sur le règne de Louis XVI.* These two works continue to have a certain interest.

39. Two of his school compositions are preserved: "De Laudibus Demosthenes" and "L'importance de l'éloquence chez l'homme." A "Discours sur le progrès des Arts dans la Grèce" had a certain effect. In 1822, Hervé presented his son with an edition of Horace (*Qvinti Horatii Flacci Opera.* Londini Aeneis Tabulis incidit Iohannes Pine MDCCXXXIII [MDCCXXXVII], 2 vols.) with this dedication: "Given to my son, Alexis, on 5 September 1822, the day when he obtained the prize of honor in Rhetoric, the first prize in Latin translation, the second prize in French composition, and four certificates of merit. Metz, 5 September 1822. The Count de Tocqueville." *Bernard Quav-*

At the end of 1826, his law studies finished, Tocqueville started on a journey to Italy and Sicily in the company of his brother, Édouard. His nomination as *juge auditeur* at Versailles, on 5 April 1827, precipitated his return to Paris.

The Machine at Law

Tocqueville spent the first months at the prefecture of his father. Following the latter's resignation, he then shared an apartment with a new friend, Gustave de Beaumont.[41]

The family Bonnin de La Bonninière originated in Touraine. It had spread into the neighboring provinces and had recently acquired the patronymic *de Beaumont*. At the beginning of the century the Count Jules de Beaumont, his wife, and their four children lived at the château de La Borde, at Beaumont-la-Chartre, in Sarthe. Jules de Beaumont was the mayor there during the Empire. It was in this setting, little different from that of Verneuil, that Gustave had spent his childhood.

The Tocquevilles devoted afternoons to reading and conversation, including among their visitors Chateaubriand, who profited particularly from his visits to work on his *Moïse*. At the home of the Beaumonts, the family read together and devoted itself to music, painting, and charitable works.[42]

---

itch, catalogue 1069, December 1986. I owe this information to the kindness of Marjorie G. Wynne, librarian of Yale University.

40. He would gain his diploma after the presentation of two theses: "De usurpationibus aut de usucapionibus" and "L'Action en rescision ou nullité." André Jardin, *Alexis de Tocqueville,* p. 70.

41. George W. Pierson indicated the importance of the influence of Beaumont in *Tocqueville and Beaumont in America* (New York: Oxford University Press, 1938), and even earlier in "Gustave de Beaumont: Liberal," *Franco-American Review* 1 (1936–1937): 307–16. More recently, Seymour Drescher has insisted on the significance of Beaumont's texts for understanding Tocqueville in an interesting appendix to *Tocqueville and Beaumont on Social Reform* (New York: Harper, 1968), pp. 201–17, "Tocqueville and Beaumont: A Rationale for Collective Study." See also Christine Dunn Henderson, "Beaumont y Tocqueville," in Eduardo Nolla, ed., *Alexis de Tocqueville. Libertad, igualdad, despotismo* (Madrid: Gota a Gota, 2007), pp. 73–99.

42. Rose Préau de la Baraudière had been called "La Providence" by the inhabitants of Beaumont-la-Charte. On her tomb is written: "She was, while alive, the mother of the poor."

Even if the Beaumont family belonged to the minor provincial nobility and could not include among its ancestors a Lamoignon de Malesherbes, the family had, like the Tocqueville family, distinguished itself in arms and was related to the Lafayette family.

In February 1826, Gustave de Beaumont was named *substitut du procureur du roi* at Versailles. Tocqueville struck up a friendship with him when he assumed his responsibility as *juge auditeur*,[43] in June 1827.

The future author of *Democracy* chose a legal career with some hesitation. He was afraid of turning into a "machine at law."[44] His first weeks of work as a magistrate showed him the deficiencies of his legal preparation and revealed a certain trouble speaking in public that he would regret all his life. He would attribute a large part of his failure in politics to this difficulty.

Gustave de Beaumont placed him under his protection. It was the beginning of a friendship that, Tocqueville would say, "was born *already old.*"[45] Heine from his perspective would compare the two friends to oil and vinegar.[46] The first letter that still exists of their correspondence goes back to the month of October 1828. It is devoted to a long reflection on *A*

43. A position without salary and with vaguely defined duties.

44. To Kergorlay, 23 July 1827, *OC,* XIII, 1, p. 108.

45. In a note from Tocqueville to Beaumont criticizing his oratorical style (YTC, CIVa).

46. "It must be said in fairness about M. de Tocqueville, who reported, that he upheld his convictions with energy; he is a man of the mind, who has little fervor and who, beneath the frozen surface, follows the arguments of his logic; consequently his speeches have a certain frigid brilliance, like sculpted ice. But what M. de Tocqueville lacks in feeling, his friend, M. de Beaumont, possesses in superabundance; and these two inseparable companions, whom we see together everywhere, in their travels, in their publications, in the Chamber of Deputies, complement each other in the best possible way. The one, the severe thinker, and the other, the man with smooth feelings, go together like a bottle of vinegar and a bottle of oil." Heinrich Heine, *Allemands et Français* (Paris: Calmann Lévy, 1881), pp. 313–14.

Another contemporary noted: "Gustave de Beaumont was as lively as he was amiable; he had solid qualities of the heart and a vivacity of spirit that gave rise to a great deal of grace and gaiety. Tocqueville, in contrast, was cold, reserved, master of himself to the point of calculating his actions as well as his relationships." Louis Passy, *Le marquis de Blosseville, souvenirs* (Évreux: Charles Hérissey, 1898), p. 107.

In the following pages, but above all in the pages of the *Democracy,* we will gain a better idea of Beaumont's decisive role in the work of his friend.

History of England From the First Invasion by the Romans to the Commence-
ment of the Reign of William the Third, by John Lingard, which Tocqueville
shared with his "dear future collaborator."[47] The two friends shared readings and together attended Guizot's course on the history of civilization in
Europe.[48]

In September 1829, Beaumont was named *substitut* for the department
of Seine. The distance that separated him from his friend did not interrupt
their friendship. Beaumont came to Versailles as soon as his work allowed.
Tocqueville now shared his apartment with Ernest de Chabrol, who took
Beaumont's place at the court of *première instance* at Versailles.

The July Revolution broke out soon after. It was going to change considerably the life of the two young magistrates.

The July Days

Although they belonged to a milieu largely hostile to the French Revolution, Tocqueville and Beaumont were not contemporaneous with the event.
As such, their ideas, without being completely opposite to those of their
relatives, were inevitably different. They witnessed the July Revolution with
more disillusionment and sadness than hatred.

In a letter to Henry Reeve,[49] Tocqueville admitted:

> Some absolutely want to make me a party man and I am not; I am given
> passions and I have only opinions, or rather I have only one passion, the
> love of liberty and human dignity. In my view, all governmental forms are

---

47. Letter of 5 October 1828, *Correspondance avec Beaumont, OC,* VIII, 1, p. 71. A
year later, Tocqueville wrote to his friend: "We are now intimately bound, bound for
life, I think" (*ibid.,* p. 89); and a little later:

> Some good works on history can still emerge from our common efforts. It goes with-
> out saying that we must develop the *homme politique* in us. And for that it is the
> history of men and, above all, the history of those who have most immediately pre-
> ceded us in the world that we must study (Letter of 25 October 1829, *ibid.,* p. 93).

48. We have the notes of Tocqueville for the lectures given between 11 April 1829 and
29 May 1830, which deal with Charlemagne and feudal society. Tocqueville also knew
the contents of the other lectures.

49. Letter to Reeve, 22 March 1837, *OC,* VI, 1, pp. 37–38.

only more or less perfect means to satisfy that holy and legitimate passion of men. I am given alternately democratic or aristocratic prejudices; I would perhaps have had one or the other, if I had been born in another century and in another country. But the chance of my birth has made it very easy for me to defend myself from both. I came into the world at the end of a long Revolution that, after destroying the old state, had created nothing lasting. The aristocracy was already dead when I was born, and democracy did not yet exist; so my instinct could not carry me blindly toward either the one or the other. I lived in a country that for forty years had tried a bit of everything without settling definitively on anything, so I wasn't easily influenced regarding political illusions. As part of the old aristocracy of my country myself, I had neither hatred nor natural jealousy against the aristocracy, and since this aristocracy was destroyed, I did not have any natural love for it either, for we are strongly attached only to what is alive. I was close enough to it to know it well, far enough away to judge it without passion. I will say as much about the democratic element. No family memory, no personal interest gave me a natural and necessary inclination toward democracy. But as for me, I had received no injury from it; I had no particular reason to love it or to hate it, apart from those provided by my reason. In a word, I was in such good equilibrium between the past and the future that I felt naturally and instinctively drawn to neither the one nor the other, and it did not take great efforts for me to look calmly at both sides.[50]

50. Beaumont expressed himself in nearly identical terms:

When I was born, a social order that was fifteen centuries old finally collapsed. [. . .] Never had such a great ruin appeared before the eyes of peoples. [. . .] Never had such a great reconstruction incited the genius of men. A new world arose on the debris of the old one; spirits were restless, passions ardent, minds in labor; all of Europe changed, [. . .] opinions, mores, laws, were swept along in a whirlpool so rapid that new institutions could scarcely be distinguished from those that no longer existed. [. . .] The origin of sovereignty had been displaced; the principles of government were changed; a new art of war had been invented, new sciences created; men were no less extraordinary than events; the greatest nations of the world took children as leaders, while old men were expelled from public affairs [. . .] soldiers without ex-

If Tocqueville exaggerated the coldness and disinterestedness with which he observed the two opposing options, he was sincere in the idea that history could just as easily have made him an *ultra* as a liberal.

Beaumont found himself in a quite similar situation. In Paris on 30 July 1830, he wrote in his memoirs: "All the men wore a tri-colored ribbon in their button hole, or a cockade on their hat. I did not have one; no one said anything to me. But when someone approached me yelling 'Long live the Charter' in a demanding tone, I gave the same cry, and it didn't cost my conscience anything to do so."[51]

---

perience triumphed over the most battle hardened groups; generals who had just come out of school overthrew powerful empires [. . .] the rule of peoples was solemnly proclaimed; and never were such strong and such glorious individuals seen. Everyone rushed into an arena that fortune seemed to open to all (*Marie, ou esclavage aux États-Unis* (Paris: Charles Gosselin, 1835), I, pp. 39–40).

51. Beaumont's unpublished memoirs on the July Revolution (YTC, AV). Beaumont summarized his thinking about the revolution as follows:

The middle class made the revolution that the people executed; but the republican party, a party recruited from all classes, led it and determined its results. I will explain:

The industrialists, tradesmen, heads of companies, small proprietors, etc., irritated by the Ministry and by the government of the king, knew that they did not want that government, but did know what they wanted in its place. They cried *Vive la Charte* because the Charter was violated. They wanted what the government did not want.

They said to the workers: "You will not work, which is to say, you will not live if this illegal state of things continues."

They said nothing more. That was indeed to say: overthrow it; and since force alone could destroy it, that was also to say: even use force. But it was not in the mores of peaceful tradesmen and tranquil industrialists to march at the head of the workers in order to lead their assaults.

Then came the men who for ten years had established a new government for when the government ended. The society, *aide-toi, le ciel t'aidera,* whose power burst forth in the newspapers, in the elections, in attacks against public officials, appeared stronger and bolder than ever. Composed in the majority of enlightened, enterprising men who were inflexible in their principles and ready to sacrifice their lives for the sanctity of their cause, they provided the leaders for the populace whose courage they regularized; and when these leaders had led the populace to victory, they were its masters; they were the masters of force from the beginning. This is how a monarchical republic emerged from the triumph of a multitude set into motion by a class whose impulse was toward the constitutional monarchy.

The following day, Tocqueville returned to the town hall of Versailles the musket and ammunition that he had received the day before as a member of the national guard and declared to Ernest de Blosseville: "There is nothing more to be done; everything is finished. At the gate of Saint-Cloud, I have just seen the convoy of the monarchy pass by, the King, the children of France, the ministers are in carriages surrounded by body guards. And well! Would you believe, the escutcheons of the royal carriages are hidden beneath mud coverings."[52]

From the time of the appointment of the Polignac government on 8 August 1829,[53] Tocqueville and Beaumont expected an event of this type. A partisan of the Bourbons, Tocqueville owed a certain loyalty to his social origins, but the accomplished deed of the change of dynasty led him in fact to discover a great fidelity to France.[54] It was far from the intention of Tocqueville and Beaumont to qualify themselves as liberals in 1830. Nonetheless, the fact of putting the honor of France as well as the principles of the Charter and of liberty before the Bourbons put them closer to liberal positions than they (and Tocqueville in particular) believed.

This loyalty to the nation rather than to the Bourbons nevertheless isolated them from their milieu. Friends and relatives withdrew from public life as the possibility of overturning the monarchy seemed more unreal, in particular after the month of August, when all officials were asked to swear an oath of loyalty to Louis-Philippe. At that moment Hippolyte de Tocqueville and Louis de Kergorlay left the army, and Hervé lost his title of peer of France.[55]

52. Louis Passy, *Le marquis de Blosseville,* p. 130.

53. This is Beaumont's opinion in his unpublished memoirs. Tocqueville wrote the same to his brother, Édouard. André Jardin, *Alexis de Tocqueville,* pp. 83–84.

54. Tocqueville would describe his feelings in this way: "Tied to the Royalists by the sharing of a few principles and by a thousand family bonds, I see myself in some way bound to a party whose conduct seems to me often not very honorable and almost always extravagant. I cannot help suffering immensely from their faults, all the while condemning them with all my power." Letter to Ernest de Chabrol, 18 October 1831, YTC, BIa2.

55. Hervé seemed to fear that the new government, suspecting his loyalty to the Bourbons, had his mail opened. During his journey in America, Tocqueville asked his sister-in-law, Alexandrine, to assure his father that his letters arrived punctually and sealed. Letter to Madame Édouard de Tocqueville, 18 October 1831, YTC, BIa2.

For their part, Tocqueville and Beaumont were confronted with a difficult choice: swear an oath to the new king or abandon their judicial careers. Tocqueville swore an oath, and justified his decision by the fear of anarchy:

> I swore an oath to the new government. I believed that by acting in this way I have fulfilled the strict duty of a Frenchman. In our current state, if Louis-Philippe were overthrown, it would certainly not be to the profit of Henry V, but of the republic and of anarchy. Those who love their country must therefore rally openly to the new power that is arising, since it alone can now save France from itself. I despise the new king; I believe his right to the throne less than doubtful, and yet I will support him more firmly, I think, than those who smoothed the way for him and who will not take long to be his masters or his enemies.[56]

When Henrion, a friend of aristocratic origin, criticized Tocqueville's decision, the latter responded in words that leave no doubt about his position:

> The morning of the ordinances I declared before the assembled tribunal that henceforth resistance seemed legitimate to me and that I would resist in my narrow sphere. When the movement went so far as to overthrow the dynasty, I hid from no one my opposition to this measure. I said that I would wage civil war if it took place. Once it was an accomplished fact, I continued to believe what I had always believed, that the strictest duty was not toward a man or a family, but toward country. The salvation of France, at the point where we were, seemed to me to be in maintaining the new king. So I promised to support him, without hiding the fact that I did not do it for him. I protested that I did not intend an oath that bound me forever to any cause other than to the interest of our country, and I

---

56. Letter to Charles Stoffels, 26 August 1830, YTC, AVII. Tocqueville swore the oath for the first time on 16 August 1830.

The conduct of Beaumont testifies to his desire to move beyond the quarrels of the moment. Thus, he opposed the policy of not applying the principle of amnesty to those who pillaged Paris on 27, 28, and 29 July, and he decided not to go forward with trials brought about by facts that seemed to him covered by the amnesty. He wrote a report on the question and defended it before the king on 14 September 1830. YTC, AV.

did not hide the fact that the moment that the new dynasty became in-compatible with that interest, I would conspire against it.[57]

It was out of these precise circumstances that the idea of the journey to America was born.[58] The plan and its realization did not take much time. On 31 October 1830, six days after Tocqueville took the oath a second time, following his nomination to the post of *juge suppléant,* the two magistrates presented to the government a proposal for a mission whose purpose was to study the American penal institutions.[59]

It involved describing and understanding the advantages and disadvantages of the two systems in use in the United States. The Pennsylvania system provided for incarceration in solitary confinement night and day as well as individual work by each person in his cell. The Auburn system, in the state of New York, provided for imprisonment in solitary confinement and work in common, but under the strict law of silence.

About his American plans, Tocqueville gave the following argument that he confided to his friend Stoffels:

> My position in France is bad on all points, at least as I see it; for either the government will consolidate itself, which is not very probable, or it will be destroyed.

---

57. Draft of a letter to Henrion, 17 October 1830, YTC, AVII.

58. See *OCB,* V, pp. 15–16. Young Tocqueville had perhaps spoken to Chateaubriand about his American projects. In a letter to Charles Stoffels of 26 August 1830 (YTC, AVII), he commented on them in this way: "If I am forced to leave my career, and if nothing necessarily keeps me in France, I have decided to flee the idleness of private life and to take up the busy existence of the traveler again for a few years. For a long time I have had the greatest desire to visit North America. I will go there to see what a great republic is. The only thing I fear is that, during that time, one will be established in France." The study of the penitentiary system is "a very honorable pretext that makes us seem particularly to merit the interest of the government, whatever it may be, and that assures us its good will upon our return." Letter of 11 October 1831 to Charles Stoffels, YTC, AVII.

59. See *Note sur le système pénitentiaire et sur la mission confiée par M. le Ministre de l'Intérieur à MM. Gustave de Beaumont et Alexis de Tocqueville* (Paris: H. Fournier, 1831).

In the first case, my situation is not very pleasant and will not be for a long while. I do not want advancement, because that would tie me to men whose intentions I suspect. So here I am, an obscure *juge suppléant,* having no way to make myself known, even in the narrow sphere in which I am enclosed; for if I become part of the opposition, as a member of the public prosecutor's office, I do not even have the honor of being removed from office; they will be content to keep me quiet by preventing me from working in court. If I support those men, I am doing something that is in accord with neither my principles nor my position. So there I am necessarily reduced to the role of a neutral, which is to say to the most pitiful role of all, especially when you occupy a lower grade. To all of that, add that the future is until now so obscure that it is impossible to say which party we should, in the interest of our country, desire to have the definitive victory.

Now, suppose that this government is overthrown; amid the disruption that will follow, I have no chance to make myself known, for I am starting too low. I still have done nothing to attract public attention. In vain would I try to do my best; this revolution would find me too young or too obscure. I would certainly warmly embrace the banner of the party that appeared to me the most just, but I would serve in its lowest ranks, which would scarcely suit me.

There is my future in France; I sketched it without exaggeration. Now, suppose that, without ceasing to be a magistrate and still maintaining my rights of seniority, I go to America; fifteen months go by; the parties become clear in France; you see clearly which one is incompatible with the grandeur and tranquility of your country; you then return with a clear and decided opinion and free of any engagement with whomsoever in the world. This journey, all by itself, has drawn you out of the most common class; the knowledge that you have acquired among so celebrated a people finally brings you out of the crowd. You know just what a vast republic is, why it is practical here, impractical there! All the points of public administration have been successively examined. Returning to France, you feel, certainly, a strength that you did not have when you left. If the moment is favorable, some publication can alert the public to your existence and fix the attention of the parties on you. If that does not happen, oh well! Your journey at least did you no harm, for you were as unknown in America as you were in France, and returning to your country you are entirely as suited to advance as if you had remained there. There, I think, is a plan that is not in all ways absurd.[60]

It is therefore understood that initially the book on the United States was considered a means: that of opening the doors of a political career for its author. But the publication that Tocqueville is referring to in the cited passage still lacked a name and substance. Moreover, the initial intention of Tocqueville and Beaumont was to publish a shared text on the political institutions and mores of the North Americans. So we are a long way from the birth of *Democracy in America* and *Marie, ou l'esclavage aux États-Unis.*

The reasons that Beaumont had for leaving France for a time were not very far from those of Tocqueville. In *Marie,* he gave the following romantic version that he put in the mouth of the protagonist:

> Toward the year 1831, a Frenchman resolved to go to America with the intention of settling there. This plan was inspired by various causes. A recent revolution had revived in his country political passions that were believed to be extinct. His sympathies and his convictions carried him toward one party; his family ties kept him in another. Thus placed between his principles and his feelings, he constantly felt some conflict; to follow the movements of his heart, he would have to stifle the voice of his reason; and if he remained faithful to his beliefs, he would offend his dearest affections.[61]

It could also be that Beaumont had refused to remove two compromising documents relating to the trial of the Baroness de Feuchères, and it has been suggested that the government sent him to the United States with the

---

60. Letter to Charles Stoffels, 4 November 1830, YTC, AVII. But, in a letter probably dating from 1835 (*OC,* XIII, 1, p. 374), Tocqueville affirmed on the contrary: "I did not go there with the idea of doing a book, but the idea of a book came to me there."

Tocqueville's letters must be used with certain precautions. The author very clearly takes into account the person who is to receive his letters. Thus, he sometimes writes to his correspondents what they expect, hiding certain information from his most intimate friends, while sharing it with acquaintances, etc.

61. Beaumont, *Marie,* I, pp. 2–3.

intention of removing him from the matter.[62] The Baroness de Feuchères was, we recall, an adventuress of English origin. She was accused of having murdered her lover, the old Prince de Condé. The person who undoubtedly profited the most from the death of the latter turned out to be Louis-Philippe himself, since his son was the direct heir of the largest portion of the wealth of the last Condé. If it is incorrect that the French government sent Beaumont to the United States for the purpose of removing him from the trial, it remains true that it was bent on including a magistrate of aristocratic origin in a trial in which the king could be implicated. By proceeding in this way, the government shielded itself from the suspicions of the legitimists and, if the judgment ever implicated the conduct of the monarch,[63] it could always turn against a lawyer who did not have the reputation of being favorable to the new regime.

America

Tocqueville and Beaumont left for America on April 2, 1831. Their baggage included dozens of letters of introduction and a few works on the United States: those of Volney and of Cooper, a history of the United States, and the book by Basil Hall. They did not need them very much. All the information that they were curious about was to be provided on site. It seemed to them that the book they planned to write upon their return had to concern America as much as democracy, and they were very impatient to know both.

During the crossing of the Atlantic, they translated one part of Basil Hall's work[64] as preparation for their research on the prisons; they learned about the history of the United States and discussed the *Cours d'économie politique* of Jean-Baptiste Say.

62. Louis André, *La mystérieuse Baronne de Feuchères* (Paris: Perrin, 1925), pp. 261–62. On the Feuchères affair, we can also consult Marjorie Bowen, *The Scandal of Sophie Dawes* (New York: Appleton, 1935); and Emile Lesueur, *Le dernier Condé* (Paris: Alcan, 1937).

63. The Beinecke Library holds, under the classification CIf, some of Beaumont's letters to his superiors on the matter of the Baroness de Feuchères.

64. A few pages of notes remain in YTC, BIf 2.9.

On the afternoon of 9 May, they reached Newport. They were in New York the next day. They would remain in the United States until 20 February 1832.[65]

Upon their arrival, Tocqueville and Beaumont discovered that the publicity that their official mission had received in the American press opened every door to them.[66] So the official study of the penitentiary system and the unofficial research on that new form of government called democracy seemed to look very promising.

Concerning democracy, the greatest difficulty was found not in America, but in France.

Once first impressions had passed, the two friends realized that their eagerness to know and understand American society required above all a real knowledge of French society, which they lacked. The purpose of their journey became more precise. It would concern a double and simultaneous intellectual journey whose subject would be France as well as America. "I will admit to you that what most prevents me from knowing what is happening on this point in America," wrote Tocqueville to his friend Blosseville, "is being almost completely ignorant of what exists in France."[67] This observation is found many times in his correspondence.

It then became imperative to contact colleagues, friends, and relatives in order to obtain the information necessary for understanding America by way of understanding France.

On this point, Tocqueville began by asking his father, Chabrol, and Blosseville for information about the French administration:

65. This is not the place to reconstitute the American itinerary in detail. Moreover, it is impossible in this matter to improve on what George W. Pierson said in *Tocqueville and Beaumont in America* (New York: Oxford University Press, 1938). I use the mention of this work to express my deep acknowledgment to Mr. Pierson for the time that he devoted to my questions and for the encouragement that he constantly lavished on me during my work.

66. "It is true that the newspapers, which deal with everything, have announced our arrival and expressed the hope that we will find active assistance everywhere. The result is that all doors are open to us and that everywhere we receive the most flattering welcome." Letter from Tocqueville to his mother, 29 April–19 May 1831, YTC, BIa2.

67. Letter of 30 October 1831, YTC, BIa2.

> You must [. . .] provide another [service] to Beaumont and to me—he
> wrote to Ernest de Chabrol—which is, perhaps you're going to laugh, to
> instruct us as fully as possible on what people think at home about this
> country. Since we left France, we have lived with Americans, either on the
> ship that carried us, or since our arrival here; as a result, we have become
> accustomed by degree, and without abrupt transitions, to the new order
> of things in the midst of which we live. We have already largely lost our
> national prejudices about this people. And yet you sense how necessary it
> is for us to know the opinions that prevail at home if we want to modify
> them and even if we desire to study particularly here what can be useful
> for enlightening minds.

About twenty questions followed concerning French ideas on American
political institutions, on the national character, on the different classes of
society, on the commercial situation, the future of the country, its position
in religious matters, etc.

> To what cause do you attribute the prosperity of this nation? Is it political
> institutions or material and industrial causes? [. . .] Do you think there
> are political parties in the United States? How far do you think the spirit
> of equality is pushed here? Is it in the mores or in the laws? What form
> do you think it takes?[68]

In order not to influence the responses of his informants, Tocqueville
decided not to share with them his impressions about America except by
chance. The first letter to his family contained a long description of the
journey and of the arrival in America, but reflections about American society had to wait until the letter to Édouard dated 28 May:

> We are very truly in another world here; political passions are only at the
> surface; the profound passion, the only one that deeply moves the human
> heart, the passion of every day, is the acquisition of wealth, and there are
> a thousand ways to acquire it without disturbing the State. You would have
> to be blind, in my opinion, to want to compare this country to Europe

---

68. Letter to Ernest de Chabrol, 18 May 1831, YTC, BIa2. Tocqueville asked him to
give the same questions to Élie de Beaumont. He also asked that the lectures of Guizot
on Roman society and the Middle Ages be sent to him.

and to adopt in one what works in another; I believed it before leaving France; I believe it more and more examining the society in the midst of which I now live; they are a people of merchants who occupy themselves with public affairs when their work leaves spare time. I hope that on our return to Europe, we will be able to say something good on this subject; perhaps no one is better placed to study a people than we are.[69]

A letter to Ernest de Chabrol, a few days after that one, returned to the same idea:

Imagine, my dear friend, if you can, a society composed of all the nations of the world: English, French, Germans . . . , everyone having a language, a belief, opinions that are different; in a word, a society without common prejudices, sentiments, ideas, without a national character, a hundred times happier than ours. More virtuous? I doubt it. There is the point of departure. What serves as a bond for such diverse elements, what makes all of that a people? Interest. There is the secret. Particular interest that pokes through at every instant, interest that, moreover, arises openly and calls itself a social theory.[70]

Only the exceptional physical conditions of the United States seemed to justify the survival of the republic and allow the free exercise of interest: "America finds itself, for the present, in such a favorable physical situation that particular interest is never contrary to general interest, which is certainly not the case in Europe."[71]

---

69. YTC, BIa2. The passage refers to Chateaubriand. In 1825, Tocqueville had written a few pages criticizing an article of Chateaubriand that had appeared in the *Journal des débats* of 24 October, and in which the latter recommended to the French the model of the American democracy. "The only task worthy of genius would have been to show us the difference that exists between American society and us," wrote Tocqueville, "and not to abuse us with a false likeness." Quoted by Antoine Rédier, *Comme disait Monsieur de Tocqueville*, p. 93.

70. Letter of 9 June 1831, YTC, BIa2. Tocqueville copied this passage into his alphabetic notebook A. This letter contains several key ideas of the book. Chabrol is also the recipient of a letter dated 26 November 1831 that contains very precise information about the American judicial system. YTC, BIa2.

71. Tocqueville added in the same letter: "This people seems to be a company of merchants, gathered for business; and the further you dig into the national character of the Americans, the more you see that they have sought the value of everything only in

At the beginning, as we see, Tocqueville was above all recalling Bodin and Montesquieu.[72] We must wait until the end of the journey to see climatic theories given a less important place. The final versions of the manuscript of *Democracy* still emphasize the decisive importance of the physical setting on American democracy, however.[73]

Tocqueville also thought that it was the exceptional physical conditions of the United States that allowed the Americans to get along without public power.[74] If a public career was closed to ambition, a thousand others were open to the Americans. In America "the entire world seems [. . .] a malleable material that man turns and shapes as he wills."[75]

The element that thwarted the harmful effects of the unlimited desire for money soon appeared clearly; it was religion. At the end of June Tocqueville wrote to his family: "Never have I felt so much the influence of religion on the mores and the social and political state of a people than since I have been in America, and it is impossible here to ignore the necessity of this force for motivating and regulating human actions."[76]

Before the multitude of sects and doctrines, the author had no doubt about the one that was suitable for democracy:

> I have always believed, you know, that constitutional monarchies would arrive at the republic; and I am persuaded as well that Protestantism will necessarily end up at natural religion. What I am saying to you is felt very deeply by many religious souls here; they are revolted at the sight of this consequence of their doctrines, and the reaction throws them into Ca-

the answer to this single question: how much money will it make?" Letter of 9 June 1831 to Ernest de Chabrol, YTC, BIa2.

72. See the letter to Ernest de Chabrol of 26 July 1831, YTC, BIa2; James T. Schleifer, *The Making of Tocqueville's "Democracy in America"* (Chapel Hill: University of North Carolina Press, 1980), pp. 45, 52–53; and George W. Pierson, *Tocqueville and Beaumont in America,* p. 126.

73. See, for example, pp. 76–77.

74. "Here, there is no public power and, truly speaking, there is no need for it." Letter of 9 June 1831 to Ernest de Chabrol, YTC, BIa2. In another letter to Chabrol on 16 June 1831, Tocqueville wrote: "As for the *government,* we are still looking for it. It doesn't really exist" (YTC, BIa2).

75. Letter of 9 June 1831 to Ernest de Chabrol, YTC, BIa2.

76. Letter to Édouard, 20 June 1831, YTC, BIa2.

tholicism, whose principle is very questionable, but where, at least, everything is linked together.[77]

Exceptional physical conditions, private interest, religion, in that it puts
a brake on the inordinate taste for material wealth—these are, from the first
weeks of the American journey, the three elements that profoundly marked
Tocqueville's arguments.

In the months that followed, natural conditions would no longer cover
physical circumstances strictly speaking, but would also include the point
of departure and the origin of the United States; interest would take various
forms: individualism, monotony, love of material enjoyments, manufacturing aristocracy, industrialization of art and of life; religion would also
be called patriotism, honor, and general ideas. But, added to a certain theory
of history, the three initial elements—physical conditions, interest and religion—would continue to form the framework of the entire system of
Democracy.

The journey led Tocqueville and Beaumont from New York to Albany
and Buffalo; it let them briefly see the great wilderness beyond Detroit, at
Pontiac and Saginaw; it took them to the Great Lakes and to Canada in
order to bring them back afterward to New England and New York. From
there, the travelers went to the west and the south. They saw Philadelphia
and Baltimore; they passed through Philadelphia again in order to see next
Cincinnati, Louisville, Nashville, Memphis, and New Orleans.[78] They returned to the north by Montgomery, Norfolk, Washington, and finally
New York.

All of this allowed scarcely any leisure. As Tocqueville wrote to Louis de
Kergorlay: "What categorizes a traveler are his questions, his research, and

77. Letter to Ernest de Chabrol, 26 October 1831, YTC, BIa2. This letter contains a
long reflection on religions in the United States.

78. Their knowledge of the south of the Union was consequently very limited.
Tocqueville recognized this in a letter to Édouard: "I am leaving America after using my
time there wisely and pleasantly. I have only a superficial idea about the *South* of the
Union, but in order to know it as well as the north it would be necessary to have remained
there six months. In general, two years are necessary to develop a complete and exact
picture of the United States. I hope, however, that I have not wasted my time." Letter
of 20 January 1832, YTC, BIa2.

not the degree of facility with which he expresses himself in the national language."[79] The two magistrates, transformed into indefatigable questioners, interrogated, took notes, read and observed.[80] Tocqueville made rough notebooks in which he noted the result of his research. Beaumont did the same and carefully recorded each of their interviews.[81]

Tocqueville's notes are not truly a travel diary, nor do they constitute the only material out of which his theory is going to emerge.[82] Reading them provides little information about his principal ideas. If you are unaware of the theoretical presuppositions of the author, the notes are sometimes uninteresting, even insignificant. The fragments of conversations, various remarks, and interviews only make some sense on the condition that they be considered not as the beginning of reflections on the United States but as stages in an intellectual process predating the American journey.

It is not by chance, or by some peculiar mental skill, that the whole book is already found in the first impressions about America.[83] Even if he wrote the opposite to some of his correspondents,[84] Tocqueville was in America as much to observe the facts that would allow him to write *Democracy* as

79. Letter to Kergorlay, 4 July 1837, *OC,* XIII, p. 460.

80. Six lists of questions exist: 1. List of forty-two questions on criminal justice. 2. List of seven questions on education. 3. Six questions on political questions. 4. Twelve questions on town rights. 5. Three questions on roads. 6. Other questions on town problems. YTC, BIIb.

81. We have the travel notes of Tocqueville, but nearly all of Beaumont's notes are lost. The few rare notes that remain show observations that are more wide-ranging and more detailed, but less theoretical in nature than those of Tocqueville. They would have been of great interest for the reconstruction of the intellectual journey of the two friends.

82. The notes of the journey to America have been published in *Voyages en Sicile et aux Etats-Unis, OC,* V, 1.

83. For example, in a letter of 29 June 1831 to Louis de Kergorlay, *OC,* XIII, 1, pp. 225–36.

84. If I ever do something [blank] about America, it will be in France, and with the documents that I am bringing back, that I will try to undertake it. I will leave America able to understand the documents that I have not been able to study yet: that is the clearest result of the journey. Moreover, on this country, I have only notes without order or coherence: detached ideas that only I have the key to, isolated facts that

to give body and substance to a certain idea of *Democracy* that he already had in mind before the American journey.[85]

The theory began to take shape by bits and pieces in the letters sent to France. "Keep this letter, I beg of you," wrote Tocqueville to his mother, "it contains details that I do not have the time to note and that I will find again later with pleasure."[86] This request was found in all of his travel correspondence.

---

remind me about a host of others. What I am bringing back of most interest are two small notebooks in which I have written word for word the conversations that I had with the most notable men of this country. This sum of paper has an inestimable value for me, but only for me who can sense the value of the questions and answers. The only, somewhat general ideas that I have expressed about America until now are found in some letters addressed to my family and to a few people in France. Even then, these were written hastily, on steamboats, or in some hole where I had to use my knees as a table. Will I ever publish anything about this country? In truth, I do not know. It seems to me that I have some good ideas; but I still do not know yet in what framework to put them, and public attention frightens me (letter of Tocqueville to his mother, 24 October 1831, YTC, BIa2).

Compare the passage quoted with this fragment from a letter to Édouard of 20 June of the same year:

In France no one doubts what America is, and we find ourselves in an excellent position to give an account of it. We come here after very serious study that has made our minds aware of or put them on the track of many ideas. We come here together so that there is a constant clash of minds. [. . .] No matter what happens, we lack neither ardor nor courage, and if some obstacle does not stop us, I hope that we will finish by bringing forth the work we have thought about for a year (YTC, BIa2).

85. In a letter published in the correspondence with Kergorlay, but perhaps addressed to Eugène Stoffels, as André Jardin has pointed out, Tocqueville confessed: "For nearly ten years, I have been thinking about part of what I explained to you just now. I was in America only to enlighten myself on this point. The penitentiary system was a pretext; I took it as a passport that would enable me to penetrate everywhere in the United States." *Correspondance avec Kergorlay, OC,* XIII, 1, p. 374.

Also see the letter to Charles Stoffels, 21 April 1830, reproduced in Appendix V of the second volume, which already advances the theory of history that is present in *Democracy.*

86. Letter of 26 April–19 May 1831, YTC, BIa2. The remark is found again in the letters addressed to his friends. Thus, in the letter to Kergorlay of 29 June 1831 ("Keep this letter. It will be interesting for me later."), *OC,* XIII, 1, p. 236; or in that of 16 July 1831, to Ernest de Chabrol ("Do not forget to keep my letters."), YTC, BIa2.

We must not forget, however, that Tocqueville did not travel alone. If, in the end, the two friends each offered to the public his own version of democracy, it is no less true that until their return to France the notion of a great work on democracy in America was elaborated in concert, in the "duel of minds" that Tocqueville mentioned several times. It is difficult in these conditions to decide on the paternity of an idea, or the origin of a citation. The final result would forever obliterate the daily debates of the two travelers.

As has sometimes been said, Beaumont had more than the effect of a catalyst on Tocqueville. He drew Tocqueville's attention to many phenomena in American society. He collaborated with energy on the writing and revision of *Democracy*. Finally he produced an admirable social novel meant to accompany the work of his friend. Beaumont's notes could have given an idea of the intellectual debate with Tocqueville. In their absence, Beaumont's criticisms of the manuscript of *Democracy*, the drafts of his own books, and the reading of his publications bring clearly to light an intelligence that was only slightly inferior to that of Tocqueville.

It is difficult to pinpoint the moment when the book project ceased to be shared. The first news from America sent by Beaumont spoke of "our great work."[87] In a letter to his mother dated 7 October, he mentioned for the first time "my plans," and the expression was found again in the correspondence that follows.[88] Between May and October, Beaumont discovered, then got to know more closely the American Indians, and as George W. Pierson noted, perhaps this is what explains the abrupt change in his plans.[89]

If family correspondence spoke with enthusiasm about the brilliant future that their works on America were to bring to the travelers, the letters addressed to colleagues remained nonetheless quite vague:

87. Gustave de Beaumont, *Lettres d'Amérique*, pp. 28, 45, 48, 66, and 92.
88. *Ibid.*, p. 159; "my work," in a letter of 26 October; and "the great work that is going to immortalize me," in a letter of 8 November.
89. In a letter of 1 August 1831, to his father and in another of 2 August, addressed to Ernest de Chabrol, Beaumont already announced his interest in the fate of the Indians. *Ibid.*, pp. 105 and 110.

You speak to me about what could be written about America, noted Tocqueville to an unknown recipient, and I do not know at all if I will ever have the occasion to publish the least thing on this subject; the general tableau of English America is an immense work absolutely beyond my strength, and from another perspective, if I abandon the idea of the whole, I no longer know to which details to pay particular attention. So I have limited myself until now to gathering a host of diverse documents and partial observations. I enjoy this work, and it interests me deeply; but will it ever be useful to me for anything? I assure you that the further I go, the more I doubt it.

But, as you say, there would be piquant new insights to present about this country. Except for about ten people in Paris who, like you, are not absorbed by the politics of the day, America is as unknown as Japan; or rather, people talk about it as Montesquieu did about Japan. The Americans *argumenti causa* are made to say and do a host of things, in honor of true principles, that the poor fellows are very innocent of, I swear.[90]

Tocqueville was obviously not interested in disclosing to his superiors that what most interested him in America was not the project officially announced, but writing about the American republic. Only Le Peletier d'Aunay seemed to have been let in on the secret: "I expected a good work from you," wrote d'Aunay to Tocqueville in August 1831, "and this field of your observations makes me certain of it. You will show us this America much more exactly than all the other travelers, beginning with Liancourt and Volney. Nothing will escape, I am sure, from the observation of your solid intelligence. On your return, give the government the report promised. But save, for your reputation, your glory, the full journey to that country."[91]

Beaumont and Tocqueville in America had different interests, but their intention was to publish their books simultaneously, as two parts of the same work. In 1831, and for some time after, their books constituted the two sides of the same coin. They would become distinct only later. The

---

90. In a draft of a letter written in Philadelphia, November 1831 (YTC, BIa2). He also hid his plans from Ernest de Chabrol (letter of 24 January 1832, YTC, BIa2).

91. Letter of Le Peletier d'Aunay, 16 August 1831, YTC, BId.

first edition of *Système pénitentiaire* still announced a joint work on America by Gustave de Beaumont and Alexis de Tocqueville, with the title *Institutions et mœurs américaines.* A month after the publication of *Système pénitentiaire,* a letter from Tocqueville to Edward Everett still suggested a collaborative work: "We are now busy, M. de Beaumont and I, composing a more general work on America."[92]

On 20 February 1832, Tocqueville and Beaumont left New York to return to France.

Tocqueville hardly considered any longer taking up the duties that he had at Versailles. He entertained other plans that he revealed in confidence to Ernest de Chabrol: "I do not know if I must withdraw entirely," he confessed, "as I am often tempted to do, or try to advance; what I see clearly at least is that I will not put on the robe of *juge suppléant* again. I will no longer be seen at Versailles, or I will be seen with another title. This point is decided (but between us)."[93]

The Penitentiary System

After returning to France at the end of March, Beaumont rejoined his family in Sarthe, while Tocqueville remained in Paris.

Beaumont began to write the report on the penitentiary system and met Tocqueville in Paris in mid-April in order to ensure his collaboration. Weeks passed. As Beaumont moved ahead preparing the report on the prisons, Tocqueville was plunged into a great despondency from which he did not want to emerge for work on any intellectual endeavor.[94] He seemed incapable of adapting to the idleness that followed the year of feverish agitation spent in North America. He accepted visiting the prison of Toulon,

92. Letter to Edward Everett, 6 February 1833, with the kind permission of the Massachusetts Historical Society (Tocqueville, Alexis de. Letter to Edward Everett, 6 February 1833. Edward Everett papers).

93. To Ernest de Chabrol, 24 January 1832, YTC, BIa2.

94. Letter of 4 April 1832 to Beaumont, *OC,* VIII, 1, pp. 111–12.

then those of Geneva and Lausanne in May and June, but the largest part of the work of writing the report fell to Beaumont.[95]

Before these journeys, Tocqueville came to the aid of his friend, Louis de Kergorlay, implicated in the adventure of the Duchess de Berry. On 9 March, for the first and last time, Tocqueville exercised his profession as a lawyer. He defended Kergorlay who, acquitted, was soon set free.[96]

The defense of one of the prisoners of the *Carlo Alberto* must not suggest that Tocqueville had changed his position about the subversive efforts to overthrow the July Monarchy. If he preferred the Bourbons, if his friendship for Kergorlay was unshakable, he remained clearly opposed to the violent expulsion of the reigning monarch. The American letters already revealed the fear of a precipitous return to Europe in case of the overthrow of the monarchy[97] and the fear of seeing the "hothead,"[98] Hippolyte, involved in such an overthrow.

As for his opinion about the *ultras,* it can be clarified by a letter in which, sensing that his older brother was tempted to take some radical decision against the July Monarchy, Tocqueville expressed himself in these terms:

Amid the chaos in which we find ourselves, I seem to see one incontestable fact. For forty years we have made immense progress in the practical understanding of the idea of liberty. Peoples, like individuals, need to become educated before they know how to act. I cannot doubt that our people advance. There are riots in the large cities, but the mass of the

95. You know what Beaumont's publications are; but there is a detail that perhaps you do not know. The first work that we published together, M. de Beaumont and I, on the American prisons, had as the sole writer, M. de Beaumont. I only provided my observations and a few notes. Although our two names were attached to that book which was, I can say more easily now, a true success, I have never hidden from my friends that M. de Beaumont was so to speak the sole author (letter of 26 June 1841, supporting Beaumont's candidacy to the Académie des sciences morales et politiques, very probably addressed to Mignet, YTC, DIIa).

96. His plea appears in *OC,* XIII, 1, pp. 321–27.

97. The idea of an exile in the United States also crossed their minds. See note j of p. 1302 of the second volume.

98. In his letter to Édouard, on 20 June 1831, Tocqueville exhorted his brother to have the utmost patience (YTC, BIa2). Also see the letter to Kergorlay of 21 June 1831, *OC,* XIII, 1, pp. 235–36.

population calmly obeys the laws; and yet the government is useless. Do you think as much would have happened forty years ago? We are harvesting the fruit of the fifteen years of liberty that we enjoyed under the Restoration. Aren't you struck to see the extreme left protest that it wants to proceed only by legal measures and, at the same time, to hear the royalists declare that they must appeal to public opinion, that public opinion alone can give strength to the throne, that it must be won over before anything else? Amid all the miseries of the present time and the fit of high fever that gave us the July Revolution, don't you find reasons to hope that we will finally reach a settled social state? I do not know if we are made to be free, but what is certain is that we are infinitely more capable of being so than forty years ago. If the Restoration had lasted ten years longer, I believe we would have been saved; the habit of legality and constitutional forms would have entirely gotten into our mores. But now, could things be put back in their place; could a second Restoration take place? I see many obstacles. The greatest of all without question is found in the personnel of the royalist party that would triumph. Never will you make the most active portion of the royalist party understand that there are concessions without which they cannot hope to govern, that to be lasting the legitimist monarchy must be national, must ally itself with the ideas of liberty or be broken by them. If the Bourbons ever regain the throne, they will make use of force, and they will fall again. Perhaps in France we have what is needed to create a government that is strong because of military glory, but not a government that is strong solely because of right. Right can indeed help to maintain a government if it is skillful, but not to protect it from its own failings.

In any case, it seems to me that the behavior of the royalists is well conceived. I am pleased to see them stand on the ground of legality, to see them work to win the majority and not to make the minority triumph by force. That fact augurs well. If they had always acted like this, they would have spared themselves and France great misfortunes. Moreover, by adopting in this way what is reasonable in the ideas of liberty, they assume in everyone's eyes a tacit commitment to respect those ideas, if they are ever the masters. Many among them become convinced by their own words, without expecting to. They acquire the habit of associating, of appealing to public opinion, all the free and constitutional habits that they never had. This spectacle reassures me a bit about the future. I hope that after so many conflicts we will succeed in saving ourselves from anarchy and despotism.[99]

The pages of a plan for a review[100] that Tocqueville and Beaumont at one time intended to establish with the participation of Blosseville, Chabrol, Montalembert, and a few others put clearly in view the political convictions of the future editors:

> They [the editors of the review] do not feel prejudices in favor of the government created by the July Revolution; they do not want to destroy it. They place themselves neither against it nor within it, but next to it, and they want to try to judge its acts without passion and without weakness. If the free expression of the national will brought the elder branch of the Bourbons back to the throne, if a restoration could take place while assuring the nation of the rights that are its due, the editors of the review would see the event with pleasure; they would consider it as a favorable measure of future social progress. But they want a restoration only on those conditions; and if it must take place in a totally other way and lead to opposite results, they would regard it as a duty to oppose it.[101]

The plan was soon abandoned, probably at the end of the summer of 1833.

---

99. Letter to Hippolyte, 4 December 1831, YTC, BIa2. In contrast, in a rough copy of a letter of August 1831, probably addressed to Dalmassy, Tocqueville noted: "Something tells me that we will not escape from civil war." YTC, BIa2.

100. See the correspondence exchanged on this subject by Tocqueville and Beaumont in *OC,* VIII, 1, pp. 119–30.

101. With the kind permission of the Library of Princeton University (General Manuscripts [MISC] Collection, Manuscripts Division. Department of Rare Books and Special Collections), reproduced in *OC,* III, 2, pp. 35–39. The same idea is found again in a letter to Mary Mottley:

> As I had foreseen and you announced a few days ago, civil war has begun in the west. The royalists will perhaps have some temporary successes, but I predict to you again that they will be crushed. How much loyal and honorable blood is going to flow! I have already read in the newspaper the name of a brave young man that I knew. He has just been miserably killed. So explain to me why in all times honor and incompetence seem to go hand in hand. Who were more brave, more loyal, and at the same time, more clumsy and more unfortunate than your Jacobites? Our French royalists are following their track exactly (3 June 1832, YTC, CIb).

When he was not yet finished with his report and not thinking only about the creation of a review, Beaumont was again faced with the shadowy affair of the Baroness de Feuchères. This time it concerned a trial for defamation by the baroness against the Rohan family, descendants of the Prince de Condé. Beaumont refused to take charge of it and explained that he knew nothing about the question, that he was working on his report, that the eighteen-month leave that had been granted to him had not yet ended.[102] The response was not long in coming. On 16 May 1832, he was removed from his duties.

Little satisfied by a profession that weighed on him, uncertain of his qualities for exercising it, Tocqueville found in the dismissal of Beaumont the pretext for honorably abandoning the legal career. As soon as he learned the news in Toulon, he presented his resignation.[103]

Once the work of drafting the report on the penitentiary system was finished, Tocqueville reviewed the text written by Beaumont, collaborated actively on the introduction, and wrote part of the notes. The two magistrates submitted their report on 10 October. *Du système pénitentiaire aux États-Unis et de son application en France* appeared in January 1833.

The First *Democracy*

The work on the penitentiary system was generally well received. Reviews noted with satisfaction the full account of the question and the impartial presentation of the advantages and disadvantages of the two systems in use in the United States. If the authors seemed to lean toward the system used in Pennsylvania, they did not seem to forget either the high cost of the construction of a penitentiary of this type or the danger of keeping the prisoners isolated in their cell night and day. In August, the Académie des sciences morales et politiques awarded the Montyon prize to *Système pénitentiaire*.

Tocqueville and Beaumont had planned to complete their American journey with a visit to England. They thought that England would offer

102. In a letter of 18 April 1832, YTC, CIf.
103. On 21 May 1832, YTC, CIc.

an image of the Americans before their departure for the United States as well as that of a society midway between aristocratic France and democratic America. They also thought that England was at the dawn of a revolution that would lead to democracy. The cholera epidemic that broke out at the end of 1831 had precipitated their return to France. Once the prison report was published, Tocqueville went to England from August 3 to September 7, 1833.[104]

"By going to England, I wanted [. . .] to flee for a time from the insipid spectacle that our country presents at this moment. I wanted to go to relieve my boredom a bit among our neighbors. And besides! Some claim that they are definitely going to begin a revolution and that one must hurry to see them as they are. So I hastened to go to England as to the final performance of a beautiful play."[105]

A few days spent on the other side of the Channel enlightened Tocqueville about his error. England was not on the eve of a revolution. Unlike the French aristocracy, the English aristocracy was open; it continued to exercise ancestral duties and the inferior classes of society could attain aristocracy by money.[106]

"The English aristocracy," wrote Tocqueville in his notes, "belongs very much by its passions and its prejudices to all the aristocracies of the world, but it is not based on birth, something inaccessible, but on the money that everyone can acquire; and this single difference allows it to resist, when all the others succumb either to peoples or to kings."[107]

A week after his arrival in London, he wrote to Beaumont: "In short, I do not recognize in anything here our America."[108] If, following these observations, England did not serve strictly speaking as a reference point for the American and French situations, it was no less one of the keys for understanding America. It is evoked throughout *Democracy*.

104. The notes of the journey to England in 1833 are published in *Voyages en Angleterre, Irlande, Suisse et Algérie, OC*, V, 2, pp. 11–43.
105. Letter to the Countess de Pisieux, 5 July 1833, YTC, CIf.
106. *OC*, V, 2, p. 36.
107. *OC*, V, 2, pp. 29–30.
108. Letter to Beaumont, 13 August 1833, *OC*, VIII, 1, p. 124.

Upon his return to Paris, Tocqueville began writing his book.[109] To do this, he settled into the attic of his parents' house, on rue de Verneuil. Beaumont, for his part, made a short journey to the Midi where his book began to take the double form of a novel and a social commentary.

In a later letter to his wife, Tocqueville would evoke the first months spent writing his book as follows:

> When I wrote *Democracy in America,* I had none of the advantages [notably a librarian at his disposal], but I had the youth, ardor, faith in a cause, and hope that allowed me to do without the kindness of librarians and the favor of archivists. Cuvier created in a garret the admirable works that earned him a beautiful house in which he set up a beautiful special room intended for the study of each of the subjects that interested him. It was a whole series of apartments each of which was as if impregnated with the particular idea that the author wanted to treat. From the moment when he was so admirably aided in his work, he did hardly anything considerable; and perhaps he sometimes came to regret the garret. But he would have found it old and cold. Those who want to return to the garret in which they passed the years of an intense and fruitful youth cannot do so. My own garret was a small room on the rue de Verneuil, where I worked in deep obscurity on the work that would bring me out of that obscurity. You are part of that memory, like all of those memories in my life that deserve to be remembered. The day was occupied by my work. Nearly every evening was spent near you.[110]

Provided with his notes on the United States, publications brought back from America, an ample correspondence with Americans and Frenchmen, his own letters, and a list of the subjects of his notes,[111] Tocqueville drew up the initial plan of his book.

---

109. James T. Schleifer has reconstructed in detail the writing of the most important chapters of *Democracy* in *The Making of Tocqueville's "Democracy in America."*

110. Letter of Tocqueville to his wife, with the only citation as "Sunday morning," YTC, CIb.

111. *"Sources manuscrites.* Subjects that can be of some interest to treat." YTC, CIIc. The list includes more or less the same questions as the first plan of the book.

The first outline included three categories: "Political society (relations between the federal and particular governments and the citizen of the Union and citizen of each state), civil society (relations of the citizens with each other), religious society (relations between God and the members of society, and of the religious sects with each other)."[112]

Tocqueville continued by specifying what should be found under each division:

> Political society.
>
> In political society there are two principles to which all the others are connected; the first, *sovereignty of the people,* democracy, whose principle divides and dissolves; the second, *federation,* whose principle unites and preserves.

He then noted, in two columns, the ideas that correspond to each principle:

> Sovereignty of the people.
>
> Democracy, no counter-balance. Tyranny of the majority—no aristocracy; difficulty of an aristocracy in America. Gentlemen farmers.
>
> Government of the majority; public opinion; stubbornness of the majority once formed—formation and working of parties.
>
> Public offices (administrative officials particularly enforce the laws between the State and individuals—judicial officials more especially the laws between individuals; the first belong to political society, the second to civil society). Public offices are small matters.—Why? *Municipal administration—Presidency of the United States—Army—Finances.*

> Elections—binding mandates.
> Town meetings.
> Convention.
> Freedom of the press—ways and effects.
> Public instruction.
> Laws—Their mobile character.
> Militia (perhaps should be carried to the other side).
> Obedience to laws. Oath

112. YTC, CVh, i, p. 23.

(Everything that precedes is nothing more than the means that the majority uses to express and to maintain itself, and those that are put to use by the minority to attack or to defend itself.)"

Under the word federation, we read the following:

Federation.
Causes for the weakness of all federal governments—especially for the United States—future of the Union—diverse interests—multiplication—Centralization—distinguish between that of the federal government and that of the states themselves—almost non-existent—the lack of centralization already felt—however less dangerous than it will become. Causes that will make it more dangerous.

Federal tax—tariff.
Canals.
Roads.
Banks of the United States.
Land sales.
Indians.
Maritime commerce, free trade.
Patents.

Show how the various Presidents since Jefferson have successively stripped the federal government of its attributions—concessions to democracy—that is to say, to the principle on the opposite side.[113]

The section with the theme society included in turn:

Civil society.
Entry. The appointment of magistrates is the work of the political powers, but since their duties are principally for the purpose of regulating the relations and the rights of citizens with each other, they belong to civil society.

Jurisdiction.
Common law.

113. YTC, CVh, 1, pp. 23–25.

Civil laws:	Slavery, equality—Negroes
	Civil state—inheritances—paternal power.
Criminal laws:	Duel—gambling—drunkenness—
	fornication—etc.
	Jury—public prosecutor's office—lawyers.
Commercial laws:	Bankruptcy.
	Interest on money.
Mores:	American character.
	Association—commerce—industry.
	To make money.
	Washington—costume of the Lyceums.[114]

Finally, religious society:

Religious society.

Nomenclature of the various sects—From Catholicism to the sect that is farthest removed from it.

Quakers, Methodists—Point out what is antisocial in the doctrines of the Quakers, Unitarians.

Relations of the sects with each other.

Freedom of religion—Toleration: from the legal aspect; from the aspect of mores.

Catholicism.

Place of religion in the political order and its degree of influence on American society.[115]

Certain ideas outlined in this first sketch would not be found again in the definitive version. The canals, roads, gambling, etc. were so many elements that would be abandoned in the process of writing.[116] Others would

114. YTC, CVh, 1, p. 26.

115. YTC, CVh, 1, pp. 26–27.

116. At the head of the bundle of drafts that bears the number 3 (copied in notebook CVh, 1) appears the following note:

Diverse and important notes. The (illegible word) must be found here. Two or three new chapters to put I do not know where.

1. Of the great men of America and in particular of Washington.

2. Of American patriotism.

be joined to the second part, such as the army, paternal power, Catholicism, the desire to make money.

The fundamental idea of the entire book, the keystone on which Tocqueville's whole theory rests, the idea for understanding the struggle between aristocracy and democracy, between a principle that divides and a principle that unites, was already evident.

Once the general lines of the work were drawn, Tocqueville attacked the work of writing in the strict sense. For this, he followed a singular system that he described in this way to Duvergier de Hauranne:

> I think what is best for me to do is to follow the method that I have already followed for writing the book that just appeared [*Old Regime*], and even for the *Democracy.* I am going to tell you about it, although it is disagreeable to talk for so long about oneself, because, knowing it, you will perhaps be able to give me some good advice. When I have whatever subject to treat, it is quasi-impossible for me to read any books that have been written on the same matter; contact with the ideas of others agitates and disturbs me to the point of making the reading of these works painful. So I refrain, as much as I can, from knowing how their authors have interpreted the facts that occupy me, the judgment that they have made of them, the diverse ideas that these facts have suggested to them (which, parenthetically, exposes me sometimes to repeating, without knowing it, what has already been said). It requires of me, on the contrary, an unbelievable effort to find the facts by myself in the documents of the time; often in this way I obtain, with immense labor, what I would have easily found by following another path. Once this harvest is gathered so laboriously, I withdraw into myself, as if into a very closed space; in a general review, I examine with an extreme attention all the notions that I have acquired by myself; I compare them, I link them, and then I make it a rule to explicate the ideas that came spontaneously to me from this long work without any consid-

---

3. Of the non-physical bonds of society in America.

4. Of public officials.

5. Of the different ways to understand the republican regime.

6. That the absolute goodness of laws {must not always be judged} by the respect that they are given by those who vote for them.

7. (Illegible word) on the influence of manufacturing on democratic liberty (YTC, CVh, 1, p. 1).

eration whatsoever for the consequences that these men or those men can draw from them. It is not that I am not extremely sensitive about the opinion of different readers; but experience has taught me that, as soon as I wanted to write with a preconceived viewpoint, to uphold a thesis, I absolutely lost all true talent, and that I was not able to do anything of value, if I did not limit myself to wanting to make clear what was most real in my impressions and in my opinions.[117]

If Beaumont informed Tocqueville in a summary way about the works that appeared on the United States, the author went forward alone and scarcely consulted any books on America, with the exception perhaps of the book by Chevalier.[118]

The writing moved ahead at a good pace. In November 1833, Tocqueville thought he would finish the part devoted to the institutions of the United States (what now constitutes the first part of the first volume of this edition) before the first of January 1834, and at one moment had the idea of publishing the first volume before the second.[119]

This plan was abandoned, and Tocqueville buckled down immediately to writing the second part, which little by little increased to an extent beyond what the author had foreseen. In addition, the part devoted to the American political institutions was reviewed and corrected several more times and, before being completed, required the aid of several collaborators.

Even as he worked relentlessly on his book, Tocqueville helped Beaumont with the writing of his.[120] Their collaboration continued throughout

---

117. Tocqueville to Duvergier de Hauranne, 1 September 1856, *OCB*, VI, pp. 332–33.

118. It is possible that he knew about several letters by Chevalier published in the *Revue des deux mondes*. See volume II, p. 898 of this edition and *OC*, VIII, 1, pp. 176, 202–3. Moreover, Tocqueville read Basil Hall's book during the crossing. He does not seem to have consulted *Society in America* by Harriet Martineau.

119. Remember that the *Democracy* of 1835 was published in two volumes.

120. The collaboration of Tocqueville on Beaumont's novel probably dated from the first moments of its development. In the manuscript of *Marie*, concerning the plan of the novel, this note is found in Tocqueville's handwriting:

Plan./
   It involves portraying a man such as he often becomes after great revolutions, whose desires are always beyond his capacities (but there must not be any ridicule, that is to say, that the one you want to portray really has a great soul, a remarkable

the whole following year, in Paris and in Sarthe. The influence of Tocqueville on the writing of *Marie* is difficult to measure. Beaumont's manuscripts bear the trace of conversations and of comments by Tocqueville, but the small number of available manuscripts does not allow us to assess the true extent of his influence.[121] Beaumont consulted his friend about certain passages of his book and even at the last moment asked for his opinion about certain fragments that were too reminiscent of Chateaubriand.[122]

---

spirit, but he aims higher than the humanity of his time); a man who, never content with his lot, has an exaggerated picture of human happiness in this world, and who, reaching the point of seeing his errors and discerning what dose of happiness life can really present, has become incapable of obtaining it and has become unsuited to society. He then looks hard and calmly at himself; convinced that he would not be able to attain the first goal of his desires, no longer capable of feeling the pleasure of reaching another one, he withdraws into the wilderness without passions, without despair, with the serenity of a strong soul that judges the greatness of its misfortunes and submits.

Perhaps here you would need a rapid and oratorical recapitulation of the reality of the things of this world and of the impossibility that he, who sees things as they are, but who has found them better in his imagination, finds of submitting . . .

You must not have him attempt love in Europe. He reconnects with love in America as to a plank of salvation, and still he misses it . . . (YTC, CIX, and *OC,* VIII, 1, p. 131).

121. In the margins of the manuscript of *Marie,* there are comments by Tocqueville, written in pencil. The latter particularly pointed out unfortunate similarities to Atala: "You cannot close your eyes to the fact that this has a great deal of similarity with Atala" (vol. II, p. 136 of *Marie*); "Here again you have to be careful about father Aubry. Perhaps I am wrong. Think about it" (vol. II, p. 151 of *Marie*); "Again, be careful here of Atala" (vol. II, p. 156 of *Marie*).

122. Thus this note from Beaumont meant for Tocqueville that is found in the manuscript of the novel:

Note for Tocqueville.

There are two passages that are reminiscent of Chateaubriand despite all the efforts that I have made to avoid it. They are at page 6 and 20. Here I am giving the passages of Chateaubriand so that you can see if it is possible to leave mine:

"The reverie of a traveler is a kind of fullness of heart and blankness of mind that allows you to enjoy your whole existence at peace. It is by thinking that we disturb the felicity that God gives us; the soul is peaceful, the mind is restless. (See *Voyages,* t. 6, p. 112.)

"I went from tree to tree, to the right and to the left indiscriminately, saying to myself: here no road to follow, no cities, no narrow houses, no presidents, republics,

At the beginning of the year 1834, Tocqueville hired an American living in Paris, Francis Lippitt,[123] to help him in the compilation of the documents that he brought back from the United States. At the house of the author's parents, Faubourg St. Germain, Lippitt compiled books and brochures, newspaper clippings and diverse documents.

Theodore Sedgwick, another American whom Tocqueville contacted when he still needed information about the United States, but whom he did not hire, seems to have played a more important role. His journal bears the traces of several interviews with Tocqueville that would exercise a clear influence on several points of *Democracy*.[124]

Once the writing of the principal part of the work was finished (only the last chapter of the second part was missing), Tocqueville had a copy of his manuscript made and circulated. In this way his brothers and his father, Gustave de Beaumont, and Louis de Kergorlay read the quasi-totality of the work. A few passages were read aloud at the evening gatherings of Madame Ancelot.[125]

----

kings." (See *Essai historique sur les Révolutions*, t. 2, p. 417, YTC, CIX and *OC*, VIII, 1, p. 145.)

123. See note a of p. 84.

124. Sedgwick met Tocqueville in the offices of the American delegation to Paris and pointed out several books that could be useful to him. His journal for the months of November and December 1833, of January and February 1834, refers several times in succession to Tocqueville (pp. 28, 29, 32, 79, 85, 98). See Sedgwick, Theodore III. Paris journal, volume 3, November 1833–July 1834, pp. 80–81, 85. Sedgwick family papers, Massachusetts Historical Society.

On 20 January 1834, for example, Sedgwick indicated that Tocqueville found that "Russia and the United States [. . .] were the only powers which presented an avenir [a future]. Both are aggrandizing—the others are stationary or diminishing" (pp. 80–81).

You find on p. 85 (Friday, 24 January 1834): "Either this day or the day before went with Tocqueville over to the legation and show [*sic*] him the books there which might assist him." On p. 98 (8 February 1834): "Tocqueville called about 11 for more information about the États-Unis." With the kind permission of the Massachusetts Historical Society.

Tocqueville also counted on the collaboration of two other American residents in Paris: Edward Livingston, head of the American representation in Paris, and Nathaniel Niles, secretary of the delegation.

125. See *OC*, VIII, 1, p. 141, and Madame Ancelot, *Un salon de Paris, de 1824 à 1864* (Paris: Dentu, 1866), p. 79. Did Guerry, a friend of Beaumont, read part of the manu-

When Édouard, on 15 June, wrote to his brother to share his *observations critiques,* only the revision of the second part remained to be done in order to complete the work. Tocqueville worked on the revision during the month of July, striking out a great deal and in some places retaining only one out of three pages of the initial draft. The same month, he contacted the publisher, Charles Gosselin, who committed to publishing the text in November. He planned a printing of five hundred copies.

On 14 August 1834, Tocqueville left Paris for the château de Gallerande, in Sarthe, and there joined Beaumont. The two friends spent their days hunting and making final corrections on their texts.

Once the work was finished, a title remained to be found.

In 1833 the book by Tocqueville and Beaumont had been announced with the title *American Institutions and Mores.*[126] Once Beaumont's project became differentiated from that of Tocqueville, the latter, in March 1834, announced to Senior the publication of a book on "American institutions."[127] Beaumont kept the term "American mores." In July, at the time of Tocqueville's arrangements with his publisher, the treatise on American institutions received the title "The Dominion of Democracy in the United States";[128] in a perhaps later note announcing the publication and contained in the drafts of the first part, we find "The Dominion of Democracy in America," while a first version of the same announcement mentioned "The Dominion of Democracy in the United States." In mid-October,

---

script? The jacket that contains the chapter on the point of departure and the one that contains the chapter on the social state bear this comment: "The copy has been sent to Guerry."

126. Tocqueville gave a very similar title to Sparks. Letter of 30 August 1833, YTC, CId.

127. *Correspondence and Conversations of Alexis de Tocqueville with Nassau William Senior* (London: H.S. King and Co., 1872), I, p. 2. In his prologue to *Marie* (p. viii), Beaumont echoes the original title of the joint work and declares: "M. de Tocqueville described the institutions; I myself tried to sketch the mores."

128. "G[osselin] asked me what the title of the work would be. I had only lightly considered it, so that I was quite embarrassed. I answered, however, that my idea was to title the book: *The Dominion of Democracy in the United States.* Since then I have thought about it, and I find the title good. It expresses well the general idea of the book and puts it in relief. What does my judge say about it?" *OC,* VIII, I, p. 141.

with the book in proofs, the publisher wrote to the author to ask him the title of his book. That is when Tocqueville chose *Democracy in America.*[129]

In the *Courier Français* of 24 December 1834,[130] Léon Faucher announced the publication of the work and reproduced a few passages from *Democracy in America.* The text appeared with this title in January 1835.[131]

The Reception of *Democracy*

If it is true that the workers in the print shop had shown Tocqueville's book particular attention and interest, the dazzling success of the *Democracy* was no less totally surprising to its author.

Tocqueville thought that the recent political tension with the United States would not fail to increase interest in and curiosity about the American continent and could therefore create a favorable situation for the success of the *Democracy.* But readers seem to have been attracted immediately by something far beyond the simple effect of timeliness. Moreover, if the indemnity affair—indemnities that the Americans had demanded from the French since the Napoleonic period—could be profitable to Tocqueville in France, such was not the case in America, where the publication of the *Democracy* was delayed until 1838.[132]

The appearance of the *Democracy* was unanimously acclaimed. Chateaubriand, Lamartine, Guizot, and Royer-Collard never tired in their praise. Very few publications met its appearance with silence. The reviews

129. Letter of 18 October 1834, copied in CVh, 2, pp. 55–56: "We do not have the title of your work, and I forgot yesterday to ask you about it. We cannot set the pages without the title."

130. Léon Faucher, "Democracy in the United States, by M. Alexis de Tocqueville (unpublished)," *Courier français,* 358, 24 December 1834.

131. On the 23rd, 27th, or 31st of the month, depending on the sources.

132. This is the opinion of Jared Sparks in his letter of 6 June 1837 to Tocqueville (YTC, CId). Sparks had contracted with a publisher in Boston for the preface and notes of an American version of the *Democracy.* He would abandon the project when he learned of the imminent appearance of another edition.

of Salvandy[133] and Sainte-Beuve[134] alone were enough to consecrate the author.[135]

"Not one of the chapters of this book," wrote Sainte-Beuve, "fails to testify to one of the best and most assured minds, to one of those minds most appropriate for political observation, a field in which we find so few striking and solid strides since the incomparable figure of Montesquieu."[136] The name of the great *légiste* also appeared from the pen of Salvandy who, in the *Journal des débats*,[137] proposed for *Democracy* the subtitle "The Spirit of American Laws."[138]

Among the number of discordant voices, the following can be cited:

> It is with a very particular predilection that this author offers for the admiration of the peoples of Europe a republic in which are found three colors, one color who are the masters, two other colors; a country of tri-

---

133. Narcise-Achille de Salvandy, "Democracy in America," *Journal des débats*, 23 March and 2 May 1835.

134. Charles-Augustin Sainte-Beuve, "Alexis de Tocqueville. De la démocratie en Amérique," *Le temps*, 7 April 1835. The first one to be astonished by the good reception of the work, Tocqueville wrote to Sainte-Beuve the next day:

> Allow me, Sir, to place even more importance on something other than on the judgment that you have made of the American democracy, that is seeing the relationship that has been established between us continue and become more frequent. I cannot keep from believing that there are many points in common between us and that a sort of intellectual and moral intimacy would not take long to prevail between you and me, if we had the occasion to know each other better (letter with the sole comment "Wednesday morning" [8 April 1835], with the kind permission of the Institut de France, Collection Spoelberch de Lovenjoul).

135. On the last day of March, Gosselin asserted to the author: "But it seems that you have created a masterpiece" (Letter to Beaumont, 1 April 1835, *OC*, VIII, 1, p. 151). The second edition was published in June, and the third at the end of the year. The fourth and fifth date from 1836. The sixth was published the following year, and the seventh in 1839.

136. *Le temps*, 7 April 1835.

137. *Journal des débats*, 23 March 1835.

138. *Le semeur* noted: "Either we are very wrong, or M. de Tocqueville greatly studied Montesquieu before studying America" (4, no. 9 [4 March 1835]: 65–68, p. 65). The commentaries of the entire French press agreed on the point. *Le national de 1834*, on 7 June 1835, described the text as "a work whose high level will be felt by all those who meditate on the current state of society in Europe, and on the future that is in store for it."

colored humanity in which the red men who are the natural masters find themselves being exterminated by the white men who are the usurpers; in which the Black men are sold jumbled together with animals in the public square. A touching example of equality, admirable evidence of independence that it is currently stylish to take as the model in Europe, to see as the standard for true perfectibility![139]

American readers, for their part, downplayed certain critical observations of the author about American society,[140] but would acknowledge the impartiality of the work and particularly its clear superiority over the commentaries of English travelers.

Foreign publications did not spare compliments. The English found in Tocqueville an abundance of arguments against the American republic[141] and recalled in reviews the precarious character of the experiment.[142] The *London and Paris Courier* of 14 January 1836 asserted on its part: "Much, indeed, has been written by Englishmen respecting America, and a good deal by visitants from the continent of Europe. But with the solitary exception of the *Démocratie en Amérique*, by M. de Tocqueville, nothing absolutely has been written by a foreigner which approaches to an accurate delineation of our political organization."

When, in December, the *Moniteur du commerce* mentioned "this excellent book that everyone has known and judged for a long time," the remark

139. *Gazette de France*, 3 and 13 February 1835. The passage quoted is found in the issue of 3 February.

140. For example, the review in *American Quarterly Review*, 19, March 1839, pp. 124–66.

141. See *Blackwood's Edinburgh Magazine*, 37, no. 230 (1835): 758–66. The commentary of the *Atheneum* is particularly critical: "rational, at times, even to dullness [. . .] a dislike of its ambitious style—its reduction of everything to theory—and its over-arrogant aim at uniting the sentenciousness of Montesquieu to the florid description of the Comte de Ségur" (394, 16 May 1835, p. 375). In a letter of 6 June 1837 (YTC, CId), Jared Sparks informed Tocqueville that the English reviews that mention the passages against democracy in Tocqueville's work had been reproduced in American publications, and that, in his opinion, this fact might diminish the desire for a quick translation of *Democracy*.

142. Among the English critiques, that of John Stuart Mill stands clearly apart. Tocqueville wrote to him, "You are [. . .] the only one who has understood me entirely" (Letter of 7 December 1835, *OC*, VI, 1, p. 302). Mill's commentary had been published in the *London Review* 30, no. 2 (1835): 85–129.

did not seem exaggerated. *Democracy* was in fashion, and the Académie des sciences morales et politiques ratified the public's interest with the Montyon prize, which bestowed on the author twelve thousand francs.

For its part, the publication of *Marie, ou l'esclavage aux États-Unis*[143] brought a success in no way inferior to that of *Democracy.*[144] Between 1835 and 1842, there would be five editions of the novel by Gustave de Beaumont. It would fall afterward, and very wrongly, into oblivion. Its reception was generally warm, though measured, although the *Quarterly Review* did not hesitate to declare it "the most interesting [book] that has ever yet been published on the subject of American society and manners by a native of the European continent."[145] Francisque de Corcelle wrote the review for the *Revue des deux mondes.*[146]

The principal failing of the book was proclaimed immediately. *Marie* had the peculiarity of being a novel and a social commentary at the same time. As such, it did not succeed in satisfying either those who love theoretical works, who preferred the *Democracy* by far, or those who read novels. The author of the review in the *Journal des débats*[147] saw this correctly when he wrote:

> There are two books in [the] book. That is its failing perhaps. The large public that wants to be amused is always afraid that it is being instructed. The rare public that seeks instruction fears being interested and moved. The readers of M. de Beaumont are indeed exposed to this double danger. He teaches the most frivolous. He captures, carries away, touches the most unsentimental and the coldest. The whole of American society is brought to life in this work that is so true that I dare not call it a novel; that is so

143. *Marie, ou l'esclavage aux États-Unis, tableau des mœurs américaines.* Paris: Charles Gosselin, 1835. 2 vols.

144. Beaumont's novel appeared in Brussels in 1835. It was translated into Spanish in 1840 and republished in 1849, and translated into Portuguese in 1847. An abridged edition was published in Germany in 1836. The second French edition dates from 1835, the third from the following year, the fourth from 1840, and the fifth and last from 1842.

145. *Quarterly Review* 53, no. 106 (1835): 289.

146. Francisque de Corcelle, "De l'esclavage aux États-Unis," *Revue des deux mondes,* 4th series, 6, 1836, pp. 227–46.

147. *Journal des débats,* 6 December 1835.

clothed in the richest and most intense colors of the imagination that I cannot call it a treatise."

Shortly after the publication of *Marie,* Beaumont abandoned the plan for a second part (announced in the notice).[148] Two years later, when he was writing *Irlande,* he seemed to care so little about his novel that he wrote to Tocqueville: "My book is my great and only passion, even more than yours is for you; I am not doing a second book, it is the first; and I am afraid of missing the mark, although I am full of zeal."[149]

England and the Second *Democracy*

Tocqueville had begun the writing of a book on America with the intention, no matter how unhelpful it might be, of making himself known for the purpose of a political career. His friend Blosseville had even used the opportunity of his review of the *Democracy* to assert, "Such books should open the way to the parliamentary tribune."[150]

But in March 1835, Tocqueville was not thinking so much about the career of a politician as about profiting from the extraordinary reputation that the appearance of his book had just given him. If the *Democracy* had not yet opened the doors of the Chamber of Deputies, it had earned him the friendship of a few prominent individuals who were going to play an important role in the writing of the second part of his book. They were Jean-Jacques Ampère, Royer-Collard, with whom Tocqueville was going to begin a profound and determinant intellectual relationship, and Corcelle.

Beaumont, Kergorlay, and Édouard de Tocqueville would form the principal trio of critics of the manuscript of the second part of the *Democracy.* The text would as well, here and there, bear the imprint of Ampère and Corcelle.

At the beginning of the year 1835, Tocqueville worked on the writing of

---

148. *Marie,* I, p. iii.
149. Letter from Beaumont to Tocqueville (15 July 1837?), *OC,* VIII, 1, p. 209.
150. *L'écho français,* 11 February 1835.

a report on pauperism[151] and planned a new journey to England. When Tocqueville and Beaumont were at the point of making important personal and professional decisions, the two friends crossed the Channel.[152]

What changes had taken place during the last two years? Was the English aristocracy capable of resisting the advance of democracy? Such were the questions that Tocqueville and Beaumont asked themselves. Their first observations concerned a strong tendency toward centralization. The point was important, and Tocqueville recognized the necessity of speaking about it in the second part of *Democracy*.[153] John Stuart Mill, Lord Minto, and Henry Reeve confirmed his impressions on this subject,[154] but it was Nassau W. Senior above all who, on the occasion of two long conversations, gave him the most detailed arguments on centralization.

> Senior tells me: The Bill for Reform of the Poor Laws is not only a bill of social economy, but is above all a political bill. Not only does it cure the plague of pauperism that torments England, but also it gives to the aristocracy the most fatal blow that it could receive. [. . .] The law has centralized the administration of the poor law; and armed with this principle, the government, to enforce the law, has appointed a certain number of commissioners or central agents who have full power in this matter in all the parishes of England. These commissioners traveled through the territory and, in order to kill the local influences that had to be centralized,

151. "Mémoire sur le paupérisme," *Mémoires de la Société académique de Cherbourg,* 1835, pp. 293–94. It is impossible to indicate the precise reason for the writing of this work, which was inspired by the work of Villeneuve-Bargemont, *Économie politique chrétienne,* and which will be mentioned again elsewhere. Tocqueville had promised a second part that he never wrote.

152. The notes and drafts of *L'Irlande* allow us to follow in a precise way the journey of Beaumont and Tocqueville to England and Ireland in 1835. Tocqueville and Beaumont left Paris on 21 April, reached Calais on the 22nd and were in London on the 24th, where they lodged at the Ship-Hotel. The next day they went to the opera to see *Anna Bolena.* They began their visits in the English capital, continuing until 24 June. From 7 July to 9 August, they visited Ireland. On the latter date, Beaumont left to visit Scotland and Tocqueville went to Southampton. On the 18th he crossed the Channel. On 23 August he was again in Cherbourg.

153. *Voyages en Angleterre, Irlande, Suisse et Algérie, OC,* V, 2, p. 49. There is also a long, unpublished conversation with Sharp (YTC, CXIb.1). Beaumont's notes contain other unpublished conversations.

154. *Ibid.,* pp. 49, 52–54.

united ten or fifteen or twenty parishes into a single administrative circumscription, that they called a union. [. . .] These unions have already
been established in this way in two thirds of England, and before long
they will be established everywhere. [. . .] The Bill transfers, as you see,
the administration of the poor law from the aristocracy to the middle
classes. And then, there you are, central administrations organized over
the whole kingdom, central administrations composed of citizens, set into
motion, not by the local aristocracy, but indeed by the central power—
and this is serious not only for granting to the central power and to the
municipal administration called a union the power to govern England,
but above all for organizing in the country an administrative power
whose center is the government and for which the justices of the peace,
prin[cipal] and essential elements of the aristocracy, are not the agents.
[. . .] I note that the result of this is, above all, that the aristocracy is
stripped to the profit of the *central power;* for the *guardians of the poor,* as
they are constituted, are agents chosen it is true by the middle class, but
essentially subordinate even in this choice and in their action to the will
of the commissioners of the government.[155]

155. YTC, CX.
Tocqueville explained the success of the democratic principle in England in this way:

General idea.
    Tocqueville said yesterday [the note is in Beaumont's hand]:
    Two elements in English society.
    The Saxon principle
    and the Norman principle.
    The Saxon principle—democratic.
    Everything that is democratic in English society dates from this time. The orga-
nization of the parish and the county—the hundreds—the representation of communal interests . . . The Normans came, which threw a layer of absolute power over
this democratic base.
    Combination of these two elements in English society.
    For a long time, the Norman fact prevailed, without destroying the Saxon prin-
ciple, which just hid and submitted.
    Today the awakening of this principle which predominates over the Norman fact
and which particularly showed itself to be superior to its adversary the day the Reform
Bill passed in Parliament (YTC, CX).

But the centralizing movement and the rise to power of the middle classes did not, for all that, imply revolution and the destruction of the aristocracy. As Tocqueville had already observed during his journey of 1833, England was very far from a revolution. At the time of this new journey, Mill confirmed his judgment:

Revolution./
[In the margin: Why no chances of violent revolution.]

I doubt that a quick and violent revolution is happening among us. All classes are very steady and know too well how to defend themselves. They are also enlightened, used to fighting and to yielding when necessary. Moreover, there is an obstacle here to general innovations and to the impulses of reform. Reform never strikes a great number of matters at once. Since everything in this country is in bits and pieces, you can only change one thing at a time, and with each change, you only attack a small number of interests. For the same reason, you excite only a small number of passions. It is rare to proceed by the path of general reform because there are few things to which you can apply the same principle in England. (J. S. Mill).[156]

From the time of his first journey to England, Tocqueville had shared this sentiment: in that country, the poor man aspires to occupy the place of the rich and can sometimes succeed. "The French spirit is to want no superior. The English spirit is to want *inferiors.*"[157]

156. YTC, CX. Cf. *OC,* V, 2, p. 47.
157. *Voyage en Angleterre, OC,* V, 2, p. 47.
Mill explained the same idea in this way:

Aristocracy in the mores./
    Aristocratic spirit./
    Spirit of equality, aristocratic spirit.
    [In the margin: The Whig who attacks the Lord honors him as a rich man.]
    Here you often find allied two sentiments that at first view seem contradictory; these are a very intense hostility toward the aristocracy and an infinite respect for the aristocrats. The privileges of the Lords are attacked, but you cannot believe what consideration there is for them as individuals, so that you see the most ardent democrat rant with an extreme exaggeration against the abusive power of an oligarchic minority and bow with humility before the Count or the Marquis of X, solely because

In *Social and Political State of France,* Tocqueville would note that the difference between the French aristocracy and the English aristocracy consists in the fact that only the English one is truly an aristocracy, that is to say a tiny part of society, having "qualities" such as blood, intelligence, money, culture, etc. In France, on the other hand, the sole quality of the aristocracy is birth, which makes it impossible for anyone to attain it. In the second part of *Democracy,* this idea would force Tocqueville to give full attention to the process of administrative centralization, inasmuch as it is the first and most powerful effect of the democratic revolution, and is capable of making its effects felt even on the English aristocracy.[158]

For Beaumont there was a totally different discovery. He who so vigorously defended the cause of the Indians and Blacks was struck by the situation of the Irish. He noted regarding them:

Moral—History.

I do not believe that the murder of nations is more legitimate than that of individuals.

I declare that in covering the history of peoples, when I see the victors and the vanquished, I can very much admire the conqueror whose value shines before my eyes; but all the sympathies of my heart are for the conquered country. As long as a subject people exists, as long as it has not entirely disappeared under conquest, I make wishes for it, I nourish hopes, I have faith in its instincts of nationality; and in my dreams I see it shaking off the chains of servitude and cleansing itself of tyranny in the blood of its tyrants. If one day I learn that this people has expired with glory, I remain faithful to it, and I weep on its tomb. For to pardon a crime because

---

he is a Count or Marquis. Here we work hard to abolish privileges, but we respect those who possess them; we find that they are clever, because they have reached the goal that everyone targets. No one has the idea of blaming them for taking a place that is due not to morality and justice, but to their privileged position. For in English society, everything is privilege (Jh. Mill, 19 May. London). (Beaumont's note. YTC, CX).

158. During their journey, which took them to several large cities of England, Tocqueville and Beaumont observed the terrible effects of industrialization, which they could already have done in part during the journey to the United States. On this subject, they knew about the book by J. B. Say and about the treatise by Villeneuve-Bargemont. The famous description of Manchester is found in *Voyage en Angleterre, OC,* V, 2, pp. 79–82.

it is successful is an odious and despicable action. It is a despicable action, commonly done.

(30 January 1836).[159]

The two friends divided subjects. To Tocqueville, America; to Beaumont, England,[160] and Beaumont intended to devote a book to the Irish cause. In 1837, he went to England for a second time and visited Ireland in order to complete his research on site. *L'Irlande, sociale, politique et religieuse* would be published in 1839.[161]

The manuscript of Beaumont's book contains criticisms in Tocqueville's hand. That of Tocqueville would be considered attentively by Beaumont before its publication. Their collaboration continued to include innumerable exchanges of ideas.[162]

The press gave *L'Irlande* a reserved reception, but the book received the approbation of English intellectuals. In October 1839, John Stuart Mill wrote to Beaumont:

159. YTC, CX.

160. Tocqueville explained this point in a letter of 5 May 1835 to his father. André Jardin, *Alexis de Tocqueville,* p. 229.

161. The second and third editions saw the light of day in 1839; the seventh and last, in 1863. The English translation appeared in 1839. The English translator took care to eliminate several passages critical of England; he summarized and altered a certain number of Beaumont's arguments.

162. Beaumont noted this idea of Tocqueville:

Brittany. Ireland.

Remarkable parallel between the province of Brittany in France and Ireland.

—Same origin.—Celtic population.

—Similarity in mores and in social state.

—Small farms in the two countries. Small-scale farming.

—Absence of luxury and no idea of material well-being; no efforts to gain it. Miserable hut in which the family pig grunts as a table companion.

—Eminently religious population, faithful—but not enlightened.

—Brittany is only separated by a river from Normandy where the taste for material well-being is so developed. In France we have England and Ireland in Normandy and Brittany.

—There is the similarity.

But differences—The Irishman is merry and fickle—The Breton melancholic and stubborn.

(Shouted by Tocqueville)

22 December (YTC, CX).

I hardly know how to express to you the degree of my estimation of your book, in as measured terms as a sober man likes to use in expressing a deliberate judgment—but this I may say, in the confidence of being rather within than beside the mark—that the book not only displays a complete and easy mastery over all the social elements and agencies at work in Ireland, over the whole great period of Irish history and Irish civilization; but that it also manifests a degree of clear comprehension and accurate knowledge of the far more complicated and obscure phenomena of *English* society, never before even *approached* by any foreigner whom I know of, and by very, *very* few Englishmen.[163]

Like *Marie, L'Irlande* would be only a half-success. This second book was also the last. At one time pushed by Tocqueville to become interested in Austria, Beaumont would cease all important intellectual work following the death of one of his sons.

The Second *Democracy*

On 26 October 1835, Tocqueville married Mary Mottley, thus formalizing a relationship that was already several years old. Beaumont and Kergorlay were witnesses.

In 1828 or 1829, at Versailles, Tocqueville had met this English woman of bourgeois origin who lived with her aunt, Mrs. Belam.[164] The correspondence of Tocqueville and his wife has almost totally disappeared. The documents that remain attest to a certain discomfort, in the family as well as among a few friends, about a marriage judged disappointing.

On 15 November the couple went to Baugy, near Compiègne, close to Édouard de Tocqueville. That is where Alexis began to work on the second part of *Democracy*. His first plan was to divide the third volume into two parts:

---

163. Letter of J. S. Mill to Beaumont, 18 October 1839, YTC, CIe.

164. Concerning Mary Mottley, few things are known. See Antoine Rédier, *Comme disait Monsieur de Tocqueville*, pp. 122–28, and André Jardin, *Alexis de Tocqueville*, pp. 50–56.

Two great divisions.
1. Influence of democracy on ideas.
2. Id. on sentiments.[165]

Then the outline became complicated:

Division to do perhaps.

Effects of democracy
1. On thought.
2. On the heart.
3. On habits.[166]

Little by little, the work took on its definitive form:

Plan of the second volume.
Sociability, sympathy, mores becoming milder, susceptibility, p. [blank] and dignity. All of that comes easily after individualism in order to demonstrate the types of relationships that can exist in a democratic society despite egoism.

The citizen, patriotism, the master and the servant, master and farmer, master and worker. All of that again comes easily after the introduction because it is principally individualism that modifies the relationships of all those people with each other.

Father, son, wife, woman, good morals. The mind is prep[ared] by what precedes to enter into families. Moreover, individualism again greatly modifies the relationships of those people.

Tone, manners, conversation, monotony of life, gravity, vanity. The chapters relating to the family have prepared the mind to descend easily into the small details of the social existence of the Americans.

Honor, ambition, revolution, military spirit, conquests, armies, perhaps a chapter that summarizes. These chapters, which perhaps I have not placed in the relative order that they should have vis-à-vis each other, elevate the mind of the reader and end the book on a high level.

There are three chapters that remain, and I do not know where to place them: Respect that is attached to all conditions, lack of susceptibilities, sentiment of dignity.

165. YTC, CVa, p. 6.
166. YTC, CVa, p. 6.

I believe, however, that they come after sociability./
Where to place equality—slavery?[167]

Individualism, which opened the book, would finally be placed at the beginning of the second part of the third volume. The idea of speaking again about slavery remained only a plan, but the principal ideas of the whole work were already present. The work of writing, with several interruptions,[168] would take four years (from November 1835 to November 1839).

In January 1836, following a division of family properties due to the death of his mother, Alexis received the château de Tocqueville and the title of count that came with it, although he would always refuse to use the title. He appeared hardly inclined in the beginning to spend much time in a cold and damp château. Various renovations that his wife would have done would be necessary before Tocqueville decided to live there for long periods. Many pages of the second *Democracy* would see the light of day there, sometimes under the critical eye of Corcelle, Beaumont, Kergorlay, or Ampère, regular guests at the château.

A large part of the first section of the book seemed finished when, in July, after the marriage of Gustave de Beaumont with Clémentine de Lafayette, Tocqueville and his wife left for Baden, in Switzerland. In November they returned to Baugy.[169] There, Tocqueville worked daily from 6:00 to 10:00 o'clock in the morning. The writing went well. Only one thing

---

167. YTC, CVa, pp. 28–30.

168. During their journey to England, Mill had begged the French visitors to contribute to the *London and Westminster Review* by writing articles on France and the United States. In 1836, Tocqueville sent Mill a first and only article on the social and political state of France before and after the Revolution, which was meant to be an introduction to a series of publications on France. "Political and Social Condition of France," *London and Westminster Review*, 25, 1836, pp. 137–69 (reproduced in *OC,* II, 1, pp. 33–66). The similarity between the first paragraphs of the article and the chapter on the philosophical method of the Americans is clear and enlightening.

169. The long stays of Tocqueville at Baugy make it difficult to measure the influence exercised by Édouard.

was missing for the author: "a good *instrument of conversation,* I needed you [Beaumont] or Louis."[170]

During the following months, Tocqueville took careful note of all the information, of every conversation that could be useful for his work. He interviewed Thiers on the problem of centralization, Kergorlay on the army, Charles Stoffels on literature. He also met an American named Robinson and a number of other people.[171]

From mid-July to mid-August the Corcelles stayed at Tocqueville. At the end of July, the Beaumonts joined the small set. In the intellectual circle thus constituted by Tocqueville only one member was missing, Louis de Kergorlay, whom he did not hesitate to call his master.[172]

In January 1838, at Baugy, Tocqueville reviewed the chapter on honor. March and April were devoted to the question of centralization, to the army and to the preparation of the fourth and last part of the book. On 15 May,

---

170. Letter of 22 November 1836 to Beaumont, *OC,* VIII, 1, p. 174. The same month, Tocqueville wrote to Kergorlay in very similar terms: "I feel the importance of this second work, which will find criticism wide-awake and will not be able to take the public by surprise. So I want to do my best. There is not a day so to speak that I do not feel your absence. [. . .] There are three men with whom I live a bit every day, Pascal, Montesquieu and Rousseau. I miss a fourth who is you." Letter of 10 November 1836, *OC,* XIII, 1, p. 418.

171. He found the time to think about the continuation of his work on pauperism and asked Beaumont to bring him all available information about the savings banks and the English pawnshops. There is a list of questions from Tocqueville for Beaumont in YTC, CXIb.13. Cf. *OC,* VIII, 1, pp. 185, 191, 193, 196, and 200. He did not find the time to choose some unpublished excerpts from *Democracy* for the *London and Westminster Review* as Mill had requested (*OC,* VIII, 1, p. 187).

Tocqueville also dedicated his efforts to two bids, one to enter the Chamber of Deputies in November and a second to get himself elected to the Académie française. These two attempts failed. Entry to the Académie des sciences morales et politiques was seen by Tocqueville only as a consolation prize that would make his entry to the Académie française more difficult. He would enter there on 24 December 1841. He published, in addition, two letters on Algeria, on 23 June and 22 August 1837, in *La presse de Seine-et-Oise.*

172. "For, after all, and without giving a useless compliment, I believe you are my master." Letter to Kergorlay, 4 September 1837, *OC,* XIII, 1, p. 472. Cf. Kergorlay's answer, 30 September, *ibid.,* p. 477. Alexis was then working on the chapters on good morals. In September, he laid down the foundations of the chapter on American manners.

Corcelle and Ampère were present for a reading of the chapter on revolutions. In July, August, and September, the last chapters took their definitive form. The last two chapters on centralization and the idea of equality grew in length and purpose. The only thing remaining was to revise the chapter on the philosophical method of the Americans and the one on general ideas.

On 19 October 1838, Tocqueville would write to Beaumont: "I have just written, my dear friend, the last word of the last chapter of my book."[173]

The revision of the whole book would occupy all of the following year. Kergorlay, who spent most of the autumn at Tocqueville [the village], came to help the author who worked to revise the first part of his book. Unsatisfied, Tocqueville had burned it.

In January 1839, Tocqueville read part of his manuscript to Chateaubriand, but confessed to Beaumont that he did not think he would be able to advance much in the revision of the whole book before the month of March. The work stretched until mid-November, the date when Tocqueville returned to Paris with a copy of his manuscript in order to have it read and approved a final time by Beaumont and Kergorlay.

Tocqueville had spoken to his correspondents about a book on "American manners." The title that tempted Tocqueville was: "The Influence of Equality on the Ideas and the Sentiments of Men." The book appeared in April 1840, however, with the same title as that of 1835.

The reception of the second part was not as unanimously laudatory as what had accompanied the appearance of the first volume. More theoretical and less descriptive, the second *Democracy* found a public little prepared for the reading of a philosophical work of such length and ambition. The criticism that appeared in this regard in *The Examiner* reflected the tone.[174]

Hunt's Merchant Magazine noted: "In our deliberate judgment, it is the most original, comprehensive, and profound treatise that has ever appeared regarding our republic."[175] The prestigious *Blackwood's Edinburgh Maga-*

---

173. *OC,* VIII, 1, p. 321.
174. *The Examiner,* 17 May 1840.
175. *Hunt's Merchant Magazine,* 3 July 1840, p. 443.

zine, acknowledging that the second part did not merit the unconditional approval given to the first, added: "It is a superstructure of theorizing without any base to support it."[176]

If favorable reviews were many—and in particular the one of John Stuart Mill must be pointed out[177]—the same judgment was found just about everywhere in the English press: "too great a disposition to theorize,"[178] or again: "Perhaps this method of generalizing facts is occasionally pushed too far."[179] The verdict seemed definitive. Tocqueville's contemporaries seemed little inclined to accept this *philosophy of democracy* that the author was offering to their understanding. The appearance of the first volume of the *Democracy* had elicited nearly seventy commentaries; that of the second brought forth scarcely half that number.

In the months immediately following the publication, Tocqueville wrote little and so to speak made no allusion to his book. Elected deputy on 2 March 1839, he intended to concern himself more with his new duties.

"Nothing has been and remains more contrary to my tastes than to accept the condition of author in this world," he wrote to Royer-Collard in 1839, explaining:

> That is entirely contrary to my way of seeing what is desirable in this life. So my firm wish, after finishing this book and whatever its fate, is to work for myself and to write no longer for the public, unless a very important and *very natural* occasion presented itself, which is not probable. I am pushed to this determination not only by the desire to set myself apart from authors strictly speaking, but also by a certain pride that persuades me that I will find no subject as grand as the one that I have just treated and that, consequently, I would be demeaning myself by taking up the pen again.[180]

176. *Blackwood's Edinburgh Magazine* 48, no. 298 (1840): 463–78, p. 463.
177. *Edinburgh Review* 145 (1840): 1–25.
178. *Dublin University Magazine* 16, no. 95 (1840): 544–63, p. 563.
179. *The New York Review* 7, no. 13 (1840): p. 234.
180. Letter to Royer-Collard, 20 November 1838, *OC,* XI, p. 74. Cf. the letter to Corcelle, 25 June 1838, *OC,* XV, 1, pp. 100–101.

The occasion would not present itself before 1852, when, forced to abandon all political activity following the coming to power of a person of whom he highly disapproved, Tocqueville decided to take up the pen again in order to remind the French of the events that had brought them liberty. That was the beginning of work on *L'Ancien régime et la révolution.*

II[181]

To Understand the Revolution

"Since, like Perrin Dandin, I am driven by the desire to judge without the power to do so, I need to keep going."[182] Tocqueville's identification with the main character of the *Plaideurs* can probably be shared by an entire generation of judges who, following the revolutions of 1789 and 1830, had to devote themselves to finding a new equilibrium for society. As Ortega remarked, the solution to the political question was above all an eminently personal problem for Tocqueville and his contemporaries.[183] Ultras and liberals, 1789 and 1793, aristocracy and democracy, liberty and equality, monarchy and republic, these were so many opposites that required a choice to be made.

In this context, where to place the author of *Democracy?* The question continues to be asked.[184] The intellectual conversation has refined his thought and made his adjectives more nuanced; that does not prevent the labels from remaining very close to those of 1835. Tocqueville is in turn called a conservative, a liberal, a conservative liberal, a liberal conservative, a Burkean conservative, a liberal *despite himself,* a liberal aristocrat, a strange liberal—in short, the confusion about his work continues.

For it to be otherwise would be difficult. The *Democracy,* which sets forth as well one of the most fascinating interpretations of the French Revolution

181. The interpretation I am offering here is necessarily limited.

182. Letter from Tocqueville to the Countess de Pisieux, 5 July 1833, YTC, CIf.

183. "Tocqueville y su tiempo," in *Meditación de Europa,* Madrid. (Revista de Occidente, 1966), pp. 135–41.

184. There are dozens of books devoted to Tocqueville's thought, but I limit myself to pointing out those of Jean-Louis Benoît, *Tocqueville moraliste* (Paris: Honoré Champion, 2004); Luis Díez del Corral, *El pensamiento político de Tocqueville* (Madrid: Alianza Editorial, 1989); Jean-Claude Lamberti, *Tocqueville et les deux démocraties* (Paris: PUF, 1983); Pierre Manent, *Tocqueville et la nature de la démocratie* (Paris: Julliard, 1982); Nicola Matteucci, *Alexis de Tocqueville* (Bologna: Il Mulino, 1990); the brief introduction to the abridged edition of *Democracy* by Dalmacio Negro (Madrid: Aguilar, 1971); and Sheldon S. Wolin, *Tocqueville Between Two Worlds* (Princeton: Princeton University Press, 2001).

ever made, attempts indeed, by using the American "mirror,"[185] to create a political philosophy capable of explaining (and producing) revolution and counter-revolution.[186]

"Placed in the middle of a rapid river," writes Tocqueville, "we obstinately fix our eyes on some debris that we still see on the bank, while the torrent carries us away and pushes us backward toward the abyss."[187] Amid this dangerous revolutionary turbulence, there is a pressing need to find a path and a bedrock somewhere; and this is what forces the author to seek an explanation for the Revolution from the very first pages of the *Democracy*.[188] If we must await *L'Ancien régime et la révolution* for Tocqueville to give a fuller and more detailed interpretation of the great historical upheaval, it is no less true that the principal lines of his theory of revolution are already present in the two *Democracies*.

Tocqueville's point of view can be somewhat roughly summarized by asserting that for him the French Revolution was neither a true revolution, nor a *French* revolution.

The Revolution was not a true revolution because authentic revolutions take place at the level of mentalities, ideas, beliefs, habits of the heart, of

185. "I did not want to do a portrait, but to present a mirror," Tocqueville confessed to Ampère. Jean-Jacques Ampère, "Alexis de Tocqueville," *Correspondant* 47 (1859): p. 322.

186. "The Revolution that reduced to dust the aristocratic society in which our fathers lived is the great event of the time. It has changed everything, modified everything, altered everything." I, p. 690, note c.

Not by chance did Tocqueville choose as a matter of fact to publish the chapter on revolutions separately, before the second volume. The chapter on revolutions undoubtedly constitutes the axis around which the whole book turns; cf. Alexis de Tocqueville, "Des revolutions dans les sociétés nouvelles," *Revue des deux mondes,* XXII, 1840, pp. 322–34.

187. I, p. 514, note o. Cf. I, p. 12, note r.

188. The unpublished texts of this edition tend to erase a certain number of differences between *Democracy* and *L'Ancien régime et la révolution.* Tocqueville is an author who treats a very small number of subjects that he considers and studies many times in each of his writings, while keeping them all interrelated, like the chapters of the same book. So in a way we have something of a *Democracy* that extends from 1835 to 1859.

all the things that, using once again the meaning of the word *mores*,[189] he designates by the term *mœurs*.[190]

Every historical change necessarily begins, according to Tocqueville, at the level of ideas. In turn, the latter transform and are transformed by the social and material conditions of a society. These, according to Tocqueville, constitute the social state of a society.[191]

> Political societies are not made by their laws, but are prepared in advance by the sentiments, beliefs, ideas, the habits of the hearts and minds of the men who are part of them, and by what nature and education have made those men. If this truth does not emerge from all parts of my book, if it does not in this sense constantly bring readers back to themselves, if it does not point out to them at every moment, without ever blatantly displaying the pretension of teaching them, the sentiments, ideas, mores that alone can lead to prosperity and public liberty, the vices and errors that on the contrary inevitably push prosperity and public liberty away, I will

189. The whole body of the ideas and the mores of a people form its character, and on this point Tocqueville recalls Montesquieu:

≠There is indeed in the bent of the ideas and tastes of a people a hidden force that struggles with advantage against revolutions and time. This intellectual physiognomy of nations, which is called their character, is found throughout all the centuries of their history and amid the innumerable changes that take place in the social state, beliefs and laws. A strange thing! What is least perceptible and most difficult to define among a people is at the same time what you find most enduring among them. Everything changes among them except the character, which disappears only with nations themselves≠ (I, p. 344, note y).

190. "So by this word I understand the whole moral and intellectual state of a people" (I, p. 466).

Montesquieu in fact remarks: "The customs of a people in slavery are part of its servitude; those of a free people are part of its liberty." *De l'esprit des lois,* book XIX, ch. XXVII, *Œuvres complètes* (Paris: Pléiade, 1951), II, p. 382. For Tocqueville, the mores of a people constitute nearly its *entire* liberty.

191. Tocqueville did not believe that he had resolved the question of knowing if ideas are the result or the cause of the social state. "Is the social state the result of ideas or are the ideas the result of the social state?" II, p. 748, note f. Ideas will act, alternately, as effect and as cause.

not have attained the principal and, so to speak, the only goal that I had in view.[192]

The social state in turn shapes the political state.[193] (Today we would speak about society and state.) This explains why, in France as in the United States,[194] the people are sovereign, for if the French do not live in a condition of liberty strictly speaking, they have already learned to think of themselves as equals.[195] The material and intellectual conditions of a society modify and are changed by ideas and sentiments; and once the social state has been changed, the legal and political institutions adapt little by little.

192. Letter to Corcelle, 17 September 1853, *OC*, XV, 2, p. 81. This is so true that a change in the law (the abolition of slavery, for example) is useless and even negative if it is not accompanied by a change in the intellectual world (the idea that the Black man is henceforth equal to the white man). In this sense Tocqueville can say that, if he had the power, he would not immediately decide on the abolition of slavery. He was convinced that, without a previous radical change in the mores, the situation of the free Black would probably be worse than the situation of the slave.

193. This term reappears from time to time (II, p. 1262, note b).

With this supposition, Tocqueville places himself at the origin of the modern social sciences. If his work attracts sociologists as well as historians, critics, and political scientists, it is because in his work the classic elements of political philosophy are beginning to separate and take form as sociology, history, or the political sciences. In the same way, if *Democracy,* and especially the second part, has not sufficiently gained the attention of researchers in the political sciences, it is undoubtedly because it requires the latter to go beyond the position of historians of ideas in order to be political philosophers for a time.

194. In the United States, the dogma of the sovereignty of the people is not an isolated doctrine that is attached neither to the habits nor to the ensemble of dominant ideas; you can on the contrary envisage it as the last link in a chain of opinions that envelops the entire Anglo-American world. Providence has given to each individual, whatever he is, the degree of reason necessary for him to be able to direct himself in the things that interest him exclusively. Such is the great maxim on which in the United States civil and political society rests: the father of the family applies it to his children, the master to his servants, the town to those it administers, the province to the town, the state to the provinces, the Union to the states. Extended to the whole of the nation, it becomes the dogma of the sovereignty of the people.

[≠So the republican principle of the sovereignty of the people is not only a political principle, but also a civil principle.≠] (I, p. 633)

195. II, p. 1033, note 1. Did Tocqueville participate in Beaumont's plan to present an essay on the influence of laws on mores and of mores on laws for the Montyon competition in 1830? See YTC, CXIb6.

"In the long run, political society cannot fail to become the expression and the image of civil society." Sovereignty of the people is born as public opinion.[196]

That is why the true revolution took place largely before 1789, accelerated by a change that was above all European in nature,[197] that began with the Reformation, continued with Bacon and Descartes, and then gave the Enlightenment universal ideas, applicable in all periods and to all parts of the world.

"[The Revolution] was just a violent and rapid process by the aid of which the political state was adapted to the social state, facts to ideas, and laws to mores,"[198] Tocqueville will repeat in the *Ancien Régime*. It was nothing more than the abrupt adaptation of the real to the ideal, or more precisely to an abstract philosophy formed from theories that had not been refined, called into question, or confirmed by political practice.

The Old Regime wanted to ignore social changes and, by preventing the slow adaptation of the political to the social, had created the conditions for its own downfall. The revolutionaries, removed from the political practice that would have led them to test and adapt their theories to the material and social circumstances of France, tried for their part to make the legal and political world conform to abstract and universal principles that were far from the social state.

A difficulty unfailingly appears, however. If the Revolution indeed had as its point of departure an intellectual movement that predated it, the vast changes whose arrival it marked cannot be completed as long as differences exist between the social and political ideas of the French and their legal and

196. "What is the sovereign rule of public [v: national] opinion to which all the English of the last [century (Ed.)] constantly declared that you must submit, if not a still obscure notion of the democratic dogma of the sovereignty of the people?" II, p. 1033, note e.

197. "The French Revolution, in my eyes, is a *European* event, and everything that happened in the same period in Europe, principally in Germany, interests me nearly as much as what [took (Ed.)] place among us" Letter to Charles Monnard, 5 October 1856. With the kind permission of the Bibliothèque cantonale et universitaire de Lausanne.

198. *L'Ancien Régime et la Révolution, OC,* II, 1, p. 66.

social institutions.[199] This raises the following question: can the Revolution end? Are France and Europe condemned to an eternal cycle of revolutions and counter-revolutions? How can you stop a revolution that is constantly unfolding?

Tocqueville observed again in 1850:

> Our country is calm and more prosperous than we could believe after such violent crises. But confidence in the future is lacking and although sixty years of Revolution have made this feeling of instability less prejudicial to social progress and less painful to us than it would be to other peoples, it has nonetheless very unfortunate results. This great nation is entirely in the state of mind of a sailor at sea or a soldier in the field. It does as little of the work of each day as possible, without worrying about tomorrow. But such a state is precarious and dangerous. Moreover, it is not peculiar to us. In all of continental Europe, except Russia, you see society in labor and the old world finally falling into ruins. Trust that all the restorations of old powers that are being made around us are only temporary happenings that do not prevent the great drama from following its course. This drama is the complete destruction of the old society and in its place the creation of I do not know what human fabric whose form the mind cannot yet clearly see.[200]

Such are the circumstances surrounding Tocqueville's project of creating a new political science that would succeed in explaining the past and the

---

199. Tocqueville noted that Napoleon, not wanting to give democratic political laws to France, had agreed to a body of social laws much more democratic than American laws and thus, very unwillingly, had accelerated the arrival of democracy. For the same reason, the primacy of the social over the political, Tocqueville asserted: "I would believe the future of liberty more assured with a government that would have many political rights and few civil rights than with a government that would have few political rights and many civil rights." (II, p. 1230, note p).

200. Letter to Edward Everett, 15 February 1850, Massachusetts Historical Society. The preface to the 1848 edition of *Democracy* (II, p. 1373) repeats the same idea.

"There is only a single [revolution], a revolution always the same across various fortunes and passions, that our fathers saw begin and that, in all probability, we will not see end" *Souvenirs, OC,* XII, p. 30.

future, the old regime and the new, or, to reuse his terminology, aristocracy and democracy.[201]

"There is a country in the world," we read in the introduction to the first volume, "where the great social revolution that I am speaking about seems more or less to have reached its natural limits; it came about there in a simple and easy way, or rather it can be said that this country sees the results of the democratic revolution that is taking place among us, without having had the revolution itself."[202]

Tocqueville intends to determine whether American society offers the sole example in the world of an exceptional situation in which the ideal easily shapes the real, in which the social state coincides with the political state, in which the entire world is "a malleable material that man turns and shapes as he wills."[203] On this strange continent, it seems that the dream of the French and of the Europeans can be realized without the need for a revolution,[204] and that their abstract, rational, and theoretical principles are real, concrete, and inductive there.

But, if the exceptional physical and intellectual conditions of America alone explain the success of democracy, there is no hope that Europe could ever know the democratic state without continual revolutions.

The first impressions of the United States, especially of the West, confirm the existence of an America that does not need revolution. The American frontier, the great wilderness that extends to the Pacific Ocean, offers a space in which ideas transform reality without encountering obstacles and

201. Tocqueville's two books thus answer the desire to elucidate first the new regime and the Revolution (*Democracy*), then *L'Ancien Régime et la Révolution*.

202. I, p. 27. The same idea appears, for example, at the beginning of the second volume: "The Americans have a democratic social state and a democratic constitution, but they have not had a democratic revolution. They arrived on the soil that they occupy more or less as we see them. That is very important." II, p. 708.

203. To Ernest de Chabrol, letter of 9 June 1831, YTC, BIa2.

204. "The Americans seemed only to have carried out what our writers had imagined; they gave the substance of reality to what we were busy dreaming" *L'Ancien Régime et la Révolution, OC*, II, 1, p. 199.

in a transparent way, so to speak.[205] Tocqueville will perfect and complicate his theory as his journey moves ahead, but the pioneer of *Democracy* especially announces the democratic man described at length in the second volume of the work.

"Everything that is good and evil in American society is found in such relief [in the West] that you would say it was one of those books published in large type to teach children to read," already notes the traveler in a letter to his mother. "Everything there is jarring and exaggerated. Nothing has yet taken its definitive place. [. . .] In the west no one has been able to make himself known or has had the time to establish his credit. Consequently democracy, without this final barrier, appears with all of its distinctive characteristics, its fickleness, its envious passions, its instability and its restless character."[206]

The pioneer is, necessarily, occupied entirely by the search for a minimum of commodities. Withdrawn from the rest of the world, isolated in his cabin, his only concern is the yield of his field on which his family's subsistence depends. Each of his movements is dictated by the necessity of the survival and the protection of his small world. His generosity toward the stranger who appears at his door is nothing more than the fruit of calculation; it comes from reason and not from the heart; it is an investment.[207] Obsession with material well-being, individualism, and interest well understood define, apparently accidentally and temporarily, life on the frontier, but they run the risk of becoming permanent conditions for the citizen of every democratic country.

So if North America does not need revolution, it is because the process of adaptation and struggle among philosophy, social state, and political condition is non-existent. Ideas and reality coincide; reason appears covered only by the clothing of the present. In order to be free and happy, it is enough for the American to want to be so.[208] No need for struggle or confrontation, no need for the complex interpenetration, necessarily slow, of

205. The first thing that the pioneer does is to clear his property, to chop down the trees, to open up his view. The first symbol of civilization is the absence of trees.
206. Letter of 6 December 1831, YTC, BIa1, pp. 54–56, and *OCB*, VII, p. 90.
207. II, p. 1289.
208. I, p. 276.

ideas with habits and laws; nowhere are there ruins, the past, and signs of the past. "The Union . . . profits from the experience of the old peoples of Europe, without being obliged, like them, to make use of the past and to adapt the past to the present; it is not forced, as they are, to accept an immense heritage handed down by its fathers, a mixture of glory and misery, of national friendships and hatreds."[209]

The United States has the privilege therefore of being able to enjoy the results of European thought without being encumbered by the heavy baggage of history. "In America," notes Tocqueville, "society seems to live from day to day, like an army in the field."[210]

Tocqueville comments on the uncommon position of the New World, which anchors it in an eternal present: "≠For the American, the past is in a way like the future: it does not exist. He sees nowhere the natural limit that nature has put on the efforts of man; according to him what is not, is what has not yet been tried.≠"[211]

The pioneer is, in a way, the last link in an historical chain that begins in Europe and ends in the American *wilderness,* where he inhabits a present

---

209. I, p. 369.
"For him [the American] the possible has hardly any limit. To change is to improve; he has constantly before his eyes the image of indefinite perfection that throws deep within his heart an extraordinary restlessness and a great distaste for the present" (II, p. 935, note b).
210. I, p. 331.
211. I, p. 643, note n.

The American inhabits a land of wonders, around him everything is constantly stirring, and each movement seems to be an improvement. So the idea of the new is intimately linked in his mind to the idea of the better. Nowhere does he see the limit that nature might have put on the efforts of man; in his eyes what is not is what has not yet been attempted (I, p. 643).

Tocqueville specifies about the frontier:

In whatever direction you looked, your eye searched in vain for the spire of a Gothic church tower, the wooden cross that marks the road, or the moss-covered doorway of the presbytery. These venerable remnants of ancient Christian civilization have not been carried into the wilderness; nothing there yet awakens the idea of the past or of the future. You do not even find places of rest consecrated to those who are no more. Death has not had the time to reclaim its sphere or mark out its field (II, p. 1346).

without limit.[212] In the American West the principal characteristics of society are also missing: "The new states of the West already have inhabitants; society still does not exist,"[213] writes Tocqueville. In the West, the only common ideas and the sole bond between the most immediate past and the present are found in the weak intellectual network created by the mail and newspapers.[214]

Is the destiny of democratic man to inhabit a world without social exchanges, an eternal cycle of death and emptiness, such as the American forest or the ocean,[215] a definitive present? You could think so. The pioneer clears an opening in the forest, cuts down the trees and in his field leaves the trunks that he does not take the trouble to uproot. He builds himself a cabin and marks with a subtle trace of history the woods that surround him. As soon as he disappears, nature takes back its domain. Then nothing more remains of the passage of man except "a few remnants falling into rot that in a bit of time will have ceased to exist."[216]

Is this the price to pay in order to live in a world without revolution?

---

212. The Indians find themselves in a quite similar situation. Beaumont writes about them: "Focused on the necessity of the present and fears of the future, the past and its memories have lost all their power over them" (*Marie*, II, p. 297). Citing Clark and Cass, Tocqueville repeats the same idea: "He [the Indian] easily forgets the past, and is not interested in the future." I, p. 527, note 7. The same thing can be said about the Black race, which has left its history in another continent.

213. I, p. 86.

214. "The only historical monuments of the United States are newspapers. If an issue happens to be missing, the chain of time is as if broken: present and past are no longer joined." I, p. 331.

215. *A Fortnight in the Wilderness*, II, p. 1339.
Also "rivers . . . are roads that respect no trails." II, p. 1353.

216. *Journey to Lake Oneida*, Volume II, p. 1301.

Sometimes man moves so quickly that the wilderness reappears behind him. The forest has only bent under his feet; the moment he passes, it rises up again. It is not unusual, while traveling through the new states of the West, to encounter abandoned dwellings in the middle of the woods; often you find the ruins of a cabin in the deepest solitude, and you are amazed while crossing rough-hewn clearings that attest simultaneously to human power and inconstancy. Among these abandoned fields, over these day-old ruins, the ancient forest does not delay growing new shoots; the animals retake possession of their realm; nature comes happily to cover the vestiges of man with green branches and flowers and hastens to make the ephemeral trace of man disappear. (I, p. 461).

The question is posed in these terms. So the new political science that Tocqueville imagines and develops in *Democracy in America* is going to have as its first objective man's return to society and to history.[217]

The Theoretician of History

It is undoubtedly difficult to find a period when the question of history attracted more attention than in the first half of the nineteenth century. Uncertainty about the future forces minds to look back: you had to try to place the Revolution in history, to assimilate it as the past, to understand it. In order to do this, liberals, like conservatives, court Clio. Politicians make history and write it; poets and novelists who claim to be historians capture imaginations and, at times, get involved in politics; all offer the world an uncommon example of political practice and political theory.

While Burke and the conservatives explain that the French Revolution was nothing more than an aberration that, far from history, broke its rhythm, the liberals concentrate their efforts on demonstrating the inevitable character of history. At first view, Tocqueville places himself on this side because he seems to follow the liberal theory of the inevitability of history and particularly the historical interpretation of Guizot.

There is no qualifying term that has been more often associated with Tocqueville, the historian-politician, than that of fatalist. Certain critics have spoken about determinism[218] or providentialism; others have sought reasons of a pedagogic nature in his use of the idea of the inevitable movement toward equality of conditions.[219] How can Tocqueville, who hates all forms of fatalism, who speaks of liberty as an almost holy thing, who asserts

---

217. Ampère said with a great deal of wisdom about *Democracy:* "In short, at the core of the whole book stirs the question of time" (*Correspondance avec Ampère, OC,* XI, p. xvi).

218. Jean-Claude Lamberti, *La notion d'individualisme chez Tocqueville* (Paris: PUF, 1970).

219. Marvin Zetterbaum, *Tocqueville and the Problem of Democracy* (Stanford: Stanford University Press, 1967), p. 17. Cf. I, pp. 10–12, note q.

that the goal of his book is to reveal very clearly that "whatever the tendencies of the social state, men can always modify them and ward off the bad tendencies while appropriating the good,"[220] how can this same Tocqueville talk at the same time about an "irresistible movement" of democracy and make it a "providential fact"?

At once simple and complex, his answer consists of saying that inevitability concerns only the arrival of social equality. With him, and with a certain number of others, this fact receives the name democracy. In the sense that, in the long run, social equality produces legal and political equality, Tocqueville's theory can be called deterministic, and the arrival of democracy is inevitable. Once intellectual equality is proclaimed (each man has the same faculties for attaining truth as another), the transformation of social and political conditions is no more than a question of time; in terms of Tocqueville's thought, it is inevitable and even desired by God.

Once you eliminate all secondary causes, Tocqueville continues, all the revolutions in the world have been and are made for the sole purpose of increasing or decreasing equality, which is the foundation or the generating fact of the revolutionary motor. Revolutions have always consisted and still consist of setting the rich against the poor and the poor against the rich.

But this determinism, which is as much logical as historical, is in no way incompatible with the passionate defense of liberty, because, for Tocqueville, the movement toward equality is independent of the development of liberty. The latter is the true human element of historical change. In other words, the inevitability of democracy, understood as the adaptation of the political state to the social state, does not determine the historical evolution of liberty: equality is as good an ally of despotism as of liberty.

So the presumption of attaining equality of social and political conditions makes the classical typology of political regimes meaningless. Whether it takes the form of public opinion or whether it presents itself as it is,

220. I, p. 694, note m.

sovereignty of the people makes possible only two types of regimes: the republican (or liberal) regime or the despotic regime, liberty or despotism. In the face of this alternative, it is man who chooses and not destiny that imposes.

This understanding of history, as Marx remarked, puts Tocqueville closer to Bossuet than to Guizot.[221] Like the bishop of Meaux, Tocqueville believes that all the facts of history obey a divine plan, the meaning of which escapes us, but one that men can predict and whose general tendencies they can discover.[222]

The action of man, says Tocqueville, always takes place within a narrow circle. It has no meaning if it is situated outside this space. Even if man is incapable of imagining what is going to follow, of reading the plans of Providence, he can, within the domain reserved to him, recognize a law of the evolution of history and of intelligence.

The final stage, that of equality, closes the cycle of history. At the beginning of history, man, isolated and savage, is equal to his fellows in barbarism. He has no need of government.

> There are few peoples who can do without government in this way. Such a state of things has never been able to subsist except at the two extremes of civilization. The savage man, who has only his physical needs to satisfy, counts only on himself. For the civilized man to be able to do the same, he must have reached the social state in which his enlightenment allows him to see clearly what is useful for him, and in which his passions do not prevent him from acting on it."[223]

So the absence of government and equality are found only at the two ends of civilization: "Savages are equal among themselves because they are

---

221. The Anglophile attitude of Guizot bothered Tocqueville, who was incapable of accepting that the model of the English revolution was applicable to France. These differences of opinion did not pass unnoticed. After the publication of the *Democracy* of 1840, Guizot wrote to his former student: "Why don't we think alike? I do not find any good reason." Roland-Pierre Marcel, *Essai politique sur Alexis de Tocqueville* (Paris: Félix Alcan, 1910, p. 319). Also see Aurelian Craiutu, *Liberalism Under Siege* (Lanham, Maryland: Lexington Books, 2003).

222. See Bossuet, *Discours sur l'histoire universelle,* part III, section II, entitled: "The revolutions of empires have particular causes that princes must study."

223. *Voyage,* pp. 89–90.

all equally weak and ignorant. Very civilized men can all become equal because they all have at their disposal analogous means to attain comfort and happiness."[224]

For Tocqueville, as we see, history is neither the progressive, rational, and necessary development of the idea of liberty, nor the advance, impossible to contain, of the middle classes, as Guizot thought. The author of *Democracy* notes a form of liberty appropriate to each period and each country.[225] Liberty understood in this way is therefore as ancient, as Madame de Staël calls it, as it is modern, as Benjamin Constant describes it. So post-revolutionary liberty is not and cannot be that of the Old Regime.[226] In the same way, a form of despotism corresponds to each period.

The novelty of Tocqueville's theory is to assert that in order to reach the final stage of history, the point at which true equality and liberty coincide, the aristocratic stage is absolutely necessary as an intermediate moment. If "it is in losing their liberty that men acquired the means to reconquer it,"[227] true liberty always requires passing by way of servitude.

This constitutes a first way to put face to face the Old Regime and democracy, to make aristocracy an inevitable moment of history, and then to move beyond it. If, in the state of barbarism, men cannot become civilized

224. "Mémoire sur paupérisme," republished in *Commentaire,* 30, 1985, p. 633.

225. "I would regard it as a great misfortune for humankind if liberty, in all places, had to occur with the same features." I, p. 513.

226. Guizot had, however, distinguished between two forms of liberty: 1. Liberty as independence of the individual, who has only his own will as law. This is the barbaric and anti-social liberty of the childhood of nations, natural liberty. 2. Liberty as independence from any will that is different and contrary to reason. Moral liberty or liberty by right. The survival of society demands the submission of all individuals to a common rule that cannot exist if natural liberty subsists to its full extent. *Journal des cours publics de jurisprudence, histoire et belles-lettres* (Paris: au bureau du journal, 1821–1822), I, pp. 248–52, lecture 23.

227. "I ≠{think that it is in losing their liberty that men acquired the means to reconquer it}≠ that it is under an aristocracy or under a prince that men still half-savage have gathered the various notions that later would allow them to live civilized, equal and free." II, p. 879, note f.

as long as they are equal,[228] it is aristocracy that, by creating a class free to dedicate itself to the works of the mind, can invent the general and universal ideas that will lead to its own destruction and to the appearance of democracy (understood as equality of conditions).

The first step toward equality was taken in the Middle Ages when peoples began to travel, to enter into contact with each other, to imitate each other. Each nation little by little lost confidence in its particular laws and in its own organization; the idea of rules common to everyone occurred to men. France placed itself at the head of these intellectual, moral, and political changes, even if the impulse that gave them birth was more European than specifically French.

If the course of history follows the change in mentalities which is, in turn, the effect and the cause of the social state,[229] and if the latter little by little transforms the political state, that is to say, laws and institutions, then it is not surprising that Tocqueville devotes the first pages of *Democracy* to philosophy.

A Philosophy of Action

Perhaps the word *philosophy* is not totally accurate when applied to the theory of Tocqueville, who said that he had a horror of philosophy and who wrote: "Philosophy is in fact only the complete exercise of thought separate from the practice of action."[230]

Tocqueville's very principle is to draw everything out of himself. He does the work of a researcher and does not neglect brochures, reports, collections of laws. But the list of works consulted in the writing of *Democracy in America* does not include books of philosophy.[231]

---

228. "If nations had begun with democratic government, I doubt they would ever have become civilized." I, p. 332.

Even industry follows this general law of evolution. The manufacturing aristocracy is the equivalent of the landed aristocracy. II, p. 980, note b.

229. Economic conditions are part of the social state, and Tocqueville judges them to be of secondary interest.

230. II, p. 739, note c.

"For no one is less philosophical than I, who preaches to you." *OCB,* VI, p. 370.

231. See Volume II, pp. 1377–95.

Tocqueville does not like philosophy. He calls it the "essence of all gibberish,"[232] and a "voluntary torment that man consented [cf. note 242 below] [. . .] to inflict on himself."[233]

The matter is clear from the beginning of the work of writing the introduction to *Democracy*. "The author of this work," we read in a draft, "wanted to write a book of politics and not of philosophy."[234]

The imperatives of the history of France forbid Tocqueville, as politician and as the author of *Souvenirs*, to forget the practical side of political theory. Thought separated from action is philosophy. For Tocqueville, reflection joined to practice constitutes the nature of what he calls his "political science."[235] This does not prevent him, however, from falling into the trap of the celebrated aphorism of Pascal: "To mock philosophy is truly to philosophize."[236]

The philosophic aspect of Tocqueville's thought appears in the form of anti-positivism.[237] "≠In all human events," he writes, "there is an immense portion abandoned to chance or to secondary causes that escapes entirely from forecasts and calculations.≠"[238]

Tocqueville's certitude about an impenetrable divine plan and his religious beliefs prevent him from falling into the sensual philosophy of the period and into positivism.[239] He accepts the existence of absolute ideas as

232. Draft of a letter to Le Peletier d'Aunay, 8 November 1831, YTC, BIa2.

233. To Charles Stoffels, 22 October 1831, YTC, BIaı, and *OCB*, VII, pp. 83–84. See *OCB*, VI, p. 370.

234. YTC, CVk, ı, p. 73.

235. Tocqueville thinks that Thomas More would not have written *Utopia* if he had been able to change the government of England. He also thinks that the Germans do philosophy because they cannot generalize their ideas in politics (II, p. 727, note b).

236. Pensée 513 (Ed. Lafuma). Cited by Luis Díez del Corral, *El pensamiento político de Tocqueville*, p. 42.

237. The predilection of Tocqueville for Plato is symptomatic: "I consider him a poor politician, but the philosopher has always appeared to me superior to all others and his aim, which consists of introducing morality as much as possible into politics, admirable." *Correspondance avec Kergorlay, OC*, XIII, ı, p. 41. Cf. *Correspondance avec Beaumont, OC*, VIII, ı, p. 292.

238. I, p. 574, note b.

239. "There is nothing so difficult to appreciate as a fact." I, p. 343.

"The world is a book entirely closed to man." I, p. 383, note m. Also see I, p. 574.

well as their unknowable character.[240] A first conclusion results: every system, every man that claims to discover absolute truth is, for that reason alone, in error; you can advance only hypotheses.

> There is no man in the world who has ever found, and it is nearly certain that none will ever be met who will find the central ending point for, I am not saying all the beams of general truth, which are united only in God alone, but even for all the beams of a particular truth. Men grasp fragments of truth, but never truth itself. This admitted, the result would be that every man who presents a complete and absolute system, by the sole fact that his system is complete and absolute, is almost certainly in a state of error or falsehood, and that every man who wants to impose such a system on his fellows by force must *ipso facto* and without preliminary examination of his ideas be considered as a tyrant and an enemy of the human species.[241]

If absolute truth existed, the constant, complex interconnections of the elements of the motor of history would cease. The consequence of this provisional nature of all intellectual study is doubt, which Tocqueville considers characteristic of man, and in particular of philosophy.[242]

On this point, he summarizes his thought in this way for Charles Stoffels:

---

240. "Of all beings, man is assuredly the one best known; and yet his prosperity or miseries are the product of unknown laws of which only a few isolated and incomplete fragments come into our view. Absolute truth is hidden and perhaps will always remain hidden." I, p. 263.

We again see the imprint of Pascal in this attitude of Tocqueville: "The final step of reason is to recognize that an infinite number of things surpass it. It is weak only if it does not go far enough to know that." Ed. Lafuma, pensée 373.

241. "The great Newton himself resembles an imbecile more by the things that he does not know than he differs from one by the things that he knows." II, p. 715, note f.

242. "I consider this doubt as one of the greatest miseries of our nature; I place it immediately after illnesses and death. But because I have that opinion of it, I do not understand why so many men impose it on themselves without cause and uselessly. That is why I have always considered metaphysics and all purely theoretical sciences, which serve for nothing in the reality of life, as a voluntary torment that man consented to inflict on himself." Letter to Charles Stoffels, 22 October 1831, YTC, BIa1 and *OCB*, VII, pp. 83–84.

When I began to think, I believed that the world was full of demonstrated truths; that it was only a matter of looking carefully in order to see them. But when I applied myself to considering things, I no longer saw anything except inextricable doubts. [. . .] I ended by convincing myself that the search for absolute, *demonstrable* truth, like the search for perfect happiness, was an effort toward the impossible. Not that there are no such truths that merit the entire conviction of man; but be assured that they are very few in number. For the immense majority of points that are important for us to know, we have only probabilities, only approximations. To despair about this is to despair about being a man; for that is one of the most inflexible laws of our nature.[243]

The creator of an idea, Tocqueville also believes, is always more uncertain of its truth than his disciples. He knows its defects; he knows the elements that can invalidate its existence. But very few men in democratic times can devote their life to the search for great intellectual truths; and if they do so, they are very much required nonetheless to use general ideas to guide their conduct.[244] It follows that the best way to avoid absolute and excessively general ideas is to force each man to occupy himself with ideas, with thinking, with feeling his way, and: "when, tired of looking for what makes his fellows act, he [man] tries hard at least to untangle what pushes himself, he still does not know what to believe. He travels across the entire universe and he doubts. He finally comes back toward himself, and obscurity seems to redouble as he approaches and wants to understand himself."[245]

As this conviction about the absence of absolute, demonstrable truths becomes deeper with Tocqueville, it seems to impose its own logic on the

243. *Ibid.,* pp. 82–83.

244. "So general ideas are only means by which the aid of which men advance toward truth, but without ever finding it. You can even say that, to a certain extent, by following this path they are moving away from it." II, p. 728, note c.

245. II, p. 840, note v.

"There is no being in the world that I know less than myself. For me, I am constantly an insoluble problem. I have a very cold head, and a reasoning, even calculating mind; and next to that are found ardent passions that sweep me along without persuading me, mastering my will, while leaving my reason free." Letter to Eugène Stoffels, 18 October 1831, OCB, V, p. 422.

writing of *Democracy:* "You know that I do not take up the pen with the settled intention of following a system and marching at random toward a goal," he observes; "I give myself over to the natural movement of my ideas, allowing myself to be led in good faith from one consequence to another. The result is that, as long as the work is not finished, I do not know exactly where I am going and if I will ever arrive."[246] The rhythm of the book becomes in fact more and more staccato; the brief chapters of the second *Democracy* turn into [*ricordi,* Italian for "souvenirs"; reference to Machiavelli's *Ricordi.*] *thoughts,* almost as if the presentation of a theory without solution required a brief and fragmentary form of writing.

So Tocqueville's philosophic ideal is the man who is feeling his way, who judges himself to be incomplete and makes doubt his natural state, while the democratic ideal is the man who can change everything because he has a blind faith in reason and in the philosophic method.

Regarding himself, the author will note for example:

> I do not need to travel across heaven and earth to find a marvelous subject full of contrast, of grandeur and infinite pettiness, of profound obscurities and singular clarity, capable at the same time of giving birth to piety, admiration, contempt, terror. I have only to consider myself. Man comes out of nothing, passes through time, and goes to disappear forever into the bosom of God. You see him only for a moment wandering at the edge of the two abysses where he gets lost.[247]

Tocqueville does not, however, share the anti-rationalism of conservative theories. What he fears in democracy is not reason, but anti-rationality. Later he will blame the *philosophes* for the same thing: "Truly speaking, some of these *philosophes* adored human reason less than their own reason. Never did anyone show less confidence in common wisdom than those men."[248]

For Tocqueville, in contrast to Guizot, the rise of the middle classes is not the arrival of political reason, but of rational individualism, which in

---

246. Letter to Mill, 19 November 1836, *OC,* VI, 1, p. 314.
247. II, p. 840.
248. *L'Ancien Régime et la Révolution, OC,* II, 1, p. 306. We could say that Tocqueville fears that the men of democracies are being transformed into little *philosophes.*

the end equates with the absence of reason. The *philosophes* understood nothing more than the voice of individual reason. As for democratic man, he runs the danger of believing that he is following his own reason when he is only blindly obeying the opinion of the majority.

The best way to avoid excesses in the matter of general ideas, the predominance of thought separated from action, is to force men to enter into practice. That is the advantage of true democracy. It forces each citizen to occupy himself in a practical way with government and moderates the tendency to create the general ideas in politics that equality produces; it provokes uncertainty in this way.

Tocqueville fears in fact that history will pass from the total predominance of action, which is characteristic of barbaric peoples who know only the practice of politics, to the triumph of theory separated from all forms of practice.[249]

But criticism of philosophy is not just a matter of methodology; it does not consist solely of blaming philosophy for a lack of connection with practice. In the drafts of *Democracy* there is a detailed reflection on the birth of general ideas.

For Tocqueville, the attempt of democracies to seek general ideas in the domain of politics arises out of an unwarranted application of the method of Descartes and Bacon to matters for which those methods are not made;

---

249. And more especially, from a simplistic philosophy characteristic of an intermediate period that wants to explain everything with a single principle and that is embodied as much in the fatalism of the theories of democratic historians as in administrative centralization.

Simplicity of means in politics is a product of human weakness. Tocqueville wants men to be able to combine a large number of means to reach an end. According to him, beauty is not in simplicity of means, but in complexity, which is nothing more than imitating God, who creates with a multiplicity of agents and places "the idea of grandeur and perfection not in executing a great number of things with the help of a single means, but in making a multitude of diverse means contribute to the perfect execution of a single thing." II, p. 740, note d.

"Centralization is not at all the sign of high civilization. It is found neither at the beginning nor at the end of civilization, but in general in the middle." II, p. 799, note e. The idea of unity is appropriate to a middle state. The echo of Pascal and of multiplicity in unity is clear.

the attempt arises out of an extension of the presumption of rationality, foreseeability, and recurrence to matters that do not have these qualities.

That is especially dangerous in the case of equality. The lack of debate about the principle of equality (which is the principle *par excellence* since it comes down to the principle of identity) ends up by imposing a structure in which reason and confrontation are lacking. Aggravated, the individual mind kills reason and its relation to practice, and with it liberty and political confrontation.

The exaltation of individual reason can break the bond between ideology, social condition, and political organization, and lead to the immobility of the social system and ultimately to the end of history. For this reason, far into the second volume and once the foundations of his criticism of democratic thought have been explained, Tocqueville can declare that what he most fears in democracies is not revolutions, but apathy.[250]

When the tendency to create philosophical systems that are separated from practice becomes general, there is also the danger that theory will not find reality adaptable; it will become always more removed from action and more utopian, and will end up by taking the place of political reality; and men, tired of facing the difficulties of action, will take refuge in theory.[251]

In this case, political theory can little by little come to resemble a religion, a doctrine applicable to all individuals and all nations, because it has considered man in an abstract way and has studied his general political rights and duties in all periods and all countries.[252] The dream of reason lives

---

250. II, p. 1150, note x.

251. This is an idea that has a very important place in the explanation of the importance of intellectuals during the Revolution, but that already appears in *Democracy*. See II, p. 727, note b.

252. The French Revolution created a body of independent ideas that were easy to transmit. Tocqueville observes that "it formed, above all particular nationalities, a common intellectual country in which the men of all nations could become citizens." *L'Ancien Régime et la Révolution, OC,* II, 1, p. 87. He also asserts that the Revolution was a religious revolution because it developed a corpus of doctrines that, like a religion, can be applied indiscriminately to all men and to all peoples, because it considered man in the abstract, like all religions, and his general political rights and obligations. *Ibid.,* pp. 88ff.

outside of time, and when it coincides with the predominance of equality over liberty, it ends up by enclosing man within the solitude of his own heart:[253] "So each person withdraws narrowly into himself and claims to judge the world from there. . . . Since they [the Americans] see that they manage without help to solve all the small difficulties that their practical life presents, they easily conclude that everything in the world is explicable, and that nothing goes beyond the limits of intelligence."[254]

Democratic man is completely immersed in tasks of a practical type, because democracy takes him away from theory and confines his activities to the economic domain; he no longer believes in anything except his own reason. This tendency, combined with the search for material well-being, takes him away from political activity and predisposes him naturally to accept the opinion of the majority.

Tocqueville notes:

As citizens become more equal and more similar, the tendency of each blindly to believe a certain man or a certain class decreases. The disposition to believe the mass increases, and more and more it is opinion that leads the world. . . . In times of equality, men, because of their similarity, have no faith in each other, but this very similarity gives them an almost unlimited confidence in the judgment of the public; for it does not seem likely to them that, since all have similar enlightenment, truth is not found on the side of the greatest number. When the man who lives in democratic countries compares himself individually to all those who surround him, he feels with pride that he is equal to each of them; but, when he comes to envisage the ensemble of his fellows and to place himself alongside this great body, he is immediately overwhelmed by his own insignificance and weakness. This same equality that makes him independent of each one of his fellow citizens in particular, delivers him isolated and defenseless to the action of the greatest number.[255]

253. "Thus, not only does democracy make each man forget his ancestors, but it hides his descendants from him and separates him from his contemporaries; it constantly leads him back toward himself alone and threatens finally to enclose him entirely within the solitude of his own heart." II, p. 884.
254. II, p. 701.
255. II, p. 718.

America, Tocqueville also says, has escaped these problems for the most part, thanks to exceptional circumstances, the intellectual influence of England, and the strength of religion.

The unusual physical conditions of the Americans, which place them in a universe that is malleable and can be transformed at will, often allow them to avoid the intellectual tensions of European societies. An American who is not satisfied with his position can always leave his home and go to the West where he can easily create a new life for himself. That is how an idea easily transforms reality, and why the forces that resist that transformation are weak.

The intellectual influence of England serves to assure the general development of thought. Tocqueville observes that, strictly speaking, the Americans do not have a literature and an intellectual class, but he does not see that condition as necessarily peculiar to democracy. How can a democracy be intellectual if the example of the United States proves the opposite? Because the Americans find their ideas and their books in Europe, just like their philosophy and their religion. They put all of that into practice in the New World. The American intellectual class is found therefore on the other side of the Atlantic. The Americans are only the part of the English population that works on the conquest of America:[256] "I consider the people of the United States as the portion of the English people charged with exploiting the forests of the New World, while the rest of the nation, provided with more leisure and less preoccupied by the material cares of life, is able to devote itself to thought and to develop the human mind in all aspects."[257]

Thus, the United States forms the non-intellectual part of a European people and constitutes a society composed solely of representatives of the middle class. Aristocracy remains on the European shore. In this way Tocqueville connects theory and practice, while avoiding having the Amer-

256. American society depends therefore on the intellectual situation of England. It follows that during its formative years, democracy in the United States does not have the following ingredient necessary for social change: the production of new ideas.

257. II, p. 768. And more particularly of the middle class: "≠America forms like one part of the middle classes of England≠" II, p. 767, note f. Also see II, p. 805, note j.

icans serve as an example of the pernicious effects of democracy that his book announces.[258] The United States certainly does not innovate in philosophy, in literature, or in the aesthetic domain, but this situation is not due to the fact that the Americans belong to a democratic society, writes Tocqueville; the reason is that they devote themselves exclusively to business,[259] or again, that they are showing only the interests and faults of the middle class.

Tocqueville believes, however, in the existence of man's natural taste for things of the mind: "The mind of man left to itself leans from one side toward the limited, the material and the commercial, the useful, from the other it tends without effort toward the infinite, the non-material, the great and the beautiful."[260]

Within the American framework, it is not impossible that an educated and free class will come about, a class that, having the necessary time and money, will be able to devote itself to intellectual work, to encourage and promote literature and the arts.[261]

Religion, the last element peculiar to the American democratic situation, prevents the Americans from falling into the error of trying to apply the principles of rationalist philosophy to matters that are not suited to such principles.[262] For Tocqueville, philosophy is liberty, all that the individual discovers thanks to his own efforts; religion, which covers all that is accepted without discussion, is servitude.[263] Excess of the first leads straight to intellectual individualism and to a state of permanent agitation that opens onto anarchy. Religion, which becomes more and more necessary as philosophy develops, can, by its excessive character, lead to intellectual dogmatism and immobility.

---

258. Thus, in the case of America, the tension between aristocracy and democracy at the level of general principles also occurs, a mechanism that we will return to. Tocqueville needed England to explain how the American model combines democratic and aristocratic principles.

259. II, pp. 786–87, note p.

260. II, p. 769, note g. We see that here, too, Pascal is not far away.

261. II, p. 772.

262. In the intellectual world, the rivalry between religion and philosophy (authority/liberty) is a variant of the opposition aristocracy/democracy. See II, p. 711, note b.

263. II, p. 724, note s.

But even if that seems paradoxical at first glance, religion, precisely for this reason, is the necessary condition for man to be able to devote himself to practical works.[264]

"For me," declares Tocqueville, "I doubt that man can ever bear complete religious independence and full political liberty at the same time; and I am led to think that, if he does not have faith, he must serve, and, if he is free, he must believe."[265] So if religious beliefs place man in relative servitude, they enclose him in the circle within which he is able to exercise his reason; and, by limiting the action of his mind to the practical circle within which it must function, they force him into action and free his intelligence by reducing his dependence on the general ideas of the majority:[266]

> A religion is a power whose movements are regulated in advance and that moves within a known sphere, and many people believe that within this sphere its effects are beneficial, and that a dogmatic religion better manages to obtain the desirable effects of a religion than one that is rational. The majority is a [illegible word] power that moves in a way haphazardly and can spread successively to everything. Religion is law, the omnipotence of the majority is arbitrariness.[267]

264. "Man needs to believe dogmatically a host of things, were it only to have the time to discuss a few others of them. This authority is principally called *religion* in aristocratic centuries. It will perhaps be named *majority* in democratic centuries, or rather *common opinion*." II, p. 720, note p.

265. II, p. 745.

266. "During centuries of fervor, men sometimes happen to abandon their religion, but they escape its yoke only to submit to the yoke of another religion. Faith changes objects; it does not die." I, p. 485. Tocqueville fears in this sense that the opinion of the majority will someday become a cult.

267. II, p. 721, note r.

> Religion is an authority (illegible word) to humanity, but manifested by one man or one class of men to all the others, who submit to it. Common opinion is an authority that is not prior to humanity and that is exercised by the generality of men on the individual.
>
> The source of these two authorities is different, but their effects come together. Common opinion, like religion, gives ready made beliefs and relieves man from the unbearable and impossible obligation to decide everything each day by himself. These

In the context of these ideas, Tocqueville asks himself whether Catholicism is the religion that suits democratic times. He is convinced that Catholicism can be proved by the philosophical method of the eighteenth century.[268] But he needs to assure the reader that the multiplication of religions is not going to lessen the importance of religious ideas and of their relation to liberty. Otherwise, it would be impossible for religion to fulfill the limiting role that Tocqueville gives it. That approach produces a difficulty however: religion is accepted rationally, as philosophy, and not as religion; it is not the result of an act of faith. Only the idea, rather unjustified, that solely "minds of the second rank" will apply to religion the principles of the philosophy of Descartes (and this will above all be the case of Protestantism[269]), seems to save Tocqueville from a clear misconception in his explanations.[270]

The intellectual anarchy that you could think is the necessary result of the daily use of the Cartesian method is, on the contrary, more characteristic of periods of revolution than of those in which democracy reigns.[271] Reason, by definition majoritarian, in the end produces characters and opinions that coincide in a certain way.

----

beliefs were originally discussed, but they are no longer discussed and they penetrate minds by a kind of pressure of all on each (II, p. 720, note p).

268. All the American sects have a core of common ideas. I, pp. 472–73.

269. "I have always believed, you know, that constitutional monarchies would arrive at the republic; and I am persuaded as well that Protestantism will necessarily end up at natural religion." Letter to Ernest de Chabrol, 26 October 1831, YTC, BIa2.

270. Tocqueville speaks of a convention that checks the spirit of innovation at the doors of religion. This idea is the result of a personal reflection, but at the beginning of the second *Democracy* he notes: "if you look very closely, you will see that religion itself reigns there much less as revealed doctrine than as common opinion." II, p. 720. Therefore the foundations of religion are not religious, but philosophic, in the sense that the author gives to that word.

"The moral dominion of the majority is perhaps called to replace religions to a certain point or to perpetuate certain ones of them, if it protects them. But then religion would live more like common opinion than like religion. Its strength would be more borrowed than its own." *Ibid.*, note p.

271. II, p. 708, note t.

Here Tocqueville seems to find in democracy a reason for optimism that does not well fit the aristocratic vision that is sometimes imputed to him. In order for the intellectual anarchy that he believes is revolutionary to disappear, the majority of citizens must exercise their reason. But the author himself recognizes that the power that directs the mass will always be aristocratic because, as he says repeatedly, it is impossible for all men to have the time and leisure necessary to occupy themselves with works of the mind.

This way of seeing allows Tocqueville to avoid the eclecticism of Cousin. Eclecticism is the government of the middle class introduced to philosophy. The ideas of Tocqueville do not combine well with this philosophy of the *juste milieu*. But if Tocqueville's aristocratic nature pushes him to reject philosophic eclecticism, it does not prevent him from constructing a philosophy of the *middle (milieu)* that is his own. He places this principle of "life in the middle" between the two excesses of reason that in his view are represented by Heliogabalus and Saint Jerome.[272]

Here it was a matter of restoring man to history and society; now it is going to be a matter of restoring him to reason.

The Reign of Total Reason

In democracies, equality reaches and penetrates every aspect of life.[273] Equality of minds, equality of conditions and sovereignty of the people

272. See II, p. 960, note k, and p. 1281, note e.

273. When Tocqueville speaks about the existence of equality in America, he means the sentiment of not being inferior to anyone and not the equal division of wealth or power. In an interesting commentary on American equality, placed in travel notebook E and from which we can quote only an extract, he explains this difference: "Men, in America as with us, are ranked according to certain categories in the course of social life; common habits, education and, above all, wealth establishes these classifications; but these rules are neither absolute, nor inflexible, nor permanent. They establish temporary distinctions and do not form classes strictly speaking; they give no superiority, even of opinion, to one man over another." YTC, BIIa, and *Voyage* (*OC,* V, 1), p. 280.

The explanation of the sentiment of equality that Beaumont gives in a note in *Marie* (I, pp. 383–90) seems equally clear on this point. But certain historians have seen in Tocqueville the model of an egalitarian society. See particularly Edward Pessen, *Jack-*

are its three constituent elements. But the reign of total reason, in which tyranny of public opinion, the pursuit of well-being, and political apathy combine and toward which the democratic regime seems to go, does not cease to frighten Tocqueville.

That is because what emerges there is a world without society, an individual without individuality, an omnipotent state that separates citizens from each other and that promotes the absence of shared ideas and sentiments;[274] in other words, a new form of despotism that, if it still lacks a name, has all the characteristics of a new state of nature.[275]

In this new despotism, society disappears and loses its power as a creator of change and protective filter of state action. The individual finds himself isolated in the face of the action of the political power that, as the expression of the social state, is also his master and his guardian. This political power, by destroying every center of resistance, finishes by coinciding with society and occupying its place,[276] until we are confronted only by either the isolated individual or individuals as an entire group: "In democracy you see only *yourself* and *all.*"[277]

This despotism is not a type of government with its own form, as Montesquieu thought. For Tocqueville, it is the negation of all political and social forms. In this, the author recognizes his debt to Rous-

---

sonian America: Society, Personality, and Politics (Homewood, Ill.: Dorsey, 1969); "The Egalitarian Myth and the American Social Reality: Wealth, Mobility and Equality in the 'Era of the Common Man,'" *American Historical Review* 76, no. 4 (1971): 898-1034; and "Tocqueville's Misreading of America, America's Misreading of Tocqueville," *Tocqueville Review* 4, no. 1 (1982): 5–22; Irving M. Zeitlin, *Liberty, Equality and Revolution in Alexis de Tocqueville* (Boston: Little, Brown and Company, 1971), 57–62.

274. "Sentiments and ideas are renewed, the heart grows larger and the human mind develops only by the reciprocal action of men on each other." II, p. 900.

275. Referring to Hobbes, Tocqueville wonders: "what is a gathering of rational and intelligent beings bound together only by force?" I, p. 389.

276. "Despotism would not only destroy liberty among these people, but in a way society." II, p. 889, note f.

277. II, p. 718, note m. Here we see Rousseau's man divided between himself and society.

seau[278] and diverges from the main current of classical liberalism by putting historical linearity in doubt. The state of nature is found as much in a final phase of history as in a pre-historic moment; it is at once pre- and post-social.

But this new condition that we have compared to the state of nature is different from the latter in an important way. By recognizing only the capacities of individual reason alone, man falls into individualistic rationalism; but at the same time, he has total confidence in common opinion, because he is pushed by the need for dogmatism that is inherent in his existence:[279] "Faith in common opinion is the faith of democratic nations. The majority is the prophet; you believe it without reasoning. You follow it confidently without discussion. It exerts an immense pressure on individual intelligence."[280]

---

278. Here [in despotism] is the final outcome of inequality, and the extreme point that closes the circle and touches our starting point. This is where all individuals again become equal, because they are nothing, and where, since the subjects have no other rule than the will of the master and the master has no other rule than his passions, the notions of good and the principles of justice disappear yet again. Everything here leads to the law of the strongest alone and consequently to a new state of nature different from the one where we began; the first was the state of nature in its purity, and the second is the fruit of an excess of corruption. Yet there is so little difference between these two states, and the contract of government is so dissolved by despotism, that the despot is the master only as long as he is the strongest; and as soon as the despot can be driven out, he has no grounds to protest against violence. The riot that ends by strangling or dethroning a sultan is an act as lawful as those by which the day before he disposed of the lives and goods of his subjects. Force alone maintained him; force alone overthrows him.

J.-J. Rousseau, *Discours sur l'origine et les fondements de l'inégalité*, in *Oeuvres complètes* (Paris: Pléiade, 1964), III, p. 191. See below, I, p. 231, note z.

279. If man was forced to prove to himself all the truths that he uses every day, he would never finish doing so; he would wear himself out with preliminary demonstrations without advancing; as he has neither the time, because of the short span of his life, nor the ability, because of the limitations of his mind, to act in this way, he is reduced to holding as certain a host of facts and opinions that he has had neither the leisure nor the power to examine and to verify for himself, but that those more clever have found or that the crowd adopts. On this foundation he builds himself the structure of his own thoughts. It is not his will that leads him to proceed in this manner; the inflexible law of his condition compels him to do so. II, p. 714.

280. II, p. 720, note p.

The common sense of the democrat operates in the narrow field in which he has some knowledge and where he is able to put that knowledge into practice. But, in the areas where men are not involved, they accept general ideas that they have not thought of themselves; and in this way, the world, except for the narrow field in which each man is enclosed, "ends up being an insoluble problem for the man who clings to the most tangible objects and who ends up lying down on his stomach against the earth out of fear that he, in turn, may come to miss the ground."[281]

Democratic despotism is therefore the exaltation of the individual and of society. It is a double state of nature in which men enter into relation with each other almost exclusively through the mathematical power of interests and through the most faithful expression of that power, which is money; in this double state of nature, society imposes its opinions on its members with a completely unheard of force.

From another perspective, the logic of reason invades the heart of man, eliminating many of his passions and modifying certain of his sentiments, transforming for example his egoism into individualism,[282] or his generosity into interest well understood. The State, for its part, by making use of the first rational principle, which is that of unity—the expression of the principle of identity that is contained in the idea of equality—and that of centralization, imposes its forms and opinions with a speed and effectiveness previously unknown.

Democratic despotism thus takes men away from political practice by leading them exclusively toward the pursuit of material well-being, which tends to separate them more and more from each other.[283] In the

281. II, p. 1370.

282. "Egoism, vice of the heart. Individualism, of the mind." II, p. 882, note d.

283. Tocqueville learned from Guizot that the barbarians of the IVth century acted in the same way: "It is not by exterminating the civilized men of the IVth century that the barbarians managed to destroy the civilization of that time. It was enough for them to come between them so to speak and by separating them to make them like strangers to one another." II, p. 896, note c.

"There is a society only when men consider a great number of objects in the same way; when they have the same opinions on a great number of subjects; when, finally, the same facts give rise among them to the same impressions and the same thoughts." I, p. 598. Also see note y on the same page.

end, "men are no longer tied together except by interests and not by ideas."[284]

By separating man from his fellows, this new form of despotism brings about a clear break in the flow of the ideas and opinions that nourish society and history. For "the circulation of ideas is to civilization what the circulation of blood is to the human body";[285] and despotism, by interrupting this movement, creates a society that is no longer composed of anything except solitary social molecules.

"In a society of barbarians equal to each other," recalls Tocqueville, "since the attention of each man is equally absorbed by the first needs and the most coarse interests of life, the idea of intellectual progress can come to the mind of any one of them only with difficulty."[286]

The old despotism was realistic. Facts were its foundation, and it made use of them. It oppressed the body, but the soul escaped its tyrannical enterprise. The new despotism has the perfidious principle of leaving the body free and oppressing the soul.[287] While the legal and political tyranny of the majority is the modern version of the old despotism, the new despotism is the mental and social tyranny of the majority, which affects the social state, habits, and mores. Thus the damage caused by the tyranny of opinion is much greater, because this new type of despotism touches on the sources of the movement of history and society, as well as on what is most proper to the individual.

284. II, pp. 708–9.
"Don't you see, on all sides, beliefs giving way to reasoning, and sentiments, to calculation?" I, p. 391.
There is, however, a profound change from one *Democracy* to the other relating to one passion, that of well-being. If Tocqueville asserts in 1835 that "there, ambition for power is replaced by the love of well-being, a more vulgar, but less dangerous passion" (I, p. 261), he will reveal all of its malignity in the 1840 part.
285. II, p. 887, note c.
286. II, p. 879, note f.
287. The new despotism has the same relation to the old as the slavery of antiquity has to the enslavement of American Blacks. The Americans of the South "have, if I may express myself in this way, spiritualized despotism and violence." I, p. 579. Ancient slavery bound the body and left the mind free; modern slavery prevents instruction and controls the mind. Thus the enormous importance of liberty of the press in democracies. See I, pp. 290–94, and II, p. 908.

In the end man could end up by no longer belonging to anything except a quasi-society of barbarians equal to each other, thus closing the cycle of history with a despotic regime that has become permanent.

Tyranny of the majority, the tyranny of the electoral voice described in the first *Democracy*, is already the triumph of individualism, that is to say the triumph of man without individuality and personality.[288] The moment of election forces the abandonment of what is specific and particular to the individual and forces him for a moment to become a unit, or, if you want, an abstraction (one man = one voice). In this way, the new form of despotism is entirely compatible with election. Men emerge from servitude to elect their tyrants and return there immediately after.[289]

In 1840, Tocqueville combines with the practical and legal tyranny of the majority the spiritual and intellectual oppression of the opinion of all, which leads in the last resort to a situation of permanent immobility and unity. If, as he remarks, "sentiments and ideas are renewed, the heart grows larger and the human mind develops only by the reciprocal action of men on each other,"[290] then common action and vitality will disappear in democracies:

> Do you not see that opinions are dividing more quickly than patrimonies, that each man is enclosing himself narrowly within his own mind, like the farm laborer in his field? . . . That sentiments become more individual each day, and that soon men will be more separated by their beliefs than they have ever been by inequality of conditions?[291]

288. By saying that tyranny of the majority is the equivalent of the state of nature, Tocqueville also repeats Madison. I, p. 425.

289. This explains why readers have been able to find in Tocqueville a critique of communist totalitarianism as well as mass society. The interest in Tocqueville's work owes a great deal to the fact that democratic despotism is more social than political, and is, in large measure, independent of the political form. The distinction between the social and the political is, however, debatable and not very clear, even if we cannot blame Tocqueville for a lack of clarity concerning a dichotomy that we are not able to express more clearly at the present time.

290. II, p. 900.

291. II, p. 1272, note t.

The inhabitant of America is forced, like every inhabitant of a new country, to acquire rapidly the habit of governing himself,[292] but this habit must be prevented from being pushed beyond its natural limits and thereby taking the form of servitude:

> Will I dare to say it amid the ruins that surround me? What I dread most for the generations to come is not revolutions.
>
> If citizens continue to enclose themselves more and more narrowly within the circle of small domestic interests and to be agitated there without respite, you can fear that they will end by becoming as if impervious to these great and powerful public emotions that disturb peoples, but which develop and renew them. When I see property become so mobile, and the love of property so anxious and so ardent, I cannot prevent myself from fearing that men will reach the point of regarding every new theory as a danger, every innovation as an unfortunate trouble, every social progress as a first step toward a revolution, and that they will refuse entirely to move for fear that they would be carried away. I tremble, I confess, that they will finally allow themselves to be possessed so well by a cowardly love of present enjoyments, that the interest in their own future and that of their descendants will disappear, and that they will prefer to follow feebly the course of their destiny, than to make, if needed, a sudden and energetic effort to redress it.
>
> You believe that the new societies are going to change face every day, and as for me, I fear that they will end by being too invariably fixed in the same institutions, the same prejudices, the same mores; so that humanity comes to a stop and becomes limited; that the mind eternally turns back on itself without producing new ideas, that man becomes exhausted in small solitary and sterile movements, and that, even while constantly moving, humanity no longer advances.[293]

Revolutions disrupt the activities of society; they suddenly make movement and social changes easy and unpredictable; finally they destroy personal wealth. It seems then that only the poor, who have nothing to lose, can court a revolution. Democracies seek the opposite, since they need a tranquil and peaceful atmosphere in which their members can concentrate

292. I, p. 650, note l.
293. II, p. 1151.

all their activity on the pursuit of their individual well-being and that of their family.[294]

In democracies, Tocqueville notes,

> since men are no longer attached to each other by any bond of castes, classes, corporations, families, they are only too inclined to become preoccupied solely with their particular interests, and are always too ready to consider only themselves and to withdraw into a narrow individualism in which every public virtue is suffocated. Despotism, far from struggling against this tendency, makes it irresistible, because despotism removes from citizens every common passion, every natural need, every need to cooperate, every occasion to act together; it walls them, so to speak, within private life. They already tended to separate themselves; it isolates them; they grew cold toward one another; it turns them into ice.[295]

So democratic despotism finishes by producing the greatest stability in society, but this stability is not desirable because it announces the immobility of death.

> Equality of conditions, giving individual reason a complete independence, must lead men toward intellectual anarchy and bring about continual revolutions in human opinions.
>
> This is the first idea that presents itself, the common idea, the most likely idea at first view.
>
> By examining things more closely, I discover that there are limits to this individual independence in democratic countries that I had not seen at first and which make me believe that beliefs must be more *common* and more *stable* than we judge at first glance.
>
> That is already doing a great deal to lead the mind of the reader there.
>
> But I want to aim still further and I am going even as far as imagining that the final result of democracy will be to make the human mind too immobile and human opinions too stable.

---

294. "Great revolutions are not more common among democratic peoples than among other peoples; I am even led to believe that they are less so. But within these nations there reigns a small uncomfortable movement, a sort of incessant rotation of men that troubles and distracts the mind without enlivening or elevating it." II, p. 780.

295. *L'Ancien Régime et la Révolution, OC,* II, 1, p. 74.

This ideas is so extraordinary and so removed from the mind of the reader that I must make him see it only in the background and as an hypothesis.[296]

Tocqueville clearly perceives the radical nature of such an idea and notes in a draft:

This idea that the democratic social state is anti-revolutionary so shocks accepted ideas that I must win over the mind of the reader little by little, and for that I must begin by saying that this social state is less *revolutionary* than is supposed. I begin there and by an imperceptible curve I arrive at saying that there is room to fear that it is not revolutionary enough. True idea, but which would seem paradoxical at first view.[297]

With this last turn, Tocqueville's thought has for its part completed its own revolution.

Dialectic of Ideas

If democratic apathy can be worse than revolutionary disorders, then the political problem abruptly changes aspect. It becomes necessary to reintroduce into society change, the circulation of ideas, intellectual movement, which does not mean revolution. It is in fact no less necessary to try to avoid revolutions, even if, in Tocqueville's eyes, temporary anarchy is preferable to permanent order.[298]

The author distinguishes between legislative instability, which concerns secondary laws, and the instability that affects the foundations of the constitution. The latter produces revolutions and causes breaks in society;[299] the former, on the other hand, is the sign of intellectual vitality. So how is

296. II, p. 1144, note q.
297. *Ibid.*
298. See II, p. 1191, note b.
299. I, pp. 635–37.
"The small shake-ups that public liberty imparts constantly to the most settled societies recall everyday the possibility of reversals and keep public prudence awake." *L'Ancien Régime et la Révolution, OC,* II, 1, p. 197. In this way, small revolutions prevent great ones.

it possible to create this first type of instability while avoiding the second? How can we bring about the circulation of ideas and sentiments that are debated and shared at the same time?

To invite men to communicate, to see each other, to exchange ideas, such is the main task of political philosophy: "So the great object of law-makers in democracies must be to create common *affairs* that *force* men to enter into contact with each other. . . . For what is society for thinking beings, if not the communication and connection of minds and hearts?"[300]

The struggle between opposing principles produces heat and the movement of ideas. It sometimes produces disorder, but it assures the circulation of the ideas and sentiments that nourish society.

Tocqueville wrote to Kergorlay:

> I compare man in this world to a traveler who is walking constantly toward an increasingly cold region and who is forced to move more as he advances. The great sickness of the soul is cold. And to combat this fearful evil, he must not only maintain the lively movement of his mind by work, but also maintain contact with his fellows and with the business of this world. Above all at this time, we are no longer allowed to live on what has already been acquired, but must try hard to continue to acquire and not rest upon ideas that would soon enshroud us as if we were asleep in the grave. But we must constantly put into contact and into conflict the ideas that we adopt and those we do not, the ideas that we had in our youth and those suggested by the state of society and the opinions of the period that has arrived.[301]

This movement and confrontation of ideas is at risk of drowning in apathy, individualism, and the obsession with well-being, first results of democracy.

---

300. II, p. 891, note k.
301. Letter to Kergorlay, 3 February 1857, *OC,* XIII, 2, p. 325.
During the last years of his life, when he was working on *Ancien Régime,* Tocqueville wrote: "I am more and more attached to my lands and my great fields, to my ocean above all, and to its serious beaches, and I feel that only there do I live happily. But even there, to be happy, some great occupation must animate my mind, and only through ideas do I see, so to speak, the physical beauties that surround me." Letter to Freslon [?], 8 October 1856, YTC, DIIIa.

The "democratic monster" that occupies so many pages of *Democracy* is the one that has made only half a revolution, that has forgotten the principle of liberty, and that has been entirely captivated by the rational character of the abstract principle of equality.[302] This democratic monster produces a political philosophy based precisely upon the social, material, and political conditions that work to promote and to ensure the existence of such a philosophy, but it does not offer the possibility of denying such a philosophy, that is to say, by political practice.

So Tocqueville aspires, in a certain way, to completing the French Revolution, to finishing it, without forgetting that fraternity is the fruit of liberty and equality, as well as of a constant tension between the two, as had been the case in 1789.

Tocqueville remarks in the *Ancien Régime:*

> It is 89, time of inexperience, undoubtedly, but of generosity, enthusiasm, virility and grandeur, time of immortal memory, toward which the view of men will turn with admiration and respect, when those who saw it and we ourselves will have long disappeared. Then the French were proud enough of their cause and of themselves to believe that they could be equal in liberty. So everywhere in the middle of democratic institutions, they placed free institutions.[303]

For the exceptional moment represented by 1789, a momentary and magnificent combination of liberty with equality, Tocqueville shows and seems to have shown all his life a quasi-religious respect, a sort of faith never denied. In this regard, Sainte-Beuve shares with Beaumont the following anecdote:

> I have always had great difficulty speaking about Tocqueville, you will have noticed it yourself; not that I do not place him very much apart and very high, but because he did not, in my opinion, completely fulfill the whole

---

302. See II, p. 1209. See *Correspondence and Conversations of Alexis de Tocqueville with Nassau William Senior from 1834 to 1859,* edited by M. C. M. Simpson (London: H. S. King, 1872), II, pp. 92–94.

303. *L'Ancien Régime et la Révolution, OC,* II, 1, p. 247.
"Democracy is liberty combined with equality." Roland-Pierre Marcel, *Essai politique sur Alexis de Tocqueville,* p. 168.

idea that his friends are allowed to have and to give of him. And then, there was always between him and me, from the beginning and long before the most recent events, a certain kernel of separation; he was of a believing nature, that is to say that, even in the realm of ideas, he had a certain religion, a certain faith. One day, at a dinner at Madame Récamier's, I saw him not being pleased with a joke about something concerning 89. I took good note of it. That form of mind impressed me, I admit, more than it attracted me, and despite friendly advances, I always remained with him on a footing more of respect than of friendship.[304]

History, according to Tocqueville, is defined as a struggle between the abstract and the concrete; thus the opposition between liberty and equality. The objective of political science is consequently to maintain these two existing principles in constant tension in such a way that no monopoly exists of equality over liberty, which would lead to despotism, and that equality does not run the risk of being carried away into anarchy by the excesses of liberty. In this sense, it is a matter of prolonging 1789.

For Tocqueville, liberty is a passion,[305] changing and impossible to define.[306] It belongs to the *order of the heart*. Equality, to use Pascal's distinction, reigns in the *order of the mind*.

When he writes to John Stuart Mill, "I love liberty by taste, equality by instinct and by reason,"[307] Tocqueville is only expressing in another way the principal elements of his thought. The taste for equality is always of a rational, mental nature. Liberty, in contrast, is a passion, a sentiment.[308]

---

304. Letter to Beaumont, 26 November 1865. With the kind permission of the Bibliothèque de l'Institut, Spoelberch de Lovenjoul.

305. "Only liberty is able to suggest to us those powerful common emotions that carry and sustain souls above themselves; it alone can throw variety into the midst of the uniformity of our conditions and the monotony of our mores; it alone can distract our minds from small thoughts and elevate the goal of our desires." *Discours de réception* at the *Académie française. OCB*, IX, p. 20.

306. "Do not ask me to analyze this sublime taste; it must be experienced." *L'Ancien Régime et la Révolution, OC*, II, 1, p. 217.

307. Letter to John Stuart Mill, June 1835 (*Correspondance anglaise, OC*, VI, p. 293). Also see *Voyages en Angleterre, Irlande, Suisse et Algérie, OC*, V, 2, p. 91.

308. "For democratic institutions I have a taste from the head, but I am aristocratic by instinct." Quoted by Antoine Rédier, *Comme disait Monsieur de Tocqueville*, p. 48.

Liberty is an individual, particular sentiment, impossible to communicate; it represents the human because it is indefinable, incomplete, always in process, always being defined, by wagering, risking, making mistakes, and beginning again. Liberty must be lived as you live your life, never ceasing to invent. Authentic democracy is the equal participation of citizens in the definition of liberty, a definition that is always complicated, disorderly, and risky. God marks out the road toward equality, but liberty is a path that man opens and that crosses always different countries.

Equality is abstract, rational, always identical to itself; it is deductive, while liberty is inductive, as within reach and clear as liberty is complicated and fleeting.

The despotic democratic regime produces an unbearable and unlimited predominance of the mind over the heart, of equality over liberty. Liberty then disappears in the face of what can be defined and what is definite, in the face of equality; the principle of equality is allowed to reign alone. That is what philosophy must avoid at all cost. That is also what constitutes the ultimate objective of *Democracy*, as Tocqueville notes in a draft: "Danger of allowing a single social principle to take without objection the absolute direction of society. General idea that I wanted to emerge from this work."[309]

If, in the plan of history, the principle of liberty must be introduced as a counterbalance to that of equality, in the political world strictly speaking[310] the struggle of ideas takes place between two great universal principles that, for Tocqueville, are called democracy and aristocracy;[311] the one

309. II, p. 740, note d.

"Do not adopt one social principle *alone* however good it seems. Do not use one form of government *alone*. Stay away from unity." II, p. 1266, note j.

In the same way, Tocqueville claims that views expressed in the French parliamentary debates have become less elevated since the victory of the liberal party and the disappearance of the opposition. I, p. 284, note c.

310. If men create laws, women create mores. A good reader of Rousseau, Tocqueville claims therefore that in America the women are superior to the men (for mores create laws). See I, p. 482, note u. Woman represents the indefinite, liberty, passions, while man represents equality, the defined, the rational.

311. The democratic social state and the aristocratic social state appear with very defined features in the letter of 1830 to Charles Stoffels. The text will be found in appendix V.

seeks to concentrate public power, the other to scatter it.[312] Once the sentiment of liberty has disappeared or is in serious danger of doing so, Tocqueville is forced to imagine institutions that can produce the conditions necessary for liberty to exist; the hope is that they will give rise to the sentiment and passion that are otherwise in danger of disappearing. In the future, liberty, according to him, will be a product of political art. Thus, if the social state moves men away from each other, the political state must unite them;[313] if society destroys the passions and tends no longer to promote anything except interest, the political state must work to maintain passions[314] and to turn away from economic well-being.[315]

312. I, p. 286.

I find that, with rare sagacity, you have indicated the conditions under which great parties, well disciplined, can exist in a free country. As you say, each of them must be the representative of one of the two great principles that eternally divide human societies, and that, to be brief, can be designated by the names aristocracy and democracy (I, p. 281, note a).

313. "The social state separates men, the political state must draw them closer./
The social state gives them the taste for well-being [v: inclines them toward the earth], the political state must raise them up by giving them great ideas and great emotions." II, p. 1262, note b.

314. In a letter to Corcelle of 19 October 1839 (*OC,* XI, 1, p. 139), Tocqueville asks: "So will we never see the wind of true political passions rise again, my dear Corcelle, those violent, hard, sometimes cruel, but great, disinterested, fruitful passions; those passions that are the soul of the only parties that I understand and to which I would feel myself willingly disposed to give my time, my fortune and my life?" Also see the speech on the question of the right to work (*OCB,* IX, p. 542).

315. There are many examples of opposition. Political liberty, we have said, implies religious beliefs:

In the moral world, therefore, everything is classified, coordinated, foreseen, decided in advance. In the political world, everything is agitated, contested, uncertain; in the one, passive though voluntary obedience; in the other, independence, scorn for experience and jealousy of all authority. Far from harming each other, these two tendencies, apparently so opposed, move in harmony and seem to offer mutual support (I, p. 70. Also see note in the same place).

Tocqueville wants to develop the sciences in aristocratic societies and the moral sciences in democracies, in order, in both cases, to counter the tendencies of the social state (II, p. 962, note n) and he wishes to promote spiritualism to stop democratic materialism:

The opposition of the social power to the force of the state, the opposition of society to the political power must also exist. For Tocqueville, as we know, the ideal instrument for achieving this situation is associations,[316] organizations of an aristocratic character that oppose the omnipotence of the majority that characterizes democracy.

Tocqueville's ideal is not the mixed regime, however. A predominating principle will always exist because men will always try to order society and the state according to the same principle.[317] Nonetheless, in order to avoid falling into despotism and omnipotence, that is to say, into the ultimate tyranny of equality (one = one), the opposite principle must always exist.

The classical mechanisms of liberalism, such as the separation of powers, the idea of rights, liberty of the press, and federalism, serve Tocqueville only to the degree that they can be used to that end.

The author of *Democracy* wants democracies to oppose a strong legislative power with a power elected for a longer period (or put in place in a permanent way, as in monarchy); this recalls the mechanism of balance and counterbalance inspired by Montesquieu. But Tocqueville demands that, within each power, concentration be balanced by an action of dispersal. If

---

If I had been born in the Middle Ages, I would have been the enemy of superstitions, for then the social movement led there.

But today, I feel indulgent toward all the follies that spiritualism can suggest.

The great enemy is materialism, not only because it is in itself a detestable doctrine, but also because it is unfortunately in accord with the social tendency (II, p. 956, note d).

316. "Sentiments and ideas are renewed, the heart grows larger and the human mind develops only by the reciprocal action of men on each other. I have demonstrated that this action is almost nil in democratic countries. So it must be created there artificially. And this is what associations alone are able to do." II, p. 900.

317. Four types of regimes (that can be despotic or free) exist: 1. Democratic social state (social equality) and democratic political state (political equality): democracy. 2. Democratic social state combined with an aristocratic political state. This regime tends toward and will arrive at democracy, for the political state finishes by being the reflection of the social state. 3. Social inequality and political equality (this is, according to Tocqueville, a chimera). 4. Social inequality and political inequality: aristocracy.

the first chamber is elected by universal suffrage, the second must be formed by indirect election. If the political power must be centralized, the administration must be decentralized to the same degree. The jury does wonders for the education of the people, but it must be guided by the judge's hand. The excesses of the majority, a constant danger in democracies, are opposed by the creation of an aristocracy of associations. And in the same way, against the associations of owners, there are the associations of workers; against the state, the society, etc.

The examples of opposition multiply throughout the book and extend from the purely political field to all aspects of intellectual life. "The most favorable moment for the development of the sciences, of literature and of the arts," Tocqueville specifies in this regard, "is when democracy begins to burst into the midst of an aristocratic society. Then you have movement amid order. Then humanity moves very rapidly, but like an army in battle, without breaking ranks and without discipline losing anything to ardor."[318]

The author of *Democracy* found this idea in Montesquieu;[319] the idea of the opposition of the three powers ends up by amounting to the opposition between the legislative power and the executive power, which in Tocqueville is the confrontation between democracy and aristocracy.[320] Nonetheless, the problem for Montesquieu, like that for all of political philosophy before him, was purely political despotism, while Tocqueville

318. II, p. 810, note q.

The sixteenth century had formed many of those fine, proud and free minds whose race was entirely lost in the theatrical splendor of the following century. Also you must have noted the superiority of the writers of the first period of the reign of Louis XIV over those of the second. The first were formed in that very short time in which feudal independence was allied for a moment with modern art and taste; the one gave grandeur, and the others the finish of details and the harmony of the whole (YTC, CIb (thoughts collected by Mary Mottley). See II, p. 1146, note l, in which the same idea is found again.)

319. As Luis Díez del Corral pointed out, Tocqueville could have had this idea from the very mouth of Guizot (*El pensamiento político de Tocqueville,* pp. 285–86, 315, 377–79). But differing from Guizot, Tocqueville does not believe that the result of the struggle between the forces of society and those of the individual is the bourgeois mentality.

320. Book XI, chapter VI of *Esprit des lois.* Also see book I, chapter 2.

points out for the first time a new form of tyranny that does not have a name, but that spreads from the political power to ideas, habits and thoughts, invading all of private and public life.[321]

There are no recipes or definitive solutions; no formula allows us to go beyond this system of opposition. The terms are in continual tension, changeable and alive. Tocqueville advances in this way between two abysses with the talent of a Malesherbes or of a Royer-Collard,[322] by adopting what is best in each condition, by maintaining a precarious equilibrium, by going along in doubt and uncertainty.

*   *   *   *   *

The objective of political philosophy is to produce among the citizens those passions that can destroy or save society, to produce that dialectic of ideas, of the abstract and the concrete, of liberty and equality, of reason and of passion, that causes small, continual revolutions.[323]

According to Tocqueville, liberty certainly cannot be defined in a negative way by obedience to laws that are the result of the compromises and struggles of two permanent and equally strong parties. The author of *Democracy* lives in a world in which one of the two powers can disappear completely and in which the best laws are capable of coexisting with a social condition similar to that of the state of nature, in which legal liberty can go hand in hand with political and intellectual despotism.

For Tocqueville, man is above all a participant in history. He is part of a vast project that he himself must work on each day. The pilot of a boat, even if he does not determine either the winds or the waves, can hoist or lower the sails; he guides his ship. He is a man who looks at the past and the future, but who cannot learn very much from history.

---

321. This sets him apart from Rousseau. See I, p. 406, note g, pp. 407 and 413.

322. See Luis Díez del Corral, *El pensamiento político de Tocqueville,* pp. 158–59, and *OCB,* VI, p. 445.

323. "As I grow older, I have more regard, I will almost say respect, for the passions. I love them when they are good, and I am not even sure about detesting them when they are bad. They are power, and power, wherever it is found, appears at its best amid the universal weakness that surrounds us." Letter to Ampère, 10 August 1841, *OC,* XI, p. 152. Also see *OCB,* VI, p. 407.

The past does not offer rules of conduct or solutions for the present; it gives sentiments, but not reasons; it creates passions and faith, but not laws; it develops tendencies, it calls for prudence, but does not offer judgments.

Nor does the history of peoples offer solutions for the present, just as *Democracy in America* does not claim to give to the French or to Europeans a theory of democracy. It is not a matter of imitating America, Tocqueville says in substance; it is a matter of understanding America. For the rest, the destiny of man is still, and is forever, in his own hands.

Eduardo Nolla
Universidad San Pablo-CEU
Madrid

Foreword to This Edition

*"The greatest effort of the government must tend toward
teaching citizens the art of doing without its help."*

—II, p. 900, note n.

Tocqueville is a classic, an author who meets Sainte-Beuve's definition of a classic, by providing "a conversation for every instance, a friendship that does not fail and will never desert you, and that offers that familiar sensation of serenity and amenity which reconciles us, as we frequently need, with other men and ourselves."[1] As befits his status as a classic author, hundreds of books and articles have been published in recent decades about Tocqueville, and dozens of editions of *Democracy in America* are printed and reprinted in the world every year.

How do you read a classic?

Stendhal defined a novel in *The Red and the Black* as "a mirror that is strolled along a main road." The same can be said of great books in general. They provide a new reflection of ourselves every time we read them, and they accompany us as we move forward in life. Tocqueville himself always traveled with the books he considered the greatest: works by Pascal, Rousseau, and Montesquieu, classics he read and read again all his life.

His favorite authors were few and old. He wrote to a friend:

> Not being able to bring my library here to keep me company, I have
> had me sent at least one volume from each of the great authors I like. I

---

1. C.-A. Sainte-Beuve. *Causeries du lundi*. Monday, 21 October 1850. Third edition. (Paris: Garnier Frères, [1857]), III, p. 55.

think they are no more than twenty-five. They all fit in a very small shelf. Almost none of them were written less than a century ago.[2]

Tocqueville had little patience for the books written by his contemporaries and maintained that he could find in a "small number of excellent books that . . . keep good company,"[3] and within himself, all he needed to generate his own works.[4]

Democracy in America is arguably Tocqueville's greatest and most enduring work. Drawing on his nine-month journey with Beaumont to the United States and influenced by the "classic" authors he carried with him as well as by his own vision, Tocqueville constructed a unique portrait of America. The very first paragraph of the working manuscript's introduction calls attention to his project's novelty:

> The work that you are about to read is not a travelogue, <the reader can rest easy>. I do not want him to be concerned with me. You will also not find in this book a complete summary of all the institutions of the United States; but I flatter myself that, in it, the public will find some new documentation and, from it, will gain useful knowledge about a subject that is more important for us than the fate of America and no less worthy of holding our attention.[5]

Rejecting the form of a travelogue, Tocqueville also wrote to his friend Ampère that he did not want to write a description of America, but rather

2. Letter to Madame de Circourt, January 11, 1854, *OC,* XVIII, pp. 141–42.

In another letter, he explains: "I have had sent to me from Paris some books I should have read a long time ago but haven't, because when I'm in good health I'm a very bad *reader* [*liseur*], particularly of new books. I must be ill or convalescing in order to pay a lot of attention to the books of my contemporaries." To Adolphe de Circourt, December 2, 1858, *OC,* XVIII, p. 509.

An explanation of abbreviations and symbols used in this edition is included in I, pp. xxxix-xli.

3. In a letter to Madame de Circourt, *OC,* XVIII, pp. 43–44: "Books are like intelligent people with no moods, no whims, no need to talk about themselves, no regrets in hearing good things being said about others; to conclude, intelligent people whom one can abandon and pick up as one wishes." *Idem.*

4. Scholars are still surprised by the small number of theory books quoted or used by Tocqueville in *Democracy in America.* In II, pp. 1377–95, the reader will find the list of works used by Tocqueville in the writing of his book.

5. In I, pp. 3–4.

a mirror—perhaps the mirror Stendhal describes—in which the readers might see themselves.[6]

For more than a century and a half, Americans and Europeans have been observing their own shifting images in Tocqueville's mirror.[7] The image is repeatedly distorted, and the aim of the exercise is far from being disinterested. We are continually rereading *Democracy in America,* never quite reaching final conclusions about it, or about Tocqueville's position.[8] With each reading, we find something new and valuable in the book, and with each reading, we continue to recognize ourselves anew in its pages.

Ortega y Gasset claimed that great books have the qualities of simultaneously being deficient and exuberant.[9] As a means of understanding the author and his intentions, they are always something of a failure, as we can never truly say we wholly comprehend either the writer or the writer's mind. At the same time, they seem to be an inexhaustible treasure trove in which we always find something that we hadn't stumbled upon before and that the author was unaware of having had the intention to say. It is in this sense that classic books are never completed, finished, or fully read, since they always seem to have something new to say.

Over a century and a half after *Democracy in America*'s publication, this non-travelogue continues to captivate us, and we continue to travel down the main road of modern democracy with Tocqueville's book in our hands.[10]

Traveling, roads, and trips; these are all very Tocquevillian things.[11]

6. See I, p. cvii, note 185.

7. "Caution: objects in this mirror may be closer than they appear!" Jean Baudrillard. *Amérique* (Paris: Grasset, 1986), p. 9.

8. For instance, the endless discussions about whether Tocqueville is a classic liberal or a conservative, an aristocrat or a democrat.

9. José Ortega y Gasset. "Comentario al *Banquete* de Platón," in *Obras completas* (Madrid: Taurus and Fundación Ortega, 2009), IX, pp. 729–57.

10. Symptomatically, Tocqueville's book was condemned to the flames in Hitler's Germany, and translations of *Democracy in America* have been published in many of the former European Communist countries since 1989.

11. See I, cxli.

Tocqueville enjoyed traveling, but did it in his own peculiar way. Beaumont writes about Tocqueville:

> A day lost or a day poorly spent were a bad day. The smallest waste of time annoyed him. He brought this passion in his travels up to the point that he never arrived in a place without previously having secured the means to leave it, which made one of his friends say that he always left before he had arrived.[12]

When Tocqueville could not travel, his favorite pastime was reading travel books, particularly if they had pictures or maps.[13] His interest in travel and travel literature is not entirely surprising; the images of travel—the journey, roads, movement, rivers, intersections—are frequently employed by Tocqueville.

He understood history as a sort of voyage, the inexorable advance of equality of conditions. Yet, equality could assume two guises: an equality consistent with freedom, or an equality compatible with despotism. America showed the promise of the first road, as well as the dangers of the second. When Tocqueville wrote his book, both paths seemed possible for France.

"One has to be at the breaking point, as we find ourselves," he explains to his friend Beaumont about the epoch they lived in, "in order to see both roads distinctively."[14]

If travel was one of Tocqueville's preoccupations, liberty was another. He wrote to John Stuart Mill in June 1835: "I love liberty by penchant, and equality by instinct and reason. These two passions that so many fake, I believe I really feel within myself, and I am ready to make great sacrifices for them."[15]

It is not surprising that he also viewed liberty as a kind of voyage or

---

12. *OCB*, V, p. 23.

13. "I very much love *good* travel books and what makes you learn about the different regions of the world. But there are few books of this kind published in French, and English books are difficult to obtain and very expensive. I am particularly curious about the new discoveries in Africa. Anything related to East Asia, Siberia, and the new conquests of Russia in the Pacific interests me much. I would very much enjoy good travel books on Siberia, with *good maps*." Letter to Adolphe de Circourt, *OC*, XVIII, p. 509.

14. In a letter dated March 23, 1853. *OC*, VIII, 3, p. 95.

15. *OC*, VI, pp. 293–94.

journey. Liberty is as much a process as a condition; it is the result of a never-ending process of discussion, debate, redefinition, movement, and change. No fixed or stable definition of it will ever be possible, and although the many manifestations of freedom share certain characteristics, freedom can never be completely uniform, for it is shaped by its context and by the individuals who exercise it. As Tocqueville observed, "I would regard it as a great misfortune for humankind if liberty, in all places, had to occur with the same features."[16]

Significantly, it is while traveling, while sailing aboard the *Havre* to America that Tocqueville finds a perfect example of liberty.

> At sea, if you don't want to quarrel, one must be the best of friends to everyone. There is no in-between. . . . The obligation of living one on top of the other and of seeing each other closely establishes a lack of discretion and a liberty for which there is no idea on land. Here, everyone acts in the middle of the multitude as if one were alone. Some read in loud voice, others play, others sing. Some write, as myself right now, while next to me a neighbor dines. Everyone drinks, eats, or cries as he wishes. Our rooms are so narrow that we exit them to dress, and except for ostensibly getting in our briefs, I don't know what part of our dressing up doesn't take place in the face of Israel. In a word, we live here on the public square, as the ancients. This is the real country of liberty, but it can only take place between four planks. That's the problem.[17]

Recreating liberty on land poses more difficulties, but liberty remained the ultimate value for Tocqueville. He did not, however, believe he could simply present American democracy as a model to be imitated elsewhere. Equality was the same all over the world, but liberty had many facets.

The greatness and enduring worth of *Democracy in America* lies, to a large extent, in the fact that Tocqueville understood that the movement that carried the modern world toward democratic regimes was a universal trend not limited by continents or traditions. Thus, it would be wrong to

16. II, p. 513. See a detailed discussion of Tocqueville's idea of liberty in I, pp. cxliii–cxlviii.

17. In a letter to his mother written on board the *Havre,* dated April 26, 1831. YTC, BIa2.

think that he was simply writing about nineteenth-century America and France.[18]

That general process of equality's movement linked the two shores of the Atlantic. Tocqueville asserted that America was not a new country, and he realized that Europe itself simultaneously became a continent when America developed into one.[19] They were both different sides of the same reality. Tocqueville writes:

> I cannot agree to separate America from Europe, despite the Ocean that divides them. I consider the people of the United States as the portion of the English people charged with exploiting the forests of the New World, while the rest of the nation, provided with more leisure and less preoccupied by the material cares of life, is able to devote itself to thought and to develop the human mind in all aspects.
>
> [<≠So I think that democracy must no more be judged by America than the different nations of Europe by one of the commercial and manufacturing classes that are found within them.≠>][20]

This is why Tocqueville refused to say that the United States was a new society. On the contrary, it was old and had all the advantages of experience and history without the burdens and difficulties of infancy. "In the United States, society has no childhood; it is born in manhood,"[21] he wrote. America had existed long before the first pilgrims had arrived on its shores. It was an idea, a project, before it became a continent:

> It was not necessity that forced them [the Puritans] to abandon their country; there they left a social position worthy of regret and a secure livelihood. Nor did they come to the New World in order to improve their situation or to increase their wealth; they tore themselves from the comforts of their homeland to obey a purely intellectual need. By exposing themselves to

18. "America was just my framework, democracy was the theme." In a letter to John Stuart Mill, November 19, 1836. *OC,* VI, p. 315.

19. Little has been written about Tocqueville's idea of Europe, but he was one of the first to understand events in France as part of trends that were, properly speaking, either European or universal movements. See I, p. cx, note 197, for example.

20. III, p. 768. And in a side note in a first version of the chapter: "America forms like one part of the middle classes of England." III, p. 767, note f.

21. I, p. 291.

the inevitable hardships of exile, they wanted to assure the triumph of *an idea.*[22]

What set apart the Europeans in America from the Europeans in Europe[23] was that, on the American continent, ideas could swiftly become real and possible.[24] Americans were able to bring to life the Europeans' dreams. The inhabitants of America traveled lightly toward the future, while Europeans advanced slowly because they had to carry with them their heavy past. As Tocqueville put it: "Admirable position of the New World where man has only himself as an enemy. To be happy and free, he only has to want to be."[25]

This explains why Americans had arrived first, before the rest of the world, at the final stage of the development of equality; that is, democracy.[26] Only the combination of the uncommon origin of the Americans, their high degree of intellectual development, their lack of aristocracy, the power of local government and associations, and the exceptional geographical conditions, among others, allowed for the existence of this ultimate form of political organization.

Had American democracy been exclusively the result of some exceptional and unrepeatable physical conditions, Europe would have had no

---

22. Tocqueville's emphasis. I, p. 54.
Another Frenchman, Crèvecœur, had thus described the Americans:

> He is an American, who, leaving behind him all his ancient prejudices and manners, receives new ones from the new mode of life he has embraced, the new government he obeys, and the new rank he holds. . . . The Americans were once scattered all over Europe; here they are incorporated into one of the finest systems of population which has ever appeared.

J. Hector Saint John de Crèvecœur. *Letters from an American Farmer* (New York: Penguin Classics, 1981), p. 70.

23. Writing to his friend Francisque de Corcelle in 1836, Tocqueville blithely explained: "In my quality as an *American,* I have developed a great disdain for the federal constitution of Switzerland." *OC,* XV, 1, p. 70. His emphasis.

24. See I, p. lxviii, note 75, and I, p. cxii, note 204.

25. I, p. 276.

26. "≠Dem[ocratic (ed.)] government, the chef-d'œuvre of civilization and enlightenment.≠" II, p. 332, note b.

chance to move toward democratic regimes and perhaps the American example would have been less interesting to Tocqueville.[27]

With these circumstances not existing in Europe, there the actions of intellectuals, mores, and laws were going to be crucial in bringing about and maintaining democracy and in educating citizens.[28] Yet, as is well known, the advance of democratic equality did not mean that America and Europe were necessarily moving toward a free democracy. In fact, many signs told Tocqueville that liberty might not be the obvious result of the democratic revolution.[29]

All this adds to the difficulty of reading Tocqueville.

We find in *Democracy* a confusing mix of America, Europe, France, United States, the ideal of a free democratic system, and the description of democratic despotism. It's not easy to find out when Tocqueville is referring to one or the other. This is why it is possible to make Tocqueville say all kinds of different and opposite things and frequently be misquoted.[30]

Democracy in America contains all of the institutional, historical, and theoretical elements that we associate with and expect in classic liberalism, such as division of powers, rights, freedom of the press, and sovereignty of the people. But it would be a mistake to look in the book for an organized and perfectly structured set of theoretical and institutional solutions for a liberal democracy. Tocqueville himself consciously attempted not to write that way. As he explained to a friend:

> I believe that the books that have made men think the most and have had the greatest influence on their opinions and actions are those in which the author hasn't attempted to tell them dogmatically what had to be thought, but rather those where he has placed their minds on the road that goes

27. "If laws and mores could do nothing without the geographical position, we are [v: we would be] lost." YTC, CVh, 4, p. 11.

28. "In order for democracy to rule there must exist citizens, people interested in public affairs, with the ability to deal with them willingly; this is a main point to which one must always return." YTC, CVe, p. 65.

29. "≠If men could remain equal only by staying free, I would have no fear for liberty.≠" YTC, CVK, 2, p. 4.

30. Or even inventing quotes that sound Tocquevillian, like the ubiquitous—and fake—"America is great because America is good. . . ."

toward the truths, and has made them find these, as if it were, by themselves.[31]

Approach *Democracy in America* keeping in mind that its author's aim was to require the reader to add and complete his book, as all classic books require, to carry it with you as a kind of travel mirror.

Read Tocqueville as Flaubert recommended reading in general to Mademoiselle de Chantepie: "Don't read as children read, to amuse yourself; or how ambitious people do, for your instruction. No. Read to live."[32]

Eduardo Nolla
Madrid, April 2011

Note on Volumes and Pagination

Although this English edition is printed in two volumes and the Liberty Fund bilingual edition comprises four, page numbers in both editions are identical.

The Spanish translation published by Trotta in Madrid in one volume also uses the same pagination.

E. N.

31. In a letter to *Corcelle, OC,* XV, 2, p. 80.

32. Gustave Flaubert: Letter to Mademoiselle Leroyer de Chantepie, dated June 6 [1857]. *Correspondance* (Paris: Bibliothèque de la Pléiade, 1980), II, p. 731.

Dilthey would later write, in a very Tocquevillian tone: "We give up constructing, we love research, but we are skeptical of the machines of systems. [. . .] We are contented dying as walkers." *Wilhelm Diltheys Gesammelte Schriften* (Leipzig: Teubner, 1924), V, p. xiv. Quoted by Luis Díez del Corral, a self-professed captive of Tocqueville's thought, in *The Rape of Europe* (London: Allen and Unwin, 1959), p. 295. My translation.

VOLUME I
(1835)

DEMOCRACY
IN AMERICA[a]

a. The drafts contain the following note, probably meant to announce the publication of the book:

Explanatory note about my position and the principal ideas that form the heart of the work./

In 1831, Messrs. Beaumont and Tocqueville received a mission from the French government for the purpose of going to the United States to study the penitentiary system there. They remained nearly one year in the United States. After returning in 1832, they published a work entitled: *Of the Penitentiary System in the United States and Its Application to France.* Since then, this work has been translated in its entirety in the United States and in Germany; a portion has been translated in England. The French Academy believed that its authors should be awarded the annual grand prize established for whoever publishes the most useful book.

M. de Tocqueville, one of the authors of the book mentioned above, is about to publish this coming October a work in two volumes that also has America as the subject. This book will be entitled *Of the Dominion of Democracy in America.*

The fact that most struck the author during his stay in the United States was the fact of equality of conditions. He believed that this primary fact had exercised and still exercised a prodigious influence on the laws, habits, mores of the Americans and dominated, so to speak, civil and political society in the United States. This struck him even more because this same fact of equality of conditions is constantly developing among all the peoples of Europe in a progressive manner.

So M. de Tocqueville thought that if someone could succeed in specifying in a very plain and very clear fashion what type of influence this fact, established in America and half-established in Europe, really exercised on society, what necessary aspect it gave to laws, what secret instincts to peoples, what cast it imparted to ideas and mores, a work not only interesting, but also useful would be written; a work, though serious in form, would nonetheless reach the minds of the greatest number of readers, because it would in some place necessarily touch on the political passions of the period and all the material interests that the political passions more or less express.

The result of these reflections has been the work that M. de Tocqueville is about to publish today and for which he gathered an enormous quantity of materials during his stay in America (YTC, CVh, 3, pp. 100–101, 99).

PART I

Introduction[a]

[The work that you are about to read is not a travelogue,[b] <the reader can rest easy>. I do not want him to be concerned with me. You will also not find in this book a complete summary of all the institutions of the United States; but I flatter myself that, in it, the public will find some new documentation and, from it, will gain useful knowledge about a subject that is

---

a. Ideas of the preface./

Irresistible movement of democracy, great fact of the modern world. Importance of this fact superior to all questions of time and of internal politics. America showing this fact come to its completion.

Goal of this work to give accurate notions about this fact; moreover, I do not judge this fact. I do not even believe that there is anything of an absolute goodness in institutions. Montesquieu . . .

Ease of criticizing me. I know that nothing will be easier than to criticize this book, if anyone ever thinks of examining it critically. You will have only to contrast certain particular facts to certain of my general ideas. Nothing is easier; there are facts and arguments for all doctrines. For you to judge me, I would like you to want to do what I did, to see an ensemble of facts and to come to a decision based on the mass of reasons. To whoever will do that and then does not agree with me, I am ready to submit. For if I am sure of having sincerely sought the truth, I am far from considering myself as certain to have found it.

To contrast an isolated fact to the ensemble of facts, a detached idea to the sequence of ideas.

It isn't that I don't have set ideas, but they are general (for there is absolute truth only in general ideas). I believe that tyranny is the greatest evil, liberty the first good. But as for knowing what is most appropriate for preventing the one and creating the other among peoples and knowing if all peoples are made to escape tyranny, that is where doubt begins (YTC, CVh, 3, pp. 96–97).

b. The criticism of this passage (YTC, CIIIb, 1, p. 7) made by Louis de Kergorlay has been published in *Correspondance avec Kergorlay* (*OC,* XIII, 1, p. 367).

3

more important for us than the fate of America and no less worthy of holding our attention.^c]

Among the new objects that attracted my attention during my stay in the United States, none struck me more vividly than the equality of conditions.^d I discovered without difficulty the prodigious influence that this primary fact exercises on the march of society; it gives a certain direction to the public mind, a certain turn to the laws; to those governing, new maxims, and particular habits to the governed.

Soon I recognized that this same fact extends its influence far beyond political mores and laws, and that it has no less dominion over civil society, than over government: it creates opinions, gives birth to sentiments, suggests customs and modifies all that it does not produce.

Therefore, as I studied American society, I saw more and more, in equality of conditions, the generating fact from which each particular fact seemed to derive, and I rediscovered it constantly before me as a central point where all of my observations came together.

Then I turned my thought back toward our hemisphere, and it seemed to me that I perceived something analogous to the spectacle that the New World offered me. I saw equality of conditions that, without having reached its extreme limits as in the United States, approached those limits

c. In a first version of the drafts:

[In the margin: I have not said everything that I saw, but I have said everything that I believed at the same time true and useful [v: profitable] to make known, and without wanting to write a treatise on America, I thought only to help my fellow citizens resolve a question that must interest us more deeply.]

I see around me facts without number, but I notice one of them that dominates all the others; it is old; it is stronger than laws, more powerful than men; it seems to be a direct product of the divine will; it is the gradual development of democracy in the Christian world. When I say "democracy" here I do not mean to speak only about a political form of government, but of a social state (YTC, CVh, 3, pp. 115–16).

d. This first paragraph differs a bit from the manuscript: "There is a fact that more than all the rest attracts the attention of the European upon his arrival on the shores of the New World. A surprising equality reigns there among fortunes; at first glance minds themselves seem equal. I was struck, like others, at the sight of this extreme equality of conditions and I discovered without difficulty . . ."

more each day; and this same democracy that reigned in American societies, appeared to me to advance rapidly toward power in Europe.[e]

From that moment, I conceived the idea of the book you are about to read.[f]

[e]. In the margin: "≠I remember that I saw something analogous in France; I think that you can usefully examine the effects in the two countries, and I conceive the idea of the book.≠" Another version is presented to the side that specifies: "≠in Europe and principally in my own country.≠"

The version not struck out in the manuscript says: ". . . appeared to me ready to take power among us." Hervé de Tocqueville remarks: "The word *ready* does not seem good to me. Besides, isn't it too absolute relative to what is still happening at the moment among us and to the government that succeeded the Restoration?"

Next to this observation, another is found, probably from Édouard de Tocqueville, brother of Alexis: "I also agree that this expression must be softened" (YTC, CIIIb, 1, p. 9).

The criticisms of Hervé de Tocqueville, father of Alexis, of Édouard and Hippolyte de Tocqueville, his brothers, and those of his friends Gustave de Beaumont and Louis de Kergorlay, made at the time of reading a copy of the manuscript of the first *Democracy*, are known to us thanks to a copy in Bonnel's hand. The latter does not identify the authors. Nonetheless, the written comments can be attributed to them without great difficulty, by taking into account tone, style, and the following facts: the observations of Louis de Kergorlay consisted of small slips of paper inserted into the manuscript (only a few of them remain relating to the introduction and to the last section of chapter X of the 1835 part); certain of his notes on the introduction have been published in the correspondence of Tocqueville and Kergorlay (cf. *OC,* XIII, 1, pp. 364–68; note that the list reproduced on p. 368 is Tocqueville's, not Kergorlay's); all comments using the *vous* form can be attributed to Beaumont, who always used *vous* with Tocqueville, in distinction to the members of Tocqueville's family and Kergorlay; finally a letter included in the critical observations (reproduced in note c for p. 142) and some sentences of the first readers of the manuscript inform us that the notes found alongside the commentaries of Hervé were written by Édouard de Tocqueville. By elimination, some remaining less interesting comments could be by Hippolyte, older brother of Alexis. Certain reflections inserted between texts seem to us to be by Alexis himself.

The whole of these commentaries are found at the Beinecke Library under the classification CIIIb. There are also a few brief commentaries by Hervé de Tocqueville for chapter IX of the second part of the first volume of 1835 under the classification YTC, CVh, 3, pp. 14–17.

[f]. At the top of the sheet appears, crossed out, the beginning of the section IMPORTANCE OF WHAT PRECEDES IN RELATION TO EUROPE, the conclusion of chapter 9 of the second part of volume I, constituting at the start the conclusion of the book (since chapter 10 was added at the last moment). This fact, as well as numerous similarities and displacements of paragraphs between the introduction and the conclusion of chapter 9, indicate that the two chapters were very likely written at the same time, probably at the end of the spring or at the beginning of the summer of 1834.

A great democratic revolution is taking place[g] among us; everyone sees it, but not everyone judges it in the same way. Some consider it as something new and, taking it for an accident, they hope still to be able to stop it; while others judge it irresistible, because it seems to them the most continuous, oldest and most permanent fact known in history.

I look back for a moment to what France was seven hundred years ago: I find it divided up among a small number of families who own the land and govern the inhabitants; at that time, the right to command is passed down with inheritances from generation to generation; men have only a single way to act on one another, force; you discover only a single source of power, landed property.

But then the political power of the clergy becomes established and is soon expanding.[h] The clergy opens its ranks to all, to the poor and to the

g. In the manuscript: ". . . is reaching completion among us."
Hervé de Tocqueville: "This sentence seems too absolute to me for the reasons that I have just enumerated a short while ago; instead of the words *reaching completion*, I would like better *seems due to take place.*"
Édouard de Tocqueville: "That is right" (YTC, CIIIb, 1, p. 9).
h. The *saints.* Men committed to the *moral* grandeur of man.

Saints taken from all classes.
Political power of the clergy that makes men of all classes arrive at the government.
[In the margin: Ascending movement of *time,* descending movement of *nobles.*]
Introduction of jurists into the government produces the same effect.
The Crusades that enervate the nobility and divide lands.
The financiers. Importance that the perpetual wars of the Middle Ages give to them. The middle classes are introduced by them into government.
Granting of freedom to the towns.
Personal estates. Tyranny toward the Jews that brings about the invention of paper wealth.
Instruction begun by the monks in the cathedrals. Religion awakens the arts. Introduction of men of letters into government. Political power of the University of Paris.
Granting of nobility that brings commoners into the government by the nobility (1270).
[In the margin: Equality penetrates finally into government by the nobility.]
Favoritism of the kings that brings men from nothing to power. Pierre de Brosse, minister after having been a barber (1275).
Laws of exclusive privileges that prevent vassals from becoming too powerful.
Introduction of towns into the Estates General (1304).
Taste for literature that opens up a new importance to men of all classes. Estab-

rich, to the commoner and to the lord; equality begins to penetrate through the Church into the government, and someone who would have vegetated as a serf in eternal slavery takes his place as a priest among nobles and often goes to take a seat above kings.

As society becomes more civilized and more stable with time, the different relationships among men become more complicated and more numerous. The need for civil laws is intensely felt. Then jurists arise; they emerge from the dark precinct of the courts and from the dusty recess of the clerks' offices, and they go to sit in the court of the prince, alongside feudal barons covered with ermine and iron.

Kings ruin themselves in great enterprises; nobles exhaust themselves in private wars; commoners enrich themselves in commerce. The influence of money begins to make itself felt in affairs of State. Trade is a new source of power, and financiers become a political power that is scorned and flattered.

Little by little, enlightenment spreads; the taste for literature and the arts reawakens; then the mind becomes an element of success; knowledge is a means of government; intelligence, a social force; men of letters reach public affairs.

As new roads to achieve power are found, however, we see the value of birth fall. In the XIth century, nobility had an inestimable value; it is pur-

---

lishment of floral games (1324).[TN 1]

Discovery of firearms that equalizes the unprotected villein with the nobleman covered in iron (1328).

The *Jacquerie.* The uprising of the bourgeois of Paris (1358).

Wars with the English that destroy or ruin the nobility.

Factions of the Armagnacs and the Burgundians that give importance to the people. The nobles use them as instruments.

Beginning of heresies. Jan Huss (1414).

Institution of permanent armies that finishes undermining feudal power (1446).

Immense commercial and personal fortunes. Jacques Coeur.

End of the Eastern Empire. Increasing influence of letters in the West (1453).

Discovery of printing toward 1440. The post in . . .

Louis XI.

Discovery of America (1492) (YTC, CVh, 1, pp. 18–20).

TRANSLATOR'S NOTE 1: Floral games were a literary competition held annually in Toulouse and elsewhere in France.

chased in the XIIIth; the first granting of nobility takes place in 1270,[j] and equality is finally introduced into government by aristocracy itself.

During the seven hundred years that have just passed, it sometimes happened that, in order to struggle against royal authority, or to take power away from their rivals, the nobles gave political power to the people.

Even more often, you saw kings make the lower classes of the State participate in government in order to humble[k] the aristocracy.

In France, kings showed themselves to be the most active and most constant of levelers. When they were ambitious and strong, they worked to raise the people to the level of the nobles, and when they were moderate and weak, they allowed[m] the people to put themselves above kings. The former helped democracy by their talents, the latter by their vices. Louis XI and Louis XIV took care to equalize everything below the throne, and Louis XV himself finally descended into the dust with his court.[n]

As soon as citizens began to own the land in ways other than by feudal tenure, and as soon as personal wealth, once known, could in turn create influence and confer power, no discoveries were made in the arts, no further

---

j. The manuscript says "1370." The correct date is indeed 1270.

k. In the manuscript: ". . . in order to pull down the aristocracy."

Hervé de Tocqueville: "Aren't the words *pull down* too absolute here?"

Édouard de Tocqueville: "Perhaps *humble* would be better" (YTC, CIIIb, 1, p. 10).

m. Hervé de Tocqueville: "I would like better: *they suffered the people*, etc" (YTC, CIIIb, 1, p. 10).

n. Hervé de Tocqueville:

There is an error here; you undoubtedly wanted to put Louis XVI, for if Louis XV prepared the Revolution by his debaucheries, you cannot deny that he was an absolute king until his last moment and his court all powerful. I do not like the word *dust* which is not of a type elevated enough for the rest of the style; one says, moreover, *fall into the dust,* but one does not say *descend into the dust.*

Édouard de Tocqueville:

I also find this sentence leaves something to be desired. I will not, however, make the same criticism as my father. It is indeed Louis XV who lost the monarchy by depriving it of all of its moral force, of its dignity and of the prestige that surrounded the throne. Only *fall into the dust* expresses a physical abasement, but it is a moral abasement that must be expressed here, by observing that Louis XV succeeded in killing the aristocracy by discrediting it by the corruption of his court (YTC, CIIIb, 1, p. 11).

improvements were introduced into commerce and industry, without also creating as many new elements of equality among men. From this moment, all processes that are found, all needs that are born, all desires that demand to be satisfied, are progress toward universal leveling. The taste for luxury, the love of war, the sway of fashion, the most superficial passions of the human heart as well as the most profound, seem to work in concert to impoverish the rich and to enrich the poor.

From the time when works of the mind became sources of strength and wealth, each development of science, each new element of knowledge, each new idea had to be considered as a germ of power put within reach of the people. Poetry, eloquence, memory, mental graces, fires of the imagination, depth of thought, all these gifts that heaven distributes at random, profited democracy, and even when they were in the possession of democracy's adversaries, they still served its cause by putting into relief the natural grandeur of man; so democracy's conquests spread with those of civilization and enlightenment, and literature was an arsenal open to all, where the weak and the poor came each day to find arms.

When you skim the pages of our history you do not find so to speak any great events that for seven hundred years have not turned to the profit of equality.

The Crusades and the English wars decimate the nobles and divide their lands; the institution of the towns introduces democratic liberty into the feudal monarchy; [<the rigors enforced against the Jews bring about the invention of paper wealth[o]>]; the discovery of firearms equalizes the villein and the noble on the field of battle; printing offers equal resources to their minds; the post comes to deposit enlightenment at the threshold of the hut of the poor as at the gate of palaces; Protestantism maintains that all men are equally able to find the way to heaven. America, which comes into sight, presents a thousand new paths to fortune and delivers the wealth and power [reserved to kings] to obscure adventurers.

If you examine what is happening in France from the XIth century every

o. In the margin: "<Letters of exchange, the most democratic of all wealth.>"

fifty years, at the end of each one of these periods, you will not fail to notice that a double revolution has taken place in the state of society. The noble will have slipped on the social ladder, the commoner will have risen; the one descends, the other ascends. Each half-century brings them closer together, and soon they are going to touch.

And this is not only particular to France. In whatever direction we cast our eyes, we notice the same revolution continuing in all of the Christian universe. [Let someone cite to me a republic or a kingdom in which the nobles of today can be compared, I would not say to the nobles of feudal times, but only to their fathers of the last century. {If France hastened the democratic revolution of which I am speaking, France did not give it birth}.

For seven hundred years, there is not a single event among Christians that has not turned to the profit of democracy, not a man who has not served its triumph. <≠The clergy by spreading enlightenment and by applying within its bosom the principle of Christian equality, kings by opposing the people to nobles, nobles by opposing the people to kings; writers and the learned by creating intellectual riches for democracy's use; tradesmen by providing unknown resources for democracy's activity; the navigator by finding democracy new worlds.≠>]

Everywhere you saw the various incidents in the lives of peoples turn to the profit of democracy; all men aided it by their efforts:P those who had in view contributing to its success and those who did not think of serving it; those who fought for it and even those who declared themselves its enemies; all were pushed pell-mell along the same path, and all worked in common, some despite themselves, others without their knowledge, blind instruments in the hands of God.

So the gradual development of equality of conditions [{democracy}] is a providential fact;q it has the principal characteristics of one: it is universal,

---

p. In the manuscript: "The Catholic priest and the sectarian, the jurist and the poet, the financier and the learned man, the manufacturer and the navigator, kings, nobles themselves, each worked for the people. The people profited from all efforts. Those who had in view . . ."

q. This sentence has not failed to provoke numerous commentaries. From it certain commentators have been able to conclude a bit quickly that Tocqueville was fatalistic. Thus François Furet ("Le système conceptuel de la Démocratie en Amèrique," in Michael Hereth and Jutta Höffken, *Alexis de Tocqueville. Zur Politik in der Demokratie,* Baden-Baden: Nomos, 1981, pp. 19–52, especially pp. 23 and 28) sees in Tocqueville the development of the idea of inevitability already present in Chateaubriand. If it is incontestable that this paragraph acknowledges a destiny of a providential nature for the idea of equality, the rest of the book, and all of Tocqueville's work, is no less a plea in favor of liberty against all forms of fatalism. Marvin Zetterbaum (*Tocqueville and the Problem of Democracy,* Stanford: Stanford University Press, 1967, pp. 15–19) attempted to resolve this contradiction by attributing to Tocqueville, in this passage, motives of the kind for persuasion and pedagogy: the latter would have insisted on the providential character of democracy in order to take advantage of the religious sentiments of the French aristocracy of the period and thus to persuade the French aristocracy not to oppose the march of democracy. Other authors, in particular Wilhelm Hennis, used a similar argument to see in Tocqueville less of a political thinker than a rhetorician (in the positive sense of the term). Without getting into a discussion of the rhetorical value of Tocqueville's work (what political discourse is not rhetorical?), it is necessary, nonetheless, to point out that in other places in the book Tocqueville sees in the inevitable character of political equality the result of social equality and of the cartesian method. This time the argument has psychological bases. If one time, even if in the middle of revolutionary disorders, men have had the experience of equality or have thought of themselves as equal, it is very difficult afterward to make them accept social inequality and political differences. So social equality is inevitable if it has existed previously, if only for a short moment, and if you accept the principle according to which social conditions determine political life.

The development of social equality remains to be explained. To understand it, it is indispensable to refer to a little known text of Tocqueville, drafted when he worked on *Democracy:* "Mémoire sur le paupérisme" (*Mémoires de la société académique de Cherbourg,* 1835, pp. 293–344, reproduced in *Commentaire* XXIII (1983): 630–36; XXIV, pp. 880–88). There Tocqueville sketches a general history of civilization. Almost literally following the Rousseau of *Discours sur l'origine de l'inégalité,* he offers a picture according to which men are equal solely when, coming out of the forests, they seek to associate together with their fellow men in order to gain sufficient food and shelter against the elements. Inequality owes its origin to ownership of territory which, in turn, produces the aristocracy.

> If you pay attention to what is happening in the world since the origin of societies, you will discover without difficulty that equality is found only at the two ends of civilization. Savages are equal to each other because they are all equally weak and ignorant. Very civilized men can all become equal because they all have at their disposal analogous means to attain comfort and happiness. Between these two extremes are found inequality of conditions, the wealth, enlightenment, power of some, the poverty, ignorance and weakness of all the others (p. 636).

The process of equality of conditions is dependent on the increase in intellectual and material needs. Tocqueville writes again:

it is lasting, it escapes every day from human power; all events, like all men, serve its development.[r]

> Men leave the plow to take up the shuttle and the hammer; from the cottage they pass into the factory; by acting in this way, they obey the immutable laws that preside over the growth of organized societies. So you can no more assign a stopping point to this movement than impose bounds on human perfectibility. The limit of the one like that of the others is known only to God (p. 634).

Equality is consequently the direct result of a law of the evolution of intelligence, and only intermediately, like all laws, a product of Providence. Finally, it must be recalled that Tocqueville is content to note here what the entire book will demonstrate and make convincing by the development of precise arguments. (See *Correspondance avec Kergorlay, OC,* XIII, 1, p. 375; according to André Jardin, this letter in reality would have been written to Eugène Stoffels.)

r. Democracy! Don't you notice that these are the waters of the flood? Don't you see them advance constantly by a slow and irresistible effort? <Already they cover the fields and the cities, they roll over the destroyed battlements of fortified castles and come to wash against the steps of thrones.> You withdraw, the waves continue their march. You flee, they run behind you. Here you are finally in your last refuge and scarcely have you sat down to take a breath when the waves have already covered the space that still separates you from them. So let us know how to face the future steadily and with open eyes. Instead of wanting to raise impotent dikes, let us seek rather to build the holy [v: tutelary] ark that must carry the human species over this ocean without shores.

But this is what hardly occupies us already placed in the middle . . .

It would be very insane to believe that we have seen the end of this great revolution. This movement continues, no one can say where it will stop. For we are already lacking terms of comparison. Conditions are more equal among us than they have ever been in any time and in any country of the world.

Thus the very grandeur of what is done prevents us from foreseeing what can still be done.

What will the probable consequences of this immense social revolution be? What new order will emerge from the debris of the one that is falling? Who can say? The men of the IVth century, witnesses to the barbarian invasions, gave themselves over, like us, to a thousand conjectures, but no one thought to foresee the universal establishment of the feudal system that followed the ruin of Rome in all of Europe. To discern effects without going back to causes, to judge what is without knowing what will be, isn't that moreover the whole of human destiny? We see that the sun changes place and that it advances constantly toward other heavens, we recognize that its movement is regulated, we feel that it obeys the hand of the Creator, but we will not be able to determine the force that makes it move and we are carried along with the sun toward a still unknown point in the universe.

In the middle of this impenetrable obscurity of the future, however, the eye sees some shafts of light. You can glimpse even now that the centuries of limited mon-

Would it be wise to believe that a social movement that comes from so far could be suspended by the efforts of a generation?[s] Do you think that

---

archy are rapidly passing and that modern societies are carried by a force superior to that of man either toward the republic or toward despotism and perhaps alternately from one to the other. As for me, I admit, in this century of liberty I fear for the future liberty of the human species. I [do not (ed.)] draw my fears from the past, which cannot be reproduced, but from the very nature of man, which does not change.

I see that by a strange oddity of our nature the passion for equality, which should decrease along with inequality of conditions, on the contrary increases as conditions become equal. In proportion [that (ed.)] the trace of hierarchies disappears, that passion alone seems to rule the human heart. Now, men [have (ed.)] two ways to be equal. They can all have the same rights or all be equally deprived of rights, and I tremble at the idea of the choice that they are going to make when I see the little care that is taken to (illegible word) [instruct? (ed.)] them, when I think how much more difficult it is to live free than to vegetate in slavery. I know that there are many honest men who are scarcely frightened by this idea and who would ask no better than to sleep peacefully in the arms of despotism while stammering some words about liberty. But my tastes, like my reason, distance me from them. Those who want thus to achieve order by way of despots hardly know what they desire. *Liberty* sometimes happens to make light of the existence of men, to be lavish with the resources of society, to disturb souls and to make beliefs waver, but despotism attacks all these things in their principle and in their [broken text (ed.)] (YTC, CVh, 3, pp. 27–30).

From the variant of this text (YTC, CVb, pp. 30–32, 26–31), the following details will be retained (pp. 29–30):

To claim to stop the march of democracy would be folly. God willing, there is still time to direct it and to prevent it from leading us to the despotism of one [v: military] man, that is to say to the most detestable form of government that the human mind has ever been able to imagine.

Sometimes liberty happens to make light of the existence of men, to be lavish with the resources of society, to disturb souls, to make beliefs waver.

But despotism attacks these very things in their principle and their essence. It prevents men from multiplying, it exhausts the source of wealth and of well-being, it confuses notions of good and evil and, by taking from man his independence [v: free will], it removes from him as much trace as it can of his divine origin. A free man often does things unworthy of himself, but a slave is less than a man.

To abhor despotism is not to do the work of a citizen, but the act of a man.

s. Hervé de Tocqueville: "The word *effort* that I advised deleting a bit above is found again here. Is the word *generation* suitable? It includes the idea of unanimity of action which will certainly not be found against democracy in the present generation" (YTC, CIIIb, 1, pp. 12–13).

after having destroyed feudalism and vanquished kings, democracy will retreat before the bourgeois and the rich?[t] Will it stop now that it has become
so strong and its adversaries so weak?

So where are we going? No one can say; for we are already lacking terms
of comparison; conditions are more equal today among Christians than
they have ever been in any time or in any country in the world; thus we are
prevented by the magnitude of what is already done from foreseeing what
can still be done.

The entire book that you are about to read has been written under the
impression of a sort of religious terror produced in the soul of the author
by the sight of this irresistible revolution that has marched for so many
centuries over all obstacles, and that we still see today advancing amid the
ruins that it has made.

It isn't necessary for God himself to speak in order for us to discover
sure signs of his will; it is enough to examine the regular march of nature and the continuous tendency of events; I know, without the Creator
raising his voice, that the stars in space follow the curves traced by his
fingers.

If long observations and sincere meditations led men of today to recognize that the gradual and progressive development of equality is at once
the past and the future of their history, this discovery alone would give this
development the sacred character of the will of God. To want to stop democracy would then seem to be struggling against God himself, and it
would only remain for nations to accommodate themselves to the social
state that Providence imposes on them.[u]

---

t. In the margin: "≠The democratic revolution that carries us along will not retreat
after having triumphed for seven hundred years over so many obstacles.≠"

u. This paragraph and the preceding one do not exist in the manuscript. In their place,
you find this: "If, to want to stop the development of democracy, is to struggle against
God himself, what then remains for men to do if not to accommodate themselves to the
social state that Providence imposes on them?"

The two new paragraphs were probably added following this suggestion by Louis de
Kergorlay:

The thought enclosed in this paragraph is very beautiful and fundamental, but unfortunately little in fashion, little spread among the public which remains more matter
of fact. I believe that to make the public see that it is a thought, that it is a sentiment,

Christian peoples seem to me to offer today a frightening spectacle.[v] The movement that sweeps them along is already so strong that it cannot be suspended, and it is not yet so rapid as to despair of directing it. Their fate is in their hands; but soon it escapes them.[w]

---

that it is something serious, it must be developed a bit more. It is one of the building blocks of your introduction. I have taken the risk of drafting the following three or four sentences as more or less encompassing what I understand as the development of your idea. So in my mind, I put this in place of your paragraph:

"Where would the hand of God be more visible than in the most immutable facts of nature? Where does man thus find other proofs of the existence and of *the will* of the divinity, than in the works of his creator, and what more sublime work could he examine than his own nature?

"So if sincere meditations led him one day to acknowledge that the progressive development of democracy is at once the past and the future of his history, this discovery alone would give to this development the sacred character of the will of our sovereign master, to all resistance against this march of our destiny that of a struggle against God himself, and that of a *duty* to the search for all that can accommodate humanity to the new social state imposed by Providence."

I do not know if you will find these sentences clear or vague, but what I want to express to you is the need for a development that elevates the soul of the reader (YTC, CIIIb, 1, pp. 23–24).

v. In the manuscript: ". . . offer today the most terrible of spectacles."
Hervé de Tocqueville: *The most terrible* here is too strong an expression, since the author says farther along that you must not yet despair of being able to direct the movement."
Édouard de Tocqueville: "The word *terrible* does not seem to me very good either; this expression which prepares for something frightening is not justified by what follows" (YTC, CIIIb, 1, p. 13).

w. It would be falling into a great error to believe that the period in which we live resembled any other and that the habitual routine of human passions could be applied to it equally. At the moment when I am speaking, the destinies of the Christian world are in suspense and nations find themselves in a position unique in their lives. The movement that carries them along is already too strong to be able to hope to stop it and not yet strong enough to despair of directing it.

At the period in which we are, what are the destinies of a man, the fortune of a law, the successes of a party? These interests of one day disappear before an interest a thousand times greater still, that touches all men and all parties equally and that must be the goal of all laws. Today the question is no longer only knowing what progress civilization will make, but what the fate of civilization will be, not what laws will regulate property, but what the very principle of property will be. It is no longer only a matter of regulating political rights, but civil rights, inheritance, paternity, marriage like the *right to vote* [v: property qualification].

To instruct democracy, to revive its beliefs if possible, to purify its mores, to regulate its movements, to substitute little by little the science of public affairs for its inexperience, knowledge of its true interests for its blind instincts; to adapt its government to times and places; to modify it according to circumstances and men; such is the first of duties imposed today on those who lead society.

A new political science[x] is needed for a world entirely new[y] [{for a unique situation, laws without precedents are needed}].

The time has passed when you struggled to conquer or to keep, not some liberty, but all liberties together, up to that of living.

Today, in a word, you must not forget, it is still much more a matter of the very existence of society than of the forms of the government.

You can no longer have anything except despotism or the *republic*.

Despotism such as our fathers never knew in any period of history, Roman or Byzantine despotism, mixture of corruption [v: plunder], barbarism, brutality and subtlety, of obsequiousness and of arrogance, no more collective resistance, no more *esprit de corps*, family *honor*, aristocratic (four illegible words). Honest men who want absolute power today do not know what they want. They will no longer have the good absolute power of the old monarchy, moderated by mores . . . but the absolute power of the Roman Empire . . . (YTC, CVh, 3, pp. 20–21, 21–22).

x. This affirmation is central and cannot be minimized. Criticism has too generally put the accent on Tocqueville as a traveler, observer of mores and institutions, historian foreshadowing the sociologist. Whereas, the objective that Tocqueville is fixed upon is above all *political*. The fact that this "science" is defined in terms that to us signal more sociology, history, or psychology must not diminish its importance. Like all political thinkers, like Montequieu or Rousseau, Tocqueville wants to try to rethink what he calls "political science" and to redefine it. He will not cease to come back to the question of the language used to designate concepts and new realities; he will introduce neologisms. It is also the meaning of the memorable speech delivered at the Academy of Moral and Political Sciences in which the author presents himself as a political theorist. It is precisely his talents as a theoretician, he thinks, that have prevented him from making a political career:

The art of writing suggests, in fact, to those who have practiced it for a long time habits of mind little favorable to the conduct of affairs. It subjugates them to the logic of ideas, when the crowd never obeys anything except that of passions. It gives them the taste for the fine, the delicate, the ingenious, the original, while it is the awful commonplaces that lead the world. (Speech delivered to the annual public meeting of the Academy of Moral and Political Sciences, *Séances et travaux de*

But that is what we scarcely consider; placed in the middle of a rapid river, we obstinately fix our eyes on some debris that we still see on the bank, while the current carries us away and pushes us backwards toward the abyss.

There is no people of Europe among whom the great social revolution[z] that I have just described has made more rapid progress than among us; but here it has always marched haphazardly.

The heads of State [{legislator}] never thought to prepare anything in advance for it; it came about despite them or without their knowledge. The most powerful, most intelligent and most moral classes of the nation did

---

l'Académie des sciences morales et politiques, XXI, 1852, p. 303; this speech has been reproduced with some omissions in *OCB,* IX, pp. 116–33).

For Tocqueville, political science is a science based on the faculties and eternal instincts of human nature; it spreads from philosophy to the civil law, from theory to written laws and to facts. Such an upside down pyramid is conceived so that the closer you get to facts, the farther you get from generalities: "There is no commentator who does not often rely upon the abstract and general truths that writers on politics have found, and the latter need constantly to base their theory on particular facts and on the studied institutions that commentators have revealed or described" (*ibid.,* p. 305). Parallel to this science exists the art of governing, politics of the practical order, able to be modified constantly. The degree of civilization of a people is always proportional to the complexity of its political science. In other words, the more civilization, the more elaborate the political science; a new world demands as well a new political science:

Among all civilized peoples, the political sciences give birth or at least give form to general ideas, from which then follow particular facts, in the middle of which politicians agitate, and the laws that they think they invent. The political sciences form around each society something like a kind of intellectual atmosphere in which the minds of the governed and of those who govern breathe, and from which both, often without knowing, sometimes without wanting to know, draw the principles of their conduct. Barbarians are the only ones where only practice is recognized in politics (*ibid.,* p. 306).

y. Hervé de Tocqueville: "I do not know if you can use the expression *for a world entirely new* while speaking of old Europe. I know well that it is a matter of the political world, but the changes there are not so abrupt that *world entirely new* applies very exactly."
Édouard de Tocqueville: "Current society is certainly entirely new by comparison with that of forty years ago" (YTC, CIIIb, 1, p. 13).
z. "The French Revolution did the same good as the Nile that fertilizes the fields of Egypt by covering them with muck" (YTC, CVh, 3, p. 97).

not try to take hold of it in order to direct it. So democracy has been abandoned to its wild instincts; it has grown up like those children, deprived of paternal care, who raise themselves in the streets of our cities, and who know society only by its vices and miseries. We still seemed unaware of its existence, when it took hold of power without warning. Then each person submitted with servility to its slightest desires; it was adored as the image of strength; when later it was weakened by its own excesses, legislators conceived the imprudent plan of destroying it instead of trying to instruct and correct it, and not wanting to teach it to govern, they thought only about pushing it away from government.

The result was that the democratic revolution took place in the material aspect of society without happening in the laws, ideas, habits and mores,[a] the change that would have been necessary to make this revolu-

a. This idea is found in the fourth lecture of Guizot's course on civilization in France. "The revolution that the last century caused to burst forth was a social revolution; it was much more concerned with changing the reciprocal situation of men than their internal and personal dispositions; it wanted to reform the society rather than the individual" (François Guizot, *Histoire de la civilisation en France* in *Cours d'histoire moderne,* Brussels: Hauman, 1839, p. 160). Tocqueville attended this course on the history of civilization in France taught by Guizot at the Sorbonne in 1829–1830. The notes for the course, from 11 April 1829 to 29 March 1830, are preserved. His correspondence indicates nonetheless that he attended the course before the month of April (see *Correspondance avec Beaumont, OC,* VIII, 1, pp. 76–77). Tocqueville, in a letter to Beaumont, dated 30 August 1829 (*OC,* VIII, 1, pp. 80–81), asserts that he has already read "most of Guizot" and that he found him so "prodigious" that he proposes to his friend to read Guizot with him during the winter. Reading Guizot enlightened him notably about the IVth century (note r from p. 12 bears a reference to the same century). Several times, furthermore, Tocqueville will allude in the *Democracy* to the eighth lecture of the *Cours.* Two years later, when he is in America, he writes to his friend and colleague Ernest de Chabrol: "We cannot find here a book that is very necessary to us for helping us analyze American society; this is the lectures of Guizot, including what he said and published three years ago on Roman society and the Middle Ages" (New York, 18 May 1831, YTC, BIa2). It is following Guizot, in the fourth lecture of the *Cours,* that Tocqueville divides his first notes on American society into civil state and social state.

Guizot did not fail to find himself in Tocqueville's work. In *De la démocratie en France (janvier 1849)* (Brussels: J. Petit, 1849), whose title alone makes explicit reference to Tocqueville, he seems to blame the latter for having taken the concept of equality and having transformed it into a universal process that pushes irremediably toward popular sovereignty while making the dominion of the middle classes disappear by its momention[b] useful. We therefore have democracy, minus what must attenuate its vices and bring out its natural advantages; and seeing already the evils that it brings, we are still unaware of the good that it can give.

When royal power, supported by the aristocracy, peacefully governed the peoples of Europe, society, amid its miseries, enjoyed several kinds of happiness, which are difficult to imagine and appreciate today.

The power of some subjects raised insurmountable barriers to the tyranny of the prince; and kings, feeling vested in the eyes of the crowd with a nearly divine character, drew, from the very respect that they caused, the will not to abuse their power.

Placed an immense distance from the people, the nobles nonetheless took the type of benevolent and tranquil interest in the fate of the people that the shepherd[c] gives to his flock; and without seeing the poor man as their equal, they watched over his lot as a trust put in their hands by Providence.

Not having conceived the idea of a social state other than their own, not imagining that they could ever be equal to their rulers, the people accepted the benefits and did not question the rights of their rulers. They loved them when they were lenient and just and submitted without difficulty and without servility to their rigors as to inevitable evils sent to them by the hand of God. Custom and mores had, moreover, established limits to tyranny and founded a kind of right in the very midst of force.

Since the noble did not think that someone would want to wrest from him the privileges that he believed legitimate, and the serf regarded his

---

tum. It is not the only time, as we will see, that Tocqueville repeats an idea of Guizot for his particular ends.

See Luis Díez del Corral, *El pensamiento político de Tocqueville* (Madrid: Alianza Universidad, 1989), pp. 353–91; Aurelian Craiutu, *Liberalism Under Siege: The Political Thought of the French Doctrinaires* (Lanham, Md.: Lexington Books, 2003), pp. 87–122.

b. Édouard de Tocqueville: "How can a revolution take place in the *material aspect* of society without the ideas, laws, habits and mores seconding it? So what then do you call the material aspect of society?" (YTC, CIIIb, 1, p. 14).

c. Hervé de Tocqueville: "I am afraid that some might respond to the author that these shepherds were really wolves. You will avoid this disadvantage by generalizing less, by putting *a portion of the nobles*" (YTC, CIIIb, 1, p. 14).

inferiority as a result of the immutable order of nature, it is conceivable that a kind of reciprocal benevolence could be established between these two classes sharing so different a fate. You then saw in society inequality, miseries, but souls were not degraded.

It is not the use of power or the habit of obedience that depraves men; it is the use of a power that they consider as illegitimate and obedience to a power that they regard as usurped and oppressive.

On one side were wealth, force, leisure and with them the pursuit of luxury, refinements of taste, pleasures of the mind, devotion to the arts; on the other, work, coarseness and ignorance.

But within this ignorant and coarse crowd, you met energetic passions, generous sentiments, profound beliefs and untamed virtues.

The social body organized in this way could have stability, power, and above all glory.

But ranks are merging; barriers raised between men are falling; estates are being divided; power is being shared, enlightenment is spreading, intellects are becoming equal; the social state is becoming democratic, and the dominion of democracy is finally being established peacefully in institutions and in mores.

Then I imagine a society where all, seeing the law as their work, would love it and would submit to it without difficulty; where since the authority of the government is respected as necessary and not as divine, the love that is felt for the head of State would be not a passion, but a reasoned and calm sentiment. Since each person has rights and is assured of preserving his rights, a manly confidence and a kind of reciprocal condescension, as far from pride as from servility, would be established among all classes.

Instructed in their true interests, the people would understand that, in order to take advantage of the good things of society, you must submit to its burdens. The free association of citizens would then be able to replace the individual power of the nobles, and the State would be sheltered from tyranny and from license.

I understand that in a democratic State, constituted in this manner, society will not be immobile; but the movements of the social body will be able to be regulated and progressive; if you meet less brilliance there than within an aristocracy, you will find less misery; pleasures will be less extreme and well-being more general; knowledge not as great and ignorance more rare; sentiments less energetic and habits more mild; there you will notice more vices and fewer crimes.[d]

If there is no enthusiasm and fervor of beliefs, enlightenment and experience will sometimes obtain great sacrifices from citizens; each man, equally weak, will feel an equal need for his fellows; and knowing that he can gain their support only on condition of lending them his help, he will discover without difficulty that for him particular interest merges with the general interest.

The nation taken as a body will be less brilliant, less glorious, less strong perhaps; but the majority of citizens there will enjoy a more prosperous lot, and the people will appear untroubled, not because they despair of being better, but because they know they are well-off.[e]

If everything was not good and useful in such an order of things, society at least would have appropriated everything useful and good that such an order can present; and men, while abandoning forever the social advantages that aristocracy can provide, would have taken from democracy all the good that the latter can offer to them.

---

d. "For nearly ten years I have been thinking a part of the things that I revealed to you just now. I was in America only to enlighten myself on this point," Tocqueville mentions to Kergorlay (?) in a letter dated from 1835 (?) (*OC,* XIII, 1, p. 374). See note q for p. 12.

A certain number of the constituent ideas of the *Democracy* already appear in a letter from Tocqueville to Charles Stoffels, dated Versailles, 21 April 1830 (that is, nearly a year before the departure for the United States). This letter is reproduced in appendix V.

e. Mass floating in the middle, inert, egoistic, without energy, without patriotism, sensual, sybaritic, that has only instincts, that lives from day to day, that becomes in turn the plaything of all the others./

Moderation without virtue, nor courage; moderation that is born from cowardice of the heart and not from virtue, from exhaustion, from fear, from egoism; tranquillity, that does not come about because you are well-off, but because you do not have the courage and the energy necessary to seek something better. Debasement of souls.

The passions of old men that end in impotence (YTC, CVh, 3, pp. 36–37).

But we, while giving up the social state of our ancestors, while throwing pell-mell their institutions, their ideas, and their mores behind us, what have we put in their place?

The prestige of royal power has vanished, without being replaced by the majesty of laws; today the people scorn authority, but they fear it, and fear extracts more from them than respect and love formerly yielded.

I notice that we have destroyed the individual existences that could struggle separately against tyranny [{but I do not see that we have created a collective strength to fulfill their function}], but I see the government that alone inherits all the prerogatives wrenched from families, from corporations or from men; so, to the sometimes oppressive but often conservative strength of a small number of citizens, the weakness of all has succeeded.

The division of fortunes has reduced the distance that separated the poor from the rich; but by coming closer together, they seem to have found new reasons to hate each other, and, eyeing one another with looks full of terror and envy, they mutually push each other away from power; for the one as for the other, the idea of rights does not exist, and force appears to them both as the only reason for the present and the sole guarantee of the future.

The poor man has kept most of the prejudices of his fathers, without their beliefs; their ignorance, without their virtues; he has accepted, as the rule for his actions, the doctrine of interest, without knowing the science of interest, and his egoism is as wanting in enlightenment as his devotion formerly was.

Society is tranquil, not because it is conscious of its strength and its well-being, but on the contrary because it believes itself weak and frail; it is afraid of dying by making an effort. Everyone feels that things are going badly, but no one has the necessary courage and energy to seek something better; we have desires, regrets, sorrows and joys that produce nothing visible or lasting, similar to the passions of old men that end in impotence.

Thus we have abandoned what the old state could present of the good, without acquiring what the current state would be able to offer of the useful; we have destroyed an aristocratic society, [and we do not think about organizing on its ruins a moral and tranquil democracy] and, stopping out of complacency amid the debris of the former edifice, we seem to want to settle there forever.[f]

What is happening in the intellectual world is no less deplorable.

f. There are two states of society that I imagine without difficulty, the one that has been, the other that could be.

We have left the virtues of the old order without taking the ideas of the new order.

We have thrown pell-mell behind us the vices and the virtues of our ancestors, their habits, their ideas, their mores, and we have put nothing in their place (YTC, CVh, 3, pp. 106–107).

ARISTOCRATIC AND MONARCHICAL SYSTEM. OUR FATHERS.
1. Love of the King.
2. (illegible word) aristocracy.
3. Individual strength against tyranny.
4. Beliefs, devotion, wild virtues, instincts.
5. Idea of duty.
6. Tranquillity of the people that arises from their not seeing anything better.
7. Monarchical immobility.
8. Strength and grandeur of the state which you reach by the constant efforts of some.

DEMOCRATIC AND REPUBLICAN SYSTEM.
1. Respect for law, idea of rights.
2. Benevolence arising from equality of rights.
3. Association.
4. Interest well understood, enlightenment.
5. Love of liberty.
6. That they know that they are well-off.
7. Orderly and progressive movement of democracy.
8. Id. by the simultaneous efforts of all.

CURRENT STATE.
1. Fear of authority that is scorned.
2. War of the poor and the rich, individual egoism without strength.
3. Equal weakness without collective power {of association}.
4. Prejudices without beliefs, ignorance without virtues, the doctrine of interest without the science, stupid egoism.
5. Taste for license.
6. Who do not have the courage to change, passions of old men (YTC, CVh, 3, pp. 110–11).

Hindered in its march or abandoned without support to its disorderly passions, democracy in France has overturned everything that it met on its way, weakening what it did not destroy. You did not see it take hold of society little by little in order to establish its dominion peacefully; it has not ceased to march amid the disorders and the agitation of battle. Animated by the heat of the struggle, pushed beyond the natural limits of his opinion by the opinions and excesses of his adversaries, each person loses sight of the very object of his pursuits and uses a language that corresponds badly to his true sentiments and to his secret instincts.

From that results the strange confusion that we are forced to witness.

I search my memory in vain; I find nothing that deserves to excite more distress and more pity than what is happening before our eyes;g it seems that today we have broken the natural bond that unites opinions to tastes and actions to beliefs; the sympathy that has been observed in all times between the sentiments and the ideas of men seems to be destroyed, and you would say that all the laws of moral analogy are abolished.

You still meet among us Christians full of zeal, whose religious souls love to be nourished by the truths of the other life; they are undoubtedly going to become active in favor of human liberty, source of all moral grandeur. [<Their hearts will open without difficulty to the holy love of country, this religion of the political world so fruitful in generous devotions.>] Christianity, which has made all men equal before God, will not be loath to see all citizens equal before the law. But, by a combination of strange events, religion is at the moment involved amid the powers that democracy is overturning, and it often happens that religion rejects the equality that it loves and curses liberty as an adversary, while, by taking liberty by the hand, religion could be able to sanctify its efforts.

Next to these religious men, I find others whose sights are turned toward the earth rather than toward heaven; partisans of liberty, not only because

g. Hervé de Tocqueville:

This expression is too strong. It takes the thought beyond the truth. What happened at the time of the imprisonment of King Jean and under the last of the Valois was of a nature to cause more distress than what is happening currently. So I would delete the words *more distress* in the sentence and I would put only: *I find nothing that deserves to excite more pity* (YTC, CIIIb, 1, pp. 15–16).

they see in it the origin of the most noble virtues, but above all because they consider it as the source of the greatest advantages, they sincerely desire to secure its dominion and to have men taste its benefits. I understand that the latter are going to hasten to call religion to their aid, for they must know that you cannot establish the reign of liberty without that of mores, nor found mores without beliefs; but they have seen religion in the ranks of their adversaries; that is enough for them; some attack religion and the others dare not defend it [all lack enlightenment or courage].

Past centuries saw base and venal souls advocate slavery, while independent spirits and generous hearts struggled without hope to save human liberty. But today you often meet men naturally noble and proud whose opinions are in direct opposition to their tastes, and who speak in praise of the servility and baseness that they have never known for themselves. There are others, in contrast, who speak of liberty as if they could feel what is holy and great in it and who loudly claim on behalf of humanity rights that they have always disregarded.

I notice virtuous and peaceful men placed naturally by their pure morals, tranquil habits, prosperity and enlightenment at the head of the populations that surround them. Full of a sincere love of country, they are ready to make great sacrifices for it. Civilization, however, often finds them to be adversaries; they confuse its abuses with its benefits, and in their minds the idea of evil is indissolubly united with the idea of the new [and they seem to want to establish a monstrous bond between virtue, misery and ignorance so that all three may be struck with the same blow[h]].

Nearby I see other men who, in the name of progress, try hard to materialize man, wanting to find the useful without attending to the just, want-

---

h. Hervé de Tocqueville: "This last thought is not very clear. Would it perhaps seem a bit gigantesque? It is a kind of irony. But is it very accurate? Who would want to strike virtue? No one, I think."

Édouard de Tocqueville: "This sentence did not fully satisfy me either. I do not see clearly why the persons in question here would desire that virtue, misery and ignorance be struck with the same blow" (YTC, CIIIb, 1, p. 16).

ing to find knowledge far from beliefs and well-being separate from virtue. These claim to be champions of modern civilization and they arrogantly put themselves at its head, usurping a place that is abandoned to them and that their unworthiness denies to them.j

So where are we?

Religious men combat liberty, and the friends of liberty attack religion; noble and generous spirits speak in praise of slavery, and base and servile souls advocate independence; honest and enlightened citizens are enemies of all progress, while men without patriotism and without mores become the apostles of civilization and enlightenment!

Have all centuries resembled ours then? Has man always had before his eyes, as today, a world where nothing is connected, where virtue is without genius,k and genius without honor; where love of order merges with the taste for tyrants and the holy cult of liberty with scorn for human laws; where conscience throws only a doubtful light upon human actions; where nothing any longer seems either forbidden, or permitted, or honest, or shameful, or true, or false?

Will I think that the Creator made man in order to leave him to struggle endlessly amid the intellectual miseries that surround us? I cannot believe it; God is preparing for European societies a future more settled and more calm; I do not know his plans, but I will not cease to believe in them because I cannot fathom them, and I will prefer to doubt my knowledge than his justice.

There is a country in the world where the great social revolution that I am speaking about seems more or less to have reached its natural limits; it came about there in a simple and easy way, or rather it can be said that this

---

j. In the margin: "≠Thus some wanted virtue and misery; others, well-being without virtue.≠"

k. Hervé de Tocqueville: "This whole sentence is very beautiful and I would very much like to let the word *genius* go by. But I cannot do so, because it expresses more than is necessary. It will be asked where is the genius in France and each person will answer: I do not know."

Édouard de Tocqueville: "After long and careful reflection, I do not share the opinion of my father. *Genius* here means intellectual superiorities and there are always some in a country" (YTC, CIIIb, 1, p. 17).

country sees the results of the democratic revolution that is taking place among us, without having had the revolution itself.

The emigrants who came to settle in America at the beginning of the XVIIth century in a way freed the principle of democracy from all those principles that it struggled against within the old societies of Europe, and they transplanted it alone to the shores of the New World. There it was able to grow in liberty and, moving ahead with mores, to develop peacefully in the laws.

It seems to me beyond doubt that sooner or later, we will arrive, like the Americans, at a nearly complete equality of conditions. From that, I do not conclude that one day we are necessarily called to draw from such a social state the political consequences that the Americans have drawn from it.[m] I am very far from believing that they have found the only form of government that democracy may take; but in the two countries the generating cause of laws and mores is the same; that is enough for us to have an immense interest in knowing what that generating cause has produced in each of them.

So it is not only to satisfy a curiosity, legitimate for that matter, that I examined America; I wanted to find lessons there from which we would be

m. Hervé de Tocqueville:

I would like the author to have added a sentence here to bring out clearly that he does not mean that the forms of the American government can be adapted to the old European societies whose conditions are so different. Alexis thinks that democracy will end by dominating everywhere, while keeping at the head of government an executive power more or less strong, more or less concentrated. He must, I think, make that understood very clearly by his reader.

Édouard de Tocqueville:

I find a great deal of accuracy in this observation. You must above all inculcate clearly in the reader the conviction that you have not returned from America with the fixed idea of adapting American institutions to Europe. So it would be good to say that you foresee the establishment of democracy and of equality of conditions which is the consequence of democracy, but *very often* with other forms and a different social organization; the character, habits and mores of the two countries being eminently dissimilar (YTC, CIIIb, 1, p. 18).

The phrase "I am very far . . . that democracy may take" does not appear in the manuscript.

able to profit. You would be strangely mistaken if you thought that I wanted to do a panegyric; whoever reads this book will be clearly convinced that such was not my purpose;[n] nor was my goal to advocate any particular form of government in general; for I am among those who believe that there is hardly ever absolute good in laws; I did not even claim to judge if the social revolution, whose march seems irresistible to me, was advantageous or harmful to humanity. I have acknowledged this revolution as an accomplished or nearly accomplished fact, and, from among the peoples who have seen it taking place among them, I sought the people among whom it has reached the most complete and most peaceful development, in order to discern clearly its natural consequences and, if possible, to see the means to make it profitable to men. I admit that in America I saw more than America;[o] I sought there an image of democracy itself, its tendencies, its character, its prejudices, its passions; I wanted to know democracy, if only to know at least what we must hope or fear from it.

In the first part of this work, I tried to show the direction that democracy, delivered in America to its tendencies and abandoned almost without con-

n. "That governments have relative goodness. When Montesquieu . . . I admire him. But when he portrays to me the English constitution as the model of perfection, it seems to me that, for the first time, I see the limit of his genius. This constitution today falls in the same [interrupted text (ed.)]" (YTC, CVh, 4, p. 91).

o. Why would I be afraid to say so? While I had my eyes fixed on America, I thought about Europe. I thought about this immense social revolution that is coming to completion among us while we are still discussing its legitimacy and its rights. I thought about the irresistible slope where [we (ed.)] are running, who knows, perhaps toward despotism, perhaps also toward the republic, but definitely toward democracy. There are men who see in the Revolution of 1789 a pure accident and who, like the traveler in the fable, sit down waiting for the river to pass. Vain illusion! Our fathers did not see it being born and we will not see it end. Its turbulent currents will flow for still many generations. More than six hundred years ago the first impulse was given.

[In the margin] Some among us consider the present state as a beginning; others, as an end. It is neither the one nor the other; it is an incident in an immense revolution that began before it and has continued since (YTC, CVh, 3, pp. 22–23; see a more or less identical fragment in YTC, CVh, 4, p. 1, and *Souvenirs, OC,* XII, p. 30).

straint to its instincts, gave naturally to laws, the course that it imparted to government, and in general the power that it gained over public affairs. I wanted to know what good and bad it produced. I sought out what precautions the Americans have used to direct it and what others they have omitted, and I undertook to discern the causes that allow it to govern society.

My goal was to portray in a second part [{third volume}] the influence that equality of conditions and the government of democracy exercise in America on civil society, on habits, ideas and mores;[p] but I begin to feel less enthusiasm[q] about accomplishing this plan. Before I can complete in this way the task that I proposed for myself, my work will have become nearly useless. Someone else will soon show readers the principal features of the American character and, hiding the seriousness of the descriptions behind a light veil, will lend truth charms with which I would not be able to adorn it.[1]

p. Although the second part had been published, probably on the recommendation of Gosselin, the publisher, with the title of the first part, Tocqueville had at one moment wanted to entitle it *Influence of Equality on the Ideas and Feelings of Men* (See letter to Mill of 14 November 1839, *Correspondance anglaise, OC,* VI, 1, p. 326).

q. In the manuscript: ". . . but each day I feel less enthusiasm . . ."

Hervé de Tocqueville: "This turn of phrase seems too explicit to me; it removes in too absolute a way the hope for a 3rd volume."

Édouard de Tocqueville: "That is very true; a sentence more or less like this would be needed: *and I give up at least at present.*

"I also do not like *my work will have become useless.* We do not know if you are speaking about the future work or this one. At least *would become useless* would be necessary" (YTC, CIIIb, 1, p. 19). The manuscript says: ". . . will have become nearly useless."

1. *At the time when I published the first edition of this work, M. Gustave de Beaumont, my traveling companion in America, was still working on his book entitled* Marie, or Slavery in the United States, *which has since appeared. The principal goal of M. de Beaumont was to bring out and make known the situation of Negroes within Anglo-American society. His work will throw a bright and new light on the question of slavery, a vital question for the united republics. I do not know if I am wrong, but it seems to me that the book of M. de Beaumont, after deeply interesting those who want to gather emotions and find descriptions there, will gain a still more solid and more lasting success among readers who, above all, desire true insights and profound truths.*[r]

r. For obvious reasons, the beginning of this note was a bit different in the first edition: "M. Gustave de Beaumont, my traveling companion in America, intends to publish during the first days of 1835, a book entitled *Marie, or Slavery in the United States.* The principal goal . . ."

I do not know if I have succeeded in making known what I saw in America, but I am sure that I sincerely desired to do so, and that I never yielded, except unknowingly, to the need to adapt facts to ideas, instead of subjecting ideas to facts.

When a point could be established with the help of written documents, I have taken care to turn to original texts and to the most authentic and most respected works.[2] I have indicated my sources in notes, and everyone will be able to verify them. When it was a matter of opinions, of political customs, of observations of mores, I sought to consult the most enlightened men. If something happened to be important or doubtful, I was not content with one witness, but decided only on the basis of the body of testimonies.

Here the reader must necessarily take me at my word. I would often have been able to cite in support of what I advance the authority of names that are known to him, or that at least are worthy to be; but I have refrained from doing so. The stranger often learns by the hearth of his host important truths, that the latter would perhaps conceal from a friend; with the stranger you ease the burden of a forced silence; you are not afraid of his indiscretion because he is passing through. Each one of these confidences was recorded by me as soon as received, but they will never emerge from my manuscripts; I prefer to detract from the success of my accounts than to add my name

2. *Legislative and administrative documents have been provided to me with a kindness the memory of which will always stir my gratitude. Among the American officials who have thus favored my research, I will cite above all Mr. Edward Livingston, the Secretary of State (now ambassador plenipotentiary to Paris). During my stay at the Congress, Mr. Livingston was nice enough to have sent to me most of the documents that I possess relating to the federal government. Mr. Livingston is one of those rare men whom you like by reading their writings, whom you admire and honor even before knowing them and to whom you are happy to owe acknowledgement.*[s]

s. This note does not appear in the manuscript of the book and no reference to it is found in the other papers of Tocqueville. At the end of the year 1834, Livingston was in Paris in a very delicate situation because of the famous affair of the American indemnities. It is possible that the note had been written in sympathy with the man whose name appears several times in the drafts as a source of information. On the affair of the indemnities and Edward Livingston, see Richard A. McLemore, *Franco-American Diplomatic Relations, 1816–1836* (Baton Rouge: Louisiana State University Press, 1941).

to the list of those travelers who send sorrows and troubles in return for
the generous hospitality that they received.

I know that, despite my care, nothing will be easier than to criticize this
book, if anyone ever thinks to examine it critically.

Those who will want to look closely at it will find, I think, in the entire
work, a generative thought that links so to speak all its parts. But the diversity of the subjects that I had to treat is very great, and whoever will
undertake to contrast an isolated fact to the whole of the facts that I cite,
a detached idea to the whole of the ideas, will succeed without difficulty.
So I would like you to grant me the favor of reading me with the same spirit
that presided over my work, and would like you to judge this book by the
general impression that it leaves, as I myself came to a decision, not due to
a particular reason, but due to the mass of reasons.

Nor must it be forgotten that the author who wants to make himself
understood is obliged to push each of his ideas to all of their theoretical
consequences, and often to the limits of what is false and impractical;[t] for
if it is sometimes necessary to step back from the rules of logic in actions,
you cannot do the same in discourses, and man finds it almost as difficult
to be inconsistent in his words as he normally finds it to be consistent in
his actions. [<This, to say in passing, brings out one of the great advantages
of free governments, an advantage about which you scarcely think. In these

t. Tocqueville is eager to emphasize that the goal of his book is the description of
models, of *ideal types* that, by definition, do not perfectly coincide with reality. He probably borrows the concept from Montesquieu, even if from Montesquieu to Tocqueville,
and later to Max Weber, differences are perceptible. The use of the idea of ideal types
(aristocracy and democracy) is of a hermeneutical nature; all attempts to make it a mechanical and automatic process would destroy one of the most remarkable aspects of
Tocqueville's theory. For the latter, the good political regime is characterized by an eternal tension between the two types, idea that points at the very same time to Pascal and
to the romanticism of the period. (See in this regard Auguste Comte, *Cours de philosophie
positive,* lesson 47; Emile Durkheim, *Montesquieu et Rousseau, précurseurs de la sociologie,*
Paris: Marcel Rivière, 1953, ch. III; Melvin Richter, "Comparative Political Analysis in
Montesquieu and Tocqueville," *Comparative Politics* I, no. 2 (1969): 129–60; Pierre Birn-
baum, *Sociologie de Tocqueville,* Paris: PUF, 1970, pp. 29–39; Gianfranco Poggi, *Images
of Society,* Stanford: Stanford University Press, 1972, pp. 2–82). Cf. note m of p. 694 of
volume I.

governments, it is necessary to talk a great deal. The need to talk forces men of State to reason, and from speeches a bit of logic is introduced into public affairs.>]

I finish by pointing out myself what a great number of readers[u] will consider as the capital defect of the work.[v] This book follows in no one's train exactly; by writing it I did not mean either to serve or to combat any party; I set about to see, not differently, but farther than parties;[w] and while they are concerned with the next day, I wanted to think about the future.[x]

u. In the manuscript: ". . . what most readers . . ."

Hervé de Tocqueville: "You must not put *most readers*. That would shock them because you seem to doubt their intelligence too much. So put *some readers* in place of *most readers*.

Édouard de Tocqueville (?): "Very right" (YTC, CIIIb, 1, pp. 19–20).

v. In the margin: "≠Why I have not put many figures and statistics. Change so rapidly. Insignificant.≠"

w. "I believe what I say, only advantage that I have over most of my contemporaries. Nothing more common than to talk of liberty, but nearly everyone wants something more or less than liberty. But I really love it and want it" (YTC, CVh, 3, p. 97).

"I am sure that my subject does not lack grandeur. If I fail it will be my fault and not the fault of my subject. In any case, I will have pointed out the path" (YTC, CVh, 3, p. 98).

x. "To point out if possible to men what to do to escape tyranny and debasement while becoming *democratic*. Such is, I think, the general idea by which my book can be summarized and which will appear on every page of the one I am writing at this moment. To work in this direction is, in my eyes, a *holy* occupation and one for which you must spare neither your money, nor your time, nor your life," writes Tocqueville to Kergorlay. 26 December 1836 (*Correspondance avec Kergorlay, OC,* XIII, 1, pp. 431–32).

CHAPTER I

Exterior Configuration of North America

North America divided into two vast regions, the one descending toward the pole, the other toward the equator.—Valley of the Mississippi.—Traces found there of global upheavals.—Coast of the Atlantic Ocean where the English colonies were founded.— Different appearance that South America and North America presented at the time of discovery.—Forests of North America.— Prairies.—Wandering tribes of natives.—Their outward appearance, their mores, their languages.—Traces of an unknown people.

North America, in its exterior configuration, presents general features that are easy to distinguish at first glance.

A kind of methodical order presided over the separation of land and waterways, mountains and valleys. A simple and majestic arrangement is revealed even in the midst of the confusion of objects and among the extreme variety of scenes.

Two vast regions divide North America almost equally.*

One is limited, in the North, by the Arctic pole; in the East, in the West, by the two great oceans. Then it advances southward and forms a triangle whose sides, irregularly drawn, finally meet below the Great Lakes of Canada.

---

* See the map placed at the end of the volume. [See pp. xliv–xlv. This map was deleted after the first editions. (ed.)]

The second begins where the first finishes and extends over the entire remainder of the continent.

The one inclines slightly toward the pole; the other, toward the equator.

The lands included in the first region descend toward the north in a slope so slight that they could almost be said to form a plateau. In the interior of this immense flatland, there are neither high mountains nor deep valleys.

There the waterways wind as if haphazardly. The rivers mingle, join together, part, meet again, vanish in a thousand swamps, are lost continually within a watery labyrinth that they have created, and only after innumerable twists and turns do they finally reach the polar seas. The Great Lakes, where this first region terminates, are not, like most of the lakes of the Old World, steeply embanked by hills and rocks; their shores are flat and rise only a few feet above sea level. So each of them forms something like a vast basin filled to the brim: the slightest changes in the structure of the globe would hurl their waters toward either the pole or the tropical sea.

The second region is more uneven and better prepared to become the permanent dwelling place of man; two long mountain ranges divide it along its length: one, named the Allegheny Mountains, follows the shores of the Atlantic Ocean; the other parallels the Pacific Ocean.

The space enclosed between these two mountain ranges includes 228,843 square leagues.[1] So its area is about six times greater than that of France.[2]

Yet this vast territory forms only a single valley that descends from the rounded summits of the Allegheny Mountains, and, without meeting any obstacles, climbs again to the peaks of the Rocky Mountains.

At the bottom of the valley flows an immense river. From all directions, waterways descending from the mountains are seen to rush toward it.

---

1. *1,341,649 miles. See* Darby's View of the United States, *p. 469. I have converted miles into leagues of 2,000 toises.*[a]

a. A *toise* equals 1,949 millimeters.

2. *France measures 35,181 square leagues.*

Formerly the French called it the Saint Louis River, in memory of the absent homeland; and the Indians, in their pompous language, named it the Father of Waters, or the Mississippi.

The Mississippi has its source at the boundaries of the two great regions that I spoke about above, near the top of the plateau that separates them.

Near the source of the Mississippi another river[3] arises that empties into the polar seas. Sometimes even the Mississippi seems uncertain of the path it should take; several times it retraces its steps, and only after slowing its pace amidst lakes and marshes does it finally settle upon its route and set its course slowly toward the south.

Sometimes calm within the clayey bed that nature has dug for it, sometimes swollen by storms, the Mississippi waters more than a thousand leagues along its way.[4]

Six hundred leagues[5] above its mouth, the river already has an average depth of 15 feet, and vessels of 300 tons go up for a distance of nearly two hundred leagues.

Fifty-seven large navigable rivers flow into it. The tributaries of the Mississippi include a river with a length of 1,300 leagues,[6] one of 900,[7] one of 600,[8] one of 500,[9] four of 200,[10] without considering an innumerable multitude of streams that rush from all directions to become lost within it.

The valley watered by the Mississippi seems to have been created for it alone; there the river dispenses good and evil at will, and seems like a god. Near the river, nature displays an inexhaustible fecundity. As you move away from its banks, plant energies fail; the soil thins; everything languishes

---

3. *The Red River.*

4. *2,500 miles, 1,032 leagues. See* Description of the United States, *by Warden, vol. I, p. 166.*

5. *1,364 miles, 563 leagues. See* id., *vol. I, p. 169.*

6. *The Missouri. See* id., *vol. I, p. 132 (1,278 leagues).*

7. *The Arkansas. See* id., *vol. I, p. 188 (897 leagues).*

8. *The Red River. See* id., *vol. I, p. 190 (598 leagues).*

9. *The Ohio. See* id., *vol. I, p. 192 (490 leagues).*

10. *The Illinois, the Saint Peter [the Minnesota (ed.)], the Saint Francis, the Des Moines.*

In the measurements above, I have taken as a measure the legal mile (statute mile) *and the postal league of 2,000 toises.*

or dies. Nowhere have the great convulsions of the earth left clearer traces than in the Mississippi Valley. The whole appearance of the country attests to the action of water. Its sterility, like its abundance, is the work of water. At the bottom of the valley, the waves of the early ocean built up huge layers of vegetable matter and then wore them down over time. On the right bank of the river you find immense plains, made smooth like the surface of a field worked over by the farmworker's roller. In contrast, the closer you get to the mountains, the more and more broken and sterile the ground becomes; the soil is pierced, so to speak, in a thousand places; and here and there primitive rocks appear, like the bones of a skeleton after time has consumed the surrounding muscles and flesh. Granite sand and stones of irregular size cover the surface of the earth; the shoots of a few plants grow with great difficulty among these obstacles; it seems like a fertile field covered by the ruins of some vast edifice. By analyzing these stones and this sand, it is in fact easy to notice a perfect analogy between their materials and those that form the dry and broken peaks of the Rocky Mountains. After pushing the earth headlong into the bottom of the valley, the water almost certainly ended up carrying along a portion of the rocks themselves; it rolled them along the nearest slopes; and, after grinding them against each other, it scattered these fragments, torn from the summits, at the base of the mountains.[b] [A]

All in all, the Mississippi Valley is the most magnificent dwelling place ever prepared by God for human habitation;[c] and yet, it can be said that it is still only a vast wilderness.[d]

On the eastern slope of the Allegheny Mountains, between the foot of the mountains and the Atlantic Ocean, stretches a long band of rocks and

---

b. In the margin: "≠For more exactitude in this picture consult and *cite* Volney. Examination of trees, nature of lands, shape of the country.≠"

c. "The general population doubles in 22 years, that of the Mississippi Valley in 10 years. 3.25% for the whole, 5% in the valley. Darby, p. 446, calculates that in 1865 the preponderance will be in the Mississippi Valley" (YTC, CVh, 1, p. 63).

d. Here Tocqueville tries to convey the sense of the English word *wilderness,* for which Beaumont had proposed *sauvagerie.* For him, throughout his book, *désert* designates the virgin forest, unexplored and not cultivated. See Roderick Nash, *Wilderness and the American Mind,* New Haven, Ct.: Yale University Press, 1973, pp. 1–7.

sand that the sea seems to have forgotten as it withdrew. This territory is, on average, only 48 leagues wide,[11] but it is 390 leagues long.[12] The soil, in this part of the American continent, lends itself to cultivation only with difficulty. Vegetation there is sparse and uniform.

On this inhospitable coast the efforts of human industry were first concentrated. On this strip of arid land were born and grew the English colonies, which would one day become the United States of America. Still today the center of power is found there, while behind, almost in secret, gather the true elements of a great people to whom the future of the continent no doubt belongs.

When Europeans landed on the shores of the Antilles and later on the coasts of South America, they thought themselves transported into the fabled regions celebrated by poets.[e] The sea sparkled with the fiery glow of the tropics. For the first time, the extraordinary transparency of the waters exposed the depth of the ocean bottom to the eyes of the navigator.[13] Here and there small perfumed islands appeared, seeming to float like baskets of flowers on the calm surface of the Ocean. In these enchanted places, all that came into view seemed prepared for the needs of man or planned for his pleasures. Most of the trees were laden with nourishing fruits, and those least useful to man charmed his vision with the vividness and variety of their colors. In a forest of fragrant lemon trees, of wild figs, of myrtle oaks, of acacias and of oleanders, all intertwined by flowering creepers, a multitude of birds unknown in Europe flashed their wings of crimson and

11. *100 miles.*

12. *About 900 miles.*

e. Hervé de Tocqueville: "Alexis thinks correctly that the description of South America must be shortened a great deal, perhaps even removed entirely. 1. Because he was not there. 2. Because South America is entirely outside of his subject" (YTC, CIIIb, 3, p. 45).

13. *The waters are so transparent in the Caribbean Sea, says Malte-Brun, vol. V, p. 726, that corals and fish are distinguishable at a depth of 60 fathoms. The ship seems to glide on air; a kind of vertigo grips the traveler whose view plunges beyond the crystalline fluid into the midst of underground gardens where shellfish and gilded fish shimmer among the clumps of fucus and the thickets of marine algae.*

azure and mingled the chorus of their songs with the harmonies of a nature full of movement and life.[f] [B]

Death was hidden under this brilliant cloak; but it was not noticed at all at that time. Moreover, in the air of these regions, there reigned I do not know what enervating influence, attaching man to the present and rendering him unmindful of the future.

North America presented another appearance; everything there was grave, serious, solemn. You could have said that it had been created to become the domain of the mind, as the other was to be the dwelling place of the senses.

A turbulent and foggy ocean enveloped its coasts; granite rocks or sandy shores girdled it; the forests that covered its banks displayed a somber and melancholy foliage; hardly anything other than pine, larch, holm oak, wild olive and laurel grew there.

After penetrating this first barrier, people entered into the shade of the central forest; there the largest trees that grow in the two hemispheres were found mixed together. The plane tree, catalpa, sugar maple, and Virginia poplar [eastern poplar][*] intertwined their branches with those of the oak, the beech and the linden.

As in forests subjected to the dominion of man, death struck here without respite; but no one took responsibility for clearing the remains that death had caused. So they piled up; time could not reduce them to dust

---

f. In the manuscript: "The objects that caught the eye in these enchanted places appeared destined to satisfy needs or to give rise to pleasures. Most of the trees produced fruits; and all of them, flowers. (The wild fig, the lemon tree, the myrtle oak and the oleander grew in dense groves. The acacia arose from the middle of the beach and scattered its fragrant remains over the shores.

The bignonias, the granadillas [passion fruit], the acacias with large pods, fifty species of creepers were thrown as) species of garlands thrown from tree to tree or branch to branch, repeating the image of the works of man in the middle of the inimitable charms of nature. A multitude of birds unknown to Europe made these flowery arches and domes of greenery sparkle with their many colors. There you heard resounding from all directions the sound of a thousand living creatures.

Death was . . ."

The published version is in Gustave de Beaumont's hand (YTC, CIIIb, 3, pp. 42–43). See note e supra, in which Tocqueville's desire to shorten this description is clear.

[*]. See Tableau des Etats-Unis, by Volney, p. 9.

quickly enough to prepare new places. But in the very midst of these remains, the work of reproduction went on without ceasing. Climbing plants and weeds of all types grew up through the obstacles; they crept along the fallen tree trunks, wormed into their dust, lifted up and broke the withered bark that still covered them, and cleared a path for their young offshoots. Thus, in a way, death there came to the aid of life. They were face to face, and seemed to want to mix and mingle their work.g

These forests concealed a profound darkness. A thousand small streams, not yet channeled by human effort, maintained an unending humidity. Scarcely any flowers, wild fruits, or any birds were seen.

Only the fall of a tree toppled by age, the cataract of a river, the bellowing of the buffalo and the whistling of the winds disturbed the silence of nature.h

East of the great river, the woods partially disappeared; in their place spread limitless prairies. Had nature, in its infinite variety, denied the seeds of trees to these fertile fields, or had the forest that once covered them been destroyed long ago by the hand of man? This is something that neither tradition nor scientific research has been able to discover.

These immense wilderness areas were not entirely without the presence of man however; for centuries, a few small tribes wandered in the shade of the forest or across the prairie lands. From the mouth of the Saint Lawrence to the delta of the Mississippi, from the Atlantic to the Pacific Ocean, these savages shared certain similarities that testified to their common origin. But they also differed from all known races.[14] They were neither white like the

---

g. Cf. *Journey to Lake Oneida*, pp. 1295–1302, in the second volume.

h. In this paragraph as in the preceding one, Tocqueville took into account the stylistic modifications suggested by Beaumont (YTC, CIIIb, 3, p. 44).

14. *Some similarities have since been discovered between the physical structure, the language and the habits of the Indians of North America and those of the Tungus, Manchus, Mongols, Tartars and other nomadic tribes of Asia. The latter occupy a position near the Bering Strait, which allows the supposition that, at a period long ago, they were able to come to people the empty American continent. But science has not yet succeeded in clarifying this*

Europeans, nor yellow like most of the Asians, nor black like the Negroes. Their skin was reddish; their hair, long and lustrous; their lips, thin; and their cheekbones, very prominent. The languages spoken by the savage tribes of America differed from each other in words, but all were bound by the same grammatical rules. On several points, these rules deviated from those that, until then, had seemed to govern the formation of human language.

The idiom of the Americans seemed to result from new combinations; it indicated on the part of its inventors an exercise of intelligence of which the Indians of today seem little capable.[C]

The social state of these peoples also differed in several respects from what was seen in the Old World: it could have been said that they multiplied freely in their wilderness, without contact with more civilized races. So among them, you found none of those doubtful and incoherent notions of good and evil, none of that profound corruption which is usually combined with ignorance and crudeness of mores among civilized nations who have descended into barbarism again. The Indian owed nothing to anyone except himself. His virtues, his vices, his prejudices were his own work; he grew up in the wild independence of his own nature.

The coarseness of common men, in civilized countries, comes not only from their ignorance and poverty, but also from their daily contact, as ignorant and poor men, with those who are enlightened and rich.

The sight of their misfortune and weakness, which is in daily contrast to the good fortune and power of certain of their fellows, excites anger and fear simultaneously in their heart; the feeling of their inferiority and dependence irritates and humiliates them. This inner state of soul is reproduced in their mores, as well as in their language; at the very same time, they are insolent and servile.

---

point. On this question, see Malte-Brun, vol. V; the works of Humboldt; Fischer, Conjectures sur l'origine des Américains; Adair, History of the American Indians.

The truth of this is easily proved by observation. The people are more coarse in aristocratic countries than anywhere else, and in opulent cities more than in the countryside.[j]

In these places, where men so rich and powerful are found, the weak and poor feel as though overwhelmed by their low condition; finding no point by which they can regain equality, they completely lose hope in themselves and allow themselves to fall below the dignity of human nature.

This unfortunate effect of the contrast in conditions is not found in savage life; the Indians, at the same time that they are all ignorant and poor, are all equal and free.[k]

At the time of the arrival of the Europeans, the native of North America was still unaware of the value of wealth and showed himself indifferent to the material well-being that civilized man obtains from it. He exhibited no coarseness however; on the contrary, an habitual reserve and a kind of aristocratic courtesy governed the way he behaved.

In peace, mild and hospitable, in war, merciless even beyond the known limits of human ferocity, the Indian risked death by starvation in order to aid a stranger who knocked at night on the door of his hut and, with his own hands, tore apart the quivering limbs of his prisoner. The most famous republics of antiquity never admired firmer courage, prouder souls, a more uncompromising love of independence than what was then hidden in the

j. Hervé de Tocqueville: "This entire paragraph is well thought out and strikingly true. But isn't it a little long? You could perhaps delete the section from the words cited above [*The truth of this,* etc. . . . (ed.)] to these: *This unfortunate effect.* It seems to me that the expression of the thought would gain in precision."

Édouard de Tocqueville: "This thought is excellent. I do not know what must be deleted or cut, but it seems to me that you must revise and rework this entire passage, perfect in thought and uneven and not very refined in style" (YTC, CIIIb, 3, p. 46). Nonetheless, Tocqueville did not modify the passage, identical in the manuscript and in the published version.

k. Note in the margin: "≠Idea of K[ergorlay (ed.)]. What makes the lower classes coarse is contact with the upper classes and the feeling of their low condition. All the savages are equal and free.≠"

wild forests of the New World.[15] The Europeans made only a small impression when landing on the shores of North America; their presence gave rise to neither envy nor fear. What hold could they have over such men? The Indian knew how to live without needs, how to suffer without complaint, and how to die singing.[16] Like all the other members of the great human family, moreover, these savages believed in the existence of a better world, and under different names worshipped God, creator of the universe. Their notions about the great intellectual truths were generally simple and philosophical.D

15. *Among the Iroquois, attacked by superior forces, says President Jefferson* (Notes sur la Virginie, *p. 148*), *one saw old men disdain to flee or to outlive the destruction of their country and to brave death, like the old Romans during the sack of Rome by the Gauls. Further along, p. 150: "There never was an instance known, he says, of an Indian begging his life when in the power of his enemies; on the contrary, that he courts death by every possible insult and provocation."*

[Documents on the Indians./

See the work entitled Historical Collections of the Indians in New England, *by Daniel Gookin, printed in 1792. It is found in the historical collections of Massachusetts, vol. 1, p. 141 [–226 (ed.)].*

Gookin says that there are people who believe that the Indians are the descendents of the ten tribes of Israel, which explains the state of barbarism and darkness in which they are found. "But this opinion [. . . (ed.) . . .], says Gookin, doth not greatly obtain. [But (ed.)] surely it is not impossible and perhaps not so improbable as many learned men think" [p. 145 (ed.)].

See as well a work entitled Key into the Language of the Indians of New England *by Roger Williams, printed in London in 1643. It is found reprinted in the collection of the historical society of Massachusetts, vol. 3, p. 203 [–238 (ed.)].]*

16. *See* Histoire de la Louisiane, *by Lepage-Dupratz;* Charlevoix, Histoire de la Nouvelle France; *Letters of R. Hecwelder [Heckewelder (ed.)],* Transactions of the American Philosophical Society, *vol. I [the* Voyages du baron de la Hontan; General History of Virginia, *by Captain John Smith;* id., *by Beverley;* History of Carolina, *by John Lawson; and* History of New York, *by William Smith];*[m] *Jefferson,* Notes sur la Virginie, *pp. 135–90. What Jefferson says carries an especially great weight, because of the personal merit of the writer, of his particular position and of the positive and exact century in which he wrote.*

[[Perhaps put in a note here the most striking features of this portrait and the discourse of Logan.}]

m. These works, included only in certain editions, do not appear at this place in the manuscript. They are, however, cited elsewhere.

Yet, no matter how primitive the people whose character we are describing may appear, it cannot be doubted that they had been preceded in the same regions by another people, more civilized and advanced in all ways.

An obscure tradition, but one widespread among most of the Indian tribes along the Atlantic coast, teaches us that long ago the dwelling place of these very bands was located west of the Mississippi. Mounds raised by human hands are still found every day along the banks of the Ohio and throughout the central valley. We are told that when you dig into the center of these monuments, you hardly ever fail to find human bones, strange instruments, weapons, implements of all sorts that are made of a metal or that recall uses unknown to the present races.[n]

The Indians of today can give no information at all about the history of this unknown people. Nor did those who lived three hundred years ago, at the time of the discovery of America, say anything from which even an hypothesis could be inferred. Traditions, those perishable and constantly recurring memorials of the primitive world, furnish no light whatsoever. It cannot be doubted, however, that thousands of people similar to us lived there. When did they come there; what was their origin, their destiny, their history? When and how did they perish? No one could say.

Strange thing! Some peoples have so completely disappeared from the earth that even the memory of their name has been blotted out; their languages are lost; their glory has faded like a sound without an echo. But I do not know if there is even one who has not at least left one tomb to mark its passage. Thus, of all the works of man, the most durable is still the one that best recounts his nothingness and his woes!

Although the vast country just described was inhabited by numerous tribes of natives, you could justly say that, at the time of discovery, it was still only a wilderness. The Indians occupied, but did not possess it. Man appropriates the soil by agriculture, and the first inhabitants of North America lived by the hunt. Their implacable prejudices, their untamed pas-

n. Cf. Conversation with Mr. Houston, December 31, 1831 (Notebook E, YTC, BIIa, and *Voyage, OC,* V, 1, p. 264). This fragment also recalls the "journal sans date" of the *Voyage en Amérique* of Chateaubriand (*Oeuvres romanesques et voyages,* Paris: Pléiade, 1969, I, pp. 710–13).

sions, their vices, and perhaps even more their wild virtues delivered them to an inevitable destruction. The ruin of these people began the day Europeans landed on their shores; it has continued constantly since then; today it reaches completion. Providence, while placing them in the midst of the riches of the New World, seemed to have given them only a short usufruct; in a way, these people were there only *waiting.* These coasts, so well prepared for commerce and industry; these rivers, so deep; this inexhaustible Mississippi Valley; this entire continent, appeared at that time as the still empty cradle of a great nation.[o]

That is where civilized men had to try to build society on new foundations. Applying, for the first time, theories until then unknown or considered inapplicable, civilized men were going to present a spectacle for which past history had not prepared the world.[p]

o. Cf. *A Fortnight in the Wilderness* (appendix II, especially p. 1354 of the second volume).

p. In this place are found remarks on the Governor, reproduced in note b of pp. 140–42.

Of the Point of Departure and Its Importance for the Future of the Anglo-Americans[a]

Usefulness of knowing the point of departure of peoples in order to understand their social state and their laws.— America is the only country where the point of departure of a great people could clearly be seen.—How all the men who came to populate English America were similar.—How they differed.—Remark applicable to all the Europeans who came to settle on the shores of the New World.— Colonization of Virginia.—Id. of New England.— Original character of the first inhabitants of New England.—Their arrival.—Their first laws.—Social contract.—Penal code taken from the law of Moses.— Religious fervor.—Republican spirit.—Intimate union of the spirit of religion and the spirit of liberty.

A man is newly born; his first years pass obscurely amid the pleasures or occupations of childhood. He grows up; manhood begins; finally the doors

---

a. *Point of departure./*

Influence of the point of departure on the future of society.

Homogeneous ideas, mores, needs, passions of the founders of American society.

Influence of the extent of the territory, of the nature of the country, of its geographic situation, of its ports, of its population, immigration from Europe, and in the West, from America itself.

The point of departure gave birth to the society as it is organized today, *primitive fact* after which come the consequences, formulated as principles (YTC, CVh, 1, p. 23).

of the world open to receive him; he enters into contact with his fellow men. Then, for the first time, you study him and think that the seeds of the vices and virtues of his mature years can be seen developing in him.[b]

If I am not mistaken, that is a great error.[c]

Go back to the beginning; examine the child even in the arms of his mother; see the exterior world reflected for the first time in the still dark mirror of his intellect; contemplate the first examples that catch his eye; listen to the first words that awaken his slumbering powers of thought; finally, witness the first struggles that he has to sustain. And only then will you understand the origin of the prejudices, the habits and the passions that are going to dominate his life. The whole man is there, so to speak, in the infant swaddled in his cradle.

Something similar happens among nations. Peoples always feel the effects of their origin. The circumstances that accompanied their birth and were useful to their development influence all the rest of their course.

If it were possible for us to go back to the elements of societies and examine the first memorials of their history, I am certain that we would be able to discover there the first cause of the prejudices, habits, dominant passions, of all that ultimately composes what is called the national character. [{There, no doubt, we would find the key to more than one historical enigma}]. There we would happen to find the explanation for customs that today seem contrary to the reigning mores; for laws that seem opposed to recognized principles; for incoherent opinions found here and there in society like fragments of broken chains that are sometimes seen still hanging

---

b. In the margin: "≠It must be very much remembered that this chapter still requires research on the laws of New England, Massachusetts, Rhode Island. See especially the *Town Officer* [Isaac Goodwin, *Town Officer: or Laws of Massachusetts Relative to the Duties of Municipal Officers*, second edition, Worcester: Dorr and Howland, 1829. (ed.)].≠"
c. In the margin:

≠Point common to all parts of the Union.
South.
West.
North. New England, sun, which is the source of all the rays that heat, light or at least color everything else.≠

from the vaults of an old edifice and that no longer hold up anything. Thus would be explained the destiny of certain peoples who seem to be dragged by an unknown force toward an end unknown even to themselves. But until now facts have been lacking for such a study. The spirit of analysis came to nations only as they grew older, and when, at last, they thought to contemplate their birth, time had already enveloped it in a mist; ignorance and pride had surrounded it with fables that hid the truth.

[Human remains are said to volatilize after death. Separated from each other, these human molecules are incorporated with other living substances. Each of us can therefore consider himself as the summary of many other individuals of the same species who have lived before him. An analogous phenomenon occurs again in the history of the formation of peoples. Moreover, since the time when the various human races began to succeed one another and to graft together, what people of the Old World is not today composed of the remnants of older nations? It is true that, in place of peoples who have ceased to exist, we have seen new peoples arise who have borrowed something from each of their precursors. From this one, its tongue; from that one, its laws; from another, its mores; from a fourth, certain opinions and prejudices. Because these elements already exist, only their combination is new. Amid all this debris of societies that slides haphazardly over the earth, there is no one who could now recapture an original type, or who would dare to trace how time has subjected an original type to changes by combining it with strange elements. Science, in such a labyrinth, provides only incomplete conclusions and vague hypotheses.]

America is the only country where we have been able to witness the natural and tranquil development of a society and where it has been possible to clarify the influence that the point of departure exercised on the future of States.[d]

---

d. Tocqueville seems not to have been satisfied with the draft of this paragraph. At the time of the correction of proofs in October 1834, he writes expressly to Beaumont to ask him what he thinks of it (*Correspondance avec Beaumont, OC,* VIII, 1, p. 144). Two corrections concerning the style were certainly suggested by Beaumont (the original version said *discern the influence* and spoke only of *tranquil development*). In relation to the same subject, Tocqueville notes in a rough draft:

At the time when European peoples descended upon the shores of the New World, the features of their national character were already well fixed; each of them had a distinct physiognomy. And since they had already reached the level of civilization that leads men to self-study, they have handed down to us a faithful picture of their opinions, mores, and laws. The men of the fifteenth century are almost as well-known to us as those of our own. So America shows us in full light what the ignorance and the barbarism of the first ages concealed from our view.

Close enough to the era of the founding of the American societies to know their elements in detail, far enough from that time to be able already to judge what these seeds produced, men in our time seem destined to see further into human events than their predecessors. Providence has put within our reach a light that our fathers lacked and has allowed us to discern the first causes of the destiny of nations that the obscurity of the past hid from them.

When, after attentively studying the history of America, you carefully

---

When the earth was given to man by the Creator, it was young, fertile, inexhaustible, but man was weak and ignorant. When he had learned to make use of the treasures that the earth enclosed in its bosom, he already covered the entire surface of the land, and he had to fight to acquire the right to have a refuge and to rest there. Then he was civilized, but the earth, like him, was old . . . Such was not the (illegible word) destiny of the men who in the fourteenth [*sic*] century found America. For them this land was like a new creation of a new universe suddenly emerging from the sea, all shining with life, youth and spring-like beauty. This new creation was being offered not to the isolated, ignorant and barbaric man of the first ages, but to men already (illegible word) with all the secrets of nature and art, united among themselves and entrusted with a civilization of fifty centuries (The copyist indicates that this page is not in the handwriting of Alexis de Tocqueville. YTC, CVh, 3, pp. 50–51).

In America Tocqueville found the history of the establishment of a people that Rousseau lacked:

In general, the most instructive part of the annals of peoples, which is the history of their establishment, is what we lack the most. Experience teaches us every day which causes give birth to the revolutions of empires, but because peoples are no longer being formed, we have hardly anything except conjectures to explain how they were formed (*Du contrat social, Œuvres complètes,* Paris: Pléiade, 1964, I, book IV, chapter IV, p. 444).

examine its political and social state, you feel deeply convinced of this truth: there is not an opinion, not a habit, not a law, I could say not an event, that the point of departure does not easily explain. So those who read this book will find in the present chapter the germ of what must follow and the key to nearly the whole book.[e]

The emigrants who came at different times to occupy the territory that the American Union covers today differed from each other in many ways; their aim was not the same, and they governed themselves according to various principles.

These men shared common features, however, and they all found themselves in an analogous situation.

The bond of language is perhaps the strongest and most durable that can unite men. All the emigrants spoke the same language; they were all children of the same people. They were born in a country troubled, for centuries, by the struggle of parties, and where the factions had been obliged, one by one, to place themselves under the protection of the laws. Their political education was shaped in this rude school, and you saw more notions of rights, more principles of true liberty spread among them than among most of the peoples of Europe. At the time of the first migrations, town government, this fertile seed of free institutions, had already entered

e. Circumstances without number, theory to make.
   Point of departure. The most important of all in my eyes, because it is the one that has had the most influence on mores; I regard mores as by far the most powerful of the three general causes. Equality. Democracy introduced in germ. *Comfort,* result of the small population and the immense resources of the country.
   Emigration, new resources equal to new needs.
   The absence of neighbors, no war, no permanent army.
   New country, no large cities, no manufacturing districts, no capital. *Men are not pressed* one against the other; popular movements less electric and less destructive./
   It is a land that presents itself with all the strength and fertility of youth.
   The discovery of America is like the complement of creation.
   America.
   In this state it is presented to man, not to the ignorant and barbaric man of the first centuries of the world, but to man already educated by an experience of 6,000 years (YTC, CVj, 2, pp. 20–21).

deeply into English habits; and with it, the dogma of the sovereignty of the people was introduced even within the Tudor monarchy.

People were then in the middle of the religious quarrels that troubled the Christian world. England had thrown itself into this new course with a sort of fury. The character of the inhabitants, which had always been grave and thoughtful, had become austere and argumentative. These intellectual struggles had greatly increased education and had stimulated deeper cultivation of the mind. While people were occupied with talk of religion, mores became more pure. All these general features of the nation were found more or less in the physiognomy of those of its sons who had come to seek a new future on the opposite shores of the ocean.

Moreover, a remark, which we will have the occasion to return to later, is applicable not only to the English but also to the French, to the Spanish, and to all the Europeans who came successively to settle the shores of the New World. All the new European colonies contained, if not the development, at least the germ, of a complete democracy. Two causes led to this result. [Among the emigrants, unlike in the old societies of Europe, neither conquerors nor conquered were seen.] It can be said in general, that, at their departure from the mother country, the emigrants had no idea whatsoever of any kind of superiority of some over others. It is hardly the happy and the powerful who go into exile, and poverty as well as misfortune are the best guarantees of equality that are known among men. It happened, however, that on several occasions great lords went to America following political or religious quarrels. Laws were made in order to establish a hierarchy of ranks there, but it was soon noticed that the American soil absolutely rejected territorial aristocracy. To clear that intractable land nothing less was required than the constant and interested efforts of the proprietor himself. The ground prepared, it was found that production was not great enough to enrich both a master and a tenant at the same time. So the land was naturally divided into small estates that the proprietor cultivated alone.[f] Now, aristocracy clings to the land; it is attached to the soil and relies upon the soil for support. It is not privileges alone that establish it; it is not birth

---

f. In the margin: "Put the details of this idea further along at democracy."

that constitutes it; it is landed property handed down by inheritance. A nation may exhibit immense fortunes and great misery; but if these fortunes are not territorial, you see poor and rich in its bosom; truly speaking, there is no aristocracy.[g]

So all the English colonies, at the time of their birth, shared a great family resemblance. All, from their beginning, seemed destined to present the development of liberty, not the aristocratic liberty of their mother country, but the bourgeois and democratic liberty of which the history of the world did not yet offer a complete model.[h]

Noticeable in the midst of this general coloration, however, were some very strong nuances that must be pointed out.

In the great Anglo-American family, two principal branches can be distinguished, one in the South, one in the North; until now, they have grown up without being completely merged.

Virginia received the first English colony. The emigrants arrived there in 1607. At this time, Europe was still singularly preoccupied with the idea that mines of gold and silver constituted the wealth of peoples. This destructive idea has done more to impoverish the European nations that embraced it and, in America, has destroyed more men than war and all bad laws put together. So it was gold seekers who were sent to Virginia,[1] men without resources and without proper behavior, whose restless and turbulent spirit troubled the early years of the colony[2] and made its progress

g. To the side, with a bracket that includes the last three sentences of the paragraph: "{Hasn't this been said a hundred times?}"

h. In the margin: "≠The great point of view of America is the development of democracy≠"

1. *The charter granted by the English crown in 1609 included, among others, the clause that the colonists would pay one-fifth of the production of gold and silver mines to the crown. See* Life of Washington, *by Marshall, vol. I, pp. 18–66.*

2. *A great portion of the new settlers, says Stith (*History of Virginia*) [pp. 167–68 (ed.)], were dissolute young men of good families, shipped off by their relatives to save them from an ignominious fate. Former servants, fraudulent bankrupts, the debauched, and other people of this type, more appropriate for pillage and destruction than for consolidating the settlement, formed the rest. Seditious leaders easily led this troop into all sorts of extravagances and excesses. See, relative to the history of Virginia, the following works:*

uncertain. Afterwards came the manufacturers and farmers, a more moral and quieter breed, but one that in hardly any ways rose above the level of the lower classes of England.[3] No noble thought, no plans that were not material, directed the foundation of these new establishments. The colony was scarcely established before slavery was introduced there;[4] that was the capital fact that would exercise an immense influence on the character, the laws and the entire future of the South.

Slavery, as we will explain later, dishonors work; into society, it introduces idleness, along with ignorance and pride, poverty and luxury. It enervates the forces of the mind and puts human activity to sleep. The influence of slavery, combined with the English character, explains the mores and the social state [{the character}] of the South.[j]

[≠Even the outward appearance of the settlers assumed the imprint of the habits of their life. The Virginian race is recognizable everywhere by its height and by the air of nobility and command that prevails among its features.≠]

In the North, completely opposite nuances were painted on this same English background. Allow me some details here.

In the English colonies of the North, better known as the New England states,[5] were combined the two or three principal ideas that today form the foundations of the social theory of the United States.

The principles of New England first spread into neighboring states;

History of Virginia from the First Settlements to the Year 1624, *by Smith.*

History of Virginia, *by William Stith.*

History of Virginia from the Earliest Period, *by Beverley, translated into French in 1707.*

3. *It is only later that a certain number of rich English proprietors came to settle in the colony.*

4. *Slavery was introduced about the year 1620 by a Dutch vessel that disembarked twenty Negroes on the banks of the James River. See Chalmer.*

j. In the travel notes and early drafts, as well as in the first drafts of the manuscript, Tocqueville's thinking tends to be oriented toward a North-South division of the United States. This understanding is modified further, particularly following the observations made by his family. Compare this note with note h of p. 77 and p. 602.

5. *The states of New England are those situated east of the Hudson; today they number six: 1. Connecticut; 2. Rhode Island; 3. Massachusetts; 4. Vermont; 5. New Hampshire; 6. Maine.*

then, one by one, they reached the most distant states and finished, if I can express myself in this way, by *penetrating* the entire confederation. Now they exercise their influence beyond its limits, over the entire American world. The civilization of New England has been like those fires kindled on the hilltops that, after spreading warmth around them, light the farthest bounds of the horizon with their brightness.

The founding of New England offered a new spectacle; everything there was singular and original.

[≠You would search the entire history of humanity in vain for an event that presented some analogy to what we are describing.[k]≠]

Nearly all colonies have had as first inhabitants either men without education and without resources, who were pushed out of the country where they had been born by poverty and misconduct, or avid speculators and business agents. There are some colonies that cannot claim even such an origin. Santo Domingo was founded by pirates; and today the English courts of justice are in charge of peopling Australia.[m]

The emigrants who came to settle the shores of New England all belonged to the comfortable classes of the mother country. Their gathering on American soil presented, from the beginning, the singular phenomenon of a society in which there were neither great lords,[n] nor lower classes, neither poor, nor rich, so to speak. [I have already said that, among the Europeans who went to America, conditions were in general largely equal, but it can be said that, in a way, these emigrants {the Puritans} carried democracy even within democracy.] In proportion, there was a greater amount of

k. In the margin: "≠Their birth has no more precedents in world history than the social and political state that we see among them today.≠"

m. To the side: "≠Union of liberty and of religion, of independence of individuals and of austerity of mores.≠"

John Quincy Adams had conversed with Tocqueville about the differences between the colonization of New England and of the states in the West and had also mentioned the importance of the "point of departure," of the way in which the United States was born (non-alphabetic notebooks 2 and 3, YTC, BIIa, and *Voyage, OC*, V, 1, p. 152).

n. Hervé de Tocqueville: "It has been said above that great lords had come to settle in America. Farther along, in chapter 4, it will be said that they founded the colony of Maryland. Beware of apparent contradictions. They will be avoided by developing the thought. This is often necessary. The author is too brief, *sometimes*" (YTC, CIIIb, 2, p. 104).

learning spread among these men than within any European nation of the present day. All, perhaps without a single exception, had received a rather advanced education; and several among them had made themselves known in Europe by their talents and knowledge. The other colonies had been founded by adventurers without families; the emigrants of New England brought with them admirable elements of order and morality; they went to the wilderness accompanied by their wives and children. But what distinguished them, above all, from all the others was the very aim of their enterprise. It was not necessity that forced them to abandon their country; there they left a social position worthy of regret and a secure livelihood. Nor did they come to the New World in order to improve their situation or to increase their wealth; they tore themselves from the comforts of their homeland to obey a purely intellectual need. By exposing themselves to the inevitable hardships of exile, they wanted to assure the triumph of *an idea.*

The emigrants, or, as they so accurately called themselves, the *pilgrims,* belonged to that English sect given the name Puritan because of the austerity of its principles. Puritanism was not only a religious doctrine, but also at several points it was mingled with the most absolute democratic and republican theories. From that had come its most dangerous adversaries. The Puritans, persecuted by the government of the mother country and, in the strictness of their principles, offended by the daily course of the society in which they lived, sought a land so barbarous and so abandoned by the world that they would still be allowed to live there as they wished and to pray to God in liberty.

A few citations will show the spirit of these pious adventurers better than anything that we could add.

Nathaniel Morton, historian of the first years of New England, begins in this way:[6]

6. New England's Memorial, *p. 13 [13–14 (ed.)], Boston, 1826. Also see the* History of Hutchinson,° *vol. II [I (ed.)], p. 440. [Also see the work entitled* An Account of the Church of Christ in Plymouth. *Collection of the Historical Society of Massachusetts, vol. IV, p. 107 [107–41 (ed.)].]*

o. Probably the appendix, *A Summary of the Affairs of the Colony of New-Plymouth,*

I have always believed, he says, that it was a sacred duty for us, whose fathers received such numerous and memorable demonstrations of divine goodness in the settlement of this colony, to perpetuate the memory of them in writing. What we have seen and what we have been told by our fathers, we must make known to our children, so that the generations to come learn to praise the Lord [(Psalms LXXVIII, 3, 4) (ed.)]; so that the lineage of Abraham, his servant, and the sons of Jacob, his chosen, keep forever the memory of the miraculous works of God (Ps. CV, 5, 6). [. . . (ed.)ᵖ . . .] They must know how the Lord brought his vine into the wil-

---

from the First Settlement until the incorporation with Massachusets-Bay &c. in one Province, pp. 449–81.

p. Tocqueville cites texts more or less freely as his times allowed. Deletions of words or sentences are not indicated. The editor has carefully corrected most of these citations; in certain cases judged to be of little importance, he has simply noted the deletions made by the author.

The first fragment from Morton says:

I have for some length of time looked upon it as a duty incumbent, especially on the immediate successors of those that have had so large experience of those many mem-orable and signal demonstrations of God's goodness, viz. The first beginners of this plantation in New England, to commit to writing his gracious dispensations on that behalf; having so many inducements thereunto, not only otherwise, but so plentifully in the sacred Scriptures, that so, what we have seen, and what our fathers have told us, we may not hide from our children, shewing to the generations to come the praises of the Lord. Psal. 78.3, 4. That especially the seed of Abraham his servant, and the children of Jacob his chosen, may remember his marvelous works (Psal. 105. 5, 6) [. . . (ed.) . . .] how that God brought a vine into this wilderness; that he cast out the heathen and planted it; and he also made room for it, and he caused it to take deep root, and it filled the land; so that it hath sent forth its boughs to the sea, and its branches to the river. Psal. 80.8, 9. And not only so, but also that He hath guided his people by his strength to his holy habitation, and planted them in the mountain of his inheritance (Exod. 15. 13.) [. . . (ed.) . . .], God may have the glory of all, unto whom it is most due; so also some rays of glory may reach the names of those blessed saints that were the main instruments of the beginning of this happy enterprise.

The second text from Morton reads:

And the time being come that they must depart, [. . . (ed.) . . .] a town called Delft Haven, [. . . (ed.) . . .] which had been their resting place [. . . (ed.) . . .] but they knew that they were pilgrims and strangers here below, and looked not much on these things, but lifted up their eyes to heaven, their dearest country, where God hath prepared for them a city, Heb. Xi, 16, and therein quieted their spirits.

When they came to the place, they found the ship and all things ready; and such

derness; how he planted it and removed the pagans; how he prepared a place for it, put its roots down deeply, and then allowed it to spread and cover the earth (Ps. LXXX, 15, 13 [Psalms LXXX, 8, 9 (ed.)]; and not only that, but also how he led his people toward his holy tabernacle, and established them on the mountain of his heritage (Exod. XV, 13). [. . . (ed.) . . .] These facts must be known, so that [. . . (ed.) . . .] God receives the honor he is due, and so that some rays of his glory can fall on the venerable names of the saints who served as his instruments.

It is impossible to read this beginning without being imbued, despite yourself, with a religious and solemn impression; you seem to inhale an air of antiquity and a kind of biblical perfume.

The conviction that animates the writer elevates his language. In your eyes, as in his, it no longer concerns a small band of adventurers going to seek their fortune across the seas; it is the seed of a great people that God comes to set down with his own hands in a predestined land.

The author continues and depicts the departure of the first emigrants in this way:[7]

> Thus, he says, they left this city (Delft-Haven) [. . . (ed.) . . .] which had been for them a place of rest; but they were calm; they knew that they were pilgrims and strangers here below. They were not attached to the

---

of their friends as could not come with them, followed after them [. . . (ed.) . . .]. One night was spent with little sleep with the most, but with friendly entertainment, and Christian discourse, and other real expressions of true Christian love. The next day [. . . (ed.) . . .] they went on board, and their friends with them, where truly doleful was the sight of that sad and mournful morning, to hear what sighs and sobs, and prayers did sound amongst them; what tears did gush from every eye, and pithy speeches pierced each others heart, that sundry of the Dutch strangers, that stood on the Keys as spectators, could not refrain from tears. [. . . (ed.) . . .] But the tide (which stays for no man) calling them away, that were thus loth to depart, their reverend pastor falling down on his knees, and they all with him, with watery cheeks commended them with most fervent prayers unto the Lord and his blessing; and then with mutual embraces, and many tears, they took their leave one of another, which proved to be the last leave to many of them.

7. New England's Memorial, *p. 23 [–24 (ed.)]*.

things of the earth, but raised their eyes toward heaven, their dear home-land, where God had prepared for them his holy city. [Heb. XI, 16 (ed.)] [. . . (ed.) . . .] They finally arrived at the port where the vessel awaited them. A great number of friends who could not leave with them had at least wanted to follow them to this port. The night went by without sleep; it passed with outpourings of friendship, with pious speeches, with ex-pressions full of a true Christian tenderness. The next day they went aboard; their friends still wanted to accompany them; then you heard deep sighs, you saw tears running from all eyes, you heard long hugs and kisses and fervent prayers that made strangers themselves feel moved. [. . . (ed.) . . .] Once the signal for departure was given, they fell on their knees, and their pastor, raising eyes full of tears toward heaven, commended them to the mercy of the Lord. Finally they took leave of each other, and pro-nounced this farewell that, for many among them, was to be the last.

The emigrants numbered about one hundred and fifty, men as well as women and children. Their goal was to found a colony on the banks of the Hudson, but, after wandering a long time on the ocean, they were finally forced to land on the arid coasts of New England, at the place where the town of Plymouth is found today. The rock where the pilgrims landed is still displayed.[8]

Says the historian I have already quoted:

But before going further, let us consider for an instant the present con-dition of these poor people and let us marvel at the goodness of God who saved them.[9]

They had now crossed the vast ocean, they were reaching the end of their journey, but they saw no friends to receive them, no dwelling to offer them shelter [. . . (ed.) . . .]; it was the middle of winter; and those who know our climate know how harsh the winters are and what furious storms then devastate our coasts. In this season, it is difficult to traverse known

---

8. *This rock has become an object of veneration in the United States. I saw fragments of it carefully preserved in several cities of the Union. Doesn't this show quite clearly that the power and greatness of man is entirely in his soul? Here is a rock touched for a moment by the feet of a few wretched individuals, and this rock becomes famous; it attracts the attention of a great people; the remains are venerated; far away, tiny pieces are shared. What has become of the threshold of so many palaces? Who worries about it?*

9. New England's Memorial, *p. 35 [–36 (ed.)].*

places, even worse to settle on new shores. Around them appeared only a
hideous and desolate wilderness, full of animals and savage men whose
level of ferocity and number they did not know. [. . . (ed.) . . .] The earth
was frozen; the land was covered with woods and thickets. Everything had
a barbarous appearance. Behind them, they saw only the immense ocean
that separated them from the civilized world. To find a little peace and
hope, they could only turn their faces toward heaven.q

You must not believe that the piety of the Puritans was only speculative,
or that it proved to be unfamiliar with the course of human concerns. Puritanism, as I said above, was almost as much a political theory as a religious
doctrine. So, scarcely are these emigrants disembarked on this inhospitable
coast that Nathaniel Morton has just described than their first concern is
to organize themselves as a society. They immediately enact an agreement
[<It is the social contract in proper form that Rousseau dreamed of in the
following century>] which* reads:[10]

q. The original text says:

But before we pass on, let the reader, with me, make a pause, and seriously consider
this poor people's present condition, the more to be raised up to admiration of God's
goodness towards them in their preservation: For being now passed the vast ocean,
and a sea of troubles before in their preparation, they had now no friends to welcome
them, no inns to entertain or refresh them [. . . (ed.) . . .] and, for the season it was
winter, and they that know the winters of the country, know them to be sharp and
violent, subject to cruel and fierce storms, dangerous to travel to known places, much
more to search unknown coasts. Besides, what could they see but a hideous and desolate wilderness, full of wild beasts and wild men? And what multitudes of them
there were, they then knew not; [. . . (ed.) . . .] all things stand in appearance with
a weather-beaten face, and the whole country full of woods and thickets, represented
a wild and savage hue; if they looked behind them, there was the mighty ocean which
they had passed, and was now a main bar and gulf to separate them from all the civil
parts of the world.

* *New England's Memorial,* p. 37 [–38. Note omitted in certain editions. (ed.)].
10. *The emigrants who created the state of Rhode Island in 1638, those who established
New Haven in 1637, the first inhabitants of Connecticut in 1639, and the founders of Providence in 1640, also began by drawing up a social contract that was submitted for approval
to all those affected,* Pitkin's History, *[vol I, (ed.)] pp. 42 [43 (ed.)] and 47.*

We, whose names follow,[r] who, for the glory of God, the development of the Christian faith and the honor of our country,[s] have undertaken to establish the first colony on these distant shores,[t] we covenant by these presents, by mutual and solemn consent, and before God, to form ourselves into a body of political society, for the purpose of governing ourselves and working for the accomplishment of our plans; and by virtue of this contract, we covenant to promulgate laws, acts, ordinances, and to establish, as needed, magistrates to whom we promise submission and obedience.

This took place in 1620. From that period on, emigration did not stop. Each year, the religious and political passions that tore apart the British Empire throughout the reign of Charles I drove new swarms of sectarians to the coasts of America. In England, the center of Puritanism continued to be located in the middle classes;[u] most of the emigrants came from within the middle classes. The population of New England increased rapidly; and, while in the mother country men were still classed despotically according to the hierarchy of ranks, the colony increasingly presented the novel spectacle of a thoroughly homogeneous society. Democracy, such as antiquity had not dared dream it, burst forth fully grown and fully armed from the midst of the old feudal society.

Content to remove the seeds of troubles and the elements of new rev-

---

r. The quoted fragment reads:

We whose names are under-written, the loyal subjects of our dread sovereign Lord, King James, by the grace of God, of Great Britain, France, and Ireland, King, Defender of the faith, &c. Having undertaken for the glory of God, and advancement of the Christian faith, and the honour of our King and country, a voyage to plant the first colony in the northern parts of Virginia; do by these presents solemnly and mutually, in the presence of God and one another, covenant and combine ourselves together into a civil body politick, for our better ordering and preservation, and furtherance of the ends aforesaid: And by virtue hereof, do enact, constitute and frame such just and equal laws, ordinances, acts, constitutions and officers, from time to time, as shall be thought most meet and convenient for the general good of the colony; unto which we promise all due submission and obedience.

s. Omitted: "our king and our country . . ."
t. The text says: "in the northern parts of Virginia."
u. Tocqueville uses the words *class* and *rank* indiscriminately.

olutions, the English government watched this heavy emigration without distress. It even encouraged it with all of its power and seemed hardly at all concerned with the fate of those who came to American soil seeking a refuge from the harshness of its laws. You could have said that the English government saw New England as a region delivered to the dreams of the imagination that should be abandoned to the free experiments of innovators.

The English colonies, and this was one of the principal causes of their prosperity, always enjoyed more internal liberty and more political independence than the colonies of other peoples; but nowhere was this principle of liberty more completely applied than in the states of New England.

It was then generally agreed that the lands of the New World belonged to the European nation that had first discovered them.

In this way, nearly the entire littoral of North America became an English possession toward the end of the sixteenth century. The means used by the British government to populate these new domains were of different kinds. In certain cases, the king subjected a portion of the New World to a governor of his choosing, charged with administering the country in his name and under his direct orders;[11] this is the colonial system adopted by the rest of Europe. At other times, he granted ownership of certain portions of the country to a man or to a company.[12] All the civil and political powers were then concentrated in the hands of one or several individuals who, under the inspection and control of the crown, sold the land and governed the inhabitants. Finally, a third system consisted of giving a certain number of emigrants the right to form a political society, under the patronage of the mother country, and to govern themselves in everything not contrary to its laws.

This method of colonization, so favorable to liberty, was put into practice only in New England.[13]

---

11. *This was the case for the state of New York.*

12. *Maryland, the Carolinas, Pennsylvania, New Jersey were in this case. See* Pitkin's History, *vol. I, pp. 13–31.*

13. *See in the work entitled:* Historical Collection of State Papers and other Authentic Documents Intended as Materials for an History of the United States of America, *by Ebenezer Hazard, printed at Philadelphia, MDCCXCII, a very large number of precious*

As early as 1628,[14] a charter of this nature was granted by Charles I to the emigrants who came to found the colony of Massachusetts.

But, in general, charters were not granted to the colonies of New England until long after their existence had become an accomplished fact. Plymouth, Providence, New Haven, the states of Connecticut and Rhode Island[15] were founded without the support and, in a sense, without the knowledge of the mother country. The new inhabitants, without denying the supremacy of the home country, did not draw on it as the source of powers; they incorporated themselves. And it was only thirty or forty years after, under Charles II, that a royal charter legalized their existence.

So it is often difficult, while surveying the first historical and legislative memorials of New England, to see the link connecting the emigrants to the country of their ancestors. At every moment you can see them performing some act of sovereignty; they name their magistrates, make peace and war, establish regulations for public order, provide laws for themselves as if they were answerable only to God alone[16] [≠later, when the colonies began to become powerful, the mother country raised the claim of defending and directing them≠].

Nothing is more singular and, at the very same time, more instructive

---

documents valuable in their contents and authenticity, relating to the early years of the colonies, among others, the different charters that were granted by the English crown, as well as the first acts of their governments.

Also see the analysis of all these charters that Mr. Story, Justice of the Supreme Court of the United States, makes in the introduction of his Commentary on the Constitution of the United States.

All these documents demonstrate that the principles of representative government and the external forms of political liberty were introduced in all the colonies almost from their birth. These principles were developed more fully in the North than in the South, but they existed everywhere.

14. See Pitkin's History, vol. I, p. 35 [36 (ed.)]. See The History of the Colony of Massachusetts, by Hutchinson, vol. I, p. 9.

15. See id., pp. 42–47 [vol. I (ed.)].

16. The inhabitants of Massachusetts, in the establishment of criminal and civil laws for proceedings and for the courts of justice, moved away from the customs followed in England: in 1650 the name of the King still did not appear at the head of judicial orders. See Hutchinson, vol. I, p. 452.

than the legislation of this period;[v] there, above all, is found the key to the great social enigma that the United States presents to the world of today.

Among these memorials, we will particularly single out, as one of the most characteristic, the law code that the small state of Connecticut gave itself in 1650.[17]

The legislators of Connecticut[18] first take charge of the penal laws; and to write them, they conceive the strange idea of drawing upon sacred texts:

"Whoever will worship a God other than the Lord," they begin by saying, "will be put to death."

Ten or twelve clauses of the same nature, borrowed word for word from *Deuteronomy, Exodus* and *Leviticus,* follow.

Blasphemy, witchcraft, adultery,[19] rape are punished with death; the same punishment is imposed on flagrant insult by a son toward his parents. In this way, the legislation of a primitive and half-civilized people was transferred to a society in which minds were enlightened and mores were mild; so the death penalty was never so common in the laws, nor so rarely applied to the guilty.

Above all, in this body of penal laws, the legislators are preoccupied with upholding moral order and standards of good behavior; they constantly enter, therefore, into the realm of conscience. There is hardly any sin that

v. "Ask Niles about the authenticity of the blue laws" (YTC, CVb, p. 33).

The laws of the first colonists of Connecticut were called blue laws. Understood in the broadest sense, the term designates the regulations for the strict observance of the Sabbath, which formerly existed throughout the American territory and which partially survive today.

Nathaniel Niles was the secretary of the American delegation in Paris from 1830 to 1833.

17. Code of 1650, *p. 28 (Hartford, 1830).*

18. *See as well in the* History *of Hutchinson, vol. I, pp. 435–56, the analysis of the penal code adopted in 1648 by the colony of Massachusetts; this code is drafted on principles analogous to that of Connecticut.*

19. *Adultery was likewise punished by death under the law of Massachusetts, and Hutchinson, vol. I, p. 441, says that several persons in fact suffered death for this crime; he cites on this subject a curious anecdote which relates to the year 1663. A married woman had relations with a young man; she became a widow and married him; several years passed; the public finally began to suspect the intimacy that had formerly existed between the spouses; they were charged under the criminal law; they were imprisoned, and both were nearly condemned to death.*

they do not manage to submit to the censure of the magistrate. The reader has been able to observe how harshly the laws punished adultery and rape. Mere flirtation between unmarried people is severely suppressed. On the guilty, the judge has the right to inflict one of three punishments: a fine, a flogging or a wedding.[20] And if the records of the old courts of New Haven are to be believed, proceedings of this nature were not rare; you find, dated May 1, 1660, a verdict with a fine and reprimand against a young woman accused of having uttered a few indiscreet words and of allowing herself to be kissed.[21] The Code of 1650 abounds in preventive measures. Laziness and drunkenness are severely punished.[22] Innkeepers cannot provide more than a certain quantity of wine to each consumer; a fine or a flogging cracks down on a simple lie when it might be harmful.[23] In other places, the legislator, completely forgetting the great principles of religious liberty that he claimed in Europe, forces, by threat of fines, attendance at divine[24] worship.[w] And he goes so far as to impose severe penalties,[25] and often death,

20. Code of 1650, *p. 48.*

It seems that sometimes judges gave these various penalties cumulatively, as you see in a decision rendered in 1643 (p. 114, New Haven Antiquities *), which declares that Marguerite Bedfort [Bedforde (ed.)], convicted of having committed reprehensible acts, will suffer the penalty of whipping and will be enjoined to marry Nicolas Jemmings [Jennings (ed.)], her accomplice.*

21. New Haven Antiquities, *p. 104 [–106 (ed.)]. Also see in the* History of Hutchinson, *vol. I, p. 435 [–436 (ed.)], several judgments as extraordinary as the former.*

22. Code of 1650, *pp. 50, 57.*

23. Id., *p. 64.*

24. Id., *p. 44.*

w. Cf. Beaumont, *Marie,* I, p. 536–37, and Tocqueville's account (appendix III).

25. *This was not particular to Connecticut. See among others the law of December 13, 1644, in Massachusetts, which sentences Anabaptists to banishment.* Historical Collection of State Papers, *vol. I, p. 538. Also see the law published on October 14, 1656, against the Quakers: "Whereas, says the law, an accursed sect of heretics called Quakers has recently arisen . . ." Clauses follow which impose a very heavy fine on captains of vessels that bring Quakers into the country. The Quakers who succeed in entering will be flogged and put into prison to work. Those who defend their opinions will first be fined, then sentenced to prison and driven from the province. Same collection, vol. I, p. 630.*

[If the Quakers banished in this way were found once again in the state, they were, once identified, condemned to death. See same collection, vol. II, p. 456, the sentencing to death of

on Christians who want to worship God according to a creed different from his own.[26] Finally, the fervor for regulations, which possesses him, sometimes leads him to deal with concerns most unworthy of him. Thus, in the same code, there is a law that prohibits the use of tobacco.[27] It must not be forgotten, moreover, that these bizarre or tyrannical laws were not at all imposed; that they were voted by the free participation of all those concerned; and that the mores were still more austere and puritanical than the laws. In the year 1649, a solemn association was formed in Boston whose purpose was to prevent the worldly luxury of long hair.[28] E

Such errors undoubtedly shame the human spirit; they testify to the infirmity of our nature, which, incapable of firmly grasping the true and the just, is most often reduced to choosing only between two excesses.

Alongside this penal legislation, so strongly stamped by narrow sectarian spirit and by all the religious passions that were excited by persecution and were still seething deep within souls, a body of political laws is found. The two are, in a way, bound together. But those political laws, written two hundred years ago, still seem very far ahead of the spirit of liberty of our age.

The general principles on which modern constitutions rest, which most of the Europeans of the seventeenth century scarcely understood and which at that time triumphed incompletely in Great Britain, were all recognized and laid down by the laws of New England. There, the intervention of the people in public affairs, the free vote of taxes, the responsibility

---

two men and a woman convicted of this crime (October 18, 1649). The woman, named Mary Dyer, received mercy, but had to attend the execution of her two accomplices with the cord around her neck.

Also see in the same collection, p. 573, a law of Plymouth: "Whereas, says this law, the Quakers sometimes obtain places to stay, [and (ed.)] horses by means of which they move rapidly from place to place and escape the searches of the legal authorities, poisoning the people with their accursed doctrines . . . [this law (ed.)] orders that the horses seized in possession of the Quakers will be confiscated."

See in general at the end of this volume the acts of the government of New Plymouth against the Quakers.]

26. In the penal law of Massachusetts, the Catholic priest who sets foot in the colony after being expelled is punished by death.

27. Code of 1650, p. 96.

28. New England's Memorial, p. 316.

of the agents of power, individual liberty, and jury trial were established without argument and in fact.

There, these generative principles receive an application and developments that not a single European nation has yet dared to give them.

In Connecticut, from the beginning, the electoral body was comprised of all citizens, and that is understood without difficulty.[29] Among this emerging people, a nearly perfect equality of means and, even more, of minds then reigned.[30]

In Connecticut, at that time, all the agents of executive power were elected, even the Governor of the state.[31]

[In Connecticut in 1650, all] The citizens older than sixteen years of age were obliged to bear arms; they formed a national militia that named its officers and had to be ready at all times to march in defense of the country.[32]

In the laws of Connecticut, as in all those of New England, you see arising and developing the town independence that still today constitutes the principle and life of American liberty.

Among most European nations, political existence began in the higher ranks of society; little by little and always incompletely, it was transmitted to the various parts of the social body.

In America, in contrast, you can say that the town was organized before the county; the county, before the state; the state, before the Union.

In New England, as early as 1650, the town is completely and definitively formed. Gathered around this town individuality and strongly attached to it are interests, passions, duties, and rights. Within the town, a real, active,

---

29. Constitution of 1638, *p. 17 [12 (ed.)]*.

30. *As early as 1641, the General Assembly of Rhode Island unanimously declared that the state government consisted of a democracy and that power rested with the body of freemen who alone had the right to make laws and to oversee their execution.* Pitkin's History, *p. 47 [46 (ed.)]*.

31. Constitution of 1638, *p. 12*.

32. Code of 1650, *p. 70*.

totally democratic and republican political life reigns. The colonies still recognize the supremacy of the mother country; the monarchy is the law of the state, but in the town, the republic is already fully alive.

The town names its magistrates of all sorts; it taxes itself; it apportions and levies the tax on itself.[33] In the New England town, the law of representation is not accepted. As in Athens, matters that touch the interests of all are treated in the public square and within the general assembly of citizens.

When you attentively examine the laws that were promulgated during these early years of the American republics, you are struck by the legislator's knowledge of government and advanced theories.

It is evident that he had a more elevated and complete idea of the duties of society toward its members than European legislators of that time and that he imposed obligations on society that society still eluded elsewhere. In the states of New England, from the start, the fate of the poor was assured;[34] strict measures were taken for maintaining roads; and officers were named to oversee them.[35] Towns had public records in which the results of general deliberations, deaths, marriages, births were inscribed;[36] clerks were appointed to maintain these records.[37] Some officers were charged with the administration of unclaimed inheritances, others, with overseeing the boundaries of legacies. The principal function of several was to maintain public peace in the town.[38]

[≠The legislation of this era announces in the mass of the people and in its leaders a civilization already well advanced; you feel that those who make the laws and those who submit to them all belong to a race of intelligent and enlightened men who have never been completely preoccupied by the material concerns of life.≠]

33. Code of 1650, *p. 80.*
34. Code of 1650, *p. 78.*
35. Id., *p. 49.*
36. *See the* History *of Hutchinson, vol. I, p. 455.*
37. Code of 1650, *p. 86.*
38. Id., *p. 40.*

The law gets into a thousand different details to provide for and to satisfy a host of social needs of which, today in France, we still have only a vague awareness. [{Nothing then in our old Europe could give the idea of a social organization as extensive and as perfect.}]

But it is in the prescriptions relating to public education that, from the very beginning, you see fully revealed the original character of American civilization.

"Whereas, says the law, Satan, enemy of humanity, finds in the ignorance of men his most powerful weapons, and it is important that the knowledge brought by our fathers does not remain buried in their grave;—whereas the education of children is one of the first interests of the State, with the help of the Lord . . ."[39] Then follow the provisions that create schools in all the towns and oblige the inhabitants, under penalty of heavy fines, to tax themselves to support them. Secondary schools are established in the same way in the most populated districts. Municipal magistrates must watch that parents send their children to school; they have the right to levy fines against those who refuse to do so. And if resistance continues, society then displaces the family, lays hold of the child and removes from the fathers the rights that nature had given to them, but that they knew so poorly how to use.[40] The reader will undoubtedly have noticed the preamble of these ordinances: in America, it is religion that leads to enlightenment; it is the observance of divine laws that brings men to liberty.

When, after thus casting a rapid glance over American society in 1650, you examine the state of Europe and particularly that of the continent

39. Id., *p. 90 [–91 (ed.)]*.[x]

x. The code of 1650 says:

It being one chiefe project of that old deluder, Sathan, to keepe men from the knowledge of the scriptures, as in former times, keeping them in an unknowne tongue, so in these latter times, by perswading them from the use of tongues, so that at least, the true sence and meaning of the originall might bee clouded with false glosses of saint seeming deceivers; and that learning may not bee buried in the grave of our forefathers, in church and commonwealth, the Lord assisting our indeavors . . . (pp. 90–91).

40. Code of 1650, *p. 38*.

around this same era, you are filled by a profound astonishment. On the European continent, at the beginning of the seventeenth century, absolute monarchy triumphed on all sides over the ruins of the oligarchic and feudal liberty of the Middle Ages. [<≠The top of the social edifice already received the lights of modern civilization, while the base still remained in the darkness of ignorance [v. of the Middle Ages].≠>] In the heart of this brilliant and literary Europe, the idea of rights had perhaps never been more completely misunderstood; never had peoples experienced less of political life; never had minds been less preoccupied by the notions of true liberty. And at that time these same principles, unknown or scorned by European nations, were proclaimed in the wilderness of the New World and became the future creed [{political catechism}] of a great people. The boldest theories of the human mind were reduced to practice in this society so humble in appearance, a society in which probably not a single statesman would then have deigned to be involved; there, the imagination of man, abandoned to its natural originality, improvised legislation without precedent. Within this obscure democracy that had still not brought forth either generals, or philosophers, or great writers, a man could stand up in the presence of a free people and give, to the acclamation of all, this beautiful definition of liberty:[41]

> Let us not be mistaken about what we must understand by our independence.[y] There is in fact a kind of corrupt liberty, the use of which is common to animals as it is to man, and which consists of doing whatever

41. Mather's Magnalia Christi Americana, *vol. II, p. 13 [vol. I, p. 113 (ed.)].*

This speech was given by Winthrop; he was accused of having committed arbitrary acts as a magistrate; after delivering the speech of which I have just given a fragment, he was acquitted with applause, and from that time on he was always re-elected Governor of the State. See Marshall, vol. I, p. 166 [167 (ed.)].

y. The original says:

Nor would I have you to mistake in the Point of your own liberty. There is a liberty of corrupt nature, which is affected by men and beasts, to do what they list; and this liberty is inconsistent with authority, impatient of all restraint; by this liberty, Sumus Omnes Deteriores; 'tis the grand enemy of truth and peace, and all the ordinances of God are bent against it. But there is a civil, a moral, a federal liberty, which is the proper end and object of authority; it is a liberty for that only which is just and good; for this liberty you are to stand with the hazard of your very lives.

you please. This liberty is the enemy of all authority; it suffers all rules with impatience; with it, we become inferior to ourselves; it is the enemy of truth and peace; and God believed that he had to rise up against it! But there is a civil and moral liberty that finds its strength in union, and that the mission of power itself is to protect; it is the liberty to do without fear all that is just and good. This holy liberty we must defend at all cost, and if necessary, at risk of our life.

I have already said enough to reveal Anglo-American civilization in its true light. It is the product (and this point of departure must always be kept in mind) of two perfectly distinct elements that elsewhere are often at odds. But in America, these two have been successfully blended, in a way, and marvelously combined. I mean the *spirit of religion* and the *spirit of liberty.*

The founders of New England were at the very same time ardent sectarians and impassioned innovators. Restrained by the tightest bonds of certain religious beliefs, they were free of all political prejudices. [{Religion led them to enlightenment; the observance of divine laws brought them to liberty.}]

From that, two diverse but not opposite tendencies resulted whose traces can easily be found everywhere, in the mores as in the laws.[z]

Some men sacrifice their friends, family, and native land for a religious opinion; you could believe that they are absorbed in the pursuit of the intellectual good that they have come to purchase at such a high price. You see them, however, seeking material riches and moral enjoyments with an almost equal fervor, heaven in the other world, and well-being and liberty in this one.

In their hands, political principles, laws, and human institutions seem to be malleable things that can be shaped and combined at will.

The barriers that imprisoned the society where they were born fall before

---

z. Variant in the margin: "≠Extreme obedience to established rules in the moral world, extreme independence, restless spirit of innovation in the political world, these are the two diverse and seemingly opposing tendencies that are revealed at each step in the course of American society.≠"

them; old opinions that for centuries ruled the world vanish; an almost limitless course and a field without horizons open. The human mind rushes toward them, sweeping over them in all directions. But having arrived at the limits of the political world, it stops by itself. In fear and trembling, it sets aside the use of its most formidable abilities, abjures doubt, renounces the need to innovate, refrains even from lifting the veil of the sanctuary, and bows respectfully before truths that it accepts without discussion. [≠After having rested awhile in the midst of the certainties of the moral order, man begins to move again and reenters the political arena with more fervor.≠]ᵃ

In the moral world, therefore, everything is classified, coordinated, foreseen, decided in advance. In the political world, everything is agitated, contested, uncertain; in the one, passive though voluntary obedience; in the other, independence, scorn for experience and jealousy of all authority.

Far from harming each other, these two tendencies, apparently so opposed, move in harmony and seem to offer mutual support.

Religion sees in civil liberty a noble exercise of the faculties of man; in the political world, a field offered by the Creator to the efforts of intelligence. Free and powerful in its sphere, satisfied with the place reserved for it, religion knows that its dominion is that much better established because it rules only by its own strength and dominates hearts without other support.

Liberty sees in religion the companion of its struggles and triumphs, the cradle of its early years, the divine source of its rights. Liberty considers religion as the safeguard of mores, mores as the guarantee of laws and the pledge of its own duration.ᶠ

[Both, taking man by the hand, guide his steps and show his way in the wilderness.]

a. In the margin: "≠There will be many things to say about that. The American political world rests upon foundations different from ours, but just as settled and certain. So you cannot say that there is more uncertainty and vagueness there than in the moral world.≠"

Reasons for Some Singularities That the Laws and Customs[b] of the Anglo-Americans Present

Some remnants of aristocratic institutions within the most complete democracy.—Why?—What is of Puritan origin and of English origin must be carefully distinguished.

[≠From whatever side I envisage the laws and mores of the Anglo-Americans, I rediscover striking traces of their origin {of the point of departure}. The reading of historians, the study of legislation, the sight of things all involuntarily lead my steps back toward the point of departure. {But I despair of making the whole extent of my idea understood by those who have not seen English America with their own eyes.}≠]

The reader must not draw from what precedes consequences that are too general and absolute. The social condition, the religion and the mores of the first emigrants undoubtedly exercised an immense influence over the destiny of their new country. It was not up to them, however, to establish a society whose point of departure was found only within themselves; no one can entirely free himself from the past. With ideas and customs that were their own, they mingled, either voluntarily or unknowingly, other customs and ideas that they got from their education or from the national traditions of their country.

So when you want to know and judge the Anglo-Americans of today, what is of Puritan origin or of English origin must be carefully distinguished.

You often encounter in the United States laws and customs that contrast with all that surrounds them. These laws seem written in a spirit opposed to the dominant spirit of American legislation; these mores seem contrary to the social state as a whole. If the English colonies had been founded in a century of darkness, or if their origin was already lost in the shadows of time, the problem would be insoluble.

---

b. In an early draft, the title said: ". . . THAT THE SOCIAL STATE OF THE ANGLO-AMERICANS PRESENTS." This section was initially at the beginning of chapter III (YTC, CVh, 3, p. 82).

I will cite a single example to make my thought understood.

The civil and criminal legislation of the Americans knows only two means of action: *prison* or *bail*.[c] The first action in proceedings consists of obtaining bail from the defendant or, if he refuses, of having him incarcerated; afterwards the validity of the evidence or the gravity of the charges is discussed.

Clearly such legislation is directed against the poor and favors only the rich.

A poor man does not always make bail, even in civil matters, and if he is forced to await justice in prison, his forced inactivity soon reduces him to destitution.[d]

A wealthy man, on the contrary, always succeeds in escaping imprisonment in civil matters; even more, if he has committed a crime, he easily evades the punishment awaiting him: after providing bail, he disappears. So it can be said that for him all the penalties of the law are reduced to fines.[42] What is more aristocratic than such legislation?[e]

In America, however, it is the poor who make the law, and usually they reserve the greatest advantages of society for themselves.

It is in England where the explanation for this phenomenon must be found: the laws I am speaking about are English.[43] The Americans have not changed them, even though they are repugnant to their legislation as a whole and to the mass of their ideas.

The thing that people change the least after their customs is their civil

---

c. "Ask Mr. Livingston about prisons and bail" (YTC, CVb, p. 33). Probably Edward Livingston. See note 2 of Tocqueville's introduction (p. 30).

d. "For prison ruins him by preventing him from working and bail makes him give up the fruit of his work.

"To develop. Opinion of Mr. Duponceau.

"Little guarantee that the poor have against the oppression of municipal magistrates.

"Unwritten law that puts justice into the hands of the privileged class of lawyers" (YTC, CVj, 2, pp. 4–5). The conversation with Mr. Duponceau is found in portable notebook 3 (YTC, BIIa, and *Voyage, OC,* V, 1, p. 182); see the conversation with [Alexander] Everett (*ibid.,* p. 95).

42. *There are certainly crimes for which there is no bail, but they are very few in number.*

e. Cf. Beaumont, *Marie,* I, pp. 197, 367–70.

43. *See Blackstone and Delolme, book I, chap. X.*

legislation. The civil laws are familiar only to jurists, that is, to those who have a direct interest in keeping them as they are, good or bad, because they know them. The bulk of the nation knows them hardly at all; they see them in action only in individual cases, grasp their tendency only with difficulty, and submit to them without thinking about it.

I have cited an example; I could have pointed out many others.

The picture that American society presents is, if I can express myself in this way, covered by a democratic layer beneath which from time to time you catch a glimpse of the old colors of the aristocracy.

CHAPTER 3

Social State of the Anglo-Americans

[Definition of the words *social state.*a/

I will speak so frequently about the social state of the Anglo-Americans that, first and foremost, I need to say what I mean by the words *social state.*

In my view, the social state is the material and intellectual condition in which a people finds itself in a given period.]

The social state is ordinarily the result of a fact, sometimes of laws, most often of these two causes together. But once it exists, it can itself be considered the first cause of most of the laws, customs and ideas that regulate the conduct of nations; what it does not produce, it modifies.b

So to know the legislation and the mores of a people, it is necessary to begin by studying its social state.c

---

a. Hervé de Tocqueville: "I do not know if this definition is very useful. It slows the transition from the second to the third chapter.

In any case, mores should be put before the other causes that modify social state. Mores come before the fact whatever it may be. They precede laws. Example: Puritan mores precede and lead to the fact of emigration."

Édouard de Tocqueville: "I do not share this opinion" (YTC, CIIIb, 2, p. 92).

b. "Among a people property is divided in a certain way, enlightenment is more or less equal, morality is more or less high, that is what I call its social state./

"In general the social state is the result of a fact predating the laws, but the laws develop its consequences and modify it" (YTC, CVh, 5, p. 9).

The social state according to Tocqueville recalls Montesquieu's concept of the general spirit of the nation (cf. *L'esprit des lois,* book XIX, chapters IV and V). On this question, see Anna Maria Battista, "Lo stato sociale democratico nella analisi di Tocqueville," *Pensiero Politico* 4, no. 3 (1973): 336–95.

c. In the margin, in pencil: "Vague, indeterminate. Perhaps examples instead of definitions."

That the Salient Point of the Social State of the Anglo-Americans Is to Be Essentially Democratic

First emigrants of New England.—Equal among themselves.—
Aristocratic laws introduced in the South.—Period of the
Revolution.—Change in the inheritance laws.—Effects produced
by this change.—Equality pushed to its extreme limits in the new
states of the West.—Intellectual equality.

Several important remarks about the social state of the Anglo-Americans could be made, but one dominates all the others.[d]

The social state of the Americans is eminently democratic. It has had this character since the birth of the colonies; it has it even more today.[e]

[≠As soon as you look at the civil and political society of the United States, you discover two great facts that dominate all the others and from

---

d. *Causes of the social state and current government of America:*

1. *Their origin:* excellent point of departure. Intimate mix of religion and of the spirit of liberty. Cold and rational race.

2. *Their geographic position:* no neighbors.

3. *Their commercial and industrial activity.* Everything, even their vices, is favorable to them now.

4. *The material good fortune* that they enjoy.

5. *The religious spirit that reigns:* republican and democratic religion.

6. The diffusion of useful knowledge.

7. Very pure morals.

8. The division into small States. They prove nothing for a large one.

9. The absence of a great capital where everything is concentrated. Care to avoid it.

10. Commercial and provincial activity that means that each person finds something to do at home (Alphabetic Notebook A, YTC, BIIa and *Voyage, OC,* V, 1, p. 207).

e. Hervé de Tocqueville:

This is too absolute. At least you should say nearly all the colonies, in order to be in agreement with page 128 (chap. 4), where you speak about the aristocratic influence long exercised to the south and west of the Hudson. This difficulty arises from chapter 2 where Alexis recognized only two political divisions of the territory, which forced him to generalize too much. Another division and a few sentences added, and everything will be fine (YTC, CIIIb, 2, p. 92). Page 128 of the copy read by Hervé and the other critics corresponds to pages 50–51 of this edition.

which the others are derived. Democracy constitutes the social state; the dogma of the sovereignty of the people, the political law.

These two things are not analogous. Democracy is society's way of being. Sovereignty of the people, a form of [v. the essence of] government. Nor are they inseparable, because democracy[f] is even more compatible with despotism than with liberty.

But they are correlative. Sovereignty of the people is always more or less a fiction wherever democracy is not established. ≠][g]

I said in the preceding chapter that a very great equality reigned among the emigrants who came to settle on the shores of New England. Not even the germ of aristocracy was ever deposited in that part of the Union. No influences except intellectual ones [{a kind of intellectual patronage}] could ever be established there. The people got used to revering certain names, as symbols of learning and virtue. The voice of certain citizens gained a power over the people that perhaps could have been correctly called aristocratic, if it could have been passed down invariably from father to son.

This happened [{north}] east of the Hudson; [{south}] southwest of this river, and as far down as Florida, things were otherwise.

---

f. With a reminder in the margin, in pencil: "Explain what is understood by democracy."

Tocqueville never arrived at a satisfactory definition of democracy. He always used the term in different senses. Harold Laski, in his introduction to *Democracy in America* (*OC,* I, p. xxx), distinguishes four; James T. Schleifer, *The Making of Tocqueville's "Democracy in America"* (pp. 263–74), identified as many as eight: inevitable development or tendency, social condition, popular sovereignty, government of the people, mobility, middle classes, equality of conditions, open society. Jean-François Sutter, in "Tocqueville et le problème de la démocratie" (*Revue internationale de philosophie* 49 (1959): 330–40), examined the reason why Tocqueville did not manage to give one single definition of democracy. Cf. the revealing letter of Louis de Kergorlay, dated January 6, 1838, a letter that Tocqueville kept with the early drafts of the second part of his book (YTC, CVg, 2, published in *Correspondance avec Kergorlay, OC,* XIII, 2, pp. 16–17).

g. In the margin: "≠Note that in this chapter the social state must never be confused with the political laws that follow from it; equality or inequality of conditions, which are facts, with democracy or aristocracy, which are laws. Reexamine from this point of view. ≠"

In most of the States situated southwest[h] of the Hudson, great English landholders had come to settle. Aristocratic principles, and with them English laws of inheritance, had been imported.[*] I have shown the reasons that prevented a powerful aristocracy from ever being established in America. But these reasons, though existing southwest[j] of the Hudson, had less power there than [{north}] east of this river. To the south, one man alone could, with the help of slaves, cultivate a large expanse of land. So in this part of the continent wealthy landed proprietors were seen; but their influence was not precisely aristocratic, as understood in Europe, because they had no privileges at all, and cultivation by slaves gave them no tenants and therefore no patronage. Nonetheless, south of the Hudson, the great landholders formed a superior class, with its own ideas and tastes and generally concentrating political activity within its ranks. It was a kind of aristocracy not much different from the mass of the people whose passions and interests it easily embraced, exciting neither love nor hate;[k] in sum, weak and

h. This word is added later. At first, the word was *south.*

[*]. Note from Jefferson.

j. Hervé de Tocqueville:

Here again the drawback of only two divisions. Alexis finds himself forced to jump abruptly from the Southwest to the South, without the connection of ideas being clear, and the differences between this Southwest and the South remain unknown. Does slavery also exist in the Southwest? Is this part entirely homogeneous with the South? If it is, why speak successively of the West and the South? If it is not, why take his example from the South alone? (YTC, CIIIb, 2, p. 93).

k. Hervé de Tocqueville:

I do not know what that means in a country where there was no people. Alexis undoubtedly meant to say an aristocracy whose habits resembled the democratic habits of other parts of the Union. The expression does not seem right, nor do those that follow: an aristocracy that embraces the passions and interests of the people cannot remain indifferent to the people. Therefore, it is not right to say that it *excited neither love nor hate.* You would have to say that it excited no jealousy at all in the other classes. Proof that it was not indifferent is that two lines lower Alexis says that it furnished all of the great men of the Revolution. But when the leaders are taken from one class of citizens, you cannot say that it inspires neither love nor hate.

not very hardy. It was this class that, in the South, put itself at the head of the insurrection; the American Revolution owed its greatest men to it.

In this period, the entire society was shaken.[m] The people, in whose name the struggle was waged, the people—now a power—conceived the desire to act by themselves; democratic instincts awoke.[n] By breaking the yoke of the home country, the people acquired a taste for all kinds of independence. Little by little, individual influences ceased to make themselves felt; habits as well as laws began to march in unison toward the same end.

But it was the law of inheritance that pushed equality to its last stage.[o]

Édouard de Tocqueville: "I agree with my father only for the last paragraph, which must absolutely be revised. How can a weak and not very hardy class lead an insurrection?" (YTC, CIIIb, 2, pp. 93–94). The author paid no attention to these criticisms; the published version is identical to that in the manuscript.

m. Hervé de Tocqueville:

This still seems to me too absolute. Society in the South had certainly been shaken, but that of New England where democracy already existed did not need to be shaken. Perhaps you should put: *the entire society received a new impulse.* Next I wonder where these people were who became a power. I see the effect perfectly without seeing the cause as clearly as I would like. It would seem from what Alexis says, page 130, that democratic instincts had won everywhere, even among those whose position should have set them most apart. Perhaps the aristocratic and rich leaders of the insurrection thought that they should recompense those who had fought under their command by granting them political rights or by extending those they already had. Once down this path, as always happens, one is not able to stop.

Édouard de Tocqueville: "Apt observation. This first paragraph must be reworked a bit" (YTC, CIIIb, 2, p. 94).

n. In the margin: "≠It was the aristocracy, if this name can be given to what was then at the head of society in America, which had armed the people and led them on the fields of battle.≠"

o. "Give me, for thirty years, a law for equal division of inheritance and liberty of the press and I will bring you a republic" (YTC, Cve, p. 63).

Tocqueville gives a privileged position to the structure of landed property in his theory. In his *Mémoire sur le paupérisme* (*Commentaire*, XXIII, 1983, p. 633), he repeats that it is the concentration of land that provoked the concentration of power and the birth of the aristocracy. The same idea often appears in the notes taken during his journey in America (conversations with Livingston, Clay, Latrobe, Sparks in YTC, BIIa, and *Voyage, OC,* V, 1, pp. 59, 87–88, 102, 109, 111–13), as well as during his journey in England

I am astonished that ancient and modern political writers have not attributed a greater influence on the course of human affairs to the laws of
landed inheritance.[1] These laws belong, it is true, to the civil order; but they
should be placed at the head of all political institutions, for they have an
incredible influence on the social state of peoples, political laws being just
the expression of the social state. In addition, the laws of inheritance have
a sure and uniform way of operating on society; in a sense they lay hold of
generations before their birth. Through them, man is armed with an almost
divine power over the future of his fellows. The law-maker regulates the
inheritance of citizens once, and he remains at rest for centuries: his work
put in motion, he can keep his hands off; the machine acts on its own power,
and moves as if self-directed toward an end set in advance.

Constituted in a certain way, the law of inheritance reunites, concentrates, gathers property and, soon after, power, around some head; in a way
it makes aristocracy spring from the soil. Driven by other principles and
set along another path, its action is even more rapid; it divides, shares, dis-

---

(*Voyages en Angleterre, Irlande, Suisse et Algérie, OC,* V, 2, pp. 52, 28, 41–42). In a letter
to Kergorlay of June 29, 1831 (*Correspondance avec Kergorlay, OC,* XIII, 1, pp. 231–33),
he explains that it is one of the particulars of American society that most surprised him.
Moreover, his interest in this question predates the journey to America. The division of
the land is already mentioned in the notes of the journey in Sicily in 1827 (*Voyage, OC,*
V, 1, pp. 43, 45). The same idea reappears in his article on the social and political state of
France before and after the Revolution of 1789, and in *L'Ancien Régime et la Révolution.*
    We know that the social consequences of the inheritance laws have been considered
by Aristotle in the *Politics* (1266b8). Montesquieu took up the question again in *De l'esprit
des lois* (book V, chapters V and VIII). Afterward the question occupied a central place
in the political considerations of the revolutionary era. The beginning of the nineteenth
century still had in mind the posthumous speech of Mirabeau (*Discours de M. de Mirabeau l'aîné sur l'égalité des partages dans les successions en ligne directe,* Imprimerie Nationale, Paris, 1791, 23 p.). Even the father of the author had treated it in one of his
publications (*De la charte provinciale,* Paris: J. J. Blaise, 1829, 62p., pp. 12–13).
    1. *By the inheritance laws, I understand all the laws whose principal end is to regulate the
disposition of property after the death of the owner.*
    *The law of entail is among this number. It is true that it also has the result of preventing
the owner from disposing of his property before his death; but it imposes the obligation on
him of keeping it only with the view of having it go intact to his inheritor. So the principal
end of the law of entail is to regulate the disposition of property after the death of the owner.
All the rest is the means used.*

seminates property and power. Sometimes people are then frightened by the rapidity of its march. Despairing of stopping its movement, they seek at least to create difficulties and obstacles before it; they want to counterbalance its action with opposing efforts; useless exertions! It crushes or sends flying into pieces all that gets in its way; it constantly rises and falls on the earth until nothing is left in sight but a shifting and intangible dust[p] on which democracy takes its seat.

When the law of inheritance allows and, even more, requires the equal division of the father's property among all the children, its effects are of two sorts; they should be carefully distinguished, even though they lead to the same end.

Due to the law of inheritance, the death of each owner leads to a revolution in property; not only do the holdings change masters, but so to speak, they change nature; they are constantly split into smaller portions. [The generations grow poorer as they succeed each other.]

That is the direct and, in a sense, the material effect of the law.[q] So in countries where legislation establishes equal division, property and particularly territorial fortunes necessarily have a permanent tendency to grow smaller. Nonetheless, if the law were left to itself, the effects of this legislation would make themselves felt only over time. Because as long as the family includes not more than two children (and the average for families in a populated country like France, we are told, is only three),[r] these chil-

<hr />

p. In the margin in pencil: "This image of dust is exaggerated and lacks precision."

q. To the side in an earlier draft: " Explanatory note and on Rodat."
Is this Rodat Claude Raudot, magistrate and friend of Tocqueville and Beaumont? We can hardly think that the author would misspell the name of someone that he knew so well. Bonnel notes "Rodat" at two places in the drafts (see note s infra). In any case, no one of this name is found in the papers and correspondence of Tocqueville.

r. Hervé de Tocqueville: "Isn't Alexis considerably underestimating the family average? At least, 4 should be put in place of 3, father, mother and two children. I do not know if the law of averages should be invoked here. The family that has only one descendant escapes from the law of division. But the family that has 5 or 6! What a progression of division of the land!" (YTC, CIIIb, 2, p. 95).

dren, sharing the wealth of their father and their mother, will be no less wealthy than each parent individually.

But the law of equal division exerts its influence not on the fate of property alone; it acts on the very soul of the proprietors, and calls their passions to its aid. These indirect effects rapidly destroy great fortunes and, above all, great estates.[s]

Among peoples for whom the inheritance law is based on the right of primogeniture, landed estates most often pass from generation to generation without being divided. That causes family spirit to be, in a way, embodied in the land. The family represents the land; the land represents the family; the land perpetuates its name, origin, glory, power and virtues.

s. Law of inheritance./
   Effect of the law of inheritance.

   1. Divides fortunes naturally. But this not very rapid, average number of children, to divide two fortunes, that of the father and that of the mother.
   2. Prevents the desire to keep them. Great effect. Destroys family spirit and substitutes individual egoism, leads to selling the land in order to have income, favors the taste for luxury, the land passes into the hands of the peasants and doesn't come out again. Conversation with Rodat (YTC, CVh, 5, p. 9).

   Law of inheritance. Its *direct effects,* its *indirect effects* (Rodat).
   So greater equality not only among peoples of European races, but also among all peoples, in all times.
   However manufacturing (YTC, CVh, 5, p. 8).

Tocqueville will devote a chapter in the second part of his book to the manufacturing aristocracy (chapter XX of volume II). On this point, this note and note d of p. 85 attest to an interest well before the voyage to England in 1835. Tocqueville had briefly visited England in 1833, but the notes of this first journey carry no trace of a particular attention to the problem of industry. It is generally agreed that his visit to Manchester, Liverpool and Birmingham in 1835 is at the origin of this interest (*Voyages en Angleterre, Irlande, Suisse et Algérie, OC,* V, 2, pp. 67, 81).

During a conversation with Tocqueville in the United States, Robert Vaux had already referred to the effects of manufacturing on the population (non-alphabetic notebooks 2 and 3, YTC, BIIa and *Voyage, OC,* V, p. 104). Beaumont, for his part, will not hesitate to affirm in the novel that he would publish in 1835: "In truth there exists in America something that resembles the feudal aristocracy. The factory is the manor; the manufacturer, the sovereign lord; the workers are the serfs" (*Marie,* I, pp. 241–42).

It is an undying witness to the past and a precious guarantee of life to come.[t]

When the inheritance law establishes equal division, it destroys the intimate connection that existed between family spirit and keeping the land; the land ceases to represent the family, for the land, inescapably divided after one or two generations, clearly must shrink continually and disappear entirely in the end. The sons of a great landed proprietor, if they are few, or if fortune favors them, can maintain the hope of not being poorer than their progenitor, but not of owning the same lands as he; their wealth will necessarily consist of other elements than his.[u]

Now, from the moment you take away from landed proprietors any great interest—arising from sentiment, memory, pride, or ambition—in keeping the land, you can be sure that sooner or later they will sell it. They have a great pecuniary interest in selling, since movable assets produce more income than other assets and lend themselves much more easily to satisfying the passions of the moment.[v]

Once divided, great landed estates are never reassembled; for the small landholder gains proportionately more revenue from his field[2] than the large landholder; so he sells it at a much higher price than the large landholder. Thus the economic calculations that brought a rich man to sell vast properties, will prevent him, with all the more reason, from buying small properties in order to reassemble large estates.[w]

What is called family spirit is often based on an illusion of individual

t. "Ask Livingston if in the United States there is still the possibility of establishing entails [in English in the text (ed.)]" (YTC, CVb, p. 33).

u. See the conversation with Mr. Latrobe (YTC, BIIa and *Voyage, OC,* V, 1, p. 109).

v. In *L'Irlande,* Beaumont will recommend the law of equal division as the way to divide property and socially weaken the English aristocracy of Ireland (see especially vol. II, pp. 191–200). Beaumont, like Tocqueville, had also observed in the United States the effects of the inheritance law (cf. in particular two letters, dated respectively July 4 and September 31, 1831, *Lettres d'Amérique,* pp. 80 and 147).

2. *I do not mean that the small landholder cultivates better, but he cultivates with more enthusiasm and care, and gains by work what he lacks in skill.*

w. In the margin: "≠The inheritance law acts much more forcefully on the destruction of landed fortunes than of fortunes in general.≠"

egoism.[x] A person seeks to perpetuate and, in a way, to immortalize himself in his great-nephews.[y] Where family spirit ends, individual egoism reverts to its true inclinations. Since the family no longer enters the mind except as something vague, indeterminate, and uncertain, each man concentrates on present convenience; he considers the establishment of the generation immediately following, and nothing more.

So a person does not try to perpetuate his family, or at least he tries to perpetuate it by means other than landed property.

Thus, not only does the inheritance law make it difficult for families to keep the same estates intact, but also it removes the desire to try and leads families, in a way, to cooperate in their own ruin.

The law of equal division proceeds in two ways: by acting on the thing, it acts on the man; by acting on the man, it affects the thing.

In these two ways it succeeds in profoundly attacking landed property and in making families as well as fortunes rapidly disappear.[3]

Surely it is not up to us, the French of the nineteenth century, daily witnesses to the political and social changes that the inheritance law brings about, to question its power. Each day we see it constantly move back and forth over our soil, toppling in its path the walls of our dwellings and de-

---

x. Hervé de Tocqueville: "I do not believe that the word *egoism* is the right word here. Egoism is only concerned with the present and does not rush toward the future. The word *pride* would seem more suitable to me."

Édouard de Tocqueville: "I find the word *egoism* good" (YTC, CIIIb, 2, p. 95).

y. Note in pencil in the manuscript that seems to speak about a first version that lacked the sentence to which this note refers: "≠Think about this. A bad inference could be drawn from it, too generalized.≠"

3. *Since land is the most secure property, there are, from time to time, wealthy men who are inclined to make great sacrifices to acquire it and who willingly lose a considerable portion of their income in order to assure the rest. But these are accidents. The love of landed property is no longer usually found except among the poor. The small landholder, who is less enlightened and who has less imagination and fewer passions than the large landholder, is generally preoccupied only with the desire to enlarge his domain; and it often happens that inheritance, marriage or turns of fortune in trade provide him the means little by little.*

So alongside the tendency that brings men to divide the land, there exists another that brings them to consolidate it. This tendency, which is enough to prevent property from being infinitely divided, is not strong enough to create great territorial fortunes, nor above all to keep them in the same families.

stroying the hedges of our fields. But if the inheritance law has already accomplished much among us, much still remains for it to do. Our memories, opinions, and habits present it with powerful obstacles.[z]

In the United States, its work of destruction is nearly finished. That is where its principal results can be studied.

English legislation on the transmission of property was abolished in nearly all the states at the time of the Revolution.

The law of entail was modified so as to interfere only imperceptibly with the free circulation of property.[a] [G]

z. Hervé de Tocqueville:

What are these obstacles? I do not know them. In France there are scarcely 2,000 families who give a double portion to the eldest son, and each day that becomes rarer. Equality of affection toward the children predominates. The law of primogeniture revolted even those who benefited from it. It was one of the most active causes of the July Revolution. So you should say what these obstacles are, because the truth of the phrase is not apparent (YTC, CIIIb, 2, p. 96).

a. [Note] "≠Here citation of Kent and analysis of Lippitt and then a remark on how the French laws on inheritance and entail are more democratic than the American laws.≠" Cf. note G.

In 1834, Tocqueville felt the need to have help in the organization and reading of American books, brochures and codes. The following advertisement is found in one of the notebooks of the copyist Bonnel:

Looking for an American from the United States who has received a liberal education, who would like to do research in the political laws and the historical works of his country and who, for two months, could sacrifice two or three hours of his time each day for this work. Choice of hours would be left to him.

Apply to M. A[lexis (ed.)]. de T[ocqueville (ed.)]. rue de V[erneuil (ed.)]. n. 49, before ten in the morning or in the afternoon between two and four.

Five copies (YTC, CVh, 2, p. 85).

This advertisement seems not to have been published. Francis Lippitt states that he was hired on the recommendation of the American delegation in Paris by Nathaniel Niles or Edward Livingston probably. In a letter to Daniel Gilman (reproduced in Daniel C. Gilman, "Alexis de Tocqueville and his book on America, sixty years after," *The Century Illustrated Monthly Magazine,* 56, May–October 1898, pp. 703–15), Francis Lippitt asserts that his work consisted of reading and summarizing books, newspaper clippings and legal collections. Theodore Sedgwick, another American who had helped the author, unquestionably had a more important role. His conversations seem to have been useful

The first generation disappeared; landed estates began to divide. As time went by, the movement became more and more rapid [as a stone thrown from the top of a tower accelerates as it moves through space]. Today, when hardly sixty years have gone by, the appearance of society is already unrecognizable; the families of the great landed proprietors are almost entirely engulfed by the common mass. In the state of New York, which had a very large number of such families, two barely stay afloat above the abyss ready to swallow them.[b] Today, the sons of these opulent citizens are businessmen, lawyers, doctors. Most have fallen into the most profound obscurity. The last trace of hereditary rank and distinction is destroyed; the law of inheritance has done its leveling everywhere.[c]

It is not that there are no rich in the United States as there are elsewhere; I do not even know of a country where the love of money holds a greater place in the human heart and where a deeper contempt is professed for the theory of the permanent equality of property.[d] But wealth circulates there with incredible rapidity, and experience teaches that it is rare to see two generations reap the rewards of wealth.[e] [{The people are like the divinity of this new world; everything emanates from and returns to them.}]

distribution of wealth

---

to Tocqueville while drafting certain points of the book. (Also see, George W. Pierson, *Tocqueville and Beaumont in America,* pp. 731–34.)

b. [Note] "≠The Livingstons and the Van Rensselaers.≠"

c. At the time of his voyage, Tocqueville met Charles Carroll, signatory of the Declaration of Independence and one of the wealthiest Americans of the time. On November 8, 1831, Tocqueville, in a draft of a letter to an unidentified recipient, noted concerning him: "[Charles Carroll], a little old man of 95 years, straight as an arrow, . . . saw all the great families disappear as a result of the new inheritance law. For sixty years he has seen their descendants grow poorer, the noble families disappear, and the democracy take hold of the power that the great landholders held in his time" (YTC, BIa2).

d. In the margin: "≠Put here, I think, the inequality arising from the accumulation of the personal wealth of *manufacturing.*≠"

e. Democracy./

What is most important for democracy, is not that there are no great fortunes; it is that great fortunes do not rest in the same hands. In this way, there are the rich, but they do not form a class. ?

Commerce, industry perhaps create larger individual fortunes in America now than sixty years ago. However, the abolition of primogeniture and entail make de-

This picture, however colored you think it is, still gives only an incomplete idea of what is happening in the new states of the West and Southwest.[f]

At the end of the last century, hardy adventurers began to penetrate the valleys of the Mississippi. This was like a new discovery of America: soon the bulk of emigration went there; you saw unknown societies suddenly emerge from the wilderness. States, whose names did not even exist a few years before, took a place within the American Union. [<≠Hardly a year passed without the republic being forced to have some new star attached to its flag.≠>] In the West democracy can be observed carried to its extreme limit. In these states, in a way improvised by chance, the inhabitants arrived but yesterday on the soil they occupy. They scarcely know each other, and each one is unaware of the history of his closest neighbor. So in this part of the American continent, the population escapes not only from the influence of great names and great wealth, but also from the natural aristocracy that arises from enlightenment and virtue. There, no one exercises the power that men grant out of respect for an entire life spent in doing good before their eyes. The new states of the West already have inhabitants; society still does not exist.

---

mocracy, its passions, interests, maxims, tastes more powerful in our time than sixty years ago.

Furthermore, equality of political rights has introduced a powerful new element of democracy.

American societies had always been democratic by their nature; the Revolution made democratic principles pass into the laws (YTC, CVe, pp. 60–61).

f. Hervé de Tocqueville:

This transition needs revision. The picture that precedes relates to the effect of the law of equal division and has no relation whatsoever to the new states of the West. I think that you should say: what we have said about the equality of fortunes and rank in the East and in the South gives only an incomplete idea of the way it is established in the *new states,* etc. Here I offer a thought. The author must not be afraid of sometimes saying a few words that recall what precedes. These are resting points for the imagination, which put it back on track, and ease the work of comparing ideas already expressed with those which are being presented (YTC, CIIIb, 2, p. 97).

But not only fortunes are equal in America; to a certain degree, equality extends to minds themselves.

I do not think there is any country in the world where, in proportion to the population, there exist so small a number of ignorant and fewer learned men than in America.

There primary education is available to every one; higher education is hardly available to anyone.

This is easily understood and is, so to speak, the necessary result of what we advanced above.

Nearly all Americans live comfortably; so they can easily gain the primary elements of human knowledge.

In America, there are few rich [≠and the rich do not form a class apart. The consequences of this fact in relation to education are of several kinds.≠]; nearly all Americans need to have an occupation. Now, every occupation requires an apprenticeship. So Americans can devote only the first years of life to general cultivation of the mind; at age fifteen, they begin a career; most often, therefore, their education concludes when ours begins. If pursued further, it is directed only toward a specialized and lucrative field; they study a field of knowledge in the way they prepare for a trade; and they take only the applications recognized to have immediate utility.

In America, most of the rich began by being poor; nearly all the men of leisure were busy men in their youth. The result is that when they could have the taste for study, they do not have the time to devote themselves to it; and when they have gained the time, they no longer have the taste.

So in America no class exists that honors intellectual work and in which the penchant for intellectual pleasures is handed down with affluence and hereditary leisure.

Both the will and the power to devote oneself to this work are therefore missing.

In America a certain middling level of human knowledge is established. All minds have approached it; some by rising, others by falling.

So you meet a great multitude of individuals who have about the same number of notions in matters of religion, history, the sciences, political economy, legislation, and government.

 Intellectual inequality comes directly from God, and man cannot prevent it from always reappearing.

But it follows, at least from what we have just said, that minds, while still remaining unequal as the Creator intended, find equal means at their disposal. Thus, today in America, the aristocratic element, always feeble since its birth, is, if not destroyed, at least weakened further; so it is difficult to assign it any influence whatsoever in the course of public affairs.

Time, events, and the laws have, on the contrary, made the democratic element not only preponderant but also, so to speak, unique. No family or group influence can be seen; often not even an individual influence, no matter how ephemeral, can be found.

[{Society there [is (ed.)] profoundly and radically democratic in its religion, ideas, habits, and passions.g}

≠For a people that has reached such a social state, mixed governments are more or less impractical; hardly any choice exists for them other than absolute power or a republic [v: sovereignty of the people].

America found itself in circumstances fortunate for escaping despotism and favorable for adopting a republic.≠]

So America presents, in its social state, the strangest phenomenon. There, men appear more equal in fortune and in mind or, in other words, more equal in strength than they are in any other country in the world and have been in any century that history remembers.

g. In the margin, with a bracket uniting this paragraph with the two preceding ones: "≠To sacrifice, I think, because all of that implies something more than the social state. Ask G[ustave (ed.)]. and L[ouis (ed.)].≠"

Political Consequences of the Social State
of the Anglo-Americans

The political consequences of such a social state are easy to deduce.

It is impossible to think that, in the end, equality would not penetrate the political world as it does elsewhere. You cannot imagine men, equal in all other ways, forever unequal to each other on a single point; so in time they will become equal in all ways.

Now I know only two ways to have equality rule in the political world: rights must either be given to each citizen or given to no one [and apart from the government of the United States I see nothing more democratic than the empire of the great lord].TN 2

For peoples who have arrived at the same social state as the Anglo-Americans, it is therefore very difficult to see a middle course between the sovereignty of all [v: of the people] and the absolute power of one man [v: of a king].

[≠So peoples who have a similar social state are faced with a frightening alternative; they must choose between the sovereignty of the people and the absolute power of a king≠].

We must not hide from the fact that the social state I have just described lends itself almost as easily to the one as to the other of these two consequences.

There is in fact a manly and legitimate passion for equality that incites men to want to be strong and esteemed. This passion tends to elevate the small to the rank of the great. But in the human heart a depraved taste for equality is also found that leads the weak to want to bring the strong down to their level and that reduces men to preferring equality in servitude to inequality in liberty. Not that peoples whose social state is democratic naturally scorn liberty; on the contrary, they have an instinctive taste for it. But liberty is not the principal and constant object of their desire; what they love with undying love is equality; they rush toward liberty by rapid impulses and sudden efforts, and if they miss the goal, they resign them-

TRANSLATOR'S NOTE 2: Here Tocqueville probably means the Sultan.

selves; but without equality nothing can satisfy them, and rather than lose it, they would agree to perish.[h]

On the other hand, when citizens are all more or less equal, it becomes difficult for them to defend their independence against the aggressions of power. Since none among them is then strong enough to struggle alone with any advantage, it is only the combination of the strength of all that can guarantee liberty. Now, such a combination is not always found.[j]

Peoples can therefore draw two great political consequences from the same social state; these consequences differ prodigiously, but they both arise from the same fact.

The first to be subjected to this fearful alternative that I have just described, the Anglo-Americans have been fortunate enough to escape absolute power. Circumstances, origin, enlightenment, and above all, mores have allowed them to establish[k] and to maintain the sovereignty of the people.[m]

h. Hervé de Tocqueville:

All of this paragraph is extremely obscure. I do not know if I understood it, but it does not seem very correct to me. Men want to be equal not in order to be strong and respected, but out of human pride, out of a more or less well understood sentiment of human dignity. Nor is it because the weak want to *draw* or rather *lower* the strong to their level that servitude is established. Servitude is a state of degradation that is never the choice of any nation or any fragment of a nation. It results from the vices of the nation from which liberty is escaping because the nation did not know how to use liberty or is cowardly enough not to know how to rid itself of a tyrant. Fatigue or cowardice, degradation or disgust, such are the causes of servitude; it does not come about because men prefer equality in servitude to inequality in liberty. Among them, it is not preference, but objection (YTC, CIIIb, 2, pp. 98–99).

j. In the version put at the disposal of the family, the sentence continues as follows: ". . . such a combination is not always found. It happens that they resign themselves without difficulty to servitude" (YTC, CIIIb, 2, pp. 100–101).

k. In another version, in the margin: ". . . mores, ≠this hidden will of God that is called chance≠, have allowed them . . ."

m. Hervé de Tocqueville: "Erase the word *establish*. The sovereignty of the aggregation of all the individuals of a nation that is called the people is not established, for this sovereignty exists by itself and everywhere. Even in Turkey, it strangles the sultan; in Spain, the Cortes is needed to sanction a change in the inheritance of the throne" (YTC, CIIIb, 2, p. 99).

CHAPTER 4

Of the Principle of the Sovereignty
of the People in America

*It dominates all of American society.—Application that the
Americans already made of this principle before their
Revolution.—Development that the Revolution gave to it.—
Gradual and irresistible lowering of the property qualification.*

When you want to talk about the political laws of the United States, you must always begin with the dogma of the sovereignty of the people.[a]

The principle of the sovereignty of the people, which is more or less always found at the base of nearly all human institutions, ordinarily remains there as if buried. It is obeyed without being recognized, or if sometimes it happens, for a moment, to be brought into the full light of day, people soon rush to push it back into the shadows of the sanctuary.

The national will is one of those terms abused most widely by schemers of all times and despots of all ages. Some have seen it expressed in votes bought from the brokers of power; others in the votes of an interested or fearful minority. There are even some who have discovered it fully formulated in the silence of the people and who have thought that from the *fact* of obedience came, for them, the *right* of command.[b]

In America, the principle of the sovereignty of the people is not hidden or sterile as it is in certain nations [a vain show and a false principle as among

---

a. *"Sovereignty of the people* and *democracy* are two perfectly correlative words; the one represents the theoretical idea, the other its practical realization" (YTC, CVh, 1, p. 22).

b. In the margin, with a bracket enclosing the entire paragraph: "≠{This seems trite to me.}≠"

certain others; it is a legal and omnipotent fact that rules the entire society; that spreads freely and reaches its fullest consequences without obstacles]; it is recognized by the mores, proclaimed by the laws; it spreads freely and reaches its fullest consequences without obstacles.

If there is a single country in the world where the true value of the dogma of the sovereignty of the people can hope to be appreciated, where its application to the affairs of society can be studied and where its advantages and dangers can be judged, that country is assuredly America.

I said before that, from the beginning, the principle of the sovereignty of the people had been the generative principle of most of the English colonies of America.

It then fell far short, however, of dominating the government of society as it does today.

Two obstacles, one external, one internal, slowed its invasive march.

It could not appear openly in the laws because the colonies were still forced to obey the home country; so it was reduced to hiding in the provincial assemblies and especially in the town. There it spread in secret.

American society at that time was not yet ready to adopt it in all its consequences. For a long time, learning in New England and wealth south of the Hudson, exercised, as I showed in the preceding chapter, a sort of aristocratic influence that tended to confine the exercise of social powers to a few hands. It still fell far short of electing all public officials and of making all citizens, voters. Everywhere the right to vote was restricted to certain limits and subordinated to the existence of a property qualification which was very low in the North and more considerable in the South.[c]

The American Revolution broke out. The dogma of the sovereignty of the people emerged from the town and took over the government;[d] all

---

c. To the side, with a note: "{Know exactly the state of things on this point.}"

d. The manuscript says: "{and occupied the throne}." A note in pencil in the margin specifies: "≠The word throne does not seem to me the right word since it concerns a republic.≠"

classes took risks for its cause; they fought and triumphed in its name; it became the law of laws.[e]

e. Of the sovereignty of the people./
   I draw a great difference between the right of a people to choose its government, and the right that each individual among this people would have to take part in the government.
   The first proposition seems to me to contain an incontestable truth; the second, a manifest error.
   I cannot acknowledge the absolute right of each man to take an active part in the affairs of his country, and I am astonished that this doctrine, so contradictory to the ordinary course of human affairs, could be proposed.
   What is more precious to man than his liberty? It is recognized, however, that society can take liberty away from one of its members who makes poor use of it.
   What is more natural [than (ed.)] to manage your own property? All peoples have recognized, however, that, before a certain age and in certain [missing word (ed.)], this control could be withdrawn, because it was thought [that (ed.)] these individuals either did not yet have or had never had the judgment necessary to make good use of this power. And would this faculty of judgment that some individuals are found to lack for conducting themselves then be granted to everyone for conducting the affairs of society? The constitutions that have apparently been founded on the doctrine that I am combating have never dared to admit all of its consequences. Even in the United States the poor man who pays no taxes obeys laws to which he has consented neither directly nor indirectly. How does that happen if the right to be involved in the affairs of government is a right inherent in the nature of man?
   So all questions of democracy and aristocracy (aristocracy as a ruling body), of monarchy and republic, are not questions of right, but questions of fact, or rather the question of fact always precedes the other. Show me a people in which all the citizens may be involved in the government and, in my eyes, this people will have the right to govern itself democratically. Imagine another, if you can, in which no class or citizen may have the required capacity; and although I hardly like the power of one man alone, I will grant that it is legitimate and will take care to live elsewhere.
   [In the margin: How so? If you recognize that some of the individuals who compose a people are incapable of taking part in its government, how even more would they be able to make a good choice? Now, if you remove some from this choice, it is no longer the people who choose. Moreover, from the moment you recognize that some can be incapable of choosing well, you must imagine a social state where no one could choose well; and then you are moving even further from the maxim that all people have the right to choose their government. Everything is reduced to this: to choose a government and to take part in government, these are two analogous products of human judgment. It is difficult entirely to concede the one while entirely refusing the other.

A change almost as rapid was carried out within the interior of society. The law of inheritance completed the dismantling of local influences.

At the moment when this effect of the laws and of the revolution began to be evident to all, victory had already been irrevocably declared in favor of democracy. Power was in fact in its hands. Even struggling against it was no longer permitted. So the upper classes submitted without a murmur and without a fight to an evil henceforth inevitable. What usually happens to powers that are in decline happened to them: individual egoism took hold of the members of the upper classes.[f] Since force could no longer be wrested from the hands of the people and since they did not detest the multitude enough to take pleasure in defying it, they came to think only of winning

---

Response:

Judgment is necessary to choose a good government. But only intelligence and experience are needed to find that an existing government is not suitable and that it should be changed.] (YTC, CVh, 5, pp. 4–6). Cf. Guizot, tenth lecture, entitled *De la représentation,* in *Journal des cours publics de jurisprudence, histoire et belles-lettres* (Paris: au bureau du journal, 1821–1822, vol. II, especially pages 131–33). Also see note c of pp. 99–100.

f. Hervé de Tocqueville:

I do not know if Alexis has grasped all the causes of this phenomenon. I indicated one in the remarks on the preceding chapter that I ask him to think about. To know if the necessity to recompense soldiers has not obligated leaders to grant them rights; perhaps even a sentiment more noble than necessity, gratitude. Afterwards, democratic appetites have grown. I see in note 2 of chapter III that only in 1786 has equal division been established in New York, from where it has spread throughout the Union. Nor do I know if individual egoism can suddenly dominate an entire class in such a way as to make it give up its most precious advantages. Something else is involved there other than just the desire to please the multitude. There is always in my mind a difficulty that I do not believe I have expressed clearly enough. In the beginning the position of the settlers in each state was identical, whether it appeared aristocratic or democratic. There was no "people"; how was "the people" formed so that there was a mass demanding concessions alongside a mass that granted them? I believe that Alexis should have said something about it in the first chapter.

Édouard de Tocqueville: "Doesn't inequality come from the lack of inheritance laws?" (YTC, CIIIb, 2, pp. 89–90).

Was Hervé thinking here of Montesquieu? Cf. *Considérations sur la cause de la grandeur des Romains et de leur décadence,* in *Œuvres complètes* (Paris: Pléiade, 1951), II, chapter XIII, p. 142.

its good will at any cost. [≠Moreover, men have at their disposal such a deep reservoir of baseness, that it is always found more or less the same in the service of all despots, whether people or king.≠] In an effort to outdo each other, the most democratic laws were then voted by the men whose interests were most damaged by them. In this way, the upper classes did not incite [{implacable}] popular passions against themselves; but they themselves hastened the triumph of the new order. So, a strange thing! The democratic impulse showed itself that much more irresistible in the states where aristocracy had more roots.

The state of Maryland, which had been founded by great lords, was the first to proclaim universal suffrage[1] and introduced the most democratic forms into its whole government.[g]

When a people begins to tamper with the electoral qualification, you can foresee that, after a more or less long delay, it will make that qualification disappear completely. That is one of the most invariable rules that govern societies. As the limit of electoral rights is pushed back, the need grows to push it further; for, after each new concession, the forces of democracy increase and its demands grow with its new power. [It is the history of the Romans buying peace with gold.[h]] The ambition of those left below the electoral qualification is aroused in proportion to the great number of those who are found above. Finally, the exception becomes the rule; concessions

1. *Amendments made to the constitution of Maryland in 1801 and 1809.*
g. Hervé de Tocqueville

The history of the great lords who founded the colony of Maryland bothers me because it implies a contradiction with what Alexis says about the original equality that was established at first in the states of the Union. I know that this contradiction is only apparent, but it leaves some suspicion in the mind. Alexis must clearly explain how and why the ideas, pretensions, etc. of these great lords were absorbed right away by the influence of the spirit of equality spread throughout the Union (YTC, CIIIb, 2, p. 108).

h. Hervé de Tocqueville: "The example does not seem to me to relate to the subject" (YTC, CIIIb, 2, p. 90). These are the very words of Montesquieu. *Considération sur les causes de la grandeur des Romains et de leur décadence,* in *Œuvres complètes* (Paris: Pléiade, 1951), II, chapter XVIII, p. 171.

follow one after the other without letup, and there is no more stopping until universal suffrage is reached.[j]

Today in the United States the principle of the sovereignty of the people has attained all the practical developments that imagination can conceive. It has been freed from all the fictions that have been carefully placed around it elsewhere; it is seen successively clothed in all forms according to the necessity of the case. Sometimes the people as a body make the laws as at Athens; sometimes the deputies created by universal suffrage represent the people and act in their name under their almost immediate supervision.

There are countries where a power, in a way external to the social body, acts on it and forces it to follow a certain path.

There are others where force is divided, being simultaneously inside and outside the society. Nothing of the sort is seen in the United States; there society acts by itself and on itself. Power exists only inside it;[k] hardly anyone may even be found who dares to conceive and especially to express the idea of seeking power elsewhere. The people participate in the composition of

---

j. In a letter to an unknown recipient, Tocqueville again takes up some arguments expressed at the time of a conversation with Charles Carroll:

> But, I replied, the Revolution over, what forced you to destroy English institutions and to establish democracy among yourselves?—"We were divided after the victory," responded Ch[arles (ed.)]. Carroll. "Each party wanted to use the people and, to gain their adherence, granted them new privileges, until finally the people became our master and showed us all the door."
>
> What do you think of this apology? Doesn't it have the air of being said in Paris toward the end of 1830 or at the very least in the course of the year of grace 1831? I am, however, a very faithful narrator (Draft of a letter of Tocqueville dated November 8, 1831, YTC, BIa2).

k. A symbol in the text refers to the following note: "Place a chapter here explaining what is called a constitution in America. Say that it is only a changing expression of the sovereignty of the people, that has nothing of the perpetual, that binds only until it is amended. Difference from what is understood by constitution in Europe, even in England.

[In the margin: Ask advice here.]"

the laws[m] by the choice of the legislators, in their application by the election of the agents of executive power. It can be said that they govern themselves, so weak and restricted is the part left to the administration, so much does the administration feel its popular origin and obey the power from which it emanates. The people rule the American political world as God rules the universe. They are the cause and the end of all things; everything arises from them and everything is absorbed by them.[H]

m. In the manuscript: "The people enter into the composition of the laws . . ." Hervé de Tocqueville:

I keep repeating the same objection, for it strikes me at every step. What is "the people" in a society where, as much as possible, ranks, fortunes, and minds approach the level of equality? Assuredly, in the New World the word *people* has none of the same meaning as among us. I believe that a sense of this must be given somewhere. Otherwise, the chapter moves along very well.

Édouard de Tocqueville: "I understand the preceding objection when it involved explaining the successive formation of American society; but here it isn't the same thing anymore. Alexis describes the government of democracy, and in this case the word *people* is appropriate and is perfectly understood. This entire passage seems remarkable to me" (YTC, CIIIb, 2, p. 90).

CHAPTER 5

Necessity of Studying What Happens in the Individual States before Speaking about the Government of the Union[a]

The following chapter is intended to examine what form government founded on the principle of sovereignty of the people takes in America, what its means of action, difficulties, advantages and dangers are.[b]

A first difficulty arises: the United States has a complex constitution. You notice two distinct societies there, bound together and, if I can explain it in this way, nested like boxes one inside the other. Two completely separate and nearly independent governments are seen: the one, habitual and undefined, which answers to the daily needs of the society; the other, exceptional and circumscribed, which applies only to certain general interests. They are, in a word, twenty-four small sovereign nations, that together form the great body of the Union.

To examine the Union before studying the state is to embark on a path strewn with difficulties. The form of the federal government in the United States appeared last; it was only a modification of the republic, a summary of political principles spread throughout the entire society before the federal government existed, and subsisting there independently of it. As I have just said, the federal government is, moreover, only an exception; the government of the states is the common rule. The writer who would like to

a. According to a rough draft (YTC, CVh, 3, p. 83), this section would at first have constituted an independent chapter.

b. In the margin: "≠Perhaps immediately after having treated the sovereignty of the people, it would be necessary to talk about election, which is its first and most complete application to the government of society.≠"

show such a picture as a whole before pointing out its details would necessarily lapse into obscurities and repetitions.

There can be no doubt that the great political principles that govern
American society today arose and developed in the *state*. So to have the key
to all the rest, the state must be understood.

The states that make up the American Union today all look the same
with regard to the external appearance of institutions. Political and administrative life there is found concentrated in three centers of action that
could be compared to the various nerve centers that make the human body
move.

At the first level is found the *town*;[TN 3] higher, the *county;* finally, the
state.

Of the Town System in America[c]

*Why the author begins the examination of political institutions
with the town.—The town is found among all peoples.—
Difficulty of establishing and maintaining town liberty.—*

TRANSLATOR'S NOTE 3: I have translated *commune,* when it refers to America, as
town rather than *township. Town* is, by far, the more common term in the United States,
especially in New England. And American historians almost unanimously use the term
town. When *commune* refers to France, I have usually left it in French, italicized.

c. When he starts on the study of the American administration, Tocqueville realizes
that he hardly knows that of his own country. In the month of October 1831, he asks
his father and two of his colleagues, Ernest de Chabrol and Ernest de Blosseville, to draw
up for him a summary sketch of the French administration. Tocqueville writes to his
father:

> Nothing would be more useful to me for judging America well than to know France.
> But it is this last point that is missing; I know in general that among us the government
> gets into nearly everything; a hundred times people have blared into my ears the word
> *centralization,* without explaining it to me. . . . If you could, my dear papa, analyze
> for me this word *centralization,* you would help me immensely (letter to his father,
> New York, 7 October 1831, YTC, BIa2).

In reply, Hervé de Tocqueville sends his son a long report bearing the title *Coup d'oeil
sur l'administration française* [*Brief View of the French Administration*]. There the former
prefect develops several of the ideas presented in *De la charte provinciale* (Paris: J. J.
Blaise, 1829, 62 pp.). After several pages devoted to description of the administration,

*Its importance.—Why the author has chosen the town
organization of New England as the principal object of
his examination.*

Not by chance do I first examine the town.

[≠The town is the first element of the societies out of which peoples
take form; it is the social molecule; if I can express myself in this way, it is
the embryo that already represents and contains the seed of the complete
being.≠]

---

the author considers in detail the problem of centralization and the way to lessen its
abuses. Hervé de Tocqueville, who fears that the autonomy of the French *communes*
[towns] will divide the country into a multitude of small republics, insists a great deal
on the fact that the King must exercise the administration and have the right to dissolve
the *conseils communaux* [town councils]. But he recognizes, nonetheless, the extreme
slowness of an excessively centralized administration and recommends the creation of
special juries for the purpose of deciding administrative questions as the most effective
means to accelerate decision making. In his response, Chabrol considers, above all, the
question of administrative jurisdiction. Macarel had in fact pointed out to him that the
majority of trials between the administration and individuals that were judged by the
conseils municipaux [municipal councils] were trials of an ordinary type that could have
been judged according to the forms of the ordinary judicial system. Chabrol also points
out that a large part of the administration still carries the trace of the centralizing concepts of the Napoleonic administration. The report of Blosseville, shorter and less precise
than the other two, allows for the shift of administrative trials to ordinary jurisdiction,
in agreement with Chabrol. (A copy of the three reports is found at Yale, under the
classification CIIIa).

For the preparation of this chapter, the report on the local administration of New
England, written by Jared Sparks for Alexis de Tocqueville, also has considerable importance. On this document and *Brief View of the French Administration,* see George
W. Pierson, *Tocqueville and Beaumont in America,* pp. 403–13. Finally, there is a note
by Beaumont that relates an interesting conversation with Sparks (in Beaumont, *Lettres
d'Amérique,* pp. 152–54). The questions posed by Tocqueville to Jared Sparks and the
responses of the latter have been published by H. B. Adams in *Jared Sparks and Alexis
de Tocqueville, Johns Hopkins University Studies in Historical and Political Science,* XVIth
series, n. 12, 1898. A rough draft with several notes for this chapter also contains numerous
references to the report of Sparks (YTC, CVb, p. 17). It is Jared Sparks who points out
to Tocqueville that Nathaniel Niles, Secretary of the American delegation in Paris and
native of New England, can be useful to him for the chapter on the town administration
of this part of the United States. It seems that, following this suggestion, Tocqueville
contacted the latter (see note v for p. 62).

The town is the only association that is so much a part of nature that wherever men are gathered together, a town takes shape by itself.

Town society exists therefore among all peoples no matter what their customs and their laws; it is man who establishes kingdoms and creates republics; the town seems to come directly from the hands of God. [≠The town is not only the first of social elements, but also the most important of all.≠] But if the town has existed ever since there have been men, town liberty is something rare and fragile.[d] A people can always establish great political assemblies, because it usually contains a certain number of men among whom, to a certain degree, enlightenment takes the place of the practice of public affairs. The town is made up of crude elements that often resist the action of the legislator. Instead of diminishing as nations become more enlightened, the difficulty of establishing town independence increases with their enlightenment. A highly civilized society tolerates the trial efforts of town liberty only with difficulty; it rebels at the sight of its numerous errors and despairs of success before having reached the final result of the experiment.

Of all liberties, town liberty, which is so difficult to establish, is also the most exposed to the encroachments of power. Left to themselves, town institutions could scarcely resist a strong and enterprising government; to defend themselves successfully, they must have reached their

d. In the margin:

Cause of its little importance. The coarse elements that it brings into use. It can hardly arise except during little developed centuries when individuality is the first need.

The town puts liberty and government within the grasp of the people; it gives them an education or creates great national assemblies.

A town system is made only with the support of mores, laws, circumstances and time.

Town liberty is the most difficult to suppress, the most difficult to create.

It is in the town that nearly all the strength of free peoples resides./

It is in the town that the liberty of peoples resides. Makes kingdoms and creates republics.≠ Cf. conversation with Mr. Gray (non-alphabetic notebooks 2 and 3, YTC, BIIa and *Voyages, OC,* V, 1, pp. 94–95).

fullest development and be mingled with national ideas and habits. Thus, as long as town liberty has not become part of the mores, it is easy to destroy; and it can become part of the mores only after existing in the laws for a long time.

Town liberty therefore escapes human effort so to speak. Consequently it is rarely created;[e] in a sense it arises by itself. It develops almost in secret[f] within a semi-barbaric society. The continuous action of laws and of mores, circumstances, and above all time succeed in its consolidation. You can say that, of all the nations of the European continent, not a single one knows town liberty.

The strength of free peoples resides in the town, however. Town institutions are to liberty what primary schools are to knowledge; they put it within the grasp of the people; they give them a taste of its peaceful practice and accustom them to its use. Without town institutions, a nation can pretend to have a free government, but it does not possess the spirit of liberty.[g] Temporary passions, momentary interests, the chance of circumstances can give it the external forms of independence; but des-

e. In his report on Algeria to the Chamber of Deputies ("Rapport fait par M. de Tocqueville sur le projet de loi relatif aux crédits extraordinaires demandés pour l'Algérie" and discussions on Algeria, *Moniteur universel*, 24, 25 May, 1, 9, 10, 11, 12 June 1847, reproduced in *OCB*, IX, pp. 423–512 and in *Écrits et discours politiques, OC*, III, 1, pp. 308–409), Tocqueville insists, nonetheless, on the necessity of creating town institutions in Algeria. He sees it as a condition of the French colonial presence in that country (*Écrits et discours politiques, OC*, III, 1, p. 352). See Seymour Drescher, *Dilemmas of Democracy: Tocqueville and Modernization* (Pittsburgh: University of Pittsburgh Press, 1968), p. 61.

f. Hervé de Tocqueville: "This does not seem to me to agree very well with what precedes. How does it develop almost in secret, if it has subsisted for a long time in the laws?" (YTC, CIIIb, 2, p. 84).

g. In his notes on the government of India, Tocqueville sees in the permanence and power of the town the reason for the survival of Hindu culture through revolution and the lack of interest in general politics: "The entire political life of the Indians withdrew into the town; the entire administration was concentrated there. As long as the town still existed, who controlled the empire was of little importance to the inhabitants. They hardly noticed the change of masters" (*Écrits et discours politiques, OC*, III, 1, p. 450).

potism, driven back into the interior of the social body, reappears sooner or later at the surface.

To make the reader understand well the general principles on which the political organization of the town and the county in the United States rests, I thought that it was useful to take one state in particular as a model, to examine in detail what happens there, and then to cast a quick glance over the rest of the country.

I have chosen one of the states of New England.

The town and the county are not organized in the same way in all the parts of the Union; it is easy to recognize, however, that throughout the Union the same principles, more or less, have presided over the formation of both.

[≠The town institutions of New England were the first to reach a state of maturity. They present a complete and uniform whole. They serve as a model for the other parts of the Union and tend more and more to become the standard to which all the rest must sooner or later conform.≠]

Now, it seemed to me that in New England these principles were considerably more developed and had attained further consequences than anywhere else. So they are, so to speak, more evident there and are thus more accessible to the observation of the foreigner.

The town institutions of New England form a complete and regular whole. They are old; they are strong because of the laws, stronger still because of the mores; they exercise a prodigious influence over the entire society.

In all these ways, they merit our attention.

Town District

The town in New England (*Township*) falls between the *canton* and the *commune* [town] in France. Generally it numbers from two to three thousand inhabitants.[1] So it is not too extensive for all its inhabitants to share

---

1. *In 1830, the number of towns, in the State of Massachusetts, was 305; the number of inhabitants 610,014; this gives an average of about 2,000 inhabitants per town.*

nearly the same interests; and on the other hand, it is populated enough to assure that elements of a good administration are always found within it.

Town Powers in New England

The people, source of all powers in the town as elsewhere.—
There they deal with principal matters by themselves.—
No town council.—The largest part of town authority
concentrated in the hands of the selectmen.*—How the selectmen*
function.—General assembly of the inhabitants of the town
*(*Town Meeting*).—Enumeration of all the town officers.—*
Offices mandatory and paid.

In the town as everywhere else, the people are the source of social powers, but nowhere else do they exercise their power more directly. In America, the people are a master who has to be pleased to the greatest possible degree.

In New England, the majority acts through representatives when the general affairs of the state must be dealt with. This was necessary; but in the town, where legislative and governmental action is closer to the governed, the law of representation is not accepted.[h] There is no town council; the body of voters, after naming their magistrates, directs them in everything that is not the pure and simple execution of the laws of the state.[2]

h. For Tocqueville, the lack of representation is the principal characteristic of the town; he gives the town a role similar to that of the small republic in the thought of Rousseau. If here he asserts that the lack of representation is a characteristic of the town across the Atlantic, in the *Ancien Régime et la Révolution* (*OC,* II, 1, pp. 119–20), he will admit that in the parish of the old regime he found the lack of political representation and other traits that he had formerly judged as belonging only to North America.

2. *The same rules do not apply to the large towns.*[j] *These generally have a mayor and a municipal body divided into two branches; but that is an exception that must be authorized by a law. See the law of 22 [23 (ed.)] February 1822, regulating the powers of the city of Boston.* Laws of Massachusetts, *vol. II, p. 588. This applies to large cities. It also frequently*

This state of things is so contrary to our ideas, and so opposed to our habits, that it is necessary to provide a few examples here for it to be well understood.

Public offices are extremely numerous and highly divided in the town, as we will see below. The largest part of administrative powers is concentrated, however, in the hands of a small number of individuals elected annually who are called selectmen.[3]

The general laws of the state have imposed a certain number of obligations on the selectmen. To fulfill them they do not need the authorization of those under their jurisdiction, and they cannot avoid their obligations without engaging their personal responsibility. State law charges them, for example, with drawing up the electoral lists in their town; if they fail to do so, they make themselves guilty of a misdemeanor. But in all things that are left to the direction of the town authority, the selectmen are the executors of the popular will, as with us the mayor is the executor of the deliberations of the town council. Most often they act on their private responsibility and, in actual practice, only carry out the implications of principles previously set down by the majority. But if they want to introduce any change whatsoever in the established order, if they desire to pursue a new undertaking, they must return to the source of their power. Suppose that it is a question of establishing a school: the selectmen convoke on a

<hr>

happens that the small cities are subject to a special administration. In 1832, the State of New York numbered 104 towns administered in this way (William's Register).

j. Hervé de Tocqueville:

Delete the note and transfer it to the end of the chapter. This note, while teaching us that the large towns have a different municipal system, interrupts, diminishes, and, in order to bring an imperfectly stated difference to our attention, diverts our interest. At the end of the chapter, a section on the municipal system of the large towns is needed. That is indispensable for the unity of the work and the satisfaction of the reader (YTC, CIIIb, 2, p. 84).

3. *Three are elected in the smallest towns; nine, in the largest. See* The Town Officer, *p. 186. Also see the principal laws of Massachusetts relative to the selectmen:*

Law of 20 February 1786, vol. I, p. 219;—24 February 1796, vol. I, p. 488;—7 March 1801, vol. II, p. 45;—16 June 1795, vol. I, p. 473;—12 March 1808, vol. II, p. 186;—28 February 1787, vol. I, p. 302;—22 June 1797, vol. I, p. 539.

given day, in a place specified in advance, the whole body of voters; there, they set forth the need that is felt; they show the means to satisfy it, the money that must be spent, the location that should be chosen. The assembly, consulted on all those points, adopts the principle, determines the location, votes the tax and puts the execution of its will into the hands of the selectmen.

Only the selectmen have the right to call the town meeting, but they can be made to do so. If ten property owners conceive a new project and want to submit it for approval by the town, they call for a general convocation of the inhabitants; the selectmen are obliged to agree to the call and only retain the right to preside over the meeting.[4]

Without a doubt, these political mores, these social customs are very far from us. At this moment I want neither to judge them nor to show the hidden causes that produce and animate them; I am limiting myself to presenting them.

The selectmen are elected annually in the month of April or May. At the same time the town meeting chooses a host of other town magistrates,[5] appointed for certain important administrative tasks.[k] Some, known as assessors, must determine the tax; others, known as collectors, must collect it. One officer, called the _constable,_ is charged with keeping the peace, supervising public places and assuring the physical execution of the laws. Another, named the town clerk, records all deliberations; he keeps minutes of the acts of the civil registry. A treasurer keeps the town funds. Add to these officers an overseer of the poor, whose duty, very difficult to fulfill, is to enforce the laws relative to the poor; school commissioners, who direct public education; road surveyors, who are responsible for all the routine tasks relating to the roadways, large and small; and you will have the list of the principal agents of town administration. But the division of offices does

---

4. *See* Laws of Massachusetts, *vol. I, p. 250; law of 23 March 1786.*
5. Ibid.
k. In the margin: "≠What makes town spirit powerful./
"Independence of the town.
"Importance of the town.
"Constant political life.
"Division of town powers.≠"

not stop there. You still find, among the town officers,[6] parish commissioners who must regulate church expenses;[m] inspectors of various kinds, some charged with directing the efforts of citizens in case of fire; others, with overseeing the harvest; these, with temporarily relieving difficulties that can arise from fencing; those, with supervising wood allotments or with inspecting weights and measures.

In all, principal offices in the town number nineteen. Each inhabitant is obligated, under penalty of a fine, to accept these different offices; but also most of these offices are paid,[n] so that poor citizens can devote their time to them without suffering a loss. The American system, moreover, does not give any fixed salary to officers. In general, each act of their administration has a value, and they are remunerated only in proportion to what they have done.[o]

---

6. *All these magistrates actually exist in practice.*

To know the details of the duties of all of these town magistrates, see the book entitled Town Officer, *by Isaac Goodwin, Worcester 1829; and the collection of the general laws of Massachusetts in 3 vols., Boston, 1823.*

m. Tocqueville learned from Goodwin that in the United States the town inhabitants were obliged to contribute to the support of a Protestant minister. This seems to him nearly the sign of a State religion, and he says so to Sparks. Apparently in agreement, Sparks answers him: "It is one of those cases in which early prejudice, habit, and accidental causes, may pervert the sense of a majority and operate against the equal rights of the whole" (H. B. Adams, *Jared Sparks and Alexis de Tocqueville,* p. 25).

n. The manuscript says: "paid, little it is true, but enough, however, so that poor citizens . . ."

o. I found myself in a Boston salon behind two respectable *gentlemen* who appeared to treat an important subject with interest:

"How much will that gain you much [*sic*]?" said one.

"It's a fairly good business," answered the other, "about one hundred dollars is given for each."

"As you say," replied the first, "that truly is a good business."

Now, it concerned nothing less than two pirates who were to be hanged the next day. One of these speakers, who was the *City Marshal,* was obliged by his position to be present at the execution and to see that everything was done according to order. The law allocated to him for his right to be present one hundred dollars for each one hanged; and he spoke of these two condemned men like a pair of cattle that he had to sell the next day at the market.

Told by the consul (alphabetic notebook B, YTC, BIIa, and *Voyage, OC,* V, 1, p. 241).

Of Town Life

*Each person is the best judge of what concerns only himself
alone.—Corollary of the principle of sovereignty of the people.—
Application that the American towns make of these doctrines.—
The New England town, sovereign in everything that concerns
only itself, subject in everything else.—Obligation of the
town toward the state.—In France, the government lends
its agents to the town.—In America, the town lends its to
the government.*

I said previously that the principle of sovereignty of the people hovers over the entire political system of the Anglo-Americans. Each page of this book will show some new applications of this doctrine.

Among nations where the dogma of the sovereignty of the people reigns, each individual forms an equal portion of the sovereign power, and participates equally in the government of the state.

Each individual is therefore considered to be as enlightened, as virtuous, as strong as any of his fellows.

So why does he obey society, and what are the natural limits of this obedience?

He obeys society, not at all because he is inferior to those who direct it, or less capable than another man of governing himself; he obeys society because union with his fellows seems useful to him and because he knows that this union cannot exist without a regulatory power.

So in all that concerns the mutual duties of citizens, he has become a subject. In all that concerns only himself, he has remained the master; he is free and is accountable for his actions only to God. Thus this maxim, that the individual is the best as well as the only judge of his particular interest and that society has the right to direct his actions only when it feels harmed by them, or when it needs to call for his support.

This doctrine is universally accepted in the United States. Elsewhere I will examine what general influence it exercises over even the ordinary acts of life; but at this moment I am talking about the towns.

The town, taken as a whole and in relation to the central government, is only an individual like any other to whom the theory I have just indicated applies.

Town liberty in the United States follows, therefore, from the very dogma of the sovereignty of the people. All the American republics have more or less recognized this independence; but among the people of New England, circumstances have particularly favored its development.

In this part of the Union, political life was born very much within the towns; you could almost say that at its origin each of them was an independent nation. When the Kings of England later demanded their share of sovereignty, they limited themselves to taking central power. They left the town in the situation where they found it; now the towns of New England are subjects; but in the beginning they were not or were scarcely so. They did not therefore receive their powers; on the contrary, they seem to have relinquished a portion of their independence in favor of the state; an important distinction which the reader must keep in mind.P

In general the towns are subject to the states only when an interest that I will call *social* is concerned, that is to say, an interest that the towns share with others.q

For everything that relates only to them alone, the towns have remained independent bodies. No one among the inhabitants of New England, I think, recognizes the right of the state government to intervene in the direction of purely town interests.r

So the towns of New England are seen to buy and sell, to sue and to defend themselves before the courts, to increase or reduce their budget

p. In the margin: "≠The dogma of sovereignty of the people, it must not be forgotten, has as its end not to make the people do all that they should want, but all that they do want.≠"

q. Cf. conversations with Sparks and Mr. Gray (non-alphabetic notebooks 2 and 3, YTC, BIIa, and *Voyage,* p. 90, 96). See also H. B. Adams, *Jared Sparks and Alexis de Tocqueville,* p. 18.

r. Earlier draft: "≠I do not believe anyone has ever dared to profess that the duty and the right of a government was to watch over the governed in such a paternal way that they could not even do what can be of harm only to themselves.≠"

without any administrative authority whatsoever thinking to oppose them.[7] [<≠This right has only a single limit. That is found in the institution of the judicial power, but we will examine it later.≠>]

As for social duties, they are required to fulfill them. Thus, if the state needs money, the town is not free to grant or to deny its cooperation.[8] If the state wants to open a road, the town does not have the right to close its territory. If it establishes a regulation concerning public order, the town must execute it. If it wants to organize education according to a uniform plan throughout the country, the town is required to create the schools desired by the law.[9] We will see, when we talk about administration in the United States, how and by whom the towns, in all these different cases, are forced to obey. Here I only want to establish the existence of the obligation. This obligation is strict, but the state government, while imposing it, only enacts a principle; for carrying out the principle, the town generally recovers all its rights of individuality. Thus, it is true that the tax is voted by the legislature, but it is the town that apportions and collects it; a school is prescribed, but it is the town that builds, funds and directs it.

In France the tax collector of the State levies the taxes of the town; in America the tax collector of the town raises the tax of the state.

With us, therefore, the central government lends its agents to the town; in America, the town lends its officers to the government. That alone makes clear to what degree the two societies differ.

Of Town Spirit in New England

Why the New England town attracts the affections of those who live there.—Difficulty met in Europe in creating town spirit.— Town rights and duties that work together in America to form this spirit.—The native land has a more distinctive

---

7. *See* Laws of Massachusetts, *law of 23 March 1786, vol. I, p. 250.*
8. Ibid., *law of 20 February 1786, vol. I, p. 217.*
9. *See the same collection, law of 2 June 1789, and 8 [10 (ed.)] March, 1827, vol. I, p. 367, and vol. III, p. 179.*

physiognomy in the United States than elsewhere.—How town
spirit is shown in New England.—What fortunate effects
it produces there.

[≠Laws act on mores; and mores, on laws. Wherever these two things do
not lend each other mutual support, there is unrest, revolution tearing apart
the society.

The legislation of New England constituted the town. Habits have completed the establishment of a true town spirit there.

The town is a center around which interests and passions gather and
where real and sustained activity reigns.≠]

In America not only do town institutions exist, but also a town spirit
that sustains and animates them.[s]

The New England town brings together two advantages that, wherever
they are found, strongly excite the interest of men—namely, independence
and power. It acts, it is true, within a circle that it cannot leave, but within
that circle its movements are free. This independence alone would already
give the town real importance even if its population and size would not
assure its importance.

You must realize that in general the affections of men go only where
strength is found. Love of native land does not reign for long in a conquered
country.[t] The inhabitant of New England is attached to his town, not so
much because he was born there as because he sees in this town a free and
strong corporate body to which he belongs and which merits the trouble
of trying to direct it.

In Europe the very people who govern often regret the absence of town
spirit; for everyone agrees that town spirit is a great element of order and
public tranquillity; but they do not know how to produce it. By making
the town strong and independent, they fear dividing social power and exposing the State to anarchy. Now, take strength and independence away

s. In the margin: "<The person who focuses his affections and his hopes on the town,
who knows how to take his place there and to participate in its governance, that person
possesses what I call town spirit.>"

t. In the margin, in pencil, on a paper glued into place: "I do not know if this thought
is very accurate. Witness, Poland."

from the town, and you will forever find there only people who are administered, not citizens.

Note, moreover, an important fact. The New England town is so constituted that it can serve as a center of strong affections, and at the same time there is nothing nearby that strongly attracts the ambitious passions of the human heart.

The officials of the county are not elected and their authority is limited. The state itself has only a secondary importance; its existence is indistinct and tranquil. To gain the right to administer it, few men agree to distance themselves from the center of their interests and to disrupt their existence.

The federal government confers power and glory on those who direct it; but the number of men who are able to influence its destiny is very small. The presidency is a high office that can hardly be attained except after reaching an advanced age. When someone reaches other high level federal offices, it is by chance in a way and after already becoming famous by pursuing another career.[u] Ambition cannot make these high offices the permanent aim of its efforts. [{The Union is a nearly ideal being that nothing represents to the mind.}][v] It is in the town, at the center of the ordinary relations of life, that the desire for esteem, the need for real interests, the taste for power and notice are focused. These passions, which so often trouble society, change character when they can operate thus near the domestic hearth and, in a way, within the family.

See with what art, in the American town, care has been taken to *scatter* power, if I can express myself in this way, in order to interest more people in public life. Apart from the voters called from time to time to perform the acts of government, how many diverse offices, how many different magistrates, who all, in the circle of their attributions, represent the powerful corporate body in whose name they act! How many men thus

---

u. The drafting of this sentence, and of the preceding one, is by Beaumont (YTC, CIIIb, 2, pp. 68–69). In this chapter, Tocqueville seems to have largely taken into account numerous stylistic suggestions made by Beaumont.

v. In pencil in the margin: "≠There again, an idea that is a bit undeveloped and that consequently lacks clarity.≠"

exploit the power of the town for their profit and are interested in it for themselves!

Nor is the American system, even as it divides municipal power among a great number of citizens, afraid to multiply town duties. In the United States people think rightly that love of country is a kind of religious cult that attaches men by observances.

In this way, town life makes itself felt at every moment as it were; it manifests itself every day by the accomplishment of a duty or by the exercise of a right. This political existence imparts a continual, but at the same time peaceful, movement to society that agitates without troubling it.[w]

The Americans are attached to the city by a reason analogous to the one that makes mountain dwellers love their country. Among them the native land has marked and characteristic features; it has a more distinctive physiognomy than elsewhere.

In general the New England towns have a happy existence. Their government suits their taste and is their choice as well. Within the profound peace and material prosperity that reign in America, the storms of municipal life are few. Leadership of town interests is easy. The political education of the people, moreover, was done a long time ago, or rather they arrived already educated on the soil they occupy. In New England, division of ranks does not exist even in memory; so there is no portion of the town tempted to oppress the other, and injustices, which strike only isolated individuals, are lost in the general contentment. Should the government exhibit some faults, and certainly it is easy to point them out, they are not obvious to view, because the government truly derives from the governed. And it is sufficient for town government to operate, whether well or poorly, for it to be protected by a kind of paternal pride. The Americans, moreover, have no point of comparison. England once ruled the colonies as a whole, but the people have always directed town affairs. So sovereignty of the

w. "Rights and duties are multiplied in the town in order to attach man by its benefits, like religion by its observances. Town life makes itself felt at every moment. Duty, flexible and easy to fulfill; social importance that that *scatters*" (YTC, CVb, p. 17).

people in the town is not only a long-standing condition, but also an original one.

The inhabitant of New England is attached to his town, because it is strong and independent; he is interested in it, because he participates in its leadership; he loves it, because he has nothing to complain about in his lot. In the town he places his ambition and his future; he joins in each of the incidents of town life; in this limited sphere, accessible to him, he tries his hand at governing society. He becomes accustomed to the forms without which liberty proceeds only by revolutions, is infused with their spirit, acquires a taste for order, understands the harmony of powers, and finally gathers clear and practical ideas about the nature of his duties as well as the extent of his rights.

Of the County in New England

The county in New England, analogous to the arrondissement
in France.—Created for a purely administrative interest.—
Has no representation.—Administered by
non-elective officials.

The American county is very analogous to the French *arrondissement*. As for the latter, an arbitrary circumscription was drawn for the former; it forms a body whose different parts have no necessary bonds with each other and for whom neither affection nor memory nor shared existence serve as attachments. It is created only for a purely administrative interest.

The town was too limited in area ever to contain the administration of justice. The county is, therefore, the primary judicial center. Each county has a court of justice,[10] a sheriff to execute the decisions of the courts, a prison that must hold the criminals.

There are needs that are felt in a more or less equal way by all the towns of a county; it was natural that a central authority was charged with providing for them. In Massachusetts, this authority resides in the hands of a

---

10. *See the law of 14 February 1821,* Laws of Massachusetts, *vol. II, p. 551.*

certain number of magistrates, appointed by the Governor of the state, with the advice[11] of his council.[12]

The county administrators have only a limited and exceptional power that applies only to a very small number of cases provided for in advance. The state and the town are sufficient for the ordinary course of things. These administrators only prepare the county budget; the legislature votes it.[13] There is no assembly that, directly or indirectly, represents the county.

So truly speaking, the county has no political existence.[x]

A double tendency is noticeable in most American constitutions, which leads the law-makers to divide executive power and to concentrate legislative power. The New England town by itself has a principle of existence that is not stripped away from it. But this existence would have to be created artificially in the county, and the usefulness of doing so has not been felt. All the towns united together have only a single representative, the state,[y] center of all national powers;[z] apart from town and national action, you could say that there are only individual powers.

Of Administration in New England[a]

In America, you do not see the administration.—Why.—
Europeans believe they are establishing liberty by taking away
some of the rights belonging to the social power; Americans, by

---

11. *See the law of 20 February 1819,* Laws of Massachusetts, *vol. II, p. 494.*
12. *The Governor's Council is an elected body.*
13. *See the law of 2 November 1781,* Laws of Massachusetts, *vol. I, p. 61.*
x. In a working note for the draft of *Ireland,* Beaumont will write:
"—In Ireland political life is in the *county,* because Ireland is aristocratic.
—In America, in the *town,* because America is democratic.
—Among us, in the *State,* because France, still *monarchical"* (Beaumont, YTC, CX).
y. In a first draft, this section was followed by that which treats the state.
z. The style of the last three sentences had been modified following remarks by Beaumont (YTC, CIIIb, 2, p. 70).
a. The manuscript mentions the following titles: "OF ADMINISTRATION IN THE UNITED STATES," "WHAT IS MEANT IN THE UNITED STATES BY ADMINISTRATION AND GOVERNMENT. THEIR MEANS OF ACTION AND THEIR ELEMENTS," and "OF EXECUTIVE POWER IN THE UNITED STATES. OF GOVERNMENT AND ADMINISTRATION."

dividing their exercise.—Nearly all of the administration strictly
speaking contained in the town, and divided among town
officers.—No trace of an administrative hierarchy is seen, either
in the town or above it.—Why it is so.— How the state happens,
however, to be administered in a uniform way.—Who is charged
with making the town and county administrations obey the
law.—Of the introduction of the judicial power into the
administration.—Result of extending the elective principle to all
officials.—Of the justice of the peace in New England.—
Appointed by whom.—Administers the county.—Ensures the
administration of the towns.—Court of sessions.—The way in
which it acts.—Who apprises it.—The right of inspection and of
complaint, scattered like all administrative functions.—
Informers encouraged by sharing fines.

What most strikes the European who travels across the United States is the
absence of what among us we call government or administration. In America, you see written laws; you see their daily execution; everything is in
motion around you, and the motor is nowhere to be seen. The hand that
runs the social machine escapes at every moment.

But just as all peoples, in order to express their thoughts, are obliged
to resort to certain grammatical forms that constitute human languages,
all societies, in order to continue to exist, are compelled to submit to a
certain amount of authority; without it, they fall into anarchy. This authority can be distributed in different ways; but it must always be found
somewhere.

There are two means to diminish the strength of authority[b] in a nation.

The first is to weaken power in its very principle, by taking from society
the right or the capacity to defend itself in certain cases; to weaken au-

---

b. Hervé de Tocqueville: "I do not like the word *authority* here very much. It seems
too generic to me to apply to the species; there is the authority of laws that cannot be
diminished, nor that of the magistrates. I would prefer *power*. It would be dropped in
the following sentence" (YTC, CIIIb, 2, p. 86 prima).

thority in this way is what, in Europe, is generally called establishing liberty.[c]

[{This method has always seemed to me barbaric and antisocial.}]

There is a second means to diminish the action of authority. This one consists not of stripping society of some of its rights or paralyzing its efforts, but of dividing the use of its powers among several hands; of multiplying officials while attributing to each all the power needed to carry out what he is meant to do. There are peoples who can still be led to anarchy by this division of the social powers; in itself, however, it is not anarchic. By sharing authority in this way, its action is made less irresistible and less dangerous, it is true; but authority is not destroyed.

The Revolution in the United States was produced by a mature and thoughtful taste for liberty, and not by a vague and undefined instinct for independence. It was not based upon passions for disorder; on the contrary, it proceeded with love of order and of legality.[d]

So in the United States, the Americans did not claim that, in a free country, a man had the right to do everything; on the contrary, social obligations more varied than elsewhere were imposed on him. They did not have the idea of attacking the power of society in its principle and of contesting its rights; they limited themselves to dividing power in its exercise. In this way they wanted to make authority great and the official small, so that society might continue to be well regulated and remain free.

There is no country in the world where the law speaks a language as

c. Édouard de Tocqueville:

I cannot understand this. How can someone think to establish liberty by taking *from society* the right to defend itself? Fine, if you had said: *by taking from the government which represents society,* etc. You wanted to say, I think, that someone thought to establish liberty by weakening the government, the governmental power. Well! That is badly expressed, for to weaken the government of a society or to weaken this society are two very different things. French society was not weak under the Convention, but the old government had just been destroyed" (YTC, CIIIb, 2, pp. 81–82).

d. In the margin of another version: "≠When democracy comes with mores and beliefs, it leads to liberty.
When it comes with moral and religious anarchy, it leads to despotism.≠"

absolute as in America, nor is there one where the right to apply the law is divided among so many hands.

Administrative power in the United States presents nothing either centralized or hierarchical in its constitution; that is why you do not see it. Power exists, but you do not know where to find its representative.

We saw above that the New England towns were not subordinate. So they take care of their own individual interests.

It is also the town magistrates who are usually charged with seeing to the execution of the general laws of the state or with executing them themselves.[14]

Apart from the general laws, the state sometimes makes general regulations concerning public order. But ordinarily it is the towns and the town officers who, jointly with the justices of the peace and according to the needs of the localities, regulate the details of social existence and promulgate prescriptions relating to public health, good order and the morality of citizens.[15]

Finally it is the municipal magistrates who, by themselves and without needing to wait for outside initiative, provide for the unexpected needs that societies often feel.[e] [16]

14. *See* The Town Officer, *particularly the words* Selectmen, Assessors, Collectors, Schools, Surveyors of Highways . . . *Example among many others: the state forbids unnecessary travel on Sunday. It is the* tythingmen, *town officers, who are especially charged with using their authority to enforce the law.*

See the law of 8 March 1792, Laws of Massachusetts, *vol. I, p. 410.*

The selectmen draw up the electoral lists for the election of the Governor and forward the result of the vote to the secretary of the republic. Law of 24 February 1796, id., vol. I, p. 488.

15. *Example: the selectmen authorize the construction of sewers, designate the locations where slaughterhouses can be built, and where certain types of business whose proximity is harmful can be established.*

See the law of 7 June 1785, vol. I, p. 193.

e. In the first draft: "≠The administration in societies where the legislative and executive powers are not concentrated in the same hands {where the principle of sovereignty of the people reigns} has only two obligations:

1. To *execute* the existing laws.

2. To provide for the unforeseen accidents of social life.≠"

16. *Example: the selectmen attend to public health in case of contagious diseases, and*

As a result of what we have just said, administrative power in Massa-chusetts is almost entirely contained within the town;[17] but it is divided there among many hands.

In the French town there is in fact only a single administrative official, the mayor.[f]

We have seen that there were at least nineteen in the New England town.

The nineteen officers do not generally depend on each other. The law has carefully drawn a circle of action around each of these magistrates. Within this circle, they have all the power needed to fulfill the duties of their office and are not under any town authority.

If you look above the town, you see scarcely a trace of an administrative hierarchy. Sometimes county officials correct a decision made by the towns or by the town magistrates,[18] but in general you can say that the adminis-trators of the county do not have the right to direct the conduct of the administrators of the town.[19] The former have authority over the latter only in things that concern the county.

----

jointly with the justices of the peace, take necessary measures. Law of 22 June 1797, vol. I, p. 539 [549 (ed.)].

17. *I say* almost, *because there are several incidents of town life that are regulated, either by a justice of the peace in their individual capacity, or by the justices of the peace assembled as a body at the county-seat. Example: it is the justices of the peace who grant licenses. See the law of 28 February 1787, vol. I, p. 297.*

f. Initially, Tocqueville wrote more specifically: "≠In the French town the mayor is only the representative of an official at a higher level than he; his power is only the reflection of a superior power, a delegation of authority; the representative must always disappear before the one who gave the mandate.≠"

18. *Example: a license is granted only to those who present a certificate of good conduct given by the selectmen. If the selectmen refuse to give this certificate, the person can complain to the justices of the peace assembled in the court of sessions, and they can grant the license. See the law of 12 March 1808, vol. II, p. 186. The towns have the right to make regulations (bylaws) and to require the observation of these bylaws by fines the level of which are fixed; but these bylaws must be approved by the court of sessions. See the law of 23 March 1786, vol. I, p. 254.*

19. *In Massachusetts, the county administrators are often called to assess the acts of the town administrators; but we will see later that they engage in this examination as a judicial power, and not as an administrative authority.*

The town magistrates and those of the county are required, in a very small number of cases stipulated in advance, to report the result of their actions to the officers of the central government.[20] But the central government is not represented by one man charged with making general regulations concerning public order or ordinances for the execution of the laws, with communicating routinely with the administrators of the county and town, with examining their conduct, with directing their actions and punishing their mistakes.

So there is no center where the lines of administrative power come together.

Then how do you manage to run society according to a more or less uniform plan? How can counties and their administrators, towns and their officers be made to obey?[g]

In the states of New England, the legislative power extends to more objects than with us. The legislator penetrates in a way to the very heart of the administration; the law gets into the smallest details. It simultaneously prescribes the principles and the means to apply them; thus it encloses the secondary bodies and their administrators within a multitude of strict and rigorously defined obligations.

As a result, if all the secondary bodies and all the officials follow the law, all parts of society proceed in a uniform way. But there still remains the

---

20. *Example: the town school committees are bound to make an annual report on the state of the school to the secretary of the republic. See the law of 10 March 1827, vol. III, p. 183.*

g. Administrative and judicial powers./

Among all nations there are two methods of executing the laws:

The *administrative* method.

The *judicial* method.

The administrative method always addresses the cause; the other, the effect. The one is direct; the other, indirect.

Example: a town makes an illegal decree.

The executive power quashes it. The judicial power prevents it from having any effects and protects those who resist it.

An obstruction arises on the public road. The executive power has it removed; the judicial power gets to the same end indirectly by fining those who caused it (YTC, CVb, pp. 19–20).

question of knowing how the secondary bodies and their officials can be forced to follow the law.

In a general way you can say that society finds at its disposal only two means to force officials to obey the laws.

It can entrust to one of the officers the discretionary power to direct all the others and to remove them from office in case of disobedience.

Or it can charge the courts with imposing judicial penalties on those who break the law.[h]

You are not always free to choose one or the other of these means.

The right of directing an official assumes the right to remove him from office, if he does not follow the orders given to him, or to promote him if he zealously fulfills all of his duties. Now, an elected magistrate can be neither removed nor promoted. Elective offices are by nature irrevocable until the end of the term. In reality, the elected magistrate has nothing either to hope or to fear except from the voters.[j] So when all public offices result from election, there can be no true hierarchy among officials, since both the right to command and the right to quell disobedience effectively cannot be given to the same man; and the power to command cannot be joined with that of rewarding and punishing.

h. Centralization. Town liberties.

In France there are two means available against the decisions of the Administration, an *administrative* means and a *judicial* means.

When an agent of the administration orders something contrary to the law, you can apply to his superior and have his decision changed.

In the same situation, you can refuse to obey, and then the question comes before the courts that decide indirectly if the official had the right to issue the order. See a discussion where these ideas are treated by Odilon Barrot. Débats [*Journal des débats* (ed.)] of 1 March 1834 (YTC, CVj, 2, pp. 26–27).

Tocqueville's papers contain an article clipped from the *Journal des débats* of the same date, relating to the discussion on 28 February 1834 on the municipal law (copied in YTC, CVj, 2, pp. 27–46). On the occasion of the debate, Barrot defends the independence of the French towns against Thiers and the government, which took a position in favor of a strict control of the mayor by the prefect.

j. "Where there is election, the supervision by the superior official of his inferior is less necessary. Elections deal with negligence; the courts, with misdeed.

Be careful to distinguish carefully what is judicial from what is administrative. *Nearly all the administration strictly speaking is concentrated in the towns; it is only a matter of having them fulfill their obligations"* (YTC, CVb, p. 6).

People who introduce election into the secondary mechanisms of their government are therefore led necessarily to make heavy use of judicial penalties as a means of administration.

This is not obvious at first glance. Those who govern see making offices elective as a first concession, and submitting elected magistrates to the decisions of judges as a second concession. They dread these two innovations equally; and because they are requested to do the first more than the second, they grant the election of the official and leave him independent of the judge. One of these two measures, however, is the only counterbalance that can be given to the other. We should be very careful about this; an elective power not submitted to a judicial power escapes sooner or later from all control or is destroyed. Between the central power and elected administrative bodies, only the courts can serve as an intermediary. They alone can force the elected official to obey without violating the right of the voter.

So in the political world, the extension of judicial power must be correlative with the extension of elective power. If these two things do not go together, the State ends by falling into anarchy or servitude.[k]

It has been noted in all times that judicial habits prepared men rather poorly for the exercise of administrative power.

The Americans took from their fathers, the English, the idea of an institution that has no analogy whatsoever with what we know on the continent of Europe: the justices of the peace.

The justice of the peace holds a middle place between a public figure and the magistrate, administrator and judge. The justice of the peace is an enlightened citizen, but not necessarily one who is versed in knowledge of the laws. Consequently, he is charged only with keeping order in society, something that requires good sense and uprightness more than knowledge. The justice of the peace brings to administration, when he takes part in it, a certain taste for forms and for publicity that makes him a highly trou-

---

k. Hervé de Tocqueville: "This sentence is abstract."

Édouard de Tocqueville: "It is very concise. I do not find it obscure" (YTC, CIIIb, 2, p. 87).

Gustave de Beaumont: "Excellent sentence. Do not listen to paternal advice" (YTC, CIIIb, 2, p. 72).

blesome instrument to despotism. But he does not appear to be a slave to those legal superstitions that make magistrates[m] little capable of governing.

The Americans appropriated the institution of justices of the peace, all the while removing the aristocratic character that distinguished it in the mother country.

The Governor[n] of Massachusetts[21] appoints, in all the counties, a certain number of justices of the peace, whose term in office lasts seven years.[22]

Among these justices of the peace, moreover, he designates three of them who form in each county what is called the *court of sessions.*

The justices of the peace individually take part in public administration. Sometimes, along with the elected officials, they are charged with certain administrative acts;[23] sometimes they form a court before which the mag-

m. Édouard de Tocqueville: "I would like there: that *generally* make magistrates little capable, etc. . . . No one must be hurt, and by allowing for exceptions, everyone applies the exception to himself; besides, I believe that there really are some" (YTC, CIIIb, 2, p. 82).

n. Édouard de Tocqueville (?):

> We have not yet heard about a governor. The reader is even totally unaware what this pompous label corresponds to in a republican country. Astonishment is redoubled when he learns that in the same country where the principle of informing [delegation? (ed.)] has penetrated everywhere, the governor appoints, in all the counties, a certain number of justices of the peace, etc.
>
> I know that further along, on page 229, you explain what the functions of the governor are, but it appears indispensable to me that you say a word about it here, since the reader is bewildered when reading this paragraph. You could, I believe, begin this paragraph more or less like this: *There is in each county a magistrate who has the title of governor. I will say further on how he gets his powers and what his attributions are.* Or better still, this could be put in a note at the bottom of the page, or simply in a note at the word governor: *head of the executive power of the county* (YTC, CIIIb, 2, pp. 82–83).

Note 21 does not exist in the manuscript.

21. *We will see further on what the Governor is; I must say at this moment that the Governor represents the executive power of the whole state.*

22. *See the Constitution of Massachusetts, chap. II, section I, paragraph 9; chap. III, paragraph 3.*

23. *Example among many others: a stranger arrives in a town, coming from a country ravaged by a contagious disease. He falls ill. Two justices of the peace, with the advice of the selectmen, can order the county sheriff to transport him elsewhere and to watch over him. Law of 22 June 1797, vol. I, p. 540.*

In general, the justices of the peace intervene in all the important acts of administrative life and give them a semi-judicial character.

istrates summarily charge the citizen who refuses to obey, or the citizen denounces the crimes of the magistrates. But it is in the court of sessions that the justices of the peace exercise the most important of their administrative functions.

The court of sessions meets twice a year at the county seat. In Massachusetts it is charged with upholding the obedience of most[24] of the public officials.[25]

Careful attention must be paid to the fact that in Massachusetts the court of sessions is simultaneously an administrative body strictly speaking and a political court.

[≠The administrative and judicial functions of the court of sessions are so often confused in practice, that it is difficult to separate them even in theory. But it is useful to do so.

<The court of sessions has attributions of two kinds. It administers the county and ensures the administration of the towns.>≠]

---

24. *I say* most *because in fact certain administrative crimes are referred to the ordinary courts. Example: when a town refuses to raise the funds needed for its schools, or to appoint the school committee, a very considerable fine is imposed. The court called* supreme judicial court *or the court of* common pleas *pronounces this fine. See the law of 10 March 1827, vol. III, p. 190. Id. When a town fails to make provision for war supplies. Law of 21 February 1822, vol. II, p. 570.*

25. *The justices of the peace, in their individual capacity,[o] take part in the government of the towns and counties. The most important acts of town life are generally undertaken only with the support of one of them.*

o. Hervé de Tocqueville:

I do not believe that the word *capacity* exactly expresses the thought of the author. Care must be taken about using words whose specific expression is made uncertain by their multiple meanings. It seems to me that, from page 189 to 193, Alexis does not say enough about how the justices of the peace participate in town administration. He must not lose sight of the fact that America is something new for most of his readers, and that they will be looking in his book still more for instructions than for reflections. I admit that here, being uninformed, my curiosity is not satisfied. I feel humiliated by my lack of knowledge, and I am annoyed that the author has assumed that I am more informed than I am. These pages must be reviewed and more precise details given about the administrative action of the justices of the peace, when they act outside of the court of sessions. Most readers do not even know how they act in England.

Édouard de Tocqueville: "Quite right. It seems to me that here the word *capacity* means *attribution*. This word would be better I believe" (YTC, CIIIb, 2, pp. 87–88).

We said that the county[26] had only an administrative existence. It is the court of sessions by itself that is in charge of the small number of interests that relate to several towns at the same time or to all the towns of the county at once, interests that consequently cannot be entrusted to any single town in particular.

When it concerns the county, the duties of the court of sessions are therefore purely administrative, and if it often introduces judicial forms into its way of proceeding, it is only as a means to inform itself,[27] and as a guarantee given to the citizens. But when the administration of the towns must be ensured, the court of sessions almost always acts as a judicial body, and only in a few rare cases, as an administrative body.

The first difficulty that presents itself is making the town itself, a nearly independent power, obey the general laws of the state.

We have seen that each year the towns must appoint a certain number of magistrates who, as assessors, apportion taxes. A town tries to evade the obligation to pay the tax by not appointing the assessors. The court of sessions imposes a heavy fine.[28] The fine is raised by head on all the inhabitants. The county sheriff, officer of the law, executes the decision. In this way, in the United States, power seems eager to hide itself carefully from sight. Administrative command is almost always veiled there as a judicial mandate; as such it is only more powerful, having in its favor the almost irresistible strength that men grant to legal forms.

This procedure is easy to follow and is easily understood. What is required of the town is, in general, clear and defined; it consists of a simple and uncomplicated act, of a principle, and not a detailed application.[29] But

---

26. *The things relating to the county and that the court of sessions attends to can be reduced to these:*

1. The building of prisons and courts of justice; 2. The proposed county budget (it is the state legislature that votes on it); 3. The apportionment of these taxes thus voted; 4. The distribution of certain licenses; 5. The establishment and repair of county roads.

27. *When it is a matter of a road, this is the way that the court of sessions, with the help of the jury, settles nearly all the difficulties of execution.*

28. *See the law of 20 February 1786, vol. I, p. 217.*

29. *There is an indirect way to make the town obey. The towns are compelled by law to keep their roads in good condition. If they neglect to vote the funds required for this main-*

the difficulty begins when it concerns securing the obedience, not of the town any longer, but of the town officers.

All the reprehensible actions that a public official can commit fall definitively into one of these categories:

He can do, without enthusiasm and without zeal, what the law requires of him.

He cannot do what the law requires of him.

Finally, he can do what the law forbids.

A court can get at the conduct of an official only in the last two cases. A positive and appreciable act is needed as grounds for judicial action.

Thus, if the selectmen fail to fulfill the formalities required by law in the case of town elections, they can be fined.[30]

But when the public official fulfills his duty without intelligence, when he obeys the instructions of the law without enthusiasm and without zeal, he is entirely beyond the reach of a judicial body.

In this case, the court of sessions, even when vested with its administrative attributions, is impotent to force him to fulfill all of his obligations. Only fear of removal can prevent these quasi-failings; and the court of sessions does not hold within itself the source of town powers; it cannot remove officials that it does not appoint.P

In order to make certain, moreover, that there is negligence or lack of zeal, the subordinate official would have to be put under constant supervision. Now, the court of sessions meets only twice a year; it does not conduct inspections; it judges only the reprehensible acts that are brought before it.

---

tenance, the town magistrate responsible for the roads is then authorized, as a matter of course, to raise the needed money. Since he is himself responsible to individuals for the bad condition of the roads, and can be sued by them before the court of sessions, it is assured that he will exercise against the town the extraordinary right given to him by the law. Thus, by threatening the officer, the court of sessions forces the town to obey. See the law of 5 March 1787, vol. I, p. 305.

30. Laws of Massachusetts, vol. II, p. 45.

p. Hervé de Tocqueville: "Que, qui, que within a few lines. I do not know why, when the thought is powerful, the style drags. It comes from repeated use of c'est que, il n'y a que; you must fight to the death against them. In a work of this type a concise and dogmatic sentence is better than a drawn-out sentence. Example: Montesquieu" (YTC, CIIIb, p. 109).

Only the discretionary power to remove public officials can guarantee the kind of enlightened and active obedience on their part that judicial suppression cannot impose.

In France we seek this last guarantee in *administrative hierarchy;* in America, they seek it in *election.*

Thus to summarize in a few words what I have just explained:

Should the public official in New England commit a *crime* in the exercise of his duties, the ordinary courts are *always* called to bring him to justice.

Should he commit an *administrative fault,* a purely administrative court is charged with punishing him, and when the matter is serious or urgent the judge does what the official should have done.[31]

Finally, should the same official be guilty of one of those intangible failings that human justice can neither define nor assess, he appears annually before a tribunal from which there is no appeal, that can suddenly reduce him to impotence [{remove him from power without even telling him why}]. His power is lost with his mandate.

Certainly this system encompasses great advantages,[q] but in its execution a practical difficulty is encountered that must be noted.

I have already remarked that the administrative tribunal that is called the court of sessions did not have the right to inspect the town magistrates; following a legal term, it can only act when it is *apprised.* But that is the delicate point of the system.

The Americans of New England have not established a public prosecutor attached to the court of sessions,[32] and you must understand how

---

31. *Example: if a town stubbornly persists in not naming assessors, the court of sessions names them, and the magistrates chosen in this way are vested with the same powers as the elected magistrates. See the law already cited of 20 February 1787.*

q. In the margin: "≠Perhaps enumerate them at this time.
Human dignity.
Legal, not *arbitrary* habits.
People at their business.≠"

32. *I say* attached to the court of sessions. *There is a magistrate, attached to the ordinary courts, who fulfills several of the functions of the public prosecutor's office.*

difficult it would have been for them to establish one. If they had limited themselves to placing a prosecutor at each county seat, and if they had not given him agents in the towns, why would this magistrate have been more informed about what was happening in the county than the members of the court of sessions themselves? If he had been given agents in each town, the power most to be feared,[*] that of administering through the courts, would have been centralized in his hands. Laws are, moreover, the daughters of habits, and nothing similar existed in English legislation.

So the Americans have divided, like all other administrative functions, the right of inspection and the right of complaint.

Under the terms of the law, the members of the grand jury must notify the court, to which they are attached, of crimes of all kinds that might be committed in their county.[33] There are certain great administrative crimes that the ordinary public prosecutor must pursue as a matter of course.[34] Most often, the obligation to have the offenders punished is imposed on the fiscal officer, charged with collecting the proceeds of the fine; thus the town treasurer is charged with pursuing most of the administrative crimes that are committed in his sight.

But above all, American legislation appeals to individual interest;[35] that is the great principle found constantly when you study the laws of the United States.

---

[*]. <≠Far from wanting to create a magistrate of this kind, the Americans have, on the contrary, such a great fear of combining too much administrative power in the same hands, that when they assign responsibility to someone for suing for administrative crimes, they hardly ever choose the most important officials.

Should a town refuse to raise the state tax, it is not the Governor who notifies the court of sessions, it is the state Treasurer. *L[aws (ed.)] of M[assachusetts (ed.)]*, vol. I, p. 209.

Should an assessor refuse to accept the functions that are granted to him, it is not the selectmen who sue, it is the town treasurer. *Id.*, vol. I, p. 218.≠>

33. *Grand juries are obliged, for example, to inform the courts about the bad condition of the roads.* Laws of Massachusetts, *vol. I, p. 308 [307–308 (ed.)]*.

34. *If, for example, the county treasurer does not provide his books.* Laws of Massachusetts, *vol. I, p. 406.*

35. *Example among many: an individual damages his vehicle or is hurt on a poorly maintained road; he has the right to ask the town or the county responsible for the road for damages before the court of sessions.* Laws of Massachusetts, *vol. I, p. 309 [307–308 (ed.)]*.

American legislators show little confidence in human honesty; but they always assume an intelligent man. So most often they rely on personal interest for the execution of laws.

Indeed, when an individual is positively and presently hurt by an administrative crime, it is understood that personal interest guarantees the lodging of a complaint.

But it is easy to foresee that, if it concerns a legal prescription that has no utility felt by an individual at the moment, even though the legal prescription is useful to society, each person will hesitate to come forward as accuser. In this way, by a kind of tacit agreement, the laws could fall into disuse.

Thrown into this extremity by their system, the Americans are forced to interest informers by calling them in certain cases to share in the fines.[36]

Dangerous measure that assures the execution of laws by debasing mores.

Above the county magistrates, there is truly no other administrative power, only a governmental power.

General Ideas on Administration in the United States

How the states of the Union differ among themselves, by the system of administration.—Town life less active and less complete

---

36. *In case of invasion or insurrection, when the town officers neglect to provide the militia with necessary equipment and supplies, the town may be fined 200 to 500 dollars (1000 to 2700 [2500 (ed.)] francs). It can easily be imagined that, in such a case, it could happen that no one would have either the interest or the desire to take the role of accuser. Consequently, the law adds:* "[the fine is] to be sued for and recovered by any person, who may prosecute for the same, [. . .(ed.). . .] one moiety to the prosecutor." *See the law of 6 March 1810, vol. II, p. 236.*

The same arrangement is found very frequently reproduced in the laws of Massachusetts.

Sometimes it is not the individual that the law incites in this way to sue public officials; it is the official who is encouraged to have the disobedience of particular individuals punished. Example: an inhabitant refuses to do the share of work assigned to him on a major roadway. The surveyor of roads must sue him; and if the surveyor has him found guilty, half of the fine comes to him. See the laws already cited, vol. I, p. 308.

as you move toward the south.—The power of the magistrate
then becomes greater; that of the voter smaller.—Administration
passes from the town to the county.—State of New York, Ohio,
Pennsylvania.—Administrative principles applicable to all the
Union.—Election of public officials or fixed term of their
offices.—Absence of hierarchy.—Introduction of judicial means
into the administration.

I previously announced that, after having examined in detail the constitution of the town and county in New England, I would cast a general
glance over the rest of the Union.

There are towns and town life in each state; but in none of the confederated states do you find a town identical to the New England town.

As you move toward the south, you notice that town life becomes less
active; the town has fewer magistrates, rights and duties; the population
there does not exercise so direct an influence on town affairs; town meetings
are less frequent and involve fewer matters. The power of the elected magistrate is therefore comparatively greater and that of the voter, smaller; town
spirit there is less awake and less powerful.[37]

You begin to see these differences in the state of New York; they are
already very apparent in Pennsylvania; but they become less striking when
you move toward the Northwest. Most of the emigrants who go to establish
the states of the Northwest come from New England, and they bring the

---

37. *See, for detail,* The Revised Statutes of the State of New York, *at part I, chap. XI,
entitled:* Of the Powers, Duties and Privileges of Towns, *vol. I, pp. 336–64.*

See in the collection entitled: Digest of the Laws of Pennsylvania, *the words* Assessors,
Collectors, Constables, Overseers of the Poor, Supervisors of highways. *And in the collection entitled:* Acts of a General Nature of the State of Ohio, *the law of 25 February
1824, relating to the towns, p. 412. And next, the particular arrangements relative to the
diverse town officers, such as:* Township's Clerks, Trustees, Overseers of the Poor, Fence
Viewers, Appraisers of Property, Township's Treasurers, Constables, Supervisors of
Highways.

administrative habits of their mother land to their adopted country. The Ohio town has much in common with the Massachusetts town.

We have seen that in Massachusetts the principle of public administration is found in the town. The town is the center where the interests and affections of men converge. But it ceases to be so the more you move toward the states where enlightenment is less universally spread and where, consequently, the town offers fewer guarantees of wisdom and fewer elements of administration. So as you move away from New England, town life passes in a way to the county. The county becomes the great administrative center and forms the intermediate power between the [central] government and the ordinary citizens.

I said that in Massachusetts county matters were directed by the court of sessions. The court of sessions is made up of a certain number of magistrates appointed by the Governor and his council. The county has no representation, and its budget is voted by the national [*sic:* state] legislature.

In the large state of New York, on the contrary, in the state of Ohio and in Pennsylvania, the inhabitants of each county elect a certain number of deputies; these deputies meet together to form a representative county assembly.[38]

The county assembly possesses, within certain limits, the right to tax the inhabitants; in this regard, it constitutes a true legislature. It simultaneously administers the county, directs the administration of the towns in several instances, and limits their powers much more strictly than in Massachusetts.[r]

These are the principal differences presented by the constitution of the town and county in the various confederated states. If I wanted to get into

38. *See* Revised Statutes of the State of New York, *part I, chap. XI, vol. I, p. 340.* Id. *chap. XII;* id., *p. 366.* Id., Acts of the State of Ohio, *law of 25 February 1824, relating to the county commissioners, p. 263. See* Digest of the Laws of Pennsylvania, *the words* County Rates, and Levies, *p. 170.*

In the state of New York, each town elects a deputy, and this deputy participates at the same time in the county administration and in that of the town.

r. In the margin: "≠Ask L[ouis (ed.)] and B[eaumont (ed.)] if it is necessary to support these generalities with notes. Here either very minutely detailed notes are needed or nothing.≠"

the details of the means of execution, there are still many other dissimi-larities that I could point out. But my goal is not to give a course in Amer-ican administrative law.

I have said enough about it, I think, to make the general principles that administration in the United States rests upon understood. These princi-ples are applied in different ways; they have more or less numerous con-sequences depending on the place; but fundamentally they are the same everywhere. The laws vary; their physiognomy changes; the same spirit an-imates them.

The town and county are not constituted in the same way everywhere; but you can say that everywhere in the United States the organization of the town and county rests on the same idea: that each person is the best judge of what concerns himself alone, and the one most able to provide for his individual needs. So the town and county are charged with looking after their special interests. The state governs and does not administer. Ex-ceptions to this principle are found, but not a contrary principle.[s]

The first consequence of this doctrine has been to have all the adminis-trators[t] of the town and county chosen by the inhabitants themselves, or at least to choose these magistrates exclusively from among the inhabitants.[*]

[≠The second, to put into their hands the administration [v. direction] of nearly all the interests of the town and county.

The state has retained the power to impose laws on all the towns and counties, but it has not put into the hands of any official the power to direct the administration in a general way.≠]

s. "To place.

Jealousy of legislatures against intermediate bodies.

In New England the justice of the peace prepares the county budget; it is the legis-lature that votes on it. In the state of New York it is a representation of the county that votes on the tax, but its power is confined to very narrow limits" (YTC, CVh, 5, p. 13).

t. Hervé de Tocqueville: "It seems to me that you cannot say as positively that these administrators are chosen by the inhabitants since you have taught us that the justices of the peace are chosen by the Governor" (YTC, CIIIb, 2, p. 111). Cf. note 48.

[*]. I say this because in the laws of Tennessee, which are probably those found among all those of Virginian descent, the justices of the peace or magistrates composing the county court (who hold their offices during good behavior) are in charge of the entire administration. I believe that it is purely and simply the English system.

Since administrators everywhere are elected or at least irrevocable, the result has been that rules of hierarchy have not been able to be introduced anywhere. So there are nearly as many independent officials as offices. Administrative power finds itself scattered among a multitude of hands.

Since administrative hierarchy exists nowhere and administrators are elected and irrevocable until the end of their term, the obligation followed to introduce courts, more or less, into the administration. From that comes the system of fines, by means of which the secondary bodies and their representatives are forced to obey the law. This system is found from one end of the Union to the other.

The power of suppressing administrative crimes or of taking administrative actions as needed has not been granted, moreover, to the same judges in all the states.

The Anglo-Americans have drawn the institution of the justices of the peace from a common source; it is found in all the states. But they have not always taken advantage of it in the same way.

Everywhere the justices of the peace take part in the administration of the towns and counties,[39] either by administering them directly or by suppressing certain administrative crimes committed in them. But in most states, the most serious of these crimes are submitted to ordinary courts.

Election of administrative officials, or irremovability from office, lack of administrative hierarchy, and introduction of judicial measures into the government of society at the secondary level are, therefore, the principal

---

39. *There are even states in the South where the magistrates*[u] *of the county courts are charged with all details of the administration. See* The Statutes of the State of Tennessee, *the art.* Judiciary, Taxes . . .

u. Hervé de Tocqueville: "If there are states where the court of sessions is charged with all details of the administration, what becomes in these states of the town spirit *so praised by the author*?

"It would seem, from the end of the chapter, that certain states are beginning to feel the disadvantage of excessive decentralization. This consideration must be weighed by the author in the following chapter" (YTC, CIIIb, 2, p. 77).

characteristics by which American administration, from Maine to Florida, is recognized.[v]

There are some states where signs of administrative centralization begin to be seen. The state of New York is the most advanced along this path.

In the state of New York, officials of the central government exercise, in certain cases, a kind of supervision and control over the conduct of the secondary bodies.[40] In certain other cases, they form a type of court of appeal for deciding matters.[41] In the state of New York, judicial penalties

---

v. "No hierarchy and no centralization, character of American administration. So in the town, more powers and more magistrates than in the French town, but all independent.

"Division of powers among those charged with making them fulfill their duties. Finally, when they are concentrated, it is in a *judicial body,* that is to say, legal and far from arbitrary [v: slave to forms]" (YTC, CVb, p. 16).

40. *Example: the running of public education is centralized in the hands of the government. The legislature appoints the members of the university, called regents; the Governor and the Lieutenant-Governor of the state are members* ex officio. *(Revised Statutes, vol. I, p. 456). The regents of the university visit the colleges and universities each year and submit an annual report to the legislature; their supervision is not illusory, for the following particular reasons: the colleges, in order to become corporations that can buy, sell and own, need a charter; but this charter is granted by the legislature only on the advice of the regents. Each year the state distributes to the colleges and academies the interest from a special fund created to encourage education. It is the regents who are the distributors of this money. See chap. XV, Public Education,* Revised Statutes, *vol. I, p. 455.*

Each year, the boards of public schools are required to send a report on conditions to the superintendent of the Republic, Id., *p. 488.*

A similar report on the number and condition of the poor must be made annually to him. Id., *p. 631.*

41. *When someone believes himself wronged by certain acts coming from the school commissioners (these are town officers), he can appeal to the superintendent of primary schools whose decision is final.* Revised Statutes, *vol. I, p. 487.*

You find here and there, in the laws of the state of New York, provisions analogous to those I have just cited as examples. But in general these tentative efforts at centralization are weak and not very productive. While the highest officials of the state were given the right to supervise and direct inferior agents, they were not given the right to reward or punish them. The same man is hardly ever charged with giving the order and with suppressing disobedience; so he has the right to command, but not the ability to make himself obeyed.

In 1830, the superintendent of schools, in his annual report to the legislature, complained that several school commissioners, despite notice from him, had not forwarded the accounts

are used less than elsewhere as an administrative measure. There, the right to bring proceedings against administrative crimes is also placed in fewer hands.[42]

The same tendency is slightly felt in several other states.[43] But, in general, you can say that the salient characteristic of public administration in the United States is to be prodigiously decentralized.

Of the State

I have talked about the towns and about administration; I still have to talk about the state and about government.

Here, I can move faster without fear of being misunderstood; what I have to say is found all sketched out in written constitutions that anyone can easily obtain.[44] These constitutions rest on a simple and rational theory.

Most of the forms that they prescribe have been adopted by all peoples who have constitutions; they have therefore become familiar to us.

So I have only to do a brief overview here. Later I will try to judge what I am about to describe.

---

they owed him. "If this omission occurs again, he added, I will be reduced to prosecuting them to the full extent of the law before the courts of competent jurisdiction."

42. *Example: the district attorney in each county is charged with suing for the recovery of all fines above 50 dollars, as long as this right has not been expressly granted by law to another magistrate.* Revised Statutes, *part I, chap. XII, vol. I, p. 383.*

43. *There are several signs of administrative centralization in Massachusetts. Example: the town school boards are charged with making an annual report to the Secretary of State.* Laws of Massachusetts, *vol. I, p. 367.*

44. *See the text of the constitution of New York.*ᵂ

w. Reproduced as an appendix in the first editions.

Legislative Power of the State

Division of the legislative body into two houses.—
Senate.—House of representatives.—
Different attributions of these two bodies.

The legislative power of the state is entrusted to two assemblies; the first is generally called the senate.

The senate is normally a legislative body; but sometimes it becomes an administrative and judicial body.

It takes part in administration in several ways depending on the different constitutions;[45] but ordinarily it enters into the sphere of executive power by taking part in the choice of officials.

It participates in judicial power by judging certain political crimes and sometimes as well by ruling on certain civil actions.[46]

Its members are always few in number.

The other branch of the legislature, usually called the house of representatives, participates in nothing related to administrative power, and takes part in judicial power only when accusing public officials before the senate.

The members of the two houses are subject almost everywhere to the same conditions of eligibility. Both are elected in the same way and by the same citizens.

The only difference that exists between them is due to the fact that the mandate of senators is generally longer than that of representatives. The second rarely remain in office more than a year; the first ordinarily hold their seats two or three years.

By granting senators the privilege of being named for several years, and by replacing them by cohort, the law has taken care to maintain, among the legislators, a nucleus of men, already used to public affairs, who can exercise a useful influence over the newcomers.

---

45. *In Massachusetts, the Senate is vested with no administrative function.*
46. *As in the state of New York.*[x]
x. See conversation with Mr. Spencer (non-alphabetic notebook 1, YTC, BIIa, and *Voyage, OC,* V, 1, p. 68).

So by the division of the legislative body into two branches, the Americans did not want to create one hereditary assembly and another elective one; they did not intend to make one into an aristocratic body, and the other into a representative of the democracy. Nor was their goal to make the first into a support for the governing power, while leaving the interests and passions of the people to the second.[y]

To divide legislative power, to slow in this way the movement of political assemblies, and to create a court of appeal for the revision of laws, such are the only advantages that result from the current constitution of the two houses in the United States.

Time and experience have shown the Americans that, reduced to these advantages, the division of legislative powers is still a necessity of the first order.

Pennsylvania alone, among all the united republics, tried at first to establish a single assembly. Franklin himself, carried away by the logical consequences of the dogma of sovereignty of the people, had worked toward this measure. The law soon had to be changed and two houses established. The principle of the division of legislative power thus received its final consecration; henceforth then, the necessity to divide legislative activity among several bodies can be considered a demonstrated truth. This theory, more or less unknown in the ancient republics, introduced into the world almost by chance, like most great truths, misunderstood among several modern peoples, has finally passed as an axiom into the political science of today.[z]

---

y. Division of administrative power, concentration of legislative power. *American principle* (important).

The legislature most often appoints *special agents* to enforce its will. Thus, power not even *regular or necessary executor* of the laws.

The Governor's veto is not a barrier to the democracy, the Governor emanating entirely from it. Only the judges are a real barrier.

Not only is power divided among several hands, but the exercise of power is divided. The Governor cannot appoint the official and direct him at the same time. *Subtle and dubious.*

The institution of the senate is a barrier to the democracy because named for a longer time; they [*sic*] are not as immediately subject to the fear of not being reelected (YTC, CVb, pp. 15–16).

z. Tocqueville, it must be remembered, was part of the commission charged with drafting the constitution of 1848. There, he defended the division of legislative power into two branches. This idea came to nothing. In his *Souvenirs* (*OC,* XII, pp. 148–87), he gives some details about it. The notes taken by Beaumont during the work of the commission offer in this regard some interesting, previously unpublished details (YTC, DIVk). Beaumont notes as follows, in a rapid and necessarily schematic fashion, Tocqueville's answers to the proposal of Marrast concerning the creation of a single chamber (25 May 1848):

> Tocqueville.—Recognizes that the cause of two chambers is lost. The state of minds is such that it would be almost dangerous to insist upon a system that [illegible word] in itself is bad only in the circumstances.
>
> —But, necessary to show how two chambers are the only institution that can perhaps make the republic viable.
> —History!
> —The United States. The Constitution of the United States must be set aside; take the thirty democratic constitutions of the United States that have same social and political state as we.
> —Now, in these 30 states the question of two chambers is an accomplished fact and an uncontested truth.
> —Is it [that this (ed.)] historical tradition is English?
> —No. Instead of following the English tradition, they broke with it. Congress began with a single assembly. Those of Massachusetts and Pennsylvania in the same way (for thirteen years in Pennsylvania); and at the end of thirteen years with a single assembly, Pennsylvania changed the system of a single assembly and adopted two chambers.
> —So in France what made opinion so hostile to single chambers?
> —It is a misunderstanding. Until now in Europe the system of two chambers was to give a special expression to two different elements, the aristocrat and the democrat; from that it was concluded that the establishment of two chambers was an aristocratic principle. This natural conclusion is correct, if it was a question of introducing the slightest element of aristocracy into the government.
> —But is the existence of two chambers in itself a fact aristocratic by nature?
> —How so! The two chambers in America are from the aristocracy!! What is it then? The two chambers are chosen by the same electors, for the same time, in the same conditions, more or less.
> —Objection that if the second chamber has no use as a counterbalance to the democracy, what purpose does it serve? Then it is a superfluity.
> —No.
> —Even logically, it can be sustained. What is logical is that the nation be all powerful; but what [more (ed.)] contrary to logic than that the sovereignty of the nation have one or two agents.
> —Now logically what purpose do two chambers serve?

Of the Executive Power of the State

What the Governor is in an American state.—What position
he occupies vis-à-vis the legislature.—What his rights and
duties are.—His dependency on the people.

The executive power of the state is represented by the Governor.[*] [≠Not
only is the Governor of each state an elected magistrate, but also he is generally elected only for a year; in this way he is tied by the shortest possible
chain to the body from which he emanates.≠]

Three principal uses.

1. Necessity in France of giving the executive power great force. But, certain considerable matters cannot be absolutely conducted by the executive power without any
everyday control. In the United States, the Senate assists the President in certain acts,
or rather controls him; treaties, choice of high officials. Body small enough to be able
to act in concert with the executive power and strong because it comes from the
people. This could be done, it is true, by [the (ed.)] *Conseil d'État.*

2. Driving impulses of democracies. Perilous and untenable situation of the executive power, in the eternal head to head of this one man and this single assembly;
eternal conflict between two wills face to face. – The only means for no conflict is
that the man always gives way to the assembly. Then no struggle.

3. The great disease of democracies is legislative intemperance, violence in proceedings, rapidity in actions. The advantage of two chambers is not to prevent
violent revolutions, but to prevent the bad government that ends up leading to
revolution.

—What means to combat the inherent vices of this single body? It is to divide it.

—Two chambers drawn from the same elements can have different thoughts
however.

—Difficulty for two or three men to dominate a country when there are two chambers. Very easy when there is only one chamber.

—Utility of two considerations of a question. But there are two considerations
only when there are two assemblies. Two readings do not mean two considerations.
It is resubmitting a judgment to those who have made it, and who will only repeat
what they judged (YTC, DIVk).

The papers of Beaumont, which contain innumerable notes on the American constitutions, are there to witness to the importance given to American constitutional history
during the discussions of the constitutional commission of 1848.

[*]. See the Constitution of Massachusetts, chap. I, part II, chap II.

It is not by chance that I have used the word *represents*. The Governor of the state in effect represents the executive power; but he exercises only some of its rights.

The supreme magistrate, who is called the Governor, is placed alongside the legislature as a moderator and adviser. He is armed with a qualified veto that allows him to stop or at least to slow the legislature's movements as he wishes. To the legislative body, he sets forth the needs of the country and makes known the means that he judges useful to provide for those needs; for all enterprises that interest the entire nation [*sic:* state], he is the natural executor of its will.[47] In the absence of the legislature, he must take all proper measures to protect the state from violent shocks and unforeseen dangers.

The Governor combines in his hands all of the military power of the state. He is the commander of the militia and chief of the armed forces.

When the power of opinion, which men have agreed to grant to the law, is not recognized, the Governor advances at the head of the physical force of the state; he breaks down resistance and reestablishes customary order.

The Governor, moreover, does not get involved in the administration of the towns and counties, or at least he participates only very indirectly by the appointment of the justices of the peace whom he cannot thereafter remove.[48]

The Governor is an elected magistrate. Care is even taken, generally, to elect him only for one or two years; in this way, he always remains narrowly dependent[a] on the majority that created him.[b]

47. *In practice, it is not always the Governor who carries out the enterprises conceived by the legislature; often, at the same time that the latter votes a principle, it names special agents to oversee its execution.*

48. *In several states, the justices of the peace are not appointed by the Governor.*

a. The manuscript says: ". . . he is tied by the shortest possible chain to the body from which he emanates."

Édouard de Tocqueville: "This sentence is absolutely unintelligible. Why? What do you mean by *the body from which he emanates?* From what body does he emanate? And how is he tied to this body by the shortest possible chain by the fact that he is named for only two years? I repeat, I do not understand this paragraph at all" (YTC, CIIIb, 2 p. 112).

b. In the manuscript, at the end of the first chapter, is a cover sheet with the title:

Of the real influence that the President exercises in the conduct of public affairs [in the margin: Real and habitual influence in foreign affairs, almost entirely personal influence in domestic affairs./Study to do.]; in it, the following fragment on the Governor is found:

> [The beginning is missing] The first of these two obligations is marked out in a clear and precise manner.
>
> The second depends essentially on the circumstances that give it birth.
>
> Among most nations, the same man or at least the same authority is charged with fulfilling these two obligations. He sees to it by himself or through his agents that order reigns, and when order begins to be disturbed, by some violent shock, some unforeseen event, he is still the one who temporarily takes the place of the missing national will and takes charge of remedying the evil.
>
> In America, it is rarely so; the Governor is only occasionally charged with the peaceful execution of the laws. His functions consist, above all, of overseeing in a general manner the state of society, of enlightening the legislative body with his advice and of providing for the accidental needs of the state.
>
> [In the margin: in a way, the Governor participates in legislative power by the veto.
>
> In executive power by the administrative council.
>
> In France it is the same man who is charged.
>
> Start with the extreme concentration of powers.
>
> There are some countries where the legislative, administrative and judicial powers are united.
>
> There are some others where the legislative power is separate from the other two. There are still others.]
>
> Thus, it is not the Governor who is charged with using his authority to see that the towns execute their duties faithfully and punctually. If the legislature orders the opening of a canal or road, it is not generally the Governor who is charged with supervising the projects. The legislative power, at the same time it votes the principle, appoints special agents to supervise the execution.
>
> But if an unforeseen danger emerges, if an enemy appears, if an armed revolt breaks out, then the Governor truly represents the executive power of the State. He commands and directs the police force.
>
> In the accidental cases that I have just enumerated, the concentration of power on a single head is an indispensable condition for the existence of societies; thus the Governor of a state in America is the sole and absolute leader of the armed force.
>
> But as for the daily, peaceful execution of the laws, powers are still divided to a degree that our imagination can scarcely conceive.
>
> [In the margin: Only it is not judicial strength that comes to add to administrative strength. It is administrative strength that comes to join with judicial strength; now, liberty never has to fear judicial strength./
>
> *Concentration* of powers and administrative *hierarchy* are two synonymous words, for where there is hierarchy you necessarily arrive at unity by moving upward.
>
> Concentration of power is not a necessity so absolute./

Of the Political Effects of Administrative
Decentralization in the United States[c]

*Distinction to establish between governmental centralization and
administrative centralization.—In the United States, no*

I am beginning to believe that it is *definitively* the judicial power that *administers.*
In America, therefore, you arrive, in a round about way, at the union of administrative
and judicial powers.]

In order to understand this part of my subject well, I take the most robust individual with whom the state would have to deal, that is to say the town, and I ask how
the town is made to obey the laws.

Here reread my town notes.

c. Letter of Édouard de Tocqueville to his brother, Alexis:

St Germain, 15 June [1834 (ed.)]./

I have read and examined your chapter very attentively, my dear friend; I send you
the notes and remarks that I have made about it, as well as some observations that I
have added to those of your father. All that you say about centralization is remarkable
and well considered, but this chapter, the last in this thick folder, will be the subject
of the most serious criticism from me.

The general tone of your work is serious, impartial, philosophical. You see things
there in too lofty a way for your expressions to reveal passion. We guess your opinion,
your sympathies, but you leave the need to conclude to the reader; you just accumulate enough facts and reasons, leading to the conclusion you desire, to carry the
reader there inevitably; that is what a tightly reasoned work should do. The author
should stay behind the curtain and be content to produce conviction without insisting
upon it and saying: as for me, here is the conclusion that I draw from all this. This
personal opinion adds nothing to the strength of reasoning, and can harm it to the
extent that this perfect impartiality that inspires confidence is no longer seen in the
author. I find, therefore, that in this last chapter you are too much on stage; you enter
the lists armed with your personal opinion; you apply your principles to France; you
enter into politics; it is no longer simply logical, clear and profound deduction from
facts and institutions attentively studied that you present to the reader, but your own
ideas about these facts, these institutions, about their consequences and their application. You judge, when the reader must be allowed to judge; you must only put all
the pieces of evidence before him. His good sense must do the rest, and it will do so
if your book is good.

Consider carefully that your book must not carry the date 1834, nor even the colors
of France; to live in posterity, it must be removed from the influences of time and
place.

To conclude: I believe that this chapter will be entirely as strong and stronger,
when you have cut from it all that reveals the polemical and when you content your-

*administrative centralization, but very great governmental
centralization.—Some unfortunate effects that result in the
United States from the extreme administrative
decentralization.—Administrative advantages of this order of
things.—The force that administers society, less steady, less
enlightened, less skillful, very much greater than in Europe.—
Political advantages of the same order of things.—In the United
States, country makes itself felt everywhere.—Support that the
governed give to the government.—Provincial institutions more
necessary as the social state becomes more democratic.—Why.*

Centralization is a word repeated constantly today, and, in general, no one tries to clarify its meaning.

Two very distinct types of centralization exist, however, that are important to know well.

Certain interests are common to all parts of the nation, such as the formation of general laws and the relationships of the people with foreigners.

Other interests are special to certain parts of the nation, such as town enterprises, for example.

To concentrate in the same place or in the same hands the power to direct the first is to establish what I will call governmental centralization.[d]

---

self with saying what centralization or rather decentralization is in America; what its effects, its action, its consequences are, without explaining what centralization has been, is still, and what has produced and produces it in France. Certainly, it is a great and interesting question, admirable to treat from the rostrum when you climb up there, but your book, which raises a host of these questions, does not argue any of them; why make an exception for this one?

Weigh these considerations.

Adieu, my dear friend, I embrace you with all my heart. Embrace *maman* for us. Alexandrine and the children are very well (YTC, CIIIb, 2, pp. 63–65).

d. "The power to have *men* and *money,* such in sum is governmental centralization" (YTC, CVb, p. 12).

Beaumont thus summarizes the intervention of Tocqueville in favor of governmental centralization during the session of the constitutional commission on 31 May 1848:

Tocqueville. Impossible to touch on centralization in its constituent and general principles.—It is centralization that has saved France. Centralization is the power given

To concentrate in the same way the power to direct the second is to establish what I will name administrative centralization.[e]

There are points at which these two types of centralization merge. But by taking, as a whole, the matters that fall more particularly in the domain of each of them, we easily manage to distinguish them.[f]

It is understood that governmental centralization acquires immense strength when it is joined with administrative centralization. In this way, it accustoms men to making a complete and continuous abstraction of their will, to obeying, not once and on one point, but in everything and every day. Then, not only does it subdue them by force, but also it captures them by their habits; it isolates them and then, within the common mass, catches hold of them, one by one.

These two types of centralization lend each other mutual aid, attract each other; but I cannot believe that they are inseparable.

Under Louis XIV, France saw the greatest governmental centralization that could be imagined, since the same man made general laws and had the power to interpret them, represented France to the outside world and acted in its name. *L'Etat, c'est moi,* he said; and he was right.[g]

---

to the State, the duty to do everything inside and outside that is of general interest and is therefore in the interest of the State. The State must do everything in the country that matters strongly to it, either in the department or in the town.

The State must not intervene in what interests only the locality (YTC, DIVk).

e. "Administrative centralization does not create strength within a nation, but despotism" (YTC, CVb, p. 25).

f. Variant: "<≠The first, which I will call governmental centralization, is the concentration in a single hand or in the same place of the great social powers. The power to *make the* general *laws* and the *strength* to force obedience to them. The direction of the foreign affairs of the State and the means to succeed in them.

The second type of centralization, which I will name administrative centralization, is the concentration in a single hand or in the same place of the power to regulate the ordinary affairs of society, to rule the diverse parts of the State in the direction of their special affairs and to be in charge of the daily details of their existence.≠>"

g. "In France the administrative power has been placed at the center, not because it was in itself more useful there, perhaps the opposite, but in order to increase political power, which is different" (YTC, CVb, p. 10).

Under Louis XIV, however, there was much less administrative centralization than today.[h]

h. In the essay on the French administration drafted in response to the request for
information from his son, Hervé de Tocqueville remarks:

> In the state of things as set up by the charter of 1814, the King is present everywhere.
> He has command over individual wills in order to unite them against the common
> danger. His action makes itself felt in all parts of the administration. Without him,
> it can do nothing; it moves if he allows; it stops when he so commands. We still do
> not know what the consequences will be of the notable changes that have taken place
> since 1830. Will not the principle of election introduced into the formation of all the
> *conseils* inspire in the provincial bodies pretensions of independence that are difficult
> to suppress; and will not this same principle applied to the nomination of officers of
> the national guard harm the passive obedience imposed on this armed force for public
> security? The newspapers that call themselves royalist ask for the reestablishment of
> the old provinces and insist daily on the creation of provincial assemblies that would
> be charged with the direction of local affairs. It is probable that these assemblies would
> tend constantly to increase their own power and that France would soon be no more
> than a vast federation, the weakest of governments, in the middle of the compact
> monarchies that surround it (YTC, CIIIe, pp. 38–39).

After having praised the effects of centralization on the accountability of the French
towns, he adds:

> The tutelage of the King is excellent because it prevents poorly planned undertakings,
> useless or superfluous expenditures and the waste of funds. But one wonders if it has
> not gone too far, or rather if it is not surrounded by too many formalities. It seems
> that a part of the things that must be submitted to the ministry of the interior could
> be decided by the provincial authority (*Ibid.,* p. 40).

And further along:

> It will be concluded from what precedes that, if centralization has become a little too
> extensive in the relations between superior and inferior authorities, it becomes dif-
> ficult to bear, above all, when it is exerted over the portion of private interests that
> are discussed and regulated administratively. In summary, it is useful to keep the
> tutelage of the administration in what concerns administrative expenditures. . . .
> Royal intervention in the affairs of the towns should be limited to the authorization
> to sell, acquire, exchange and borrow. Then again, small loans could be authorized
> by the prefect (*Ibid.,* pp. 41–42).

It is difficult to establish the precise influence that the report of the author's father,
the letters of Chabrol and Blosseville, the conversations and correspondence with Sparks
had on the formation of Tocqueville's ideas on centralization. If all of this material was
able to help him clarify several points, it seems that his ideas on centralization date at
least from the first days of his journey on American territory.

In a letter to his father of 3 June 1831, that is, four months before asking for help,

In our time, we see a power, England, where governmental centralization is carried to a very high degree; the State there seems to move like a single man; at will, it rouses immense masses, gathers and delivers, wherever it wants, the utmost of its strength.

England, which has done such great things for the last fifty years, does not have administrative centralization.

For my part, I cannot imagine that a nation could live or, above all, prosper without strong governmental centralization.

Tocqueville already referred to centralization: "All that there is of good in centralization seems to be as unknown as what there is of bad; no central idea seems to regulate the movement of the machine" (*OCB*, VII, p. 21). The theme is found again a month later in a letter also addressed to his father:

> Here, moreover, the central government is hardly anything. It is involved only with what relates to the state as a whole; the localities arrange their affairs all by themselves. That is how they have made the republic practicable. Everywhere individual ambition finds a small center of action at hand where its activity is exercised without danger for the state. I imagine that if the Bourbons, instead of fearing the organization of the towns, had sought little by little, from the beginning of the Restoration, to give importance to the localities, they would have had less difficulty struggling against the mass of passions that were raised against them (Albany, 4 July 1831, YTC, BIa2).

Two months before meeting Sparks, 29 June 1831, he had written to Louis de Kergorlay in nearly identical terms (*Correspondance avec Kergorlay, OC*, XIII, I, pp. 233–34). See George W. Pierson, *Tocqueville and Beaumont* in *America*, p. 363; and James T. Schleifer, *The Making of Tocqueville's "Democracy in America,"* pp. 122–23. See note q for p. 150.

Tocqueville returns to this subject in his report on Algeria (*Écrits et discours politiques, OC*, III, 1, especially pp. 331–38). There he denounces an excess of administrative centralization and a lack of political centralization. Algeria opens to Tocqueville a potential for political creativity in which he envisions using the theoretical tools forged in America. More than once, Tocqueville encounters in French Africa situations entirely similar to those at the beginning of the American colonies. His intervention in parliament retains a certain transatlantic flavor easy to detect. The project of buying land in Algeria with Kergorlay, which would come to nothing, is there to attest to his interest in the colony. See the reports and parliamentary interventions, published in the *Moniteur Universel*, 24 and 25 May, and 1, 9, 10, 11, and 12 June 1847 (reproduced in *OCB*, IX, pp. 423–512, and in *Écrits et discours politiques, OC*, III, 1, pp. 308–409). His travel notes and other writings on Algeria also contain numerous references to centralization and to other American subjects. Cf. note f for p. 1210 of volume II.

But I think that administrative centralization is suitable only to enervate the peoples who submit to it, because it constantly tends to diminish the spirit of citizenship in them.[j] Administrative centralization, it is true, succeeds in gathering at a given time and in a certain place all the available forces of a nation, but it is harmful to the multiplication of those forces. It brings the nation victory on the day of battle and over time reduces its power. So it can work admirably toward the passing greatness of a man, not toward the lasting prosperity of a people.[k] [<≠I see there an element of despotism, but not of lasting national strength [in pencil: that would be].≠>]

You must be very careful; when someone says that a State is unable to act because it has no centralization, he is, without knowing it, almost always talking about governmental centralization.[m] The German empire, it is said repeatedly, has never been able to gain all that it possibly could from its forces. Agreed. But why? Because national force has never been centralized there; because the State has never been able to compel obedience to its general laws; because the separate parts of this great body have always had the right or the possibility to refuse their support to the agents of the common authority, even in what concerned all citizens; in other words, because there was no governmental centralization. The same remark applies to the Middle Ages. What produced all the miseries of feudal society was that the power, not only to administer, but also to govern, was divided among a thousand hands and fragmented in a thousand ways; the absence of any governmental centralization then prevented the nations of Europe from moving with energy toward any goal.

j. In the manuscript: ". . . to diminish the number of citizens. . . ."
k. In the manuscript: ". . . the greatness of a man, but not that of the State." Gustave de Beaumont:

False idea. Administrative centralization, by the effects that are concerned here, can work toward the greatness of the State just as toward that of a man, for this greatness can depend on a great battle that might have been lost without administrative centralization. Only, it is an obstacle to lasting greatness. As I do not know if the author agrees and do not know what idea he will adopt, I am not occupying myself with the writing (YTC, CIIIb, 2, p. 76).

m. The same idea appears in Beaumont, *Irlande,* vol. II, pp. 157–59.

[≠Moreover, like nearly all the harmful things of this world, administrative centralization is easily established and, once organized, can hardly ever be destroyed again except with the social body itself.[n]

When all the governmental force of a nation is gathered at one point, it is always easy enough for an enterprising genius to create administrative centralization. We ourselves have seen this phenomenon take place before our eyes. The Convention had centralized government to the highest degree, and Bonaparte needed only to will it in order to centralize the administration. It is true that for centuries in France our habits, mores and laws had always worked simultaneously toward the establishment of an intelligent and enlightened despotism.[*]

Once administrative centralization has lasted for a time, should the power that established it sincerely desire to destroy it, that same power almost always finds itself unable to bring about its ruin.

In fact, administrative centralization assumes a skillful organization of authority; it forms a complicated machine in which all the gears fit together and offer mutual support.

When the law-maker undertakes to scatter this administrative power that he has concentrated in a single place, he does not know where to begin, because he cannot remove one piece of the mechanism without disrupting the whole thing. At each moment, he sees that either nothing must be changed or everything; but what hand, so foolhardy, would dare to smash with one blow the administrative machinery of a great people?

To attempt it would be to invite disorder and confusion into the State.

The art of administration is assuredly a science, and peoples do not have more innate knowledge than individuals do. Delivered to itself without any transition, society would almost entirely cease to be administered.

Moreover, one of the greatest misfortunes of despotism is that it creates in the soul of the men submitted to it a kind of depraved taste for tranquillity and obedience, a sort of self-contempt, that ends by making them

---

n. In the margin: "≠Perhaps all of that to delete as irrelevant.≠"

[*]. "≠Truthfully, in France, the provinces have never *administered* themselves; it was always the authority of one man that was exercised and that regulated, directly or indirectly, all the affairs of society. Only, the administrative range was limited; the Revolution of 1789 just extended it.≠"

indifferent to their interests and enemies of their own rights. In nothing, however, is it more necessary for the governed themselves to show a definite and sustained will.

Nearly all the passionate and ambitious men who talk about centralization lack a real desire to destroy it. What happened to the Praetorians happens to them; they willingly suffer the tyranny of the emperor in the hope of gaining the empire. So decentralization, like liberty, is something that the leaders of the people promise, but that they never deliver. In order to gain and keep it, nations can count only on their own efforts; and if they themselves do not have a taste for it, the evil is without remedy.

Surprisingly, the same corporations, in whose name the power of self-administration has been passionately claimed, are often seen to accept without enthusiasm the portion of power granted to them and to show themselves almost eager to lay it down again, like a useless and heavy burden. ≠]o

We have seen that in the United States no administrative centralization existed. Scarcely a trace of hierarchy is found there. Decentralization there has been carried to a point that no European nation could bear, I think, without a profound uneasiness, and that, even in America, produces unfortunate effects. But, in the United States, governmental centralization exists to the highest degree. It would be easy to prove that national [*sic: state*] power is more concentrated there than it has been in any of the old monarchies of Europe. Not only is there just a single body in each state that makes laws; not only is there just a single power able to create political life around it; but in general, the Americans have avoided bringing together numerous district or county assemblies for fear that these assemblies would be tempted to move beyond their administrative attributions and hinder the movement of the government. In America the legislature of each state is faced by no power capable of resisting it. Nothing can stop it in its tracks, neither privileges, nor local immunity, nor personal influence, not even the authority of reason, for it represents the majority that claims to be the only

---

o. In the margin: "<{To review the part on centralization and perhaps shorten it. Advice of Beau[mont (ed.)].}>"

instrument of reason. So it has no limit to its action other than its own will. Next to it and close at hand is found the representative of the executive power who, with the aid of physical force, has to compel the discontent to obey.P

Weakness is found only in certain details of governmental action.

The American republics do not have a permanent armed force to suppress minorities, but up to now minorities there have never been reduced to starting a war; and the need for an army has not yet been felt.q Most often, the state uses town or county officials to act upon the citizens. Thus, for example, in New England, it is the town assessor who apportions the tax; the town tax collector levies it; the town treasurer makes sure that the tax revenue goes into the public treasury; and complaints that arise are submitted to the ordinary courts. Such a way to collect taxes is slow and awkward; at every instant it would hinder the movement of a government that had great pecuniary needs. In general, for everything essential to its exis-

p. In the manuscript: "Next to it and close at hand is found an executive power, absolute head of physical force, to compel the minorities to obedience."

q. In a letter to Ernest de Chabrol, Tocqueville explained:

All the offices, like all the registers, have been open to us, but as for the government, we are still looking for it. It does not really exist at all. The legislature regulates everything that is of general interest; the municipalities have the rest.

The advantage of this arrangement is to interest each locality very actively in its own affairs and greatly to feed political activity. But the disadvantage, even in America, seems to me to be to deprive the administration of any kind of uniformity, to make general measures impossible and to give to all useful enterprises a character of instability that you cannot imagine.

We are, above all, in a position to notice these effects of the lack of centralization in what relates to the prisons: nothing fixed, nothing certain in their discipline; men replace each other; with them, the systems; the methods of administration change with each administrator, because no central authority exists that can give everything a common direction.

The United States must thank heaven that until now they have been placed in such a way that they have no need for standing armies, for police or for skillful and sustained foreign policy. If one of these three needs ever presents itself, you can predict without being a prophet that they will lose their liberty or concentrate power more and more (Auburn, 16 July 1831, YTC, BIa2).

tence, you would want the government to have officials of its own, chosen and removable by it, and to have ways to move ahead rapidly; but it will always be easy for the central power, organized as it is in America, to introduce more energetic and effective means of action, as needed.[*]

So it is not, as is often repeated, because there is no centralization in the United States, that the republics of the New World will perish.[r] It can be asserted that the American governments, very far from not being centralized enough, are centralized too much; I will prove it later. Each day the legislative assemblies devour some of the remains of governmental powers; they tend to gather them all unto themselves, just as the Convention did.[s] The social power, thus centralized, constantly changes hands, because it is subordinate to popular power. Often it happens to lack wisdom and foresight, because it can do everything. That is where the danger to it is found. So it is because of its very strength, and not as a result of its weakness, that the social power is threatened with perishing one day.[t]

[*]. The creation of paid and standing military bodies to suppress or to prevent insurrections has already happened in Massachusetts and in Pennsylvania. See *Federalist*, p. 115 [No. 28 (ed.)].

r. Variant in a draft: ". . . but because the central power is constantly in different hands and is subordinated to popular power, a power eminently variable by nature and, for this reason, incapable of governing society for long" (YTC, CVb, p. 1).

s. In a first version, under a paper glued into place: "{Executive power is nothing while remaining in their hands. This is, moreover, an inherent weakness in completely [uncertain reading (ed.)] democratic government. See the *Federalist*, p. 213 [No. 48 (ed.)].}"

t. In the margin:

≠When a people renounces the centralization of power, the need for administrative courts is felt; now, I admit that it is always with terror that I see the administration and the judicial system concentrated in the same hands. Of all tyrannies, the worst is the one that covers itself in legal forms. Administrative courts, once subservient, seem to me one of the most fearsome instruments of despotism.≠

Recall the words of Montesquieu: "No tyranny is more cruel than the one you exercise under the cloak of the laws and with the colors of justice: when, so to speak, you drown the unfortunate on the very plank on which they were saved." *Considérations sur les causes de la grandeur des Romains et de leur décadence,* in *Œuvres complètes* (Paris: Pléiade, 1951), II, chapter XIV, p. 144. Cf. note o for p. 1228 of the second volume.

Administrative decentralization produces several diverse effects in America.

We have seen that the Americans had almost entirely isolated administration from government; in that, they seem to me to have gone beyond the limits of healthy reason, because order, even in secondary things, is still a national interest.[49]

The state has no administrative officials of its own, who are placed in permanent posts at different points of the territory and to whom it can give a common impulse; the result is that it rarely attempts to establish general rules of public order. Now, the need for these rules makes itself sharply felt. The European often notices their absence. This appearance of disorder, which reigns on the surface, persuades him, at first view, that there is complete anarchy in the society; it is only by examining things in depth that he corrects his error.

[This absence of national (v: central) administration often prevents the different states from engaging in certain undertakings of a general interest, the execution of which would present great difficulties if handed over to the localities and left to temporary and special agents. Besides, it is always to be feared that, without a permanent authority to centralize and supervise, the work, once done, might self-destruct.

As for differences that would make themselves felt between the administrative principles of one portion of the territory and those of another, differences that would be very great in Europe are not noticeable in America. The states are not so vast as to present examples; and above all, their population is too perfectly homogeneous and too enlightened for these differences to be lasting. All the counties, moreover, are forced to obey general laws that are the same for each of them.

49. *The authority that represents the state, even when it does not itself administer, must not, I think, relinquish the right to inspect local administration. I suppose, for example, that a government agent, placed at a set post in each county, might refer crimes that are committed in the towns and in the county to the judiciary. In this case, would not orderly organization be more uniformly followed without compromising the independence of the localities? Now, nothing like this exists in America. Above the county courts, there is nothing; and in a way, only by chance are these courts made officially aware of administrative crimes that they must suppress.*

≠I recognize as well that in America the views that direct the administration are rarely permanent. It is difficult to decentralize administrative power without putting a portion of it back into the hands of the people; and the people never proceed except by momentary efforts and sudden impulses.

I come to the great objection that has been made from time immemorial to the system of administrative decentralization, the objection that encompass [*sic*] all of the others.≠

The partisans of centralization in Europe . . .]

Certain enterprises interest the entire state and yet cannot be carried out because there is no national [*sic:* state] administration to direct them. Abandoned to the care of the towns and counties, left to elected and temporary agents, they lead to no result or produce nothing lasting.

The partisans of centralization in Europe maintain that governmental power administers the localities better than they would be able to administer themselves. Perhaps that is true, when the central power is enlightened, and the localities are not; when it is active, and they are passive; when it is in the habit of taking action, and they are in the habit of obeying. You can even understand that the more centralization increases, the more this double tendency grows; and the capacity of the one and incapacity of the other become more striking.

But I deny that this is so when the people are enlightened, alert to their interests, and accustomed to consider them as they do in America.

I am persuaded, on the contrary, that in this case the collective strength of the citizens will always be more powerful for producing social well-being than the authority of the government.

I admit that it is difficult to indicate with certainty how to awaken a people who are asleep, how to give them the passions and enlightenment that they lack. To persuade men that they should take charge of their own affairs is, I am aware, a difficult enterprise. Often it would be less awkward to interest them in the details of court etiquette than in the repair of their town hall [{and I would conclude, if you want, that there are certain nations [v: peoples] who cannot do without despotism.}].

But I also think that when the central administration claims to replace completely the free participation of those who have the primary interest, it is mistaken or wants to deceive you.

A central power, as enlightened, as skillful as can be imagined, cannot by itself encompass all the details of the life of a great people. It cannot, because such a task exceeds human power. When, on its own, it wants to create and put into operation so many different mechanisms, it either contents itself with a very incomplete result or exhausts itself in useless efforts.

Centralization easily manages, it is true, to subject the outward actions of men to a certain uniformity that is ultimately loved for itself, apart from the things to which it is applied; like the devout who worship the statue, forgetting the divinity it represents. Centralization succeeds without difficulty in imparting a steady appearance to everyday affairs; in skillfully dictating the details of social order; in suppressing slight disturbances and small transgressions; in maintaining society in a *status quo* which is not exactly either decadence or progress; in keeping a kind of administrative somnolence in the social body that administrators customarily call good order and public tranquillity.[50] In a word, it excels at preventing, not at doing. When it is a matter of profoundly shaking society or moving it rapidly, centralization loses its strength. As soon as its measures need the support of individuals, you are totally surprised by the weakness of this immense machine; it suddenly finds itself reduced to impotence.

Then sometimes centralization, in desperation, tries to call citizens to its aid. But it says to them: "You will act as I want, as long as I want, and exactly in the way that I want. You will take charge of these details without aspiring to direct the whole; you will work in the shadows, and later you will judge my work by its results." Under such conditions you do not gain the support

---

50. *China seems to me to offer the most perfect symbol of the type of social well-being that can be provided by a very centralized administration to the people who submit to it. Travelers tell us that the Chinese have tranquillity without happiness, industry without progress, stability without strength, physical order without public morality. Among them, society functions always well enough, never very well. I imagine that when China opens to Europeans, the latter will find there the most beautiful model of administrative centralization that exists in the universe.*

of human will, which requires liberty in its ways, responsibility in its actions. Man is made so that he prefers remaining immobile to moving without independence toward an unknown end.[u]

[During the almost forty years that we in France have completed the system of administrative centralization, what great improvement has been introduced into the state of the civilization of the people? Who would compare our social progress to that of the English during the same period? But, centralization does not exist in England.]

I will not deny that in the United States you often regret the lack of those uniform rules that seem constantly to watch over each of us.

From time to time, great examples of unconcern and of social negligence are found there. Here and there crude blemishes appear that seem completely at odds with the surrounding civilization.

Useful undertakings that require constant care and rigorous exactitude in order to succeed often end up being abandoned; for in America, as elsewhere, the people proceed by momentary efforts and sudden impulses.[v]

The European, accustomed to finding an official constantly at hand who gets involved in nearly everything, becomes used to these different mechanisms of town administration with difficulty. In general it can be said that the small details of social order that make life pleasant and easy are neglected in America; but the guarantees essential to man in society exist there as much as everywhere else. Among the Americans, the force that administers the State is much less stable, less enlightened, less skillful, but is one hundred times greater than in Europe. When all is said and done, there is no country in the world where men make as many efforts to create social well-being. I know of no people who have managed to establish schools so numerous and so effective; churches more appropriate to the religious needs of the inhabitants; town roads better maintained. So, in the United States, do not look for uniformity and permanence of views, minute attention to

u. To the side, in the manuscript: "≠Louis advises placing this elsewhere, but where?≠"

v. In the margin: "≠{The small details of} social {order} are generally neglected, but in short the guarantees essential to man in society exist as much in America as everywhere else.≠"

details, perfection in administrative procedures.[51] What is found there is the image of strength, a little wild, it is true, but full of power; of life, accompanied by accidents, but also by activities and efforts.[x]

I will admit, moreover, if you want, that the villages and counties of the United States would be administered more profitably by a central authority that was located far from them and remained unknown to them, than by officials drawn from within. I will acknowledge, if you insist, that more security would reign in America, that wiser and more judicious use of social resources would be made there, if the administration of the entire country were concentrated in a single hand. The political advantages that the Americans gain from the system of decentralization would still make me prefer it to the opposite system.

51. *A talented writer who, in a comparison between the finances of the United States and those of France, proved that the mind could not always make up for knowledge of facts, rightly reproaches the Americans for a type of confusion that prevails in their town budgets; and, after giving the model of a departmental budget in France, he adds: "Thanks to centralization, admirable creation of a great man [which is slandered without knowing it (ed.)], municipal budgets, from one end of the kingdom to the other, those of the largest cities, like those of the most humble towns, show the same order and method."ʷ That, certainly, is a result that I admire; but I see most of these French towns, whose accounts are so perfect, plunged into a profound ignorance of their true interests and given over to an apathy so invincible, that society there seems rather to vegetate than to live; on the other hand, I notice in these same American towns, whose budgets are not drawn up according to methodical or, above all, uniform plans, an enlightened, active, enterprising population; there I gaze upon a society always at work. This spectacle astonishes me; for in my eyes the principal end of a good government is to produce the well-being of peoples and not to establish a certain order in the midst of their misery. So I wonder if it would not be possible to attribute to the same cause the prosperity of the American town and the apparent disorder of its finances, the distress of the French town and the perfection of its budget. In any case, I distrust a good that I find intermingled with so much evil, and I am easily consoled about an evil that is offset by so much good.*

w. Sébastien L. Saulnier, "Nouvelles observations sur les finances des États-Unis, en réponse à une brochure publié par le Général La Fayette," *Revue Britannique*, n. s., 8, October 1831, pp. 195–260), p. 239. On this article and the polemic over American finances, see note j for pp. 349–50.

x. "The admirable effect of republican governments (where they can subsist) is not to present a glimpse of *regularity,* of *methodical order* in the administration of a people, but the *picture of life.* Liberty does not carry out each of its enterprises with the same perfection as intelligent despotism, but in the long run, it produces more than intelligent despotism" (pocket notebook 3, YTC, BIIa, and *Voyage, OC,* V, I, p. 184).

So what, after all, if there is an authority always at the ready, [{that muzzles dogs [v: waters public walkways] during the heat wave, that breaks up river ice during the winter}] that makes sure that my pleasures are peaceful, that flies before my steps to turn all dangers aside without the need for me even to think about them; if this authority, at the same time that it removes the smallest thorn from my route, is absolute master of my liberty and life; if it monopolizes movement and existence to such a degree that everything around it must languish when it languishes, sleep when it sleeps, perish if it dies?

There are such nations in Europe where the inhabitant considers himself a sort of settler, indifferent to the destiny of the place where he lives. The greatest changes occur in his country without his participation; he does not even know precisely what happened; he surmises; he has heard about the event by chance. Even more, the fortune of his village, the policing of his street, the fate of his church and his presbytery have nothing to do with him; he thinks that all these things are of no concern to him whatsoever, and that they belong to a powerful stranger called the government. [v: At each moment, you think you hear him say: what concern is this to me; it is the business of the authorities to provide for all of this, not mine.] As for him, he enjoys these benefits like a usufructuary, without a sense of ownership and without ideas of any improvement whatsoever. This disinterestedness in himself goes so far that if his own security or that of his children is finally compromised, instead of working himself to remove the danger, he crosses his arms to wait until the entire nation comes to his aid. Moreover, this man, even though he has so completely sacrificed his own free will, likes to obey no more than anyone else. He submits, it is true, to the will of a clerk; but, like a defeated enemy, he likes to defy the law as soon as power withdraws. Consequently, you see him oscillate constantly between servitude and license.

When nations have reached this point, they must modify their laws and mores or perish, for the source of public virtues has dried up; subjects are still found there, but citizens are seen no more.

I say that such nations are prepared for conquest. If they do not vanish from the world stage, it is because they are surrounded by similar or inferior nations. It is because within them there still remains a kind of indefinable patriotic instinct, I do not know what unthinking pride in the name that the nation carries. It is because there still remains I do not know what vague memory of past glory, not precisely linked to anything, but enough to impart an impulse of preservation as needed.

You would be wrong to reassure yourself by thinking that certain peoples have made prodigious efforts to defend a native land where, so to speak, they lived as strangers. Be very careful here, and you will see that in that case religion was almost always their principal motive.

For them, the duration, glory or prosperity of the nation had become sacred dogmas, and by defending their native land, they also defended this holy city in which they were all citizens.

The Turkish populations have never taken any part in the direction of the affairs of society; they accomplished immense enterprises, however, as long as they saw the triumph of the religion of Mohammed in the conquests of the Sultans. Today religion is disappearing; despotism alone remains for them; they are in decline.[y]

y. Original version in one of the drafts:

There are peoples living under despotism who have a great sentiment of nationality, however; you see them making immense sacrifices to save a native land where they live without interests and without rights.

But then be very careful here; for them, it is always religion which takes the place of patriotism.

For them, the duration, glory or prosperity of the nation is a religious dogma. By defending their country, they defend this holy city in which they are all citizens.

The Turkish populations have never taken any part in the direction of the affairs of society. They accomplished immense things, however, as long as they saw the triumph of the religion of Mohammed in the conquests of the Sultan. Today religion is disappearing; only despotism remains for them, and they are in decline.

The Russian, who does not even have an interest in the land on which he was born, is one of the bravest soldiers of Europe; and he burns his house and harvest to ruin the enemy. But it is the Holy Empire that he defends, and when he dies for his country, heaven opens and his reward is ready.

Despotic governments are made formidable when the peoples they direct are transformed by a religious enthusiasm. Then the unity of power, instead of harming the social power, does nothing more than direct it; nations in this condition have the strength of free peoples, without the disadvantages of liberty. Forces are combined and there is a single direction. Their impact is nearly irresistible. . . . Then a strange thing happens: the harder and more oppressive the government, the more it does

Montesquieu, by giving despotism a strength of its own, gave it, I think, an honor that it did not deserve. Despotism, all by itself, can sustain nothing lasting. When you look closely, you notice that what made absolute governments prosper for a long time was religion, and not fear.

No matter what, you will never find true power among men except in the free participation of wills.[z] Now, in the world, only patriotism or re-

----

great things; the more unfortunate the nation, the more it makes the effort to protect a soil that it does not possess; the less these men cling to life, the better they defend it. It is not with this world in view that religious people act in this way; and the more miserable they are, the more easily they die. . . .

Montesquieu, by giving despotism a lasting strength, gave it an honor that it does not deserve. Despotism is something so bad by nature that, all by itself, it can neither create nor maintain anything. Fear, all by itself, can only serve for a while.

When you look closely, you notice that what makes absolute governments last and act is religion, and not fear; religion, principle of strength that they use, but that is not in them. When a nation still enslaved ceases to be religious, there is no human means to keep it bundled together for long.

In summary, I am profoundly convinced that there is no lasting strength except in the collaboration of human wills. So to apply this force to the preservation of societies, men must have an interest in this world or the other (YTC, CVe, pp. 55–57).

Tocqueville defends the preeminence of social and intellectual habits over laws; it is therefore inevitable that he finds Montesquieu's idea of despotism based far too much on legal criteria. The author seems to be more concerned with the problems envisioned by Montesquieu than with the solutions he proposes, which does not, for all that, reduce the influence of the author of *Esprit des lois*. Nonetheless, Kergorlay denies a stylistic influence of Montesquieu on his friend ("Étude littéraire sur Alexis de Tocqueville," *Correspondant* 52 (1861): 758–59): "I would not go so far as to say that Tocqueville never, at any period of his literary life, sought in Montesquieu some models to follow. But it was only in a quite secondary manner, not very lasting and not very effective." On the other hand, Kergorlay recognizes the influence of Pascal, Voltaire and La Bruyère. On the influence of Montesquieu, see Melvin Richter, "Modernity and Its Distinctive Threats to Liberty: Montesquieu and Tocqueville on New Forms of Illegitimate Domination," in Michael Hereth and Jutta Höffken, eds., *Alexis de Tocqueville. Zur Politik in der Demokratie*, Baden Baden: Nomos, 1981, pp. 362–98.

z. Édouard de Tocqueville: "How did Louis XIV, Peter the Great, Frederick, Bonaparte, not give great power to their nations? And with them what became of the free collaboration of wills?" (YTC, CIIIb, 2, p. 113).

ligion can make the totality of citizens march for long toward the same goal.

It does not depend on the laws to revive beliefs that are fading; but it does depend on the laws to interest men in the destinies of their country. It depends on the laws to awaken and to direct that vague patriotic instinct that never leaves the human heart, and, by linking it to thoughts, passions, daily habits, to make it into a thoughtful and lasting sentiment. And do not say that it is too late to try; nations do not grow old in the same way that men do. Each generation born within the nation is like a new people who comes to offer itself to the hand of the law-maker.

What I admire most in America are not the *administrative* effects of decentralization, but its *political* effects. In the United States, country makes itself felt everywhere. It is an object of solicitude from the village to the whole Union. The inhabitant becomes attached to each of the interests of his country as to his very own. He glories in the glory of the nation; in the successes that it achieves, he believes that he recognizes his own work, and he rises with them; he rejoices in the general prosperity that benefits him. For his country, he has a sentiment analogous to that you feel for your family, and it is even by a kind of egoism that he is interested in the State.

Often the European sees in the public official only force; the American sees the law. So it can be said that in America, a man never obeys a man, but obeys justice or the law.

Consequently, he has conceived an often exaggerated, but almost always salutary opinion of himself. Without fear, he relies on his own powers that seem to him all sufficient. An individual conceives the idea of some enterprise; even if this enterprise has some direct connection with the well-being of society, it does not occur to him to address himself to public authority to gain its support. He makes his plan known, offers to carry it out, calls other individual powers to his aid, and struggles hand-to-hand against all obstacles. Often, doubtlessly, he succeeds less than if the State took his place; but in the long run the general result of all of these individual undertakings surpasses by a great deal what the government would be able to accomplish.[a]

a. The example was provided to Tocqueville by Mr. Quincy, President of Harvard

Since administrative authority is placed next to the administered, and in a way represents them, it excites neither jealousy nor hate. Since its means of action are limited, each person feels that he cannot rely on it alone.

So when the administrative power intervenes within the circle of its attributions, it does not find itself alone, as in Europe. No one believes that the duties of individuals have ceased because the public representative happens to act. On the contrary, each person guides, supports and sustains him.

By joining the action of individual powers with the action of social powers, you often succeed in doing what the most concentrated and energetic administration would be unable to carry out.[1]

I could cite many facts to support what I am advancing; but I prefer to present only one and to choose the one I know best.

In America, the means put at the disposal of authority to uncover crimes and to pursue criminals are few.

Police control does not exist; passports are unknown. Officers of the court in the United States cannot be compared to ours. The agents of the public prosecutor's office are few; [they do not communicate with each other;] they do not always have the right to initiate legal proceedings; preliminary investigation is rapid and oral. I doubt, however, that, in any country, crime as rarely escapes punishment.

The reason for it is that everyone believes himself interested in providing proof of the crime and in catching the offender.

I saw, during my stay in the United States, the inhabitants of a county, where a great crime had been committed, spontaneously form committees for the purpose of pursuing the guilty party and delivering him to the courts.

In Europe, the criminal is an unfortunate who is fighting to hide from the agents of power; the population in a way helps in the struggle. In America, he is an enemy of the human species, and he has all of humanity against him.

University, 20 September 1831 (non-alphabetic notebooks 1 and 2, YTC, BIIa, and *Voyage, OC*, V, 1, pp. 89–90).

I believe provincial institutions useful to all peoples; but none seems to me to have a more real need for these institutions than the one whose social state is democratic.

In an aristocracy, a certain order is sure to be maintained in the midst of liberty.

Since those who govern have a great deal to lose, order has a great interest for them.

In an aristocracy, it can be said as well that the people are sheltered from the excesses of despotism, because organized forces are always found, ready to resist the despot.

A democracy without provincial institutions possesses no guarantee against similar evils.

How can a multitude that has not learned how to make use of liberty in small things, be made to support it in larger ones?

How to resist tyranny in a country where each individual is weak, and where individuals are united by no common interest?

So those who are afraid of license and those who fear absolute power must equally desire the gradual development of provincial liberties.[b]

I am convinced, moreover, that there are no nations more at risk of falling under the yoke of administrative centralization than those whose social state is democratic.

Several causes lead to this result, but among others, these:

The permanent tendency of these nations is to concentrate all governmental power in the hands of the single power that directly represents the people, because, beyond the people, nothing more is seen except equal individuals merged into a common mass.

---

b. Once a man has contracted the habit of obeying a foreign and arbitrary will in nearly all the actions of his life, and notably in those that come closest to the human heart, how do you expect him to conceive a true taste for great political liberty and independence in general actions?

Town institutions not only give *the art of using great political liberty,* but they bring about *the true taste* for liberty. Without them, the taste for political liberty comes over peoples like childish desires or the hotheadedness of a young man that the first obstacle extinguishes and calms (YTC, CVh, 1, pp. 1–2; the same fragment is found, almost word for word, in YTC, CVe, p. 61).

Now, when the same power is already vested with all the attributes of government, it is highly difficult for it not to try to get into the details of administration [{so you often see democratic peoples simultaneously establish liberty and the instruments of despotism}]; and it hardly ever fails to find eventually the opportunity to do so. We have witnessed it among ourselves.

[≠If we shift our view to times closer to us, we see a strange confusion prevailing in most of the States of Europe. Kings descend into the administration of {the narrowest communal interests}.≠]c

In the French Revolution,d there were two opposing movements that must not be confused: one favorable to liberty, the other favorable to despotism.e

c. In the margin: "≠That is, you have wanted to make a city without citizens, a republic with subjects [v: servants] submitted to a clerk [v: and transform servants of a clerk into republicans] [v: and place the spirit of liberty in the very midst of servitude]." On the idea of citizenship as participation, see Doris S. Goldstein, "Alexis de Tocqueville's Concept of Citizenship," *Proceedings of the American Philosophical Society* 108, no. 1 (1964): 39–53.

d. "Ask Mr. Feuillet if there is a book that can give basic ideas about the French constitution in 1789" (YTC, CVb, p. 33). Feuillet was the librarian at the Bibliothèque Royale. See note v for pp. 1110–13 of the second volume.

e. Of centralization./

When you speak about centralization you are constantly struggling in the shadows because you have not made the distinction that I established above between governmental centralization and administrative centralization.

You blame or praise without knowing why.

There are people who cite as one of the advantages of centralization the establishment of the present system where everything ends at a supreme court. As one of the proofs of the evils caused by decentralization, they cite the old system of *parlements*. They do not see that the system of *parlements* was a gross abuse and not a natural consequence of the system of decentralization. If there is one thing in the world that is a national necessity, it is the unity of law. For the law to be *one*, two things are needed: 1. that it comes from a single authority, 2. that it is interpreted by a single authority. For to interpret the law is, in a way, to make it again. That is how all the American republics have understood it.

A judicial system where seventeen sovereign courts can interpret the same law at the same time, on the same question, in seventeen different ways is a political monstrosity.[1] For a nation to bear such a division of the judicial system without itself dividing, all the real power in the nation must be in hands other than judicial ones. That is what happened in France, where the King easily made his will prevail over the courts in all things that essentially concerned politics and acutely interested the State, and where he let anarchy reign only on secondary points that did not matter much to the general course of public affairs. That was a necessary cure, but one almost as bad as the illness. Interpretation, instead of being made by a central judicial power, was made by a (illegible word) council [v: power]. France of the old regime, already much too centralized relative to several objects, was evidently not centralized enough on the former. And when the partisans of decentralization stand on this ground, they are wrong. They defend what they should concede at the beginning.

What has caused our greatest misfortunes in France is that there is a host of excellent principles that we have never known and felt except by their exaggerated consequences. Strange thing! We have often experienced the abuse of the thing, without knowing the thing itself.[2]

Decentralization is among this number. Apart from our continental situation, which has always made us feel more acutely the need for the concentration of power, decentralization has never appeared to us other than as a division of the essential rights of sovereignty, that is, as the most active agent of oppression and anarchy. Today, we have not learned better; the word decentralization represents in our mind only a multitude of small sovereigns, judging with sovereignty, dispensing justice, coining money. And for us, it is even quite difficult to place this power, divided in this way, in hands other than those of an envious, haughty, exclusive aristocracy. Iudex irae. England, on the contrary, alone among all the peoples of Europe, had the good fortune that, from the beginning, the part of the central power was largely established. In that country, the system of decentralization, contained right away within true limits, awakens only ideas of order, prosperity and glory. The system of decentralization made and still makes the strength of England. England had strong and despotic kings at a time when royalty was too crude to want to take charge of everything. The kings created governmental centralization; the mores and the social state, administrative decentralization.

Moreover, we must not be mistaken about this. It is democratic governments that arrive most quickly at administrative centralization while losing their political liberty. Aristocracies struggle an infinitely longer time, because the power of resistance is greater in each of the parts of the social body organized in this way.

1. The American Union, which is a confederation, is more centralized on this point than was the *absolute monarchy of France.*

2. Thus in France, when the King intervened in the administration of justice, the abuse of governmental centralization was pointed out; when, on the contrary, the courts were free to establish judicial anarchy, all minds felt the abuse of administrative decentralization. But no one perceived the precise limits of the one and the other" (YTC, CVe, pp. 57–60, and BIIb, pp. 6–8).

In the old monarchy, the King alone made the law.

Below the sovereign power were found some remnants, half destroyed, of provincial institutions. These provincial institutions were incoherent, poorly ordered, often absurd. In the hands of the aristocracy, they had sometimes been instruments of oppression.

The Revolution has declared itself against royalty and provincial institutions at the same time. It has mingled in the same hatred all that had preceded it, absolute power and what could temper its rigors; it has been simultaneously republican and centralizing.

This double character of the French Revolution is a fact that the friends of absolute power have laid hold of with great care. When you see them defend administrative centralization, do you think that they are working in favor of despotism? Not at all; they are defending one of the great conquests of the Revolution.[K] In this way, they can remain a man of the people and an enemy of the rights of the people, secret servant of tyranny, and declared friend of liberty.[f]

I have visited the two nations that have developed the system of provincial liberties to the highest degree, and I have heard the voice of the parties dividing these nations.

In America, I found men who secretly longed to destroy the democratic institutions of their country. In England, I found others who openly attacked the aristocracy; I did not meet a single one who did not view provincial liberty as a great good.[g]

In these two countries, I saw the ills of the State imputed to an infinity of diverse causes, but never to town liberty.

I heard citizens attribute the greatness or the prosperity of their native land to a multitude of reasons; but I heard all of them put provincial liberty in the first rank and list it at the head of all the other advantages.

When men, who are naturally so divided that they do not agree on either religious doctrines or on political theories, fall into agreement on a single

f. The manuscript indicates that Tocqueville at one moment considered the possibility of placing here a section entitled OF THE EXCELLENCE OF TOWN INSTITUTIONS.

g. To the side: "≠Aristocrats and democrats, royalists and republicans.≠"

fact, a fact that they can best judge, since it occurs everyday before their eyes, am I to believe that this fact might be wrong?

Only peoples who have only a few or no provincial institutions deny their utility; that is, only those who do not know the thing at all, speak ill of it.

CHAPTER 6[a]

Of the Judicial Power in the United States and Its Action on Political Society[b]

The Anglo-Americans have kept all the characteristics that distinguish the judicial power among other peoples.—They have,

a. This chapter and the following one are not found in the copy read by friends and family, which suggests that they were included belatedly in the project. From the beginning of the voyage, Tocqueville, as a lawyer, showed a lively interest in how the American judicial power functioned. Notebook F of his travel notes is devoted exclusively to civil and criminal law in America (YTC, BIIa, and *Voyage, OC,* V, 1, pp. 296–335); and in the first plans of the book (YTC, CVh, 1, pp. 20–31) the judicial power, as well as the civil and criminal laws, occupy an important place. Beyond the notebook cited, a great number of commentaries on the American judicial power appear in the other notebooks of the travel diaries and in the correspondence. There are certain indications that Tocqueville had in particular asked his friend, Élie de Beaumont, judge at Versailles, for information about the French judicial power. We recall that Tocqueville used this method of comparing the situation in France with that in the United States when he considered centralization. A letter from Tocqueville to another magistrate, Ernest de Chabrol, dated November 26, 1831 (YTC, BI a2) contains, along with a description of the American jurisdictional organization, a reference to an earlier note on justices of the peace; the note was a reflection made in a letter (apparently lost) addressed to Élie de Beaumont. Another possible source of information is mentioned in a rough draft: "Speak to Mr. Livingston about the American judicial system" (YTC, CVh, 3, p. 10).

b. Judicial power./

The most original and most difficult part to understand of all the American constitution. Elsewhere there have been confederations, a representative system, a democracy; but no where a judicial power organized as that of the Union.

How the judicial power of the Union is conservative without harming that great principle of the necessity of a single dominating principle in constitutions. It slows, it cannot stop the people, because the latter by changing the constitution can always arrive at what they desire.

How all the laws that challenge the judicial power in America are truly destructive of order and of liberty (YTC, CVh, 5, p. 40).

however, made it into a great political power.—How.—
How the judicial system of the Anglo-Americans differs
from all others.—Why American judges have the right to
declare laws unconstitutional.—How American judges
exercise this right.—Precautions taken by the law-maker
to prevent abuse of this right.

I have thought that a separate chapter must be devoted to the judicial power. Its political importance is so great that it seemed to me that talking about it in passing would diminish it in the eyes of readers.

There have been confederations elsewhere than in America; we have seen republics in places other than on the shores of the New World; the representative system is adopted in several States in Europe; but I do not think that until now any nation in the world has constituted the judicial power in the same way as the Americans.[c]

[≠The Americans have established the judicial power as counterbalance and barrier to the legislative power. They have made it a political power of the first order.≠]

What is most difficult for a foreigner to understand in the United States is the judicial organization. There is, so to speak, no political event in which he does not hear the authority of the judge invoked; and he naturally concludes that in the United States the judge is one of the premier political powers. Then when he comes to examine the constitution of the courts, he discovers at first view only judicial attributions and habits. In his eyes, the magistrate seems never to get into public affairs except by chance; but this very chance recurs daily.

When the Parlement of Paris made remonstrances and refused to register an edict, when on its own it summoned a corrupt official to appear before it, the political action of the judicial power could be recognized. But nothing similar is seen in the United States. [{The American judge never enters

c. "≠In my eyes, the constitution of the judicial power forms the newest and most original portion of the entire political system of the Americans≠" (YTC, CVh, 4, pp. 16–17).

into direct conflict [v: is never found battling] with the political powers strictly defined.}]

The Americans have kept all the characteristics by which the judicial power is customarily recognized. They have enclosed it exactly within the circle where it habitually moves.

The first characteristic of the judicial power, among all peoples, is to serve as arbiter. For the courts to take action, a case must be brought. For there to be a judge, there must be proceedings. As long as a law does not give rise to a case, the judicial power has no occasion to get involved with it. The judicial power is there, but it doesn't see the law. When a judge, as part of a trial, attacks a law relating to the trial, he extends the circle of his attributions, but he does not go beyond them, since in a way he must judge the law in order to be able to judge the trial. When he delivers a verdict on a law, outside of a trial, he goes completely beyond his sphere and enters into that of the legislative power.

The second characteristic of the judicial power is to deliver a verdict concerning particular cases and not concerning general principles. Should a judge, while deciding a particular question, make it certain that each of the consequences of the same principle is struck down in the same way, the principle becomes sterile. While destroying the general principle in this way, he remains within the natural circle of his action. But should a judge directly attack the general principle and destroy it without having a particular case in view, he goes beyond the circle where all peoples have agreed to enclose him; he becomes something more important, perhaps more useful than a magistrate, but he ceases to represent the judicial power.

The third characteristic of the judicial power is to be able to act only when it is called upon, or, following the legal expression, when it is apprised. This characteristic is not found as generally as the other two. I believe, however, that, despite exceptions, it can be considered as essential. By its nature, the judicial power is passive; to stir, it must be put in motion. Someone denounces a crime before it and it punishes the guilty; someone calls upon it to redress an injustice and it redresses it; someone submits an act to it and it interprets it; but it does not go on its own to pursue criminals, seek out injustice and examine facts. In a way the judicial power would do violence to this passive nature if it took initiative on its own and set itself up as censor of the laws.

[<Two things must not be confused. The same man can be vested with political and judicial powers without thereby mingling political and judicial power. The mind sees them as distinct in the very midst of the confusion of actions. When the Parlement of Paris issued decisions, registered edicts and made regulations for public order, it formed only a single body; but within it three different powers were easily distinguished>.]

The Americans have kept these three distinctive characteristics for the judicial power. The American judge can deliver a verdict only when there is a lawsuit. He can never get involved except in a particular case; and to act he must always wait to be apprised.

So the American judge perfectly resembles the magistrates of other nations. He is vested, however, with an immense political power [that the latter do not have. His power forms the most formidable barrier to the encroachments of the legislature].

What causes that? He moves within the same circle and uses the same means as other judges; why does he possess a power that the latter do not have?

The cause is this single fact: the Americans have recognized the right of judges to base their decisions on the *constitution* rather than on the *laws*. In other words, they have allowed them not to apply laws that would appear unconstitutional to them.

I know that a similar right has sometimes been claimed by the courts of other countries; but it has never been granted to them. In America, it is recognized by all powers; no party, not even a man is met who contests it.

The explanation for this must be found in the very principle of American constitutions.

In France, the constitution is, or is considered to be, an immutable work.[d] No power can change anything in it; such is the accepted theory.[e] [L]

---

d. In the margin: "≠The oath is therefore a very rational consequence of very absurd principles.≠"

e. In the margin, with a mark: "≠Is this true?≠"

In England, Parliament is recognized to have the right to modify the constitution. In England, therefore, the constitution can change constantly, or rather it does not exist at all. Parliament is, at the same time, the legislative body and the constituent body.M

In America, political theories are simpler and more rational.

An American constitution is not considered to be immutable, as in France; it cannot be modified by the ordinary powers of society, as in England. It forms a work apart that, representing the will of all the people, binds legislators as well as ordinary citizens; but it can be changed by the will of the people following established forms and in cases for which provisions have been made.

So in America, the constitution can vary; but as long as it exists, it is the source of all powers. Predominant force resides in it alone.

It is easy to see how these differences must influence the position and rights of the judicial body in the three countries that I have cited.

If, in France, the courts could disobey the laws on the grounds that they found them unconstitutional, the constituent power would actually be in their hands, since they alone would have the right to interpret a constitution whose terms no one could change. They would therefore take the place of the nation and would dominate society, at least in so far as the inherent weakness of the judicial power would allow them to do so.f

f. If the French judge had the right to disregard the laws on the grounds that they are unconstitutional, not only would he usurp the constituent power, but also he would escape from all constraint, for in France the courts are answerable only to themselves. Political jurisdiction is introduced only against the principal organs of the government. Therefore the judge, while becoming a political power, would continue to be answerable only to a judicial power, which implies an obvious confusion in all ideas.

In America the judge interprets the constitution, but his opinion is not necessarily followed; he takes a place naturally among the principal political powers, but he answers for his actions to a central political court. He cannot shield either his actions [v. opinions] or his person from the control of society.

In the United States political jurisdiction is a weapon always hanging over the head of the magistrate, a weapon all the more formidable because by his position the judge is the habitual censor of those who are called to deliver his decision.

So the high prerogatives granted to American magistrates never put them beyond

I know that by denying judges the right to declare laws unconstitutional, we indirectly give the legislative body the power to change the constitution, since it no longer encounters a legal barrier that stops it. But better to grant the power to change the constitution of the people to men who imperfectly represent the will of the people, than to others who represent only themselves.

It would be still more unreasonable to give English judges the right to resist the will of the legislative body, because Parliament, which makes the law, makes the constitution as well, and because, as a result, a law cannot

---

the reach of the majority; and their independence is not such that there is not always a single dominant power in society before which all must definitively submit. Judicial power slows the people; it cannot stop them.

When you examine the constitution of the different powers that govern society, you easily discover that the weakest of all is the judiciary when it finds itself abandoned solely to it own resources.[1] The legislature relies on the moral force that belongs to the whole nation; the executive power has its right to initiate and the physical strength of its agents; but the magistracy represents only the authority of reason. The judicial power only becomes formidable when united with another power. There is no more powerful agent of tyranny in the world than the body of magistrates when it joins its action with that of a despot. Because it then delivers to him the only thing that force alone cannot create: the support of the law [in the margin, with a bracket: a commonplace]. Then human liberty does not know where to flee and comes to expire at the very door of the temple of laws. In America the magistrate cannot seek the principle of power outside of himself. The executive power would willingly come to his aid; but it [is (ed.)] without influence. The people would be able to offer him more real help, but the people often see him only as an inconvenient censor. The American judge is therefore isolated among the crowd. To the passions that swirl around him, to the impetus of public opinion, he can only oppose his word; he commands only as long as they want to obey.

It must be remarked, moreover, that in the United States the judge could only get involved in politics through the unconstitutionality of laws. When the people act within the circle drawn by the constitution, whatever the nature of their acts, the judge is reduced to silence. Actually the American magistrates do not have the right to constrain the will of the people; they can only force the people not to be unfaithful to their will and not to fall into self-contradiction.

If, against the view of the majority and after public opinion has had the time to come to a decision, the magistrate persists in his refusal, the people can always change or clarify the terms of the constitution. And immediately resistance ceases along with the motive or the pretext that gave it birth.

1. Don't I previously say the opposite? (YTC, CVh, 5, pp. 16–19).

in any case be called unconstitutional when it issues from the three powers.

Neither of these two arguments applies to America.

In the United States, the constitution dominates the legislators as well as ordinary citizens. It is, therefore, the highest law and cannot be modified by a law. So it is right that the courts obey the constitution in preference to all laws [and by doing so, they do not make themselves masters of society since the people, by changing the constitution, can always reduce the judges to obedience. So American judges refuse without hesitation to apply laws that seem to them contrary to the constitution]. This follows from the very essence of the judicial power: to choose from among legal provisions those that bind him most strictly is in a way the natural right of the magistrate.

In France, as well, the constitution is the highest law, and judges have an equal right to base their decisions on it. But by exercising this right, they would not be able to avoid encroaching upon another right still more sacred than theirs: that of the society in whose name they act. Here ordinary reason must yield to reason of state.g

In America, where the nation can always reduce magistrates to obedience by changing its constitution, a similar danger is not to be feared. On this point, therefore, politics and logic are in agreement, and the people as well as the judges equally retain their privileges.

When a law that the judge considers contrary to the constitution is invoked before the courts of the United States, he can refuse to apply it. This power is the only one particular to the American magistrate, but a great political influence follows from it.

There are, in fact, very few laws that can by nature escape judicial analysis for long, for there are very few of them that do not harm an individual interest, and that litigants cannot or must not cite before the courts.

Now, from the day when the judge refuses to apply a law in a trial, it

g. "In France {during the Restoration}, we have often seen the executive power seek to reduce judicial authority, while the democratic party sought with all its efforts to raise it up. It seems to me that on both sides they acted against themselves" (YTC, CVh, 5, pp. 26–27).

instantly loses part of its moral force. Those who have been wronged by the law are then alerted that a way exists to escape the obligation to obey it; trials multiply, and it becomes powerless. Then one of these two things happens: the people change the constitution or the legislature revokes its law.

So the Americans have given their courts an immense political power; but by forcing them to challenge laws only by judicial means, they have greatly diminished the dangers of this power.

If the judge had been able to challenge laws in a theoretical and general fashion; if he had been able to take the initiative and censure the legislator, he would have burst upon the political scene. Having become the champion or the adversary of one party, he would have called upon all the passions that divide the country to join in the struggle. But when the judge challenges a law in an obscure debate and on a particular application, he partially conceals the importance of the challenge from the eyes of the public. His decision intends only to strike an individual interest; the law is harmed only by chance.

The law censured in this way, moreover, is not destroyed; its moral force is lessened, but its material effect is not suspended. Only little by little, and under the repeated blows of jurisprudence, does it finally succumb. [{If the law were challenged directly it would triumph or succumb in a day.}]

Furthermore, it is easily understood that by charging individual interest with provoking the censure of laws, by intimately linking the trial of the law to the trial of a man, you assure that legislation will not be lightly challenged. In this system legislation is no longer exposed to the daily aggression of parties. By pointing out the mistakes of the legislator, you obey a real need; you start with a definite and appreciable fact, since it must serve as the basis for a trial.

I do not know whether the way in which the American courts act, at the same time that it is most favorable to public order, is not most favorable to liberty as well.

If the judge could challenge the legislators only head on, there are times when he would be afraid to do so; there are other times when partisan spirit would push him daily to dare to do so. Thus the laws would be challenged when the power from which they came was weak, and you would submit to them in silence when that power was strong. That is to say that the laws would often be challenged when respect for them would be most useful, and would be respected when oppression in their name would become easy.[h]

But the American judge is led onto political terrain despite himself. He judges the law only because he has a trial to judge and cannot avoid judging the trial. The political question that he must resolve is linked with the interest of the litigants, and he cannot refuse to settle it without committing a denial of justice. By fulfilling the strict duties imposed on the profession of magistrate, he performs the act of a citizen. It is true that judicial censure, exercised by the courts on legislation, cannot be extended in this way to all laws without distinction, for there are some that can never give rise to this kind of clearly formulated dispute that is called a trial. And when such a dispute is possible, it is still conceivable that there will be no one who wants to submit it to the courts.

The Americans have often felt this drawback, but they have left the remedy incomplete for fear of making it dangerously effective in all cases.

Enclosed within its limits, the power granted to the American courts to rule on the unconstitutionality of laws still forms one of the most powerful barriers that has ever been raised against the tyranny of political assemblies.[j]

---

h. Note: "≠This is what happened particularly at the time of the constitution of the year VIII. The senate was established as overseer of the other powers, and it had to denounce to the legislative bodies attacks against the constitution. We know that it refrained from doing so on any occasion. Under Napoleon's son, this very senate could perhaps have hindered the legal course of government.≠"

j. "≠The absence of administrative centralization is more a fortunate circumstance than the result of the wisdom of the law-maker. But the judicial power in the United States is a barrier raised by design against the omnipotence of the majority. It can be considered as the only powerful or real obstacle that the American laws have placed before the steps of the people≠" (YTC, CVh, 4, pp. 16–17).

"Judicial power in general./

"Utility of the judicial power to oppose the encroachments of popular power. See Kent, vol. 1, p. 275" (YTC, CVh, 5, p. 41).

Other Powers Granted to American Judges

In the United States, all citizens have the right to accuse public
officials before ordinary courts.—How they exercise this right.—
Art. 75 of the French constitution of the year VIII.—
The Americans and the English cannot understand
the sense of this article.

I do not know if I need to say that among a free people, like the Americans, all citizens have the right to accuse public officials before ordinary judges, and that all judges have the right to condemn public officials, it is so natural a thing.

To allow the courts to punish agents of the executive power when they violate the law is not giving the courts a particular privilege. To forbid them to do so is taking away a natural right.

It did not appear to me that in the United States, by making all officials responsible to the courts, the forces of government had been weakened.

It seemed to me, on the contrary, that the Americans, by acting in this way, had increased the respect that is owed to those who govern, the latter being much more careful to avoid criticism.

Nor did I observe in the United States that many political trials were instituted, and it is easily explained. A trial is always, whatever its nature, a difficult and costly enterprise. It is easy to accuse a public man in the newspapers, but it is not without grave motives that someone decides to bring him before the law. So to bring legal proceedings against an official, it is necessary to have just grounds of complaint; and officials hardly provide such grounds when they fear having proceedings brought.

This does not result from the republican form that the Americans have adopted, for the same experience can occur every day in England.

These two peoples did not believe that their independence had been assured by allowing the principal agents of power to be put on trial. Instead, they thought that they succeeded in guaranteeing liberty, much more by small trials, placed daily within the reach of the least citizen, than by great proceedings that were never used or were used too late.

In the Middle Ages, when it was very difficult to reach criminals, judges, when they got hold of some of them, often inflicted terrible punishments on these unfortunates; this did not reduce the number of those guilty. Since then, we have discovered that by making justice both more certain and milder, we have made it more effective at the same time.

The Americans and the English think that arbitrariness and tyranny must be treated like theft: make it easier to take legal action and make the penalty more mild.

In the year VIII of the French Republic, a constitution appeared whose article 75 was worded thus: "The agents of the government, other than the ministers, cannot have legal proceedings instituted against them for facts relating to their functions, except by virtue of a decision of the *Conseil d'État;* in this case, the proceedings take place before the ordinary courts."

The constitution of the year VIII passed from the scene, but not this article, which remained after it [{and we are still so inexperienced in the art of [being (ed.)] free.}]; and it is still used every day to oppose the just complaints of citizens.

[{But this is particular to France.}]

I have often tried to explain the sense of this art. 75 to some Americans or Englishmen, and it has always been very difficult for me to succeed in doing so.

What they noticed first was that the *Conseil d'État,* in France, was a high court seated at the center of the kingdom; there was a kind of tyranny in sending all complainants before it as a preliminary step.

But when I tried to make them understand that the *Conseil d'État* was not a judicial body at all, in the ordinary sense of the term, but an administrative body, whose members were dependent on the King; and that the King, as sovereign, after ordering one of his servants, called prefect, to commit a wrongful act, could order, as sovereign, another of his servants, called councilor of the *Conseil d'État,* to prevent someone from having the first punished; when I showed them the citizen harmed by the order of the prince, reduced to asking the prince himself for the authorization to seek justice, they refused to believe in such enormities and accused me of lying and of ignorance.

Often, in the old monarchy, the *parlement* ordered the arrest of the public official who made himself guilty of a crime. Sometimes the royal authority, intervening, had the procedure annulled. Despotism then showed itself openly, and people, while obeying, submitted only to force.

So we have retreated far from the point reached by our fathers; for we allow, under the color of justice, and consecrate, in the name of law, deeds that violence alone imposed on them.

CHAPTER 7

Of Political Jurisdiction in the United States[TN 4]

What the author understands by political jurisdiction.—How political jurisdiction is understood in France, England and the United States.—In America, the political judge concerns himself only with public officials.—He orders dismissals rather than punishments.—Political jurisdiction, customary method of government.—Political jurisdiction, as understood in the United States, is, despite its mildness, and perhaps because of it, a very powerful weapon in the hands of the majority.

[≠Political jurisdiction is a violation of the great principle of the separation of powers; you resort to it as an extreme measure to reach certain guilty individuals.≠]

I understand by political jurisdiction the decision delivered by a political body temporarily vested with the right to judge.

In absolute governments, it is useless to give judgments extraordinary forms. The prince, in whose name the accused is prosecuted, is master of the courts as of everything else, and he has no need to seek a guarantee beyond the idea that is held of his power.[a] The only fear that he can imagine

TRANSLATOR'S NOTE 4: For this chapter, there is no totally satisfactory way to translate *jugement politique.* The most direct translation, *political judgment,* is extremely ambiguous. For want of a better alternative, I have decided to use the traditional translation, *political jurisdiction,* since the chapter has to do with the right of a political body, in particular circumstances, to bring to trial, to judge and to punish a public figure.

a. In the margin:

It was necessary to give the superior political power control of all powers for the *unity* of government, and for that it was necessary to give the legislature the entirely administrative power to *dismiss* or the entirely judicial power to *judge.*

is that not even the external appearances of justice are kept, and that his authority is dishonored in the desire to assert it.

But in most free countries, where the majority can never act on the courts as an absolute prince would, judicial power is sometimes placed temporarily in the hands of the very representatives of society. Temporarily mixing powers in this way is preferred to violating the necessary principle of the unity of government. England, France and the United States have introduced political jurisdiction into their laws; it is curious to examine how these three great peoples have turned it to good account.

In England and in France, the chamber of peers forms the highest criminal court[1] of the nation. It does not judge all political crimes, but it can do so.

Alongside the chamber of peers is another political power, vested with the right to accuse. On this point, the only difference that exists between the two countries is this: in England, the members of the House of Commons can accuse whomever they choose before the Lords; while in France the deputies can only prosecute the ministers of the King in this way.[b]

In these two countries, moreover, the chamber of peers finds all the penal laws at its disposal for striking the delinquents.

In the United States, as in Europe, one of the two branches of the legislature is vested with the right to accuse, and the other with the right to judge. The representatives denounce the guilty party; the Senate punishes him.

But a matter can be *referred* to the Senate only by the *representatives;* and before the Senate, the representatives can accuse only *public officials.* Therefore the Senate has a more limited competence than the French court of

---

On the other hand, it was very dangerous to liberty and humanity to vest a political power with the most formidable rights of a judicial body.

From that the mixed American system. Political jurisdiction more than dismissal, less than a ruling.

1. *The court of Lords in England furthermore forms the last appeal in certain civil matters. See Blackstone, book III, chap. IV.*

b. In the margin: "I find nothing in Blackstone that justifies this distinction. However I think it is correct."

the peers, and the representatives have a broader right to accuse than our deputies.

But here is the greatest difference that exists between America and Europe. In Europe, political courts can apply all the provisions of the penal code. In America, when they have removed from the guilty party the public character with which he was vested, and have declared him unworthy to hold any political offices whatsoever in the future, their right is exhausted, and the task of the ordinary courts begins.

I suppose that the President of the United States has committed a crime of high treason.

The House of Representatives accuses him; the senators decide his removal. Afterward he appears before a jury that alone can take away life or liberty.

This succeeds in throwing a bright light on the subject that occupies us.

By introducing political jurisdiction into their laws, Europeans wanted to reach great criminals whatever their birth, rank or power in the State. To achieve that, they temporarily united, within a great political body, all the prerogatives of the courts.

The legislator is then transformed into a magistrate; he can establish the crime, classify and punish it. By giving him the rights of the judge, the law imposed all of the judge's obligations on him, and bound him to the observation of all the forms of justice.

When a political court, French or English, has a public official as a defendant and delivers a verdict condemning him, by doing so, it removes him from office and can declare him unworthy to hold any office in the future. But here the dismissal and political interdiction are a consequence of the decision and not the decision itself.

So in Europe, political jurisdiction is more a judicial act than an administrative measure.

The opposite is seen in the United States, and it is easy to be persuaded that political jurisdiction there is more an administrative measure than a judicial act.

It is true that the decision of the Senate is judicial in form; to make it, the senators are obliged to conform to the solemnity and customs of the procedure. It is also judicial by the grounds on which it is based; the Senate is, in general, obliged to base its decision on a crime of the common law. But it is administrative in its objective.

If the principal aim of the American law-maker had really been to arm a political body with a great judicial power, he would not have restricted its action to the circle of public officials, for the most dangerous enemies of the State may hold no office at all. This is true above all in republics, where the favor of parties is the first of powers, and where someone is often much stronger when not legally exercising any power.

If the American law-maker had wanted to give society itself, like judges, the right to prevent great crimes by fear of punishment, he would have put at the disposal of the political courts all the resources of the penal code. But he only provided them with an incomplete weapon that cannot reach the most dangerous of criminals. For what use is a judgment of political interdiction against someone who wants to overturn the laws themselves?

The principal aim of political jurisdiction in the United States is, therefore, to withdraw power from someone who is making poor use of it, and to prevent the same citizen from being vested with power in the future. That, as we see, is an administrative act that has been given the solemnity of a judgment.

So in this matter, the Americans have created something mixed. They have given all the guarantees of political jurisdiction to administrative dismissal, and they have removed from political jurisdiction its greatest rigors.

This point settled, everything closely follows; we then discover why the American constitutions submit all civil officials to the jurisdiction of the Senate, and exempt the military whose crimes are, however, more to be feared [{in republics}]. In the civil order, the Americans have, so to speak, no removable officials; some are irremovable; others hold their rights by a mandate that cannot be abrogated. So to remove them from power, they must all be judged.ᶜ But military officers depend on the head

c. To the side: "≠Action of the two systems.

"French system more effective, more dangerous.

"American system more *just,* more rational in the *separation* of power. Less effective in times of crisis, more everyday.≠"

of State, who himself is a civil officer. By reaching the head of State, they strike them all with the same blow.[2]

Now, if we come to compare the European and American systems in the effects that each produces or can produce, we discover differences no less noticeable.

In France and in England, political jurisdiction is considered as an extraordinary weapon that society should use only to save itself in moments of great peril.

We cannot deny that political jurisdiction, as understood in Europe, violates the conservative principle of the separation of powers and constantly threatens the life and liberty of men.

Political jurisdiction in the United States strikes only an indirect blow at the principle of separation of powers. It does not threaten the existence of citizens; it does not, as in Europe, hang over all heads, since it strikes only those who, by accepting public offices, subject themselves to its rigors in advance.

It is simultaneously less to be feared and less effective.

Moreover, the law-makers of the United States did not consider it as an extreme remedy for the great ills of society, but as a customary means of government.

From this point of view, it perhaps exercises more real influence over the social body in America than in Europe. You must not in fact be fooled by the apparent mildness of the American legislation regarding political jurisdiction. It must be noted, in the first place, that in the United States the court that delivers these judgments is composed of the same elements and is subject to the same influences as the body charged with accusing; this gives an almost irresistible impulse to the vindictive passions of parties. If political judges, in the United States, cannot order punishments as severe as those ordered by political judges in Europe, there is less chance of being acquitted by them as a result. Conviction is less to be feared and more certain.

Europeans, by establishing political courts, had as their principal object

---

2. *Not that his rank can be taken from an officer, but he can be removed from his command.*

to *punish* the guilty; Americans, to *remove* them from power. Political jurisdiction in the United States is a preventive measure in a way. So judges there must not be bound by very exact criminal definitions.

Nothing is more frightening than the vagueness of American laws, when they define political crimes strictly speaking. The crimes that will justify the conviction of the President, says the Constitution of the United States, section IV, art. I [*sic:* Article II, Section 4], are "Treason, Bribery, or other high Crimes and Misdemeanors." Most of the state constitutions are even more obscure.

"Public officials, says the constitution of Massachusetts,[d] will be condemned for their culpable behavior and for their bad administration.[3] All officials who put the State in danger by bad administration, corruption or other misdemeanors, says the constitution of Virginia, are impeachable by the House of Delegates." There are constitutions that, in order to let an unlimited responsibility weigh upon the public officials, specify no crime.[4]

But what makes the American laws in this matter so formidable arises, I dare say, from their very mildness.

We have seen that in Europe the dismissal of an official, and his political interdiction, were consequences of the penalty, and that in America it was the penalty itself. The result is this. In Europe, the political courts are vested with terrible rights that sometimes they do not know how to use; and it happens that they do not punish for fear of punishing too much. But in America, they do not back away from a penalty that humanity does not bemoan. To condemn a political enemy to death, in order to remove him from power, is in everybody's eyes a horrible assassination. To declare an adversary unworthy to possess this same power and to take it away from him, while leaving him his life and liberty, can appear as the honest outcome of the struggle.

---

d. The Massachusetts Constitution reads: "The senate shall be a court with full authority to hear and determine all impeachments made by the house of representatives, against any officer or officers of the commonwealth, for misconduct and mal-administration in their offices."

3. *Chap. 1, sect. II, § 8.*

4. *See the constitutions of Illinois, Maine, Connecticut and Georgia.*

Now, this judgment, so easy to decide, is nonetheless the height of misfortune for the ordinary man among those to whom it is applied. Great criminals will undoubtedly defy its empty rigors; ordinary men will see in it a decision that destroys their position, stains their honor, and that condemns them to a shameful inaction worse than death.

So the less formidable political jurisdiction in the United States seems, the greater the influence it exercises on the course of society. It does not act directly on the governed, but it makes the majority entirely master of those who govern. It does not give the legislature an immense power that could be exercised only in a day of crisis; it allows the legislature to have a moderate and regular power that can be used every day. If the power is less, on the other hand, its use is more convenient and its abuse easier.

By preventing political courts from ordering judicial punishments, the Americans seem to me therefore to have avoided the most horrible consequences of legislative tyranny, rather than tyranny itself. And all things considered, I do not know if political jurisdiction, as it is understood in the United States, is not the most formidable weapon ever put in the hands of the majority.

When the American republics begin to degenerate, I believe that it will be easy to recognize; it will be enough to see if the number of cases of political jurisdiction increases.[N]

CHAPTER 8

Of the Federal Constitution

Until now I have considered each state as forming a complete whole, and I have shown the different mechanisms that the people put in motion there, as well as the means of action that they use. But all these states that I have envisaged as independent are, in certain cases, forced to obey a supreme authority, which is that of the Union. The time has come to examine the portion of sovereignty that has been conceded to the Union, and to cast a rapid glance over the federal constitution.[1]

Historical Background of the Federal Constitution[a]

Origin of the first Union.—Its weakness.—Congress
summons the constituent power.—Interval of two years that

---

1. *See the text of the federal Constitution.* [In Appendix in the first editions (ed.)]
a. In the margin: "≠Where to find the *outline* of the first federation?
"Bad result of the first federation. See *Federalist,* p. 60 [No. 15 (ed.)].≠"
The *Federalist* is, without any doubt, the work that Tocqueville cites most often. Its decisive influence on the drafting of this chapter must be recognized, even if such an influence on the whole book is difficult to define and remains to be determined. When Tocqueville reads the *Federalist,* he certainly has in mind, and at hand, Montesquieu and Rousseau. He rediscovers many of their ideas in the American work. An initial examination of the citations taken from the work seems to indicate that, above all, Tocqueville found in it a confirmation of his own ideas. This does not mean, as has often been asserted, that he intentionally omitted citations of the text in other chapters. If undeniable similarities exist between the American text and the *Democracy,* they demonstrate the result of a shared origin of ideas between the two texts more than a direct influence of the first book on the second. Another important work concerning information on the political organization of the United States is the commentaries on the Constitution by Justice Joseph Story. In a letter to Francis Lieber of May 9, 1840, Story, apparently

passes between this moment and that when the
new Constitution is promulgated.

[≠I am not among those who profess a blind faith in legal prescriptions
and who think that it is sufficient to change the laws of a people in order
to modify easily their social and political state. Laws act only in two ways,
either by their long duration, when a power superior to society manages to
impose them over many years, or by their perfect harmony with the mores,
habits and civilization of the people. In this last case, the laws are only the
conspicuous and legal manifestation of a preexistent fact.[b]

But I admit that when laws are found to be in harmony with the needs
{the social state} of a country, its mores and its habits, their effect is often
something of a miracle.

---

unable to recognize the significance of the *Democracy,* judges that Lieber's knowledge
of the American political system is much superior to that of Tocqueville; according to
Story, Tocqueville simply took his ideas from the *Federalist* and from Story's own book
on the American Constitution (*Life and Letters of Joseph Story,* Boston: Charles C. Little
and James Brown, 1851, vol. II, p. 330). John W. Henry Canoll ("The Authorship of
Democracy in America," *Historical Magazine* 8, no. 9 (1864): 332–33), who reports the
words of Mgr. Alexander Vattemare, asserts that the American author who had a direct
influence on Tocqueville's thought is John C. Spencer. According to Canoll, Tocqueville
would have shown Spencer a plan of his work; the latter would have reviewed and criticized it and, after numerous interviews, would have given the canvas of the *Democracy*
to the author.

b. In the margin:

≠The government of the United States is not truly speaking a *federal* government,
it is a *national* government whose powers are limited. *Important.*/

Mixture of *national* and *federal* in the constitution. See *Federalist,* p. 166 [No. 28
(ed.)]./

The Union enters most profoundly into the government of the United States by
the right to invalidate laws that are contrary to vested rights. Note that it is the federal
judicial power alone that acts in this case./

[To the side: I am not among those who believe that there is a force in the laws
that commands obedience to such an extent that all the present and all the future of
a people depend on its legislation./

You could deal with the principles of *union,* from complete independence, *league,*
confederation, to finally *national* government.≠]

No country on earth more than America has ever given a greater example of the power of laws on the life of political society.≠]

The thirteen colonies that simultaneously threw off the yoke of England at the end of the last century had, as I have already said, the same religion, the same language, the same mores, nearly the same laws; they struggled against a common enemy. So they must have had strong reasons to unite closely together, and to be absorbed into one and the same nation.

But each of them, having always had a separate existence and a government close at hand, had created particular interests as well as customs; and each found repugnant a solid and complete union that would have made its individual importance disappear within a common importance. From that, two opposing tendencies: one that led the Anglo-Americans to unite; the other that led them to separate.

As long as the war with the mother country lasted, necessity made the principle of union prevail. And, although the laws that constituted the union were defective, the common bond continued to exist in spite of them.[2]

But as soon as peace was concluded, the vices of the legislation[c] became clear; the State seemed to dissolve all at once. Each colony, having become an independent republic, seized full sovereignty. The federal government, condemned by its very constitution to weakness, and no longer supported by the feeling of public danger, saw its flag abandoned to the outrages of the great peoples of Europe. At the same time, it could not find sufficient resources to stand up to the Indian nations and to pay the interest on debts contracted during the war for independence. About to perish, it officially declared its own impotence and summoned the constituent power.[3]

---

2. *See the articles of the first confederation formed in 1778. This federal constitution was adopted by all the States only in 1781.*

Also see the analysis that the Federalist *makes of this constitution, from No. 15 to No. 22 inclusive, and Mr. Story in his* Commentaries on the Constitution of the United States, *pp. 85 [84 (ed.)]–115.*

c. Hervé de Tocqueville: "I do not know if you shouldn't say: *of the constitution*" (YTC, CIIIb, 3, pp. 9–10).

3. *Congress made this declaration on February 21, 1787.*

If ever America was capable of rising for a few moments to the high level of glory that the proud imagination[d] of its inhabitants would like constantly to show us, it was at this supreme moment when the national power had, in a way, just abdicated authority.

For a people to struggle energetically to conquer its independence is a spectacle that every century has been able to provide. The efforts made by the Americans to escape from the yoke of the English have, moreover, been much exaggerated. Separated from their enemies by 1,300 leagues of ocean, aided by a powerful ally, the United States owed their victory to their position much more than to the merit of their armies or to the patriotism of their citizens.[e] Who would dare to compare the American war to the wars of the French Revolution, and the efforts of the Americans to ours? France, the object of attacks from the whole of Europe, without money, credit, allies, threw one-twentieth of its population before its enemies, with one hand putting out the conflagration that devoured its bowels and with the other carrying the torch abroad.[f] But what is new in the history of societies is to see a great people, warned by its legislators that the gears of government are grinding to a halt, turn its attention to itself, without rushing and without fear; sound the depth of the trouble; keep self-control for two whole years, in order to take time to find the remedy; and, when this remedy is indicated, voluntarily submit to it without costing humanity either a tear or a drop of blood.

When the insufficiency of the first federal constitution made itself felt, the excitement of the political passions that had given birth to the revolution was partially calmed, and all the great men that it had created still lived. This was double good fortune for America. The small as-

---

d. The manuscript says: ". . . that the vain imagination . . ."

Hervé de Tocqueville: "I would cross out the word *vain* in order not to shock the Americans among whom the book should have a great deal of success" (YTC, CIIIb, 3, p. 10).

e. In the margin: "≠If you want to know what a people can do for its independence, it is not America that you must look at.≠"

f. Hervé de Tocqueville: "If you keep this paragraph, you must suppress this last sentence which is declamatory, vague and could be interpreted as praise for violence in the manner of Thiers" (YTC, CIIIb, 3, p. 10).

sembly,[4] which charged itself with drafting the second constitution, included the best minds and most noble characters that had ever appeared in the New World. George Washington presided over it.[h]

This national commission, after long and mature deliberations, finally offered to the people for adoption the body of organic laws that still governs the Union today. All the states successively adopted it.[5] The new federal government began to operate in 1789, after two years of interregnum. So the American Revolution finished precisely at the moment when ours began.

4. *It was composed of only 55*[g] *members. Washington, Madison, Hamilton, the two Morrises were part of it.*

g. The manuscript says 39, which indicates the number of delegates to the convention approving the proposed constitution on September 17, 1787.

h. Great men of the early times of the republic./

Their enlightenment. Their true patriotism. Their high character. Convention that made the federal Constitution. Few prejudices that were met there; constant struggle against provincial prejudices. Sincere love of republican liberty, but courageous and constant struggle against the bad passions of the people.

Character of Washington. Still more admirable for his courage in struggling against popular passions than for what he did for liberty. The gods are disappearing!

A separate chapter on Washington. Washington has been admired for not having wanted to become a dictator, for having returned to the crowd. . . . Ignorance about the true state of things; historical memories badly applied.

Cincinnatus. Washington could not reasonably think to dominate. But *admirable* in his resistance to the exaggerations of popular opinion; there is his superiority; there is the culminating point.

Washington could not rise by arms (absurd), but by popular favor. And he did not seek it out for a moment.

Why did Washington, who in the end during his lifetime lost the majority, become more than a man after his death? (YTC, CVe, pp. 61–62).

In a bundle of notes where Tocqueville had gathered information for new chapters, the following title is found: OF THE GREAT MEN OF AMERICA AND OF WASHINGTON IN PARTICULAR (YTC, CVh, 1, p. 1).

5. *It was not the legislators who adopted it. The people named deputies for this express purpose. In each of these assemblies the new Constitution was the object of thorough discussion.*

Summary Picture of the Federal Constitution[j]

*Division of powers between federal sovereignty and that of the
states.—The government of the states remains the normal law;—
the federal government, the exception.*

A first difficulty must have presented itself to the minds of the Americans.
It was a question of sharing sovereignty in such a way that the different
states that formed the Union continued to govern themselves in everything
that related only to their internal prosperity, and that the whole nation,
represented by the Union, did not cease to be a body and to provide for all
its general needs. A complex question, difficult to resolve.[k]

It was impossible to set in advance, in an exact and complete manner,
the portion of power that had to revert to each of these two governments
that were going to share sovereignty.

Who would be able to anticipate in advance all the details of the life of
a people?

The duties and rights of the federal government were simple and easy
enough to define, because the Union had been formed for the purpose of
meeting a number of great general needs. The duties and rights of the
government of the states were, on the contrary, numerous and complicated,
because this government penetrated into all the details of social life.

So the attributions of the federal government were defined with great
care,[m] and everything that was not included in the definition was declared
to be part of the attributions of the government of the states. Thus, the

j. Union./

The Union has an artificial sovereignty; the states, a natural sovereignty; cause of
difference in real strength (perhaps subtle)./

Power of the Union in what concerns it: The Union has more extensive and more
essential prerogatives, in what concerns it, than a number of States forming only a
single body have had (YTC, CVh, 1, p. 51).

k. In the margin: "I believe that the principle of the unity of the American people
regarding the matters provided for in the Constitution—principle rich in consequences
and which you come back to constantly—must be placed at the beginning of this part
(I do not know where)."

m. ≠Here there was a principle that was supposed to dominate the whole matter:

government of the states remained the normal law; the federal government was the exception.[6]

But it was anticipated that, in practice, questions could arise relative to the exact limits of this exceptional government, and that it would be dangerous to abandon the solution of these questions to the ordinary courts established in the different states, by the states themselves. So a high federal court,[7] a single tribunal, was created; one of its attributions was to maintain the division of powers between the two rival governments as the Constitution had established it.[8]

The Union has only a circumscribed sovereignty, but within this circle it forms only one and the same people.[1]

(You could define the Union as a people who does not enjoy all the rights of sovereignty.) Within this circle the Union is sovereign. This set forth and accepted, the rest is easy; for from the origin of societies, this point is agreed: that a people has the right to have all that involves its security and independence judged by its own courts.

Now, since the Union, for the particular matters indicated by the Constitution, forms only one people, the above rule was as applicable to it as to all others.

Nothing more was involved than determining what its interests were within the circle of its existence, traced by the Constitution.

1. Some restriction has indeed been put on these principles by introducing the states as independent powers in the Senate and by making them vote separately in the House of Representatives in the case of election of the President. But these are exceptions. The opposite principle predominates≠ (YTC, CVb, p. 20).

6. *See amendments to the federal Constitution.* Federalist, *No. 32. Story [*Commentaries *(ed.)], p. 711. Kent's* Commentaries, *vol. I, p. 364.*

Note indeed that, whenever the Constitution has not reserved to Congress the exclusive right to regulate certain matters, the states can do so, while waiting for Congress to choose to take charge of them. Example: Congress has the right to pass a general bankruptcy law; it doesn't do so; each state could pass one in its own way. This point was established, moreover, only after discussion before the courts. It is only jurisprudence.

7. *The action of this court is indirect, as we will see later.*

8. *This is how the* Federalist, *in No. 45 [p. 200], explains this division of sovereignty between the Union and the particular states:*

The powers delegated by the proposed Constitution to the federal government are few and defined. Those which are to remain in the state governments are numerous and indefinite. The former will be exercised principally on external objects, as war, peace, negotiation, and foreign commerce. [. . . (ed.) . . .] The powers reserved to the several states will

Attributions of the Federal Government

Power granted to the federal government to make peace, war, to establish general taxes.—Matter of internal political policy with which it can be involved.—The government of the Union, more centralized on some points than was the royal government under the old French monarchy.

Peoples in relation to one another are only individuals. Above all, a nation needs a single government to appear with advantage in regard to foreigners.

So the Union was granted the exclusive right to make war and peace; to conclude treaties of commerce; to raise armies, to equip fleets.[9]

The necessity of a national government does not make itself as strongly felt in the direction of the internal affairs of society.

Nonetheless, there are certain general interests for which only a general authority can usefully provide.

The Union was left the right to regulate all that relates to the value of money; it was charged with the postal service; it was given the right to open

---

extend to all the objects which, in the ordinary course of affairs, concern the lives, liberties, and properties of the people, and the internal order, improvement, and prosperity of the state.

I will often have the occasion to cite the Federalist *in this work. When the proposal that has since become the Constitution of the United States was still before the people, and submitted for adoption, three men who were already celebrated and have since become even more famous, John Jay, Hamilton and Madison, joined together for the purpose of making the advantages of the proposal clear to the nation. With this idea, they published, in the form of a newspaper, a series of articles that together form a treatise. They gave the newspaper the name* Federalist, *which has remained the title of the work.*

The Federalist[n] *is a fine book that, though particular to America, should be familiar to the statesmen of all countries.*

n. James T. Schleifer has identified the English edition used by Tocqueville. It was the one published in Washington by Thomson & Homans, in 1831. In his notes, Tocqueville also cites a French edition of 1792 (probably that of Buisson, Paris).

9. See *Constitution, sect. VIII. Federalist, Nos. 41 and 42. Kent's* Commentaries, *vol. I, p. 207 and following. Story [*Commentaries *(ed.)], pp. 358–82;* id., *pp. 409–26.*

the great avenues of communication that had to unite the various parts of the territory.[10]

The government of the different states was generally considered free in its sphere, but it could abuse this independence and compromise the security of the entire Union through imprudent measures. For these rare cases, defined in advance, the federal government was permitted to intervene in the internal affairs of the states.[11] That explains how, while still recognizing in each of the confederated republics the power to modify and change its legislation, each was, nevertheless, forbidden to make retroactive laws and to create bodies of noblemen within its midst.[12]

Finally, since the federal government had to be able to fulfill the obligations imposed on it, it was given the unlimited right to levy taxes.[13]

When you pay attention to the division of powers as the federal constitution has established it; when, on the one hand, you examine the portion of sovereignty that the particular states have reserved to themselves and, on the other, the share of power that the Union took, it is easily discovered that the federal law-makers had formed very clear and very sound ideas about what I earlier called governmental centralization.[o]

The United States forms not only a republic, but also a confederation.[p] But the national authority there is, in several respects, more centralized than it was in the same period under several of the absolute monarchies of Europe. I will cite only two examples.

---

10. *There are also several other rights of this type, such as that to pass a general law on bankruptcy, to grant patents. . . . What made the intervention of the whole Union necessary in these matters is felt well enough.*

11. *Even in this case, its intervention is indirect. The Union intervenes through its courts, as we will see further on.*

12. *Federal Constitution, sect. X, art. 1.*

13. *Constitution, sect. VIII, IX and X. Federalist, Nos. 30–36, inclusive.* Id., *41, 42, 43, 44. Kent's* Commentaries, *vol. I, pp. 207 and 381. Story,* id., *pp. 329–514.*

o. In a variant of the manuscript: "≠You can even say that the necessity of governmental centralization was better understood by them than it was in several of the monarchies of Europe.≠"

p. Throughout the book, Tocqueville uses the words *federation* and *confederation* with not much precision.

France counted thirteen sovereign courts that, most often, had the right to interpret the law without appeal. It possessed, in addition, certain provinces called *pays d'États* that could refuse their support, after the sovereign authority, charged with representing the nation, had ordered the raising of a tax.

The Union has only a single court to interpret the law, as well as a single legislature to make the law; a tax voted by the representatives of the nation obligates all the citizens. So the Union is more centralized on these two essential points than the French monarchy was; the Union, however, is only a collection of confederated republics.

In Spain, certain provinces[q] had the power to establish their own customs system, a power that, by its very essence, stems from national sovereignty.

In America, Congress alone has the right to regulate commerce among the states. So the government of the confederation is more centralized on this point than that of the kingdom of Spain.

It is true that, in the end, you arrived at the same point, since in France and in Spain the royal power is always able to execute, by force if necessary, what the constitution of the kingdom denied it the right to do. But I am talking here about theory.

Federal Powers

After having enclosed the federal government within a clearly drawn circle of action, it was a matter of knowing how to make it work.

q. In the manuscript: "each province."

Legislative Powers[r]

[DIFFERENCE BETWEEN THE CONSTITUTION OF THE SENATE AND
THAT OF THE HOUSE OF REPRESENTATIVES]

*Division of the legislative body into two branches.—Differences
in the way the two houses are formed.—The principle of the
independence of the state triumphs in the formation of the
Senate.—The dogma of national sovereignty, in the composition
of the House of Representatives.—Singular effects that result
from this, that constitutions are logical only when peoples
are young.*

In the organization of the powers of the Union, the plan that was traced in advance by the particular constitution of each of the states was followed on many points.

The federal legislative body of the Union was composed of a Senate and a House of Representatives.

The spirit of conciliation caused different rules to be followed in the formation of each of these assemblies.

I brought out above that, when the Americans wanted to establish the federal constitution, two opposing interests found themselves face to face. These two interests had given birth to two opinions.

Some wanted to make the Union a league of independent states, a sort of congress where the representatives of distinct peoples would come to discuss certain points of common interest.

Others wanted to unite all the inhabitants of the old colonies into one and the same people, and give them a government that, although its sphere would be limited, would be able to act within this sphere, as the one and only representative of the nation. The practical consequences of these two theories were very different.

Thus, if it was a matter of organizing a league and not a national government, it was up to the majority of the states to make laws, and not up

r. In the manuscript: "legislative power."

to the majority of the inhabitants of the Union. For each state, large or small, would then conserve its character of independent power and would enter into the Union on a perfectly equal footing.

On the contrary, from the moment when the inhabitants of the United States were considered to form one and the same people, it was natural that only the majority of the citizens of the Union made the law.

Understandably, the small states could not consent to the application of this doctrine without completely abdicating their existence in what concerned federal sovereignty; for, from co-regulating power, they would become an insignificant fraction of a great people. The first system would have granted them an unreasonable power; the second nullified them.

In this situation, what almost always happens when interests are opposed to arguments happened: the rules of logic were made to bend. The lawmakers adopted a middle course that forced conciliation of two systems theoretically irreconcilable.

The principle of the independence of the states triumphed in the formation of the Senate;[s] the dogma of national sovereignty, in the composition of the House of Representatives.[t]

s. Senate./

The constitution of the Senate is the least *logical* and the least *rational* part of the Constitution of the United States. That is what Hamilton remarks in the *Federalist*. All of his discussion on this point shows great distress to see this system introduced, though he considers it a necessity given the state of opinion.

The equal representation of the states in the Senate goes directly against the principle of the Constitution to create a *national,* not a *federal* government.

In practice, however, I believe few disadvantages result from this anomaly. Once the majority is well and *constitutionally* established in the House of Representatives, a power *enormously popular* by its nature, the Senate is forced to go along.

You could be astonished to see the Senate charged with participating in a treaty. . . . But this power, though not expressed in all constitutions, exists in fact among all free peoples, even in monarchies.

In America, as among us, all the preliminary negotiations are done, moreover, by the executive power acting alone. It is the treaty itself that needs the support of the Senate (YTC, CVh, 1, pp. 42–43).

t. "Political assemblies./

"The more numerous they are, the more prone they are to the oligarchical direction of some members. See *Federalist,* p. 235 [No. 58 (ed.)].

Each state had to send two senators to Congress and a certain number of representatives,[u] in proportion to its population.[14]

Today, as a result of this arrangement, the state of New York has forty representatives in Congress and only two senators; the state of Delaware, two senators and only one representative. So in the Senate, the state of Delaware is the equal of the state of New York, while the latter has, in the House of Representatives, forty times more influence than the first. Thus, it can happen that the minority of the nation, dominating the Senate, entirely paralyzes the desires of the majority, represented by the other chamber; this is contrary to the spirit of constitutional governments.

All this shows clearly how rare and difficult it is to link all the parts of legislation together in a logical and rational manner.

In the long run, time always gives birth to different interests and consecrates diverse rights in the same people. Then, when it is a question of establishing a general constitution, each of these interests and rights serves as so many natural obstacles that are opposed to following all of the consequences of any one political principle. So only at the birth of societies can you be perfectly logical in the laws. When you see a people enjoy this advantage, do not rush to conclude that they are wise; instead, think that they are young.

"January 30, 1832, Washington. Small number of the members of Congress" (YTC, CVe, p. 51; this note is not reproduced in *Voyage, OC,* V, 1).

u. "Ask Mr. Livingston or other Americans at the nomination of the King what the current rule of *apportionment* for the representatives is" (YTC, CVb, p. 34).

14. *Every ten years, Congress again fixes the number of deputies that each state must send to the House of Representatives. The total number was 69 [65 (ed.)] in 1789; it was 240 in 1833. (American Almanac, 1834, p. 194 [124 (ed.)].)*

The Constitution had said that there would not be more than one representative for 30,000 inhabitants; but it did not set a lower limit. Congress has not believed that it had to increase the number of representatives in proportion to the growth of the population. By the first law that dealt with this subject, April 14, 1792 (see Laws of the United States by Story, vol. I, p. 235), it was decided that there would be one representative for 33,000 inhabitants. The last law, which occurred in 1832, set the number at 1 representative for 48,000 inhabitants. The population represented is composed of all free men and three-fifths of the number of slaves.

At the time when the federal Constitution was formed, only two interests positively opposed to each other existed among the Anglo-Americans: the interest of individuality for the particular states, and the interest of union for the whole people. It was necessary to come to a compromise.

You must recognize, nonetheless, that up to now this part of the Constitution has not produced the evils that could be feared.

All the states are young;[v] they are near each other; they have homogeneous mores, ideas and needs; the difference that results from their greater or lesser size is not sufficient to give them strongly opposed interests. So the small states have never been seen to join together in the Senate against the plans of the large. There is, moreover, such an irresistible force in the legal expression of the will of an entire people that, when the majority expresses itself in the organ of the House of Representatives, the Senate, facing it, finds itself quite weak.

Beyond that, it must not be forgotten that it did not depend on the American law-makers to make one and the same nation out of the people to whom they wanted to give laws. The aim of the federal Constitution was not to destroy the existence of the states, but only to restrain it. So, from the moment when a real power was left to those secondary bodies (and it could not be taken from them), the habitual use of constraint to bend them to the will of the majority was renounced in advance. This said, the introduction of the individual strengths of the states into the mechanism of the federal government was nothing extraordinary. It only took note of an existing fact, a recognized power that had to be treated gently and not violated.

v. Hervé de Tocqueville: "I would prefer *new*, for if they are young in terms of establishment, they are old in terms of civilization" (YTC, CIIIb, 3, p. 12).

Another Difference between the Senate and the House of Representatives[w]

The Senate named by the provincial legislators.—
The representatives, by the people.—Two levels of election
for the first.—A single one for the second.—Length of the
different mandates.—Attributions.

The Senate differs from the other chamber not only by the very principle of representation, but also by the mode of election, by the length of mandate and by the diversity of attributions.

The House of Representatives is named by the people; the Senate, by the legislators of each state.

The one is the product of direct election; the other, of indirect election.

The mandate of representatives lasts only two years; that of the senators, six.

The House of Representatives has only legislative functions; it participates in judicial power only by accusing public officials. The Senate participates in the making of laws; it judges political crimes that are referred to it by the House of Representatives; it is, in addition, the great executive council of the nation. Treaties, concluded by the President, must be validated by the Senate; his choices, to be definitive, need to receive the approval of the same body.[15]

w. In the manuscript: "OTHER DIFFERENCES BETWEEN . . ."
15. *See* Federalist, *Nos. 52–66, inclusive. Story* [Commentaries *(ed.)], pp. 199–314. Constitution, sect. II and III.*

Of Executive Power[16]

Dependence of the President.—Elective and accountable.—
Free in his sphere; the Senate oversees him and does not direct
him.—The salary of the President fixed at his entry into
office.—Qualified veto.

The American law-makers had a difficult task to fulfill: they wanted to create an executive power that depended on the majority and yet was strong enough by itself to act freely in its sphere.[x]

The maintenance of the republican form required that the representative of the executive power be subject to the national will.

The President is an elective magistrate. His honor, goods, liberty, life answer continually to the people for the good use that he will make of his power. While exercising his power, moreover, he is not completely independent. The Senate watches over him in his relations with foreign powers, as well as in the distribution of positions; so he can be neither corrupted nor corrupt.

The law-makers of the Union recognized that the executive power could not fulfill its task usefully and with dignity, if they did not succeed in giving it more stability and strength than it had been granted in the particular states.

---

16. Federalist, *Nos. 67–77, inclusive. Constitution, art. 2. Story* [Commentaries *(ed.)*], p. 315, pp. 515–80. Kent's Commentaries *[vol. I (ed.)]*, p. 255 [235 *(ed.)*].

x. The President and in general the executive power of the Union./
  Some advantages of a strong executive power:

1. It executes the *constitutional* desires of the legislatures with more skill and sagacity than they would be able to do themselves.
2. It is a barrier against the abuse of their power; it prevents their omnipotence from degenerating into tyranny (see, on the subject of the requisite conditions for the creation of a sufficient executive power, the *Federalist*, pp. 301 and 316 [No. 70 (ed.)]).

To divide the executive power, to subordinate its movements to the desires of a council, is to diminish its accountability.

It was necessary to liberty that the President depended on the national will. He is elective, not inviolable (YTC, CVh, 1, p. 53).

The President was named for four years and could be re-elected. With a future, he had the courage to work for the public good and the means to implement it.

The President was made the one and only representative of the executive power of the Union. Care was even taken not to subordinate his will to those of a council: a dangerous measure that, while weakening the action of the government, lessens the accountability of those who govern. The Senate has the right to strike down some of the acts of the President, but it can neither force him to act, nor share the executive power with him.

The action of the legislature on the executive power can be direct; we have just seen that the Americans took care that it was not. It can also be indirect.

The chambers, by depriving the public official of his salary, take away a part of his independence; it must be feared that, masters of making laws, they will little by little take away the portion of power that the Constitution wanted to keep for him.

This dependence of the executive power is one of the vices inherent in republican constitutions. The Americans have not been able to destroy the inclination that leads legislative assemblies to take hold of government,[y] but they have made this inclination less irresistible.

---

y. In the manuscript: "The Americans have not been able to destroy the inclination [v: tendency], but they have made it less irresistible [v: rapid]."
Gustave de Beaumont:

On this page there is an error of style. *Executive power* is taken here in a double sense; first, as presenting the idea of the persons who govern, and then, as including the idea of the administration itself. This word can indeed be used in this double sense, but not in places so close together, because it sows confusion in the mind. That is so true that, when we read: The Americans have not been able to destroy the inclination to drag the *executive power* into the legislative assemblies . . . , we think we are going to see the President of the United States brought into the House of Representatives, because you were speaking about him a moment before under the name executive power. This is certainly not the thought of the author, since he means, on the contrary, that the legislative assemblies are always led toward taking hold of the executive power. I would put: *The Americans have not been able to destroy the inclination that leads legislative assemblies to take hold of power, but . . .* " (YTC, CIIIb, 3, pp. 51–52).

The salary of the President is fixed, at his entry into office, for the entire time that his leadership lasts. In addition, the President is armed with a qualified veto that permits him to stop the passage of laws that would be able to destroy the portion of independence that the constitution left to him. There can only be an unequal struggle, however, between the President and the legislature, since the latter, by persevering in its intentions, always has the power to overcome the resistance that opposes it. But the qualified veto at least forces it to retrace its steps; it forces the legislature to consider the question again; and this time, it can no longer decide except with a two-thirds majority of those voting. The veto, moreover, is a kind of appeal to the people; the executive power pleads its cause and makes its reasons heard. Without this guarantee, it could be oppressed in secret. But if the legislature perseveres in its intentions, can it not always overcome the resistance that opposes it? To that I will answer that in the constitution of all peoples, no matter what its nature, there is a point where the law-maker is obliged to rely on the good sense and virtue of the citizens. This point is closer and more visible in republics, more removed and more carefully hidden in monarchies; but it is always found somewhere. There is no country where the law can foresee everything and where the institutions must take the place of reason and mores.

How the Position of the President of the United States Differs from That of a Constitutional King in France

The executive power, in the United States, limited and exceptional, like the sovereignty in the name of which it acts.—The executive power in France extends to everything, like the sovereignty there.—The King is one of the authors of the law.—The President is only the executor of the law.—Other differences that arise from the duration of the two powers.—The President hampered in the sphere of executive power.—The King is free there.—France, despite these differences, resembles a republic more than the Union does a monarchy.—Comparison of the number of officials who depend on the executive power in the two countries.

The executive power plays such a great role in the destiny of nations that I want to stop for an instant here in order to explain better what place it occupies among the Americans.

In order to conceive a clear and precise idea of the position of the President of the United States, it is useful to compare it to that of the King in one of the constitutional monarchies of Europe.[z]

---

z. Dissimilarity and similarity between the President and the King of England. *Federalist*, pp. 295 and 300 [No. 69 (ed.)].

America.
1. Elective magistrate.
2. Subject to the courts, accountable.
3. Qualified veto.
4. Commands the militia, but only in time of war.
5. Cannot pardon in case of impeachment.
6. He cannot *adjourn* the legislature except in a case allowed.
7. He can make treaties only with two-thirds of the Senate.
8. He can only appoint to office with the advice and consent of the Senate.
9. He can prescribe no rule concerning commerce and monetary system of the country.
10. He has no ecclesiastical jurisdiction whatsoever.

In this comparison, I will attach little importance to the external signs of power; they fool the observer more than they help.

When a monarchy is gradually transformed into a republic, the executive power there keeps titles, honors, respect, and even money, long after it has lost the reality of power. The English, after having cut off the head of one of their kings and having chased another from the throne, still knelt to speak to the successors of these princes.

On the other hand, when republics fall under the yoke of one man, power continues to appear simple, plain and modest in its manners, as if it had not already risen above everyone. When the emperors despotically disposed of the fortune and the life of their citizens, they were still called Caesar when spoken to, and they went informally to have supper at the homes of their friends.

So we must abandon the surface and penetrate deeper.

Sovereignty, in the United States, is divided between the Union and the states; while among us, it is one and compact. From that arises the first and greatest difference that I notice between the President of the United States and the King in France.

In the United States, executive power is limited and exceptional,[a] like

---

England.
1. Hereditary.
2. Inviolable.
3. Absolute veto.
4. At all times and throughout the kingdom.
5. In all cases.
6. He can always *prorogue* and *dissolve* Parliament.
7. He alone makes treaties. He is the only representative of England abroad.
8. He appoints to all offices, even creates offices, and beyond that can confer a multitude of graces, either *honorary* or *lucrative.*
9. On certain points he is the arbiter of commerce; he can establish markets, regulate weights and measures, strike money, set an embargo.
10. He is the head of the national church (YTC, CVh, 1, pp. 58–59).

a. Édouard de Tocqueville:

How is the sovereignty represented by the executive power (that is the national sovereignty) limited and exceptional? That can only be applied to the executive power, which is in fact very limited.

Upon reflection, I understand the thought. As we saw in the preceding chapter,

the very sovereignty in whose name it acts; in France, it extends to everything, like the sovereignty there.

The Americans have a federal government; we have a national government.

This is a primary cause of inferiority that results from the very nature of things; but it is not the only one. The second in importance is this: strictly speaking, sovereignty can be defined as the right to make laws.

The King, in France, really constitutes one part of the sovereign power, since laws do not exist if he refuses to sanction them. In addition, he executes the law.

The President also executes the law, but he does not really take part in making the law, since, by refusing his consent, he cannot prevent it from existing. So he is not part of the sovereign power; he is only its agent.

Not only does the King, in France, constitute one portion of the sovereign power, but he also participates in the formation of the legislature, which is the other portion. He participates by naming the members of one chamber and by ending at his will the term of the mandate of the other. The President of the United States takes no part in the composition of the legislative body and cannot dissolve it.

The King shares with the Chambers the right to propose laws.

The President has no similar initiative.

The King is represented, within the Chambers, by a certain number of agents who set forth his views, uphold his opinions and make his maxims of government prevail.

The President has no entry into Congress; his ministers are excluded as he is, and it is only by indirect pathways that he makes his influence and his opinion penetrate this great body.

---

the Union was granted, by the Constitution, only a limited power, very defined and perhaps exceptional. But, it seems to me, the President does not represent only this portion of sovereignty that has been attributed to the federal government; he also represents the entire sovereignty of the country, its internal as well as external will; in a word, he is the instrument of national sovereignty (YTC, CIIIb, 3, pp. 1–2).

So the King of France operates as an equal with the legislature, which cannot act without him, as he cannot act without it.

The President is placed beside the legislature, as an inferior and dependent power.

In the exercise of executive power strictly speaking, the point on which his position seems closest to that of the King in France, the President still remains inferior due to several very great causes.

First, the power of the King in France has the advantage of duration over that of the President. Now, duration is one of the first elements of strength. Only what must exist for a long time is loved and feared.

The President of the United States is a magistrate elected for four years. The King in France is a hereditary leader.

In the exercise of executive power, the President of the United States is constantly subject to jealous oversight. He prepares treaties, but he does not make them; he designates people for offices, but he does not appoint them.[17]

The King of France is the absolute master in the sphere of executive power.

The President of the United States is accountable for his actions. French law says that the person of the King of France is inviolable.

But above the one as above the other stands a ruling power, that of public opinion. This power is less defined in France than in the United States; less recognized, less formulated in the laws; but, in fact, it exists there. In America, it proceeds by elections and by decisions; in France, by revolutions. Hence France and the United States, despite the diversity of their constitutions, have this point in common: public opinion is, in effect, the dominant power.[b] So the generative principle of the laws is, in actual fact, the

---

17. *The Constitution had left it doubtful whether the President was required to ask the advice of the Senate in the case of removal, as in the case of nomination of a federal official. The* Federalist, *in No. 77, seemed to establish the affirmative; but in 1789, Congress decided with all good reason that, since the President was accountable, he could not be forced to use agents that did not have his confidence. See Kent's* Commentaries, *vol. I, p. 289.*

b. In the margin: "≠This fact, the sovereignty of the people, the capital point common to the two countries, gives a similarity to their constitutions despite the diversity of the laws.≠"

same among the two peoples, although its developments are more or less free, and the consequences that are drawn from it are often different. This principle, by its nature, is essentially republican. Consequently, I think that France, with its King, resembles a republic more than the Union, with its President, resembles a monarchy.

In all that precedes, I have been careful to point out only the main points of difference. If I had wanted to get into details, the picture would have been still more striking. But I have too much to say not to want to be brief.

I remarked that the power of the President of the United States, in his sphere, exercises only a limited sovereignty, while that of the King, in France, acts within the circle of a complete sovereignty.

I could have shown the governmental power of the King in France surpassing even its natural limits, however extensive they were, and penetrating into the administration of individual interests in a thousand ways.

To this cause of influence, I could join that which results from the great number of public officials, nearly all of whom owe their mandate to the executive power. This number has surpassed all known limits among us; it reaches 138,000.[18] Each of these 138,000 nominations must be considered as an element of strength. The President does not have an absolute right to appoint to public positions, and those positions hardly exceed 12,000.[19]

18. *The sums paid by the State to these various officials amount annually to 200,000,000 francs.*

19. *Each year in the United States an almanac, called the* National Calendar, *is published; the names of all the federal officials are found there. The* National Calendar *of 1833 furnished me with the figure I give here.*

It would follow from what precedes that the King of France has at his disposal eleven times more places than the President of the United States, although the population of France is only one and a half times greater than that of the Union.

Accidental Causes That Can Increase
the Influence of the Executive Power

External security that the Union enjoys.—Cautious policy.—
Army of 6,000 soldiers.—Only a few ships.—The President
possesses some great prerogatives that he does not have the
opportunity to use.—In what he does have the opportunity
to execute, he is weak.

If the executive power is less strong in America than in France, the cause must be attributed to circumstances perhaps more than to laws.

It is principally in its relations with foreigners that the executive power of a nation finds the opportunity to deploy skill and force.

If the life of the Union were constantly threatened, if its great interests were found involved daily in those of other powerful peoples, you would see the executive power grow in opinion by what would be expected of it and by what it would execute.

The President of the United States is, it is true, the head of the army, but this army is composed of 6,000 soldiers;[c] he commands the fleet, but the fleet numbers only a few vessels; he directs the foreign affairs of the Union, but the United States has no neighbors. Separated from the rest of the world by the ocean, still too weak to want to dominate the sea, they have no enemies; and their interests are only rarely in contact with those of the other nations of the globe.

This demonstrates well that the practice of government must not be judged by theory.

The President of the United States possesses some nearly royal prerogatives that he does not have the opportunity to use; and the rights that, up to now, he is able to use are very circumscribed. The laws allow him to be strong; circumstances keep him weak.

On the contrary, circumstances, still more than the laws, give royal authority in France its greatest strength.

---

c. 4,000 in the manuscript.

In France, the executive power struggles constantly against immense obstacles and disposes of immense resources to overcome them. It increases with the greatness of the things that it executes and with the importance of the events that it directs, without thereby modifying its constitution.

Had the laws created it as weak and as circumscribed as that of the Union, its influence would soon become very much greater.

Why the President of the United States, to Lead Public Affairs, Does Not Need to Have a Majority in the Chambers

It is an established axiom in Europe that a constitutional King cannot govern when the opinion of the legislative chambers is not in agreement with his.

Several Presidents of the United States have been seen to lose the support of the majority of the legislative body, without having to leave power, nor without causing any great harm to society.

I have heard this fact cited to prove the independence and strength of the executive power in America. A few moments of reflection are sufficient, on the contrary, to see there the proof of its weakness.

A European King needs to obtain the support of the legislative body to fulfill the task that the constitution imposes on him, because this task is immense. A European constitutional King is not only the executor of the law; the care of its execution so completely devolves onto him that, if the law is against him, he would be able to paralyze its force. He needs the chambers to make the law; the chambers need him to execute it; they are two powers that cannot live without each other; the gears of government stop at the moment when there is discord between them.

In America, the President cannot stop the making of laws; he cannot escape the obligation to execute them. His zealous and sincere support is undoubtedly useful, but it is not necessary to the course of government. In everything essential that he does, he is directly or indirectly subject to the legislature; where he is entirely independent of it, he can hardly do anything. So it is his weakness, and not his strength, that allows him to live in opposition to the legislative power.

In Europe, there must be agreement between the King and the Chambers, because there can be a serious struggle between them. In America, agreement is not required, because the struggle is impossible.

Of the Election of the President

The danger of the system of election increases in proportion to the extent of the prerogatives of the executive power.—The Americans can adopt this system because they can do without a strong executive power.—How circumstances favor the establishment of the elective system.—Why the election of the President does not make the principles of government change.— Influence that the election of the President exercises on the fate of secondary officials.

The system of election, applied to the head of the executive power among a great people, presents some dangers that experience and historians have sufficiently pointed out.

Consequently, I do not want to talk about it except in relation to America.

The dangers feared from the system of election are more or less great, depending on the place that the executive power occupies and its importance in the State, depending on the method of election and the circumstances in which the people who elect are found.

Not without reason, the elective system, applied to the head of State, is criticized for offering such a great lure to individual ambitions and inflaming them so strongly in the pursuit of power that often, when legal means are no longer sufficient, they appeal to force when right happens to desert them.

It is clear that the greater the prerogatives of the executive power, the greater the lure; also, the more the ambition of the pretenders is excited, the more it finds support among a host of men of lesser ambition who hope to share power after their candidate has triumphed.[d]

d. The wording of this paragraph is a bit different in the manuscript. The published version was suggested by Beaumont (YTC, CIIIb, 3, pp. 52–53).

The dangers of the elective system increase therefore in direct proportion to the influence exercised by the executive power in the affairs of the State.

The Polish revolutions should not be attributed only to the elective system in general, but to the fact that the elected magistrate was the head of a large monarchy.[e]

So before discussing the absolute goodness of the elective system, there is always an intervening question to resolve, that of knowing if the geographic position, laws, habits, mores and opinions of the people among whom you want to introduce it allow you to establish a weak and dependent executive power. To want the representative of the State to be simultaneously armed with great power and elected is, to my mind, to express two contradictory desires. For my part, I know only one way to make hereditary royalty change to a state of elected power. Its sphere of action must be contracted in advance; its prerogatives gradually reduced; and little by little, the people accustomed to living without its aid. But the republicans of Europe are hardly concerned with this. Since many among them hate tyranny only because they are the objects of its rigors, the extent of executive power does not offend them; they attack only its origin, without noticing the tight bond that links these two things.

No one has yet been found who cared about risking his honor and his life to become President of the United States, because the President has only a temporary, limited and dependent power. Fortune must put an immense prize at stake in order for desperate players to enter the lists. [≠For my part, I would prefer to be *Premier Ministre* in France than President of the Union.≠] No candidate, until now, has been able to raise ardent sympathies and dangerous popular passions in his favor.[f] The reason is simple. Once at the head of the government,[g] he can distribute to his friends nei-

---

e. Cf. Rousseau, *Considérations sur le gouvernement de Pologne,* chapters VIII and XIV.

f. Hervé de Tocqueville: "Carefully check if this paragraph agrees well with what the author says in the chapters on the crisis [of election] and on re-election. You must be careful about even the appearance of contradiction. Later you talk about intrigues, about the efforts of the President to get himself re-elected and about the development of his power in this regard" (YTC, CIIIb, 3, p. 13).

g. In the manuscript: ". . . the President has only a few places . . ."

Hervé de Tocqueville: "These sentences are in clear opposition to what the author

ther much power, nor much wealth, nor much glory; and his influence in the State[h] is too weak for factions to see their success or their ruin in his elevation to power.

Hereditary monarchies have a great advantage. Since the particular interest of a family is continually tied in a close way to the interest of the State, there is never a single moment when the latter is left abandoned to itself. I do not know if in these monarchies public affairs are better conducted than elsewhere; but at least there is always someone who takes charge for good or ill, depending on his capacity.[j]

In elective States, on the contrary, at the approach of the election and a long time before it happens, the gears of government no longer function, in a way, except by themselves. The laws can undoubtedly be put together so that the election takes place at one go and rapidly, and the seat of executive power never remains vacant so to speak; but no matter what is done, an empty place exists mentally despite the efforts of the law-maker.

At the approach of the election, the head of the executive power thinks only of the struggle to come; he no longer has a future; he can undertake nothing, and pursues only languidly what someone else perhaps is going to achieve. "I am so near the moment of my retirement," wrote President Jefferson on 21 [28 (ed.)] January 1809 (six weeks before the election), "that I no longer take part in public affairs except by expressing my opinion. To me, it seems just to leave to my successor the initiation of measures that he will have to execute and for which he will have to bear responsibility."

On its side, the nation has its eyes focused only on a single point; it is occupied only with overseeing the birth about to take place.

---

says on pages 346 and 347. Moreover, can one say that a man has only a few places to distribute when 20,000 nominations depend on him in a machine as simple as the American organization?" (YTC, CIIIb, 3, p. 14).

h. Cf. non-alphabetic notebook 1, conversation with John (?) Livingston (YTC, BIIa, and *Voyage, OC,* V, 1, p. 60).

j. "In France, for society to work, social power must be not only *centralized,* but also *stable.*

"Power can be centralized in an assembly; then it is *strong,* but not *stable.* It can be centralized in a man. Then it is less strong, but more stable" (YTC, Cve, p. 64).

The more vast the place occupied by the executive power in the leadership of public affairs, the greater and more necessary is its habitual action, and the more dangerous such a state of things is. Among a people who have contracted the habit of being governed by the executive power, and with even more reason, of being administered by it, election cannot help but produce a profound disturbance.

In the United States, the action of the executive power can slow down with impunity, because this action is weak and circumscribed.

When the head of government is elected, a lack of stability in the internal and external policies of the State almost always follows. That is one of the principal vices of this system.

But this vice is felt more or less, depending on the portion of power granted to the elected magistrate. In Rome, the principles of government never varied, although the consuls were changed annually, because the Senate was the directing power; and the Senate was an hereditary body. In most of the monarchies of Europe, if the King were elected, the kingdom would change faces with each new choice.

In America, the President exercises a fairly great influence on affairs of State, but he does not conduct them; the preponderant power resides in the whole national representation. Therefore, the mass of people must be changed, and not only the President, in order for the maxims of policy to change. Consequently, in America, the system of election, applied to the head of the executive power, does not harm the steadiness of government in a very tangible way.

The lack of steadiness is an evil so inherent in the elective system, moreover, that it still makes itself keenly felt in the President's sphere of action, no matter how circumscribed.

Mr. Quincy Adams, when he took power, dismissed most of those appointed by his predecessor; and of all the removable officials that the federal administration uses, I do not know of a single one who was left in office by General Jackson in the first year that followed the election.[k]

k. This paragraph, which does not appear in the manuscript, is included in the edition of 1835 and eliminated from the sixth and later editions, following a letter from John Quincy Adams, dated June 12, 1837:

The Americans thought correctly that the head of the executive power, in order to fulfill his mission and bear the weight of full responsibility, had to remain free, as much as possible, to choose his agents himself and to remove them at will;[m] the legislative body watches over rather than directs

---

The truth is that I never dismissed a single individual named by my predecessor. It was a principle of my administration to dismiss no person from office but for misconduct, and there were in the course of four years that I presided, only two persons dismissed from civil executive office, both of them for gross official misdemeanors. My successor it is true did pursue a different principle. He dismissed many subordinate officer executive [*sic*] not however so generally as the remainder of the paragraph in your book, which I have cited, supposes. He left in office many of those who had been appointed by his predecessors, and would probably have left many more but for the influences by which he was surrounded (YTC, CId).

On December 4, 1837, Tocqueville answers from Paris:

I receive with great pleasure the complaint that you very much wanted to address to me relating to a sentence in my book that concerns you. You can be assured that this sentence will disappear in the sixth edition which is supposed to appear, I believe, this winter. I am delighted that you have given me this occasion to please you and to correct an error that I regret having made. The fact you complain about and that you say is inaccurate had been affirmed to me in America itself (my notes prove it) by a man on whose veracity I thought I could count (YTC, CId, and *OC*, VII, pp. 67–68). See, in the non-alphabetic notebooks 2 and 3, the second conversation with Mr. Walker (YTC, BIIa, and *Voyage, OC*, V, 1, p. 130).

m. In the manuscript:

The legislative body therefore interferes only very little in the choices of men to whom public positions are entrusted. It limits itself to supervising the President; it does not direct him. What is the result? At each election, a complete replacement takes place in the federal administration. [In the margin: This happened only under Quincy Adams and under Jackson.] There is not an employee so lowly who can claim to escape from the result of the vote. His place belongs in advance to the friends of the new power. People in the constitutional monarchies of Europe complain about seeing the fate of the secondary employees of the administration depend on the fate of the ministers. It is still much worse in States where the head of government is elected. Of the [blank (ed.)] revocable officials employed by the federal administration, I do not think that there was a single one that General Jackson left in place the first year that followed his election. The reason for this difference is easily understood. In monarchies, the ministers, in order to come to power and remain there, have no need to extend the circle of their influence very far; as long as they obtain the majority in the chambers, it is enough. But to bring about his election or reelection, the President needs to reach the popular masses; and in order to succeed in that, he must not neglect the President. From that it follows that at each new election, the fate of all federal employees is as if in suspense.

---

a single means of action. Each election, therefore, brings to public affairs a new administration whose education is completed at the expense of the administered. As for the individual misfortunes that result . . .

(In the margin) *False,* for to bring about election and reelection of the deputies, the ministers need the same means.

Hervé de Tocqueville:

Here is a piece that Alexis proposes to delete. But it contains views and a fact worth keeping; perhaps it could be modified in the following way:

After the sentence: *The legislative body therefore interferes only very little in,* I would like a short note that explained how the legislative body intervenes in nominations. The flaw in this explanation is that something is missing.

A complete replacement takes place in the administration. Here a note at the bottom of the page where you will say that, because this replacement has taken place at the election of the last two Presidents, it may be believed that this precedent will be followed by their successors (YTC, CIIIb, 3, p. 14).

Gustave de Beaumont:

I would very much hesitate to delete the piece crossed out. Possibly it contains some ideas and opinions that need to be revised and modified. But as a whole it is very interesting and will be especially for the public, because it touches on a question *extremely exciting* to the *personal interests* of all public officials.

The contrast between the President and the ministers does not exist; they are in an analogous position in the sense that the ministers of a French monarchy have an interest in bringing their weight to bear on the least agents, in order to gain the majority in the chambers from the electoral body. And they cannot remain ministers if they do not have this majority, just as the President will not be elected if he does not gain it.

But here is the difference: a minister cannot think of dismissing everyone in order to remain minister; and if he wanted to do it, he would not be able to do so. Because public opinion, on which he depends, would never understand that the *end* justified the *means.* It is the opposite when it is a matter, for a man, of being head of the State (YTC, CIIIb, 3, pp. 53–54).

Édouard de Tocqueville:

Whatever your decision regarding this piece, I will make several observations; first this sentence: *to remove them at will* is trite. But the most serious flaw in this piece is to present a striking contradiction to what you said a few sentences earlier. Here you say that all the employees are replaced at the coming into office of the President and that he is obligated, in the machinery he puts in motion, *to reach the popular masses,* without neglecting a *single means of action.* While you say, p. 324, that no one cares about *risking his honor and his life to become President,* that no candidate

In the constitutional monarchies of Europe, the complaint is that the destiny of the obscure agents of the administration often depends on the fate of the ministers. It is even worse in States where the head of government is elected. The reason for this is simple. In constitutional monarchies, ministers replace each other rapidly; but the principal representative of the executive power never changes, which contains the spirit of innovation within certain limits. So administrative systems there vary in the details rather than in the principles; one cannot be suddenly substituted for another without causing a kind of revolution. In America, this revolution takes place every four years in the name of law.

As for the individual misfortunes that are the natural consequence of such legislation, it must be admitted that the lack of stability in the lot of officials does not produce in America the evils that would be expected elsewhere. In the United States, it is so easy to make an independent living that to remove an official from an office that he holds sometimes means taking away the comforts of life, but never the means to sustain it.

I said at the beginning of this chapter that the dangers of the mode of election, applied to the head of the executive power, were more or less great, depending on the circumstances in which the people who elect are found.

Efforts to reduce the role of the executive power are made in vain. There is something over which this power exercises a great influence, whatever the place that the laws have given it. That is foreign policy; a negotiation can hardly be started and successfully carried through except by a single man. [{Physical force can only be adequately put in motion [v: directed] by a single will.}]

The more precarious and perilous the position of a people, the more the need for consistency and stability makes itself felt in the direction of foreign

---

has been able to raise *ardent sympathies in his favor* and that he can attach to his cause neither *personal interest* nor party interest, that he has only a few *places* to distribute *to his friends.*

How then do you say afterwards, p. 330, that *the place of the lowliest employee belongs in advance to the friends of the new power,* and that General Jackson did not leave a single official in place? And again, page 346, *the positions he has at his disposal,* etc. (YTC, CIIIb, 3, p. 3).

affairs, and the more dangerous the system of election of the head of State becomes.

The policy of the Americans in relation to the whole world is simple; you would almost be able to say that no one needs them, and that they need no one. Their independence is never threatened.

So among them, the role of executive power is as limited by circumstances as by laws. The President can frequently change his views without having the State suffer or perish.

Whatever the prerogatives with which the executive power is vested, the time that immediately precedes the election and the time while it is taking place can always be considered as a period of national crisis.

The more the internal situation of a country is troubled and the greater its external perils, the more dangerous this moment of crisis is for it. Among the peoples of Europe, there are very few who would not have to fear conquest or anarchy every time that they chose a new leader.

In America, society is so constituted that it can maintain itself on its own and without help; external dangers are never pressing. The election of the President is a cause for agitation, not for ruin.

Mode of Election

Skill which the American law-makers have demonstrated in the choice of the mode of election.—Creation of a special electoral body.—Separate vote of special electors.—In what case the House of Representatives is called to choose the President.—What has happened in the twelve elections that have taken place since the Constitution has been in force.

Apart from the dangers inherent in the principle, there are many others that arise from the very forms of election and that can be avoided by the care of the law-maker.[n]

---

n. The draft of this passage has been corrected by Gustave de Beaumont (YTC, CIIIb, 3, p. 55).

When a people gather in arms in the public square to choose a leader, it exposes itself not only to the dangers presented by the elective system itself, but also to all those of civil war which arise from such a method of election.

When Polish laws made the choice of the king depend on the *veto* of a single man, they invited the murder of this man or created anarchy in advance.

As you study the institutions of the United States and look more attentively at the political and social situation of this country, you notice a marvelous accord there between fortune and human efforts. America was a new country; but the people who lived there had already long made use of liberty elsewhere: two great causes of internal order. Furthermore, America had no fear of conquest. The American law-makers, taking advantage of these favorable circumstances, had no difficulty in establishing a weak and dependent executive power; having created it so, they could make it elective without risk.

Nothing remained for them to do except to choose, from among the different systems of election, the least dangerous; the rules that they drew up in this respect completed admirably the guarantees that the physical and political constitution of the country already provided.

The problem to solve was to find a mode of election that, while still expressing the real will of the people, little excited their passions and kept the people in the least possible suspense. First, they granted that a *simple* majority would make the law. But it was still very difficult to obtain this majority without having to fear delays that they wanted to avoid above all.

It is rare, in fact, to see a man get the majority of votes on the first try from among a large population. The difficulty increases still more in a republic of confederated states where local influences are much more developed and more powerful.

A way to obviate this second obstacle presented itself: to delegate the electoral powers of the nation to a body that represented it.

This mode of election made a majority more probable; for the fewer the electors, the easier it is for them to agree among themselves. It also presented more guarantees for a good choice.

But should the right to elect be entrusted to the legislative body itself, the usual representative of the nation; or, on the contrary, must an electoral college be formed whose sole purpose would be to proceed to the naming of the President?[o]

The Americans preferred this last option. They thought that the men sent to make ordinary laws would only incompletely represent the wishes of the people relating to the election of the first magistrate. Being elected, moreover, for more than a year, they could represent a will that had already changed. They judged that, if the legislature was charged with electing the head of the executive power, its members would become, long before the election, the objects of corrupting maneuvers and the playthings of intrigue; while special electors, like jurors, would remain unknown in the crowd until the day when they must act and would only appear at one moment to deliver their decision.

So they established that each state would name a certain number of electors,[20] who would in turn elect the President. And, since they had noticed that assemblies charged with choosing heads of government in elective countries inevitably became centers of passions and intrigue, that sometimes they took hold of powers that did not belong to them, and that often their operations, and the uncertainties that followed, lasted long enough to put the State in danger, they decided that the electors would all vote on a set day, but without meeting together.[21]

The mode of election in two stages made a majority probable, but did not guarantee it, for it could be that the electors would differ among themselves as those who named them would have differed.

In this case, the Americans were led necessarily to take one of three measures: it was necessary to have new electors named, or to consult once again those already named, or finally to refer the choice to a new authority.

o. Gustave de Beaumont: "335, 336, 337, 338, etc. . . . All these pages seem excellent to me and I very strongly urge the author not to make the corrections that are advised by *imprudent* friends" (YTC, CIIIb, 3, pp. 55–56).

20. *As many as the members they send to Congress. The number of electors for the election of 1833 was 288 (*The National Calendar *[1833] [p. 19 (ed.)]).*

21. *The electors of the same state meet; but they send to the seat of the central government the list of individual votes and not the result of the majority vote.*

The first two methods, apart from the fact that they were not very certain, led to delays and perpetuated an always dangerous excitement.

So they settled on the third and agreed that the votes of the electors would be transmitted in secret to the president of the Senate. He would count the votes on the day fixed and in the presence of the two houses. If no candidate had gained a majority, the House of Representatives would itself proceed immediately to the election; but they took care to limit its right. The Representatives could only elect one of the three candidates who had obtained the largest number of votes.[22]

As you see, only in a rare case, difficult to foresee in advance, is the election left to the ordinary representatives of the nation; and even then, they can only choose a citizen already designated by a strong minority of the special electors; a happy combination, that reconciles the respect owed to the will of the people with the rapidity of execution and the guarantees of order required by the interest of the State. Yet, by making the House of Representatives decide the question, in case of division, the complete solution of all difficulties had still not been achieved; for the majority in the House of Representatives could in turn be doubtful, and this time the Constitution offered no remedy. But by establishing required candidates, by restricting their number to three, by relying on the choices of some enlightened men, it had smoothed all the obstacles[23] over which it could have some power; the others were inherent in the elective system itself.p

22. *In this circumstance, it is the majority of the states, and not the majority of the members, that decides the question. So that New York does not have more influence on the deliberation than Rhode Island. Thus the citizens of the Union, considered as forming one and the same people, are consulted first; and when they cannot agree, the division by states is revived, and each of the latter is given a separate and independent vote.*

That again is one of the strange things that the federal constitution presents and only the clash of opposing interests can explain.

23. *In 1801, however, Jefferson was named only on the thirty-sixth ballot.*

p. Tocqueville writes to Corcelle:

There is a piece of your work that particularly pleased me a great deal. It is where you indicate, as a remedy for the excesses of democracy, election by stages. In my opinion that is a capital idea that must be introduced very prudently and that is very

During the forty-five years the federal Constitution has existed, the United States has already elected its President twelve times.

Ten elections were done immediately, by the simultaneous vote of the special electors seated at different points of the territory.

The House of Representatives has used the exceptional right with which it is vested in case of division only twice. The first, in 1801, was at the time of the election of Jefferson; and the second, in 1825, when Quincy Adams was named.

Election Crisis

The moment of the election of the President can be considered a moment of national crisis.—Why.—Passions of the people.— Preoccupation of the President.—Calm which follows the agitation of the election.

I have talked about the favorable circumstances in which the United States was found for adopting the elective system, and I have shown the precautions taken by the law-makers to reduce its dangers. The Americans are used to having all kinds of elections. Experience has taught them what level of agitation they can reach and where they must stop. The vast extent of their territory and the distribution of the inhabitants make a collision

---

important to introduce gradually to the thinking of those who love liberty and the equality of men. I firmly believe, without yet saying it as strongly as I think it, that different stages of election form the most powerful and perhaps the only means that democratic peoples have to give the direction of society to the most skillful, without making them independent of everyone else (Letter of October 1835 (?) *Correspondance avec Corcelle, OC,* XV, I, p. 57. Cf. *Souvenirs, OC,* XII, pp. 188–90).

In the report that he did as a member of the Commission charged with the revision of the constitution ("Rapport fait à l'Assemblée législative au nom de la Commission chargée d'examiner les propositions relatives à la révision de la constitution . . . ," *Moniteur Universel,* July 9, 1851, pp. 1943–1945, and *OCB,* IX, pp. 574–606), Tocqueville praises the American system of indirect election of the President. He sees there a way to avoid revolutions as well as the temptation to resort to dictatorship. In a letter of 1853 (partially reproduced in *OCB,* VI, pp. 212–20), he will share with W. R. Greg, English essayist and ardent defender of free trade, extremely lucid views on French electoral laws under the monarchy and the republic.

among the different parties less probable and less perilous than anywhere else. Until now, the political circumstances in which the nation has found itself during elections have not presented any real danger. [<Finally, the power of the President is so dependent and so limited that the passions of the candidates and those of their partisans can never be either very ardent or very long-lasting.>]

But the moment of the election of the President of the United States can still be considered a period of national crisis.

The influence that the President exercises on the course of public affairs is undoubtedly weak and indirect, but it extends over the entire nation; the choice of President has only a moderate importance for each citizen, but it matters to all citizens. Now, an interest, however small, assumes a character of great importance from the moment it becomes a general interest.

Compared to a king of Europe, the President has certainly few means to create partisans for himself; nonetheless, the places he has at his disposal are numerous enough^q for several thousands of the voters to be either directly or indirectly interested in his cause.

In the United States as elsewhere, moreover, parties feel the need to gather around a man, in order to be more easily understood by the crowd. So they generally use the name of the candidate for President as a symbol; in him, they personify their theories. Thus, parties have a great interest in determining the election in their favor, not so much for making their doctrines triumph with the help of the elected President, as for showing, by his election, that these doctrines have won the majority.

Long before the fixed moment arrives, the election becomes the greatest and, so to speak, the sole matter that preoccupies minds. Factions redouble their ardor [the administration finds itself attacked from all directions; {slanders, insults, rantings of all types are thrown lavishly against it}]; all the artificial passions that can be imagined, in a happy and tranquil country, are stirred up at this moment in full view.

---

q. Hervé de Tocqueville: "Check if that agrees with page 324 where it is said: *no candidate, until now, has been able to raise, etc.*" (YTC, CIIIb, 3, p. 15).

On his side, the President is absorbed by the care to defend himself. He no longer governs in the interest of the State, but in that of his re-election; he grovels before the majority; and often, instead of resisting its passions, as his duty requires, he runs ahead of its caprices.

As the election approaches, intrigues become more active; agitation, more intense and more widespread. The citizens divide into several camps, each taking the name of its candidate. The entire nation falls into a feverish state; the election is then the daily story of the public papers, the subject of individual conversations, the goal of all moves, the object of all thoughts, the sole interest of the moment. [≠The danger certainly is more apparent than real.≠]

It is true that as soon as fortune has decided, this ardor dissipates; everything becomes calm, and the river, once overflowing, retreats peacefully to its bed. But shouldn't we be astonished that the storm could arise? [<For the choice that so strongly preoccupied the nation can influence its prosperity and its dreams only in a very indirect way; the passions that arose did not find their source in those real interests and penchants [doubtful reading (ed.)] that so profoundly trouble the human heart [v: society] [v: stirring the deepest levels of the human heart and turning society upside down to be satisfied]. For the election of the President of the United States cannot put into play any of those dangerous human passions that find their source in profound beliefs or in great positive interests.>]

Of the Re-election of the President

When the head of the executive power is eligible for re-election, it is the State itself that schemes and corrupts.—Desire to be re-elected that dominates all the thoughts of the President of the United States.—Disadvantage of re-election, special to America.—The natural vice of democracies is the gradual subservience of all powers to the slightest desires of the majority.—The re-election of the President favors this vice.

Were the law-makers of the United States wrong or right to allow the re-election of the President?[r]

To prevent the head of the executive power from being re-elected seems, at first glance, contrary to reason.[s] We know what influence the talents or character of one man exercise over the destiny of an entire people, especially in difficult circumstances and in times of crisis. Laws that forbid citizens to re-elect their primary magistrate would deny them the best means of ensuring the prosperity of the State or of saving it. You would, moreover, arrive at this bizarre result, that a man would be excluded from the government at the very moment when he would have finally proved that he was capable of governing well.[t]

These reasons are certainly powerful; but can't they be opposed by still stronger ones?[u]

---

r. In the *Souvenirs,* Tocqueville reproaches himself for having supported, in the committee to draft the Constitution of 1848, Beaumont's proposal that urged that a president leaving office not be re-elected. "On this occasion, we both fell into a great error that, I am very afraid, will have very damaging consequences," wrote Tocqueville in March 1851 (*Souvenirs, OC,* XII, p. 190). The impossibility of being re-elected was, we know, one of the reasons that pushed Louis Napoleon to the *coup d'état.*

s. In the margin: "≠Eight years, term indicated by experience.≠" See note y p. 229.

t. In the margin: "≠1. The great end of the laws is to mingle individual interest and State interest.

2. Weakening of the executive power, capital vice to avoid in republics.≠"

u. Variant:

<The great object of the laws [v: of the law-maker] must always be intimately to mingle individual interest and State interest. Certainly laws can never reach such a

Intrigue and corruption are the natural vices of elective governments. But when the head of the State can be re-elected, these vices spread indefinitely and compromise the very existence of the country. When an ordinary candidate wants to succeed by intrigue, his maneuvers can only be

---

degree of perfection, but it can be said that the more difficult it is to separate these two interests, the better the laws.

If the President were not eligible for re-election, he would have only one goal, to leave a great recollection in the memory of men and to return to private life surrounded by the respect as well as the love of his fellow citizens. To obtain this goal, he could hardly follow another path than to govern well; for at the bottom of the human heart, there is a secret instinct that constantly calls out that the approval of the present [v: the sincere approval of contemporaries] and the admiration of posterity belong to virtue alone.

In place of this entirely non-material and distant interest, the American laws have given the President a positive and current interest that, if not contrary to, is at least distinct from that of the State.

The President has naturally two goals to pursue: to govern well and to be re-elected. I know you will stop me here by saying: the two interests are the same, for the only way to be re-elected is to govern well. This argument is far from satisfying to me; it goes back to the argument that the majority is not subject to error, that it has neither prejudice to be flattered nor passions to be inflamed, that favor [added: and intrigue] have no hold on it, a proposition that cannot be sustained and that does not merit the effort to refute. It is incontestable that there are two ways for the President to be re-elected. The first, it is true, consists of governing well, but that is within reach of only great souls. Even then, success is always uncertain. Washington had lost the majority when he voluntarily removed himself from public activities. The second, easier and more within the reach of ordinary minds, is to buy partisans at any cost, to make offices the recompense for services rendered to the President, not to the country, to exploit public power in favor of individual interests, and to turn all laws into a combination of personal and party interests.

It is impossible to examine the ordinary course of public affairs in the United States without noticing that the desire to be re-elected dominates the thoughts of the President, that the entire policy of his administration focuses on this point, that his slightest declarations are subordinated to this end, that above all, as the moment of crisis nears, the interest of the State becomes more and more incidental to him and re-election becomes his principal interest.

By allowing re-election of the President, the Americans introduced intrigue and corruption [v: a new element] into government.>

≠That is still not the most frightening result of the system of re-election. Certain physicians believe that when each man comes into the world, he already has the seed of the illness that one day will kill him. This remark may be applied to government.≠

Each government . . .

extended over a circumscribed space. When, on the contrary, the head of
the State himself gets into the fray, he borrows for his own use the strength
of the government.[v]

In the first case, it is one man with his limited means; in the second, it
is the State itself with its immense resources that schemes and corrupts.

The ordinary citizen who uses reprehensible maneuverings to gain
power can harm public prosperity only in an indirect manner; but if the
representative of the executive power enters the lists, concern for the government becomes, for him, something of secondary interest; the main interest is his election. Negotiations, like laws, are, for him, nothing more
than electoral schemes; positions become recompense for services rendered,
not to the nation, but to its leader. Even if the action of the government
would not always be contrary to the interest of the country, it would at
least no longer serve it. Yet the action of the government is undertaken for
its use alone.

It is impossible to consider the ordinary course of affairs in the United
States, without noticing that the desire to be re-elected dominates the
thoughts of the President; that the entire policy of his administration leads
to this point; that his smallest steps are subordinated to this end; that above
all, as the moment of crisis approaches, individual interest replaces general
interest in his mind.

So the principle of re-election makes the corrupting influence of elective
government more widespread and more dangerous. It tends to degrade the
political morality of the people and to replace patriotism with cleverness.

In America, it attacks the sources of national existence even more
fundamentally.

Every government carries within itself a natural vice that seems attached
to the very principle of its life; the genius of the law-maker is to discern

---

v. Hervé de Tocqueville: "Isn't Alexis drawing too excited a picture there, relative to
what precedes? He tried hard in several places to show us that the President has only
limited means at his disposal. Here he exalts his strength and his immense resources.
Perhaps the imagination of the author has sought to prove too much, for fear of not
proving enough" (YTC, CIIIb, 3, p. 16).

this well.ʷ A State can overcome many bad laws, and the evil they cause is often exaggerated. But every law whose effect is to develop this seed of death cannot miss becoming fatal in the long run, even if its bad effects do not immediately make themselves felt.

The principle of ruin in absolute monarchies is the unlimited and unreasonable expansion of royal power. A measure that removes the counterweight that the constitution left to this power would therefore be radically bad, even if its effects seemed unnoticeable for a long time.

In the same way, in countries where democracy governs and where the people constantly draw everything to themselves, laws which make their action more and more immediate and irresistible attack, in a direct way, the existence of the government.

The greatest merit of the American law-makers is to have seen this truth clearly and to have had the courage to put it into practice. [{The greatest glory of this people is to have known how to appreciate it and to submit themselves to it.}]

They understood that beyond the people there needed to be a certain number of powers that, without being completely independent of the people, nonetheless enjoyed in their sphere a fairly large degree of liberty; so, though forced to obey the permanent direction of the majority, they could nevertheless struggle against its caprices and refuse its dangerous demands.

To this effect, they concentrated all the executive power of the nation in one pair of hands; they gave the President extensive prerogatives, and armed him with a veto, to resist the encroachments of the legislature.ˣ

---

w. Cf. Montesquieu, *De l'esprit des lois,* particularly books II and VIII.

x. Hervé de Tocqueville:

This locution seems contradictory to what has been said and repeated earlier about the slight power of the President. Isn't it to be feared that Alexis will be accused of reducing or augmenting this power as his theory requires? Perhaps this chapter has the fault of not coming to a conclusion. It is clear that the author blames re-election, and I believe he is right. What would he want in its place? Four years in office are very few.

Édouard de Tocqueville:

It doesn't seem to me that there is a contradiction here. They armed the President with great power and *took from him the will to make use of it.* That is why this power, strong in appearance, is weak in reality.

But by introducing the principle of re-election, they have partially destroyed their work. They have granted great power to the President, and have taken from him the will to use it.

Not re-eligible, the President was not independent of the people, for he did not cease being responsible to them; but the favor of the people was not so necessary to him that he had to bend in all cases to their will.

Re-eligible (and this is true above all in our time when political morality is becoming lax and when men of great character are disappearing), the President of the United States is only a docile instrument in the hands of the majority. He loves what it loves, hates what it hates; he flies ahead of its will, anticipates its complaints, bends before its slightest desires. The law-makers wanted him to lead the majority, and he follows it.

Thus, in order not to deprive the State of the talents of one man, they have rendered his talents almost useless; and to arrange for a resource in extraordinary circumstances, they have exposed the country to daily dangers.[y]

Of the Federal Courts[24]

Political importance of the judicial power in the United States.—Difficulty in treating this subject.—Utility of the judicial system in confederations.—What courts could the Union

---

Everything has its advantages and disadvantages. Here Alexis presents those of the principle of election, without claiming, by doing so, that it must be destroyed (YTC, CIIIb, 3, pp. 17–18).

y. "In my opinion the President of the United States should be chosen for a longer term and not be re-eligible" (YTC, CVh, 1, p. 58).

24. *See ch. VI entitled* "Of the Judicial Power in the United States." *This chapter shows the general principles of the Americans in the matter of the judicial system. Also see the federal Constitution, art. 3.*

See the work with the title: The Federalist, *Nos. 78–83 inclusive.* Constitutional Law, Being a View of the Practice and Jurisdiction of the Courts of the United States, *by Thomas Sergeant.*

*See Story [*Commentaries *(ed.)], pp. 134–62, 489–511, 581–668. See the organic law of September 24, 1789, in the collection entitled:* Laws of the United States, *by Story, vol. I, p. 53.*

[Kent's Commentaries, *vol. I, p. 275 [273 (ed.)] and following.]*

use?—Necessity of establishing federal courts of justice.—
Organization of the federal judicial system.—The Supreme
Court.—How it differs from all the courts of justice that we know.

I have examined the legislative power and the executive power of the Union. It still remains for me to consider the judicial power.

Here I must reveal my fears to readers.

The judicial institutions exercise a great influence on the destiny of the Anglo-Americans; they hold a very important place among political institutions properly so called. From this point of view, they particularly merit our attention.

But how to make the political action of the American courts understood, without entering into some of the technical details of their constitution and of their forms; and how to get into the details without discouraging, by the natural dryness of such a subject, the curiosity of the reader? How to remain clear and still be concise?

[<So I have said only what I believed indispensable for someone to judge the political action of courts within the confederation.> So often, I have assumed the reader's pre-existent ideas on the administration of justice among the people of the English race; even more often I counted on him searching in the sources that I point out in order to fill out my ideas. In a word, I have said only what I believed indispensable for someone to be able to understand the political action of the federal courts.]

I do not flatter myself that I have escaped these different dangers. Men of the world will still find that I go on too long; legal specialists will think that I am too brief. But that is a disadvantage connected to my subject in general and to the special matter that I am treating at this moment.

The greatest difficulty was not to know how the federal government would be constituted, but how obedience to its laws would be assured.

Governments generally have only two means to overcome the efforts of the governed to resist them: the physical force that they find within themselves; the moral force that the decisions of the courts bestow on them.

A government that would have only war to enforce obedience to its laws would be very close to its ruin. One of two things would probably happen to it. If it were weak and moderate, it would use force only at the last extremity and would let a host of incidents of partial disobedience go by unnoticed; then the State would fall little by little into anarchy.

If it were audacious and powerful, it would resort daily to the use of violence, and soon you would see it degenerate into pure military despotism. Its inaction and its action would be equally harmful to the governed.

The great object of justice is to substitute the idea of law for that of violence; to place intermediaries between the government and the use of physical force.

The power of opinion generally granted by men to the intervention of the courts is something surprising. This power is so great that it is still attached to judicial form when the substance no longer exists; it gives flesh to the shadow.

The moral force with which the courts are vested renders the use of physical force infinitely rarer, substituting for it in most cases; and when, finally, physical force must be exerted, its power is doubled by the moral force that is joined with it.

A federal government, more than another government, must desire to obtain the support of the judicial system, because it is weaker by its nature; and efforts at resistance can more easily be organized against it.[25] If it always and immediately had to resort to the use of force, it would not be adequate to its task.[z]

---

25. *It is federal laws that most need courts, and yet federal laws have least accepted them. The cause is that most confederations have been formed by independent states that had no real intention of obeying the central government; and, while giving it the right to command, they carefully reserved to themselves the ability to disobey.*

z. The great interest of the law-maker is to substitute as many intermediaries as possible between man and the use of physical force. All men have known propensities, based on known needs, interests and passions. The natural inclination of man will always be to gain for himself what he desires, or to avoid what displeases him, by the shortest and most effective of all means: physical force. It does not depend on the laws to prevent men, absolutely and in all cases, from using physical force. But it does depend on them to reduce the occasions greatly. For that, the *legal* means of action and of resistance must be multiplied. Reduced in this way to using force only in extremely rare circumstances, or for satisfying clearly evil passions, man will renounce the use of *violence* almost completely. That is why, where the agents of the administration are *open to attack* before the courts, administrative power is more respected within the circle of its attributions, and revolts are more rare.

To make citizens obey its laws, or to repel the aggressions that would be directed against it, the Union therefore had a particular need for courts.

But what courts could it use? Each state already had a judicial power organized within it. Would it be necessary to resort to these courts? Would it be necessary to create a federal judicial system? It is easy to prove that the Union could not adapt to its use the judicial power established in the states.

It is undoubtedly important to the security of each person and to the liberty of all that the judicial power should be separated from all the others; but it is no less necessary to national existence that the different powers of the State have the same origin, follow the same principles and act in the same sphere, in a word, that they are *correlative* and *homogeneous.* No one, I imagine, has ever thought to have crimes committed in France judged by foreign courts in order to be more certain of the impartiality of the magistrates.

The Americans form only a single people, in relation to their federal government. But in the midst of this people, political bodies, dependent on the national government on certain points and independent on all the others, have been allowed to continue to exist; they have their particular origins, their own doctrines and their special means of action. To entrust the enforcement of the laws of the Union to courts instituted by these political bodies, was to deliver the nation to foreign judges.

When the American Union had only ≠war to make the different states obey, it was not obeyed at all; and if the Union had wanted to be, it would have enveloped America in a series of violent scenes. From the moment when it was able to use the courts [text interrupted (ed.)]≠ There is such a social state[1] where power, to exist, needs the prompt and passive obedience of its agents. (This is the case of several European nations.) Then, it avoids the legal impediments that would hamper its march and prefers to risk insurrections more than trials. But the closer you get to this situation, the further you get from civilization. In Turkey, where there is only a single intermediary between obedience and revolt, either you submit to the Sultan or you strangle him.

1. There are governments for which the rapidity of enforcement is a condition of life (YTC, CVb, pp. 21–22).

Cf. note m for p. 90, where Hervé de Tocqueville also refers to strangling the Sultan of Turkey. For Montesquieu and his entire period, the government of this country was the best possible example of oriental despotism.

Even more, each state is not only a foreigner in relation to the Union, but it is also a daily adversary, since the sovereignty of the Union can only be lost to the profit of that of the states.

So by having the laws of the Union applied by the courts of the individual states, the nation would be delivered, not only to foreign judges, but also to partial judges.

It was not their character alone, moreover, that made the state courts incapable of serving a national end; it was above all their number.

At the moment when the federal Constitution was formed, there were already in the United States thirteen supreme courts of justice from which there was no appeal. Today they number twenty-four. How to accept that a State can endure when its fundamental laws can be interpreted and applied in twenty-four different ways at once! Such a system is as contrary to reason as to the lessons of experience.

So the law-makers of America agreed to create a federal judicial power, in order to apply the laws of the Union and to decide certain questions of general interest which were carefully defined in advance.

All of the judicial power of the Union was concentrated in a single tribunal called the Supreme Court of the United States. But to facilitate the dispatch of affairs, inferior courts were added to assist and were charged with judging with sovereign power cases of little importance or with ruling on more important disputes in the first instance. The members of the Supreme Court were not elected by the people or the legislature; the President of the United States had to choose them with the advice of the Senate.

In order to make them independent of the other powers, they were made irremovable, and it was decided that their salary, once fixed, would be beyond the control of the legislature.[26]

---

26. *The Union was divided into districts; in each*[*] *of these districts a federal judge was seated. The court where this judge presided was called the district court.*

In addition, each of the judges of the Supreme Court must travel annually over a certain part of the territory of the Republic, in order to decide certain more important cases on site; the court over which this magistrate presides was given the name circuit court.

It was easy enough to proclaim the establishment of a federal judicial system in principle, but a host of difficulties arose the moment its attributions had to be set.

Way of Determining the Jurisdiction[TN 5] of the Federal Courts

Difficulty of determining the jurisdiction of the various courts in confederations.—The courts of the Union given the right to determine their own jurisdiction.—Why this rule attacks the portion of sovereignty that the individual states reserved to themselves.—The sovereignty of these states limited by laws and

---

Finally, the most serious matters must come, either directly or on appeal, before the Supreme Court where all the judges of the circuit courts gather once each year to hold a formal session.

The jury system was introduced in federal courts, in the same way as in state courts, and in similar cases.

There is hardly any analogy at all, as you see, between the Supreme Court of the United States and our Cour de cassation. *The Supreme Court can be apprised of a case in the first instance, and the* Cour de cassation *can be only in the second or third instance.*[a] *The Supreme Court indeed forms, like the* Cour de cassation, *a single court charged with establishing a uniform jurisprudence; but the Supreme Court judges fact as well as law, and decides itself, without sending the matter to another court; two things that the* cour de cassation *cannot do.*

See the organic law of September 24, 1789, Laws of the United States, *by Story, vol. I, p. 53.*

[*]. "≠See, for the organization, the organic law of 1789, *Kent's Commentaries,* vol. I, p. 273 and following. *Sargent's* [*sic: Sergeant's*] *Constitutional Law.*≠"

a. In the manuscript: "only in the third instance."

Gustave de Beaumont:

This is inexact. The *Cour de cassation* can be apprised of any judgment or decision made in the *last resort;* and many judgments are made in the last resort without having been appealed. Such are judgments about simple offenses, judgments of the justices of the peace not exceeding 50 francs; id. of courts of the first instance not exceeding 1,000 francs, etc. You must say in the *second or third instance* (YTC, CIIIb, 3, pp. 28–29).

Translator's Note 5: *Compétence,* in relation to the courts, has a more narrowly legal, a more restricted meaning in French than *competence* would have in English; the English word *jurisdiction* is closer to the meaning.

by the interpretation of laws.—The individual states thus risk a
danger more apparent than real.

A first question arose. The Constitution of the United States set up, face to face, two distinct sovereignties, represented in terms of judicial structure by two different court systems; no matter what care was taken to establish the jurisdiction of each of these two court systems, you could not prevent frequent conflicts between them. Now, in this case, who would have the right to establish jurisdiction?

Among peoples who form only one and the same political society, when a question of jurisdiction arises between two courts, it is usually brought before a third that serves as arbiter.

This is easily done because, among these peoples, questions of judicial jurisdiction do not have any relation to questions of national sovereignty.

But above the highest court of an individual state and the highest court of the United States, it was impossible to establish any kind of court that was not either one or the other.

So one of these two courts had to be given the right to judge in its own case and to take or accept cognizance of the matter in dispute. This privilege could not be granted to the various courts of the states; that would have destroyed the sovereignty of the Union in fact, after having established it in law; for interpretation of the Constitution would soon have given back to the individual states the portion of independence that the terms of the Constitution took away from them.

By creating a federal court, the desire had been to remove from the courts of the states the right to settle, each in its own way, questions of national interest and, by doing so, to succeed in shaping a uniform body of jurisprudence for the interpretation of the laws of the Union. The goal would not have been reached at all if the courts of the individual states, while abstaining from judging cases considered federal, had been able to judge them by pretending that they were not federal.

The Supreme Court of the United States was therefore vested with the right to decide all questions of jurisdiction.[27]

---

27. *Moreover, to make the cases of jurisdiction less frequent, it was decided that, in a very*

That was the most dangerous blow brought against the sovereignty of the states. It thus found itself limited not only by the laws, but also by the interpretation of the laws; by a known limit and by another that was unknown; by a fixed rule and by an arbitrary one. It is true that the Constitution had set precise limits to federal sovereignty; but each time this sovereignty is in competition with that of the states, a federal court must decide.

The dangers, moreover, with which this way of proceeding seemed to menace the sovereignty of the states were not as great in reality as they appeared to be.

We will see further along that, in America, real strength resides more in the provincial governments than in the federal government. Federal judges sense the relative weakness of the power in whose name they act; and they are more likely to abandon a right of jurisdiction in cases where it is granted to them by law, than they are led to claim it illegally.

Different Cases of Jurisdiction

The matter and the person, bases of federal jurisdiction.—
Proceedings against ambassadors,—against the Union,—against
an individual state.—Judged by whom.—Proceedings that arise
from the laws of the Union.—Why judged by the federal
courts.—Proceedings relating to breach of contracts judged by the
federal judicial system.—Consequence of this.

After having recognized the means to set federal jurisdiction, the lawmakers of the Union determined the cases in which that jurisdiction must be exercised.

---

large number of federal cases, the courts of the individual states would have the right to decide concurrently with the courts of the Union; but then the losing party would always have the right to appeal to the Supreme Court of the United States. The Supreme Court of Virginia contested the right of the Supreme Court of the United States to hear an appeal of its decisions, but unsuccessfully. See Kent's Commentaries, vol. I, pp. 300, 370, and following. See Story's Commentaries, p. 646, and the organic law of 1789, Laws of the United States, vol. I, p. 53.

They acknowledged that there were certain litigants who could only be judged by the federal courts, no matter what the subject of the proceedings.

They then established that there were certain proceedings that could only be decided by these same courts, no matter what the qualification of the litigants.

So the person and the matter became the two bases of federal jurisdiction.

Ambassadors represent nations friendly to the Union; everything that involves ambassadors involves in a way the entire Union. When an ambassador is party to a legal proceeding, the proceeding becomes an affair that touches on the welfare of the nation; it is natural that a federal court decides.

The Union itself can be the subject of proceedings; in this case, it would have been contrary to reason as well as to the custom of nations, to bring it for judgment before courts representing a sovereignty other than its own. It is for the federal courts alone to decide.

When two individuals, belonging to two different states, have a legal proceeding, you cannot, without disadvantage, have them judged by the courts of one of the two states. It is safer to choose a court that cannot incite the suspicion of any of the parties, and the court that very naturally presents itself is that of the Union.

When the two litigants are no longer isolated individuals, but states, this reason for equity is joined by a political reason of the first order. Here the status of the litigants gives a national importance to all proceedings; the smallest litigious issue between two states involves the peace of the entire Union.[28]

Often the very nature of the proceedings must serve as a rule of juris-

---

28. *The Constitution says as well that the proceedings that can arise between a state and the citizens of another state will be under the jurisdiction of the federal courts. Soon the question arose of knowing if the Constitution meant all proceedings that can arise between a state and the citizens of another state, whether the ones or the others were* plaintiffs. *The Supreme Court decided affirmatively; but this decision alarmed the individual states who feared being brought despite themselves, for the slightest reason, before the federal court system. So an amendment was introduced to the Constitution, by virtue of which the judicial power of the Union could not extend to judging the cases that had been* initiated *against one of the United States by the citizens of another. See Story's* Commentaries, *p. 624.*

diction. Thus all questions that are related to maritime commerce must be settled by federal courts.[29]

The reason is easy to point out: nearly all these questions get into an estimation of the law of nations. From this perspective, they essentially involve the whole Union in relation to foreigners. Since the sea, moreover, does not fall into one judicial circumscription rather than another, only the national court system can have a claim on legal proceedings that have a maritime origin.

The Constitution has enclosed in a single category nearly all the proceedings that, by their nature, must be under the jurisdiction of the federal courts.

In this regard, the rule that it indicates is simple, but it comprises in itself alone a vast system of ideas and a multitude of facts.

The federal courts, it says, must judge all proceedings that *arise in the laws of the United States.*

Two examples will make the thought of the law-maker perfectly clear.

The Constitution forbids the states the right to make laws on the circulation of money; despite this prohibition, a state makes such a law. Interested parties refuse to obey it, understanding that it is contrary to the Constitution. The matter must be brought before a federal court, because the grounds for the case are drawn from the laws of the United States.

Congress establishes a tariff law. Difficulties arise over the understanding of this law. Again, the matter must be presented before the federal courts, because the cause for the proceeding is in the interpretation of a law of the United States.

This rule is in perfect agreement with the bases adopted for the federal Constitution.

The Union, as constituted in 1789, had, it is true, only a limited sovereignty, but the desire was that, within this circle, the Union formed only one and the same people.[30] Within this circle, it is sovereign. This point

29. *Example: all acts of piracy.*

30. *A few restrictions were certainly placed on this principle by introducing the individual states as independent powers in the Senate, and by having them vote separately in the House of Representatives in the case of election of the President; but these are exceptions. The opposite principle is the dominant one.*

set forth and accepted, all the rest becomes easy; for if you recognize that the United States, within the limits posed by their Constitution, form only one people, the rights belonging to all peoples must surely be granted to them.

Now, since the origin of societies, this point is agreed upon: each people has the right to have all questions relating to the enforcement of its own laws judged by its courts. But you answer: the Union is in the singular position that it forms one people only relative to certain matters; for all others, it is nothing. What is the result? At least for all the laws that relate to these matters, the Union has the rights that would be granted to complete sovereignty. The real point of difficulty is knowing what those matters are. This point settled (and we have seen above, while treating jurisdiction, how it was settled), no question truly speaking remains; for once you have established that a proceeding was federal, that is, came within the portion of sovereignty reserved to the Union by the Constitution, it naturally followed that a federal court alone would decide.

So whenever someone wants to attack the laws of the United States, or invoke them in self-defense, it is the federal courts that must be addressed.

Thus, the jurisdiction of the courts of the Union expands or contracts depending on whether the sovereignty of the Union itself expands or contracts.

We have seen that the principal aim of the law-makers of 1789 had been to divide sovereignty into two distinct portions. In one, they placed the direction of all the general interests of the Union; in the other, the direction of all the interests particular to some of its parts.

Their principal concern was to arm the federal government with enough power for it to be able to defend itself, within its sphere, against the encroachments of the individual states.

As for the latter, the general principal adopted was to leave them free in their sphere. Within that sphere, the central government can neither direct them nor even inspect their conduct.

I have indicated in the chapter on the division of powers that this last principle had not always been respected. There are certain laws that an individual state cannot enact, even though the laws apparently involve only that state.

When a state of the Union enacts a law of this nature, the citizens who are harmed by the execution of this law can appeal to the federal courts.[b]

Thus, the jurisdiction of the federal courts extends not only to all the proceedings that have their source in the laws of the Union, but also to all those that arise in the laws that the individual states have enacted unconstitutionally.

The states are forbidden to promulgate *ex post facto* laws in criminal matters; the man who is sentenced by virtue of a law of this type can appeal to the federal judicial system.

The Constitution also forbids the states to make laws that can destroy or alter rights acquired by virtue of a contract (*impairing the obligations* [*sic: obligation*] *of contracts*).[31]

From the moment when an individual believes that he sees a law of his state that harms a right of this type, he can refuse to obey and appeal to the federal justice system.[32]

b. "Other defect of federal jurisdiction. The federal courts can only be apprised by an individual interest. Now, what would happen if a state passed an unconstitutional act that harmed only the sovereignty of the Union? Nearly impossible case" (YTC, CVh, I, pp. 50–51).

31. *It is perfectly clear, says Mr. Story, p. 503, that every law that expands, contracts or changes in whatever way the intention of the parties, such as result from the stipulations contained in a contract, impairs this contract. In the same place, this same author carefully defines what federal jurisprudence understands by a contract. The definition is very broad. A concession made by a state to an individual and accepted by him is a contract, and cannot be taken away by the effect of a new law. A charter granted by the state to a company is a contract, and binds the state as well as the concessionary. The article of the Constitution that we are speaking about therefore assures the existence of a great portion of* vested rights, *but not all. I can very legitimately own a property without its having passed into my hands by a contract. Its possession is for me a vested right, and this right is not guaranteed by the federal constitution.*

32. *Here is a remarkable example cited by Mr. Story, p. 508. Darmouth [*Dartmouth (ed.)*] College, in New Hampshire, had been founded by virtue of a charter granted to certain individuals before the American Revolution. Its administrators formed, by virtue of this charter, a constituted body, or, following the American expression, a corporation. The legislature of New Hampshire believed it necessary to change the terms of the original charter and transferred to new administrators all the rights, privileges and immunities that resulted from this charter. The former administrators resisted and appealed to the federal court, which agreed to hear the case, understanding that, since the original charter was a true contract between the state and the concessionaries, the new law could not change the disposition of this charter without violating the vested rights of a contract and consequently violating article I, section X, of the Constitution of the United States.*

To me, this disposition seems to attack the sovereignty of the state more profoundly than all the rest.[c]

The rights granted to the federal government, for ends clearly national, are defined and easy to understand. Those that are indirectly conceded to it by the article that I have just cited are not easily felt, and their limits are not easily traced. There is, in fact, a multitude of political laws that act upon the existence of contracts, and that could therefore furnish grounds for encroachment by the central power.

The Federal Courts' Way of Proceeding

Natural weakness of the judicial system in confederations.— Efforts that law-makers must make to place, as much as possible, only isolated individuals and not states before the federal courts.—How the Americans succeeded in doing this.—Direct action of the federal courts on ordinary individuals.—Indirect attack against states that violate the laws of the Union.—The decision of the federal judicial system does not destroy provincial law; it enervates it.

I have made known the rights of the federal courts; it is no less important to know how they are exercised.

The irresistible strength of the judicial system, in countries where sovereignty is not divided, comes from the fact that, in those countries, the courts represent the entire nation in a contest with a single individual who has been struck by a judgment. To the idea of law is joined the idea of the force that supports the law.

But in countries where sovereignty is divided, it is not always so. There, the judicial system most often finds itself facing, not an isolated individual,

c. In a first version: "≠. . . than all the rest. But it is so difficult to calculate in advance the impact of laws, that it is not unusual to see the most numerous assemblies consecrate long discussions to uninteresting points, while an article that will lead to the most characteristic effect of the law is precisely the one that passes unnoticed and is revealed only by experience.≠"

but a fraction of the nation. Its moral power and its physical power are diminished as a result.

So in federal States, the judicial system is naturally weaker; and the one subject to trial, stronger.

The law-maker, in confederations, must constantly work to give the courts a position analogous to the one they occupy among peoples who have not divided sovereignty. In other words, his most constant efforts must strive toward having the federal judicial system represent the nation, and having the one subject to trial represent an individual interest.

A government, whatever its nature, needs to act on the governed in order to force them to give the government what it is owed; it needs to take action against them in order to defend itself from their attacks.

As for the direct action of the government on the governed, in order to force them to obey the law, the Constitution of the United States saw to it that the federal courts, acting in the name of these laws, never had any dealing except with individuals (and that was its highest achievement). In fact, since it had been declared that the confederation formed only one and the same people within the circle drawn by the Constitution, the government, created by this Constitution and acting within its limits, was, as a result, vested with all the rights of a national government, the principal one being to have its injunctions reach ordinary citizens without an intermediary. So when the Union levied a tax, for example, it did not have to apply to the states to collect it, but to each American citizen, according to his share. In turn, the federal judicial system charged with assuring the enforcement of this law of the Union, had to condemn not the recalcitrant State, but the taxpayer. Like the judicial system of other peoples, it found only an individual facing it.[d]

Note that here the Union itself has chosen its adversary. It has chosen a weak one; it is entirely natural that he succumbs.

But when the Union, instead of attacking, is reduced to defending itself, the difficulty increases. The Constitution recognizes the power of the states

d. In the margin: "≠In this, the judicial power only follows the laws of its nature which lead it to judge only on particular cases. Only a political court can break a legislative measure.≠"

to make laws. These laws can violate the rights of the Union. Here, necessarily, the Union finds itself in conflict with the sovereignty of the state that enacted the law. Nothing remains except to chose, from among the means of action, the least dangerous. This means was indicated in advance by the general principles that I stated before.[33]

You see that, in the case that I have just supposed, the Union would have been able to cite the state before a federal court that would have declared the law void; this would have followed the most natural course of ideas. But, in this way, the federal judicial system would have found itself directly facing a state, something it wanted to avoid as much as possible.

The Americans have thought that it was nearly impossible for a new law, in its execution, not to harm some individual interest.

It is on this individual interest that the authors of the federal constitution rely to attack a legislative measure about which the Union could complain. To this individual interest, they offer a protection.

A state sells lands to a company; one year later, a new law disposes of the same lands in another way, and thus violates the part of the Constitution which forbids changing rights vested by contract. When the one who bought by virtue of the new law presents himself in order to take possession, the owner, who holds his rights from the former law, brings an action before the courts of the Union and has the title of the new owner voided.[34] Therefore, in reality, the federal judicial system is grappling with the sovereignty of the state; but it attacks that sovereignty only indirectly and on an application of detail. It thus strikes the law in its consequences, not in its principle. It does not destroy the law; it enervates it.

A final hypothesis remained.

Each state formed a corporation that had a separate existence and separate civil laws; consequently, it could sue or be sued before the courts. A state could, for example, bring suit against another state.

In this case, it was no longer a matter for the Union of attacking a provincial law, but of judging a case in which a state was a participant. It was

33. *See the chapter entitled: "Of the Judicial Power in America [in the United States (ed.)]."*

34. *See* Kent's Commentaries, *vol. I, p. 387.*

a case like any other; only the status of the litigants was different. Here the danger noted at the beginning of this chapter still exists. But this time it cannot be avoided; it is inherent in the very essence of federal constitutions that they will always result in creating, in the midst of the nation, individuals powerful enough to make it difficult to use the judicial system against them.

Elevated Rank That the Supreme Court Occupies among the Great Powers of the State

No other people have constituted a judicial power as great as the Americans.—Extent of its attributions.—Its political influence.—The peace and the very existence of the Union depend on the wisdom of seven federal judges.

When, after examining the organization of the Supreme Court in detail, you come to consider all of the attributions that it has been given, you easily discover that never has a more immense judicial power been constituted among any people.

The Supreme Court is placed higher than any known court, both by the *nature* of its rights and by the *type* of those subject to trial.

In all the civilized nations of Europe, the government has always shown a great reluctance to allow the ordinary judicial system to decide questions that involve the government itself. This reluctance is naturally greater when the government is more absolute. As liberty increases, on the contrary, the circle of the attributions of the courts is always going to widen; but not one of the European nations has yet thought that every judicial question, of no matter what origin, could be left to judges of ordinary law.

In America, this theory has been put in practice. The Supreme Court of the United States is the one and only national court.

It is charged with the interpretation of laws and of treaties; questions relating to maritime trade, and all those generally relating to the law of nations, are exclusively within its competence. You can even say that its attributions are almost entirely political, although its constitution is entirely judicial. Its unique purpose is to have the laws of the Union enforced. And the Union determines only the relations of the government with the governed and of the nation with foreigners; nearly all of the relations of citizens among themselves are governed by the sovereignty of the states.

To this first cause of importance, another still greater must be added. In the nations of Europe, only individuals are subject to trial before the courts; but you can say that the Supreme Court of the United States makes sovereigns appear before it. When the bailiff, climbing the steps of the court, comes to proclaim these few words: "The State of New York versus the State of Ohio," you feel that you are not within the realm of an ordinary court of justice. And when you consider that one of these litigants represents a million men, and the other, two million, you are astonished at the responsibility that weighs upon the seven judges whose decision is going to delight or sadden such a large number of their fellow citizens.

In the hands of seven federal judges rest unceasingly the peace, prosperity, the very existence of the Union. Without them, the Constitution is a dead letter. To them, the executive power appeals in order to resist the encroachments of the legislative body; the legislature, to defend itself against the undertakings of the executive power; the Union, to make the states obey; the states, to repulse the exaggerated pretensions of the Union; public interest against private interest; the spirit of conservation against democratic instability. Their power is immense; but it is a power of opinion. They are omnipotent as long as the people consent to obey the law; they can do nothing once the people scorn the law. Now, the power of opinion is the most difficult one to exercise, because it is impossible to know its limits exactly. Often it is as dangerous to fall short, as to go beyond those limits.

So the federal judges must be not only good citizens, learned and upright men, qualities necessary for all magistrates, but they must also be statesmen; they must know how to discern the spirit of the times, to brave the obstacles that can be overcome, and to change direction when the current threatens to carry away, with them, the sovereignty of the Union and the obedience due to its laws.

The President can fail without having the State suffer, because the President has only a limited duty. Congress can go astray without having the

Union perish, because above Congress resides the electoral body that can change the spirit of Congress by changing its members.

But if imprudent or corrupt men ever came to compose the Supreme Court, the confederation would have to fear anarchy or civil war.

But make no mistake; the root cause of the danger is not in the constitution of the court, but in the very nature of federal governments. We have seen that nowhere is it more necessary to constitute a strong judicial power than among confederated peoples, because nowhere are individual existences, which can struggle against the social body, greater and in better condition to resist the use of the physical force of the government.

Now, the more necessary it is that a power be strong, the more scope and independence it must be given. The more extensive and independent a power, the more dangerous is the abuse that can be made of it. So the origin of the evil is not in the very constitution of this power, but in the very constitution of the State that necessitates the existence of such a power.

How the Federal Constitution Is Superior to the State Constitutions

How the Constitution of the Union can be compared to those of the individual states.—The superiority of the federal Constitution must be attributed particularly to the wisdom of the federal law-makers.—The legislature of the Union less dependent on the people than those of the states.—The executive power freer in its sphere.—The judicial power less subject to the desires of the majority.—Practical consequences of this.—The federal law-makers have mitigated the dangers inherent in democratic government; the law-makers of the states have heightened these dangers.

The federal Constitution differs essentially from the constitutions of the states in the purpose that it intends, but it is highly similar in the means to achieve this purpose. The object of government is different, but the forms of government are the same. From this special point of view, they can usefully be compared.

I think that the federal Constitution is superior to all of the state constitutions. This superiority stems from several causes.

The present Constitution of the Union was formed only after those of most of the states; so the Union could profit from acquired experience.

You will be convinced, nonetheless, that this cause is only secondary, if you consider that, since the establishment of the federal Constitution, the American confederation has increased by eleven new states, and that these new states have nearly always exaggerated rather than mitigated the defects existing in the constitutions of their precursors.

The great cause of the superiority of the federal Constitution is in the very character of the law-makers.

At the time when it was formed, the ruin of the American confederation seemed imminent; it was obvious to all, so to speak. In this extremity, the people chose, perhaps not the men they loved most, but those they respected most.

I have already pointed out above that nearly all the law-makers of the Union had been remarkable by their enlightenment and more remarkable still by their patriotism.

They had all risen in the midst of a social crisis, during which the spirit of liberty had constantly to struggle against a strong and dominating authority. When the struggle ended, and while the excited passions of the crowd were, as usual, still fixed on combating dangers that for a long time no longer existed, these men had stopped; they had cast a calmer and more penetrating eye on their country; they had seen that a definitive revolution was accomplished, and that henceforth the perils that threatened the people could only arise from the abuses of liberty.[e] What they thought, they had the courage to say, because deep in their hearts they felt a sincere and passionate love for this very liberty; they dared to speak of limiting it, because they were certain of not wanting to destroy it.[35]

e. In the manuscript: "of their power {of their liberty}."

35. *In this period, the celebrated Alexander Hamilton, one of the most influential framers of the Constitution, was not afraid to publish the following in the* Federalist, *No. 71 [p. 307]. He said:*

Most of the constitutions of the states give a term of one year to the house of representatives and two years to the senate. In this way the members of the legislative body are tied constantly and in the closest way to the slightest desires of their constituents.

The law-makers of the Union thought that this extreme dependence of the legislature distorted the principal effects of the representative system, by placing in the people themselves not only the source of powers, but also the government.

They increased the length of the electoral mandate in order to allow the deputy greater use of his free will.

The federal Constitution, like the different constitutions of the states, divided the legislative body into two branches.

But in the states, these two parts of the legislature were composed of the same elements and followed the same mode of election. As a result, the

----

There are some," he said, "who would be inclined to regard the servile pliancy of the executive to a prevailing current, either in the community or in the legislature, as its best recommendation. But such men entertain very crude notions, as well of the purposes for which government was instituted, as of the true means by which the public happiness may be promoted.

The republican principle demands that the deliberate sense of the community should govern the conduct of those to whom they entrust the management of their affairs; but it does not require an unqualified complaisance to every sudden breeze of passion, or to every transient impulse which the people may receive from the arts of men, who flatter their prejudices to betray their interests.

It is a just observation that the people commonly intend *the public good. This often applies to their very errors. But their good sense would despise the adulator who should pretend that they always reason right about the* means *of promoting it. They know from experience that they sometimes err; and the wonder is that they so seldom err as they do, beset as they continually are by the wiles of parasites and sycophants, by the snares of the ambitious, the avaricious, the desperate, by the artifices of men who possess their confidence more than they deserve it, and of those who seek to possess rather than to deserve it.*

When occasions present themselves in which the interests of the people are at variance with their inclinations, it is the duty of the persons whom they have appointed to be the guardians of those interests to withstand the temporary delusion in order to give them time and opportunity for more cool and sedate reflection. Instances might be cited in which a conduct of this kind has saved the people from very fatal consequences of their own mistakes, and has procured lasting monuments of their gratitude to the men who had courage and magnanimity enough to serve them at the peril of their displeasure.

passions and will of the majority emerged as easily and found an organ and an instrument as rapidly in one as in the other of the houses. This gave a fierce and hasty character to the making of laws.

The federal Constitution also had the two houses come out of the votes of the people; but it varied the conditions of eligibility and the mode of election. So, if one of the two legislative branches did not represent interests different from those represented by the other, as in certain nations, at least it represented a higher wisdom.

To be a Senator you had to have reached a mature age; and a small assembly, itself already elected, was charged with the election.

Democracies are naturally led to concentrate all social force in the hands of the legislative body. The latter, being the power that comes most directly from the people, is also the one that most partakes of the omnipotence of the people.

So, in the legislative body, you notice an habitual tendency that leads it to gather all kinds of authority within itself.

This concentration of powers, at the same time that it singularly harms the good management of public affairs, establishes the despotism of the majority.

The law-makers of the states have frequently surrendered to these democratic instincts; those of the Union always fought courageously against them.

In the states, executive power is placed in the hands of a magistrate who appears to be placed alongside the legislature, but who, in reality, is only a blind agent and passive instrument of its will. From where would he draw his strength? In the length of his term in office? Generally, he is named for only one year. In his prerogatives? He has, so to speak, none at all. The legislature can reduce him to impotence by granting the execution of its laws to special committees drawn from its midst. If it wanted, it could, in a way, nullify him by taking away his salary.

The federal Constitution has concentrated all the rights of the executive power, as well as all of its responsibility, in a single man. It gave the President a four-year term; it assured him his salary during the entire length of his term in office; it created a group of supporters for him and armed him with a qualified veto. In a word, after carefully drawing the sphere of executive power, it sought, within this sphere, to give the executive power as strong and as free a position as possible.

The judicial power, of all the powers, is the one that, in the state constitutions, remained least dependent on the legislative power.

Nonetheless, in all the states, the legislature retained the authority to set the salaries of judges, which necessarily subjected the former to immediate legislative influence.

In certain states, judges are appointed only for a time, which again removes a large part of their strength and freedom.

In others, legislative and judicial powers are entirely mixed. The Senate of New York, for example, serves as the highest court of the state for certain trials.

The federal Constitution has, on the contrary, carefully separated the judicial power from all the others. In addition, it made judges independent by declaring their salaries fixed and making their office irrevocable.

The practical consequences of these differences are easy to see. It is clear to all attentive observers that the affairs of the Union are conducted infinitely better than the particular affairs of any state.

The federal government is more just and more moderate in its action than the state governments. There is more wisdom in its views, more continuity and intelligent design in its projects, more skill, steadiness and firmness in the execution of its measures.

A few words suffice to summarize this chapter.

Two principal dangers menace the existence of democracies:

The complete subservience of the legislative power to the will of the electoral body.

The concentration, in the legislative power, of all the other powers of government.

The law-makers of the states favored the development of these dangers. The law-makers of the Union did what they could to make them less to be feared.

What Distinguishes the Federal Constitution of the United States of America from All Other Federal Constitutions

The American confederation outwardly resembles all confederations.—Its effects are different, however.— What causes that?—How this confederation stands apart from all others.—The American government is not a federal government, but an incomplete national government.[f]

The United States of America has not presented the first and only example of a confederation. Without mentioning antiquity, modern Europe has furnished several. Switzerland, the German Empire, the Dutch Republic have been or still are confederations.

When you study the constitutions of these different countries, you notice with surprise that the powers they confer on the federal government are more or less the same as those granted by the American Constitution to the government of the United States. Like the latter, they give the central power the right to make war or peace, the right to raise an army, to levy taxes, to provide for general needs and to regulate the common interests of the nation.

Among these different peoples, however, the federal government has almost always remained deficient and weak, while that of the Union conducts public affairs with vigor and ease.

Even more, the first American Union could not continue to exist because of the excessive weakness of its government. Yet this government, so weak,

---

f. In the margin: "Temporary alliance, *league.*
"Lasting alliance, confederation.
"*Limited* [v: incomplete] national government.
"*Complete* national government.
"The Union is not a confederation [v: federal government], but an incomplete national government."

had received rights as extensive as the federal government of today. You can even say that in certain respects its privileges were greater.[g]

So several new principles are found in the current Constitution of the United States that are not striking at first, but make their influence profoundly felt.

This Constitution, which at first sight you are tempted to confuse with previous federal constitutions, rests as a matter of fact on an entirely new theory that must stand out as a great discovery in the political science of today.

In all the confederations that have preceded the American confederation of 1789, peoples who combined for a common purpose agreed to obey the injunctions of a federal government; but they retained the right to command and to supervise the execution of the laws of the Union at home.

The American states that united in 1789 agreed not only that the federal government could dictate laws to them, but also that the federal government itself would execute its laws.

In the two cases, the right is the same; only the exercise of the right is different. But this single difference produces immense results. [Such is the power of laws over the fate of societies.][h]

In all the confederations that have preceded the American Union of today, the federal government, in order to provide for its needs, applied to the individual governments. In the case where the prescribed measure displeased one of them, the latter could always elude the need to obey. If it was strong it appealed to arms; if it was weak, it tolerated a resistance to the laws of the Union that had become its own, pretended weakness and resorted to the power of inertia.

Consequently, one of these two things has constantly happened: the

g. "The old constitution gave Congress great power to command the different states (illegible word) in order to compel them other than by war. It established a *league* among independent states, not a *federal government*" (YTC, CVh, 1, p. 47).

h. Hervé de Tocqueville: "I believe that this paragraph could be deleted. It develops an idea that springs from what precedes and comes naturally to the mind of the reader. By removing it, the pace will be faster. Be careful about slowing the pace by reflections, when they are not absolutely necessary. The last sentence of the paragraph is a useless commonplace" (YTC, CIIIb, 3, p. 22).

most powerful of the united peoples, taking hold of the rights of the federal authority, has dominated all the others in its name;[36] or the federal government has been left to its own forces. Then anarchy has become established among the confederated peoples, and the Union has fallen into impotence.[37]

In America, the Union governs not the states, but ordinary citizens. When it wants to levy a tax, it does not apply to the government of Massachusetts, but to each inhabitant of Massachusetts. Former federal governments faced peoples; the Union faces individuals. It does not borrow its strength, but draws upon its own. It has its own administrators, courts, officers of the law, and army.

Certainly the national [*sic:* state] spirit, collective passions, provincial prejudices of each state still strongly tend to diminish the extent of federal power so constituted, and to create centers of resistance to the will of the federal power. Limited in its sovereignty, it cannot be as strong as a government that possesses complete sovereignty; but that is an evil inherent in the federal system.

In America, each state has far fewer opportunities and temptations to resist; and if the thought occurs, the state can act on it only by openly violating the laws of the Union, by interrupting the ordinary course of justice, and by raising the standard of revolt. In a word, it must suddenly take an extreme position, something men hesitate to do for a long time.

In former confederations, the rights granted to the Union were causes of war rather than of power, since these rights multiplied its demands without augmenting its means of enforcing obedience. Consequently, the real weakness of federal governments has almost always been seen to grow in direct proportion to their nominal power.

---

36. *This is what was seen among the Greeks under Philip, when this prince took charge of enforcing the decree of the Amphictyons. This is what happened to the republic of the Netherlands, where the province of Holland has always made the law. The same thing is still going on today among the Germans. Austria and Prussia are the agents of the Diet and, in its name, dominate the entire confederation.*

37. *It has always been so for the Swiss confederation.—Were it not for the jealousy of its neighbors, Switzerland, for several centuries, would no longer exist.*

This is not so for the American Union; the federal government, like most ordinary governments, can do everything that it has the right to do.

The human mind invents things more easily than words; this is what causes the use of so many incorrect terms and incomplete expressions.[j]

Several nations form a permanent league and establish a supreme authority that, without acting on ordinary citizens as a national government could, nonetheless acts on each of the confederated peoples, taken as a group.

This government, so different from all the others, is given the name federal.

Next, a form of society is found in which several peoples truly blend together as one for certain common interests, and remain separate and only confederated for all the others.

Here the central power acts without intermediary on the governed, administering and judging them as national governments do, but it acts this way only within a limited circle. Clearly that is no longer a federal government; it is an incomplete national government. So a form of government, neither precisely national nor federal, is found. But here things have stopped, and the new word needed to express the new thing does not yet exist.[k]

Because this new type of confederation was unknown, all unions have arrived at civil war, or slavery, or inertia. The peoples who composed them have all lacked either the enlightenment to see the remedy to their ills, or the courage to apply them.

j. Hervé de Tocqueville: "In my opinion, this paragraph and the four following must be deleted and replaced by one or two sentences. It is long and a bit heavy; its importance does not justify its defects. I therefore advise pruning the grammatical discussion and quickly going straight to the paragraph: *Because this new type of confederation was unknown* . . ."

Édouard de Tocqueville: "I cannot share this opinion. This reflection seems very profound to me. Moreover, if you went to the paragraph beginning *Because this new type* . . . , it would have absolutely no sense, since it relates only to the deleted paragraph" (YTC, CIIIb, 3, p. 22).

k. In the margin: "≠The thing is new [v: other], but an old word is still needed to designate it.≠"

The first American Union had also lapsed into the same faults.

But in America, the confederated states, before achieving independence, had been part of the same empire for a long time; so they had not yet contracted the habit of complete self-government, and national prejudices had not been able to become deeply rooted. Better informed than the rest of the world, they were equal to each other in enlightenment; they only weakly felt the passions that ordinarily, among peoples, resist the extension of federal power; and these passions were fought against by the greatest citizens. The Americans, at the same time that they felt the evil, resolutely envisaged the remedy. They corrected their laws and saved the country.

Of the Advantages of the Federal System in General, and of Its Special Utility for America[m]

Happiness and liberty that small nations enjoy.—Power of large nations.—Large empires favor the developments of civilization.—That strength is often the first element of prosperity for nations.—The purpose of federal systems is to combine the advantages that peoples gain from the largeness and the smallness of their territory.—Advantages that the United States derives from this system.—The law yields to the needs of the populations; the populations do not yield to the necessities of the law.—Activity, progress, taste for and practice of liberty among the American peoples.—The public spirit of the Union is only the sum of provincial patriotism.—Things and ideas circulate freely within the territory of the United States.— The Union is free and happy, like a small nation; respected, like a large one.

Among small nations, society keeps its eye on everything; the spirit of improvement gets down to the smallest details. Since the weakness of the people profoundly tempers their ambition, their efforts and resources are

m. In the margin: "Perhaps this chapter should be shifted to the place where I will talk about the future of the Union."

almost entirely focused on their internal well-being and are not likely to be wasted on the empty illusion of glory. Since the capacities of each one are generally limited, desires are limited as well. The mediocrity of wealth makes conditions nearly equal; and mores have a simple and peaceful air. Thus, considering everything and taking into account various degrees of morality and enlightenment, more comfort, population and tranquillity are usually found in small nations than in large ones.

When tyranny establishes itself within a small nation, it is more troublesome than anywhere else; acting inside a smaller circle, it extends to everything within this circle. Unable to undertake some great objective, it is busy with a multitude of small ones; it appears both violent and meddlesome. From the political world, which is strictly speaking its domain, it penetrates into private life. After dictating actions, it aspires to dictate tastes; after governing the State, it wishes to govern families. But that rarely happens; as a matter of fact, liberty forms the natural condition of small societies. There, government offers too little attraction to ambition, and the resources of individuals are too limited, for sovereign power to be easily concentrated in the hands of one man.[n] Should it happen, it is not difficult for the governed to unite together and, by a common effort, to overthrow the tyrant and the tyranny at the same time. [≠Liberty is, moreover, something so natural and so easy within a small nation that abuse can hardly be brought about.≠]

So small nations have at all times been the cradle of political liberty. It has happened that most of them have lost this liberty by growing larger, which clearly reveals that liberty is due to the small size of a people and not to the people themselves.

The history of the world provides no example of a large nation that remained a republic for long;[38] this has led men to say that the thing was impractical. As for me, I think that it is very imprudent for man to want to limit the possible and to judge the future; the real and the present elude

n. In the margin: "≠The power of one man easily succeeds in putting itself above the law and the interest of all.≠"

38. *I am not speaking here about a confederation of small republics, but of a large consolidated republic.*

him every day, and he finds himself constantly surprised by the unexpected in the things he knows best. What can be said with certainty is that the existence of a large republic will always be infinitely more at risk than that of a small one.[o]

All the passions fatal to republics grow with the extent of the territory, while the virtues that serve to support them do not increase in the same measure.[p]

The ambition of individuals increases with the power of the State; the strength of parties, with the importance of the end that they have in mind; but love of country, which must combat these destructive passions, is not stronger in a vast republic than in a small one. It would even be easy to prove that love of country there is less developed and less powerful. Great riches and profound poverty, large cities, depravity of mores, individual egoism, complexity of interests are so many perils that almost always result from the large size of the State. Several of these things do not harm the existence of a monarchy; some can even work toward its duration. In monarchies, moreover, government has a strength of its own; it makes use of the people and does not depend on them; the more numerous the people, the stronger the prince. But to these dangers, republican government can oppose only the support of the majority. Now, this element of strength is not proportionately more powerful in a vast republic than in a small one. Thus, while the means of attack constantly increase in number and power, the strength of resistance remains the same. It can even be said that it decreases, for the more numerous the people and the more varied the nature

o. "I suspect that this doctrine that presents small States to us as the only ones that are suitable for republican forms will be refuted by experience. Perhaps it will be recognized that in order to establish a republic in which justice reigns, the republic must be large enough so that local egoism is never able to harm the whole, nor corrupt the major part of those who lead it; so that on every question you will always be sure to find in the councils a majority free of particular interests and capable of making solely the principles of justice prevail."

Jefferson to Davernois [d'Ivernois (ed.)], 6 February 1795. (YTC, CVh, 5, p. 2). Citation from Louis P. Conseil, editor. *Mélanges politiques et philosophiques extraits des mémoires et de la correspondance de Thomas Jefferson* (Paris: Paulin, 1833), vol. I, pp. 407–9.

p. The wording of this sentence comes from Beaumont (YTC, CIIIb, 3, p. 34).

of minds and interests, the more difficult it is, as a result, to form a compact majority.

[≠Republican government is fragile by nature. It lasts much more because of the weakness of the attacks directed against it than because of a strength of its own [v: its own power]. It relies only on a certain sentiment of order, virtue and moderation on the part of the governed. The immoderate desires of parties, great riches and great poverty, vast cities, and the profound corruption of mores that they engender, constantly threaten the existence of republics. Now, all of these things are found only among large nations alone. A government that has the source of its power outside of the people can continue to exist for a long time, whatever the opinions of the people; but a republican government has strength only in the support of the majority; the more numerous the people, the harder to form a majority. Here my reasoning is based only upon a numerical calculation.≠]

We have been able to note, moreover, that human passions acquired intensity, not only from the greatness of the end that they wanted to attain, but also from the multitude of individuals who felt them at the same time. There is no one who does not find himself more moved in the middle of an agitated crowd that shares his emotion than if he were to feel it alone. In a large republic, political passions become irresistible, not only because the objective that they pursue is immense, but also because millions of men experience those political passions in the same way and at the same moment.

So it is permissible to say that, in general, nothing is so contrary to the well-being and to the liberty of men as large empires.

Large States have particular advantages, however, that must be recognized.

In them, the desire for power is more passionate among common men than elsewhere. So too the love of glory there is more developed among certain souls who find in the applause of a great people an objective that is worthy of their efforts and appropriate for raising them, in a way, above themselves. There, thought in all fields is given a more rapid and powerful impetus; ideas circulate more freely; large cities are like vast intellectual centers where all the lights of the human mind come to shine and combine.

This fact explains for us why large nations bring more rapid progress to enlightenment and to the general cause of civilization than small ones.q It must be added that important discoveries often require a development of national strength of which the government of a small people is incapable; among large nations, the government has a greater number of general ideas; it is more completely free from the routine of antecedents and from local egoism. There is more genius in its conceptions, more boldness in its ways of doing things.

Internal well-being is more complete and more widespread among small nations as long as they remain at peace; but a state of war is more harmful to them than it is to large nations. In the latter, great distance from the borders sometimes allows most people to remain far from danger for centuries. For them, war is more a cause of discomfort than of ruin. [≠Large nations are at war more than small ones, but all things considered, among the large ones, there are more men at peace.≠]

Moreover, in this matter as in many others, there is a consideration that predominates over all the rest: that of necessity.

If there were only small nations and not any large ones, humanity would certainly be freer and happier; but the existence of large nations cannot be avoided.

This introduces into the world a new element of national prosperity, which is strength. What good is it for a people to present a picture of comfort and liberty, if they are exposed each day to devastation or conquest? What good is it that they have manufacturing and commerce, if another people commands the seas and establishes the law for all markets? Small nations are often miserable, not because they are small, but because they are weak; large nations prosper, not because they are large, but because they are strong. So for nations, strength is often one of the first conditions of happiness and even of existence. Because of that, barring particular circumstances, small peoples always end up being violently united with large ones or uniting with them on their own. I know of no condition more deplorable than that of a people able neither to defend itself nor to be self-sufficient.

q. This sentence and the preceding one have been corrected by Beaumont (YTC, CIIIb, 3, pp. 34–35).

The federal system has been created to unite the various advantages that result from the large and the small sizes of nations.[r]

It is enough to look at the United States of America to see all the good that comes to those who adopt this system.

Among large centralized nations, the legislator is forced to give laws a uniform character that does not allow for the diversity of places and mores; never learning about individual cases, he can only proceed by general rules. Men are then obliged to bend to the necessity of legislation, for legislation cannot adapt to the needs and mores of men; this is a great cause of trouble and misery.[s]

This disadvantage does not exist in confederations. The congress regulates the principal actions of social existence; all the detail is left to the provincial legislatures.

You cannot imagine to what degree this division of sovereignty serves the well-being of each of the states that compose the Union. In these small societies, not preoccupied by the need to defend themselves or to expand, all public power and all individual energy are turned toward internal improvements.[t] The central government of each state, situated close to the governed, is alerted daily to needs that make themselves felt. Consequently, each year new plans are presented; these plans, discussed in town assemblies or the state legislature and then reproduced in the press, excite universal

---

r. Rousseau made the following recommendation to the Poles: "Apply yourselves to expanding and perfecting the system of federative governments, the only one that unites the advantages of large and small States" (*Considérations sur le gouvernement de Pologne,* chapter V, in *Œuvres complètes,* III, Paris: Pléiade, 1964, p. 971). The same idea is set forth at the beginning of *Jugement sur le projet de paix perpétuelle,* and it appears in a note at the end of chapter XV of book III of the *Contrat social (ibid.,* p. 431). The advantages of the federal form had been equally praised by Montesquieu in the first chapter of book IX of *Esprit des lois* (in *Oeuvres complètes,* Paris: Pléiade, 1951, II, p. 369).

s. Cf. conversation with Mr. Bowring (*Voyage en Angleterre, OC,* V, 2, p. 35).

t. "≠Nevertheless, the greatest difficulty is not to find some peoples who know how to manage their own affairs, but to find some with this habit who can understand federal sovereignty and submit to it≠" (YTC, CVh, 4, p. 4).

interest and the zeal of the citizens. This need to improve agitates the American republic constantly and does not trouble them; there, ambition for power is replaced by the love of well-being, a more vulgar, but less dangerous passion. It is an opinion generally shared in America that the existence and duration of republican forms in the New World depend on the existence and the duration of the federal system. A great part of the miseries engulfing the new States of South America is attributed to the desire to establish large republics there, instead of dividing sovereignty.[u]

As a matter of fact, it is incontestable that in the United States the taste and the practice of republican government were born in the towns and within the provincial assemblies. In a small nation such as Connecticut,[v] for example, where the important political matter is opening a canal or laying out a roadway, where the state has no army to pay nor war to sustain, and where the state can give to those who lead it neither wealth nor much glory, you can imagine nothing more natural and more appropriate to the nature of things than a republic. Now, this same republican spirit, these mores and these habits of a free people, after being born and developing in the various states, are then applied easily to the whole country. In a way, the public spirit of the Union is itself only a summary of provincial patriotism. Each citizen of the United States transfers, so to speak, the interest inspired in him by his small republic to the love of the common native land. By defending the Union, he defends the growing prosperity of his district, the right to direct its affairs, and the hope of winning acceptance there for the plans for improvement that are to enrich him himself: all things that ordinarily touch men more than the general interests of the country and the glory of the nation.

u. Hervé de Tocqueville: "All that precedes is very good. A thought however: Isn't the well-being that, for the states of the Union, results from the division of sovereignty disturbed by the vices of their democratic organization that Alexis had pointed out?"

Édouard de Tocqueville: "It seems to me that this can only be related to the whole. It is certain that the United States, as they are constituted, enjoy an enormous prosperity, and that the nations of the South are in anarchy" (YTC, CIIIb, 3, p. 24).

v. In the first version, the state cited was Massachusetts.

On the other hand, if the spirit and the mores of the inhabitants make them more suitable than others to cause a large republic to prosper, the federal system has made the task much less difficult. The confederation of all the American states does not show the usual disadvantages of numerous human agglomerations. The Union is a large republic in terms of expanse; but in a way, it can be likened to a small republic, because of the small number of matters that concern its government. Its acts are important, but rare. Since the sovereignty of the Union is hindered and incomplete, the use of this sovereignty is not dangerous to liberty. Nor does it excite those immoderate desires for power and reputation that are so deadly to great republics. Since everything there does not necessarily end up at a common center, you see neither vast cities,[w] nor enormous wealth, nor great poverty, nor sudden revolutions. Political passions, instead of spreading instantaneously like a firestorm over the whole surface of the country, are going to break against the individual passions and interests of each state.

Within the Union, however, ideas and things circulate freely, as among one and the same people. Nothing stops the rise of the spirit of enterprise. Its government draws upon talents and enlightenment. Within the boundaries of the Union, as within the interior of a country under the same empire, a profound peace reigns. Outside, the Union ranks among the most powerful nations of the world; it offers to foreign trade more than eight hundred leagues of coastline. Holding in its hands the keys to a whole world, it enforces respect for its flag in the far reaches of the seas.[x]

w. Hervé de Tocqueville: "And New York which is so large?
Édouard de Tocqueville: "New York, it seems to me, is only a large city and not a metropolis, in the true meaning of this word" (YTC, CIIIb, 3, p. 24).

x. Hervé de Tocqueville: "This peroration is beautiful, but isn't Alexis making America into too much of an El Dorado? It must not be forgotten that he thinks himself obliged to disenchant us in the following chapters. Two sentences here appear too strong to me: that of the profound peace that reigns within the interior—two recent examples have shown that this peace is easily troubled—and that of respect for the flag, which exists only because the European nations wish it or do not agree to humiliate it. Not with its small fleet would America force the maritime powers to respect its flag."

Édouard de Tocqueville: "Alexis shows in several places what the future dangers of the American government are, and what its weak side is at the present time. But, if one judges it now as a whole, one can say, as in the last sentence, '*The Union is free and happy,* etc.'" (YTC, CIIIb, 3, pp. 24–25).

The Union is free and happy like a small nation, glorious and strong like a large one.[y]

What Keeps the Federal System from Being within the Reach of All Peoples; And What Has Allowed the Anglo-Americans to Adopt It

There are, in all federal systems, inherent vices that the law-maker cannot fight.—Complication of all federal systems.— It requires from the governed the daily use of their intelligence.— Practical knowledge of the Americans in the matter of government.—Relative weakness of the government of the Union, another vice inherent in the federal system.—The Americans have made it less serious, but have not been able to destroy it.—The sovereignty of the individual states weaker in appearance, stronger in reality than that of the Union.—Why.— So among confederated peoples, there must be natural causes of union, apart from the laws.—What these causes are among the Anglo-Americans.—Maine and Georgia, 400 leagues apart, more naturally united than Normandy and Brittany.—That war is the principal danger to confederations.—This proved by the very example of the United States.—The Union has no great wars to fear.—Why.—Dangers that the peoples of Europe would run by adopting the federal system of the Americans.

[Of all beings, man is assuredly the one best known; and yet his prosperity or miseries are the product of unknown laws of which only a few isolated and incomplete fragments come into our view. Absolute truth is hidden and perhaps will always remain hidden.] The law-maker sometimes succeeds, after a thousand efforts, in exercising an indirect influence on the destiny of nations, and then his genius is celebrated. While often, the geo-

---

y. See the conversation with Mr. MacLean (non-alphabetic notebooks 2 and 3, YTC BIIa, and *Voyage, OC,* V, 1, p. 127).

graphic position of the country, over which he has no influence; a social state that was created without his support; mores and ideas, whose origin is unknown to him; a point of departure that he does not know, impart to society irresistible movements that he struggles against in vain and that carry him along as well.

The law-maker resembles a man who plots his route in the middle of the sea. He too can navigate the ship that carries him, but he cannot change its structure, raise the wind, or prevent the ocean from heaving under his feet.

I have shown what advantages the Americans gain from the federal system. It remains for me to explain what allowed them to adopt this system; for not all peoples are able to enjoy its benefits.

Accidental vices arising from the laws are found in the federal system; these can be corrected by law-makers. Others are encountered that are inherent in the system; these could not be destroyed by the peoples who adopt it. So these peoples must find within themselves the strength to withstand the natural imperfections of their government.

Among the vices inherent to all federal systems, the most visible of all is the complication of means that they use. This system necessarily brings two sovereignties face to face. The law-maker succeeds in making the movements of these two sovereignties as simple and as equal as possible, and he can enclose both of them within clearly defined spheres of action. But he cannot make it so that there is only one of them, nor prevent them from being in contact at some point.

[The federal system of the United States consists of combining two governments: one, provincial; the other, national.

It is already not so easy to find a people who have the taste and, above all, the habit of provincial government. I have already remarked earlier that, among enterprises that can be attempted, certainly one of the most difficult was to persuade men to attend to their own affairs. It follows that the federal system is hardly ever established except among nations who, independent of one another for a long time, have naturally contracted this taste and these habits to a high degree. Notably, this is what happened in the United States. Before the Revolution, they all recognized the authority of the mother country, but each of them had its individual government as well and did not depend on its neighbor.

Nonetheless, the great difficulty is not finding some peoples who know how to run their own affairs, but finding some who can understand federal sovereignty and submit to it.]

So no matter what is done, the federal system rests on a complicated theory whose application requires, in the governed, the daily use of the light of their reason.[z]

In general, only simple conceptions take hold of the mind of the people. An idea that is false, but clear and precise, will always have more power in the world than a true, but complicated, idea. It follows that parties, which are like small nations within a large one, are always quick to adopt, as a symbol, a name or a principle that often represents only very incompletely the end that they propose and the means that they employ. But without this symbol, they would be able neither to subsist nor to stir. Governments that rest only on a single idea or single sentiment, easy to define, are perhaps not the best, but they are assuredly the strongest and the most durable.

On the contrary, when you examine the Constitution of the United States, the most perfect of all known federal constitutions, you are alarmed by the many varieties of knowledge and by the discernment that it assumes among those whom it must govern. The government of the Union rests almost entirely on legal fictions. The Union is an ideal nation that exists only in the mind so to speak; intelligence alone reveals its extent and its limits.

Once the general theory is well understood, the difficulties of application remain; they are innumerable, for the sovereignty of the Union is so entangled with the sovereignty of the states that it is impossible at first

---

z. In the fourth lecture of his course on civilization in Europe, Guizot insisted on this point:

The federative system, logically the most simple, is in fact the most complex; in order to reconcile the degree of independence, of local liberty, that it allows, with the degree of general order, of general submission that it requires and assumes in certain cases, a very advanced civilization is clearly required. . . . The federative system is therefore the one that clearly requires the greatest development of reason, of morality, of civilization, in the society to which it applies (*Histoire générale de la civilisation en Europe,* Brussels, Société belge de Librairie, 1839, lesson IV, p. 41).

glance to perceive their limits. Everything is by convention and by artifice in such a government, and it can only suit a people accustomed, for a long time, to running their own affairs, a people among whom political knowledge has penetrated to the lowest levels of society. I have never admired the good sense and practical intelligence of the Americans more than in the way in which they escape the innumerable difficulties that arise from their federal constitution. I almost never met a common man in America who did not, with surprising ease, discriminate between the obligations arising from the laws of Congress and those originating in the laws of his state, and who, after distinguishing the matters that were among the general attributions of the Union from those that the local legislature had to regulate, could not indicate the point at which the jurisdiction of the federal courts began and the limit at which that of the state courts ended.

The Constitution of the United States resembles those beautiful creations of human industry that shower glory and wealth on those who invent them, but that remain sterile in other hands.

This is what Mexico has demonstrated in our times.

The inhabitants of Mexico, wanting to establish the federal system, took as a model and almost completely copied the federal constitution of the Anglo-Americans, their neighbors.[39] But while importing the letter of the law, they could not at the same time import the spirit that gives it life. So they are seen constantly encumbered by the mechanism of their double government. The sovereignty of the states and that of the Union, leaving the circle that the constitution had drawn, penetrate each other daily. Still today, Mexico is constantly dragged from anarchy to military despotism, and from military despotism to anarchy.

[But even if a people were advanced enough in civilization and versed enough in the art of government to submit intelligently to so complicated a political theory, it would still not mean that the federal system could meet all their needs.

There is, in fact, a vice inherent in this system that will manifest itself no matter what is done. That is the relative weakness of the government of the Union.]

39. *See the Mexican constitution of 1824.*

The second and more destructive of all the vices, which I regard as inherent in the federal system itself, is the relative weakness of the government of the Union.

The principle on which all confederations rest is the division of sovereignty. Law-makers make this division hardly noticeable; they even hide it from view for awhile, but they cannot keep it from existing. Now, divided sovereignty will always be weaker than complete sovereignty.

In the account of the Constitution of the United States, we saw how artfully the Americans, while enclosing the power of the Union within the limited circle of federal governments, succeeded in giving it the appearance and, to a certain extent, the strength of a national government.

By acting in this way, the law-makers of the Union reduced the natural danger of confederations; but they were not able to make it disappear entirely.

The American government, it is said, does not address itself to the states; it applies its injunctions directly to the citizens and bends them, separately, to the work of the common will.

But if federal law collided with the interests and prejudices of a state, should it not be feared that each of the citizens of this state would believe himself interested in the cause of the man who refuses to obey? When all the citizens of the state found themselves thus harmed at the same time and in the same way by the authority of the Union, the federal government would seek in vain to isolate them in order to combat them. They would instinctively feel that they must unite to defend themselves, and in the portion of sovereignty left for their state to enjoy, they would find an organization already prepared. Fiction would then disappear and give way to reality, and you would be able to see the organized power of one part of the territory joining battle with the central authority.

[This is, moreover, the spectacle most recently presented by South Carolina. The regulations of the United States concerning the tariff had become completely unpopular in Carolina; the state legislature took the initiative and suspended the enforcement of the federal law. This result is inevitable. When the interest or passions of men are left a powerful means of satisfaction, you can be assured that legal fictions will not long prevent them from noticing and making use of that means. ≠This is so well understood even in America that, no matter how large certain states already are, care has been taken not to create district assemblies that could represent a collective resistance. The legislature never has to make anything obey, other than towns, without links to each other. ≠

Former federal constitutions obliged the states to *act.* The Constitution of the United States only obliges them to *allow action,* an essential difference that makes resistance very rare; for it is very much easier to refuse to act than to prevent someone else from acting. But once what you resolved simply to endure reaches a certain level of pain, the reluctance that men have to take initiative does not take long to disappear, and the precaution of the law-maker is found wanting.

The principle of federal law is that the Court of the United States must endeavor to judge only individuals. In this way, it does [not (ed.)] generally attack the laws of the states, which reduces the danger of a collision between the two sovereignties. But if, in a particular interest, it violates an important state law, or harms a general state principle or interest, the precautions of the law-maker are again useless; and the struggle, real if not obvious, is between the harmed state, represented by a citizen, and the Union, represented by its courts. The Constitution gives the Union . . . [text of note 40 (ed.)].

It is enough, moreover, to see in what a persuading and conciliatory manner the federal government calls for the execution of laws, in order to judge that, despite appearances and the efforts of the law-maker, the federal government constantly finds itself facing not individuals, but sovereigns.

It is even easy to go further, and it must be said with the famous Hamilton in the *Federalist* that of the two sovereignties, the stronger is assuredly the sovereignty of the state.

You can even go further . . . [cf. infra (ed.)] . . .]

I will say as much about the federal judicial system. If, in a particular trial, the courts of the Union violated an important state law, the real, if not obvious, struggle would be between the harmed state, represented by a citizen, and the Union, represented by its courts.[40]

---

40. *Example: The Constitution gave the Union the right to have unoccupied lands sold for its benefit. I suppose that Ohio claims this same right for those that are enclosed within its*

You must have little experience in the ways of this world to imagine that, after leaving the passions of men a means of satisfaction, you will always prevent them, with the aid of legal fictions, from noticing and making use of that means.

So the American law-makers, while making the struggle between the sovereignties less probable, did not destroy the causes.

You can even go further and say that they were not able to secure preponderance to the federal power in case of conflict.[a]

They gave the Union money and soldiers, but the states retain the love and the prejudices of the people.

The sovereignty of the Union is an abstract thing connected to only a small number of external matters. The sovereignty of the states is felt by all the senses; it is understood without difficulty; every moment, it is seen in action. One is new; the other was born with the people themselves.

The sovereignty of the Union is a work of art. The sovereignty of the states is natural; it exists by itself, without effort, like the authority of the father of a family.

The sovereignty of the Union touches men only through a few general interests; it represents an immense and distant country, a vague and indefinite sentiment. The sovereignty of the states envelops each citizen in a way and catches him every day by details. It is the state that takes responsibility

---

borders, under the pretext that the Constitution only meant territory not yet submitted to the jurisdiction of any state; and that consequently Ohio itself wanted to sell the lands. The judicial question would be posed, it is true, between the buyers who held their title from the Union and the buyers who held their title from the state, and not between the Union and Ohio. But if the court of the United States ruled that the federal buyer was in possession, and the courts of Ohio maintained the holdings of his competitor, then what would become of the legal fiction?

a. With a bracket that goes from this paragraph to the one that ends with the words "that carry them toward peace":

To note.

I say the same thing with more development in the last chapter on the future. Ask for advice?"

Hervé de Tocqueville: "Do not put it here. One can do without it."

Édouard de Tocqueville: "The more I reread the passage, the more I regret that there is a question of deleting it, even more because I have not read the one that it repeats" (YTC, CIIIb, 3, p. 25).

for guaranteeing his prosperity, his liberty, his life; at every moment, it influences his well-being or his misery. The sovereignty of the states rests on memories, on habits, on local prejudices, on the egoism of province and of family; in a word, on all the things that make the instinct for native land so powerful in the heart of man. How can its advantages be doubted?

Since the law-makers cannot prevent the occurrence of dangerous collisions between the two sovereignties that are brought face to face by the federal system, their efforts to turn confederated peoples away from war must be joined with particular dispositions that carry them toward peace.

It follows that the federal pact cannot exist for long if, among the peoples to whom it applies, a certain number of conditions for union are not found that make this common life easy for them and facilitate the task of government.

Thus, to succeed, the federal system needs not only good laws, but also favorable circumstances.

All peoples who have been seen to form a confederation have had a certain number of common interests that serve as the intellectual bonds of the association.

But beyond material interests, man still has ideas and sentiments. For a confederation to last for a long time, there must be no less homogeneity in the civilization than in the needs of the diverse peoples who constitute it. The civilization of a *canton* in Vaud compared with that of a *canton* in Uri is like the XIXth century compared with the XVth; so Switzerland has never truly had a federal government. The union among the different *cantons* exists only on the map; and that would be clearly seen if a central authority wanted to apply the same laws over the whole territory.[b]

b. Before the 1836 visit, Tocqueville probably went to Switzerland in 1829 and 1832 (Cf. Luc Monnier, "Tocqueville et la Suisse," in *Alexis de Tocqueville. Livre du centenaire,* Paris: Editions du C.N.R.S., 1960, pp. 101–13).

André Jardin indicates that in his view Tocqueville must have visited Switzerland at least five times between 1823 and 1836. The notes of the voyage to Switzerland in 1836 are known to us thanks to the text published in the *Oeuvres complètes,* Beaumont edition. André Jardin ("Tocqueville et la décentralisation," in *La décentralisation, VI colloque d'histoire,* Aix-en-Provence: Publication des Annales de la Faculté des Lettres, 1961, pp. 89–117, 97) has nonetheless remarked that certain similarities between these notes

[There are men who pretend that one of the advantages of federal constitutions is to allow each portion of the same empire to live entirely in its own way, without ceasing to be united. That is true, if confederation means a kind of offensive and defensive league, by means of which different peoples unite to repel a common danger and remain strangers to each other for everything else. But if, among confederated peoples, you want to create a common existence and a true national government, it is absolutely necessary that their civilization be homogeneous in nature. This necessity makes itself felt even much more in confederations than in monarchies, because in order to be obeyed, government has much more need for the support of the governed in the first than in the second.

The federal system allows and favors diversity in laws dealing with specifics, which is a great good; but it often resists uniformity in general laws, which is a great evil.]

In the United States there is a fact that admirably facilitates the existence of the federal government. The different states not only have more or less the same interests, the same origin and the same language, but also the same degree of civilization; this almost always makes agreement among them easy. I do not know if there exists any European nation, however small, that, in its different parts, does not present a less homogeneous face than the American people whose territory is as large as half of Europe.

From the state of Maine to the state of Georgia, there are about four hundred leagues. However, less difference exists between the civilization of Maine and that of Georgia than between the civilization of Normandy and that of Brittany. So Maine and Georgia, placed at two extremities of a vast

---

and *Democracy* lead to the thought that these texts, published by Beaumont as dating from 1836, are perhaps the fruit of an earlier voyage (*Voyages en Angleterre, Irelande, Suisse et Algérie, OC,* V, 2, pp. 173–88). In his "Rapport fait à l'Académie des sciences morales et politiques sur l'ouvrage de M. Cherbuliez, entitled *De la démocratie en Suisse"* (*Séances et travaux de l'Académie des sciences morales et politiques,* XII, 1848, pp. 97–119, reproduced as an appendix to *Democracy* beginning with the twelfth edition), Tocqueville comments on the Swiss confederation in terms entirely similar to those of this chapter, and concludes that Switzerland possesses the most ineffective federal constitution that could exist.

empire, naturally find more real ease in forming a confederation, than Normandy and Brittany, which are separated only by a stream.

With these opportunities, which the mores and habits of a people offer to the American law-makers, are joined others that arise from the geographic position of the country. It is principally to the latter that the adoption and maintenance of the federal system must be attributed.[c]

[Despite all these obstacles, I believe federal governments still more appropriate for maintaining internal peace and for favoring, over a vast empire, the peaceful development of social well-being, than for struggling with advantage against foreign enemies.

It is the difficulty that confederations find in sustaining great wars that makes so many peoples incapable of enduring federal government.]

The most important of all the actions that can mark the life of a people is war. In war, a people acts as a single individual vis-à-vis foreign peoples; it fights for its very existence.

As long as it is only a question of maintaining peace within the interior of a country and of favoring prosperity, skill in the government, reason among the governed, and a certain natural attachment that men almost always have for their country can easily suffice. But for a nation to be able to wage a great war, the citizens must impose numerous and painful sacrifices on themselves. To believe that a large number of men will be capable of submitting themselves to such social exigencies, is to know humanity very badly. [Were the necessity of war to be universally acknowledged, the natural inclination of the human mind is to reject the annoying conse-

---

c. In the margin:

≠General ideas./
    Insular position of the Union.
    Indians, nothing. 4,000 soldiers. Attacked from a distance, defended close by./
    Impossibility of taxes. *Federalist./*
    Difficulties over the militias in the War of 1812./
    Inability of the large nations of Europe to live federally./
    Fortunate Americans.≠

quences of the principle that it previously accepted. So once the principle of war is accepted, an authority capable of forcing individuals to bear its consequences must be found somewhere.]

It follows that all peoples who have had to wage great wars have been led, almost despite themselves, to augment the forces of the government. Those who have not been able to succeed in doing so have been conquered. A long war almost always puts nations in this sad alternative; their defeat delivers them to destruction, and their triumph, to despotism.

[There is a great nation in Europe where the forces of society [v: governmental forces] are centralized in such a way that in case of war, a drumbeat assembles the entire nation, so to speak, around its leader, like the inhabitants of a village. This nation, apart from its courage, must have a great advantage over others for waging war; on several occasions, therefore, we have seen it dominate all of Europe by force of arms.

The fact is that to draw from people the enormous sacrifices of men and money that war requires and to concentrate, in one place and at a given time, all national forces, nothing less is required than the efforts of complete sovereignty.

Now, the inevitable evil of confederations, I have already said, is the division of sovereignty. In the federal system, not only is there no administrative centralization or anything approaching it, but also governmental centralization itself exists only very incompletely. That is always a great cause of weakness when it is a question of defense against peoples among whom governmental centralization exists.

In the federal Constitution of the United States . . . [cf. infra (ed.)]].

So, in general, it is during a war that the weakness of a government is revealed in a most visible and dangerous manner; and I have shown that the inherent vice of federal governments was to be very weak.

In the federal system, not only is there no administrative centralization or anything approaching it, but also governmental centralization itself exists only incompletely. That is always a great cause of weakness, when defense is necessary against peoples among whom governmental centralization is complete.

In the federal Constitution of the United States, of all federal constitutions, the one where the central government is vested with the most real strength, this evil still makes itself acutely felt. [The law gives Congress, it is true, the right to take all measures required by the interest of the country, but the difficulty is to exercise such a right. If Congress, pressed by urgent needs, comes to impose on the governed sacrifices equal to the dangers, the discontent of those individuals who suffer does not fail to find a place of support in the sovereignty of the states, or at least in the ambition of those who lead the states and who, in turn, want the support of the malcontents. The states that do not want to wage war, or to whom the war is useless or harmful, easily find in the interpretation of the Constitution the means to refuse their support. The physical and, above all, the moral force of the nation is considerably reduced by it, for even the possibility of such an event renders the federal government weak and slow to act; it fills the government with hesitations and fears and prevents it from even attempting all that it could do.

"It is evident," says Hamilton in the *Federalist,* no. 12, "from the state of the country, from the habits of the people, from the experience we have had on the point itself that it is impracticable to raise any very considerable sums by direct taxation." The direct tax is in fact the most visible and bur-densome of taxes; but at the same time, it is the only one that can always be resorted to during a war.]

A single example will allow the reader to judge.

The Constitution gives Congress the right to call the state militias into active duty when it is a matter of suppressing an insurrection or repelling an invasion. Another article says that in this case the President of the United States is the Commander in Chief of the militia.

At the time of the War of 1812, the President ordered the militias of the North to move toward the national borders; Connecticut and Massachusetts, whose interests were harmed by the war, refused to send their contingents.

The Constitution, they said, authorizes the federal government to use the militias in cases of *insurrection* or *invasion;* but in the present situation there was neither insurrection nor invasion. They added that the same Constitution that gave the Union the right to call the militias into active service, left the states the right to appoint the officers. It followed, according to them, that even in war, no officer of the Union had the right to command the militias, except the President in person. But this was a matter of serving in an army commanded by someone other than him.

These absurd and destructive doctrines received not only the sanction of the Governors and the legislature, but also that of the courts of justice of these two states; and the federal government was forced to find elsewhere the troops that it needed.[41]

[A fact of this nature proves, better than all that I could say, the inability the American Union would have to sustain a great war, even with the improved organization that the 1789 Constitution gave it.

Allow for a moment the existence of such a nation in the midst of the aggressive peoples of Europe where sovereignty is unified and omnipotent, and the relative weakness of the American Union will become for you a proven and plain truth.]

So how is it that the American Union, all protected as it is by the relative perfection of its laws, does not dissolve in the middle of a great war? It is because it has no great wars to fear.[e]

[In general, we must give up citing the example of the United States to prove that confederations can sustain great wars, for the Union has never had a single one of this nature.

Even that of 1812, which the Americans speak about with such pride, was nothing compared to the smallest of those that the ambition of Louis XIV or the French Revolution brought about in Europe. The reason is simple.]

Placed in the center of an immense continent, where human industry

---

41. Kent's Commentaries, *vol. I, p. 244. Note that I have chosen the example cited above from the time after the establishment of the current Constitution. If I had wanted to go back to the period of the first confederation, I would have pointed out even more conclusive facts. [[Nothing more miserable can be imagined than the way the central government conducted the War of Independence and yet]] Then true enthusiasm reigned in the nation; the Revolution was represented by an eminently popular man; and yet, in that period, Congress had no resources at all, so to speak. Men and money were needed at every moment; the best laid plans failed in the execution; and the Union, always at the brink of perishing, was saved much more by the weakness of its enemies than by its own strength.*[d]

d. At first, the text of this note was found before "[In general . . .]."

e. In the beginning, note 41 was found at this place in the manuscript.

can expand without limits, the Union is almost as isolated from the world as if it were enclosed on all sides by the ocean.[f]

Canada numbers only a million inhabitants; its population is divided into two enemy nations. The rigors of climate limit the extent of its territory and close its ports for six months of the year.

From Canada to the Gulf of Mexico, there are still a few, half-destroyed, savage tribes that six thousand soldiers[g] drive before them.

In the South, the Union at one point touches the empire of Mexico; probably great wars will come from there one day [if the Anglo-Americans and the Mexicans each continue to form a single, unified nation. In Mexico, in fact, there is a numerous population that, different from its neighbors by language, religion, habits and interest [broken text (ed.)]]. But, for a long time still, the little developed state of its civilization, the corruption of its mores and its poverty will prevent Mexico from taking an elevated rank among nations. As for the great powers of Europe, their distance makes them little to be feared.[O]

So the great happiness of the United States is not to have found a federal constitution that allows it to sustain great wars, but to be so situated that there are none to fear.

No one can appreciate more than I the advantages of the federal system. There I see one of the most powerful devices favoring prosperity and human liberty. I envy the fate of nations permitted to adopt it. But I refuse, nonetheless, to believe that confederated republics could struggle for long, with equal strength, against a nation where governmental power would be centralized.

The people who, in the presence of the great military monarchies of Europe, would come to divide sovereignty, would seem to me to abdicate, by this fact alone, its power and perhaps its existence and its name.

Admirable position of the New World where man has only himself as an enemy. To be happy and free, he only has to want to be.

---

f. In the margin, with a bracket that includes this paragraph and the two following: *"To note.*
I also say part of all of this at the *future. Quid?"*
g. The figure 4,000 appears in the manuscript as well as in a few other places.

PART II

Until now, I have examined the institutions, I have surveyed the written laws, I have depicted the current forms of political society in the United States.

But above all institutions and beyond all forms resides a sovereign power, that of the people, which destroys or modifies institutions and forms as it pleases.

I have yet to make known by what paths this power, which dominates the laws, proceeds; what its instincts, its passions are; what secret motivating forces push, slow or direct it in its irresistible march; what effects its omnipotence produces, and what future is reserved for it.[a]

a. In the margin:

≠Of freedom of the press.
Of associations.
Of parties.
Of elections. Democratic choices. Electoral mores.
Democratic omnipotence, omnipotence of the majority.
Its tyrannical effects. Political demoralization.
Its counterweights in the *laws*,[1] in the *mores* and in the *local circumstances*.
Jury.

1. Judicial power, above all that of the Union, in that it prevents retroactive laws. Lack of administrative centralization.≠

277

CHAPTER I

How It Can Be Strictly Said That in the United States It Is the People Who Govern

In America, the people name the one who makes the law and the one who executes it; the people themselves form the jury that punishes infractions of the law. Institutions are democratic not only in their principle, but in all their developments as well; thus the people name their representatives *directly* and generally choose them *every year,* in order to keep them more completely dependent. So it is really the people who lead, and, although the form of the government is representative, clearly the opinions, prejudices, interests, and even the passions of the people cannot encounter any lasting obstacles that can prevent them from appearing in the daily leadership of society.

In the United States, as in all countries where the people rule, the majority governs in the name of the people.[b]

This majority is composed principally of peaceful citizens who, either by taste or by interest, sincerely desire the good of the country. In constant motion around them, parties seek to draw them in and gain their support.[c]

b. In the margin: "≠An action external to society exercised on society resembles the medicine that often aids nature but still more often harms it. Despotism often appears useful, but I mistrust its benefits.≠"

c. Cf. note a of p. 402.

Of Parties in the United States

*A great division among parties must be made.—Parties that
differ among themselves like rival nations.—Parties strictly
speaking.—Difference between great and small parties.—In
what times they arise.—Their different characters.—America
had great parties.—It no longer has them.—Federalists.—
Republicans.—Defeat of the Federalists.—Difficulty of
creating parties in the United States.—What is done to
succeed in creating them.—Aristocratic or democratic
character that is found in all parties.—Struggle of
General Jackson against the Bank.*

First I must establish a great division among parties.

There are countries so vast that the different populations living there,
though united under the same sovereignty, have contradictory interests that
give rise to a permanent opposition among them. Then, the various portions of the same people do not form parties strictly speaking, but distinct
nations; and if civil war happens to break out, there is a conflict between
rival peoples rather than a struggle between factions.

[≠What I call truly a party is a gathering of men who, without sharing the bond of a common birth, view certain points in a certain
way.≠]

But when citizens differ among themselves on points that interest
all portions of the country equally, such as the general principles of
government, for example, then what I will call truly parties are seen to
arise.

Parties are an evil inherent in free governments; but they do not have the same character and the same instincts in all periods of time.

There are periods of time when nations feel tormented by such great ills that the idea of a total change in their political constitution occurs to their mind. There are other periods when the malaise is even more profound and when the social state itself is compromised. That is the time of great revolutions and great parties.

Between these centuries of disorders and miseries, you find others when societies are at rest and when the human race seems to catch its breath. In truth, that is still only outward appearance. The march of time does not stop for peoples any more than for men; both advance each day toward an unknown future; and when we believe them stationary, it is because their movements escape us. They are men who are walking; to those who are running, they seem immobile.

[<Similar to the hand that marks the hours; everyone can tell the path it has already followed, but the hand must be watched for a long time to discover that it is moving.>]

Be that as it may, there are periods when the changes that take place in the political constitution and social state of peoples are so slow and so imperceptible, that men think they have arrived at a final state; the human mind then believes itself firmly seated on certain foundations and does not look beyond a certain horizon.

This is the time of intrigues and of small parties.

What I call great political parties are those that are attached to principles more than to their consequences, to generalities and not to particular cases, to ideas and not to men. In general, these parties have more noble traits, more generous passions, more real convictions, a more candid and bold appearance than the others. Here, particular interest, which always plays the greatest role in political passions, hides more cleverly behind the veil of public interest; sometimes it even manages to hide from the view of those whom it arouses and brings into action.

Small parties, on the contrary, are generally without political faith. Since they do not feel elevated and sustained by great objectives, their character is stamped by an egoism that occurs openly in each of their acts. They get worked up from a cold start; their language is violent, but their course is timid and uncertain. The means they use are miserable, like the very end that they propose. That is why, when a time of calm follows a violent revolution, great men seem suddenly to disappear and souls withdraw into themselves.

Great parties turn society upside down; small ones trouble it; the ones tear it apart and the others deprave it. [<Both have a common trait, however: to reach their ends, they hardly ever use means that conscience approves completely. There are honest men in nearly all parties, but it can be said that no party should be called an honest man.>] The first sometimes save society by shaking it up; the second always disturb it to no profit.

America had great parties; today they no longer exist. From that it has gained a great deal in happiness, but not in morality.[a]

a. The ideas of this paragraph and the three preceding ones are found again almost literally in a note of 14 January 1832 from Notebook E of the American journey (YTC, BIIa, and *Voyage, OC*, V, 1, pp. 260–61) and in a nearly identical note from pocket notebooks 4 and 5 (YTC, BIIa, and *Voyage, OC*, V, 1, pp. 197–98). The last paragraph continues in this way:

> I do not know of a more miserable and more shameful spectacle in the world than the one presented by the different coteries (they do not deserve the name parties) that divide the Union today. Within them, you see stirring, in full view, all the petty and shameful passions that ordinarily take care to hide deep within the human heart. As for the interest of the country, no one considers it; and if someone speaks about it, it is a matter of form. The parties put it at the head of their articles of association, just as their fathers did, in order to conform to long-standing usage. It has no more relation to the rest of the work than the license of the king that our fathers printed on the first page of their books.
>
> It is pitiful to see what a flood of coarse insults, what petty, malicious gossip, and what coarse slanders fill the newspapers that all serve as organs of the parties; with what shameless contempt for social proprieties, they bring the honor of families and the secrets of the domestic hearth before the court of opinion each day.

In a letter dated 1 October 1858 and addressed to William R. Greg (*OCB*, VI, pp. 455–56), Tocqueville comments on an article by the latter on political parties ("The State of the Parties," *National Review* 7, no. 13 (1858): 220–43). He notes as well another danger tied to the absence of great political parties:

> When there are no more great parties, well bound together by shared interests and passions, foreign policy hardly ever fails to become the primary element of parliamentary activity. . . . Now, I regard such a state of things as contrary to the dignity

When the War of Independence finally ended and it was a matter of establishing the foundations of the new government, the nation found itself divided between two opinions. These opinions were as old as the world, and they are found under different forms and given various names in all free societies. One wanted to limit popular power; the other, to expand it indefinitely.

Among the Americans, the struggle between these two opinions never took on the violent character that has often marked it elsewhere. In America, the two parties were in agreement on the most essential points. Neither one had to destroy an old order or turn an entire social state upside down in order to win. Consequently, neither one bound a large number of individuals' lives to the triumph of its principles. But they touched upon nonmaterial interests of the first order, such as love of equality and of independence. That was enough to arouse violent passions.

The party that wanted to limit popular power sought, above all, to apply its doctrines to the Constitution of the Union, which earned it the name *Federalist.*

The other, which claimed to be the exclusive lover of liberty, took the title *Republican.*[b]

---

and security of nations. Foreign affairs, more than all other matters, need to be treated by a small number of men, *with consistency,* in secret.

And further on he adds:

I find that, with rare sagacity, you have indicated the conditions under which great parties, well disciplined, can exist in a free country. As you say, each of them must be the representative of one of the two great principles that eternally divide human societies, and that, to be brief, can be designated by the names aristocracy and democracy.

b. The history of the Federalists and the Republicans owes a great deal to a conversation with Mr. Biddle, President of the Bank of the United States (non-alphabetic notebooks 2 and 3, YTC, BIIa, and *Voyage, OC,* V, 1, pp. 122–23). The idea that, in America, there are no real parties had already appeared in April 1831, in a conversation with Mr. Schermerhorn on the *Havre,* during the crossing of the Atlantic (notebook E, YTC, BIIa, and *Voyage, OC,* V, 1, pp. 292–93). Beaumont will report this conversation to his father in a letter of 16 May 1831 (*Lettres d'Amérique,* p. 40), and will mention it in *Marie* (I, p. 360).

On Tocqueville's theory of parties, see especially Nicola Matteucci, "Il problema de partito politico nelle riflessioni d'Alexis de Tocqueville," *Pensiero politico* 1, no. 1 (1968):

America is the land of democracy. So the Federalists were always a minority; but they counted in their ranks nearly all the great men who had emerged from the War of Independence, and their moral power was very extensive. Circumstances, moreover, favored them. The ruin of the first confederation made the people afraid of falling into anarchy, and the Federalists profited from this temporary frame of mind. For ten or twelve years, they led affairs and were able to apply, not all of their principles, but some of them; for, day by day, the opposing current became too violent for anyone to dare to struggle against it.

In 1801, the Republicans finally took possession of the government. Thomas Jefferson was named President; he brought them the support of a celebrated name, a great talent, and an enormous popularity.

The Federalists had only survived thanks to artificial means and with the aid of temporary resources; the virtue or talents of their leaders, as well as the good fortune of circumstances, had brought them to power. When the Republicans, in turn, gained power, the opposing party was as if enveloped by a sudden flood. An immense majority declared against it, and the party found itself at once in such a small minority that it immediately gave up hope. From that moment, the Republican or Democratic party has marched from conquest to conquest and has taken possession of the entire society.

The Federalists, feeling defeated, without resources, and finding themselves isolated within the nation, divided; some joined the victors; others put down their banner and changed their name. They entirely ceased to exist as a party a fairly great number of years ago.

The transitional period when the Federalists held power is, in my opinion, one of the most fortunate events that accompanied the birth of the great American union. The Federalists struggled against the irresistible inclination of their century and country. Their theories, however excellent or flawed, had the fault of being inapplicable as a whole to the society that the Federalists wanted to govern; so what happened under Jefferson would

39–92; and Gerald M. Bonetto, "Alexis de Tocqueville's Concept of Political Parties," *American Studies,* 22, no. 2 (1981): 59–79.

have happened sooner or later. But at least their government let the new republic have time to get established and allowed it afterward to bear, without difficulty, the rapid development of the doctrines that they had fought. A great number of their principles ended up, moreover, being accepted into the creed of their adversaries; and the federal Constitution, which still continues to exist in our time, is a lasting monument to their patriotism and wisdom.[c]

So today great political parties are not seen in the United States. Parties that threaten the future of the Union abound there; but none exist that appear to attack the present form of government and the general course of society. The parties that threaten the Union rest, not on principles, but on material interests. In the different provinces of so vast an empire, these interests constitute rival nations rather than parties.[d] That is how the North

c. Parties./

.-.-.- great parties that shared the first times of the Union .-.-.- but their principles are found again. That one of the two, it is true, attained an immense superiority. That from there came the miserable party spirit of today. Principles no longer being in question, but men, or at least principles forced to hide behind interests and men. Analogous example in France. There was grandeur in the struggle of the liberal party with the royalist party. But since the first triumphed, there is only pettiness in the debates that stir within it (YTC, CVh, 4, p. 35).

d. Gustave de Beaumont:

Is this a theory safe from criticism? So you call *great parties* only those that rest on a political theory, and you deny this name to those that have *immense interests* for their base. That is arbitrary.

I see clearly that the *moral* and political consequences of the different parties are not the same. They are parties nonetheless.

Do you get out of it well by saying: these are *rival nations rather than parties?*

But the parties concerned (for example, those for and against free trade) are not only from province to province, but also in each province, from citizen to citizen.

It would have been more correct, I believe, to establish a distinction between *great* parties that have political theories as objectives and *great* parties that are tied to material interests. Certainly America, turned upside down and threatened with dissolution by the question of free trade, has within it *great parties;* though different from ours, they are no less great. Note that these parties would be powerful among us, if we did not have others. After all, the developments of the author lead to the same result (YTC, CIIIb, 2, pp. 57–58).

was recently seen to uphold the system of commercial tariffs, and the South, to take arms in favor of free trade. The sole reason is that the North engages in manufacturing and the South in agriculture,[e] and the restrictive system works to the profit of the one and to the detriment of the other.

For lack of great parties, the United States swarms with small ones, and public opinion splinters infinitely on questions of details. The pain that is taken there to create parties cannot be imagined; it is not an easy thing to do in our time.[f] In the United States, there is no religious hatred, because religion is universally respected and no one sect is dominant; no class hatred, because the people are everything and no one still dares to struggle against them; finally there are no public miseries to exploit, because the material state of the country offers such an enormous scope to industry that leaving man to himself is enough for him to work wonders. But [particular] ambition must indeed succeed in creating parties, because it is difficult to throw someone who holds power out of office for the sole reason that you want to take his place. So all the skill of politicians consists of forming parties. A politician, in the United States, seeks first to discern his interest and to see what analogous interests could be grouped around his; then he busies himself finding out if, by chance, a doctrine or principle exists in the world that could be placed conveniently at the head of the new association, to give it the right to come into being and to circulate freely. It amounts to what would be called the license of the king that our fathers used to print on the first sheet of their works and incorporated into the book, even though it was not part of it.[g]

e. The manuscript says: ". . . and the South only in producing and the restrictive system . . ."

Édouard de Tocqueville: "Economists will find that this term *only in producing* is incorrect. Manufacturers being producers, like farmers or makers of sugar" (YTC, CIIIb, 2, p. 51).

f. "Cite the birth of the masons and the anti-masons to show how parties form and recruit in the United States" (YTC, CVh, 4, p. 35). See the story of the freemason Morgan in Beaumont, *Marie,* I, pp. 353–55.

g. In the manuscript: ". . . had no relation to the object of the book."

Gustave de Beaumont: "I beg your pardon; all the licenses of the king were related to the book and to its objective. So say: *that our fathers used to print on the first sheet of their works and incorporated into the book, even though it was not part of it*" (YTC, CIIIb, 2, p. 59).

This done, the new power is introduced into the political world.

To a foreigner, nearly all the domestic quarrels of the Americans seem, at first view, incomprehensible or childish, and you do not know if you should pity a people who seriously keeps itself busy with such miseries or envy it the good fortune of being able to keep busy in that way.

But when you come carefully to study the secret instincts that govern factions in America, you easily discover that most of them are more or less linked with one or the other of the two great parties that have divided men since free societies have existed. As you enter more profoundly into the intimate thought of these parties, you notice that some of them work to narrow the use of public power, others, to expand it.

I am not saying that American parties always have as their open aim, or even as their hidden aim, making aristocracy or democracy prevail in the country. I am saying that aristocratic or democratic passions are easily found at the bottom of all the parties, and, although hidden from view, they form the tender spot and the soul of the parties.

I will cite a recent example. The President attacks the Bank of the United States. The country is aroused and divided; the enlightened classes generally side with the Bank; the people favor the President. Do you think that the people knew how to discern the reasons for their opinion in the middle of the twists and turns of such a difficult question, where experienced men hesitate? Not at all. But the Bank is a great establishment that has an independent existence; the people, who destroy or raise all powers, can do nothing to it; that astonishes them. Amid the universal movement of society, this immobile point shocks their sight, and they want to see if they cannot succeed in getting it moving like the rest.

Of the Remnants of the Aristocratic Party in the United States

*Secret opposition of the rich to democracy.—They withdraw into
private life.—Taste that they show inside their residences for
exclusive pleasures and luxury.—Their simplicity outside.—
Their affected condescension for the people.*

Sometimes among a people divided by opinions, when the equilibrium among parties is broken, one of them acquires an irresistible preponderance. It crushes all obstacles, overwhelms its adversary and exploits the entire society to its profit. The vanquished, then despairing of success, hide or fall silent. A universal immobility and silence develop. The nation seems united by the same idea. The conquering party stands up and says: "I have brought peace to the country; you owe me thanks."

But beneath this apparent unanimity, profound divisions and a real opposition are still hidden.

This is what happened in America. When the democratic party gained preponderance, you saw it take exclusive possession of the leadership of public affairs. Since then, it has not ceased to model the mores and laws after its desires.[h]

Today you can say that, in the United States, the wealthy classes of society are almost entirely out of public affairs, and that wealth, far from being a right, is a real cause of disfavor and an obstacle to reaching power.

So the rich prefer abandoning the contest to sustaining an often unequal struggle against the poorest of their fellow citizens. Not being able to take a rank in public life analogous to the one they occupy in private life, they

---

h. There is an often very effective means to reestablish peace in a country divided by opinion; it is to give so complete a preponderance to one of the parties that the other disappears or falls into silence. Experience has proved that this was buying peace at a high price. When Ferdinand and Isabella chased the Moors from Spain, they made a great cause of internal troubles disappear; but they impoverished the country and delivered a blow to its industry from which it has never recovered.

The democratic party acted in the same way in America. Once in power, it took exclusive possession of the leadership of public affairs and modeled the mores and laws after its desires (YTC, CVh, 4, pp. 40–41).

abandon the first in order to concentrate on the second. In the middle of the State, they form something like a society apart with its own tastes and enjoyments.

The rich man submits to this state of things as to an evil without remedy; with great care, he even avoids showing that it wounds him. So you hear him publicly praise the sweet pleasures of republican government and the advantages of democratic forms. For, next to hating their enemies, what is more natural to men than flattering them?

Do you see this opulent citizen? Wouldn't you say, a Jew of the Middle Ages who is afraid of arousing suspicion of his wealth? His attire is simple; his gait is modest. Within the four walls of his dwelling, he adores luxury; into this sanctuary, he lets only a few chosen guests that he arrogantly calls his equals. You meet no nobleman in Europe who appears more exclusive in his pleasures than he, more envious of the slightest advantages that a privileged position assures. But here he is, leaving his house, to go to work in a tiny, dusty room that he occupies in the business center of the city, where everyone is free to come to meet him. Along his path, his shoemaker happens by, and they stop. They begin to converse with each other. What can they be saying? These two citizens are dealing with the affairs of the State, and they will not part without shaking hands.

At the bottom of this enthusiasm for convention and in the midst of these obsequious forms toward the dominant power, it is easy to notice in the rich a great disgust for the democratic institutions of their country. The people are a power that they fear and despise. If, one day, the bad government of democracy led to a political crisis, if monarchy ever presented itself in the United States as something feasible, you would soon discover the truth of what I am advancing.

The two great weapons that parties use to succeed are newspapers and associations.[j]

---

j. "General picture. A mass, not impassioned, wanting the good. In the middle of it, parties that seek to create a majority to *legalize* their ideas" (YTC, CVh, 4, p. 40).

CHAPTER 3

Of Freedom of the Press in the United States

Difficulty of limiting freedom of the press.—Particular reasons
that certain peoples have for valuing this liberty.—Freedom of
the press is a necessary consequence of the sovereignty of the
people as it is understood in America.—Violence of the language
of the periodical press in the United States.—The periodical press
has its own instincts; the example of the United States proves
it.—Opinion of the Americans about the judicial suppression of
the crimes of the press.—Why the press is less powerful in the
United States than in France.

Freedom of the press not only makes its power felt over political opinions, but also over all of the opinions of men. It modifies not only laws, but also mores. In another part of this work, I will seek to determine the degree of influence that freedom of the press has exercised over civil society in the United States; I will try to discern the direction it has given to ideas, the habits it has imparted to the mind and sentiments of the Americans.[a] For now, I only want to examine the effects produced by freedom of the press in the political world.

[{The greatest problem of modern societies is to know how to use freedom of the press.} I love freedom of the press enough to have the courage to say everything that I think about it.]

I admit that to freedom of the press I do not bring that complete and instantaneous love that is given to things supremely good by their nature.

---

a. See chapter VI of the second part of the second volume.

[I do not see freedom of the press in the same way that I consider *patriotism* or *virtue,* for example.][b] I love it much more from consideration of the evils it prevents than for the good things that it does.[c]

If someone showed me an intermediate position where I could hope to stand firm between complete independence and total subservience of thought, I would perhaps take my position there; but who will find this intermediate position?[d] You start from license of the press, and you march in rank order; what do you do? First, you submit writers to juries. But the juries acquit them, and what was only the opinion of an isolated man becomes the opinion of the country. So you have done too much and too little. You have to move further. You deliver authors to permanent magistrates; but judges are obliged to hear before condemning. What someone was afraid to avow in a book, is proclaimed with impunity in the defense plea. Thus, what was said obscurely in one account is found repeated in a thousand others. The expression is the external form, and, if I can express myself in this way, the body of the thought; but it is not the thought itself. Your courts arrest the body, but the soul escapes them and subtly slips through their hands. So you have done too much and too little; you must

b. Gustave de Beaumont: "Patriotism is a virtue, so there is no alternative. Moreover, why compare a political institution to a virtue? If you want to make your comparison with a political institution that you consider as essentially and absolutely good, begin by searching your mind. Is there a principle, an institution that appears so to you? Why don't you take individual liberty?" (YTC, CIIIb, 2, p. 60).

c. Hervé de Tocqueville:

> In general the author should stay in the background in order to allow only his book to speak. His opinions should be appreciated by the reader because of a deduction of the ideas that the work develops. If you depart from this rule, it must at least be in the briefest possible way. I believe that the two paragraphs, the one beginning with the words *I admit,* the second with the words *I love it,* could be deleted. They have the disadvantage of delineating the author too openly, but without giving this picture very clear contours. There is a bit of obscurity both in the thought and in its expression. My proposition accepted, you will pass immediately to the paragraph that begins with the words: *if someone"* (YTC, CIIIb, 2, pp. 42–43).

The phrasing of the last sentence of this paragraph is by Beaumont (YTC, CIIIb, 2, p. 60). In the manuscript, it finishes this way: "*. . . from consideration of the evils that follow its ruin than for the good things that it does.*"

d. The manuscript says *a marker.* Beaumont suggested putting *an intermediate position* (YTC, CIIIb, 2, p. 60).

continue to move.[e] Finally you abandon writers to censors. Very good; we are getting closer. But isn't the political rostrum free? So you still haven't done anything. I am wrong; you have made things worse. Would you, by chance, take thought for one of those material powers that grow with the number of their agents? Would you count writers like soldiers in an army? In contrast to all material powers, the power of thought often increases with the small number of those who express it. The spoken word of a powerful man, which spreads alone through the passions of a silent assembly, has more power than the confused cries of a thousand orators. And if only someone can speak freely in a single public place, it is as if he has spoken publicly in each village. So you must destroy the freedom to speak as well as to write. This time, here you are at your destination: everyone is quiet. But where have you arrived? You began from the abuses of liberty, and I find you under the feet of a despot.

You have gone from extreme independence to extreme servitude without finding, on such a long journey, a single place where you could rest.

Some peoples, apart from the general reasons that I have just set forth, have particular reasons that must attach them to freedom of the press.

In certain nations claiming to be free, each of the agents of power can violate the law with impunity, and the constitution of the country does not give the oppressed the right to complain to the judicial system. Among these peoples, the independence of the press must no longer be considered as one of the guarantees, but as the sole remaining guarantee for liberty and for the security of the citizens.

So if the men who govern these nations spoke about taking independence away from the press, the whole people could respond to them: Allow

e. This reflection is similar to the one that appears in the discussion about Malesherbes and freedom of the press in *Essai sur la vie, les écrits et les opinions de M. de Malesherbes* (Paris: Treuttel et Würtz, 1819–1821, I, pp. 179–83) of Count Boissy-d'Anglas. On the general ideas of this chapter, see the conversation with Spencer (non-alphabetic notebook 1, YTC, BIIa, and *Voyage, OC,* V, 1, pp. 69–70), and Beaumont, *Lettres d'Amérique,* p. 101.

us to prosecute your crimes before ordinary judges, and perhaps then we will consent not to appeal to the court of opinion.[f]

In a country where the dogma of sovereignty of the people openly reigns, censorship is not only a danger, but also a great absurdity.[g]

When you grant each person a right to govern society, you must recognize his capacity to choose between the different opinions that trouble his contemporaries and to appreciate the different facts, the knowledge of which can guide him.

So sovereignty of the people and freedom of the press are two entirely correlative things. Censorship and universal suffrage are, on the contrary, two things that contradict each other and that cannot exist together for long in the political institutions of the same people. Among the twelve million men who live within the territory of the United States, *not a single one* has yet dared to propose limiting freedom of the press.

When I arrived in America, the first newspaper that came before my eyes contained the following article, which I translate faithfully:

> Throughout the whole of this affair, the tone and language of Jackson [the President] was that of a heartless despot, alone intent on preserving his power. Ambition is his crime and will yet prove his curse. Intrigue is his vocation, and will yet overthrow and confound him. Corruption is his element and will yet react upon him to his utter dismay and confusion. He has been a successful as well as a desperate political gangster, but the hour of retribution is at hand; he must disgorge his winnings, throw away his false dice, and seek the hermitage, there to blaspheme and execrate his folly, for to repent is not a virtue within the capacity of his heart to obtain (*Vincennes Gazette*).

f. "Freedom of the press is the sole guarantee for a people who cannot attack the agents of power through the courts, something seen among us. If the men who govern us allow us to prosecute their misdeeds and crimes before ordinary judges, perhaps we will consent not to attack their absurdities and their vices before the court of public opinion" (YTC, CVh, 3, p. 93).

g. In the margin: "≠After the people themselves, the press is the most irresistible power that exists in America.≠"

Many men in France imagine that the violence of the press among us is due to the instability of the social state, to our political passions and to the general malaise that follows. So they are constantly waiting for a time when, after society has regained a tranquil footing, the press in turn will become calm. As for me, I would willingly attribute the extreme ascendancy that the press has over us to the causes indicated above; but I do not think that these causes influence its language much. The periodical press seems to me to have its own instincts and passions, apart from the circumstances in which it works. What happens in American really proves it for me.

America is perhaps at this moment the country in the world that contains within it the fewest seeds of revolution. In America, nevertheless, the press has the same destructive tastes as in France, and the same violence without the same reasons for anger. [<≠Most often it feeds on hate and envy; it speaks more to passions than to reason; it spreads falsehood and truth all jumbled together.≠>] In America, as in France, the press is an extraordinary power, a strange mixture of good and evil; liberty cannot live without it and order can hardly be maintained with it.[h]

What must be said is that the press has much less power in the United States than among us. Nothing, however, is rarer in that country than seeing a judicial proceeding directed against the press. The reason is simple: the Americans, while accepting among themselves the dogma of sovereignty of the people, have applied it sincerely. They did not have the idea of establishing, with elements that change every day, constitutions that endured forever. So to attack existing laws is not criminal, as long as you do not want to evade them by violence.

They believe, moreover, that the courts are powerless to moderate the press; that because the flexibility of human languages constantly escapes judicial analysis, crimes of this nature in a way slip out of the hand that reaches out to seize them. They think that to be able to act effectively on the press, a court would have to be found that was not only devoted to the

---

h. Variant: "The American press, like ours, is a power that you can speak ill of in quiet and that you bow before in public, that you can fight by surprise, but that no power can attack head on" Cf. note o of p. 78.

existing order, but was also able to stand above the public opinion that stirs around it, a court that judged without allowing publicity, ruled without justifying its decisions, and punished the intention even more than the words. Whoever had the power to create and to maintain such a court would waste his time pursuing freedom of the press; for then he would be absolute master of society itself and would be able to rid himself of writers and their writings at the same time. In the matter of the press, therefore, there is really not a middle ground between servitude and license. To reap the inestimable advantages that freedom of the press assures, you must know how to submit to the inevitable evils that it produces. Wanting to gain the first while escaping from the second is to give yourself over to one of these illusions that usually delude sick nations when, tired by struggles and exhausted by efforts, they seek the means to allow hostile opinions and opposite principles to coexist at the same time on the same soil.

The little power of newspapers in America is due to several causes; here are the principal ones:

The freedom to write, like all other freedoms, is that much more to be feared, the newer it is. A people who has never heard the affairs of State treated in front of it believes the first popular orator who appears. Among the Anglo-Americans, this liberty is as old as the founding of the colonies. Moreover, the press, which knows so well how to inflame human passions, cannot create those passions by itself. [{What feeds freedom of the press, what gives it a hold on human will are political passions.}] Now, in America, political life is active, varied, even agitated, but it is rarely troubled by profound passions; rarely do the latter arise when material interests are not jeopardized, and in the United States these interests prosper. To judge the difference that exists on this point between the Anglo-Americans and us, I have only to glance at the newspapers of the two peoples. In France, the commercial advertisements occupy a very limited space; even the news items are few; the vital part of a newspaper is where the political discussions are found. In America, three quarters of the immense newspaper put before your eyes are filled by advertisements; the rest is usually occupied by political news or simple stories; only now and then, in an obscure corner, do you notice one of those heated discussions that among us are the daily food of the reader.

Every power augments the action of its forces as their control is centralized; that is a general law of nature that examination demonstrates to the observer and that an even more certain instinct has always shown to the least of despots.

In France, the press combines two distinct types of centralization.

Nearly all of its power is concentrated in the same place and, so to speak, in the same hands, for the organs of the press are very few in number.

Constituted in this way, in the middle of a skeptical nation, the power of the press is necessarily almost without limit. It is an enemy with which a government can reach a shorter or longer truce; but it is difficult for a government to live in confrontation with the press for long.

Neither one nor the other of the two types of centralization that I have just spoken about exists in America.

The United States has no capital.[j] [≠In America the press is even less centralized than the government it attacks.≠] Enlightenment, like power, is disseminated in all the parts of this vast country. There, the beams of human intelligence, instead of coming from a common center, cut across each other in all directions; the Americans have placed the general direction of thought nowhere, any more than they have that of public affairs.

That is due to local circumstances that do not depend on men. But here are the ones that come from the laws:

In the United States, there are no licenses for printers, no stamps or registration for newspapers; the rule of surety bonds is unknown.

As a result, the creation of a newspaper is a simple and easy undertaking; a few[k] subscribers suffice for the journalist to cover his expenses. The

---

j. In the manuscript: "is fortunate enough not to have a capital."

Hervé de Tocqueville: "I would remove *fortunate enough*. With a single phrase, the author comes to a decision offhandedly on a question that is very susceptible to controversy. That is at least unnecessary" (YTC, CIIIb, 2, p. 45).

k. In the manuscript a blank indicates that Tocqueville thought about putting here the precise number of subscribers. Following this sentence you find: "The most reliable reports put it at [blank (ed.)] in 1832."

number of periodical or semi-periodical writings in the United States therefore surpasses all belief. The most enlightened Americans attribute the little power of the press to this incredible scattering of its forces. It is an axiom of political science in the United States that the only means to neutralize the effects of newspapers is to multiply their number. I cannot imagine that a truth so obvious has not yet become more common among us. I understand without difficulty that those who want to make revolutions with the aid of the press try to give it only a few powerful organs; but what I absolutely cannot conceive is that the official partisans of the established order and the natural supporters of existing laws believe that, by concentrating the press, its action can be attenuated. The governments of Europe seem to me to act toward the press in the same way that knights used to act toward their enemies. They had noticed from their own experience that centralization was a powerful weapon, and they wanted to provide it to their enemy, most probably to gain more glory in resisting him.

In the United States, there is hardly any small town without its newspaper. It can be easily understood that, among so many combatants, neither discipline nor unity of action can be established. Therefore each one raises his banner. Not that all the political newspapers of the Union are lined up for or against the administration; but they attack and defend it in a hundred different ways. So in the United States newspapers cannot establish those great waves of opinions that rise up or overwhelm the most powerful dikes. This division of the forces of the press produces still other no less remarkable effects. Because the creation of a newspaper is so easy, everyone can do it. On the other hand, competition means that a newspaper cannot hope for very great profits; this prevents great industrial talents from getting involved in enterprises of this type. Even if newspapers were a source of riches, they are so excessively numerous that there would not be enough talented writers to run them. So in general journalists in the United States do not have a very high [social] position; their education is only rudimentary; and the turn of their ideas is often vulgar. Now, in all things the majority makes the law; it establishes certain behaviors to which each person then conforms. The ensemble of these common habits is called a spirit;[m] there is the spirit of the bar, the spirit of the court. The spirit of the journalist, in France, is to discuss in a violent, but elevated and often eloquent way, the great interests of the State; if this is not always so, it is because every rule has its exceptions. The spirit of the journalist, in America, is to attack in a coarse way, unaffectedly and without art, the passions of those whom he addresses, to leave principles behind in order to grab men, to follow men in their private life, and to lay bare their weaknesses and their vices [treat the secrets of the domestic hearth and the honor of the marital bed].

Such an abuse of thought must be deplored. Later I will have the opportunity to inquire into what influence newspapers have on the taste and morality of the American people; but I repeat that at the moment I am only dealing with the political world. You cannot hide from the fact that the political effects of this license of the press contribute indirectly to the maintenance of public tranquillity. The result is that men who already have an elevated position in the opinion of their fellow citizens do not dare to write in the newspapers; and they thereby lose the most formidable weapon that they could use to stir popular passion to their profit.[1] The result is, above all, that the personal views expressed by journalists have no weight, so to speak, in the eyes of readers. What readers seek in a newspaper is knowledge of facts; only by altering or misrepresenting these facts can a journalist gain some influence for his opinion.

Reduced to these resources alone, the press still exercises an immense power in America. It makes political life circulate in all parts of this vast territory. Always watchful, the press constantly lays bare the secret

---

m. In the manuscript: "what is called a spirit."
Gustave de Beaumont:

I do not like that. Here is how I would conceive the sentence: I would delete *what is called a spirit,* which is certainly bad (there are many other things that are called a *spirit,* without counting the author) and I would say: in all, there is what is called the *spirit of the thing.* There is the *spirit of the bar,* the *spirit of the court.* Journalism also has its own. In France it consists . . ." (YTC, CIIIb, 2, p. 62).

1. *They write in newspapers only in the rare cases when they want to address the people and speak in their own name; when, for example, slanderous charges have been spread about them, and they want to reestablish the true facts.*

motivating forces of politics and compels public men, one by one, to appear before the court of opinion. It rallies interests around certain doctrines and formulates the creed of parties. Through the press, interests
speak together without seeing each other, agree without having contact.
When a large number of the organs of the press manage to follow the
same path, their influence eventually becomes nearly irresistible; and public opinion, always struck from the same side, ends by yielding to their
blows.

In the United States, each newspaper individually has little power; but
the periodical press, after the people, is still the first of powers.[A]

That the Opinions Established under the Dominion of Freedom of the Press in the United States Are Often More Tenacious Than Those That Are Found Elsewhere under the Dominion of Censorship.[n]

In the United States, democracy constantly leads new men to the leadership
of public affairs; so the government has little coherence and order in its
measures. But the general principles of government there are more stable
than in many other countries, and the principal opinions that rule society
are more lasting. When an idea, whether sound or unreasonable, takes hold
of the mind of the American people, nothing is more difficult than to erad-
icate it.

The same fact has been observed in England, the European country in
which, for a century, the greatest freedom of thought and the most invincible prejudices have been seen.

I attribute this effect to the very cause that, at first view, should seemingly
prevent it, freedom of the press. Peoples among whom this freedom exists
are attached to their opinions by pride as much as by conviction. They love
them because they seem sound to them, and also because they have chosen

n. In the margin: "≠But this is due to the political institutions and not to freedom
of the press.≠"

them. And they hold them not only as something true, but also as something of their own.

There are still several other reasons.

A great man has said that *ignorance is at the two ends of knowledge.*° Perhaps it would have been more true to say that deep convictions are found only at the two ends, and that doubt is in the middle. In fact, you can consider human intelligence in three distinct and often successive states.

A man strongly believes, because he adopts a belief without going deeper. When objections appear, he doubts. Often he succeeds in resolving all these doubts; and then he begins to believe again. This time, he no longer grasps truth haphazardly and in the shadows; but he faces it and walks directly toward its light.[2]

When freedom of the press finds men in the first state, it leaves them for yet a long time with this habit of believing strongly without reflection; only it changes the object of their unthinking beliefs each day. So, over the whole intellectual horizon, the mind of man continues to see only one point at a time; but this point is constantly changing. This is the time of sudden revolutions. Woe to the generations that are the first suddenly to allow freedom of the press!

Soon, however, the circle of new ideas is nearly covered. Experience arrives, and man is plunged into doubt and a universal distrust.

You can be assured that the majority of men will always stop at one of these two states. The majority will believe without knowing why, or will not know exactly what should be believed.

As for the other type of thoughtful and self-confident conviction that is born out of knowledge and arises from the very midst of the agitations of doubt, it will never be granted except in response to the efforts made by a very small number of men to attain it.

---

o. Pascal, *Pensées,* number 83 in Lafuma edition.

2. *Still, I do not know if this thoughtful and self-confident conviction ever elevates man to the degree of ardor and devotion that dogmatic beliefs inspire.*

Now, it has been observed that, in centuries of religious fervor, men sometimes changed belief; while in centuries of doubt, each one stubbornly kept his belief. This is how things happen in politics, under the rule of freedom of the press. Since all social theories, one by one, have been contested and fought, those who are attached to one of them keep it, not so much because they are sure that it is good, as because they are not sure that there is a better one.

In these centuries, you do not risk death as easily for your opinions; but you do not change them. And, at the very same time, fewer martyrs and fewer apostates are found.

To this reason, add another still more powerful. When opinions are doubted, men end up being attached solely to instincts and to material interests, which are much more visible, more tangible and more permanent by their nature than opinions are.

To know whether democracy or aristocracy governs better is a very difficult question to decide. But clearly democracy hinders one man and aristocracy oppresses another.P

That is a self-evident truth; there is no need to discuss it; you are rich and I am poor.

[≠When, as often happens, freedom of the press is combined with sovereignty of the people, the majority is sometimes seen to decide clearly in favor of an opinion. Then, the opposite opinion no longer has a way to be heard; those who share it fall silent, while their adversaries triumph out loud.

Suddenly there is an unimaginable silence of which we Europeans can have no idea. Certain thoughts seem suddenly to disappear from the memory of men. Then freedom of the press exists in name, but in fact censorship

p. In the manuscript: "that democracy hinders you and aristocracy oppresses me."
Gustave de Beaumont: "It is not the author's intention to enter on stage and to appear as a proletarian crushed by the aristocrats. So this form must be dropped; say: *But clearly democracy hinders one man and aristocracy oppresses another.* Then you could finish by saying: *You are rich and I am poor.* Why? Because then it is clearly seen that this is only a convention of language" (YTC, CIIIb, e, pp. 63, 54).

reigns, a censorship a thousand times more powerful than that exercised by power./

Note. I know of no country where freedom of the press exists less than in America on certain questions. There are few despotic countries where censorship does not concern the form rather than the substance of thought. But in America there are subjects that cannot be touched upon in any way≠].

CHAPTER 4

Of Political Association in the United States

*Daily use that the Anglo-Americans make of the right of
association.—Three types of political associations.—How the
Americans apply the representative system to associations.—
Dangers that result for the State.—Great convention of 1831
relating to the tariff.—Legislative character of this
convention.—Why the unlimited exercise of the right of
association is not as dangerous in the United States as
elsewhere.—Why it can be considered necessary there.—
Utility of associations among democratic peoples.*

Of all the countries in the world, America has taken greatest advantage of
association and has applied this powerful means of action[a] to the greatest
variety of objectives.

Apart from permanent associations created by the law, known as towns,
cities and counties, a multitude of others owe their birth and development
only to individual wills.

The inhabitant of the United States learns from birth that he must depend on himself in the struggle against the ills and difficulties of life; he
looks upon social authority only with a defiant and uneasy eye, and calls
upon its power only when he cannot do without it. This begins to be noticed as early as school where children, even in their games, submit to their

---

a. Variant: "≠Of all the countries in the world, America is where government is least
centralized. It is also the one that has taken greatest advantage of association. There is a
correlation between these two things.≠"

own rules and punish their own infractions.[b] The same spirit is found in all the actions of social life. An obstruction occurs on the public road; the way is interrupted; traffic stops; the neighbors soon get together as a deliberative body; out of this improvised assembly will come an executive power that will remedy the difficulty, before the idea of an authority pre-dating that of those interested has occurred to anyone's imagination. If it is a matter of pleasure, the Americans will associate to give more splendor and order to the festival. Lastly, they unite to resist entirely intellectual enemies: together they fight intemperance. In the United States, they associate for purposes of public security, commerce and industry, [pleasure], morality and religion. There is nothing that human will despairs of achieving by the free action of the collective power of individuals.

Later I will have the opportunity to speak about the effects that association produces in civil life.[c] At the moment, I must stay within the political world.

[≠After the press, association is the great means that parties use to get into public affairs and to gain the majority.

In America the freedom of association for political ends is unlimited. The freedom of assembly in order to discuss together the views of the association is equally unlimited.≠]

Once the right of association is recognized, citizens can use it in different ways.

An association consists only of the public support that a certain number of individuals give to such and such doctrines and of the promise that they make to work in a particular way toward making those doctrines prevail. Thus the right to associate almost merges with freedom to

---

b. "So how to move hearts and develop love of country and its laws? Dare I say? By the games of children; by institutions, pointless in the eyes of superficial men, but which form cherished habits and invincible attachments" (Rousseau, *Considérations sur le gouvernement de Pologne,* chapter I, in *Œuvres complètes* [Paris: Pléiade, 1964], III, p. 955).

c. In the margin: "≠Perhaps the chapter should begin here and what precedes should be kept for the chapter on ordinary associations?≠"

write;[d] but the association already has more power than the press. When an opinion is represented by an association, it is forced to take a clearer and more precise form. It counts its partisans and involves them in its cause. The latter learn to know each other, and their ardor increases with their number. The association gathers the efforts of divergent minds into a network and vigorously pushes them toward a single, clearly indicated goal [<even if it did not provide material means of action, its moral force would still be very formidable>].

The second level in the exercise of the right of association is the power to assemble. When a political association is allowed to locate centers of action at certain important points of the country, its activity becomes greater and its influence more extensive. There, men see each other; the means of action combine; opinions are expressed with the force and heat that written thought can never attain.

Finally, in the exercise of the right of association in political matters, there is a last level. The partisans of the same opinion can meet in electoral colleges and name representatives to go to represent them in a central assembly. Strictly speaking, this is the representative system applied to a party.

So, in the first case, men who profess the same opinion establish a purely intellectual bond among themselves; in the second, they meet in small assemblies that represent only a fraction of the party; finally, in the third, they form, so to speak, a separate nation within the nation, a government within the government.[e] Their representatives, similar to the representatives of the majority, represent in themselves alone the whole collective force of their partisans; just like the representatives of the majority, they arrive with an

d. In the manuscript: "This type of association almost merges with freedom of the press."

Hervé de Tocqueville: "This sentence lacks clarity. The idea is not well developed, and its expression is not good. What is an association that merges with a liberty, a material thing with something not material?" (YTC, CIIIb, 2, p. 48).

e. Note in the margin: "≠Government within the government. Printing there [illegible word (ed.)]. See conversation with Ingersol [Ingersoll (ed.)].≠" It concerns Charles J. Ingersoll. See George W. Pierson, *Tocqueville and Beaumont in America*, pp. 480–82.

appearance of nationhood and all the moral power that results from that. It is true that, unlike the representatives of the majority, they do not have the right to make laws; but they have the power to attack the laws that exist and to formulate in advance those that should exist.

I assume a people who is not perfectly used to the practice of liberty or among whom deep political passions are stirring. Alongside the majority that makes the laws, I put a minority that only attends to *preambles* and stops at *plans of action;* and I cannot keep myself from believing that public order is exposed to great hazards [<≠for man is made in such a way that, in his mind, there is only a step, the easiest of all to take, between proving that something is good and doing it.≠>]

Between proving that one law is better in itself than another, and proving that it must be substituted for the other, there is certainly a great distance. But where the minds of enlightened men see a great distance remaining, the imagination of the crowd no longer sees any. There are times, moreover, when the nation is almost equally divided between two parties, each claiming to represent the majority. If, next to the governing power, a power arises whose moral authority is almost as great, can we believe that it will limit itself for long to speaking without acting?

Will it always stop before the metaphysical consideration that the purpose of associations is to lead opinions and not to force them, to recommend law and not to make it?

The more I contemplate the principal effects of the independence of the press, the more I am convinced that among modern peoples independence of the press is the capital and, so to speak, the constituent element of liberty. So a people who wants to remain free has the right to require that the independence of the press be respected at all cost. But the *unlimited* freedom of association in political matters cannot be completely confused with the freedom to write. The first is both less necessary and more dangerous than the second. A nation can set limits on the first without losing control over itself; sometimes it must set limits in order to continue to be in control.

In America, the freedom of association for political ends is unlimited.

An example will show, better than all I could add, the degree to which it is tolerated.

You recall how the question of the tariff or free trade has stirred minds up in America. The tariff favored or attacked not only opinions, but also very powerful material interests. The North attributed a portion of its prosperity to the tariff; the South, nearly all of its misfortunes. It can be said that, for a long time, the only political passions that have agitated the Union have arisen from the tariff.

In 1831, when the quarrel was most bitter, an obscure citizen of Massachusetts thought to propose, in the newspapers, that all the enemies of the tariff send deputies to Philadelphia, in order to consult together about the ways to reestablish free trade. In a few days, the proposal circulated from Maine to New Orleans due to the power of the printed word. The enemies of the tariff adopted it ardently. They met everywhere and named deputies. Most of these were men who were known, and some of them were famous. South Carolina, seen afterward to take up arms in the same cause, sent sixty-three delegates on its behalf. The first of October 1831, the assembly, which, following the American habit, had taken the name "convention," formed in Philadelphia; it numbered more than two hundred members. The discussions were public and, from the first day, took on an entirely legislative character. The deputies examined the extent of congressional powers, the theories of free trade, and finally the various provisions of the tariff. At the end of ten days, the assembly dispersed after having drafted an address to the American people. This address stated: 1. that Congress did not have the right to pass a tariff and that the existing tariff was unconstitutional; 2. that the lack of free trade was not in the interest of any people, and particularly not the American people.

It must be recognized that, until now, unlimited freedom of association in political matters has not produced, in the United States, the harmful results that could perhaps be expected elsewhere. There, the right of association is an English import, and it has existed in America since the beginning. Today, the use of this right has passed into the habits and into the mores. [{perhaps today it has even become a necessary guarantee against parliamentary tyranny as well}].

In our time, freedom of association has become a necessary[f] guarantee

f. The manuscript reads "almost necessary."

against the tyranny of the majority.[g] In the United States, once a party has become dominant, all public power passes into its hands; its particular friends hold all posts and have the use of all organized forces. Not able to break through the barrier that separates them from power, the most distinguished men of the opposite party must be able to establish themselves outside of it; with its whole moral strength, the minority must resist the material power that oppresses it. So one danger is set against another more to be feared.

The omnipotence of the majority appears to me to be such a great peril for the American republics that the dangerous means used to limit it still seem good to me.

Here I will express a thought that will recall what I said elsewhere about town liberties. There are no countries where associations are more necessary, to prevent the despotism of parties or the arbitrariness of the prince, than those where the social state is democratic. Among aristocratic nations, secondary bodies form natural associations that stop the abuses of power.[h] In countries where such associations do not exist, if individuals cannot artificially and temporarily create something that resembles those natural associations, I no longer see any dike against any sort of tyranny; and a great people can be oppressed with impunity by a factious handful of individuals or by a man.

[≠There is a cause that is hardly suspected and that, in my view, renders political associations less dangerous in America than elsewhere; it is uni-

g. Cf. note a for p. 402.

h. Aristocracy to democracy./

Aristocracies are *natural* associations that need neither enlightenment nor calculations to resist the great national association that is called the government. As a result they are more favorable to liberty than democracy is. It is possible for associations to be formed in a democracy, but by dint of enlightenment and talents; and they are never enduring. In general, when an oppressive government has been able to form in a democracy, it finds itself facing only isolated men and no collective forces. Hence its irresistible strength. What gives the judicial system that immeasurable force over the person on trial? It has the use of the forces of the entire society against one man. Extreme example of the power of association and the weakness of isolation (YTC, CVh, 1, p. 82).

versal suffrage. In Europe, associations act in two ways: by the material strength that their organization brings to them, or by the moral power given to them by the support of the majority that they always claim to represent. In the United States this last element of strength is lacking. In countries where universal suffrage is allowed, there is never a doubtful majority, because no party can establish itself as the representative of those who did not vote.

Thus, in America, associations can never pretend to represent the majority; they only aim to convince it. They do not want to act, but to persuade; in that, above all, they are different from the political associations of Europe.≠]

The meeting of a great political convention (for there are conventions of all types) can often become a necessary measure. Even in America, such a meeting is a serious event, one that the friends of their country can only contemplate with fear.

This was seen very clearly in the convention of 1831, where all the efforts of the distinguished men who were part of the assembly tended to moderate its language and to limit its objectives. Probably, the convention of 1831 exercised, in fact, a great influence on the mind of the discontented and prepared them for the open revolt that took place in 1832 against the commercial laws of the Union.

You cannot conceal the fact that, of all liberties, the unlimited freedom of association, in political matters, is the last one that a people can bear.[j] If unlimited freedom of association does not make a people fall into anarchy, it puts a people on the brink, so to speak, at every moment. This

---

j. Nations are not able in all periods of their history to bear the same degree of freedom of association. You find some peoples among whom the relative positions and the strength of parties make certain associations dangerous; among others, despotism has taken care to keep men in such great ignorance that they do not understand what can be done by associating together. Only time and the gradual development of free institutions can teach them.

The society that cannot take the right of association away from citizens without destroying itself is, therefore, sometimes required to modify it, depending on the times and mores (YTC, CVh, 3, pp. 92–93).

See José María Sauca Cano, *La ciencia de la asociación de Tocqueville* (Madrid: Centro de Estudios Constitucionales, 1995).

liberty, so dangerous, offers guarantees on one point, however; in countries where associations are free, secret societies are unknown. In America, there are agitators, but not conspirators.

Different Ways in Which the Right of Association Is Understood in Europe and in the United States, and the Different Use That Is Made of That Right

After the liberty of acting alone, the liberty most natural to man is to combine his efforts with the efforts of his fellows and to act in common. So to me, the right of association seems almost as inalienable by nature as individual liberty. The legislator would not want to destroy it without attacking society itself. But if there are some peoples among whom the liberty to unite together is only beneficial and fruitful in prosperity, there are also others who, by their excesses, distort it and turn an element of life into a cause of destruction. It seemed to me that a comparison of the different paths that associations follow, in countries where the liberty is understood and in those where this liberty turns into license, would be useful both to governments and to parties.

Most Europeans still see the association as a weapon that is hastily made to try out immediately on the field of battle.

They join together for the purpose of talking, but the next thought, that of acting, preoccupies all minds. An association is an army; they talk in order to take stock and to come to life; and then they march on the enemy. In the eyes of those who compose the association, legal resources can appear to be means, but they are never the only means of success.

That is not the way the right of association is understood in the United States. In America, citizens who form the minority join together, first, to determine their number and, in this way, to weaken the moral dominion of the majority; the second objective of those associated is to test and, in this way, to discover the arguments most suitable for making an impression on the majority; for they always hope to attract the majority and then, in its name, to have the use of power. [≠So in America, the purpose of associations is to convince and not to compel.≠]

Political associations in the United States therefore are peaceful in their objective and legal in their means; and when they claim to want to triumph only through law they are, in general, speaking the truth.

On this point the noticeable difference between the Americans and us is due to several causes.

In Europe parties exist that differ so much from the majority that they can never hope to gain their support; and these very parties believe they are strong enough by themselves to struggle against the majority. When a party of this type forms an association, it does not want to convince, but to fight. In America, men[k] who are so removed from the majority by their opinion can do nothing against the power of the majority; all others hope to win it over.

So the exercise of the right of association becomes dangerous in proportion to how impossible it is for great parties to become the majority. In a country like the United States, where opinions differ only by nuances, the right of association can, so to speak, remain unlimited.

What still leads us to see, in freedom of association, only the right to make war against those governing, is our inexperience in liberty. When a party gains strength, the first idea that comes to its mind, as to that of a man, is the idea of violence. The idea of persuasion only comes later; it arises from experience.

The English, who are divided among themselves in so profound a way, rarely abuse the right of association, because they have used it longer.

In addition, among us, such a passionate taste for war exists that no undertaking, however insane, even if it must turn the State upside down, lacks adherents who see themselves as glorious for dying on the field of battle.

But of all the causes in the United States that work together to moderate the violence of political association, perhaps the most powerful is universal suffrage. In countries where universal suffrage is accepted, the majority is never in doubt, because no party can reasonably set itself up as the representative of those who have not voted. So the associations know, and everyone knows, that they do not represent the majority. This results from

k. The manuscript reads: "the parties."

the very fact of their existence; for, if they represented the majority, they would change the law themselves instead of asking for its reform.

The moral force of the government they are attacking is greatly increased; theirs, much weakened.

In Europe, there is hardly any association that does not claim to represent or believe it represents the will of the majority. This claim or this belief prodigiously increases their strength, and serves marvelously to legitimate their actions. For what is more excusable than violence in order to gain victory for the oppressed cause of right?

Thus, in the immense complication of human laws, sometimes extreme liberty corrects the abuses of liberty, and extreme democracy prevents the dangers of democracy.

In Europe, associations consider themselves, in a way, the legislative and executive council of the nation that cannot speak for itself; starting from this idea, they act and command. In America, where, in everyone's eyes, associations represent only a minority of the nation, they talk and petition.

The means used by associations in Europe agree with the end that they propose.

Since the principal end of these associations is to act and not to talk, to fight and not to persuade, they are led naturally to adopt an organization that is not at all civil and to introduce military habits and maxims. Thus you can see them centralize the control of their forces, as much as possible, and deliver the power of all into the hands of a very small number of men.[m]

The members of these associations respond to an order like soldiers at war; they profess the dogma of passive obedience, or rather, by uniting together, they have at one stroke made the complete sacrifice of their judgment and free will. Thus, within these associations, a tyranny often reigns that is more unbearable than the one exercised within the society in the name of the government that is attacked.

This greatly diminishes their moral force. In this way, they lose the sacred

---

m. In the margin: "≠They use legal resources as a stopgap means and not as the means.≠"

character attached to the struggle of the oppressed against the oppressors. For how can he who, in certain circumstances, consents to obey slavishly a few of his fellows, to surrender his will to them and to submit even his thoughts to them, how can that man possibly claim that he wants to be free?

The Americans have also established a government within associations. But, if I can express myself in this way, it is a civil government. Individual independence plays a role. As in society, all men there march at the same time toward the same end. But no one is forced to march exactly in the same path. No one sacrifices his will and his reason; but his will and his reason are applied to making the common enterprise succeed.

CHAPTER 5

Of the Government of
Democracy in America

I know that I am walking here on fiery ground. Each of the words of this chapter must in some respects offend the different parties dividing my country. I will, nonetheless, express my whole thought.

In Europe, we have difficulty judging the true character and permanent instincts of democracy, because in Europe there is a struggle between two opposite principles. And we do not know precisely what should be attributed to the principles themselves or to the passions that the conflict has produced.

It is not the same in America. There, the people dominate without obstacles; there are no dangers to fear or wrongs to revenge.

So, in America, democracy is given over to its own inclinations. Its pace is natural, and all its movements are free. That is where it must be judged. And for whom would this study be interesting and profitable, if not for us, who are dragged along each day by an irresistible movement and who march blindly, perhaps toward despotism, perhaps toward the republic, but definitely toward a democratic social state?

Of Universal Suffrage

I said previously that all the states of the Union had allowed universal suffrage. It is also found among populations situated at different levels of [{civilization}] the social scale. I have had the opportunity to see its effects in various places and among races of men made nearly strangers to each other by their language, their religion, or their mores, in Louisiana as in New England, in Georgia as in Canada. I noted that, in America, universal suffrage was far from producing all the good and all the evil that are expected in Europe, and that, in general, its effects were other than those supposed.[a]

Of the Choices of the People and of the Instincts of American Democracy in Its Choices

In the United States the most outstanding men are rarely called to the leadership of public affairs.—Causes of this phenomenon.—The envy that animates the lower classes in France against the upper classes is not a French sentiment, but democratic.—Why, in America, distinguished men often move away on their own from political careers.

Many people in Europe believe without saying, or say without believing, that one of the great advantages of universal suffrage is to call men worthy of public confidence to the leadership of public affairs.[b] It is said that a people cannot govern itself, but always sincerely wants the good of the State, and its instinct hardly ever fails to point out those who are animated by the same desire and who are most capable of holding power.[c]

I must say that, for me, what I saw in America does not authorize me to think that this is so. Upon my arrival in the United States, I was struck

---

a. Marginal note: "≠For that I do not know what to do. The interests that divide men are innumerable, but truth is singular and has only one way to come about.≠"

b. "≠What is most important to a nation is not that those who govern are men of talent, but that they have no interests contrary to the mass of their fellow citizens≠" (YTC, CVh, 4, p. 90).

c. Repetition of an argument from Montesquieu, who asserts in chapter II of book II of the *Esprit des lois:*

> The people are admirable for choosing those to whom they must entrust some part of their authority. In order to decide they have only things that they cannot ignore and facts that are tangible. . . . But would they be able to conduct a matter, to know the places, the occasions, the moments, how to profit from them? No, they will not. . . . The people, who have enough capacity to understand the management of others, are not fit to manage by themselves (*Œuvres complètes* [Paris: Pléiade, 1951], II, pp. 240–41. Cf. note e for p. 93).

with surprise to find out how common merit was among the governed and how uncommon it was among those governing.[d] Today it is a constant fact in the United States that the most outstanding men are rarely called to public office, and we are forced to recognize that this has occurred as democracy has gone beyond all its former limits. Clearly the race of American statesmen has grown singularly smaller over the past half century.

Several causes of this phenomenon can be indicated.

It is impossible, no matter what you do, to raise the enlightenment of the people above a certain level. Whatever you do to make human learning more accessible, improve the methods of instruction and make knowledge more affordable, you will never be able to have men learn and develop their intelligence without devoting time to the task.

So the greater or lesser facility that the people have for living without working sets the necessary limit to their intellectual progress. This limit is further away in certain countries, closer in certain others; but for there to be no limit, it would be necessary for the people not to have to be occupied with the material cares of life; that is, for them no longer to be the people.[e] So it is as difficult to imagine a society in which all men are very enlightened, as a State in which all citizens are rich; these are two correlative difficulties. I will admit without difficulty that the mass of citizens very sincerely wants the country's good. I go even further, and I say that, in general, the lower classes of society seem to me to mingle fewer calculations of personal interest with this desire than do the upper classes; but what they always more or less lack is the art of judging the means while sincerely desiring the end.

d. Why, when civilization spreads, do prominent men decline in number? Why, when learning becomes the privilege of all, do great intellectual talents become more rare? Why, when there are no more lower classes, are there not more upper classes? Why, when understanding of government reaches the masses, are great geniuses missing from the leadership of society? America clearly poses these questions. But who will be able to resolve them? (pocket notebook 3, 6 November 1831, YTC, BIIa, and *Voyage, OC,* V, 1, p. 188).

e. "As the cares of material life demand less time, the development of the intelligence of the people will be greater. The one concerned with none of these cares will always have an intellectual advantage over those who are obliged to be concerned with them" (YTC, CVh, 4, p. 37).

What long study, what diverse notions are necessary to get an exact idea of the character of a single man! There the greatest geniuses go astray, and the multitude would succeed! The people never find the time and the means to give themselves to this work. They must always judge in haste and attach themselves to the most salient objects. As a result, charlatans of all types know very well the secret of pleasing the people, while their true friends most often fail. [<In most of the states of the Union I saw positions occupied by men who had succeeded in gaining them only by flattering the slightest passions and bowing before the smallest caprices of the people.>]

Moreover, it is not always the capacity to choose men of merit that democracy lacks, but the desire and the taste.

The fact must not be concealed that democratic institutions develop the sentiment of envy in the human heart to a very high degree, not so much because they offer each person the means to become equal to others, but because these means constantly fail those who use them. Democratic institutions awaken and flatter the passion for equality without ever being able to satisfy it entirely. Every day, at the moment when people believe they have grasped complete equality, it escapes from their hands and flees, as Pascal says,[f] in an eternal flight. People become heated in search of this good, all the more precious since it is close enough to be known, but far enough away not to be savored. The chance to succeed rouses the people; the uncertainty of success irritates them. They get agitated, grow weary, become embittered. Then, everything that is in some way beyond them seems an obstacle to their desires, and there is no superiority, however legitimate, that they do not grow tired of seeing.

Many people imagine among us that the secret instinct that leads the lower classes to keep the upper classes away from the leadership of public affairs as much as they can is found only in France. That is an error: the instinct that I am speaking about is not French, it is democratic. Political circumstances have been able to give it a particular character of bitterness, but they did not give birth to it.

In the United States, the people have no hatred for the upper classes of society; but they feel little goodwill toward them and carefully keep them

---

f. *Pensées,* number 390 in the Lafuma edition.

out of power; they do not fear great talents, but they appreciate them little.g In general, you notice that everything that arises without their support gains their favor with difficulty.

While the natural instincts of democracy lead the people to keep distinguished men away from power, an instinct no less strong leads the latter to remove themselves from a political career in which it is so difficult for them to remain entirely themselves, and to operate without debasing themselves. This thought is very ingenuously expressed by Chancellor Kent. The celebrated author about whom I am speaking, after giving great praise to the part of the Constitution that grants the nomination of judges to the executive power, adds: "The fittest men would probably have too much reservedness of manners, and severity of morals, to secure an elec-

g. Here Tocqueville seems to invoke the difference that Guizot and most of the *Doctrinaires* establish between democracy, the political form that destroys the legitimate inequality of intelligence and virtue existing among men and that leads to the despotism of the greatest number, and representative government that divides power according to reason. "Representative government therefore is not that of the numerical majority pure and simple, it is that of the majority of those who are capable (*des capables*)," writes François Guizot (*Journal des cours publics,* Paris: au bureau du journal, 1821–1822, vol. I, lecture 7, p. 98). If Tocqueville radically rejects Guizot's conclusion that makes the middle class the most capable class, his problem remains nonetheless the same: how to make the best govern? This question, which marks the entire history of political thought, had been explained in this way by Tocqueville to Louis de Kergorlay: "The most rational government is not the one in which *all* those interested take part, but the one that the most enlightened and most moral classes of society lead" (Letter from Yonkers, 29 June 1831, *Correspondance avec Kergorlay, OC,* XIII, 1, p. 234). Four years later, just after the publication of the first part of his book, Tocqueville wrote to Mill:

> It is much less a matter for the friends of democracy to find the means to make the people govern than to make the people choose those most capable of governing, and to give the people enough authority over the latter for the people to be able to direct the whole of their conduct and not the detail of actions or the means of execution. That is the problem. I am deeply persuaded that on its solution depends the future fate of modern nations (letter of 3 December 1835, *Correspondance anglaise, OC,* VI, 1, pp. 303–4).

Tocqueville, however, seems only to repeat what Mill had written in his review of the first part of *Democracy:* "The best government [. . .] must be the government of the wisest" (John Stuart Mill, "De Tocqueville on Democracy in America," *London and Westminster Review,* 30, 1835, pp. 110–11). See Luiz Díez del Corral, "Tocqueville and the Political Thought of the Doctrinaires," *Alexis de Tocqueville. Livre du centenaire* (Paris: Editions du CNRS, 1960), pp. 57–70.

tion resting on universal suffrage" (*Kent's Commentaries,* vol. I, p. 272 [273 (ed.)].) This was published without contradiction in America in the year 1830.

This demonstrated to me that <u>those who regard universal suffrage as a guarantee for good choices are under a complete illusion.</u> Universal suffrage has other advantages, but not that one.

Of the Causes That Can Partially Correct These Democratic Instincts

Opposite effects produced on peoples as on men
by great perils.—Why America saw so many remarkable men
at the head of its public affairs fifty years ago.—
Influence that enlightenment and mores exercise on the choices of
the people.—Example of New England.—States of
the Southwest.—How certain laws influence the choices of
the people.—Indirect election.—Its effects on the
composition of the Senate.

When great perils threaten the State, you often see people happily choose the citizens most appropriate to save them.

It has been remarked that, in pressing danger, man rarely remains at his usual level; he rises well above, or falls below. The same thing happens to peoples themselves. Extreme perils, instead of elevating a nation, sometimes finish demoralizing it; they arouse its passions without guiding them; and, far from enlightening its mind, they trouble it. The Jews still slit their own throats amid the smoking ruins of the Temple. But, among nations as among men, it is more common to see extraordinary virtues arise from very present dangers. Then great characters appear like those monuments, hidden by the darkness of night, that suddenly stand out against the glow of a fire. Genius is no longer averse to reappearing on its own, and the people, struck by their own dangers, temporarily forget their envious passions. Then, it is not uncommon to see celebrated names emerge from the electoral urn. I said above that in America the statesmen of today seem[h] greatly inferior to those who appeared at the head of public affairs fifty years ago. This is due not only to laws, but also to circumstances. When America fought for the most just of causes, that of one people escaping from the yoke of another people; when it was a matter of having a new nation emerge in the world, all souls rose to reach the lofty goal of their efforts. In this general excitement, superior men courted the people and the people, embracing them, placed them at their head. But such events are rare; judgment must be based on the ordinary course of things.

If temporary events sometimes succeed in combating the passions of democracy, enlightenment and, above all, mores exercise a no less powerful and more enduring influence on its inclinations. This is clearly noticed in the United States.

In New England, where education and liberty are the daughters of morality and religion, where society, already old and long settled, has been able to form maxims and habits, the people, while escaping from all the superiorities that wealth and birth have ever created among men, have become used to respecting and submitting to intellectual and moral superiorities without displeasure; consequently, you see democracy in New England make better choices than anywhere else.

In contrast, as you descend toward the south, in the states where the social bond is less ancient and less powerful, where instruction is less widespread, and where the principles of morality, religion, and liberty are less happily combined, you notice that talents and virtues become more and more rare among those governing.

When, finally, you enter the new states of the Southwest, where the social body, formed yesterday, still presents only an agglomeration of adventurers or speculators, you are astounded to see what hands hold the public power, and you wonder by what force independent of legislation and men the State can grow and society prosper there.

h. The manuscript says "were."

There are certain laws of a democratic nature, however, that succeed in partially correcting these dangerous democratic instincts.

When you enter the House chamber in Washington, you feel struck by the vulgar aspect of the great assembly. Often your eye searches in vain for a celebrated man within the assembly. Nearly all its members are obscure persons, whose names bring no image to mind. They are, for the most part, village lawyers, tradesmen, or even men belonging to the lowest classes. In a country where instruction is nearly universal, it is said that the representatives of the people do not always know how to write correctly.[j]

[<If they speak, their language is usually without dignity and the ideas they express are devoid of scope and loftiness.>]

Two steps from there opens the Senate chamber, whose narrow enclosure contains a large portion of the famous men of America. You notice hardly a single man there who does not evoke the idea of recent celebrity. They are eloquent lawyers, distinguished generals, skilled magistrates, or known statesmen. All the words that issue from this [august] assembly would do honor to the greatest parliamentary debates of Europe.

What causes this bizarre contrast? Why is the nation's elite found in this chamber rather than in the other? Why does the first assembly gather so many vulgar elements, while the second seems to have a monopoly of talents and enlightenment? Both come from the people, however; both are

---

j. The manuscript says: "the representatives of the people do not know . . ."

Elections./

When the right to vote is *universal,* and deputies are *paid* by the State, the choices of the people can descend and stray to a singular degree.

Two years ago, the inhabitants of the district in which Memphis is the capital, sent to the House of Representatives of Congress an individual named David Crockett, who has no education, can scarcely read, has no property, no fixed abode, but spends his life hunting, selling his game to make a living, and living constantly in the woods. His competitor was a man of talent and moderate wealth who lost. Memphis, 20 December 1831 (YTC, BIIa, notebook E, and *Voyage, OC,* V, 1, pp. 274–75).

the result of universal suffrage, and, until now, no voice has been raised in America to maintain that the Senate might be the enemy of popular interests. So what causes such an enormous difference? I see only a single fact that explains it. The election that produces the House of Representatives is direct; the one producing the Senate is subject to two stages. The universality of citizens names the legislature of each state, and the federal Constitution, transforming each of these legislatures into electoral bodies, draws from them the members of the Senate. So the Senators express the result of universal suffrage, though indirectly. For the legislature, which names the Senators, is not an aristocratic or privileged body that derives its electoral right from itself; it is essentially dependent on the universality of citizens. In general it is elected by them annually, and they can always direct its choices by remaking it with new members. But it is sufficient for the popular will to pass through this chosen assembly in order, in a sense, to be transformed and to emerge clothed in more noble and more beautiful forms. So the men elected in this way always represent exactly the governing majority of the nation; but they represent only the elevated thoughts that circulate in its midst, the generous instincts that animate it, and not the small passions that often trouble it and the vices that dishonor it.

It is easy to see a moment in the future when the American republics will be forced to multiply the use of two stages in their electoral system, under pain of getting miserably lost among the pitfalls of democracy.[k]

I will have no difficulty in admitting it; I see in indirect election the only means to put the use of political liberty within reach of all classes of the people. Those who hope to make this means the exclusive weapon of one party, and those who fear this means, seem to me to be equally in error.

k. On the contrary, the seventeenth amendment to the American Constitution, approved 31 May 1913, establishes direct election of Senators, by regularizing in large part a preexisting situation, by which the second voters committed themselves to scrupulously following the desires expressed by the votes of the first voters.

Influence That American Democracy Has Exercised on Electoral Laws[m]

The rarity of elections exposes the State to great crises.—
Their frequency keeps it in a feverish agitation.—
The Americans have chosen the second of these two evils.—
Variableness of the law.—Opinion of Hamilton,
Madison and Jefferson on this subject.

When election recurs only at long intervals, the State runs the risk of upheaval at each election.

Parties[n] then make prodigious efforts to grasp a fortune that comes so rarely within reach; and since the evil is almost without remedy for candidates who fail, everything must be feared from their ambition driven to despair. If, in contrast, the legal struggle must soon be renewed, those who are defeated wait.

When elections follow one another rapidly, their frequency maintains a feverish movement in society and keeps public affairs in a state of constant change.

Thus, on the one hand, there is a chance of uneasiness for the State; on the other, a chance of revolution; the first system harms the goodness of government, the second threatens its existence.

The Americans have preferred to expose themselves to the first evil rather than to the second. In that, they have been guided by instinct much more than by reasoning, since democracy drives the taste for variety to a passion. The result is a singular mutability in legislation.

Many Americans consider the instability of the laws as a necessary consequence of a system whose general effects are useful.[o] But there is no one

m. In the margin: "I believe this small chapter decidedly bad. Hackneyed ideas."
n. "Political men" in the manuscript. The change was suggested by Beaumont (YTC, CIIIb, 2, p. 30).
o. Democracy-Aristocracy./
    Legislative instability in America./
    I have just found one of the strongest proofs of this instability in the laws of Massachusetts (the most stable state in the Union).

in the United States, I believe, who pretends to deny that this instability exists or who does not regard it as a great evil.

Hamilton, after having demonstrated the utility of a power that could prevent or at least slow the promulgation of bad laws, adds: "It may perhaps be said that the power of preventing bad laws includes that of preventing good ones. . . . But this objection will have little weight with those who can properly estimate the mischiefs of that inconstancy and mutability in the laws, which *form the greatest blemish in the character and genius of our governments"* (*Federalist*, No. 73.)p

"[The] facility and excess of lawmaking," says Madison, "seem to be the diseases to which our governments are most liable" (*Federalist*, No. 62).

Jefferson himself, the greatest democrat who has yet emerged from within the American democracy, pointed out the same perils.

> The instability of our laws is really a very serious disadvantage, he says. I think that we will have to deal with that by deciding that there would always be an interval of a year between the proposal of a law and the definitive vote. It would then be discussed and voted, without being able to change a word, and if circumstances seemed to require a more prompt resolution, the proposed law could not be adopted by a simple majority, but by a two-thirds majority of both houses.[1]

From 1803 to 1827, the administrative attributions of the Court of Sessions were changed many times in order to convey them to the Court of Common Pleas. See *Laws of Massachusetts,* vol. II, p. 98 (YTC, CVb, p. 24). The quotations included in the text follow.

p. This paragraph and the one preceding belonged to chapter VII of this second part (p. 407).

1. *Letter to Madison, 20 December 1787, translation of Mr. Conseil.*q

q. The second sentence reads differently in the French translation of Conseil (volume I, pp. 310–18; the citation is found on page 318).

Of Public Officials under the Dominion
of American Democracy

*Simplicity of American officials.—Lack of official dress.—All
officials are paid.—Political consequences of this fact.—In
America, there is no public career.—What results from that.*

Public officials in the United States remain mixed within the crowd of
citizens; they have neither palaces, nor guards, nor ceremonial dress [but
they are all paid]. This simplicity of those who govern is due not only to
a particular turn of the American spirit, but also to the fundamental principles of the society.

In the eyes of the democracy, government is not a good, but a necessary
evil. A certain power must be accorded to officials; for, without this power,
what purpose would they serve? But the external appearances of power are
not indispensable to the course of public affairs; they needlessly offend the
sight of the public.

Officials themselves are perfectly aware that, by their power, they have
not obtained the right to put themselves above others, except on the condition of descending, by their manners, to the level of all.

I can imagine nothing plainer in his ways of acting, more accessible to
all, more attentive to demands, and more civil in his responses, than a public
figure in the United States.

I like this natural look of the government of democracy;[r] in this internal

---

r. In the manuscript: "I like this simple look . . ."
Hervé de Tocqueville:

I am afraid that a bit of the enthusiasm of a young man may be seen in this admiration
for American simplicity. In our old Europe, there is often a need to catch the imagination by a certain pomp, and the simplicities of Louis-Philippe have attracted as
much scorn as his villainies. The author is bold to pronounce himself categorically
against one of the most general ideas. When you have this boldness, you must at least
try to justify your opinion by an example whose truth is striking and perceptible to
everyone. At the end of the second paragraph, which finishes with the words *solely
to his own merit,* the example would have to be cited of jurors in tail coats who are
more imposing than magistrates in red robes (YTC, CIIIb, 2, pp. 24–25).

strength that is attached more to the office than to the official, more to the man than to the external signs of power, I see something manly that I admire.

As for the influence that official dress can exercise, I believe that the importance that it must have in a century such as ours is greatly exaggerated. I have not noticed that in America the official, by being reduced solely to his own merit, was greeted with less regard and respect in the exercise of his power.[s]

From another perspective, I strongly doubt that a particular garment leads public men to respect themselves when they are not naturally disposed to do so; for I cannot believe that they have more regard for their outfit than for their person.

When, among us, I see certain magistrates treat parties brusquely or address them with false courtesy, shrug their shoulders at the means of defense and smile with complacency at the enumeration of charges, I would like someone to try to remove their robe, in order to discover if, finding themselves dressed as simple citizens, they would not be reminded of the natural dignity of the human species.[t]

No public official in the United States has an official dress, but all receive a salary.[u]

Still more naturally than what precedes, this follows from democratic principles. A democracy can surround its magistrates with pomp and cover them with silk and gold without directly attacking the principle of its existence. Such privileges are temporary; they are attached to the position, and not to the man. But to establish unpaid offices is to create a class of rich and independent officials, to form the kernel of an aristocracy. If the

---

s. In the margin: "≠I do not even know if a particular costume does not make what is lacking in the one wearing it, more salient in the eyes of the public.≠"

t. Hervé de Tocqueville: "I believe this paragraph should be removed. It would be good if the book were to be read only by the French; but as it will probably be sought out by foreigners, I do not know if it is suitable to expose our base acts to them" (YTC, CIIIb, 2, p. 25).

u. This paragraph is missing in the 1835 edition. It appears in the manuscript, but the wording is a bit different.

people still retain the right to choose, the exercise of the right then has necessary limits.

When you see a democratic republic make paid officials unsalaried, I believe that you can conclude that it is moving toward monarchy. And when a monarchy begins to pay unsalaried offices, it is the sure sign that you are advancing toward a despotic state or toward a republican state.[v]

So the substitution of salaried offices for unpaid offices seems to me to constitute, in itself alone, a true revolution.

I regard the complete absence of unpaid offices as one of the most visible signs of the absolute dominion that democracy exercises in America. Services rendered to the public, whatever they may be, are paid there; moreover, each person has, not only the right, but also the possibility of rendering them.

If, in democratic States, all citizens can gain positions, not all are tempted to try to obtain them. It is not the conditions of candidacy, but the number and the capacity of the candidates that often limit the choice of the voters.[w]

For peoples among whom the principle of election extends to everything, there is no public career strictly speaking. In a way men reach offices only by chance, and they have no assurance of remaining there. That is true above all when elections are annual. As a result, in times of calm,

---

v. Public offices./

Little power of officials, their large number, their dependence on the people, little *stability* in their position, the mediocrity of their emoluments, the ease of making a fortune in another way, fact that few capable persons aspire to the leadership of society, except in times of crisis.

Disposition that tends to make government less skillful, but that assures liberty./

Every position that demands a certain apprenticeship and a special knowledge must usually be poorly filled in America. Who would want to prepare at length to gain what a caprice or even the ordinary order of things can take away from you from one moment to another?" (YTC, CVh, I, pp. 4–5).

w. This paragraph does not appear in the manuscript. The following note is found in the margin: "≠Influence of election and of repeated election on the personnel of officials. More public careers in ordinary times. Example of the Romans ready for anything because elected.≠"

public offices offer little lure to ambition. In the United States, it is men of moderate desires who commit themselves to the twists and turns of politics. Great talents and great passions generally move away from power, in order to pursue wealth; and often someone takes charge of leading the fortune of the State only when he feels little capable of conducting his own affairs.

The great number of vulgar men who occupy public offices must be attributed to these causes as much as to the bad choices of democracy. In the United States, I do not know if the people would choose superior men who bid for their votes, but it is certain that the latter do not bid for them.

Of the Arbitrariness of Magistrates[2] under the Dominion of American Democracy[x]

Why the arbitrariness of magistrates is greater under absolute monarchies and in democratic republics than in limited monarchies.—Arbitrariness of magistrates in New England.

There are two types of government in which a great deal of arbitrariness is joined with the action of magistrates; it is so under the absolute government of one man and under the government of democracy.[y]

2. *Here, I understand the word* magistrate *in its broadest sense; I apply it to all those who are charged with executing the laws.*

x. "Put this chapter next to the one that deals with the despotism of the majority. Despotism and arbitrariness are two. For this chapter, see pocket notebook number 3, p. 15. All the main ideas are there. To find examples" (YTC, CVh, 4, p. 74). See the note for 14 October 1831, pocket notebook 3, YTC, BIIa, and *Voyage, OC,* V, 1, p. 183.

y. Hervé de Tocqueville: "Yes, there can be a great deal of arbitrariness under the absolute government of one man. Under the regular government of democracy there is free will and not arbitrariness, which is very different. I observe that despotism as the author depicts it exists only in Turkey, but is found to this extent in no other European State" (YTC, CIIIb, 2, p. 27). Hervé repeats this same observation about arbitrariness in other places (YTC, CIIIb, 2, pp. 27 and 34).

This same result comes from almost analogous causes.

In despotic States, no one's fate is assured, not that of public officials any more than that of simple individuals. The sovereign, always holding in his hand the life, fortune and sometimes the honor of the men he employs, thinks that he has nothing to fear from them; and he leaves them great freedom of action, because he thinks he is assured that they will never use that freedom against him.

In despotic States, the sovereign is so in love with his power that he fears the constraint of his own rules; and he loves to see his agents go more or less haphazardly in order to be sure never to find among them a tendency contrary to his desires.

Nor in democracies does the majority fear that power will be used against it, because every year it can remove power from the hands of those to whom power has been confided. Able at every moment to make its will known to those who govern, the majority prefers to abandon them to their own efforts rather than to bend them to an invariable rule that, by limiting those who govern, would in a sense limit the majority itself.

You even discover, looking closely, that under the dominion of democracy, the arbitrariness of the magistrate must be still greater than in despotic States.

Hervé de Tocqueville:

This entire chapter is very obscure and the mind must work to follow the connection of ideas. That comes about partly because the author sometimes used certain words that do not exactly have the meaning that he wants to give them. Starting with the title, the word *arbitrariness* loses meaning, because arbitrariness is commonly understood as the action of a power that is placed or puts itself above the law, and acts without concern for legal prescriptions. Such is not the type of action of magistrates in America. The law leaves infinitely more to their judgment than anywhere else. But there is no arbitrariness there. I propose to put, in place of *arbitrariness, the free will of magistrates,* etc. Next, I do not know why the author struggles so much to tell us about despotic government, which is not in his subject, and throws himself into abstract though ingenious definitions in order to tell us a truth that could be expressed with less difficulty, to know that the Americans leave great latitude and great freedom of action to their magistrates, because frequent elections banish all fear of the abuse that they could make of it (YTC, CIIIb, 2, pp. 26–27).

In these States, the sovereign can punish in a moment all the misdeeds that he notices, but he cannot flatter himself that he notices all the misdeeds that he should punish. In democracies, on the contrary, the sovereign is simultaneously omnipotent and omnipresent. You see, therefore, that American officials are much freer within the circle of action that the law traces for them than any official in Europe. Often the Americans limit themselves to showing officials the end toward which they must aim, leaving them with the authority to choose the means.

In New England, for example, the duty to draw up the jury list is referred to the *selectmen* of each town. The only rule that is stipulated is this: they must choose the jurors from among those citizens who enjoy the right to vote and who are of good reputation.[3]

In France, we would believe the lives and liberty of men at risk if we confided the exercise of so fearsome a right to an official, whoever he was.

In New England, these same magistrates can have the names of drunkards posted in taverns and, by penalty of a fine, prevent the occupants from providing them with wine.[4]

Such a censorial power would outrage people in the most absolute monarchy; here, however, people submit without difficulty.

Nowhere has the law left a larger portion of arbitrariness than in democratic republics, because there does not seem to be any reason to fear arbitrariness. You can even say that, as the right to vote expands and as the term in office becomes more limited, the magistrate becomes freer.

---

3. *See the law of 27 February 1813.* General Collection of the Laws of Massachusetts, vol. II, p. 331. *It must be said that afterward the jurors are drawn by lot from the lists.*

4. *Law of February 28, 1787. See* General Collection of the Laws of Massachusetts, vol. I, p. 302. *Here is the text:*

> *That the selectmen in each town shall cause to be posted up in the houses and shops of all taverners, innholders and retailers [. . . (ed.) . . .] a list of the names of all persons reputed common drunkards, [. . . (ed.) . . .] or common gamesters, misspending their time and estate in such houses. And every keeper of such house or shop, after notice given him, as aforesaid, that shall be convicted, [. . . (ed.) . . .] of entertaining or suffering any of the persons, in such a list, to drink or tipple, or game, in his or her house, [. . . (ed.) . . .] or of selling them spirituous liquor, as aforesaid, shall forfeit and pay [the sum of thirty shillings (ed.)].*

That is why it is so difficult to have a democratic republic become a monarchy. The magistrate, while ceasing to be elective, usually keeps the rights and preserves the customs of the elected magistrates. Then you arrive at despotism.[z]

Only in limited monarchies does the law, while drawing a circle of action around public officials, still take care at the same time to guide them at each step. The reason for this fact is easy to state.

In limited monarchies, power is divided between the people and the prince. Both are interested in having the position of the magistrate stable.

The prince does not want to put the fate of officials back into the hands of the people, for fear that the officials will betray his authority; on their side, the people are afraid that the magistrates, placed in absolute dependence on the prince, will help to crush liberty; so, in a way, the magistrates are made to depend on no one.

The same reason that leads the prince and the people to make the official independent, leads them to seek guarantees against the abuse of his independence, so that he does not turn against the authority of the one or the liberty of the other. Both agree, therefore, on the need to trace in advance a line of conduct for the public official, and find it in their interest to impose rules on him that are impossible for him to evade.

z. This idea is found in Montesquieu, who asserts: "There is no authority more absolute than that of a prince who succeeds the republic: for he finds himself with all the power of the people who were not able to limit themselves" (*Considérations sur les causes de la grandeur des Romains et de leur décadence,* chapter XV, in *Oeuvres complètes,* Paris: Pléiade, 1951, II, p. 150). In the *Republic* (Book VIII, 564), Plato had already noted that extreme liberty would necessarily be followed by extreme subjection.

Administrative Instability in the United States

*In America, the actions of society often leave fewer traces than
the actions of a family.—Newspapers, the only historical
memorials.—How extreme administrative instability
harms the art of governing.*

Men hold power only for an instant and then are lost in a crowd that, itself, changes face every day; as a result, the actions of society in America often leave less trace than the actions of a simple family.[a] Public administration there is, in a way, oral and traditional. Nothing is put in writing, or what is put in writing flies away with the slightest wind, like the leaves of the Sybil, and disappears forever.

The only historical memorials of the United States are newspapers. If an issue happens to be missing, the chain of time is as if broken: present and past are no longer joined. I do not doubt that in fifty years it will be more difficult to gather authentic documents about the details of the social existence of the Americans of today, than about the administration of the French of the Middle Ages; and if an invasion of barbarians happened to surprise the United States, it would be necessary, in order to know something about the people who live there, to resort to the history of other nations.

Administrative instability began by entering into habits; I could almost say that today each person has ended up by acquiring the taste for it. No one is worried about what was done before. No method is adopted; no collection is assembled; no documents are gathered, even when it would be easy to do so. When by chance someone has them in his possession, he hardly holds onto them. Among my papers, I have original pieces that were given to me in the offices of the public administration in order to answer some of my questions. In America, society seems to live from day to day, like an army in the field. Yet, the art of administration is definitely a science;

---

a. Variant: "<≠. . . a singular instability in the course of administrative affairs. No one finishes what he began; no one hopes to finish what he begins.≠>"

and all sciences, to progress, need to link together the discoveries of different generations as they succeed each other. One man, in the short space of a life, notices a fact, another conceives an idea; this one invents a method, that one finds a formula; humanity gathers along the way these various fruits of individual experiences and forms the sciences. It is very difficult for American administrators to learn anything from one another. Therefore, they bring to the conduct of society the knowledge that they find widespread in society, but not the learning that is their own.[b] So democracy, pushed to its extreme limits, harms progress in the art of governing.[c] From this perspective, it is better suited to a people whose administrative education is already formed than to a people who are inexperienced novices in public affairs.

This, moreover, does not relate uniquely to administrative science.[d] Democratic government, which is based upon such a simple and natural idea, always supposes the existence of a very civilized and learned society.[5] At first you would think it contemporaneous with the earliest ages of the world; looking more closely, you easily discover that it could have come about only during the last.[e]

[If nations had begun with democratic government, I doubt they would ever have become civilized.]

b. In the margin: "≠Dem[ocratic (ed.)] government, the chef-d'oeuvre of civilization and enlightenment.≠"

c. "Legislative instability in America, its effects, its causes./

"*Mutability of public officials.* Madison proves very ingeniously that this mutability, apart from its recognized ill effects, diminishes the responsibility of officials. New proposition, *Federalist,* p. 271 [No. 63 (ed.)]" (YTC, CVb, p. 25).

"After the electoral system, a small chapter on legislative and administrative instability in America is absolutely necessary. Show how, since nothing has any follow-up, no one can finish what he began. In this way responsibility diminished instead of increased, as is believed (*Federalist,* p. 268 [No. 62 (ed.)])" (YTC, CVh, 4, p. 27).

d. On Tocqueville and the science of administration, see Roland Drago, "Actualité de Tocqueville (Tocqueville et l'administration)," *Revue des sciences morales et politiques,* 139, 1984, pp. 633–49.

5. *It is unnecessary to say that here I am talking about democratic government applied to a people and not to a small tribe.*

e. In the margin: "Is this clear and developed enough? Ask G[ustave (ed.)] and L[ouis(ed.)]?"

Of Public Expenses under the Dominion
of American Democracy

In all societies, citizens are divided into a certain
number of classes.—Instinct that each of these classes brings to
the management of the finances of the State.—Why public
expenses must tend to increase when the people govern.—
What renders the lavish expenditures of democracy less to fear in
America.—Use of public monies under democracy.

Is democratic government economical? First of all, we must know to what we mean to compare it.

The question would be easy to resolve if we wanted to establish a parallel between a democratic republic and an absolute monarchy [v: despotic State]. We would find that public expenditures in the first are more considerable than in the second.[f] But this is the case in all free States, compared to those that are not free. It is certain that despotism ruins men more by preventing them from being productive, than by taking the fruits of production from them; it dries up the source of wealth and often respects acquired wealth. Liberty, in contrast, gives birth to a thousand times more goods than it destroys, and, among nations that know liberty, the resources of the people always increase faster than taxes.[g]

---

f. In chapter VIII of book III of the *Social Contract* (*Contrat social*), Rousseau had asserted, on the contrary, that the democratic form was the least costly.

g. Édouard de Tocqueville:

This entire paragraph seems to me to leave much to be desired. The first sentence presents, with the tone of affirmation, a proposition that is in no way evident; there have been and there still are very economical absolute monarchies; witness Austria, Prussia today. What I criticize most in this piece is that you seem to confuse two perfectly distinct things: the comparatively high level of public expenses and the sources of wealth; it is certain that generally the latter must increase with liberty; as for the reduction of public expenses, that is less sure. All that one can say is that, with an absolute government, economy can never be permanent because a prodigal prince may succeed an economical prince, but this economical prince can be found and is found often enough. So I would propose softening the beginning of this paragraph

What is important to me at this moment is to compare free peoples, and among the latter to note what influence democracy exercises on the finances of the State.

Societies, just as organized bodies do, follow certain rules in their formation that they cannot evade. They are composed of certain elements that are found everywhere and in all times.

It will always be easy to divide each people ideally into three classes.

The first class will be composed of the rich. The second will include those who, without being rich, live well-off in all things. The third will contain all those who have only few or no properties and who live particularly from the work provided to them by the first two classes.

The individuals included in these different categories can be more or less numerous, depending on the social state [added: and the laws]; but you cannot make these categories cease to exist.

It is evident that each of these classes will bring its own distinctive instincts to the handling of the finances of the State.

Suppose that the first makes the laws. Probably it will be little concerned with economizing public monies, because a tax that happens to strike a considerable fortune only takes what is superfluous and produces an effect that is little felt.[h]

---

and finishing the first page as follows: Still this principle can have some exceptions, *but what is beyond doubt is that despotism ruins peoples much more by preventing them from being productive than by taking the fruits of production from them.* That way the two ideas are distinct (YTC, CIIIb, 2, pp. 6–7).

h. Édouard de Tocqueville:

This proposition can be and will be contested; in most States, the rich are not so *rich* as to be indifferent to the total amount of the tax that strikes their fortune. I do not even know if they have ever been seen to be so; and in France in the time of the great lords and great fortunes, it was the rich who screamed the most when taxes were increased. So this paragraph is applicable only to the class of courtiers that one tried hard to confuse with all of the nobility, but that had never been more than a very small portion. All the nobles of the provinces and the rich who did not dissipate their income at the court desired economy in finances and saw public expenses increase with great disgust (YTC, CIIIb, 2, p. 7).

Assume, on the contrary, that the middle classes alone make the law. You can count on the fact that they will not be lavish with taxes, because there is nothing so disastrous as a heavy tax that happens to strike a small[j] fortune.

It seems to me that, among free governments, the government of the middle classes must be,[k] I will not say the most enlightened, nor, especially, the most generous, but the most economical.[m]

Now I suppose that the last class is exclusively charged with making the law; I clearly see the chance for public expenses to increase instead of decrease, and this for two reasons.

Since the greatest portion of those who in that case vote the law have no taxable property, all the money expended in the interest of society seems to be only to their profit, never to their harm; and those who have some bit of property easily find the means to fix the tax so that it hits only the rich and profits only the poor, something that the rich cannot do in their case when they are in control of the government.

So countries in which the poor[6] would exclusively be charged with mak-

j. Hervé de Tocqueville: "The word *small* is badly used applying to the middle class. *Mediocre* or something equivalent should be used" (YTC, CIIIb, 2, p. 11).

k. In the manuscript: ". . . the government of the middle classes is the most economical . . ."

Gustave de Beaumont: "I find the assertion presented in much too strong a form. Theoretically that appears true to me. And yet it is only a theory. I would put 'seems to be so by *its nature*'" (YTC, CIIIb, 2, pp. 20–21).

m. Hervé de Tocqueville:

The assertion of the author is contradicted by the example of France. Never has more been wasted, never have there been larger budgets than since the middle class has governed. I will observe in passing that the government of the middle class is, at bottom, only a small aristocracy on a larger scale. Attached to democracy by number, to aristocracy by the insolence and harshness of the parvenu, this government would be well able to have the vices of both. I urge Alexis to reflect on this again (YTC, CIIIb, 2, p. 11).

6. *You clearly understand that here, as in the rest of the chapter, the word poor has a relative sense and not an absolute meaning. The poor of America, compared with those of Europe, could frequently appear rich; you can correctly call them the poor, however, when you contrast them to those of their fellow citizens who are richer than they.*[n]

n. Hervé de Tocqueville:

ing the law could not hope for great economy in public expenditures; these expenditures will always be considerable, either because taxes cannot reach those who vote, or because they are fixed so as not to reach them. In other words, the government of democracy is the only one in which the one who votes the taxes can escape the obligation to pay them.

You will object in vain that the well understood interest of the people[o] is to handle the fortune of the rich carefully, because it would not take long for the people to feel the effects of any difficulties caused. But isn't it also the interest of kings to make their subjects happy, and that of the nobles to know how to open their ranks opportunely? If long-term interest could prevail over the passions and needs of the moment, there would never have been tyrannical sovereigns or exclusive aristocracies.

You will stop me here, saying: Who ever imagined charging the poor alone with making the law? Who! Those who have established universal suffrage. Is it the majority or the minority that makes the law? Undoubtedly the majority; and if I prove that the poor always make up the majority, won't I be correct to add that in countries where the poor are called to vote, they alone make the law?

Now, it is certain that until now, among all the nations of the world, the greatest number has always been composed of those who had no property, or of those whose property was too limited for them to be able to live comfortably without working. So universal suffrage really gives the government of society to the poor.

The poor must be deleted everywhere; on the one hand, it does not present a sufficiently clear idea and, on the other hand, does not agree with the condition in America of the class that the author wants to indicate. He says further along that this class lives in affluence, and an effort must always be made to connect ideas to America. Without that, there would be no unity in the composition. I would put here in place of *poor, the country in which the last class that I named,* etc.

To the side, in the handwriting of Alexis de Tocqueville according to the copyist: "The word *poor* has a relative, not an absolute meaning. The American poor could often appear rich compared to those of Europe. But they [above: count as] are always the poor [above: the class of the poor] if you compare them to those of their fellow citizens who are richer than they" (YTC, CIIIb, 2, p. 12).

o. The manuscript says "the lower classes."

The unfortunate influence that popular power can sometimes exercise over the finances of the State made itself clear in certain democratic republics of antiquity, in which the public treasury was exhausted to help indigent citizens, or to give games and spectacles to the people.

It is true to say that the representative system was almost unknown in antiquity.P Today, popular passions arise with more difficulty in public affairs; you can, however, count on the fact that, in the long run, the delegate will always end by conforming to the spirit of his constituents and by making their propensities as well as their interests prevail.

[This same tendency is even more noticeable in England with the poor tax, the only tax that is established by the people, that profits only them, and that has a democratic origin and object.]

The profusions of democracy are, moreover, less to be feared the more people become property owners, because then, on the one hand, the people have less need for the money of the rich and, on the other hand, they encounter more difficulties establishing a tax that does not hit them. From this perspective, universal suffrage would be less dangerous in France than in England, where nearly all taxable property is gathered in a few hands. America, where the great majority of citizens own property, is in a more favorable situation than France.

Still other causes can raise the sum of public expenditures in democracies.q

When the aristocracy governs, the men who conduct State affairs escape all needs by their very position; content with their lot, they ask above all

---

p. Of the principle of representation./

    It is the principle of representation that eminently distinguishes modern republics from ancient republics.

    Partially known in antiquity however. See *Federalist,* p. 273 [No. 63 (ed.)].

    Superiority that it gives to the modern ones, practicability of the republic.

    It tends to be weakened more and more in America.

    Frequency of elections. Dependence of power on the people. Binding mandates. Public vote (YTC, CVh, 1, pp. 5–6).

q. In the manuscript, what follows forms a section entitled: OTHER CAUSES THAT MAKE PUBLIC EXPENDITURES RISE HIGHER UNDER DEMOCRATIC GOVERNMENT THAN UNDER OTHERS.

for power and glory from society; and, placed above the anonymous crowd of citizens, they do not always see clearly how the general welfare necessarily works toward their own grandeur. It is not that they see the sufferings of the poor without pity; but they cannot feel the miseries of the poor as though they shared them themselves. As long as the people seem to be content with their own fortune, these men consider themselves satisfied and expect nothing more from the government. Aristocracy thinks more about maintaining than improving.[r]

When, on the contrary, public power is in the hands of the people, the sovereign power seeks everywhere for something better, because it has a sense of unease.

The spirit of amelioration then extends to a thousand different objects; it gets down to infinite details and is applied, above all, to types of amelioration that cannot be achieved except by paying; for it is a matter of improving the condition of the poor who cannot help themselves.

In addition there exists in democratic societies an agitation without a specific aim; a sort of permanent fever reigns there that turns toward all kinds of innovation, and innovations are nearly always costly.

---

r. In the manuscript: "When the aristocracy governs society, the only necessary care it has for the people is to prevent an uprising against it."

Hervé de Tocqueville:

This sentence is harsh though true. But let us not forget that the violent acts of the Revolution came from the fact that this truth had penetrated the people too deeply. Let us not once again put on the foreheads of the upper classes this mark that has been so deadly to them. It is more than useless for Alexis to alienate himself from these classes. So this sentence must be cut or softened. It can be cut without disadvantage to what follows. Then the chapter would begin in this way: *When the governing power is placed in the people, the spirit of amelioration is extended to a host of objects.*

If Alexis absolutely does not want to sacrifice it, this must be inserted: *The aristocracy has often been reproached for not having a care for the people,* etc. Then it is not he who pronounces and condemns; he is only reporting an opinion current in the world.

Édouard de Tocqueville: "This observation seems just to me" (YTC, CIIIb, 2, pp. 13–14).

Gustave de Beaumont: "Idea much too absolute that is suitable to modify" (YTC, CIIIb, 2, p. 21).

In monarchies and in aristocracies, the ambitious flatter the natural taste that carries the sovereign power toward fame and power, and they often push it therefore toward great expenditures.

In democracies, where the sovereign power is needy, you can hardly gain its good will except by increasing its well-being; that can hardly ever be done except with money.[s]

Moreover, when the people themselves begin to reflect on their position, a host of needs arises that they had not felt at first and that can only be satisfied by turning to the resources of the State. As a result, public expenses seem generally to increase with civilization, and you see taxes rise as enlightenment spreads.[t]

Finally, a last cause often makes democratic government more expensive than another. Sometimes the democracy wants to economize on its expenditures, but it cannot succeed in doing so, because it does not have the art of being economical.

As the democracy frequently changes views and, still more frequently, changes agents, it happens that enterprises are poorly conducted or remain incomplete. In the first case, the State makes expenditures disproportionate

---

s. In the margin: *"Isn't this subtle?"*

t. In the manuscript, this paragraph finishes in this way: ". . . taxes generally increase with enlightenment; and public expenses with civilization which should seemingly make them almost unnecessary."

Hervé de Tocqueville: "This is nothing less than clear [*sic*]. I do not understand why civilization should make public expenses nearly unnecessary."

Édouard de Tocqueville: "Nor do I" (YTC, CIIIb, 2, p. 14).

Hervé de Tocqueville:

Here are two divisions of the chapter devoted to generalities. But the author comes to no conclusion, and the reader will not fail to complain about it. He proves very well that democratic government is and must be expensive. But he does not arrive at the application that is indispensable to justify a theory. Is American democratic government proportionately more expensive than another; are public expenditures higher there? Not only must the author say so, but he must also explain why, give certain examples. If he has refrained because he is going to do so later, he must indicate it here. It is impossible for this division to end in this way, in a vague way.

Édouard de Tocqueville: "That is very true" (YTC, CIII b, 2, p. 14).

to the grandeur of the end that it wishes to achieve; in the second, it makes unproductive expenditures.

Of the Instincts of American Democracy in Determining the Salaries of Officials

In democracies, those who institute large salaries do not have the chance to profit from them.—Tendency of the American democracy to raise the salaries of secondary officials and to lower those of principal officials.—Why this is so.— Comparative picture of the salary of public officials in the United States and in France.

One great reason leads democracies, in general, to economize on the salaries of public officials.

In democracies, since those who institute the salaries are very numerous, they have very little chance ever to get them.

In aristocracies, on the contrary, those who institute large salaries almost always have a vague hope to profit from them. These salaries are capital that they create for themselves, or at the very least resources that they prepare for their children.

It must be admitted, however, that democracy appears to be very parsimonious only toward its principal agents.

In America, officials of secondary rank are paid more than elsewhere, but high officials are paid much less. [{There are states in which the Governor receives less money as a salary than one of our sub-prefects.}]

These opposite effects are produced by the same cause; the people, in both cases, set the salaries of public officials. They think about their own needs, and this comparison guides them. Since they themselves live in great comfort, it seems natural to them that those who are serving them share it.[7] But when it is time to set the lot of the great officers of the State, this rule escapes them, and they proceed only haphazardly.

---

7. *The comfort in which secondary officials live in the United States is also due to another*

The poor man does not have a clear idea of the needs that the superior classes of society may feel. What would appear to be a modest sum to a rich man, appears to be a prodigious sum to the poor man who contents himself with what's necessary; and he considers that the Governor of the state, provided with his two thousand *écus,* should still be happy and excite envy.[8]

If you try to make him understand that the representative of a great nation must appear with a certain splendor in the eyes of foreigners, he will understand you at first. But when, thinking about his simple dwelling and about the modest fruits of his hard labor, he thinks about all that he could do with this very salary that you judge insufficient, he will find himself surprised and almost frightened by the sight of such riches.

Add that the secondary official is nearly at the level of the people, while the other towers above them. So the first can still excite their interest, but the other begins to arouse their envy.

This is seen very clearly in the United States, where salaries seem in a way to decrease as the power of the officials grows greater.[9]

---

cause. This one is foreign to the general instincts of democracy: every type of private career is highly productive. The State would not find secondary officials if it did not agree to pay them well. So it is in the position of a commercial enterprise, obliged, whatever its tastes for economy, to sustain a burdensome competition.

8. *The state of Ohio, which has a million inhabitants, gives the Governor only 1,200 dollars in salary or 6,504 francs.*

9. *To make this truth clear to all, it is sufficient to examine the salaries of some of the agents of the federal government.*[11] *I thought the salary attached, in France, to the analogous office should be placed in juxtaposition, in order for the comparison to enlighten the reader.*

United States
Treasury Department

Attendant	*3,734 fr.*
The lowest paid clerk	*5,420 fr.*
The highest paid clerk	*8,672 fr.*
Chief Clerk	*10,840 fr.*
Secretary of State [sic: of the Treasury]	*32,520 fr.*
The President	*135,000 fr.*

Under the dominion of aristocracy, on the contrary, high officials receive very large emoluments, while lower level ones often have hardly enough on which to live. It is easy to find the reason for this fact in causes analogous to those that we have indicated above.[w]

If the democracy does not imagine the pleasures of the rich man or envies them, the aristocracy from its perspective does not understand the miseries of the poor man; or rather it is unaware of them. The poor man is not, strictly speaking, similar to the rich man; he is a being of another species. So the aristocracy worries very little about the fate of its lower level agents. It raises their salaries only when they refuse to serve for too small a price.

The parsimonious tendency of democracy toward principal officials has caused great economical propensities to be attributed to democracy that it does not have.

It is true that democracy gives scarcely what is needed to live honestly to those who govern it, but it spends enormous sums to relieve the needs

---

France
Ministry of Finance

Attendant of the Minister	*1,500 fr.*
The lowest paid clerk	*1,000 to 1,800 fr.*
The highest paid clerk	*3,200 to 3,600 fr.*
Chief Clerk	*20,000 fr.*
Minister	*80,000 fr.*
The King	*12,000,000 fr.*

Perhaps I was wrong to take France as the point of comparison. In France, where, daily, democratic instincts increasingly penetrate the government, you already notice a strong tendency that leads the Chambers to raise small salaries and above all to lower the large ones.[v] Thus the Minister of Finance, who, in 1834, receives 80,000 fr., received 160,000 under the Empire; the general directors of finance, who receive 20,000, then received 50,000.

u. In various articles about public expenditures in the United States and in France, which we will speak about later (see note j for p. 349), comparisons of this type abound.

v. "Ask Mr. Livingston if apart from the *clerks* in the American Treasury Department, there are still lower paid employees" (YTC, CVh, 3, p. 11).

w. Hervé de Tocqueville: "I ask for the deletion of this paragraph and the following for the reason that I gave on page 135. They are, moreover, superfluous and entirely unnecessary, because the author is not treating aristocracy. In addition, they are written with a bitterness against the aristocracy that cannot come from the pen of Alexis and that will bring his impartiality into question" (YTC, CIIIb, 2, p. 15). Cf. note r for p. 338.

or to facilitate the pleasures of the people.[10] That is a better use of the tax revenue, not an economy.

In general, democracy gives little to those who govern and a great deal to the governed. The opposite is seen in aristocracies where the money of the State profits above all the class that leads public affairs.

Difficulty of Discerning the Causes That Lead the American Government to Economy[x]

[≠In the silence of his study, the observer draws up general rules, and he believes that he has grasped the truth. But a fact, the first cause of which is often lost in the night, appears in his thoughts, and it seems to him that truth is escaping from him.≠]

The man who searches among facts for the real influence exercised by laws on the fate of humanity is exposed to great errors, for there is nothing so difficult to appreciate as a fact.

One people is naturally thoughtless and enthusiastic; another, reflective

---

10. *See among other items, in American budgets, what it costs for the support of the poor and for free education.*

In 1831, in the state of New York, the sum of 1,200,000 francs was spent for the support of the poor. And the sum devoted to public education was estimated to amount to 5,420,000 francs at least (William's New York Annual Register, *1832, pp. 205 and 243*).

The state of New York in 1830 had only 1,900,000 inhabitants, which is not double the population of the département du Nord.

x. Former title: THAT REASONS TAKEN FROM THE MORES OF A PEOPLE OFTEN DISRUPT OR MODIFY GENERAL ARGUMENTS.

Hervé de Tocqueville:

The title [This concerns the definitive title (ed.)] of this division does not seem good to me for two reasons. First, it establishes a sort of contradiction with the preceding chapters, which established that democratic government is not economical; then the difficulty is suddenly resolved in the chapter. I propose changing this title and putting: OF THE CAUSES FOR THE ECONOMY OF THE AMERICAN GOVERNMENT FOR CERTAIN OBJECTS. As for the rest, the chapter is very good. I will make only one observation to which I do not attach great importance; the author assumes preliminary knowledge in his reader. He reasons as if the reader already knew that the Americans like neither the luxury of festivals, nor that of buildings (YTC, CIIIb, 2, p. 16).

and calculating. This is due to their physical constitution itself or to distant causes that I do not know.[y]

You see peoples who love show, noise and pleasure, and who do not regret spending a million that goes up in smoke. You see others who value only solitary pleasures and who seem ashamed to appear contented.

In certain countries, a great price is attached to the beauty of buildings. In certain others, no value whatsoever is placed on objects of art, and what has no return is scorned. Finally, there are some in which fame is loved, and others in which money is placed before all else.

Apart from the laws, all these causes influence in a very powerful way the management of the finances of the State.

If the Americans have never happened to spend the people's money on public festivals, it is not only because, among them, the people vote the tax; it is because the people do not like to enjoy themselves.

If they reject ornament in their architecture and prize only material and real advantages, it is not only because they are a democratic nation, but also because they are a commercial people.

The habits of private life are continued in public life; and among the Americans the economies that depend on institutions and those that follow from habits and mores must be clearly distinguished.[z]

y. Fragment of a first version in the manuscript:

≠There is indeed in the bent of the ideas and tastes of a people a hidden force that struggles with advantage against revolutions and time. This intellectual physiognomy of nations, which is called their character, is found throughout all the centuries of their history and amid the innumerable changes that take place in the social state, beliefs and laws. A strange thing! What is least perceptible and most difficult to define among a people is at the same time what you find most enduring among them. Everything changes among them except the character, which disappears only with nations themselves.≠

z. In the margin: "≠The beginning of the chapter does not exactly correspond to the end. The beginning contains a general idea on national character; the end contains a clear and precise observation on what gives the Americans their character.≠"

[Influence of the Government of Democracy on the Tax Base {and on the Use of the Tax Revenues}][a]

[The form of government greatly influences the tax base. The instinct of the aristocracy[b] leads it to handle the producer carefully {and to burden the consumer} because the aristocracy holds the sources of wealth. It is the opposite for the democracy, which willingly takes on the producer and han-

a. "The advice of L[ouis (ed.)]. is that the ideas of this chapter are questionable, that in any case they are presented too succinctly and in a superficial way" (YTC, CVh, 3, p. 90).

A first version of this part is found in YTC, CVh, 3, pp. 74–80; it presents numerous differences from the manuscript version. Notably, the opening of this draft states:

> I know that minds are much preoccupied with comparing the expenses of the United States with ours. If such were not the disposition of the public, I would not have done this chapter. For I am convinced that such a comparison is necessarily incomplete and, consequently, unproductive and that, were it complete, the truth would not be self-evident. It can be useful only to those who are looking for figures to support their ideas and not to those who want truth to emerge from figures (p. 74).

b. Hervé de Tocqueville:

> I do not believe the word *aristocracy* is very applicable here. The same thing would happen in a democracy in which the governing party was, in the majority, composed of owners of landed properties, large or small.
>
> This division has the same fault as one of the preceding ones; it leaves the reader almost completely wanting in terms of facts. We see clearly that the Americans have not wanted one tax, but you do not say what taxes they do want. A detailed account of this subject would be useless. But at least it would be necessary to tell us the nature of the taxes and to justify, with examples, the truth of the theory that the author is establishing. If by chance in America there was no contribution based on land, as I believe, and the producer was thus treated very carefully, then the chapter would come crashing down and it would have to be revised. I have a vague memory of having heard that there were only indirect taxes in America, and we know that indirect taxes weigh particularly on the consumer. I believe that the customs duties are the principal revenue of the American government (YTC, CIIIb, 2, pp. 16–17).

dles the consumer carefully, because the resources of the people[c] scarcely reach the level of the ordinary prices of objects of consumption.

Among the English, land has not been taxed and indirect taxes have been multiplied. All the exemptions have been made in favor of the rich, while taxes that hit only the poor have always continued to grow. In America, when the legislature attempted to establish a tax on fermented liquors, a revolt ensued and in 1794 the legislature was forced to repeal the law.[*]

Only the despotism of one man is indifferent to the tax base. Its instinct leads it only to strike the taxpayer most able to give and least able to resist.][d]

[Influence of Democratic Government on the Use of Tax Revenues]

[The partisans of democracy claim that the government of democracy is more economical than any other, and I think they are mistaken. If they said, instead, that, of all governments, democratic government is the one that generally makes best use of tax revenues, they would put themselves, I believe, on their true ground.

c. Édouard de Tocqueville:

This sentence is completely unintelligible to me; the resources of the people hardly reach the level of the price of *the most ordinary objects of consumption* would seem understandable, but the thought still would not seem sound to me. Here you fall, I think, into the fault, almost inevitable for a European, of using the word *people* for low people or populace. Well, even in France the resources of the people, of the mass, often reach beyond the price of ordinary consumer objects, that is to say, food and clothing; with greater reason, can you say that in America, where the greatest comfort reigns for the mass, in such a country can you say that the *people* willingly take on the producer? I do not believe it, for they would be taking on themselves as consumers. The more economical the price of production, the more the objects of consumption fall within reach of the people; and when the latter have tasted these consumer objects, the objects become needs for them (YTC, CIIIb, 2, p. 9).

[*]. See Marshall, *Life of Washington,* and Pitkin.

d. Cf. Montesquieu, *De l'esprit des lois,* book XIII, chapter XIV, in *Oeuvres complètes* (Paris: Pléiade, 1951), II, pp. 467–68, and Rousseau, *Discours sur l'économie politique,* in *Oeuvres complètes* (Paris: Pléiade, 1964), III, pp. 241–78.

I spoke above about the squanderings of democracy {bread and spectacles the Romans of the decline would say}, but such excesses are rare and are ordinarily found during the centuries when enlightenment is weak and corruption very great. If the government of democracy levies more considerable sums on society than another government, it generally uses public monies for objects of a more certain and more extensive utility and uses them to relieve more real needs.[e] Incontestably, democracies have never built the palace of Versailles, nor based the political world on money as the aristocracy of England has done.[f]

Apart from its direct influence on the object of public expenditures, the government of democracy exercises still another influence, no less great, on how they are handled. Democratic institutions tend to make habits simpler and to remove, if not the taste for luxury and ostentation, the usual appendage to the inequality of fortunes, at least the possibility of indulging in that taste. As a result of this general spirit of the nation, expenditures are made on more modest and more economical plans.[g]

e. In the margin, under a paper glued into place: "≠It uses it for schools, for roads, for measures of order and health.≠"

f. To the side:

≠Democracy shows itself parsimonious toward its agents.

This is due to two causes.

The first is that the poor man, who then makes the law, measures by his own scale the needs of those who serve him. What appears to be a modest sum to a rich man, appears to be a prodigious sum to him who has nothing; and he feels that a public official [v: the Governor of the state], with his puny salary, should still be happy and excite envy. The second is that since those who institute the salaries are very numerous under the dominion of democracy, they have very little chance to get them.

This parsimony of democracy for the principal ones among its agents gives an illusion about its economical inclinations. But if it limits itself to giving public officials what is needed to live, it spends enormous sums to relieve the needs {to establish free schools} or to facilitate the pleasures of the people {to aid the poor}. It is a better use of the tax revenue, but not an economy. In general, democracy gives little to those who govern and a great deal to the governed, against aristocratic governments where the money .-.-.-. above all the class that .-.-.-. public affairs.≠

g. In the margin, under a paper glued into place: "Perhaps put at the end of the chapter, the chapter on mores placed above."

In all that precedes I have kept to subjects as a whole and not to details. I happened to notice many times in America that public expenditures were not applied to the most useful objects or that they were made without economy; but it appeared to me that these were particular cases and that they should be blamed much less on a natural tendency of the government of democracy than on the poor choice of its agents. For, of all masters, the people are assuredly the worst served.][h]

h. Hervé de Tocqueville:

I do not believe this idea developed enough. This last division of the chapter presents a great imperfection in my eyes. The good faith of the author leads him to admit that several facts in America contradict his theory. In several of the preceding divisions, facts, unstated, did not support the theory. Here, in certain respects, they are opposed to it. Alexis has too much wisdom not to sense that by operating thus, he gives a wide scope to criticism. Overall, he has changed his way of writing, and I regret it. In the first volume, facts led naturally to theory that seemed a natural consequence. Here theory precedes facts, and sometimes does without them; that is dangerous. The reader willingly submits to the author's opinion when it seems to be a deduction, so to speak, from facts, because then the author does not seem to want to impose his opinion. It would be otherwise if it preceded facts and, above all, if facts were lacking to support it. Then the intelligence of the author exercises over that of the reader a sway to which the latter does not always adapt and against which he sometimes takes a strong stand. I acknowledge with great pleasure that this last chapter is very well written and that it contains new and ingenious insights. But this merit does not compensate for the disadvantage of the absence of facts to support the theory.

In my opinion, every time Alexis is led to develop general insights, he must hasten to connect them to America. Without that, his work would lose its unity of composition, which is a major disadvantage in works of the mind. The reader glimpses in this case two aims without being able to set exactly the limits of each of the things that relate to each other; and a kind of confusion arises in his mind that forces him to a tedious effort that displeases him.

I have conscientiously examined if the paragraphs on aristocracy are necessary to establish a useful parallel between it and democracy. I am convinced of the opposite. Not only are they unnecessary, but they come as irrelevant, because aristocracy is in no way within the author's subject. There is no point, without a pressing need, in turning the upper classes against him. Alexis has been carried away by his natural frankness and also by a generous sentiment, that of knowing how to put himself above the prejudices of his class. All that he says was appropriate when the aristocracy was powerful. At present, I believe that one must abstain from doing it. I do not need to expand on the reasons.

Can the Public Expenditures of the United States Be Compared with Those of France[j]

Two points to be established in order to appreciate the extent of public expenses: national wealth and taxation.—Fortune and expenses in France are not known exactly.—Why you cannot hope to know fortune and expenses in the Union.—Research of the author to learn the total amount of taxes in Pennsylvania.— General signs by which you can recognize the extent of the expenses of a people.—Result of this examination for the Union.

Some have been much occupied recently with comparing the public expenditures of the United States with ours. All of these efforts have been without result, and a few words will suffice, I believe, to prove that it must be so.

To the side, written by Alexis, according to the copyist: "and that it (three illegible words) it would not have (illegible word) at State expense to buy the younger branches of certain families as the English aristocracy did" (YTC, CIIIb, 2, pp. 17–19).

Édouard de Tocqueville:

> *General observation.* This entire chapter needs, in my opinion, to be altered. Economic questions are not treated in it with enough assurance; there are several propositions that can be questioned. Certain thoughts are inadequately developed. All in all, I do not find this chapter at the same level as the preceding ones. The author here does not seem to be as perfectly in control of his subject (YTC, CIIIb, 2, p. 10).

j. This section does not exist in the manuscript; it does not appear in the criticisms of family and friends. It seems to have been included following a polemic on the economy of republican government, in which the United States was generally taken as the example. In September 1831, Sebastien L. Saulnier, official voice of the government, prefect of police and editor of the *Revue Britannique,* published "Rapprochements entre les dépenses publiques de la France et celles des États-Unis" (*Revue Britannique,* n.s., VI, 1831, pp. 272–324, reprinted in various publications), in which he claimed that the United States had an extremely expensive form of government and that American finances were consequently in chaotic condition. Since the moment for discussion in the Chamber of Deputies of the proposed budget for 1832 was at hand, Lafayette saw in this article an attempt on the part of the government to influence the parliamentary debate. He solicited the opinions of James Fenimore Cooper and of General Bernard, following which

In order to be able to appreciate the extent of public expenses among a people, two operations are necessary: first, you must learn the wealth of this people, and then what portion of this wealth they devote to State expenditures. The person who researches the total amount of taxes without showing the extent of the resources that must provide them, would be pursuing unproductive work; for it is interesting to know not the expenditure, but the relation of the expenditure to the revenue.

The same tax that a wealthy taxpayer easily bears will succeed in reducing a poor man to poverty.

The wealth of peoples is made up of several elements: real estate holdings form the first, personal property constitutes the second.[k]

---

he published a brochure that circulated among the deputies (*Le général Lafayette à ses collègues de la Chambre des députés,* Paris: Paulin, 1832, 68 pp.) The letter of Cooper had been published separately, in English (*Letter of J. Fenimore Cooper to Gen. Lafayette, on the expenditure of the United States of America,* Paris: Baudry, December 1831, pp. 50, iii, and also in the *Revue des deux mondes,* n.s., V, January 1832, pp. 145–82). Saulnier answered with two new writings: "Nouvelles observations sur les finances des États-Unis, en réponse à une brochure publiée par le Général Lafayette" (*Revue Britannique,* n.s., VIII, pp. 195–260), and a letter to the editor of the same review (n.s., IX, November 1833, pp. 164–94). In 1834, Francisque de Corcelle published an article, "Administration financière des États-Unis" (*Revue des deux mondes,* 3rd series, I, 1834, pp. 561–84), with new statistics obtained from an inquiry into the American financial system done by Edward Livingston. New data, Corcelle argued, would demonstrate that the Americans paid lower taxes than the French. The article by Corcelle had probably attracted Tocqueville's attention, because he wrote to D. B. Warden on 21 July 1834 (YTC, CId), asking him for "the brochures of Bernard, Lafayette and Cooper." Regarding this, the following note is also found in the drafts: "Brochure of General Bernard and of Mr. Cooper on the finances of the United States appeared in the middle of 1831. I believe that General Lafayette's aide-de-camp published something on the same subject" (YTC, CVh, 4, pp. 21–22). See note 51 for p. 156.

k. In the 1835 edition: "The wealth of peoples is made up of several elements: population is the first; real estate holdings form the second, and personal property constitutes the third.

"Of these three elements, the first is easily discovered. Among civilized peoples you can easily reach an exact count of the citizens; but it is not the same with the other two. It is difficult to . . ."

The correction is probably due to a criticism from Nassau William Senior in a letter to Tocqueville of 17 February 1835:

I cannot think that population is an element of wealth. It may rather be said to be an element of poverty. The wealth or poverty of the *people* of a country depends on

It is difficult to know the extent of land suitable for cultivation that a nation possesses and its natural or acquired value. It is still more difficult to estimate all of the personal property that a people has at its disposal. Personal property, because of its diversity and amount, eludes almost all efforts of analysis.

Consequently we see that the oldest civilized nations of Europe, even those in which the administration is centralized, have not yet established the state of their wealth in any precise way.

In America, no one has even conceived the idea of trying. And how could you think to succeed in this new country where society has not yet peacefully and finally settled down, where the national government does not find at its disposal, as ours does, a multitude of agents whose efforts can be simultaneously commanded and directed; where, finally, statistics are not studied, because no one is found who has the power to gather the documents or the time to look through them?

So the constituent elements of our calculations cannot be obtained. We do not know the comparative wealth of France and of the Union. The wealth of the one is not yet known, and the means to establish that of the other do not exist.

But, for a moment, I agree to put aside this necessary term of comparison; I give up knowing the relationship of tax to revenue, and I limit myself to wanting to establish what the taxes are.

The reader is going to recognize that by narrowing the circle of my research, I have not made my task easier.

I do not doubt that the central administration of France, aided by all the officials at its disposal, might succeed in discovering exactly the total amount of direct or indirect taxes that weigh upon the citizens. But this

---

the proportion between their numbers and the aggregate wealth of that country. Diminish their numbers, the wealth remaining the same, and they will be, individually, richer. The people of Ireland, and indeed of England, would be richer if they were fewer. I do call a country like China, where there is an immense population, individually poor, a rich country, though the aggregate wealth of China is greater than the aggregate wealth of Holland, where the population is, comparatively, individually rich (*Correspondence and Conversations of Alexis de Tocqueville with Nassau William Senior,* London: Henry S. King & Co., 1872, I, p. 4).

work, which an individual cannot undertake, the French government itself has not yet finished, or at least it has not made the results known. We know what the State expenses are; the total of the departmental expenses is known; we do not know what happens in the French towns. So no one can say, as of now, what amount public expenditures in France total.

If I now return to America, I notice difficulties that become more numerous and more insurmountable. The Union makes public the exact amount of its expenses; I can obtain for myself the individual budgets of the twenty-four states that constitute the Union; but who will teach me what the citizens spend for the administration of the county and of the town?[11]

Federal authority cannot extend to forcing the provincial governments to enlighten us on this point; and if these governments themselves wanted to lend us simultaneously their support, I doubt that they would be able to satisfy us. Apart from the natural difficulty of the enterprise, the political

---

11. *The Americans, as you see, have four types of budgets: The Union has its; the states, counties, and towns have theirs as well. During my stay in America, I did extensive research to know the total amount of public expenditures in the towns and in the counties of the principal states of the Union. I was able easily to obtain the budget of the largest towns, but it was impossible for me to get that of the small towns. So I cannot form any exact idea of town expenditures. For what concerns the expenditures of the counties, I possess some documents that, though incomplete, are perhaps the kind that are worthy of the reader's curiosity. I owe to the goodness of Mr. Richards, former[m] mayor of Philadelphia, the budgets of thirteen counties of Pennsylvania for the year 1830, those of Lebanon, Center, Franklin, Fayette, Montgomery, Luzerne, Dauphin, Butler, Alleghany [Allegheny (ed.)], Columbia, Northumberland, Northampton, Philadelphia. In 1830, there were 495,207 inhabitants. If you cast your eyes on a map of Pennsylvania, you will see that these thirteen counties are dispersed in all directions and subject to all the general causes that can influence the state of a country; so that it would be impossible to say why they would not provide an exact idea of the financial state of the counties of Pennsylvania. Now, these very counties spent, during the year 1830, 1,808,221 francs, which yields 3.64 fr. per inhabitant. I calculated that each of the same inhabitants, during the year 1830, devoted to the needs of the federal Union 12.70 fr., and 3.80 fr. to those of Pennsylvania; the result is that in the year 1830 the same citizens gave to society, to meet all public expenditures (except town expenditures), the amount of 20.14 fr. This result is doubly incomplete, as you see, because it applies only to a single year and to one part of public expenses; but it has the merit of being certain.*

m. The word "former" appears only after the first editions.

organization of the country would still conflict with the success of their efforts. The magistrates of the town and of the county are not appointed by administrators of the state, and do not depend on them. So it may be believed that if the state wanted to obtain the information we need, it would meet great obstacles in the carelessness of the lower level officials it would be forced to use.[12]

Useless, moreover, to try to find out what the Americans would be able to do in such a matter, because certainly until now they have done nothing.

So today in America or in Europe not a single man exists who can teach us what each citizen of the Union pays annually to meet the expenses of society.[13]

12. *Those who have wanted to establish a parallel between the expenditures of the Americans and ours have clearly felt that it was impossible to compare the total of the public expenditures of France to the total of the public expenditures of the Union; but they have sought to compare detached portions of these expenditures. It is easy to prove that this second way of operating is no less defective than the first.*

To what will I compare, for example, our national budget? To the budget of the Union? But the Union is occupied with far fewer objects than our central government, and its expenses must naturally be much less. Will I contrast our departmental budgets to the budgets of the individual states that make up the Union? But in general the individual states attend to more important and more numerous interests than the administration of our departments; so their expenditures are naturally more considerable. As for the budgets of the counties, you find nothing in our system of finance that resembles them. Will we add expenditures made there to the budget of the state or to that of the towns? Town expenditures exist in the two countries, but they are not always analogous. In America, the town assumes several needs that in France are left to the department or to the State. How, moreover, must town expenditures in America be understood? The organization of the town differs depending on the states. Will we take as the rule what happens in New England or in Georgia, in Pennsylvania or in the state of Illinois?

It is easy to see, between certain budgets of two countries, a sort of analogy; but since the elements that constitute them always differ more or less, you cannot establish a serious comparison between them.

13. *Should you succeed in knowing the precise sum that each French or American citizen pays into the public treasury, you would still have only one part of the truth.*

Governments ask not only money from the taxpayers, but also personal efforts that have a monetary value. The State raises an army; apart from the balance that is charged to the entire nation to supply it, the soldier must still give his time, which has a greater or lesser value depending on the use that he would make of it if he remained free. I will say as much about the service of the militia. The man who is part of the militia temporarily devotes a precious

Let us conclude that it is as difficult to compare fruitfully the social expenditures of the Americans with ours, as it is to compare the wealth of the Union to that of France. I add that it would even be dangerous to attempt it. When statistics are not based on rigorously true calculations, they mislead rather than guide. The mind is easily led astray by the false air of exactitude that statistics conserve even in their discrepancies, and it rests untroubled in the errors that it thinks are cloaked in the mathematical forms of truth.

So let us abandon numbers and try to find our proof elsewhere.

Does a country present an aspect of material prosperity; after paying the State, does the poor man still have resources and the rich man superfluity; do both appear satisfied with their lot, and do they still seek to improve it each day, so that industry never lacks capital and capital in turn does not lack industry? Lacking positive documents, it is possible to resort to such indicators to know if the public expenses that burden a people are proportionate to its wealth.

The observer who kept to this evidence would undoubtedly judge that the American of the United States gives to the State a less significant portion of his income than the Frenchman.

But how could you imagine that it would be otherwise?

---

time to public security, and really gives to the State what he fails to acquire for himself. I have cited these examples; I would have been able to cite many others. The government of France and that of America collect taxes of this nature; these taxes burden the citizens. But who can appreciate with exactitude their total amount in the two countries?

This is not the last difficulty that stops you when you want to compare the public expenditures of the Union to ours. The State has certain obligations in France that it does not assume in America, and reciprocally. The French government pays the clergy; the American government leaves this concern to the faithful. In America, the State takes care of the poor; in France, it leaves them to the charity of the public. We give all our officials a fixed salary; the Americans allow them to collect certain fees. In France, service charges occur only on a small number of roads; in the United States, on nearly all roads. Our roads are open to travelers who can travel on them without paying anything; in the United States there are many toll roads. All these differences in the way in which the taxpayer acquits himself of the expenses of the society make comparison between the two societies very difficult; for there are certain expenditures that the citizens would not make or that would be less, if the State did not take it upon itself to act in their name.

One part of the French debt is the result of two invasions; the Union has nothing to fear about that. Our position obliges us as a rule to keep a numerous army under arms; the isolation of the Union allows it to have only 6,000 soldiers. We maintain nearly 300 ships; the Americans have only 52[14] of them. How could the inhabitant of the Union pay to the State as much as the inhabitant of France?

So there is no parallel to establish between the finances of countries so differently placed.

It is by examining what happens in the Union, and not by comparing the Union with France, that we can judge if American democracy is truly economical.

I cast my eyes on each of the various republics that form the confederation, and I discover that their government often lacks perseverance in its designs, and that it does not exercise continuous surveillance over the men it employs. From this I naturally draw the conclusion that it must often spend the money of the taxpayers uselessly, or devote more of their money than necessary to its undertakings.

I see that, faithful to its popular origin, it makes prodigious efforts to satisfy the needs of the lower classes of society, to open the paths to power to them, and to spread well-being and enlightenment among them. It supports the poor, distributes millions each year to the schools, pays for all services, and generously recompenses its least important agents. If such a means of governing seems useful and reasonable to me, I am forced to recognize that it is expensive.

I see the poor man who leads public affairs and has national resources at his disposal; and I cannot believe that, profiting from State expenditures, he does not often drag the State into new expenditures.

So I conclude, without resorting to incomplete figures and without wanting to establish risky comparisons, that the democratic government of the Americans is not, as is sometimes claimed, an inexpensive govern-

---

14. *See the detailed budgets of the Ministry of the Navy in France, and for America, the* National Calendar *of 1833, p. 228.*[n]

n. The budget of the American navy is found on pages 290–91. On page 228, the list of warships is found; the total is 53 (Tocqueville seems to have eliminated from the list a barge, a small unarmed galley with about twenty oars aboard).

ment; and I am not afraid to predict that, if great difficulties came one day to assail the peoples of the United States, you would see taxes among them rise as high as in most of the aristocracies or monarchies of Europe.

Of the Corruption and Vices of Those Who Govern in Democracy; Of the Effects on Public Morality That Result from That Corruption and Those Vices

In aristocracies, those who govern sometimes seek to corrupt.— Often, in democracies, they prove to be corrupt themselves.—In the first, vices directly attack the morality of the people.—In the second, vices exercise an indirect influence on the morality of the people that is still more to be feared.

Aristocracy and democracy mutually reproach each other with facilitating corruption; it is necessary to distinguish.

In aristocratic governments, the men who come to public affairs are rich men who only want power. In democracies, the statesmen are poor and have their fortune to make.

It follows that, in aristocratic States, those who govern are not very open to corruption and have only a very moderate taste for money, while the opposite happens among democratic peoples.

But, in aristocracies, since those who want to arrive at the head of public affairs have great riches at their disposal, and since the number of those who can make them succeed is often circumscribed within certain limits, the government finds itself, in a way, up for sale.[o] In democracies, on the

o. Hervé de Tocqueville:

It is clear that in this picture the author has England in view, but all aristocracies are not like that of England, which, however omnipotent it is, needs the people. There were other aristocracies, such as that of Venice and I believe that of Berne, that were self-sufficient, the people remaining outside; was corruption at work in the last ones? The author cites a mixed government rather than a clear-cut aristocracy. Some would probably object to him about it; to avoid it I would like him to put: "in aristocracies *in which the popular vote is necessary*" (YTC, CIIIb, 2, p. 5).

contrary, those who aspire to power are hardly ever rich, and the number of those who contribute to gaining power is very great. Perhaps, in democracies, men are for sale no less, but there are hardly any buyers, and, besides, too many people would have to be bought at once to achieve the end. [≠As a result of this difference, in democracies corruption acts upon those who govern and in aristocracies upon the governed. In the one, public officials are corrupted; in the other, the people themselves.≠

Thus, corruption finds some way to be exercised in the two governments: its object alone varies.]

Among the men[p] who have occupied power in France during the past forty years, several have been accused of having made a fortune at the expense of the State and its allies; a reproach that was rarely made to the public men of the old monarchy. But, in France, there is almost no example of someone buying the vote of an elector for money,[q] while this is notoriously and publicly done in England.

[In aristocracies corruption is generally exercised in order to gain power. In democracies it is linked to those who have gained power. So in demo-

---

p. In the manuscript: "Nearly all the men . . ."
Édouard de Tocqueville (?):

That reproach was not addressed to anyone during the fifteen years of the Restoration. I do not know if it was generally addressed to Bonaparte's ministers, M. de Talleyrand excepted, although it was addressed to his generals. So we are left then with the ministers of the Republic and, above all, those of the Directory. A great number of the ministers of the Restoration entered power poor and still remain so. So you cannot with justice say: *during the past forty years nearly all the men,* etc. Couldn't you say: "Nearly all the men who have occupied power after the establishment of the French republic and during its existence, that is to say, when citizens, until then obscure and poor, suddenly found themselves carried to the head of public affairs, nearly all these men, I say, have been accused . . ."? (YTC, CIIIb, 2, p. 4).

Hervé de Tocqueville: "In this paragraph what Alexis says is not true. Most of the ministers since the Directory were beyond suspicion of mischief, and several ministers under the old regime were regarded as great knaves" (YTC, CIIIb, 2, p. 5).

q. Hervé de Tocqueville: "It is true that they are rarely bought for cash money, but often enough by the lure of places or other advantages, which is a corruption that differs only by the means. The government candidate at Cherbourg had promised the same place of *juge de paix* to 15 persons" (YTC, CIIIb, 2, p. 6).

cratic States corruption harms the public treasury more than the morality of the people. It is the opposite in aristocracies.]

I have never heard it said that in the United States someone used his riches to win over the governed; but I have often seen the integrity of public officials called into question. Still more often I have heard their success attributed to low intrigues or to guilty maneuvers.

[It must be said, moreover, that the result is not as fearsome in America as it would be in Europe.

Great robberies can only be practiced among powerful democratic nations in which the government is concentrated in few hands and in which the State is charged with executing immense enterprises.][r]

So if the men who lead aristocracies sometimes seek to corrupt, the heads of democracies are corrupted themselves. In the one, the morality of the people is directly attacked; in the other, an indirect action is exerted on the public conscience that must be feared even more.

Among democratic peoples, those who head the State are almost always exposed to deplorable suspicions; so they give the support of the government, in a way, to the crimes of which they are accused. Thus they present dangerous examples to still struggling virtue, and provide glorious comparisons to hidden vice.

You would say in vain that dishonest passions are met at all levels; that they often accede to the throne by the right of birth; that deeply despicable men can thus be found at the head of aristocratic nations as well as within democracies.

This response does not satisfy me. In the corruption of those who gain power by chance, something crude and vulgar is disclosed that makes it contagious to the crowd; on the contrary, there reigns, even in the deprav-

---

r. Édouard de Tocqueville (?): "What, so the United States is not a *powerful democratic nation?* And then the word *robbery* seems inadmissible to me in an elevated style; *great misappropriations* or *great embezzlements* is needed. Finally, how can power be concentrated in few hands in a *democratic nation?* That to me would seem impossible. This small paragraph must be revised" (YTC, CIIIb, 2, pp. 4–5).

What follows this paragraph, until the end of the section, does not exist in the manuscript.

ities of great lords, a certain aristocratic refinement, an air of grandeur that often prevents its spread.[s]

The people will never penetrate the dark labyrinth of court spirit; it will always be difficult for them to discover the baseness hidden beneath the elegance of manners, the pursuit of taste, and the grace of language. But to rob the public treasury or to sell State favors for money, that the first wretch understands and can claim to be able to do in turn.

What is to be feared, moreover, is not so much the sight of the immorality of the great as that of immorality leading to greatness. In democracy, simple citizens see a man who emerges from their ranks and who in a few years achieves wealth and power; this spectacle excites their surprise and envy; they try to find out how the one who was their equal yesterday is today vested with the right to lead them. To attribute his elevation to his talents or his virtues is uncomfortable, for it means admitting that they themselves are less virtuous and less skillful than he. So they place the principal cause in some of his vices, and often they are right to do so. In this way, I do not know what odious mixture of the ideas of baseness and power, of unworthiness and success, of utility and dishonor comes about.

s. "There, I confuse two things: corruption and embezzlements.

"There is corruption when you seek to obtain something which is not your due by sharing some stake with the one who gives it.

"There is corruption on the part of the candidate who pays for the votes of the voter.

"There is corruption on the part of the individual who obtains a favor from an official for money.

"But when officials draw for their own account from the State treasury, it is not corruption; it is *theft*" (YTC, CVh, 4, p. 88).

Of What Efforts Democracy Is Capable

The Union has fought for its existence only a single time.—
Enthusiasm at the beginning of the war.—Cooling at the end.—
Difficulty of establishing conscription or registration of sailors in
America.—Why a democratic people is less capable than another
of great sustained efforts.

I forewarn the reader that here I am speaking about a government that follows the real will of the people, and not about a government that restricts itself only to commanding in the name of the people.

There is nothing so irresistible as a tyrannical power that commands in the name of the people, because, while vested with the moral power that belongs to the will of the greatest number, it acts at the same time with the decisiveness, promptitude and tenacity that a single man would have.

It is quite difficult to say what degree of effort a democratic government is capable of in time of national crisis.

A great democratic republic has never been seen until now. It would be an insult to republics to give this name to the oligarchy that reigned over France in 1793.[t] The United States alone presents this new spectacle.

Now, since the Union was formed a half-century ago, its existence has been put in question only once, at the time of the War of Independence. At the beginning of this long war, there were extraordinary acts of enthusiasm for serving the country.[15] But as the struggle continued, you saw individual egoism reappear. Money no longer arrived at the public treasury; men no longer presented themselves for the army; the people still wanted independence, but they drew back from the means to obtain

---

t. Variant in the margin, under a paper glued into place: "The name republic given to the oligarchy of 1793 has never been anything except a bloody veil behind which was hidden the tyranny of some and the oppression of all."

15. *One of the most singular, in my opinion, was the resolution by which the Americans temporarily renounced the use of tea. Those who know that men generally cling more to their habits than to their life will undoubtedly be astonished by this great and obscure sacrifice obtained from an entire people.*

it.[*] [≠This languor of public spirit, the only motivating force [doubtful reading (ed.)] of democracies, put the liberty of America in danger several times, and yet the nature of the country alone and its expanse made conquest impossible.≠] "Tax laws have in vain been multiplied; new methods to enforce the collection have in vain been tried," says Hamilton in the *Federalist* (No. 12):

> the public expectation has been uniformly disappointed, and the treasuries of the States have remained empty. The popular system of administration, inherent in the nature of popular government, coinciding with the real scarcity of money incident to a languid and mutilated state of trade, has hitherto defeated every experiment for extensive collections, and has at length taught the different legislatures the folly of attempting them.

Since this period, the United States has not had to sustain a single serious war.

To judge what sacrifices democracies know how to impose on themselves, we must therefore await the time when the American nation will be forced to put into the hands of its government half of the revenue of its property, like England, or must throw one twentieth of its population all at once onto the field of battle, as France did.

In America, conscription is unknown; men are enrolled there for money. Forced recruitment is so contrary to the ideas and so foreign to the habits of the people of the United States that I doubt that anyone would ever dare to introduce it in the laws. What is called conscription in France assuredly is the heaviest of our taxes; but, without conscription, how would we be able to sustain a great continental war?

The Americans have not adopted English impressment. They have nothing that resembles our registration of sailors. The navy, like the merchant marine, recruits by voluntary enlistments.

Now, it is not easy to conceive that a people could sustain a great maritime war without resorting to one of the two means indicated above. Consequently, the Union, which has already fought with glory at sea, has never

[*]. See the *Life of Washington* by Marshall.

had large fleets, and the cost of manning the small number of its ships has always been very expensive.

I have heard American statesmen admit that the Union will have difficulty maintaining its rank on the seas, if it does not resort to impressment or to registration of sailors; but the difficulty is to force the people, who govern, to bear impressment or registration of sailors.[u]

Incontestably, free peoples, when in danger, generally display an infinitely greater energy than those who are not free, but I am led to believe that this is true, above all, for free peoples among whom the aristocratic element predominates.[v]

Democracy seems to me much more appropriate for leading a peaceful society, or for making a sudden and vigorous effort as needed, than for braving for a long time the great storms in the political lives of peoples. The reason for it is simple. Men expose themselves to dangers and privations out of enthusiasm, but they remain exposed for a long time only from reflection. In what is called instinctive courage itself, there is more calculation than we think; and although, in general, passions alone bring about the first efforts, efforts continue with the result in mind. You risk a portion of what is dear in order to save the rest.[w]

u. On the back of the page: "≠Difficulty of establishing conscription as in France. Even *impressment* does not exist, though of English origin. Impossibility, however, of navy without impressment. See opinion Gallatin, non-alphabetic notebook 1, p. 25.≠" See YTC, BIIa, and *Voyage, OC,* V, 1, p. 62.

v. In a first version: "It is not that the first impulse of democracy is often to assist the evil. Nothing is more impetuous than the movements of democracy, but enthusiasm, like all the other passions, soon burns itself out. In men [who (ed.)] expose themselves to dangers for a long time and submit to great sacrifices to attain an end, there is a great mixture of passion and calculation."

w. Hervé de Tocqueville:

The entire paragraph preceding these words is very well put, and yet I have an observation to make that does not seem unimportant. Free countries make more efforts when in danger, because love of country predominates there more than in monarchies; this point granted, it seems that the devotion to public things should be greater in democracies than in aristocracies, for the author has proved well in the preceding chapters that democratic government is the one in which the people

Now, this clear perception of the future, based on learning and experience, must often be missing in democracy. The people feel much more than they reason; and if the present difficulties are great, the fear is that they will forget the greater difficulties that perhaps await them in case of defeat.

Still another cause must make the efforts of a democratic government less long-lasting than the efforts of an aristocracy.

The people not only see less clearly than the upper classes what can be hoped or feared in the future, but the people also suffer the troubles of the present quite differently from the upper classes. The nobleman, by exposing his person, runs as many chances for glory as perils. By giving the State the greater part of his income, he temporarily deprives himself of some of the pleasures of his wealth. But, for the poor man, death has no prestige, and the tax that bothers the rich man often attacks the poor man's sources of life.

This relative weakness of democratic republics in time of crisis is perhaps the greatest obstacle opposing the establishment of such a republic in Europe. For the democratic republic to survive without difficulty among a European people, it would have to be established at the same time among all the other European peoples.

I believe that the government of democracy must, in the long run, increase the real forces of society; but it cannot assemble all at once, at one place, and at a given moment, as many forces as an aristocratic government or an absolute monarchy. If a democratic country remained under republican government for a century, you can believe that at the end of the century it would be richer, more populated and more prosperous than neighboring despotic States; but during this century, it would have run the risk several times of being conquered by them.

---

are attached to the State by the most bonds; I know that there is nothing to bring up against the fact. But here the fact appears to me in contradiction with the theory, and the author, with Montesquieu. Perhaps it would be necessary for him to develop his idea a bit more. The following paragraph begins, moreover, to explain it well (YTC, CIIIb, 1, p. 110).

Of the Power That American Democracy
Generally Exercises over Itself

That the American people only go along with something in the long run, and sometimes refuse to do what is useful for their well-being.—Ability that the Americans have to make mistakes that can be corrected.

This difficulty that democracy has in vanquishing passions and silencing the needs of the moment with the future in mind is noticeable in the United States in the smallest things.

The people, surrounded by flatterers [and sycophants], succeed with difficulty in triumphing over themselves. Every time you want them to impose a privation or discomfort on themselves, even for an end their reason approves, they almost always begin by refusing. The obedience that Americans give to laws is rightly praised. It must be added that in America legislation is made by the people and for the people. So in the United States, the laws appear favorable to those who, everywhere else, have the greatest interest in violating it. Thus, it may be believed that a bothersome law, which the majority felt had no present utility, would not be put into effect or would not be obeyed.

In the United States, no legislation exists relating to fraudulent bankruptcies. Would it be because there are no bankruptcies? No, on the contrary, it is because there are many of them. The fear of being prosecuted as a bankrupt surpasses, in the mind of the majority, the fear of being ruined by bankruptcies; and in the public conscience there is a sort of culpable tolerance for the crime that each person condemns individually.

In the new states of the Southwest, the citizens almost always take justice into their own hands, and murders[x] happen constantly. That stems from the habits of the people being too rough and enlightenment being spread

---

x. In the manuscript: "are more frequent than fistfights among us." The expression had been unanimously rejected by the readers: YTC, CIIIb, 1, p. 107 (Édouard de Tocqueville?), p. 105 (Gustave de Beaumont), and CIIIb, 2, p. 1 (Hervé de Tocqueville).

too little in these wilderness areas for anyone to feel the utility of giving the law some force. There they still prefer duels[y] to trials.

Someone[z] said to me one day, in Philadelphia, that nearly all crimes in America were caused by the abuse of strong liquors that the lower classes could use at will, because it was sold to them at a very low price. "Why," I asked, "don't you put a duty on brandy?" "Our legislators have often considered it," he replied, "but it is a difficult undertaking. They fear a revolt; and besides, the members who voted for such a law would very surely not be reelected." "So," I responded, "among you, drinkers are the majority, and temperance is unpopular."

When you point out these things to statesmen, they simply respond: Let time pass; feeling the evil will enlighten the people and will show them what they need. This is often true. If democracy has more chances to make a mistake than a king or a body of nobles, it also has more chances to return to the truth, once enlightenment comes; within a democracy there are generally no interests that are contrary to the interest of the greatest number and that fight reason. But democracy can only gain the truth by experience, and many peoples cannot wait for the results of their errors without perishing.

So the great privilege of the Americans is not only to be more enlightened than others, but also to have the ability to make mistakes that can be corrected.

Add that, in order to profit easily from the experience of the past, democracy must already have reached a certain degree of civilization and enlightenment.

We see some peoples whose first education has been so perverted, and whose character presents such a strange mixture of passions, of ignorance and erroneous notions about everything, that they cannot by themselves discern the cause of their miseries; they succumb to evils that they do not know.

---

y. Édouard de Tocqueville (?): "The word *duel* does not apply well to a half-civilized people. Couldn't you say: the majority still prefers *fights* to trials?" (YTC, CIIIb, 1, pp. 107–8).

z. Mr. Washington Smith (in pocket notebook 3, 25 October 1831, YTC, BIIa, and *Voyage, OC,* V, 1, p. 184). See George W. Pierson, *Tocqueville and Beaumont in America,* p. 459.

I have traveled across vast countries formerly inhabited by powerful Indian nations that today no longer exist; I have lived among already mutilated tribes that, everyday, see their number decline and the splendor of
their savage glory disappear; I have heard these Indians themselves foretell
the final destiny reserved to their race. There is no European, however, who
does not see what would have to be done to preserve these unfortunate
peoples from inevitable destruction. But they do not see it; they feel the
misfortunes that, each year, accumulate on their heads, and they will perish
to the last man while rejecting the remedy. Force would have to be used to
compel them to live.

We are astonished to see the new nations of South America stir, for a
quarter century, amid constantly recurring revolutions; and each day we
expect to see them recover what is called their *natural state*. But who can
assert that today revolutions are not the most natural state of the Spanish
of South America? In this country, society struggles at the bottom of an
abyss from which it cannot escape by its own efforts.

The people who inhabit this beautiful half of a hemisphere seem obstinately bound to eviscerate themselves; nothing can divert them. Exhaustion makes them come to rest for an instant, and rest soon brings them
back to new furies. When I consider them in this alternating state of miseries and crimes, I am tempted to believe that for them despotism would
be a benefit.

But these two words will never be found united in my thought.

Of the Manner in Which American Democracy
Conducts the Foreign Affairs of the State

*Direction given to the foreign policy of the United States by
Washington and Jefferson.—Nearly all the natural defects of
democracy make themselves felt in the conduct of foreign affairs,
and its qualities are felt little there.*

We have seen that the federal Constitution places the permanent leadership
of the foreign interests of the nation in the hands of the President and of

the Senate,[16] which to a certain extent puts the general policy of the Union outside of the direct and daily influence of the people. So we cannot say in an absolute manner that, in America, it is democracy that conducts the foreign affairs of the State.

There are two men who gave the policy of the Americans a direction that is still followed today; the first is Washington, and Jefferson is the second.

Washington said, in this admirable letter addressed to his fellow citizens that forms the political testament of this great man:

> The great rule of conduct for us in regard to foreign nations is, in extending our commercial relations, to have with them as little *political* connection as possible. So far as we have already formed engagements, let them be fulfilled with perfect good faith. Here let us stop.
>
> Europe has a set of primary interests, which to us have none, or a very remote relation. Hence she must be engaged in frequent controversies, the causes of which are essentially foreign to our concerns. Hence therefore it must be unwise in us to implicate ourselves, by artificial ties, in the ordinary vicissitudes of her politics, or the ordinary combinations and collisions of her friendships, or enmities.
>
> Our detached and distant situation invites and enables us to pursue a different course. If we remain one People, under an efficient government, the period is not far off, when we may defy material injury from external annoyance; when we may take such an attitude as will cause the neutrality we may at any time resolve upon to be scrupulously respected; when belligerent nations, under the impossibility of making acquisitions upon us, will not lightly hazard the giving us provocation; when we may choose peace or war, as our interest guided by justice shall Counsel.
>
> Why forego the advantages of so peculiar a situation? Why quit our own to stand upon foreign ground? Why, by interweaving our destiny with

---

16. *"[The President],"* says the Constitution, art. 2, sect. II, paragraph 2, *"shall have Power, by and with the Advice and Consent of the Senate, to make Treaties." The reader must not lose sight of the fact that the term of Senators lasts six years, and that, chosen by the legislators of each state, they are the result of indirect election.*

that of any part of Europe, entangle our peace and prosperity in the toils of European Ambition, Rivalship, Interest, Humour or Caprice?

'Tis our true policy to steer clear of permanent Alliances with any portion of the foreign world. So far, I mean, as we are now at liberty to do it; for let me not be understood as capable of patronizing infidelity to existing engagements (I hold the maxim no less applicable to public than to private affairs, that honesty is always the best policy). I repeat it, therefore, let those engagements be observed in their genuine sense. But, in my opinion, it is unnecessary and would be unwise to extend them. Taking care always to keep ourselves, by suitable establishments, on a respectable defensive posture, we may safely trust to temporary alliances for extraordinary emergencies.

Previously Washington had expressed this excellent and sound idea: "The Nation, which indulges towards another an habitual hatred, or an habitual fondness, is in some degree a slave. It is a slave to its animosity or to its affection."

The political action of Washington always aimed to follow his maxims. He succeeded in keeping his country at peace, when all the rest of the universe was at war, and he established as a point of doctrine that the well understood interest of Americans was never to take part in the internal quarrels of Europe.

Jefferson went still farther, and he introduced to the policy of the Union this other maxim: "That the Americans should never ask for privileges from foreign nations, so that they are never obligated themselves to grant such privileges."[*]

These two principles, which due to their obvious soundness were easily grasped by the crowd, have extremely simplified the foreign policy of the United States.

Not mixing into Europe's affairs, the Union has, so to speak, no foreign interests to discuss, for it does not yet have powerful neighbors in America [{it had to be grossly and groundlessly provoked in 1812 for it to consider taking up arms}]. Placed by its situation as much as by its will outside the

---

[*]. Washington had already indicated this maxim, but Jefferson put it into practice and introduced it into the ideas and mores of his country.

passions of the Old World, the Union does not have to protect itself from them anymore than to espouse them. As for the passions of the New World, they are still hidden in the future.

[The Union grows constantly larger; it appears different each year, for its prosperity has something revolutionary about it. So the clear interest of the Union, which changes daily, is not to create lasting ties. Ties useful today could soon hamper its course and compromise its future.]

The Union is free from previous commitments; so it profits from the experience of the old peoples of Europe, without being obliged, like them, to make use of the past and to adapt the past to the present;[a] it is not forced, as they are, to accept an immense heritage handed down by its fathers, a mixture of glory and misery, of national friendships and hatreds. The foreign policy of the United States is eminently one of wait-and-see; it consists much more of refraining from action than of doing.

So it is very difficult to know, for now, what skill American democracy will develop in the conduct of the foreign affairs of the State.[b] On this point, its adversaries as well as it friends must suspend their judgment.

As for me, I will have no difficulty in saying: it is in the leadership of the foreign interests of society that democratic governments seem to me decidedly inferior to others.[*] In democracy, experience, mores, and edu-

a. In the margin: "≠America appears amid the civilized world with the strength of {youth and the experience of mature age.}≠" Cf. conversation with Mr. Latrobe, 3 November 1831 (non-alphabetic notebooks 2 and 3, YTC, BIIc, and *Voyage, OC,* V, 1, p. 120).

b. To the side: "≠So we must wait until matters become complicated and difficulties appear in order to be able to judge the degree to which American democracy will be capable of conducting the public affairs of society.≠"

Tocqueville's short experience at the head of the Ministry of Foreign Affairs, from June to October 1849, confirmed his fears about the inferiority of democracies in foreign affairs (see his *Souvenirs, OC,* XII, p. 246). On this question, see Stephen A. Garrett, "Foreign Policy and the Democracies: De Tocqueville Revisited," *Virginia Quarterly Review* 48, no. 4 (1972): 481–500.

[*]. ≠Note, moreover, that the federal Constitution places the permanent leadership of the foreign interests of the nation in the hands of the President and the Senate, which to a certain extent places the general policy of the Union outside the daily influence of the democracy.≠

cation almost always end by creating the sort of everyday practical wisdom and the skill in the small events of life that is called good sense. Good sense suffices for the ordinary routine of society; and among a people whose education is already accomplished, democratic liberty applied to the internal affairs of the State produces greater good than the evil that can be caused by the errors of democratic government. But it is not always so in the relations of one people with another.

Foreign policy requires the use of almost none of the qualities that belong to democracy and, on the contrary, demands the development of nearly all those qualities that it lacks. Democracy favors the growth of the internal resources of the State; it spreads comfort, develops public spirit; strengthens respect for law in the different classes of society; all things that have only an indirect influence on the position of a people vis-à-vis another. But only with difficulty can democracy coordinate the details of a great undertaking, settle on one plan and then follow it stubbornly across all obstacles. It is little capable of devising measures in secret and patiently awaiting their result. These are the qualities that belong most particularly to a man or to an aristocracy. Now, in the long run it is precisely these qualities that make a people, like an individual, predominate in the end.

If, on the contrary, you pay attention to the natural defects of aristocracy,[c] you will find that the effect that these defects can produce can be felt hardly at all in the leadership of the foreign affairs of the State. The capital vice for which the aristocracy is reproached is to work only for itself alone

c. Hervé de Tocqueville:

It is absolutely necessary to add the words *in internal administration* in order to establish clearly the division between internal and external, so that the author cannot be accused of praising here the institution that he blamed above. In fact, history proves that the aristocracy, very strong externally, because it is led solely by the interest of the State, commits many mistakes internally, because its personal interest misleads it. The aristocracy of Rome had been absolute in regard to the plebeians. That of France committed enormous mistakes, and that of England for fifty years has not been much wiser (YTC, CIIIb, 2, p. 3).

and not for the mass. In foreign policy, it is very rare for the aristocracy to have an interest distinct from that of the people.

The inclination that leads democracy in policy matters to obey sentiments rather than reasoning, and to abandon a long developed plan for the satisfaction of a momentary passion, clearly revealed itself in America when the French Revolution broke out. The simplest insights of reason would suffice then, as today, to make the Americans understand that it was not in their interest to get engaged in the struggle that was going to cover Europe in blood, and from which the United States could suffer no harm.

The sympathies of the people in favor of France came out with such violence, however, that nothing less was required to prevent a declaration of war against England than the unyielding character of Washington and the immense popularity that he enjoyed.[d] And yet, the efforts made by the austere reason of this great man to combat the generous but unthinking passions of his fellow citizens very nearly deprived him of the only recompense that he had ever expected, the love of his country. The majority pronounced against his policy; now, the whole people approve it.[17]

If the Constitution and public favor had not given Washington the leadership of the foreign affairs of the State, the nation would certainly have done then precisely what it condemns today.[e]

---

d. In the margin: "{see the *History* of Pitkin.}"

17. *See the fifth volume of the* Life of Washington *by Marshall. "In a government established as that of the United States," he says, page 314, "the chief executive, whatever his firmness, cannot long present a barrier to the torrent of popular opinion; and the popular opinion that then prevailed seemed to lead to war. In fact, in the session of Congress held at this time, it was seen very frequently that Washington had lost the majority in the House of Representatives. Outside, the violence of the language used against him was extreme; in a political meeting, some were not afraid to compare him indirectly with the traitor Arnold (p. 265). Those who belonged to the opposing party," says Marshall again (p. 353), "claimed that the partisans of the administration were an aristocratic faction that was submissive to England and, wanting to establish a monarchy, was therefore the enemy of France; a faction whose members constituted a kind of nobility, that had shares of the Bank as titles, and that was so afraid of any measure that could influence its capital, that it was insensitive to the insults that both the honor and the interest of the nation demanded to be rejected."*

e. Cf. note h for p. 190.

Nearly all the peoples who have acted strongly on the world, those who have conceived, followed and executed great designs, from the Romans to the English, were led by an aristocracy; and how can you be surprised [≠when you see the part that must be attributed to the continuous effect of the same will in human events≠]?

In this world, what is most steady in its views is an aristocracy. The mass of people can be seduced by its ignorance or its passions. You can catch the mind of a king unawares and make him vacillate in his plans; and, besides, a king is not immortal. But an aristocratic body is too numerous to be won over, too few in number to yield easily to the intoxication of unthinking passions. An aristocratic body is a firm and enlightened man who does not die.[f]

f. The Pennsylvania Historical Society retains a commentary by Tocqueville on the question of French indemnities in the United States and American foreign policy. (This document had been catalogued by mistake as belonging to *Democracy in America.*) The reference to the correspondence of Livingston and the possibility that the latter had not yet left France when Tocqueville wrote his commentary led to the thought that these pages date from April or the beginning of May 1835, that is, a few months after the publication of the first part of the book. Nor is there any indication in the Yale Collection that allows a relationship to be established between these pages and the manuscript of the work. Perhaps documents in the hands of the Commission charged with the edition of Tocqueville's works would be able to offer some decisive information as to the origin of this commentary. This text, to an unknown recipient, is part of the collection of manuscripts of Ferdinand Dreer, even though the catalogue of the collection, edited by Dreer himself (*A Catalogue of the Collection of Autographs formed by Ferdinand Julius Dreer,* Philadelphia: printed for private distribution, 1890, 2 vols.), mentions no document of Tocqueville. This unedited manuscript had been utilized by William E. Lingelbach, in his commentary "American Democracy and European Interpreters," *Pennsylvania Magazine of History and Biography* 61, no. 1 (January 1937): 1–25 (in pages 8 and 9).

Here is the text:

First here is what the *Constitution* says. Then I will examine the commentaries and the *practice.*

The second section of Article II of the constitution reads: "*[The President] shall have Power, by and with the Advice and Consent of the Senate, to make Treaties, provided two thirds of the Senators present concur; and he shall nominate, and by and with the Advice and Consent of the Senate, shall appoint Ambassadors.*"

In section three of the same Article, you read: "*[The President] shall receive Ambassadors and other public Ministers.*"

Commentaries.

I consulted the three most respected commentaries. They are the *Federalist,* work published by three of the principal draftsmen of the federal Constitution, the commentaries of Chancellor Kent, and those of Justice Story.

[In the margin: *Federalist,* No. 43–64, vol. 2.

Story's *Commentaries,* pp. 556 and 576.]

Here are the doctrines that result. I will put my authorities in the margin.

The Senate of the United States is an assembly vested with a double character; it is at the same time a legislative body and an administrative body. In the first case, its deliberations are public; they are secret in the other case. The Senate in its quality of administrative body is charged jointly with the President with making treaties. As such it would clearly have the right to take part in negotiations,[1] but it has been wisely admitted in practice that the Senate had to leave to the President, *sole intermediary of the nation with foreign ministers,* the right to start, direct, and provisionally conclude treaties. They are afterward submitted to the Senate, which approves, rejects or modifies them, depending on its views.

It was a great question in the United States to know if a treaty concluded in this way still had to be submitted to Congress or if it bound the nation *ipso facto.*

The House of Representatives declared in 1796[2] that when the enforcement of certain clauses required the passage of a law, Congress had the right, in regard to this law, to deliberate on the treaty itself. Washington in a message that same year refused to recognize such a power in Congress.

This opinion of Washington, says Kent, *seems to have become the prevailing one in America. The House of Representatives in 1816 had the occasion to show that it shared it.* To a certain degree, this opinion explains the language of General Jackson; it served him as pretext and support for saying [that (ed.)] France would fail to meet its *agreements* if the Chamber of Deputies rejected the treaty.

It is clear to me from the texts, and from the commentaries that I have just cited, as well as from what I learned myself in America, that the Constitution and practice made the President of the United States the usual and sole representative of the nation vis-à-vis foreigners. Ministers address themselves to him alone; all words and all pieces pass through him to reach the Senate.

Now, if President Jackson by his message, which is after all only the speech of an official, did not involve the American nation in a quarrel with the French nation, at least it is certain that, as an individual, he gravely offended France. Can France, respecting its honor, continue to accept this man as the *sole and necessary intermediary* between itself and the American nation, at least until this man has given some honorable explanations? I do not think so, neither as an individual, nor as a Frenchman.

Far from President Jackson appearing disposed during three months to retract his outrageous insinuations, his conduct has continued to be more and more arrogant. His letter to Mr. Livingston indicated that with pleasure he would have seen the

Ambassador of the United States immediately leave France at the moment when passports had been offered to him.

In summary, I think that the Chamber, by adopting the principle of the law, by agreeing to separate (which is not already to act like Louis XV) the American nation from its President, the Chamber, I say, can do nothing less than declare that it only acted in this way because it was persuaded that the ministers will not accredit any diplomatic agent close to the President of the United States except in the case that the latter would give a satisfactory explanation for his words.

By acting in this way, only a temporary embarrassment in relations can result, since the term of the President expires in two years.

1. Mr. Story says, p. 558: "The Senate has very rarely, if ever, been consulted before the clauses of the treaty were settled; the treaty was then submitted to the Senate for ratification."

2. See *Kent's Commentaries,* vol. I, p. 267.

With the kind permission of the Pennsylvania Historical Society.

The edition of the *Federalist* cited here by Tocqueville is probably the French translation, in two volumes, published by Buisson, which appeared in Paris in 1792. See note n for p. 193.

What Are the Real Advantages That American Society Gains from the Government of Democracy?

[Before beginning this chapter I feel the need to explain myself. I do not want my thought enclosed within limits that I have not set.

When I speak generally about the advantages of {that a country can gain from} the government of democracy, I am not talking only about the government that democracy has provided for itself in America, but about all types of government that emanate from democracy.

Every time that the government of a people is the sincere and permanent

a. Édouard de Tocqueville:

I criticize this whole chapter for being very favorable to the government of democracy at the expense of other governments. It seems to me that America is too young, that its society is too new and, you could even say, still too incomplete to draw arguments so positively advantageous to the government that it is attempting; it cannot be denied that the basis of your thought in this chapter seems to be sympathetic to American institutions; now, it would be unfortunate if someone were to believe that you came back from America American, following the usual inclination of men, and of Frenchmen above all, who greatly admire what they go to seek far away, while deprecating what is found at home. So I believe it would perhaps be good to show democratic government a little less favorably and make a bit more use of the dubitative form, perhaps to be a bit more severe as well about the bad things and the vicious aspects of this government, which would make your impartiality emerge more fully; finally, remove all the expressions that seem like those of a young man and that do not constitute true warmth of style (YTC, CIIIb, 1, pp. 101–2).

expression of the will of the greatest number, that government, whatever the forms, is democratic.[b]

So democracy can rule over a unified nation as over a confederation, in a monarchy as in a republic.

I admit that of all governments the one that seems to me most natural to democracy is republican government. When the social state of a people turns toward democracy, the republic becomes for them a probable consequence of this social state; but I do not believe that it is a necessary consequence.

If the majority of all the citizens do violence to the instincts of equality that are natural to them and, favoring order and governmental stability, consent to vest the attributes of executive power in a family or a man who, while still leading, depends on them, there is nothing in that that shocks reason. So the rule of all and the government [v: the administration] of one man can be seen at the same time. I confess that this much reduces royal majesty, but the time is coming when, if kings do not want to take the places left [v: still offered] to them, they will no longer find any to take.][c]

Before beginning the present chapter, I feel the need to remind the reader of what I have already pointed out several times in the course of this book.

The political constitution of the United States seems to me one of the forms that democracy can give to its government; but I do not consider American institutions as either the only or the best that a democratic people should adopt.

So by making known what good things the Americans gain from the government of democracy, I am far from claiming or thinking that such advantages can only be obtained with the help of the same laws.

b. To the side: "To retouch all of this small chapter. *According to L[ouis (ed.)],* my purpose is not seen clearly enough. One doesn't know if this isn't a carefully phrased remark in favor of despotism or of L[ouis (ed.)]. P[hilippe (ed.)]."

c. This fragment also appears in YTC, CVh, 3, pp. 38–39, accompanied (p. 38) by the following comment in the margin: "All of this preamble seems to me of questionable utility, because the thought that led to writing it does not emerge clearly. As I am going to say things favorable to democracy, I am afraid that someone might suppose that I wanted to praise the *American republic,* and given this fear, I wanted to extend what I said about America to democracy in general. But I do not know if my intention is grasped."

Of the General Tendency of Laws under the Dominion of American Democracy, and Of the Instinct of Those Who Apply Them

The vices of democracy are immediately apparent.—Its advantages are seen only in the long run.—American democracy is often clumsy, but the general tendency of its laws is beneficial.—Public officials, under American democracy, have no permanent interests that differ from those of the greatest number.—What results from that.

The vices and weaknesses of the government of democracy are easily seen; they are demonstrated by obvious facts, while its salutary influence is exerted in an imperceptible and, so to speak, hidden way. Its drawbacks are striking at first sight, but its qualities are revealed only in the long run.

The laws of American democracy are often defective or incomplete; it happens that they violate vested rights or sanction dangerous ones. Were they good, their frequency would still be a great evil. All of this is seen at first glance.

So why do the American republics live on and prosper?

In laws, the end that they seek must be carefully distinguished from the way in which they move toward that end; their absolute goodness, from goodness that is only relative.[d]

---

d. In legislation, three things must be carefully discerned: 1. its *general tendency,* 2. its *perfection* (once its direction is given), and 3. the *manner* in which it is executed. A perfect law would be the one that would have the most useful tendency, that would move toward this end by the most skillful and most effective provisions, and that would be executed by the best agents. But this perfection is hardly ever found.

The laws of democracy are decidedly defective in the last two objects. But I am tempted to believe that they are superior in the first, and in this way I explain their general result, which often seems in general contradiction to reason and daily experience. See the example of England (YTC, CVh, 4, pp. 77–78).

I suppose that the purpose of the legislator is to favor the interests of the few at the expense of those of the many; his measures are devised in a way to obtain the result that he wants in the least time and with the least possible effort. The law will be well made; its aim, bad. It will be dangerous in proportion to its very effectiveness.

The laws of democracy tend, in general, toward the good of the greatest number, for they emanate from the majority of all citizens; the majority can be mistaken, but cannot have an interest against itself.

Those of aristocracy tend, on the contrary, to monopolize wealth and power in the hands of the few, because the aristocracy by its nature always forms a minority.

So we can say, in a general way, that the purpose of democracy, in its legislation, is more useful to humanity than the purpose of aristocracy in its legislation.

But its advantages end there.

Aristocracy is infinitely more skillful in the science of lawmaking than democracy can be. Having self-control, aristocracy is not subject to passing impulses; it has long-term plans that it knows how to develop until the favorable opportunity presents itself. Aristocracy proceeds skillfully; it knows the art of bringing together at the same time, toward the same point, the collective force of all its laws.

Not so with democracy; its laws are nearly always defective or ill-timed.

[In the eyes of the world, laws badly made or made at the wrong time discredit the legislative spirit of democracy.]e

---

e.

DEMOCRACY.

Imperfect laws. Succession of laws, a great evil.

Incapable or vice-ridden officials, but not having an interest contrary to the greatest number.

Laws badly made or made [v: interpreted] wrong on purpose, that is what discredits the legislative spirit of democracy.

ARISTOCRACY.

Tendency of laws contrary to the interests of the greatest number.

Capable and honest officials, but having an interest contrary to the greatest number and acting either with their consent or without their knowledge.

Less wisdom in each effort, but a greater result produced by the sum of efforts.

So the means of democracy are more imperfect than those of aristocracy. Democracy, without wanting to, often works against itself; but its end is more useful.

Imagine a society that nature, or its constitution, had organized in a way to bear the transient effect of bad laws, a society that, without perishing, can await the result of the *general tendency of the laws;*[f] and you will understand that, of all governments, the government of democracy, despite its flaws, is still the most appropriate to make this society prosper.

This is precisely what happens in the United States; here I repeat what I have already expressed elsewhere: the great privilege of the Americans is to be able to make mistakes that can be corrected.

I will say something analogous about public officials.

It is easy to see that American democracy is often wrong in its choice of the men to whom it confides power; but it is not as easy to say why the State prospers in their hands.

Note first that, in a democratic State, if those who govern are less honest or less capable, the governed are more enlightened and more attentive.

In democracies, the people, constantly occupied as they are with their affairs and jealous of their rights, prevent their representatives from departing from a certain general line drawn by the interest of the people.

If democracy could direct the spirit of legislation and aristocracy could make the laws.

This tie that binds men with or without their knowledge to the consequences of the principle that they accepted is one of the greatest miseries and greatest humiliations of our nature (YTC, CVh, 4, p. 75).

f. Hervé de Tocqueville:

If a society made only bad laws, the effect of these laws would be to bring about bad tendencies, and everything would go to the devil.

This subject is extremely abstract, and needs to be reviewed and considered again. I believe that the difficulty comes from the fact that Alexis seems to assume that most of the American laws are bad; I imagine that it is the opposite. Without that, the system that the author puts forth would not be tenable (YTC, CIIIb, 1, p. 93).

Note too that if the democratic magistrate exercises power worse than another, he generally holds it for less time.g

But there is a more general and more satisfying reason than the latter.

It is undoubtedly important for the good of nations that those who govern have virtues and talents; but perhaps it is even more important to them that those who govern have no interests contrary to the mass of the governed; for, in this case, virtues could become nearly useless, and talents, destructive.

I said it was important that those who govern have no interests contrary to or different from the mass of the governed; I did not say it was important that they had interests similar to those of *all* the governed, for I am not aware that such a thing has yet been seen.

The political form has not yet been found that equally favors the development and the prosperity of all the classes that make up society. These classes have continued to form like so many distinct nations in the same nation, and experience has proved that it was nearly as dangerous to put the fate of the others completely in the hands of any one of them as to make one people the arbiter of the destiny of another people. When the rich alone govern, the interest of the poor is always in danger; and when the poor make the laws, the interest of the rich runs great risks. So what is the advantage of democracy? The real advantage of democracy is not, as some have said, to favor the prosperity of all, but only to serve the well-being of the greatest number.

Those charged, in the United States, with leading public affairs are often

g. Hervé de Tocqueville:

In my view, that is the true, often noted reason why, in the republics of antiquity, the more clearly it was noticed that officials abused their power, the more the term of office was shortened. Thus, in Athens the archons for life were reduced to ten years, and then to one year. In Rome, the power of the consuls, which lasted only one year, was much less dangerous than that of the tribunes, which lasted five years; the dictatorship, despite its omnipotence, only became dangerous to liberty when it dared to go beyond the limit of six months that had been set by law (YTC, CIIIb, 1, p. 94).

Here, as elsewhere, Hervé uses arguments taken from Montesquieu (cf. chapter III of book II of *L'esprit des lois*).

inferior in capacity and morality to the men whom aristocracy would bring to power; but their interest merges and is identified with that of the majority[h] of their fellow citizens. So they can commit frequent infidelities and serious errors, but they will never systematically follow a tendency hostile to this majority; and they can never impart an exclusive and dangerous direction to the government.

The bad administration of a magistrate, under democracy, is moreover an isolated fact that has influence only during the short term of the administration. Corruption and incompetence are not common interests that can bind men together in a permanent way.

A corrupt or incompetent magistrate will not combine his efforts with another magistrate for the sole reason that the latter is, like him, incompetent and corrupt; and these two men will never work in unison to make corruption and incompetency flower among their descendants. On the contrary, the ambition and the maneuvering of the one will serve to unmask the other. In democracies, the vices of the magistrate are, in general, entirely personal.

But public men, under the government of aristocracy, have a class interest that, if it sometimes merges with the interest of the majority, often remains distinct from it. This interest forms a common and lasting bond among these public men; it invites them to unite and to combine their efforts toward an end that is not always the happiness of the greatest number. It not only links those who govern with each other; it also links them with a considerable portion of the governed, for many citizens, without holding any office, are part of the aristocracy.

So the aristocratic magistrate finds a constant support in society, at the same time that he finds one in government.

This common objective that, in aristocracies, unites magistrates with the interest of a part of their contemporaries, also identifies them with and, so to speak, subjects them to future races. They work for the future as well as for the present. So the aristocratic magistrate is pushed simultaneously toward the same point, by the passions of the governed, by his own, and I could almost say by the passions of his posterity.

h. In the manuscript: "of the greatest number."

How can we be surprised if he doesn't resist? Consequently, in aristocracies we often see even those not corrupted by class spirit dragged along by it and unknowingly made to adapt society little by little to their own use and to prepare it for their descendants.

I do not know if an aristocracy has ever existed as liberal as that of England, and that has, without interruption, provided the government of the country with men as worthy and as enlightened.

It is easy to recognize, however, that in English legislation the good of the poor has often ended by being sacrificed to that of the rich,[j] and the

j. This sentence provoked the immediate reaction of two English readers. In a letter of 17 February 1835, Nassau Senior remarked:

> I do not think that in England the wealth of the poor has been sacrificed to that of the rich. As far as my investigations extend, the wages of the English labourer are higher than those of any labourer. He has no landed property, because it is more profitable to him to work for another than to cultivate; but this depends on the same ground which makes it more profitable to work for a cotton manufacturer than to make stockings for his own use. It is a part of the division of labour, of which la grande culture is only an instance (*Correspondence and Conversations of Alexis de Tocqueville and Nassau William Senior,* London: Henry S. King & Co., 1872, I, pp. 4–5).

Tocqueville replied:

> It seems to me that you give to the expression *le bien du pauvre* a confined sense that was not mine: you translate it *wealth,* a word especially applied to money. I meant by it all that contributes to happiness: personal consideration, political right, easy justice, intellectual enjoyments, and many other indirect sources of contentment. I shall believe, till I have proof of the contrary, that in England the rich have gradually monopolized almost all the advantages that society bestows upon mankind. Taking the question in your own restricted sense, and admitting that a poor man is better paid when he works on another man's land than when he cultivates his own, do you not think that there are political, moral, and intellectual advantages, which are a more than sufficient and, above all, a permanent compensation for the loss that you point out? (letter of 21 February 1835, *ibid.,* p. 7).

He replied in slightly different terms to Basil Hall, officer in the English navy and author of the controversial work on the United States *Travels in North America in the Years 1827 and 1828:*

> You reproach me for having said *that the interests of the poor were sacrificed in England to those of the rich.* I confess that this thought, exposed in so few words, thrown out in passing, without commentary, naturally tends to present a meaning much more absolute than what I intended to give it, and my intention has always been to modify

rights of the greatest number to the privileges of a few. Therefore, within England today all the greatest extremes of fortune are present together, and miseries are found there that nearly equal its power and glory.[k]

In the United States, where public officials have no class interest to insist upon, the general and continuous course of government is beneficial, even though those who govern are often lacking in skill and sometimes contemptible.

So there is, at the heart of democratic institutions, a hidden tendency that often makes men work toward the general prosperity, despite their vices or errors, while in aristocratic institutions a secret inclination is sometimes uncovered that, despite talents and virtues, carries them toward contributing to the miseries of their fellows. In this way, in aristocratic governments, public men can do evil without wanting to do so, and in democracies, they can produce good without thinking to do so.[m]

---

it when I would be able to revise my work. What I principally wanted to say is that England is a country where wealth is the *necessary preliminary* to a multitude of things that elsewhere can be obtained without it. So that in England there is a multitude of careers that are much more closed to the poor than they are in several other countries. This would still require a great number of explanations to be well understood. I am obliged to postpone them until the moment when I will have the pleasure of seeing you again. Château de Baugy, 19 June 1836. With the kind permission of the library of Princeton University (General Manuscripts [MISC] Collection, Manuscripts Division, Department of Rare Books and Special Collections). See note d for pp. 819–21 of volume II.

k. In the manuscript: "Thus England today has reached a level of misery that nearly equals its power . . ."

Hervé de Tocqueville: "The word *England* presents too absolute an idea that reason immediately contests. I believe that it would be necessary to put: *the lower class in England has reached,* etc." (YTC, CIIIb, 1, p. 95).

m. The world is a book entirely closed to man.

So there is at the heart of democratic institutions a hidden tendency that carries men toward the good [v: to work toward general prosperity] despite their vices and errors; while in aristocratic institutions a secret inclination is sometimes uncovered that, despite talents and virtues, leads them to contribute to the miseries of the greatest number of their fellows.

If a hidden force independent of men did not exist in democratic institutions, it would be impossible to explain satisfactorily the peace and prosperity that reign within certain democracies (YTC, CVh, 4, p. 76).

[If it were not so, who could understand what happens among men?

We would see some peoples enjoy a greater mass of well-being and prosperity than other peoples and, when we came to examine the detail of their government, we would find something to correct in each of its actions.

Other peoples would have something more than the usual state of human miseries as their share, and their public affairs would seem wisely conducted.

So is prosperity in the world the reward of error and folly; are miseries the recompense for skill and wisdom?/

This involuntary obedience of man to his own laws seems to me one of the great miseries of our nature.

Who could say within what narrow limits what we call our free will is exercised? Man obeys first causes of which he is unaware, secondary causes that he cannot foresee, a thousand caprices of his fellows; in the end, he puts himself in chains and binds himself forever to the fragile work of his hands.][n]

Of Public Spirit in the United States[o]

*Instinctive love of country.—Thoughtful patriotism.—Their
different characters.—That peoples must tend with all their
might toward the second when the first disappears.—Efforts that
the Americans have made to succeed in doing so.—The interest of
the individual intimately bound to that of the country.*

There exists a love of country that has its source principally in the unthinking, disinterested and indefinable sentiment that binds the heart of the man to the places where the man was born. This instinctive love is mingled with

n. In the first chapter of the *Social Contract,* Rousseau asserts that if man is born free, he finds himself everywhere in chains. The image is customary at that time.

o. To the side: "{Mr. Parier [?(ed.)] will leave blank what I} enclosed in lines." (It probably involves the copyist of the manuscript. Here and there fragments in his hand are found in the manuscript.)

the taste for ancient customs, with respect for ancestors, and the memory of the past; those who experience it cherish their country as one loves the paternal home. They love the tranquillity that they enjoy there; they are fond of the peaceful habits that they contracted there; they are attached to the memories that it offers, and even find some sweet pleasure in living there in obedience. Often this love of country is intensified even more by religious zeal, and then you see it accomplish miracles. It is itself a kind of religion; it does not reason, it believes; it feels; it acts. Some peoples have been found who have, in some way, personified the country and have caught sight of it in the prince. So they have transferred to him a part of the sentiments that compose patriotism; they have boasted about his triumphs and have been proud of his power. There was a time, under the old monarchy, when the French felt a sort of joy in feeling themselves given, without recourse, to the arbitrariness of the monarch, and said with pride: "We live under the most powerful king in the world."[p]

Like all unthinking passions, this love of country encourages great episodic efforts rather than continuity of efforts. After saving the State in time of crisis, it often leaves it to decline amid peace. [≠This love of country is found in the cradle of societies; it presides during the early ages of peoples.≠]

When peoples are still simple in their mores and firm in their beliefs; when society rests gently upon an old order of things, whose legitimacy is uncontested, you see this instinctive love of country reign.[q]

There is another love of country more rational than that one; less generous, less ardent perhaps, but more fruitful and more durable; this one arises from enlightenment; it develops with the help of laws; it grows with the exercise of rights; and it ends up merging, in a way, with personal interest. A man understands the influence that the well-being of the country has on his own; he knows that the law allows him to contribute to bringing

p. Hervé de Tocqueville: "All of this piece is charming; nonetheless the words *caught sight of* are not good" (YTC, CIIIb, 1, p. 95).

q. "If God had granted me the power to change societies at will, and if I found along my way a people who had remained in this state, I would hesitate a long time, I admit, before trying to draw them out of that state" (YTC, CVh, 3, p. 5).

this well-being into being, and he interests himself in the prosperity of his country, first as something useful to him and then as his work.

But sometimes, in the life of peoples, a moment occurs when ancient customs are changed, mores destroyed, beliefs shaken, the prestige of memories has vanished, yet when enlightenment has remained incomplete and political rights poorly guaranteed or limited. Then men no longer see the country except in a weak and doubtful light; they no longer locate it either in the soil, which in their eyes has become an inanimate land, or in the customs of their ancestors, which they have been taught to regard as a burden; or in religion, which they doubt; or in the laws, which they do not make, or in the legislator, whom they fear and scorn. So they see it nowhere, not under its own features any more than under any other, and they withdraw into a narrow and unenlightened egoism. These men escape prejudices without recognizing the empire of reason; they have neither the instinctive patriotism of monarchy, nor the thoughtful patriotism of the republic; but they have stopped between the two, in the middle of confusion and misery.

What is to be done in such a state? Go back. But peoples do not return to the sentiments of their youth any more than men to the innocent tastes of early years; they can regret them, but not make them come again. So it is necessary to move ahead and hasten to unite, in the eyes of the people, individual interest and the interest of the country, for disinterested love of country flies away never to return.[r]

---

r. I see in Europe an innumerable multitude that finds itself entirely excluded from the administration of its country. I think at first that these men, seeing themselves reduced to such a state [v: bondage] are going to become indignant, but no, they rejoice in it.

For my part, what I most reproach despotism for are not its rigors. I would pardon it for tormenting men if it did not *corrupt* them. Despotism creates in the soul of those who are subjected to it a blind passion for tranquillity, a kind of depraved taste for obedience, a sort of inconceivable self-contempt that ends up making them indifferent to their interests and enemies of their own rights.

Then they wrongly persuade themselves that by losing in this way all the privileges of civilized man, they escape all his burdens and evade all his duties. So they feel free and count in society like a lackey [v: valet] in the house of his master; and think that they have only to eat the bread that is left for them, without concerning themselves about the cares of the harvest.

I am surely far from claiming that to reach this result we must suddenly grant the exercise of political rights to all men; but I say that the most powerful means, and perhaps the only one remaining to us, to interest men in the fate of their country, is to make them participate in its government. Today, civic spirit seems to me inseparable from the exercise of political rights; and I think that from now on, we will see the number of citizens in Europe increase or decrease in proportion to the extension of these rights.

How is it that in the United States, where the inhabitants arrived yesterday on the soil that they occupy, where they brought neither customs, nor memories; where they meet for the first time without knowing each other; where, to put it in a word, the instinct for native land can hardly exist; how is it that each person is involved in the affairs of his town, of his district, and of the entire State as his very own? Because each person, in his sphere, takes an active part in the government of society.

The common man in the United States has understood the influence that general prosperity exercises over his own happiness, an idea so simple and yet so little known by the people. He has, moreover, become accustomed to regarding this prosperity as his work. So, in public fortune, he sees his own, and he works for the good of the State, not only by duty or by pride, but I would almost dare to say by cupidity.

When a man has reached this point, I will call him, if you want, a peaceful inhabitant, an honest settler, a good family man. I am ready for everything, provided that you do not force me to give him the name of citizen.

I am surely far from claiming that the exercise of political rights can be suddenly granted to all men. But I say that civic spirit is nearly inseparable from the exercise of political rights. So the number of citizens always increases or decreases in a country in proportion to the extension of these rights, and where the exercise can be granted to all, the development of civic spirit is nearly without limits (YTC, CVh, 1, pp. 2–4).

A note dated 1840, when Tocqueville was a deputy and was occupied in the Chamber with the electoral issue, specified, however: "As for electoral reform, here is my sentiment. The mode of election: I absolutely refuse all lowering of the electoral qualification or equivalent additions.—I do not want a more *radical* election law, but a more *moral* one—an electoral system that makes corruption by patronage more difficult—1840." Note reproduced in Pierre Roland-Marcel, *Essai politique sur Alexis de Tocqueville,* Paris: Félix Alcan, 1910, p. 211.

[He values his rights as a citizen as his rights as a proprietor, and he takes an interest in the State as in his cottage or in the field that his labors have made fruitful.]

It is not necessary to study the institutions and the history of the Americans to know the truth of the preceding; the mores alert you to it well enough. The American, taking part in all that is happening in this country, believes it is in his interest to defend all that you criticize there; for it is not only his country that you then attack, it is himself. Consequently, you see his national pride resort to all the artifices and descend to all the puerilities of individual vanity.

[An American in his country resembles a lover of gardens on his grounds. Don't you admire this rock? Is there anything more graceful than the contour of this stream? Aren't these trees planted well and to good effect? Whatever you say, do not hope to satisfy him. The reason is simple. You admire what is good, and he admires his work.]

There is nothing more annoying in the experience of life than this irritable patriotism of the Americans. The foreigner would gladly agree to praise a great deal in their country; but he would want them to allow him to find fault with something, and that is what they absolutely refuse.

So America is a country of liberty, where, to hurt no one, the foreigner must not speak freely about individuals, nor the State, nor the governed, nor those who govern, nor public enterprises, nor private enterprises, about nothing in fact that you find there, except perhaps for climate and soil; even then you find some Americans ready to defend the one and the other as if they had taken part in their formation.[s]

Today it is necessary to know how to make up your mind and dare to

s. American patriotism is already mentioned in the first letter that Tocqueville sent to his family during his voyage to the United States: "These people seem to me to stink of national pride; it pokes through all of their politeness" (Letter to his mother, 26 April 1831, YTC, BIa2; this sentence does not appear in the edition of Tocqueville's works done by Beaumont). Beaumont, on his side, writes in his novel: "The writers, in the United States, who want to find readers are obliged to praise all that belongs to the Americans, even their rigorous climate, about which they can assuredly change nothing. In this way, Washington Irving, despite all of his intelligence, believes himself forced to admire the temperate heat of the summers and the mildness of the winters in North America" (*Marie*, I, pp. 360–61).

choose between the patriotism of all and the government of a few, for you cannot at the same time combine the social strength and activity given by the first with the guarantees of tranquillity sometimes provided by the second.

Of the Idea of Rights in the United States

There are no great peoples without the idea of rights.—What is the way to give the people the idea of rights.—Respect for rights in the United States.—What gives rise to it.

After the general idea of virtue, I do not know any more beautiful than that of rights, or rather, these two ideas merge. The idea of rights is nothing more than the idea of virtue introduced into the political world.

With the idea of rights, men have defined what license and tyranny were. Enlightened by it, each person has been able to show himself independent without arrogance and submissive without servility. The man who obeys violence yields and abases himself; but when he submits to the right of command that he acknowledges in his fellow, he rises, in a way, above even the one commanding him. There are no great men without virtue; without respect for rights, there is no great people. You can almost say that there is no society; for what is a gathering of rational and intelligent beings bound together only by force?[t]

t. In the world there are two kinds of respect for rights that must not be confused; one, unthinking, arises from custom and grows stronger in ignorance. What for a long time has been powerful and strong is respected, and the right to command is judged by the fact of command. This respect for rights only guarantees the existence of the strong, not that of the weak. Where it reigns, there is tranquillity, but there is no liberty; neither prosperity nor independence is found.

Authority based on this instinctive respect for (illegible word) [v: {for rights}] is absolute as long as no one contests its right; the day it is disputed, it is reduced almost to nothing.

There is another kind of respect for rights. The latter is reciprocal and guarantees the privileges of the subject as well as those of the prince. This respect for rights was based on reason and experience. Once it reigns in society, it is very difficult to destroy it.

I wonder what way there is today to inculcate men with the idea of rights and to make it apparent to their senses, so to speak; and I only see a single one; it is to give all of them the peaceful exercise of certain rights. You see that clearly with children, who are men, except for strength and experience. When a child begins to move among external objects, instinct leads him to put everything that comes within reach to his own use; he has no idea of the property of others, not even that of existence; but as he is informed about the cost of things and as he discovers that things can, in turn, be taken from him, he becomes more circumspect and ends by respecting in his fellows what he wants them to respect in him.

What happens to the child concerning toys, happens later to the man concerning all the objects belonging to him. Why in America, country of democracy par excellence, does no one raise against property in general the complaints that often resound in Europe? Is it necessary to say? In America there are no proletarians. Each person, having an individual possession to defend, recognizes in principle the right of property.

In the political world, it is the same. In America the common man has conceived a high idea of political rights, because he has political rights; he does not attack the rights of others, so that no one violates his. And while in Europe this same man has no regard even for the sovereign authority, the American submits without murmuring to the power of the least of his magistrates.

This truth appears even in the smallest details of the existence of peoples. In France, there are few pleasures exclusively reserved for the upper classes of society; the poor man is admitted almost everywhere the rich man is able

---

[In the margin: The one is a sentiment rather than an idea. The other is based on an idea rather than on a sentiment. The one is instinctive; the other is rational.]

But there are centuries when peoples, having lost the habit of respecting what they do not know, still have not learned to know what they must respect. Then peoples are tormented by a profound illness, tossing and turning without rest, like a sick man stretched out aboard ship on his unsteady sickbed; there are even some who perish during this transition [from (ed.)] custom to reason.

[In the margin: You could more easily turn a river back upon its source than make this instinctive respect for rights reappear.]

I wonder what the way is . . . (YTC, CVh, 3, pp. 11–13).

to enter. Consequently you see him conduct himself with decency and respect all that is useful for the enjoyments that he shares. In England, where wealth has the privilege of pleasure, like the monopoly of power, the complaint is that when the poor man succeeds in getting furtively into the place destined for the pleasures of the rich man, he loves to cause pointless damage. Why be astonished by this? Care has been taken so that he has nothing to lose.

The government of democracy makes the idea of political rights descend to the least of citizens, as the division of property puts the idea of the right of property in general within reach of all men. That is one of its greatest merits in my view.

I am not saying that it is an easy thing to teach all men to use political rights; I am only saying that, when it is possible, the effects that result are great.

And I add that if there is a century when such an enterprise must be attempted, that century is our own.

Don't you see that religions are growing weaker and that the divine notion of rights is disappearing? Don't you find that mores are becoming corrupted and that, with them, the moral notion of rights is fading away?

Don't you see, on all sides, beliefs giving way to reasoning, and sentiments, to calculation? If, in the midst of this universal disturbance, you do not succeed in linking the idea of rights to personal interest, which offers itself as the only fixed point in the human heart, what will you have left for governing the world, if not fear?[u]

---

u. It is because I see the rights of governments disputed, that I think it necessary to hasten to give rights to those governed.

It is because I see democracy triumphing, that I want to regulate democracy.

[In the margin: If morality was strong enough by itself, I would not regard it as so important to rely on what is useful.

If the idea of what is just was more powerful, I would not speak so much about the idea of what is useful.]

You say to me that, since morality has become lax, new rights will be new items for the passions of today; that since governments are already weak, new rights will give new weapons to their enemies to use against them; that democracy is already too strong in society without further introducing it into government.

So when you say to me that laws are weak, and the governed, turbulent; that passions are intense, and virtue, powerless, and that in this situation you must not think about increasing the rights of democracy, I answer that, because of these very things, I believe you must think about it; and in truth, I think that governments have still more interest in it than society does, for governments perish, and society cannot die.[v] However, I do not want to abuse the example of America.

In America, the people were vested with political rights in a period when it was difficult for them to make poor use of those rights, because the citizens were few and had simple mores. While growing, the Americans have not increased the powers of democracy; rather they have extended its sphere. [That is an invaluable advantage.]

It cannot be doubted that the moment when political rights are granted to a people who have, until then, been deprived of them is a moment of crisis, a crisis often necessary, but always dangerous.

The child inflicts death when he is unaware of the value of life; he takes property from others before knowing that someone can rob him of his. The common man, at the moment when he is granted political rights, finds himself, in relation to his rights, in the same position as the child vis-à-vis all of nature. In this case the celebrated phrase [of Hobbes] applies to him: *Homo puer robustus.*[w]

I will answer that it is because I see that morality is weak that I want to put it under the safeguard of interest; it is because I see governments impotent that I would like to accustom the governed to respecting them; it is [broken text (ed.)] (YTC, CVh, 4, p. 30).

v. To the side: "≠I am not saying that political rights must be granted as of today to the universality of citizens; I am saying the unlimited extension of rights is the end toward which you must always tend.≠"

w. Tocqueville cites *De Cive* (see the critical edition of Howard Warrender, Oxford: Clarendon Press, 1983, p. 33), but what precedes the citation is more similar to *Discours sur l'origine de l'inégalité* (*Oeuvres complètes,* Paris: Pléiade, 1964, III, pp. 153–54), in which Rousseau, who cites the same fragment, reproaches Hobbes for not knowing that ethical values are born with society and are not a product preceding society. Tocqueville pointed out in this same part of the chapter that a society cannot survive if its only bond is force and its only government, fear; on this point, this also makes him closer to Rousseau than to Hobbes. This proximity of ideas must not hide divergences on the concept of rights, which has scarcely any place in the theory of Rousseau.

This truth is even revealed in America. The states in which citizens have enjoyed their rights for the longest time are those in which the citizens know best how to make use of their rights.

It cannot be said too much. There is nothing more fruitful in wonders than the art of being free; but there is nothing harder than apprenticeship in liberty. It is not the same with despotism. Despotism often presents itself as the repairer of all the misfortunes suffered; it is the support of legitimate rights, the upholder of the oppressed, and the founder of order. Peoples fall asleep amid the temporary prosperity that it brings forth; and when they awaken, they are miserable. Liberty, in contrast, is usually born amid storms; it is established painfully in the midst of civil discord, and only when it is already old can its benefits be known.

Of the Respect for the Law in the United States[x]

Respect of the Americans for the law.—Paternal love that they feel for it.—Personal interest that each one finds in increasing the power of the law.

It is not always possible to call the whole people, either directly or indirectly, to the making of the law; but it cannot be denied that, when it is practicable, the law thereby acquires a great authority. This popular origin, which often harms the goodness and wisdom of the legislation, contributes singularly to its power.[y]

In the expression of the will of an entire people, there is a prodigious strength. When it comes clearly to light, even the imagination of those who would like to fight against it is as though overwhelmed.

x. Title in the manuscript: OF THE POINT OF VIEW FROM WHICH THE PEOPLE CONSIDER THE LAW IN THE UNITED STATES.

y. In the margin: "≠There are two types of moral force:

"The one because the law conforms to justice and to reason.

"The other because it conforms to the will of the greatest number./

"The law draws its moral force from two sources.

"The one is reason; the other is the consent of the greatest number.≠"

The truth of this is well known by parties.

Consequently, you see them contest the majority wherever they can. When they lack the majority of those who voted, they place it among those who have abstained from voting; and when, even there, the majority escapes them, they find it among those who do not have the right to vote.

In the United States, except for slaves, servants, and the poor provided for by the towns, there is no one who is not a voter and who, as such, does not indirectly contribute to the law. So those who want to attack the laws are reduced to doing conspicuously one of two things; they must either change the opinion of the nation, or trample its will underfoot.

Add to this first reason another more direct and more powerful, that in the United States each person finds a kind of personal interest in having everyone obey the laws; for the one who is not part of the majority today will perhaps be among its ranks tomorrow; and this respect that he now professes for the will of the legislator, he will soon have the occasion to demand for his own will. So, however annoying the law, the inhabitant of the United States submits without trouble, not only as a work of the greatest number, but also as his own; he considers it from the point of view of a contract to which he would have been a party.

So in the United States, you do not see a numerous and always turbulent crowd who, seeing the law as a natural enemy, only looks upon it with fear and suspicion. On the contrary, it is impossible not to see that all classes show a great confidence in the legislation that governs the country and feel a kind of paternal love for it.

I am wrong in saying all classes. In America, since the European scale of powers is reversed, the rich find themselves in a position analogous to that of the poor in Europe; they are the ones who often distrust the law. I have said it elsewhere: the real advantage of democratic government is not to guarantee the interests of all, as has sometimes been claimed, but only to protect those of the greatest number. In the United States, where the poor man governs, the rich have always to fear that he will abuse his power against them.

This disposition of the mind of the rich can produce a muted discontent; but society is not violently troubled by it; for the same reason that prevents the rich man from giving his confidence to the legislator prevents him from defying his commands. He does not make the law, because he is rich; and he does not dare to violate it, because of his wealth. In general, among civilized nations, only those who have nothing to lose revolt. Therefore, if the laws of democracy are not always respectable, they are nearly always respected; for those who generally violate the laws cannot fail to obey the laws that they have made and from which they profit, and the citizens who could have an interest in breaking them are led by character and by position to submit to whatever the will of the legislator is. Moreover, the people, in America, not only obey the law because it is their work, but also because they can change it when by chance it injures them; they submit to it first as an evil that they imposed on themselves, and then as a temporary evil.

Activity That Reigns in All Parts of the Political Body in the United States; Influence That It Exercises on Society

It is more difficult to imagine the political activity that reigns in the United States than the liberty or equality that is found there.—The great movement that constantly agitates the legislatures is only an episode, a prolongation of this universal movement.—Difficulty that the American has occupying himself only with his own affairs.—Political agitation spreads into civil society.—Industrial activity of the Americans coming in part from this cause.—Indirect advantages that society gains from the government of democracy.

When you pass from a free country into another that is not, you are struck by a very extraordinary spectacle: there, everything is activity and movement; here, everything seems calm and immobile. In the one, the only question is improvement and progress; you would say that society, in the other, having gained all good things, aspires only to rest in order to enjoy them. The country that gets so worked up to be happy is, however, generally richer and more prosperous than the one that seems so satisfied with its lot. And in considering the one and the other, you have difficulty imagining how so many new needs make themselves felt each day in the first, while so few seem to be experienced in the second.[z]

If this remark is applicable to free countries that have retained monarchical form and to those in which aristocracy dominates, it is very much more applicable to democratic republics. There, it is no longer a portion of the people that sets out to improve the state of society; the whole people take charge of this concern. It is a matter of providing for the needs and conveniences not only of a class, but of all classes at the same time.[a]

It is not impossible to imagine the immense liberty that the Americans enjoy. You can also have an idea of their extreme equality, but what you cannot understand, without having already witnessed it, is the political activity that reigns in the United States.

Scarcely have you landed on American soil than you find yourself in the middle of a sort of tumult; a confused clamor arises on all sides; a thousand voices reach your ear at the same time; each one expresses various social needs. Around you, everything stirs: here, the people of a neighborhood have gathered to know if a church should be built; there, some are working on choosing a representative; farther along, the deputies of a district go as fast as they can to the city, in order to see to certain local improvements; in another place, it is the farmers of the village who abandon their fields to go to discuss the plan of a road or of a school. Some citizens assemble for the sole purpose of declaring that [{freemasonry menaces the security of the State}] they disapprove of the government's course; while others gather

z. In the margin: "<≠What is even much more surprising is that often [v: sometimes] the people who do nothing to improve their lot, find themselves as satisfied with their destiny as the people who stir themselves to make theirs better. The second wonders that one can be so happy in the midst of so much misery; and the first, that one can go to so much trouble to become happy.≠>"

a. In the margin: "≠A European would be very unhappy if you forced him to pursue well-being with so much effort.

"It is difficult to believe that men are happy when they make so much effort to become happier.

"It is the story of the rich tradesman who dies of boredom when he is forced to abandon his business.≠"

to proclaim that the men in office are the fathers of the country. Here are still others who, seeing drunkenness as the principal source of the evils of the State, come to pledge solemnly to give an example of temperance.[1]

The great political movement that constantly agitates American legislatures, the only one that is noticed outside, is only an episode and a sort of prolongation of the universal movement that begins in the lowest ranks of the people and then reaches, one by one, all classes of citizens. You cannot work harder to be happy.

It is difficult to say what place political concerns occupy in the life of a man in the United States. To get involved in the government of society and to talk about it, that is the greatest business and, so to speak, the only pleasure that an American knows. This is seen even in the smallest habits of his life; women themselves often go to public assemblies and, by listening to political speeches, relax from household cares. For them, clubs replace theatrical entertainments to a certain point. An American does not know how to converse, but he discusses; he does not discourse, but he holds forth. He always speaks to you as to an assembly; and if he happens by chance to get excited, he will say: Gentlemen, while addressing his interlocutor.

In certain countries, the inhabitant accepts only with a kind of repugnance the political rights that the law grants him; dealing with common interests seems to rob him of his time, and he loves to enclose himself within a narrow egoism exactly limited by four ditches topped by hedges.

In contrast, from the moment when the American would be reduced to attending only to his own affairs, half of his existence would be taken away

---

1. *Temperance societies*[b] *are associations whose members pledge to abstain from strong liquor. At the time of my visit to the United States, temperance societies already counted more than 270,000 members, and their effect had been to diminish, in the state of Pennsylvania alone, the consumption of strong liquors by 500,000 gallons annually.*

b. See chapter V of this part (p. 365) and *Écrits sur le système pénitentiaire en France et à l'étranger* (*OC,* IV, 1), pp. 327–28, appendix VII of *Système pénitentiaire.*

from him; he would feel an immense emptiness in his days, and he would become unbelievably unhappy.[2]

I am persuaded that if despotism ever succeeds in becoming established in America, it will have even more difficulties overcoming the habits that liberty has engendered than surmounting the love of liberty itself.

This constantly recurring agitation that the government of democracy has introduced into the political world passes afterward into civil society. Everything considered, I do not know if that is not the greatest advantage of democratic government, and I praise it much more for what it causes to be done than for what it does.

Incontestably the people often direct public affairs very badly; but the people cannot get involved in public affairs without having the circle of their ideas expand, and without seeing their minds emerge from their ordinary routine. The common man who is called to the government of society conceives a certain esteem for himself. Since he is then a power, very enlightened minds put themselves in the service of his. People speak to him constantly in order to gain his support, and by seeking to deceive him in a thousand different ways, they enlighten him. In politics, he takes part in enterprises that he did not conceive, but that give him a general taste for enterprises. Every day new improvements to make to common property are pointed out to him, and he feels the desire to improve his personal property arise. Perhaps he is neither more virtuous nor more happy, but he is more enlightened and more active than his predecessors. I do not doubt that democratic institutions, joined with the physical nature of the country, are the cause, not direct, as so many people say, but indirect of the prodigious movement of industry that is noticed in the United States. It is not the laws that give birth to it, but the people learn to produce it by making the law.[d]

---

2. *The same fact was already observed in Rome under the first Caesars.*

Montesquieu remarks somewhere[c] that nothing equaled the despair of certain Roman citizens who, after the agitations of a political existence, returned suddenly to the calm of private life.

c. Probably in *Considérations sur les causes de la grandeur des Romains et de leur décadence,* chapter XI, in *Œuvres complètes,* Paris: Pléiade, 1951, II, p. 131.

d. In the margin: "≠Superiority of the strength of the people which is worth more

When the enemies of democracy claim that one man does what he undertakes better than the government of all, it seems to me that they are right. The government of one man, supposing equality of enlightenment on both sides, brings more consistency to its enterprises than that of the multitude; it shows more perseverance, more of an idea of the whole, more perfection in details, a more correct discernment in the choice of men. [{So a republic is not administered as well as a monarchy, supposing equality of enlightenment on both sides.}] Those who deny these things have never seen a democratic republic, or have judged only on a small number of examples. Democracy, even when local circumstances and the dispositions of the people allow it to persist, does not offer the sight of administrative regularity and methodical order in government; that is true. Democratic liberty does not execute each of its enterprises with the same perfection as intelligent despotism; often it abandons them before gaining the fruit, or chances dangerous ones; but in the long run it produces more than despotism; it does not do each thing as well, but it does more things. Under its dominion, it is, above all, not what the public administration executes that is great, but what is executed without it and outside of it. Democracy does not give the people the most skillful government, but it does what the most skillful government is often impotent to create; it spreads[e] throughout the social body a restless activity, a superabundant force, an energy that never exists without it and that, if only circumstances are favorable, can bring forth wonders. Those are its true advantages.

In this century, when the destinies of the Christian world appear to be in suspense, some hasten to attack democracy like a powerful enemy, while it is still growing; others already adore it as a new god coming out of nothingness; but both know only imperfectly the object of their hate or their desire; they fight in the shadows and strike only at random.

---

than the government. It is difficult to make the people listen to reason, but when they hear it, they advance toward reason with a much stronger step and with a much more powerful effort. Criminal investigation in America. Smuggling.≠"

e. The manuscript adds: "in a way unknowingly."

What do you ask of society and its government? We must understand one another.

Do you want to give the human spirit a certain nobility, a generous fashion of envisioning the things of this world? Do you want to inspire in men a sort of contempt for material goods? Do you desire to bring about or to maintain profound convictions and prepare great devotions?

Is it a matter for you of polishing mores, of elevating manners, of making the arts shine? Do you want poetry, fame, and glory?

Do you claim to organize a people in a way to act strongly on all others? Do you intend it to attempt great undertakings, and, whatever the result of its efforts, to leave an immense trace in history?

If such, in your view, is the principal object that men must propose for themselves in society, do not opt for the government of democracy; it would not lead you surely to the goal.

But if it seems useful to you to divert the intellectual and moral activity of man toward the necessities of material life, and to use it to produce well-being; if reason appears to you more profitable to men than genius; if your object is not to create heroic virtues, but peaceful habits; if you like to see vices more than crimes, and prefer to find fewer great actions, on the condition of encountering fewer cases of heinous crimes; if, instead of acting within the bosom of a brilliant society, it is enough for you to live in the midst of a prosperous society; if, finally, in your view, the principal object of a government is not to give the entire body of the nation the most strength or the most glory possible, but to provide for each of the individuals that make up the society the most well-being and to avoid the most misery; then equalize conditions and constitute the government of democracy.[f]

If there is no more time to make a choice, and a force superior to men is already carrying you, without consulting your desires, toward one of

f. See appendix V of this edition, particularly pp. 1369–71.

these two governments, seek at least to derive from it all the good that it can do; and knowing its good instincts, as well as its bad inclinations, endeavor to limit the effect of the second and to develop the first.[g]

g. Note in the manuscript at the end of the chapter: "≠Perhaps, in place of these generalities, it would be better to develop this single idea that if the government of democracy is not favorable to the first part of the picture, it has the advantage of serving the well-being of the greatest number.

"Perhaps put all this at the end of the advantages of democracy like a kind of summary.≠"

CHAPTER 7

Of the Omnipotence of the Majority in the United States and Its Effects[a]

a. Hervé de Tocqueville:

Before beginning the notes on this chapter, I want to make two general reflections:

1. Isn't there a kind of contradiction between this chapter and the last paragraph of page 3 of the second volume, where the author expresses himself this way: "In the United States, as in all countries where the people rule, the majority governs in the name of the people. This majority is composed principally of a mass of men who, either by taste or by interest, sincerely desire the good of the country; agitating around this quite peaceful mass, parties work to draw it toward them and gain its support"?

2. I do not know if this chapter is well placed in the book. In one of the preceding chapters, entitled *Of the Right of Association,* the author says, p. 67: "In our time, the right of association has become a guarantee against the tyranny of the majority."

The logical order of ideas demands that the disadvantages be cited before the remedy. I observe, moreover, that the author must revise the sentence I have just transcribed and make it less absolute, if he does not want it to harm singularly the effect of the chapter on omnipotence (YTC, CIIIb, 1, pp. 81–83).

It seems that the idea of the tyranny of the majority is mentioned for the first time on the occasion of a conversation with Sparks, 29 September 1831 (non-alphabetic notebooks 1 and 2, YTC, BIIa, and *Voyage, OC,* V, 1, p. 96). John Stuart Mill, following Tocqueville, will take up this expression again and use it in his famous essay *On Liberty.* Nonetheless, as Joseph Hamburger points out ("Mill and Tocqueville on Liberty," in John M. Robson and M. Laine, eds., *James and John Stuart Mill. Papers of the Centenary Conference,* Toronto: University of Toronto Press, 1976, pp. 111–25), if Mill uses the term, the consequences he derives from it are quite far removed from those of Tocqueville. H. O. Pappe as well is skeptical about the possible influence of Tocqueville on Mill ("Mill and Tocqueville," *Journal of the History of Ideas* 25, no. 2 (1964): 217–44).

Ludovic, the protagonist in *Marie,* also insists on the sway of opinion in America (I, pp. 165, 172–74, and 203).

*Natural strength of the majority in democracies.—Most of the
American constitutions have artificially increased this natural
strength.—How.—Binding mandates.—Moral dominion of the
majority.—Opinion about its infallibility.—Respect for its
rights.—What augments it in the United States.*

The very essence of democratic governments is that the dominion of the majority be absolute; for, in democracies, nothing outside of the majority can offer resistance.

Most of the American constitutions have also sought to augment this natural strength of the majority artificially.[1]

Of all political powers, the legislature is the one that most willingly obeys the majority. The Americans have wanted the members of the legislature to be named *directly* by the people, and for a *very short* term, in order to force them to submit not only to the general views, but also to the daily passions of their constituents.

They have taken the members of the two houses from the same classes and named them in the same way; in this way, the movements of the legislative body are almost as rapid and no less irresistible than those of a single assembly.[c]

1. *We have seen, at the time of the examination of the federal Constitution, that the law-makers of the Union made contrary efforts.*[b] *The result of these efforts was to make the federal government more independent in its sphere than the government of the states. But the federal government is scarcely in charge of anything except foreign affairs; the state governments really run American society.* Is this still the case today?

b. ≠So in democratic republics the majority forms a true power. And after it, the body that represents it. The political body that best represents the majority is the legislature. To augment the prerogatives of this body is to augment the power of the majority.

Nonetheless, this power of the majority can be moderated in its exercise by the efforts of the law-maker. The authors of the federal Constitution worked in this direction. They sought to hinder the march of the majority. In the individual states, one tried hard, in contrast, to make the march of the majority more rapid and more irresistible≠ (YTC, CVh, 5, p. 14).

c. Hervé de Tocqueville: "If this is so, we do not see clearly why the American constitutions created two houses; it is probable that there is something too absolute in the author's phrasing" (YTC, CIIIb, 1, p. 83).

Within the legislature thus constituted, the Americans gathered together nearly the entire government.

At the same time that the law increased the strength of powers that were naturally strong, it weakened more and more those that were naturally weak. It gave to the representatives of the executive power neither stability nor independence; and, by subjecting them completely to the caprices of the legislature, it took from them the little influence that the nature of democratic government would have allowed them to exercise.[d]

In several states, the law delivered the judicial power to election by the majority; and in all, it made the existence of the judicial power dependent, in a way, on the legislative power, by leaving to the representatives the right to fix the salaries of judges annually.[e]

Customs have gone still further than the laws.

In the United States, a custom is spreading more and more that will end by making the guarantees of representative government empty; it happens very frequently that the voters, while naming a deputy, trace a plan of conduct for him and impose on him a certain number of definite obligations from which he cannot deviate in any way. Except for the tumult, it is as if the majority itself deliberated in the public square.

Several particular circumstances in America also tend to make the power of the majority not only predominant, but irresistible.

The moral dominion of the majority is based in part on the idea that there is more enlightenment and wisdom in many men combined than in one man alone, more in the number than in the choice of legislators. It is the theory of equality applied to minds. This doctrine attacks the pride of

---

d. "In America executive power is nothing and can do nothing. The entire strength of government is entrusted to society itself, organized under the most democratic form that has ever existed. In America all danger comes from the people; it is never born outside" (YTC, CVh, 5, p. 21).

e. "Importance of the judicial power as barrier to democracy, its weakness. See *Federalist*, p. 332 [No. 78 (ed.)]".

"In most states, judges are dependent upon the legislature for their salaries; in several, elected by the legislature or by the people. Growing causes of tyranny" (YTC, CVe, p. 64). Cf. conversations with Mr. Storer, Spencer, and Judge MacLean (non-alphabetic notebooks 1, 2 and 3, YTC, BIIa, and *Voyage, OC,* V, 1, pp. 69, 124 and 127).

man in its last refuge. Consequently the minority admits it with difficulty and gets used to it only with time. Like all powers, and perhaps more than any other, the power of the majority thus needs to last in order to seem legitimate. When it is beginning to be established, it makes itself obeyed by force; only after living under its laws for a long time do you begin to respect it.

The idea that the right to govern society belongs to the majority because of its enlightenment was carried to the soil of the United States by the first inhabitants. This idea, which alone would be enough to create a free people, has today passed into the mores, and you find it in the least habits of life.

The French, under the old monarchy, held as a given that the king could do no wrong;[f] and when he happened to do something wrong, they thought that the fault was with his advisors. This facilitated obedience marvelously. You could murmur against the law, without ceasing to love and respect the law-maker. Americans have the same opinion about the majority.

The moral dominion of the majority is based as well on the principle that the interests of the greatest number must be preferred to those of the few. Now, it is easily understood that the respect professed for this right of the greatest number naturally increases or decreases depending on the state of the parties. When a nation is divided among several great irreconcilable interests, the privilege of the majority is often unrecognized, because it becomes too painful to submit to it.

If a class of citizens existed in America that the legislator worked to strip of certain exclusive advantages, held for centuries, and that he wanted to bring down from an elevated position and restore to the ranks of the multitude, it is probable that the minority would not easily submit to his laws.

But since the United States was populated by men equal to each other,

f. Hervé de Tocqueville: "I do not know why Alexis applies to the old monarchy the principle that the king could do no wrong. The Charter of 1814 and that of 1830 have this principle as a basis" (YTC, CIIIb, 1, p. 83).

no natural and permanent dissidence is yet found among the interests of the various inhabitants.g

There is such a social state in which the members of the minority cannot hope to attract the majority because to do so it would be necessary to abandon the very object of the struggle that the minority wages against the majority. An aristocracy, for example, cannot become a majority while preserving its exclusive privileges, and it cannot allow its privileges to slip away without ceasing to be an aristocracy. [In these countries, it is almost impossible for the moral power of the majority ever to succeed in being recognized by all.]

In the United States, political questions cannot be posed in as general and absolute a way, and all parties are ready to recognize the rights of the

g. Majority./

The moral dominion of the majority is established with more difficulty than another because it is based upon ideas of equality shocking to many minds that have not become accustomed to it.

Like all other empires, it is lost by abuse. Tyranny of the majority leads to appeals by minorities to physical force. From that, confusion, anarchy and the despotism of one man. The American republics, far from raising the fear of anarchy at the present moment, raise only the fear of despotism of the majority; anarchy will come only as a consequence of this tyranny.

There is such a social state in which the minorities can never become majorities, without losing enormously or even ceasing to be. In these countries, the dominion of the majority can only be established with great difficulty and can only be maintained with even more difficulty. France in this case./

In America, the dominion of the majority will be overturned not because it lacks strength, but wisdom. The government is centralized in such a way that the governing majority is omnipotent. It will lack not physical force, but moral force. In all power exercised by the people, there is something variable, something of scant wisdom.

I would like someone to explain to me what is meant when this banal phrase is put forth: that an entire people cannot completely go beyond the limits of reason.

It is undoubtedly rare for an entire people to go beyond those limits. But what generally does the will of the people mean? A majority; but what is a majority taken as a whole if not an individual who has opinions and, most often, interests contrary to another individual called the minority?

Now, if you admit that an individual vested with omnipotence can abuse it against his adversaries, why would you not admit the same thing for the majority? As for me, I see only God who can be vested with omnipotence without disadvantage (YTC, CVj, 2, pp. 2–3).

majority, because all hope one day to be able to exercise those rights to their profit.

So in the United States the majority has an immense power in fact and a power of opinion almost as great; and once the majority has formed on a question, there is, so to speak, no obstacle that can, I will not say stop, but even slow its course and leave time for the majority to hear the cries of those whom it crushes as it goes.

The consequences of this state of affairs are harmful and dangerous[h] for the future.

How the Omnipotence of the Majority in America Increases the Legislative and Administrative Instability That Is Natural to Democracies

*How the Americans increase legislative instability,
which is natural to democracy, by changing the legislator
annually and by arming him with an almost limitless power.—
The same effect produced in the administration.—In America a
force infinitely greater, but less sustained than in Europe is
brought to social improvements.*

I spoke previously of the vices that are natural to the government of democracy; there is not one of them that does not grow at the same time as the power of the majority.

And, to begin with the most obvious of all.

Administrative instability is an evil inherent in democratic government, because it is in the nature of democracies to bring new men to power. But this evil is greater or lesser depending on the power and the means of action granted to the legislator.

In America sovereign power is handed over to the authority that makes the laws. That authority can rapidly and irresistibly abandon itself to each of its desires, and every year it is given other representatives. That is to say, what has been adopted is precisely the combination that most favors dem-

h. The manuscript says: ". . . very harmful and highly dangerous for the future."

ocratic instability and that allows democracy to apply its changeable will to the most important objects. [≠We have seen under the National Assembly and the Convention how, by granting omnipotence to the legislative body, the natural instability of law in republics increased more. These extreme consequences of a bad principle cannot recur in the same way in America because American society is not in revolution as French society then was and because there has been a long apprenticeship in liberty in America.≠]

America today is, therefore, the country in the world where laws have the shortest duration. Nearly all the American constitutions have been amended during the last thirty years. So, during this period, there is no American state that has not modified the principle of its laws.ʲ

As for the laws themselves, it is sufficient to glance at the archives of the different states of the Union to be persuaded that in America the activity of the legislator never flags.ᵏ Not that the American democracy is by nature more unstable than another, but in the formation of the laws, it has been given the means to follow the natural instability of its inclinations.[2]

The omnipotence of the majority and the rapid and absolute manner in which its will is executed in the United States not only make the law unstable, but also exercise the same influence on the execution of the law and on the action of public administration.

Since the majority is the only power important to please, the works that it undertakes are ardently supported; but from the moment when its at-

j. In this place in the manuscript three paragraphs are found that Tocqueville will later add to chapter V of this second part. (It concerns the passage that begins with: "Many Americans consider . . ." and that concludes with the citation of Number 73 of the *Federalist*, pp. 322–23.)

k. To the side: "≠The omnipotence of the majority is not the first cause of the evil, but it infinitely increases it.≠"

2. *The legislative acts promulgated in the state of Massachusetts alone, from 1780 to today, already fill three thick volumes. It must be noted as well that the collection of which I speak was revised in 1823, and that many former or pointless laws were discarded. Now, the state of Massachusetts, which is no more populated than one of our departments, can pass for the most stable state in the entire Union, and the one that puts the most coherence and wisdom into its enterprises.*

tention goes elsewhere, all efforts cease; whereas in the free States of Europe, in which administrative power has an independent existence and an assured position, the will of the legislator continues to be executed, even when he is occupied by other objects.

In America, much more zeal and activity is brought to certain improvements than is done elsewhere.

In Europe, an infinitely smaller, but more sustained social force is applied to the same things.

[I saw some striking examples of what I am advancing in a matter that I had particular occasion to examine in the United States.]

Several years ago some religious men undertook to improve the condition of prisons. The public was roused by their voice, and the regeneration of criminals became a popular undertaking.

Then new prisons arose. For the first time, the idea of reforming the guilty penetrated the jail at the same time as the idea of punishing him. But the happy revolution that the public joined with so much fervor and that the simultaneous efforts of citizens made irresistible could not be accomplished in one moment.

Alongside some new penitentiaries, the development of which was hastened by the desire of the majority, the old prisons still existed and continued to house a great number of the guilty. The latter seemed to become more unhealthy and more corrupting as the new ones became more reforming and healthier. This double effect is easily understood: the majority, preoccupied by the idea of founding the new establishment, had forgotten the one that already existed. By each person averting his eyes from the object that no longer attracted the regard of the master, supervision had ceased. At first the salutary bonds of discipline were seen to relax and then, soon after, to break. And alongside the prison, lasting monument of the mildness and enlightenment of our time, was found a dungeon that recalled the barbarism of the Middle Ages.

[In France, it would be very difficult to find prisons as good and as bad as in the United States.]

Tyranny of the Majority[m]

How the principle of sovereignty of the people must be understood.—Impossibility of conceiving a mixed government.— The sovereign power must be somewhere.—Precautions that must be taken to moderate its action.—These precautions have not been taken in the United States.—What results.

I regard as impious and detestable this maxim that in matters of government the majority of a people has the right to do anything, and yet I consider that the will of the majority is the origin of all powers. Do I contradict myself?

A general law exists that has been made, or at least adopted, not only by the majority of such or such people, but by the majority of all men. This law is justice.

So justice forms the limit of the right of each people [to command].

A nation is like a jury charged with representing universal society and with applying justice, which is its law. Should the jury, which represents society, have more power than the very society whose laws it applies?[n]

So when I refuse to obey an unjust law, I am not denying the right of the majority to command; I am only appealing from the sovereignty of the people to the sovereignty of the human race.

m. Title in the manuscript: TYRANNICAL EFFECTS OF THE OMNIPOTENCE OF THE MAJORITY.

Concerning the idea of tyranny of the majority, Morton Horwitz ("Tocqueville and the Tyranny of the Majority," *Review of Politics,* 28, 1966, pp. 293–307) defends the idea that Tocqueville, when speaking of the majority in numerical terms, is thinking about France, not about America, and that he thinks about America only when he considers the moral tyranny of the majority. Also see David Spitz, "On Tocqueville and the Tyranny of Public Sentiment," *Political Science* 9, no. 2 (1957): 3–13.

n. In the margin: "≠Its effects:

on actions,

on words,

on character and thoughts.

"That it is by the abuse of the strength of their government and not by its weakness that the American republics are threatened with perishing.≠"

There are men who are not afraid to say that, in objects that concern only itself, a people could not go entirely beyond the limits of justice and reason, and that we should not be afraid, therefore, to give all power to the majority that represents a people. But that is the language of a slave.

So what is a majority taken as a whole, if not an individual who has opinions and, most often, interests contrary to another individual called the minority. Now, if you admit that an individual vested with omnipotence can abuse it against his adversaries, why would you not admit the same thing for the majority? Have men, by gathering together, changed character? By becoming stronger, have they become more patient in the face of obstacles?[3] As for me, I cannot believe it; and the power to do everything that I refuse to any one of my fellows, I will never grant to several.[o]

Not that I believe that, to preserve liberty, several principles can be mixed together in the same government, in a way that truly opposes them to each other.

The government called mixed has always seemed to me a chimera. Truly

---

3. *No one would want to maintain that a people is not able to abuse strength vis-à-vis another people. Now, parties are like small nations within a large one; in relation to each other, they are like foreigners.*

If you agree that a nation can be tyrannical toward another nation, how can you deny that a party can be so toward another party?

o. Democracy./

Tyranny of democracy. Confusion of all powers in the hands of the *assemblies.* Weakness of the executive power to react against these assemblies of which it is only an instrument. See very curious article of the *Federalist* on this subject, p. 213 [No. 48 (ed.)]; *id.,* p. 205 [No. 46 (ed.)]; *id.,* p. 224 [No. 51 (ed.)]./

Moreover, that is a required result of the rule of democracy. There is strength only in the people; there can only be strength in the constitutional power that represents the people./

In America the executive and judicial powers are absolutely dependent upon the legislative power. It fixes their salaries in general, modifies their organization; and nothing is provided for them to be able to resist its *encroachments* [word in English in the original (ed.)]. *Federalist,* p. 205 [No. 46 (ed.)]./

Necessity of taking measures to avoid the abuse of all powers, even those that seem most legitimate. *Federalist,* p. 223 [No. 51 (ed.)] (YTC, CVb, pp. 25–26).

speaking, there is no mixed government (in the sense that is given to this term), because, in each society, you eventually discover a principle of action that dominates all the others.

England of the last century, which was particularly cited as an example of this sort of government, was an essentially aristocratic State, although some large elements[p] of democracy were found within it; for the laws and the mores there were established in such a way that eventually the aristocracy would always predominate and lead public affairs as it willed.

The error arose because, seeing the interests of the great constantly in conflict with those of the people, only the struggle was considered, instead of paying attention to the result of this struggle, which was the important point. When a society truly comes to have a mixed government, that is a government equally divided among contrary principles, it enters into revolution or dissolves.[q]

So I think that a social power superior to all others must always be placed somewhere, but I believe liberty is in danger when this power encounters no obstacle that can check its course[r] and give it time to moderate itself.

Omnipotence in itself seems to me something bad and dangerous.[s] Its

p. The manuscript says, on the other hand: "some democratic institutions."
This paragraph makes direct reference to Montesquieu. Cf. note n of p. 28.
q. If here Tocqueville denies the existence of mixed government, he is, nonetheless, about to explain in the following paragraphs his theory of a social and political organization in which every principle must necessarily be opposed by another. (The idea has been mentioned in the editor's introduction.)
r. In the manuscript: "that can, if not entirely stop, at least check its course . . ."
s. "Despotism is at the two ends of sovereignty, when one man rules and when the majority governs. Despotism is attached to omnipotence, whoever the representative may be" (YTC, CVe, p. 65).
Guizot defends a similar idea:

> The partisans of divine right had said: there is only one God; so there should be only one king, and all power belongs to him because he is the representative of God. The partisans of sovereignty of the people have said: there is only one people; so there should be only one legislative assembly; for it represents the people. In both cases the error is the same, and it leads equally to despotism. There is only one God and there

exercise seems to me beyond the power of man, whoever he may be; and I see only God who can, without danger, be all powerful, because his wisdom and his justice are always equal to his power. So there is no authority on earth so respectable in itself, or vested with a right so sacred, that I would want to allow it to act without control or to dominate without obstacles. So when I see the right and the ability to do everything granted to whatever power, whether called people or king, democracy or aristocracy, whether exercised in a monarchy or a republic, I say: the seed of tyranny is there and I try to go and live under other laws.

What I most criticize about democratic government as it has been organized in the United States, is not its weaknesses as many people in Europe claim, but on the contrary, its irresistible strength.[t] And what repels me the

---

is only one people, that is certain; but this God is nowhere on earth, for neither one man nor the whole people is God, knows his law perfectly and wants it constantly. So no *de facto* power should be unique, for unity of the *de facto* power assumes complete *de jure* power which no one possesses or can possess (*Journal des cours publics,* Paris: au bureau du Journal, 1821–1822, II, p. 293).

In another place, Guizot refers to Pascal for his argument: *"'Unity that is not multiple,'* says Pascal, *'is tyranny.'* From that follows the necessity for two chambers" (*ibid,* p. 17). The principle of Guizot's representative system is nothing other than the destruction of all absolute power. This principle requires the provision of the jury, freedom of the press, the division of powers and the organization of the legislative power into two chambers. These elements are repeated in Tocqueville's theory.

t. How democracy leads to tyranny and will succeed in destroying liberty in America. See the beautiful theory presented on this point in the *Federalist,* p. 225 [No. 51 (ed.)]. It is not because powers are not concentrated; it is because they are too concentrated that the American republics will perish. The tyranny of one man will appear more tolerable than the tyranny of the majority.

"A good government implies two things: first, fidelity to the object of government, which is the happiness of the people; secondly, a knowledge of the means by which that object can be best attained. Some governments are deficient in both these qualities; most governments are deficient in the first. [I (ed.)] Scruple not to assert that, in the American governments, too little attention has been paid to the last. The federal Constitution avoids this error." *Federalist,* p. 268 [No. 62 (ed.)].

Tendency of republics to make the executive power only a passive agent, without any strength whatsoever, *id.,* p. 207 [No. 47 (ed.)] (YTC, CVb, p. 26).

most in America is not the extreme liberty that reigns there; it is the slight guarantee against tyranny that is found.[u]

When a man or a party suffers from an injustice in the United States, to whom do you want them to appeal? To public opinion? That is what forms the majority. To the legislative body? It represents the majority and blindly obeys it. To the executive power? It is named by the majority and serves it as a passive instrument. To the police? The police are nothing other than the majority under arms. To the jury? The jury is the majority vested with the right to deliver judgments. The judges themselves, in certain states, are elected by the majority. However iniquitous or unreasonable the measure that strikes you may be, you must therefore submit to it [or flee. <What is that if not the very soul of tyranny under the forms of liberty?>].[4]

u. "≠It is very much easier to contest a principle than its consequences. You easily prove to a king that he does not have the right to sacrifice the interest of the State to his own, but when the majority oppresses you, you are forced to recognize its right before attacking the use of that right≠" (YTC, CVh, 4, p. 81).

4. *In Baltimore, at the time of the War of 1812, a striking example was seen of the excesses to which the despotism of the majority can lead.[v] At this time the war was very popular in Baltimore. A newspaper that was strongly against the war aroused the indignation of the inhabitants by its conduct. The people gathered, broke the presses, and attacked the newspaper office. Some wanted to call the militia, but it did not answer the call. In order to save the unfortunate journalists, who were threatened by the public furor, it was decided to put them in jail, like criminals. This precaution was useless; during the night, the people gathered again; the magistrates were unable to get the militia to come; the prison was forced open; one of the journalists was killed on the spot; the others were left for dead; the guilty, brought before a jury, were acquitted.*

I said one day to an inhabitant of Pennsylvania: "Please explain to me why, in a state founded by Quakers and renowned for its tolerance, emancipated Negroes are not allowed to exercise the rights of citizens. They pay taxes; isn't it just that they vote?"—"Don't insult us, he answered, by thinking that our legislators have committed such a gross act of injustice and intolerance."—"So, among you, Blacks have the right to vote?"—"Undoubtedly."—"Then, how come at the polling place this morning, I did not see a single one in the crowd?"—"This is not the fault of the law," the American said to me; "Negroes, it is true, have the right to present themselves at elections, but they abstain voluntarily it seems."—"That is very modest of them."—"Oh! it isn't that they refuse to go, but they are afraid that they will be mistreated there. Among us, it sometimes happens that the law lacks force when the majority does not support it. Now, the majority is imbued with the greatest prejudices against Negroes, and magistrates do not feel they have the strength to guarantee to the latter the rights that the legislator has conferred."—"What! the majority which has the privilege of making the law, also wants to have that of disobeying the law?"

v. Mr. Cruse, editor of a newspaper in Baltimore, told this anecdote to Tocqueville

Suppose, in contrast, a legislative body composed in such a way that it represents the majority, without necessarily being the slave of the majority's passions; an executive power that has a strength of its own; and a judicial power independent of the two other powers; you will still have a democratic government, but there will no longer be hardly any chances for tyranny.

[{If the effects of this tyranny are not felt more in America, it is because America is a new country where political passions are still not very deep and where so vast a field for human activity is presented that interests are rarely opposed to each other.}]

I am not saying that at the present time in America tyranny is frequently practiced; I am saying that no guarantee against tyranny is found there, and that the causes for the mildness of government must be sought in circumstances and in mores, rather than in laws.[w]

Effects of the Omnipotence of the Majority on the Arbitrariness of American Public Officials

Liberty that American law leaves to officials within the circle that it draws.—Their power.

Arbitrariness must be carefully distinguished from tyranny. Tyranny can be exercised by means of the law itself, and then it is not arbitrary; arbitrariness can be exercised in the interests of the governed, and then it is not tyrannical.[x]

(note of 4 November 1831, pocket notebook 3, YTC, BIIa, and *Voyage, OC*, V, 1, pp. 187–88). The interlocutor of the other conversation is George Washington Smith (conversation of 24 October 1831, alphabetical notebook B, YTC, BIIa, and *Voyage, OC*, V, 1, pp. 246–47).

w. "≠The omnipotence of the majority seems to me the most serious disadvantage attached to democratic governments and the source of their greatest dangers≠" (YTC, CVh, 4, p. 81).

x. In the manuscript: "≠Arbitrariness must be carefully distinguished from tyranny, and tyranny from arbitrariness. Arbitrariness can be not tyrannical, and tyranny can be not arbitrary. In the United States there is almost never arbitrariness, but sometimes there is tyranny.≠"

To the side: "≠When Louis XIV regulated by himself and with sovereign power the

Tyranny usually makes use of arbitrariness, but if necessary it knows how to do without it.

In the United States, the omnipotence of the majority, at the same time that it favors the legal despotism of the legislator, also favors the arbitrariness of the magistrate. Because the majority has absolute control over making the law and supervising its execution, and has equal control over those governing and those governed, it regards public officials as its passive agents and willingly relies on them to take care of serving its designs. So the majority does not enter in advance into the details of the duties of public officials and scarcely takes the trouble to define their rights. It treats them as a master would treat his servants, if, having their behavior always in view, he could direct or correct their conduct at every moment.

In general, the law leaves American officials much more free than ours within the circle that is drawn around them. Sometimes the majority even allows them to go outside of this circle. Guaranteed by the opinion of the greatest number and strong because of their support, they then dare things that a European, accustomed to the spectacle of arbitrariness, still finds astonishing. In this way, habits being formed within liberty that, one day, will be able to become destructive to it.

Of the Power Exercised by the Majority in America over Thought

In the United States, when the majority has irrevocably settled on a question, it is no longer discussed.—Why.—Moral power that the majority exercises over thought.—Democratic republics immaterialize despotism.

When you come to examine how thought is exercised in the United States, you notice very clearly to what extent the power of the majority surpasses all the powers that we know in Europe.

---

commercial rights [doubtful reading (ed.)] of his subjects, he committed an arbitrary but not a tyrannical act.

"When the National Assembly ordered [blank space in the manuscript (ed.)], it committed a tyrannical act but not an arbitrary act.≠"

Thought is an invisible and almost imperceptible power that scoffs at all tyrannies [that scoffs amid chains and executioners. {You could say of it what Malherbe said of death: it does not stop at the gates of the Louvre any more than at the door of the poor man}].*y* Today, the most absolute sovereigns of Europe cannot prevent certain ideas hostile to their authority from circulating silently within their States and even within their courts. It is not the same in America; as long as the majority is uncertain, people speak; but as soon as the majority has irrevocably decided, everyone is silent, and friends as well as enemies then seem to climb on board together. The reason for this is simple. There is no monarch so absolute that he can gather in his hands all of society's forces and vanquish opposition in the way that a majority vested with the right to make and execute laws can [at will, vested with the right and the force].

A king, moreover, has only a physical power that acts on deeds and cannot reach wills; but the majority is vested with a strength simultaneously physical and moral, which acts on the will as well as on actions and which at the same time prevents the deed and the desire to do it.

I know of no country where, in general, there reigns less independence of mind and true freedom of discussion than in America.

There is no religious or political theory that may not be freely preached in the constitutional States of Europe and that does not penetrate into the others [{and I do not know of} ≠a European people so powerful and so strong that it is not forced from time to time to hear hard truths. It is not this way in America.≠]; for there is no country in Europe so subject to a single power that someone who wants to speak the truth does not find some support capable of insuring him against the results of his independence. If he has the misfortune to live under an absolute government, he often has the people for him; if he lives in a free country, he can find shelter, as needed, behind royal authority. The aristocratic part of society sustains him in democratic countries, and democracy in the others. But within a democracy organized as that of the United States, only a single power

---

y. In *Consolation à Monsieur Du Périer, gentilhomme d'Aix-en-Provence, sur la mort de sa fille.*

is found, a single element of strength and success, and nothing outside of it.[z]

In America, the majority draws a formidable circle around thought. Within these limits, the writer is free; but woe to him if he dares to go beyond them. It isn't that he has to fear an auto-da-fé, but he is exposed to all types of distasteful things and to everyday persecutions. A political career is closed to him; he has offended the only power that has the ability to open it to him. Everything is denied him, even glory. Before publishing his opinions, he believed he had some partisans; it seems to him that he has them no longer, now that he has revealed himself to all; for those who censure him speak openly, and those who think as he does, without having his courage, keep quiet and distance themselves. He gives in; finally, under the daily effort, he yields and returns to silence, as though he felt remorse for having told the truth.

Chains and executioners, those are the crude instruments formerly used by tyranny; but today civilization has perfected even despotism itself, which seemed however to have nothing more to learn.

Princes had, so to speak, materialized violence; the democratic republics of today have made violence as entirely intellectual as the human will that it wants to constrain. Under the absolute government of one man, despotism, to reach the soul, crudely struck the body; and the soul, escaping from these blows, rose gloriously above it; but in democratic republics, tyranny does not proceed in this way; it leaves the body alone and goes right to the soul. The master no longer says: You will think like me or die; he says: You are free not to think as I do; your life, your goods, everything remains with you; but from this day on you are a stranger among us. You will keep your privileges as a citizen, but they will become useless to you. If you aspire to be the choice of your fellow citizens, they will not choose you, and if you ask only for their esteem, they will still pretend to refuse it to you. You will remain among men, but you will lose your rights to humanity. When you approach your fellows, they will flee from you like an impure being. And those who believe in your innocence, even they will

---

z. In the margin: "<≠Base circumlocutions of the Federalists.≠>"

abandon you, for people would flee from them in turn. Go in peace; I spare your life, but I leave you a life worse than death.

Absolute monarchies had dishonored despotism. Let us be careful that democratic republics do not rehabilitate it, and that, while making despotism heavier for some, they do not, in the eyes of the greatest number, remove its odious aspect and its degrading character.

Among the proudest nations of the Old World, books have been published that intended faithfully to portray the vices and absurdities of their contemporaries. La Bruyère lived at the palace of Louis XIV when he composed his chapter on the great, and Molière criticized the court in the plays that he had performed before the courtiers. But the dominating power in the United States does not understand being played in this way. The slightest reproach wounds it; the smallest biting truth shocks it, and everything from the forms of its language to its most solid virtues must be praised. No writer, no matter how famous, can escape this obligation to heap praise upon his fellow citizens. So the majority lives in perpetual self-adoration; only foreigners or experience can bring certain truths to the ears of Americans.

If America has not yet had great writers, we do not have to look elsewhere for the reasons: literary genius does not exist without freedom of the mind, and there is no freedom of the mind in America.[a]

The Inquisition was never able to prevent the circulation in Spain of books opposed to the religion of the greatest number. The dominion of the majority does better in the United States: it has removed even the thought of publishing such books. Unbelievers are found in America, but unbelief finds, so to speak, no organ there.[b]

---

a. Cf. chapter XIII of the first part of the second volume.

b. The ideas of this paragraph were suggested to Tocqueville by a doctor in Baltimore, Mr. Stuart (non-alphabetic notebooks 2 and 3, YTC, BIIa, and *Voyage, OC,* V, 1, p. 115).

A note on a slip of paper attests to Tocqueville's dissatisfaction concerning this part of the chapter:

I have put two distinct ideas within the same expressions, which is a great defect./

That tyranny in America acts directly on the soul and does not torment the body results from two causes:

You see governments that strive to protect morals by condemning the authors of licentious books. In the United States, no one is condemned for this kind of work; but no one is tempted to write them. It is not that all citizens have pure morals, but the majority is steady in its morals.

Here, the use of power is undoubtedly good. I am, consequently, speaking only about the power itself. This irresistible power is an unremitting fact, and its good usage is only an accident. [Doesn't the majority in Paris acquire a taste for the filth that sullies our theatres daily?]

Effect of Tyranny of the Majority on the National Character of the Americans; Of the Courtier Spirit in the United States

Until now the effects of tyranny of the majority are felt on mores more than on the running of society.—They arrest the development of men of great character.—Democratic republics organized like those of the United States put the courtier spirit within reach of the greatest number.—Evidence of this spirit in the United States.—Why there is more patriotism among the people than among those who govern in their name.

The influence of what precedes is still felt only weakly in political society; but its harmful effects are already noticeable on the national character of the Americans. I think that the small number of outstanding men who appear today on the political stage must be attributed, above all, to the

---

1. Because it is exercised by a *majority* and not by a *man*. A man, never able to obtain the voluntary support of the mass, cannot inflict on his enemy the moral torment that arises from isolation and public scorn. He is forced to act *directly* in order to reach his enemy.

2. Because in fact mores have become milder and that despotism has been perfected and *intellectualized*.

This same note also exists in YTC, CVh, 3, p. 59; (the copyist indicates that the original is not in Tocqueville's hand).

always increasing action of the despotism of the majority in the United States.

When the American Revolution broke out, outstanding men appeared in large number; then public opinion led and did not tyrannize over wills. The famous men of this period, freely joining the movement of minds, had a grandeur of their own; they shed their brilliance on the nation and did not derive it from the nation.

In absolute governments, the great who are near the throne flatter the passions of the master and willingly bow to his caprices. But the mass of the nation does not lend itself to servitude; it often submits out of weakness, habit or ignorance, sometimes out of love of royalty or the king. We have seen peoples take a type of pleasure or pride in sacrificing their will to that of the prince and, in this way, give a kind of independence of soul to the very act of obedience. Among these peoples much less degradation than misery is found. There is, moreover, a great difference between doing what you do not approve or pretending to approve what you do; the one is done by a weak man, but the other belongs only to the habits of a valet.[c]

In free countries, in which each person is more or less called to give his opinion on matters of State; in democratic republics, in which public life is constantly mingled with private life, in which the sovereign is approachable from all sides, and in which it is only a matter of raising one's voice to reach the sovereign's ear, many more people are found who seek to bank on the sovereign's weaknesses and to live at the expense of the sovereign's passions, than in absolute monarchies. Not that men there are naturally worse than elsewhere, but temptation is stronger and is offered to more people at the same time. A much more general debasing of souls results.

Democratic republics put the courtier spirit within reach of the greatest number and make it penetrate into all classes at the same time. It is one of the principal reproaches that can be made against them.

c. The manuscript says "lackey."
Hervé de Tocqueville: "Trivial expression that, moreover, attacks an entire class that at present is no less proud than another" (YTC, CIIIb, 1, p. 87).

That is true, above all, in democratic states organized like the American republics, in which the majority possesses such absolute and irresistible dominion, that, in a way, you must renounce your rights as a citizen and, so to speak, your position as a man when you want to deviate from the road marked out by the majority.

Among the immense crowd, in the United States, that pushes into a political career, I saw very few men who showed this virile candor, this manly independence of thought, that often distinguished Americans in former times and that, wherever it is found, forms the salient feature of great characters. At first view, you would say that in America minds have all been formed on the same model because they so exactly follow the same paths. Sometimes, it is true, the foreigner will encounter some Americans who deviate from the rigor of the formulas; these Americans happen to deplore the vice of the laws, the variableness of democracy and its lack of enlightenment; often they even go so far as to notice the defects that are spoiling the national character, and they indicate the measures that could be taken to correct those defects. But no one, except you, is listening to them; and you, to whom they confide these secret thoughts, you are only a passing foreigner. They willingly give you truths that are useless to you, and, coming into the public square, they use another language.

If these lines ever reach America, I am sure of two things: first, that readers will all raise their voices to condemn me; second, that many among them will absolve me deep down in their conscience.[d]

I have heard country spoken about in the United States. I have encountered true patriotism among the people; I have often searched in vain for these two things among those who lead the people. This is easily understood

---

d. Democracy./

The greatest moral evil that results from the dominion of democracy is that it puts the courtier spirit within reach of everyone.

[In the margin: Here the character of courtiers.]

In democratic republics the number of courtiers is immense; the only difference from monarchies is that these are courtiers with bad taste.

The Americans have only two means to gain the truth, the *voice* of foreigners and *experience* (YTC, CVe, pp. 62–63).

by analogy: despotism depraves the one submitted to it much more than the one who imposes it. In absolute monarchies, the king often has great virtues; but the courtiers are always vile.

[≠What I blame democratic republics for is putting the courtier spirit within reach of such a large number.≠]

It is true that courtiers, in America, do not say: Sire and Your Majesty, a grand and capital difference; but they talk constantly about the natural enlightenment of their master. They do not raise the question of knowing which one of the virtues of the prince most merits adoration; for they assert that he possesses all virtues, without having acquired them and, so to speak, without wanting to do so. They do not give him their wives and daughters so that he would deign to elevate them to the rank of his mistresses; but by sacrificing their opinions to him, they prostitute themselves.

Moralists and philosophers in America are not forced to envelop their opinions in veils of allegory; but, before hazarding an annoying truth, they say: We know that we are speaking to a people too far above human weaknesses ever to lose control of itself. We would not use such language, if we did not address men whose virtues and enlightenment make them alone, among all others, worthy of remaining free.

How could those who flattered Louis XIV do better?

As for me, I believe that in all governments, whatever they are, baseness will attach itself to strength and flattery to power. And I know only one way to prevent men from degrading themselves: it is to grant to no one, with omnipotence, the sovereign power to debase them.

That the Greatest Danger to the American Republics Comes from the Omnipotence of the Majority

*Democratic republics risk perishing by the bad use of
their power, and not by powerlessness.—The government
of the American republics more centralized
and more energetic than that of the monarchies of Europe.—
Danger that results.—Opinion of Madison and
of Jefferson on this subject.*

Governments usually perish by powerlessness or by tyranny. In the first case, power escapes from them; in the other, it is wrested from them.[e]

Many men, seeing democratic States[f] fall into anarchy, have thought that government in these States was naturally weak and powerless. The truth is that, once war has flared up there among the parties, government loses its effect on society. But I do not think that the nature of a democratic power is to lack strength and resources; I believe, on the contrary, that it is almost always the abuse of its forces and the bad use of its resources that make it perish. Anarchy is almost always born out of its tyranny or its lack of skill, but not out of its powerlessness.

Stability must not be confused with strength, the greatness of something

e. Washington, 15 January 1832.
   There are two ways for a government to perish:

   1. By lack of power (like the first Union, for example).
   2. By bad use of power, like all tyrannies.

   It is by this last evil that the American republics will perish.
   The first mode is more rapid than the second. The latter is no less certain (YTC, BIIb, p. 13).

This note does not appear in YTC, CVe and has not been published in *Voyage, OC,* V, 1. YTC, BIIb, and YTC, CVe are two different copies of the same original, but copy BIIb, which is later, contains texts that do not appear in the first copy.
   f. The manuscript says "free States."

with its duration. In democratic republics, the power that leads[5] society is not stable, for it often changes hands and objectives. But, wherever it goes, its strength is nearly irresistible.

The government of the American republics seems to me as centralized and more energetic than that of the absolute monarchies of Europe. So I do not think that they will perish from weakness.[6]

If liberty is ever lost in America, it will be necessary to lay the blame on the omnipotence of the majority that will have brought minorities to despair and will have forced them to appeal to physical force. Then you will see anarchy, but it will arrive as a consequence of despotism.

President James Madison expressed the same thoughts (see the *Federalist,* No 51.)

> It is of great importance in a republic not only to guard the society against the oppression of its rulers, but to guard one part of the society against the injustice of the other part. [. . . (ed.) . . .] Justice is the end of government. It is the end of civil society. It ever has been and ever will be pursued until it is obtained, or until liberty be lost in the pursuit.
>
> In a society under the forms of which the stronger faction can readily unite and oppress the weaker, anarchy may as truly be said to reign as in a state of nature, where the weaker individual is not secured against the violence of the stronger; and as, in the latter state, even the stronger individuals[g] are prompted, by the uncertainty of their condition, to submit to a government which may protect the weak as well as themselves; so, in the former state, will the more powerful factions or parties be gradually induced, by a like motive, to wish for a government which will protect all parties, the weaker as well as the more powerful. It can be little doubted that if the State of Rhode Island was separated from the Confederacy and left to itself, the insecurity of rights under the popular form of government

---

5. *Power can be centralized in an assembly; then it is strong, but not stable. It can be centralized in a man; then it is less strong, but it is more stable.*

6. *It is useless, I think, to warn the reader that here, as in all the rest of the chapter, I am speaking, not about the federal government, but about the individual governments of each state that the majority leads despotically.*

g. In the manuscript: "the strongest individuals."

within such narrow limits would be displayed by such reiterated oppressions of factious majorities that some power altogether independent of the people would soon be called for by the voice of the very factions whose misrule had proved the necessity of it.

[In another place he said: "[The] facility of lawmaking seems to be the disease to which our government is most liable."]

Jefferson also said: "The executive power, in our government, is not the only, and perhaps not the principal object of my concern. The tyranny of legislators is now and will be for many years to come the most formidable danger. That of the executive power will come in its turn, but in a more distant period."[7]

In this matter, I like to cite Jefferson in preference to all others, because I consider him the most powerful apostle democracy has ever had.[j]

---

7. *Letter from Jefferson to Madison, 15 March 1789.*[h]

h. In Conseil's edition, vol. I, pp. 340–41. Tocqueville quotes correctly from the French, but in the English Jefferson speaks about the "tyranny of the legislatures," not of the "legislators."

j. Édouard de Tocqueville: "In this chapter, very well written moreover and of great interest, you completely avoid the defect for which I reproached you in the notes for the preceding chapter. Here you coldly judge democracy, without admiration and without weakness; you tell the truth about it, all the while recognizing its qualities and its advantages" (YTC, CIIIb, 1, p. 90).

CHAPTER 8

Of What Tempers Tyranny of the Majority in the United States

Absence of Administrative Centralization

The national majority does not have the idea of doing everything.—It is forced to use town and county magistrates in order to carry out its sovereign will.

Previously I distinguished two types of centralization; one, I called governmental, and the other administrative.[a]

Only the first exists in America; the second is almost unknown there.

If the power that directs American societies found these two means of government at its disposal, and combined, with the right to command everything, the ability and the habit of carrying out everything by itself; if, after establishing the general principles of government, it entered into the details of application, and after regulating the great interests of the country,

---

a. In America, there are a thousand natural causes that so to speak work by themselves toward moderating the omnipotence of the majority. The extreme similarity that reigns in the United States among all the interests, the material prosperity of the country, the diffusion of enlightenment and the mildness of mores, which is the necessary consequence of the progress of civilization, greatly favor the leniency of government.

I have already pointed out the different causes; the time has come to examine what barriers the institutions themselves have carefully raised against the power from which they derive.

Previously I distinguished . . . (YTC, CVh, 4, p. 15).

it could reach as far as individual interests, liberty would soon be banished from the New World.[b]

But, in the United States, the majority, which often has the tastes and instincts of a despot, still lacks the most advanced instruments of tyranny.

In none of the American republics has the central government ever taken charge of anything other than a small number of objects whose importance attracted its attention. It has never undertaken to regulate the secondary things of society. Nothing indicates that it has ever even conceived the desire to do so. The majority, while becoming more and more absolute, has not increased the attributions of the central power; it has only made it omnipotent in its sphere. Thus despotism can be very heavy at one point, but it cannot extend to all.[c]

Besides, however carried away the national majority may be by its passions; however ardent it is in its projects, it cannot in all places, in the same way, and in the same moment, make all citizens yield to its desires.[d] When the central government that represents the national majority

b. In the manuscript, the paragraph is written as follows: "The Americans must consider themselves fortunate that this is so: if the majority in the United States found the one, like the other, in its hands in order to compel obedience to its will, and if it combined, with the right to do everything, the ability and the habit of carrying everything out by its agents, its power would be, so to speak, without limits."

c. In notes taken by Beaumont for the writing of *Marie,* this is found in Tocqueville's hand:

In the American republics the central government has never taken charge except of a small number of objects whose importance attracted its attention. It has never undertaken to direct the administration of the towns and counties [v: secondary things]. It does not seem ever to have conceived the desire to do so. Becoming more and more absolute has allowed the rule of the majority to regulate these objects with more sovereign authority, but has not increased the number of objects in its sphere. So despotism can be great, but it cannot extend to everything (YTC, Beaumont, CIX).

d. Two causes.

1. Splitting up of sovereignty.
2. Splitting up of administration.

Tyranny can be very great but it cannot be popular.

The Union cannot present a tyrannical majority. Each state could do it, but town administrations (illegible word).

has given orders as a sovereign, it must rely, for the execution of its command, on agents who often do not depend on it and that it cannot direct at every moment. So the municipal bodies and county administrations form like so many hidden reefs that slow or divide the tide of popular will. Were the law oppressive, liberty would still find a refuge in the way in which the law would be executed; the majority cannot get into the details, and, if I dare say so, into the puerilities of administrative tyranny. The majority does not even imagine that it can do so, for it is not entirely aware of its power. It still knows only its natural strength and is unaware of how far art could extend its limits.

This merits reflection.[e] If a democratic republic like that of the United States ever came to be established in a country where the power of one man had already established administrative centralization and introduced it into habits, as well as into laws, I am not afraid to say that, in such a republic, despotism would become more intolerable than in any of the absolute monarchies of Europe. It would be necessary to look to Asia in order to find something comparable.

The national majority finding itself opposed in its designs in this way by the majority of the inhabitants of a city or of a district, and tyranny [v: despotism] which can be very great at some points cannot become general.

If the majority rules the state, it also rules the town and the county; and since these two majorities can be opposed in their designs, liberty always finds some refuge, and despotism which can be irresistibly exercised at several points of the territory cannot become general, however (YTC, CVh, 3, pp. 53–54).

Tocqueville here is quite close to the idea that Madison expresses in Number 10 of the *Federalist,* that the best barrier against tyranny is the great extent of the republic. Nonetheless there is no reference to this Number of the *Federalist* in the drafts.

e. Hervé de Tocqueville: "I observe generally that in the whole work the author makes extremely frequent use of this way of expressing himself.

"This chapter needs to be reviewed. I would in addition like the author to put there what he said about associations as barriers to omnipotence. That would be better placed here than in the chapter on associations where you speak about the remedy before indicating the malady" (YTC, CIIIb, 1, p. 71).

Of the Spirit of the Jurist in the United States, and How It Serves as Counterweight to Democracy[f]

Usefulness of trying to find out what the natural instincts of the spirit of the jurist are.—Jurists, called to play a great role in the society that is trying to be born.—How the kind of work that jurists devote themselves to gives an aristocratic turn to their ideas.—Accidental causes that can oppose the development of these ideas.—Facility that the aristocracy has in uniting itself with jurists.—Advantage that a despot could draw from the jurists.—How the jurists form the only aristocratic element that is by nature able to combine with the natural elements of democracy.—Particular causes that tend to give an aristocratic

f. Influence exercised by the judicial power on the power of the majority./

When you examine political society in the United States, you notice at first glance only a single principle that seems to bind all the parts strongly together: the people appear as the sole power. Nothing seems able to oppose their will or to thwart their designs.

But here is a man who appears in a way above the people; he does not get his mandate from them; he has, so to speak, nothing to fear from their anger, nor anything to hope from their favor. He is vested, however, with more power than any one of the representatives of the people; for, with a single blow, he can strike with sterility the work emanating from the common will (YTC, CVh, 1, pp. 14–15).

Rousseau (*Du contrat social,* book II, chapter VII), not wanting to limit the sovereignty of the people in any way, had to put the legislator outside of the political process. Tocqueville, who acknowledged absolute sovereignty in no power, makes the legislator a decisive element of political life.

Several conversations with American lawyers and jurists persuaded the author of the foremost role that lawyers and jurists play in political life. Cf. the conversation with Edward Everett of 24 January 1832 (non-alphabetic notebooks 2 and 3, YTC, BIIa, and *Voyage, OC,* V, 1, p. 151); the conversation with Mr. Latrobe of 30 October 1831 (*ibid.,* p. 110) and more especially the conversation with Mr. Gallatin of 10 June 1831 (non-alphabetic notebook 1, YTC, BIIa, and *Voyage, OC,* V, 1, p. 61), where the idea that lawyers constitute a body that serves as a counterweight to democracy is mentioned; the conversations with John C. Spencer of 17 and 18 July 1831 (*ibid.,* pp. 68–69), on the conservative effects of the American legal mentality. When Tocqueville takes up the argument again, he is also thinking of Blackstone (Cf. *Correspondence and Conversations of Alexis de Tocqueville with Nassau William Senior,* II, p. 44). Also see Gino Gorla, *Commento a Tocqueville. L'idea dei diritti* (Milan: Dott. A Guiffrè Editore, 1948, pp. 259–68).

turn to the spirit of the English and American jurists.—The American aristocracy is at the lawyers' bar and on the judges' bench.—Influence exercised by jurists on American society.— How their spirit enters into the legislatures, into the administration, and ends by giving the people themselves something of the instinct of magistrates.

[≠I said elsewhere that the American magistracy was vested with a great political power; it remains for me to see how it tends to exercise its power.

American judges are named by the executive power {or by the legislature}; they are hardly ever chosen by the people.

But had you made judges chosen directly by the people, by making them irremovable, you would have given them instincts entirely different from those of the people.

From the moment when a public official is vested with an office for life, he takes a personal interest in society remaining immobile. If he is not always the enemy of progress, he is definitely the enemy of revolutions, and if this official is a man of the law, he is naturally carried by education to prize stability and he becomes attached to stability by inclination.

In fact, in what could be called the spirit of the jurist there is something singularly aristocratic.

Whoever will not allow himself to be preoccupied by a fact but by the ensemble of facts, not by a particular period but by the succession of times, will easily discover this tendency in the spirit of the jurist.≠]

When you visit the Americans and study their laws, you see that the authority that they have given to jurists and the influence that the Americans have allowed them to take in government form today the most powerful barrier to the errors of democracy. To me this effect seems due to a general cause that it is useful to try to determine, because it can recur elsewhere.

Jurists have been mixed up in all the movements of political society in Europe for five hundred years. Sometimes they have served as instruments of the political powers; sometimes they have used the political powers as instruments. In the Middle Ages, jurists cooperated wonderfully in extending the domination of kings; since then, they have worked powerfully to restrict this very power. In England, they were seen to unite intimately with the aristocracy; in France they revealed themselves as its most dangerous enemies. So do jurists yield only to sudden and momentary impulses, or, depending on circumstances, do they more or less obey instincts that are natural to them and that always recur? I would like to clarify this point; for jurists are perhaps called upon to play the first role in the political society trying to be born.

Men who have made law their specialty have drawn from this work habits of order, a certain taste for forms, a sort of instinctive love for the regular succession of ideas, that make them naturally strongly opposed to the revolutionary spirit and to the unthinking passions of democracy.

[{This effect is larger or smaller depending on how you study the law.

In countries like France, where all legislation is written [the jurist (ed.)] contracts the taste for what is regular and legal.}

≠Furthermore, in countries where the law of precedents rules, such as England and America, the taste and respect for what is old are almost always merged in the soul of the jurist with the love of what is legal.

It is not the same in countries where, as in France, the whole legislation is found written in codes.

The English jurist tries to determine what has been done; the French jurist, what the intention was. The first wants≠ evidence; the second, arguments. The one wants decisions; the other wants reasons. [Cf. infra (ed.)]]

The special knowledge that jurists acquire while studying the law assures them a separate rank in society. They form a sort of privileged class among intelligent people. Each day they rediscover the idea of this superiority in the exercise of their profession; they are masters of a necessary science, the knowledge of which is not widespread; they serve as arbiters among citizens, and the habit of leading the blind passions of the litigants toward the goal gives them a certain contempt for the judgment of the crowd. Add that they naturally form a *corps*. It isn't that they agree among themselves and head in concert toward the same point; but the community of study and unity of methods link their minds, as interest could unite their wills.

So you find hidden at the bottom of the soul of jurists a portion of the tastes and habits of the aristocracy. Like the aristocracy, they have an instinctive propensity for order, a natural love of forms; like the aristocracy, they conceive a great distaste for the actions of the multitude and secretly despise the government of the people.g

I do not want to say that these natural tendencies of jurists are strong enough to bind them in an irresistible way. What dominates jurists, as all men, is particular interest, and above all the interest of the moment.

There is a kind of society where men of the law cannot take a rank in the political world analogous to the one that they occupy in private life; you can be sure that, in a society organized in this way, the jurists [despite their natural tastes] will be very active agents of revolution. But then you must try to determine if the cause that leads them to destroy or to change arises among them from a permanent disposition or from an accident. It is true that jurists singularly contributed to overturning the French monarchy in 1789.h It remains to be known if they acted in this way because they had studied the laws, or because they could not contribute toward making them.j

g. The manuscript says: ". . . always scorn the people."
Hervé de Tocqueville:

I do not know if jurists inwardly scorn the government of the people, but definitely they never express this scorn; because they are sure that the ease with which they handle words will always open a role for them in the government of the people. In general, of all classes, jurists are the one in which vanity is the most developed by popular successes. This vanity directs their outwardly expressed opinions and is the foundation of their actions.

This vanity has much less effect when they have an established position as in America, but it will always be formidable when they have a position to establish, or when superiorities are found that offend them, which will always happen in a monarchy where absolute equality cannot be found and where they are too numerous for the places and for the influence that reasonably can be given to them (YTC, CIIIb, 1, p. 76).

h. Hervé de Tocqueville: "They contributed even more to overturning the Restoration, although a part of their desires was fulfilled" (YTC, CIIIb, 1, p. 77).

j. Hervé de Tocqueville: "There is a gap here. Alexis throws himself toward another order of ideas before going deeply enough into those that precede. One or two more paragraphs are necessary here in order to explain more clearly the motives for the conduct of the jurists in 1789 and 1830" (YTC, CIIIb, 1, p. 77).

Five hundred years ago, the English aristocracy put itself at the head of the people and spoke in their name; today it upholds the throne and makes itself the champion of royal authority.[k] The aristocracy, however, has instincts and tendencies that are its own.

You must also guard against taking isolated members of the corps for the corps itself.

In all free governments, of whatever form, you will find jurists among the first ranks of all parties. This same remark is also applicable to the aristocracy. Nearly all the democratic movements that have agitated the world have been led by nobles.

An elite body can never be sufficient for all the ambitions that it contains; there are always more talents and passions than posts, and you do not fail to find a large number of men there who, not able to grow great quickly enough by using the privileges of the corps, seek to grow great by attacking its privileges.

So I do not claim that a period will come when *all* jurists, or that in *all* times, most jurists must appear as friends of order and enemies of change.

I am saying that in a society where jurists occupy without dispute the elevated position that belongs to them naturally, [and with all the more reason in the society where they occupy the first rank] their spirit will be eminently conservative and will show itself to be antidemocratic.[m]

When the aristocracy closes its ranks to jurists, it finds in them enemies

---

k. Hervé de Tocqueville: "That is not exact; the English aristocracy only makes itself the champion of its privileges and of those of the clergy" (YTC, CIIIb, 1, pp. 77–78).
m. Édouard de Tocqueville:

The sense of this paragraph must necessarily be changed, for this reflection could apply to all those of ambition, to all agitators, to all the anarchists of the world, as well as to jurists. There is no revolutionary who, reaching the first rank, does not reveal a *conservative* spirit, that is to say, who does not want to *conserve* this rank, that speaks for itself. So you must not, after saying that jurists do not have anarchic tendencies, give as proof their conduct and their passions that from this paragraph are precisely those of the anarchists of all times and in all places. Couldn't you say: *I am saying that in a society where jurists will occupy without dispute the rank that legitimately belongs to them, their spirit,* etc? (YTC, CIIIb, 1, pp. 68–69).

all the more dangerous because, below the aristocracy in wealth and power, they are independent of the aristocracy by their work and feel themselves on its level by their enlightenment.

But every time the nobles have wanted to share some of their privileges with the jurists, these two classes have found it very easy to join together and have, so to speak, discovered themselves to be of the same family.

I am equally led to believe that it will always be easy for a king to make jurists the most useful instruments of his power.[n]

There is infinitely more natural affinity between men of the law and the executive power than between them and the people, although jurists often have to overthrow the first; just as there is more natural affinity between the nobles and the king than between the nobles and the people, even though you have often seen the superior classes of society combine with the others to struggle against royal power. [Jurists often fear the king, but they always despise the people.]

What jurists love above all things is the sight of order, and the greatest guarantee of order is authority. It must not be forgotten, moreover, that if they prize liberty, they generally put legality much above it; they fear tyranny less than arbitrariness and, provided that the legislator himself sees to taking independence away from men, they are more or less content.

So I think that the prince who, in the presence of an invasive democracy, would seek to break down the judicial power in his States and to diminish the political influence of jurists, would commit a great error. He would let go of the substance of authority in order to seize its shadow.

I do not doubt that it would be more profitable for him to introduce jurists into the government. After entrusting despotism to them in the form

n. Hervé de Tocqueville:

As for me, I believe that this will always be a nearly insoluble problem for a king. It would be necessary that near the sovereign there were neither court, nor in the State any great superiority that offended the vanity of the jurists. One objects that they love Louis-Philippe. That comes from the contempt that he inspires in them and that precisely makes each one of them believe he has the right to consider himself above Louis-Philippe, though he is the king. Alexis must take care not to be caught in a paradox, as much here as in what follows (YTC, CIIIb, 1, p. 78).

of violence, perhaps he would rediscover it in their hands with the features of justice and the law.

[As for me, I would never advise any people to leave to the courts the care of guaranteeing its liberty. I would be afraid that the courts would sacrifice it to monarchs or to themselves. This care concerns great political assemblies.]

The government of democracy is favorable to the political power of jurists. When the rich man, the nobleman and the prince are excluded from government, the jurists arrive there by right, so to speak; for then they are the only enlightened and skillful men that the people can choose outside of themselves.[o]

If jurists are led naturally toward the aristocracy and the prince by their tastes, they are led naturally toward the people by their interest.

Thus, jurists love the government of democracy, without sharing its tendencies and without imitating its weaknesses, double cause to be powerful by democracy and over democracy.

The people, in a democracy, do not distrust jurists, because they know that the interest of jurists is to serve their cause; they listen to them without anger, because they do not assume that jurists have an ulterior motive.[p] In fact, jurists do not want to overturn the government that democracy has established, but they strive constantly to lead it along a path that is not its own and by means that are foreign to it. The jurist belongs to the people by his interest and by his birth and to the aristocracy by his habits and his tastes; he is like the natural liaison between these two, like the link that unites them.

The body of jurists forms the only aristocratic element that can mingle with the natural elements of democracy without effort and combine with them in a happy and enduring way. I am not unaware of the faults inherent

o. "≠In America the second guarantee of liberty is found in the constitution of the judicial power. The absence of administrative centralization is a happy circumstance more than a result of the wisdom of the law-maker. But the judicial power in the United States is a barrier raised by design against the omnipotence of the majority. You can consider it as the only powerful or real obstacle that the American laws have placed in the path of the people≠" (YTC, CVh, 4, pp. 16–17).

p. In the margin: "≠It is to jurists that democracy owes the ability to govern.≠"

in the spirit of jurists; without this mixture of the spirit of jurists with the democratic spirit, I doubt, however, that democracy could govern society for long, and I cannot believe that today a republic could hope to maintain its existence, if the influence of jurists in public affairs did not increase in proportion to the power of the people.

This aristocratic character that I see in the spirit of jurists is still more pronounced in the United States and in England than in any other country. This is due not only to the study of the law made by English and American jurists, but also to the very nature of legislation and to the position that these interpreters occupy among these two peoples.

The English and the Americans have kept the law of precedents, that is, they continue to draw from the opinions and legal decisions of their fathers the opinions that they must have in matters of the law and the decisions they must render.

So with an English or American jurist, the taste and respect for what is old is nearly always mingled with love of what is regular and legal.

This has still another influence on the turn of mind of jurists and consequently on the course of society.

The English or American jurist seeks what has been done; the French jurist, what you must have wanted to do; [the first, evidence; the second, arguments] the one wants judgments, the other wants reasons.

When you listen to an English or American jurist, you are surprised to see him so often cite the opinion of others, and to hear him speak so little about his own, while among us the contrary happens.

No affair that the French lawyer agrees to handle is so small that he treats it without introducing a system of his own ideas; and he will examine even the constituent principles of the law so that the court be pleased in this regard to have the boundary marker of a disputed inheritance moved back about six feet.

This sort of abnegation of his own sense made by the English and American jurist in order to rely on the sense of his fathers; this type of servitude, in which he is obliged to maintain his thought, must give the spirit of the jurist more timid habits and make him acquire more stationary tendencies in England and America than in France [for a fact is very much more immobile than an idea or an argument].

Our written laws are often difficult to understand, but everyone can read them; in contrast, there is nothing more obscure to the common people and less accessible to them than legislation founded on precedents. This need for the jurist in England and in the United States, this high idea of his knowledge, separate him more and more from the people, and end by putting him in a class apart. The French jurist is only a learned man, but the English or American man of the law in a way resembles the priests of Egypt; like them, he is the sole interpreter of an occult science.

The position that the men of the law occupy in England and in America exercises an influence no less great on their habits and their opinions. The aristocracy of England, which has taken care to draw to its bosom everything that had some natural analogy to it, has given a very great portion of consideration and power to jurists. In English society jurists are not at the first rank, but they consider themselves content with the rank that they occupy. They form something like the junior branch of the English aristocracy, and they love and respect their seniors, without sharing all their privileges. So the English jurists combine with the aristocratic interests of their profession the aristocratic ideas and tastes of the society in which they live.

Therefore in England, above all, you can see in relief the type of jurist that I am trying to paint: the English jurist esteems the laws, not so much because they are good as because they are old; and, if he sees himself reduced to modifying them on some point in order to adapt to the changes that societies are subjected to by time, he resorts to the most incredible subtleties in order to persuade himself that, by adding something to the work of his fathers, he is only developing their thought and completing their efforts. Do not hope to make him recognize that he is an innovator; he will consent to go to absurd lengths before admitting himself guilty of such a great crime. In England was born this legal spirit that seems indifferent to the heart of things in order to pay attention only to the letter, and that would rather go beyond reason and humanity than go beyond the law.

English legislation is like an ancient tree on which jurists have constantly grafted the strangest shoots, in the hope that, while producing different fruits, they will at least blend their foliage with the venerable stock that supports them.

In America, there are no nobles nor men of letters, and the people distrust the rich. So jurists form the superior political class and the most intellectual portion of society.[q] Thus, they could only lose by innovating: this adds a conservative interest to the natural taste that they have for order.

If you asked me where I place the American aristocracy, I would answer without hesitating that it is not among the rich who have no common bond that gathers them together. The American aristocracy is at the lawyers' bar and on the judges' bench.[r]

The more you think about what happens in the United States, the more you feel persuaded that in this country the body of jurists forms the most powerful and, so to speak, the sole counterweight of democracy.

In the United States you easily discover how appropriate the spirit of the jurist is, by its qualities, and I will say even by its faults, for neutralizing the vices inherent in popular government.

When the American people allow themselves to be intoxicated by their passions, or abandon themselves to the impetus of their ideas, jurists make them feel an almost invisible brake that moderates and stops them. To their democratic instincts, jurists secretly oppose their own aristocratic tendencies; to their love of novelty, the jurists' superstitious respect for what is old; to the immensity of their designs, the jurists' narrow views; to their disdain for rules, the jurists' taste for forms; and to their hotheadedness, the jurists' habit of proceeding slowly.

The courts are the most visible organs that the body of jurists uses to act upon democracy.

The judge is a jurist who, apart from the taste for order and rules that he acquired in the study of law, draws the love of stability also from his irremovability from office. His legal knowledge had already assured

---

q. In the margin: "≠Perhaps put here the large piece added at Baugy.≠"

r. I am not saying that the aristocratic spirit in the United States is found only among jurists; the rich in America, as everywhere else, certainly have great instincts for order and preservation. But they do not form a corps; they are not united together by shared habits, ideas, tastes. There is no intellectual bond that gathers their collective strength; they do not make a corps. The people distrust them and do not mix them into public affairs, while the jurists, who have more or less the same instincts as the rich, do not cause the people any fear (YTC, CVj, 2, pp. 17–18).

him an elevated position among his fellows; his political power really places him in a rank apart, and gives him the instincts of the privileged classes.

Armed with the right of declaring laws unconstitutional, an American magistrate enters constantly into public affairs.[1] He cannot force the people to make laws, but at least he compels them not to be unfaithful to their own laws and to remain consistent.

I am not unaware that a secret tendency exists in the United States that leads the people to reduce the judicial power; in most of the particular state constitutions, the government, at the request of two legislative houses, can remove judges from the bench. Certain constitutions make the members of the courts *elective* and submit them to frequent reelection.[t] I dare to predict that sooner or later these innovations will have harmful results and that one day you will see that by diminishing the independence of the magistrates in this way you have attacked not only the judicial power but also the democratic republic itself.

It must not be believed, moreover, that in the United States the spirit of the jurist is enclosed only within the courtrooms; it extends well beyond.

Jurists, forming the only enlightened class that the people do not distrust, are naturally called to occupy most of the public offices. They fill the legislatures and are at the head of administrations, so they exercise a great influence on the formation of the law and on its execution. Jurists are obliged, however, to yield to the current of political opinion that carries them along; but it is easy to find indications of what they would do if they were free. The Americans, who have innovated so much in their political laws, have introduced only slight changes, and with great difficulty, into their civil laws, although several of these laws are strongly repugnant to their social state.[u] That is because in matters of civil law the majority is

1. *See in the first volume what I say about the judicial power.*[s]

s. The first part of the book, as the reader remembers, was published in two volumes.

t. A lawyer from Montgomery, in Alabama, had, on 6 January 1832, drawn the attention of the author to this fact (nonalphabetic notebooks 1 and 2, YTC, BIIa, and *Voyage, OC,* V, 1, pp. 140–41).

u. Tocqueville considers this question in the last pages of chapter II of the first part of the first volume.

always obliged to rely on jurists; and the American jurists, left to their own choice, do not innovate.

It is a very strange thing for a Frenchman to hear the complaints that arise in the United States against the jurists' stationary spirit and their prejudices in favor of what is established.

The influence of the spirit of the jurist extends still farther than the precise limits that I have just traced.[v]

There is hardly any political question in the United States that sooner or later does not turn into a judicial question. From that, the obligation that the parties find in their daily polemics to borrow ideas and language from the judicial system. Since most public men are or have formerly been jurists, they make the habits and the turn of ideas that belong to jurists pass into the handling of public affairs. The jury ends up by familiarizing all classes with them. Thus, judicial language becomes, in a way, the common language; so the spirit of the jurist, born inside the schools and courtrooms, spreads little by little beyond their confines; it infiltrates all of society, so to speak; it descends to the lowest ranks, and the entire people finishes by acquiring a part of the habits and tastes of the magistrate.

In the United States, the jurists form a power that is little feared, that is scarcely noticed, that has no banner of its own, that yields with flexibility to the exigencies of time and gives way without resistance to all the movements of the social body. But this power envelops the entire society, pen-

v. It is easy to notice, if you look closely, that in all the states of the Union, the judicial power exercises a great influence over political affairs. But this influence is visible, above all, in the action of the federal courts. You know that the Constitution of the United States predominates over the particular constitutions just as the latter in turn predominate over simple laws. Now, I said elsewhere that the Constitution of the United States forbids the provincial legislatures to introduce retroactive provisions into their penal laws and to damage certain vested rights. To take these two courses of action away from the particular states was to wrest from them the very weapons of tyranny. So every time that legislators pass laws of this type, they are attacked as unconstitutional before the federal courts. The federal judicial system then comes to put itself as a disinterested arbiter between the majority that wants to oppress and the individual that it oppresses.[1] It interposes itself among the local passions whose ardor can be compared only to those fraternal hatreds about which Tacitus speaks.

1. I do not know if that is true in as absolute a way as I indicate. To research. See notably Story, p. 498 (YTC, CVh, 5, pp. 22–23).

etrates into each of the classes that compose society, works on society in secret, acts constantly on society without society's knowledge and ends by shaping society according to its desires.

Of the Jury in the United States Considered as a Political Institution[w]

The jury, which is one of the modes of sovereignty of the people, must be put in harmony with the other laws that establish this sovereignty.—Composition of the jury in the United States.— Effects produced by the jury on the national character.— Education that it gives to the people.—How it tends to establish the influence of magistrates and to spread the spirit of the jurist.

Since my subject has led me naturally to talk about the judicial system in the United States, I will not abandon this matter without dealing with the jury.

w. Jury./
  The jury is at the very same time an energetic means to make the people rule and the most effective means to teach them to rule./
  Since I am on the judicial system, I want to talk about the jury./
  Democratic or aristocratic, but never monarchical, always republican./
  [In the margin: As for me, I find that when you deal with the jury the political point of view absorbs all others so to speak; the jury is above all a political institution; it is from this point of view that you must always judge it.] There would be a book to do on the ways in which the Americans make the responsibility of the jury apply in criminal and civil matters, but here I only want to consider it from the political point of view (YTC, CVh, 5, p. 31).

These and other ideas had been sketched by Tocqueville in two notes dated respectively 11 October 1831 and 12 January 1832 (pocket notebooks 3, 4 and 5, YTC, BIIa, and *Voyage, OC,* V, 1, pp. 181–82, 201–2). The travel notebooks contain numerous references to the jury, especially notebook F, which is dedicated exclusively to civil and criminal law in America. On the role of the jury in civil matters, see the conversation of 21 September 1831 with Senator Francis Gray and the conversation with a lawyer from Montgomery (nonalphabetic notebooks 2 and 3, YTC, BIIa, and *Voyage, OC,* V, 1, pp. 91 and 142). During his journey, Tocqueville attended a hearing in a *circuit court* (George W. Pierson, *Tocqueville and Beaumont in America,* chapter XXVIII).
  Tocqueville considers that mores and circumstances act as well against tyranny of the majority. These two other obstacles to the power of the majority are set forth in chapter IX, which initially concluded the work. See note a on p. 277 and note e on p. 452.

Two things must be distinguished: the jury as a judicial institution and as a political institution.

If it was a matter of knowing to what extent the jury, and above all the jury in civil matters, serves the good administration of justice, I would admit that its usefulness could be contested.

The institution of the jury was born in a society that was little advanced, where hardly anything was submitted to the courts except simple questions of fact; and it is not a simple task to adapt the jury to the needs of a very civilized people, when the relationships among men are singularly multiplied and have taken on a complicated and intellectual character.[2]

My principal goal, at this moment, is to envisage the political side of the jury; another path would take me away from my subject. As for the jury considered as a judicial means, I will say only two words. When the English adopted the institution of the jury, they were a half-barbaric people; they have since become one of the most enlightened nations of the globe, and their attachment to the jury has seemed to increase with their enlightenment. They emerged from their territory, and we have seen them spread across the universe. Some formed colonies; others, independent States. The body of the nation kept the king; several of the emigrants founded powerful republics. But everywhere the English equally advocated the institution of

2. *It would be something quite useful and curious to consider the jury as a judicial institution, to appreciate the effects that it produces in the United States and to try to find out in what way the Americans have made use of it. You could find in the examination of this question alone the subject of an entire book and a book interesting for France. You would try to find out there, for example, what portion of American institutions relative to the jury could be introduced among us and with the help of what gradual process. The American state that would provide the most light on this subject would be the state of Louisiana. Louisiana contains a mixed population of French and English. The two sets of law are found there face to face like the two peoples and combine little by little with each other. The most useful books to consult would be the collection of the laws of Louisiana in two volumes, entitled* Digeste des lois de la Louisiane; *and perhaps even more a course-book on civil procedure written in the two languages and entitled:* Traité sur les règles des actions civiles, *printed in 1830 in New Orleans, published by Buisson. This work presents a special advantage; it provides to the French an accurate and authentic explanation of English legal terms. The language of the law forms something like a separate language among all peoples, and among the English more than among any other.*

the jury.[3] They established it everywhere or hastened to reestablish it. A judicial institution that thus obtains the votes of a great people over a long succession of centuries, that is zealously reproduced at all periods of civilization, in all climates and under all forms of government cannot be contrary to the spirit of justice.[4]

[<Justice is one of the first needs of men, and there is no prejudice that can stifle it for long.>]

But let us leave this subject. It would singularly narrow your thought to limit yourself to envisioning the jury as a judicial institution; for, if it exercises a great influence on the outcome of trials, it exercises a very much greater one on the very destinies of society. So the jury is before all else a political institution. You must always judge it from this point of view.

I understand by jury a certain number of citizens taken at random and vested temporarily with the right to judge.

3. *All the English and American jurists are unanimous on this point. Mr. Story, Justice of the Supreme Court of the United States, in his [very fine] treatise on the federal Constitution returns again to the excellence of the institution of the jury in civil matters:* "The inestimable privilege of a trial by Jury in civil cases [is (ed.)]," *he says,* "a privilege scarcely inferior to that in criminal cases, which is conceded by all persons to be essential to political and civil liberty" *(Story, book III, ch. XXXVIII [p. 654 (ed.)]).*

4. *If you wanted to establish the utility of the jury as judicial institution, you would have many other arguments to offer, and among others the following:*

As you introduce jurors into affairs, you can without inconvenience diminish the number of judges; this is a great advantage. When judges are very numerous, each day death creates a gap in the judicial hierarchy and opens new places for those who survive. So the ambition of the magistrates is continually in suspense and makes them naturally depend on the majority or on the man who appoints to empty posts: then you advance in the courts like you gain rank in the army. It is a state of things entirely contrary to the good administration of justice and to the intentions of the legislator. You want the judges to be irremovable so that they remain free; but what good is it that no one can take their independence away from them if they willingly sacrifice it themselves?

When judges are very numerous, it is impossible not to find many incompetent men among them: for a great magistrate is not an ordinary man. Now, I do not know if a half-enlightened court is not the worst of all combinations in order to attain the ends that are set when establishing the courts of justice.

As for me, I would prefer to abandon the decision in a trial to ignorant jurors led by a skillful magistrate, than to leave it to judges, the majority of whom would have only an incomplete knowledge of jurisprudence and of the laws.

To apply the jury to the suppression of crime appears to me to introduce into the government an eminently republican institution. Let me explain.

The institution of the jury can be aristocratic or democratic, depending on the class from which you take the jurors; but it always retains a [an eminently] republican character, in that it places the real direction of society in the hands of the governed or of a portion of them, and not in the hands of those governing.

Force is never more than a fleeting element of success; soon after force comes the idea of right. A government reduced to being able to reach its enemies only on the field of battle would soon be destroyed. The true sanction of political laws is therefore found in the penal laws and if the sanction is lacking, the law sooner or later loses its force. So the man who judges in a *criminal court* is really the master of society. Now, the institution of the jury puts the people themselves, or at least a class of citizens, on the judge's bench. So the institution of the jury really puts the leadership of society into the hands of the people or of this class.[5]

In England, the jury is recruited from among the aristocratic portion of the nation. The aristocracy makes the laws, applies the laws and judges the infractions of the laws.[B] Everything is in accord: consequently England truly speaking forms an aristocratic republic. In the United States, the same system is applied to the whole people. Each American citizen is a voter and eligible for office and jury.[C] The system of the jury, such as it is understood in America, seems to me as direct and as extreme a consequence of the dogma of sovereignty of the people as universal suffrage. These are two equally powerful means to make the majority rule.

All the sovereigns who have wanted to draw the sources of their power from within themselves and lead society instead of letting themselves be led by society have destroyed the institution of the jury or have enervated

---

5. *An important remark must be made however:*

The institution of the jury, it is true, gives to the people a general right of control over the actions of the citizens, but it does not provide them with the means to exercise this control in all cases or in an always tyrannical manner.

When an absolute prince has the right to have crimes judged by his appointees, the fate of the accused is so to speak fixed in advance. But were the people resolved to condemn, the composition of the jury and its lack of accountability would still offer some favorable chances to the innocent.

it. The Tudors imprisoned jurors who would not condemn, and Napoleon had jurors chosen by his agents.

[It was the Bourbons who, in the year 1828, really reestablished among us the institution of the jury by making chance the principal arbiter of the choice of jurors. I cannot in this matter prevent myself from admiring the singular connection of events in this world. Bonaparte, who pretended to hold his right from the national will, made a law directly contrary to the sovereignty of the people, and the Bourbons, who said they held their right from themselves, returned the sanction to the hands of the people.[x]

The law of 1828 was, without the knowledge of those who passed it, an immense advance[y] made toward republican institutions in France. You would have noticed it clearly if the Restoration had not rushed headlong into an abyss. The jury thus emancipated would have been sufficient to bind the government little by little to the desires of the middle classes without having had the need to resort to force, because the majority of jurors was always found among the middle classes.]

However evident most of the preceding truths may be, they do not strike all minds, and often, among us, there still seems to be only a confused idea of the institution of the jury. If someone wants to know what elements should make up the list of jurors, the discussion is limited to considering the enlightenment and capacity of those called to be a part of the list, as if it was only a matter of a judicial institution. In truth, that seems to me to be preoccupied with the least portion of the subject. The jury is before all else a political institution; it should be considered as a mode of sovereignty of the people; it must be entirely rejected when you rule out the

x. To the side: "<*In note if included.*

"≠The cause for it is that the first attached more value to absolute power than to the right to exercise it [v: the appearance] while the second still preferred the aspect of the thing to the thing itself≠ {have the right to do everything rather than to use it.}>"

y. Édouard de Tocqueville:

"I would like an *immense step* instead of an *immense advance,* because a *step* may not be an *advance* and it is still very doubtful that it is one in this case. In any case I do not think that you wish to express yourself in this regard or that you should.

"This expression of *advance,* moreover, implies blame for the Bourbons who granted it without knowing, that is to say against their will. While the word *step* cannot include this sense" (YTC, CIIIb, 1, p. 66).

sovereignty of the people, or must be put in harmony with the other laws that establish this sovereignty. The jury forms the part of the nation charged with ensuring the execution of the laws, as the legislative houses are the part of the nation charged with making the laws; and for society to be governed in a fixed and uniform manner, it is necessary that the list of jurors be expanded or restricted with the list of voters. This is the point of view that, in my opinion, must always attract the principal attention of the legislator. The rest is so to speak secondary.

I am so persuaded that the jury is before all else a political institution that I still consider it in this way when it is applied to civil matters. [This can seem extraordinary at first glance. Here are my reasons for doing so.]

Laws are always shaky as long as they do not rely on mores; mores form the only resistant and enduring power among a people.

When the jury is reserved for criminal affairs, the people see it act only from time to time and in particular cases; they get used to doing without the jury in the ordinary course of life, and they consider it as a means and not as the only means for obtaining justice.[6]

When, on the contrary, the jury is extended to civil affairs, its application comes into view at every moment; then it touches all interests; each person comes to contribute to its action; in this way it enters into the customs of life; it bends the human spirit to its forms and merges so to speak with the very idea of justice.

So the institution of the jury, limited to criminal affairs, is always at risk; once introduced into civil matters, it stands up against time and the efforts of men. If you had been able to remove the jury from the mores of the English as easily as from their laws, the jury would have completely succumbed under the Tudors. So it is the civil jury that really saved the liberties of England.

In whatever manner you apply the jury, it cannot fail to exercise a great

---

6. *This is true for all the more reason when the jury is applied only to certain criminal affairs.*

influence on the national character, but this influence increases infinitely the more you introduce it into civil matters.

The jury, and above all the civil jury, serves to give the mind of all citizens a part of the habits of mind of the judge; and these habits are precisely those that best prepare the people to be free.

It spreads in all classes respect for the thing judged and for the idea of right. Remove these two things, and the love of independence will be nothing but a destructive passion.

It teaches men the practice of equity. Each person, by judging his neighbor, thinks that he can be judged in his turn. That is above all true of the jury in civil matters: there is hardly anyone who fears one day being the object of a criminal proceeding; but everyone can have a civil trial.

The jury teaches each man not to retreat from responsibility for his own actions; a manly disposition, without which there is no political virtue.

It vests each citizen with a sort of magistracy; it makes all feel that they have duties to fulfill toward society and that they enter into its government. By forcing men to get involved in something other than their own affairs, it combats individual egoism, which is like the rust of societies [{that ruins nations more than armies do}].

The jury serves unbelievably to form the judgment and to augment the natural enlightenment of the people. That, in my opinion, is its greatest advantage. You must consider it as a free school, always open, where each juror comes to be instructed about his rights, where he enters into daily communication with the most learned and most enlightened members of the upper classes, where the laws are taught to him in a practical way, and are put within the reach of his intelligence by the efforts of the lawyers, the advice of the judge and the very passions of the parties. I think that the practical intelligence and good political sense of the Americans must be attributed principally to the long use that they have made of the jury in civil matters.

I do not know if the jury is useful to those who have legal proceedings, but I am sure that it is very useful to those who judge them. I regard it as one of the most effective means that a society can use for the education of the people.

What precedes applies to all nations; but here is what is special to the Americans, and in general to democratic peoples.

I said above that in democracies the jurists, and among them the magistrates, form the only aristocratic body that can moderate the movements of the people. This aristocracy is vested with no physical power; it exercises its conservative influence only over minds. Now, it is in the institution of the civil jury that it finds the principal sources of its power.

In criminal trials, where society struggles against a man, the jury is led to see in the judge the passive instrument of the social power, and it distrusts his advice. Moreover, criminal trials rest entirely on simple facts that good sense easily comes to appreciate. On this ground, judge and juror are equal.

It is not the same in civil trials; then the judge appears as a disinterested arbiter between the passions of the parties. The jurors view him with confidence, and they listen to him with respect; for here his intelligence entirely dominates theirs. He is the one who lays out before them the diverse arguments that have fatigued their memory and who takes them by the hand to lead them through the twists and turns of procedure; he is the one who confines them to the point of fact and teaches them the answer that they must give to the question of law. His influence over them is almost without limits.

Is it necessary to say finally why I am so little moved by arguments drawn from the incapacity of jurors in civil matters?

In civil trials, at least whenever it is not a matter of questions of fact, the jury has only the appearance of a judicial body.

The jurors deliver the decision that the judge has rendered. They lend to this decision the authority of the society that they represent and he, the authority of reason and the law.D

In England and in America, judges exercise an influence over the fate of criminal trials that the French judge has never known. It is easy to understand the reason for this difference: the English or American magistrate has established his power in civil matters; afterward he is only exercising it in another theater; he is not gaining it there.

There are cases, and they are often the most important ones, where the

American judge has the right to deliver a verdict alone.[7] He then finds himself, by happenstance, in the position where the French judge usually finds himself; but his moral power is very much greater: the memories of the jury still follow him, and his voice has almost as much power as that of the society of which the jurors were the organ.

His influence extends even well beyond the courtroom: in the diversions of private life as in the labors of political life, in the public square as within the legislatures, the American judge constantly finds around him men who are used to seeing in his intelligence something superior to their own; and, after being exercised in trials, his power makes itself felt in all the habits of mind and even on the very souls of those who have participated with him in judging.

So the jury, which seems to diminish the rights of the magistracy, really establishes its dominion, and there is no country where judges are as powerful as those where the people share their privileges.

With the aid of the jury in civil matters, above all, the American magistracy makes what I have called the spirit of the jurist enter into the lowest ranks of society.

Thus the jury, which is the most energetic means to make the people rule, is also the most effective means to teach them to rule.[z]

---

7. *Federal judges almost always decide alone questions that touch most closely on the government of the country.*

z. Among Beaumont's documents relative to the discussion of the constitutional committee of 1848, the following note is found, which gives an account of an intervention by Tocqueville concerning the jury: "Tocqueville sees a disadvantage in an immediate, absolute and general application of the jury in civil matters. Singular mixture sometimes of fact and law. Necessity of very enlightened public mores. Greater necessity of a more capable jury because of the difficulty of functions. Who says jury says *suppression* in nearly all cases of the double degree of jurisdiction. Great difficulty in leading the jury" (YTC, Beaumont, DIVk).

CHAPTER 9

Of the Principal Causes That Tend to Maintain the Democratic Republic in the United States[a]

The democratic republic[b] survives in the United States. The principal goal of this book has been to make the causes of this phenomenon understood.

The flow of my subject carried me, despite myself, close to several of these causes that I pointed out only from afar in passing. I could not deal with others. And those that I was allowed to expand upon have been left behind as if buried under details.

So I thought that before going further and speaking about the future, I had to gather together in a narrow scope all the reasons that explain the present.

In this type of summary I will be brief, for I will take care to recall only very summarily to the reader what he already knows, and among the facts that I have not yet had the occasion to put forth, I will choose only the principal ones.

I thought that all the causes that tend to maintain the democratic republic[c] in the United States could be reduced to three:[d]

---

a. At first this chapter was the last in the book; the tenth was added later.

Melvin Richter ("The Uses of Theory: Tocqueville's Adaptation of Montesquieu," in *Essays in Theory and History,* Cambridge: Harvard University Press, 1970, pp. 74–102) compares the method of Tocqueville in this chapter with that followed by Montesquieu in *Esprit des lois.*

b. In the manuscript: "A large democratic republic . . ."

c. The manuscript says: ". . . the large democratic republic . . ."

d. ≠Of the three causes the least influential is that of laws and it is, so to speak, the only one that depends on man. Peoples cannot change their position and the first

The particular and accidental situation in which Providence placed the Americans forms the first;

The second results from laws;

The third follows from habits and mores.

Of the Accidental or Providential Causes That Contribute to Maintaining the Democratic Republic in the United States[e]

The Union does not have neighbors.—No large capital.—The Americans have had the good fortune of birth in their favor.— America is an empty country.—How this circumstance serves powerfully to maintain the democratic republic.—Manner in which the wilderness of America is populated.—Eagerness of the Anglo-Americans to take possession of the empty wilderness areas of the New World.—Influence of material well-being on the political opinions of the Americans.

---

conditions of their existence. A nation can in the long run modify its habits and its mores, but a generation cannot succeed in doing so. It can only change the laws. [In the margin: But what can the best laws do without circumstances and mores?] Now, of the three causes that we are speaking about, the least influential is precisely that which results from laws. So not only does man not exercise power around himself, but he possesses so to speak none over himself and remains almost completely a stranger to his own fate≠ (YTC, CVh, 4, p. 19).

e. At first this part was entitled: *What Tends {to Moderate the Omnipotence of the Majority in America} to Make the Democratic Republic Practicable in America.* The first sentences of the initial draft show that this part was a continuation of that on the tyranny of the majority: "≠The causes that tend to moderate the omnipotence of the majority in the United States and to make the democratic republic practicable arise from the particular circumstances in which the country is or was, from laws and from mores.≠"

A note in the margin specifies: "≠To put immediately after the omnipotence of the majority what serves more particularly as a counterweight to it and then what in general favors the republic, for the omnipotence of the majority, which is the greatest obstacle to maintaining republics, is not the only one.≠"

There are a thousand circumstances[f] independent of the will of men that make it easy to have the democratic republic in the United States. Some are known, others are easy to make known: I will limit myself to explaining the principal ones.

The Americans do not have neighbors,[g] consequently no great wars, financial crisis, ravages, nor conquest to fear; they need neither heavy taxes nor a numerous army, nor great generals; they have almost nothing to fear from a plague more terrible for republics than all the others put together, military glory.

How to deny the incredible influence that military glory exercises on the spirit of the people? General Jackson, whom the Americans have twice chosen to put at their head, is a man of violent character and middling capacity; nothing in all the course of his career had ever proved that he had the qualities necessary to govern a free people; consequently, the majority of the enlightened classes of the Union have always been opposed to him. So who put him in the President's seat and still keeps him there? The memory of a victory won by him, twenty years ago, under the walls of New Orleans; now, this victory of New Orleans is a very ordinary feat of arms which cannot be of much interest for long except in a country where no battles are fought; and the people who allow themselves to be thus carried away

f. James T. Schleifer (*The Making of Tocqueville's "Democracy in America*," p. 61) noted that the meaning of the word "circumstances" appreciably narrows from the drafts to the final version and ends by designating only physical circumstances. It can be added, in the same way, that the importance of the influence of climate, as has been seen elsewhere, is manifestly greater in the drafts and manuscript than in the final version.

During his journey, as the correspondence attests, Tocqueville accorded a great importance to climatic conditions: "When you see men who tell you that climate does nothing to the constitution of peoples, assure them that they are mistaken. We saw the French of Canada: they are a tranquil, moral, religious people; in Louisiana we left other French who were restless, dissolute, lax in everything. Between them was 15 degrees of latitude; that is in truth the best reason that I can give for the difference" (Letter to Ernest de Chabrol of 16 January 1832, YTC, BIa2). Also see *Correspondance avec Kergorlay, OC,* XIII, 1, pp. 225–36 and a letter of 1829, before the American journey, in *Correspondance avec Beaumont, OC,* VIII, 1, pp. 93–94.

g. For Rousseau, the absence of conflicts with neighbors constitutes one of the conditions for the existence of a good body of laws (*Du contrat social,* book II, chapter X, in *Oeuvres complètes,* Paris: Pléiade, 1964, III, p. 389). Jefferson often repeated the same idea.

by the prestige of glory is, certainly, the coldest, most calculating, least military and, if I can put it this way, the most prosaic of all the peoples of the world.[*] h

America has no large capital[1] whose direct or indirect influence is felt over the whole extent of the territory; I consider this one of the first causes for maintaining republican institutions in the United States.j In cities, you can hardly prevent men from consulting each other, from getting worked

[*]. {which has not prevented one of our compatriots who became American forty years ago} ≠During our visit to America a medal was struck in honor of G[ener (ed.)]al. J[ackson (ed.)] having as an inscription: "quod Caesar fecit Jackson superavit," which could have seemed a pleasant jest, but the author did not intend it as a joke. It is true that this unfortunate flatterer was a former French republican, a very ardent enemy of kings and the vices of the royal court [Edmond-Charles Genêt (ed.)].≠

h. This paragraph appears almost literally in a note of 1 November 1831 (pocket notebook 3, YTC, BIIa, and *Voyage, OC,* V, 1, p. 186). Tocqueville and Beaumont met Andrew Jackson on 19 January 1832. The evening spent at the White House seems hardly to have impressed the two Frenchmen favorably. Nor did it modify their opinion about the American President. Beaumont gave an account of this visit in a letter to his mother (*Lettres d'Amérique,* pp. 210–11). Also see George W. Pierson, *Tocqueville and Beaumont in America,* pp. 663–66.

1. *America does not yet have a large capital, but it already has three large cities. In 1830, Philadelphia numbered 161,000 inhabitants, and New York 202,000. The lower classes who inhabit these vast cities form a populace more dangerous than even that of Europe. It is made up first of all of emancipated Negroes, who are condemned by law and opinion to a state of hereditary degradation and misery. Also in its midst is found a multitude of Europeans pushed daily by misfortune and loose behavior to the shores of the New World; these men bring to the United States our worst vices, and they have none of the interests that could combat the influence of those vices. Inhabiting the country without being citizens, they are ready to take advantage of all the passions that agitate the country; consequently we have for some time seen serious riots break out in Philadelphia and New York. Such disorders are unknown in the rest of the country, which is not worried about them, because until now the city population has not exercised any power or any influence on the rural population.*

I regard the large size of certain American cities and above all the nature of their inhabitants, however, as a genuine danger that threatens the future of the democratic republics of the New World, and I am not afraid to predict that it is there that they will perish, unless their government succeeds in creating an armed force that, while remaining subject to the will of the national majority, is nevertheless independent of the people of the cities and can repress their excesses.

j. Compare chapter VIII of book II of *Ancien Régime et la Révolution* (*OC,* II, 1, pp. 139–40), where Tocqueville cites the Marquis de Mirabeau and Montesquieu on the same theme. Later, the great anti-metropolitan will be Rousseau (*Du contrat social,* book III, chapter XIII, *Oeuvres complètes,* Paris: Pléiade, 1964, III, p. 427).

up together, from making sudden and impassioned resolutions. Cities form like great assemblies of which all the inhabitants are members. The people exercise a prodigious influence over their magistrates there, and often the people execute their will there without intermediary.

So to subject the provinces to the capital is to put the destiny of the whole empire, not only in the hands of a portion of the people, which is unjust, but also to put it in the hands of the people acting by themselves, which is very dangerous. So the preponderance of capitals strikes a grave blow at the representative system. It makes modern republics succumb to the fault of the ancient republics which all perished from not knowing this system.

It would be easy for me to enumerate here a great number of other secondary causes that have favored the establishment and assure the maintenance of the democratic republics in the United States. But in the middle of this host of fortunate circumstances, I see two principal ones, and I hasten to point them out.

I have already said previously that I saw in the origin of the Americans, in what I called their point of departure, the first and most effective of all the causes to which the present prosperity of the United States could be attributed. The Americans have had the good fortune of birth in their favor: long ago their fathers imported to the land that they inhabit equality of conditions and intellectual equality, from which the democratic republic was bound to emerge one day as if from its natural source. This is still not all; with a republican social state, they passed on to their descendants the habits, ideas and mores most appropriate to make the republic flourish. When I think about what this original fact produced, I seem to see the whole destiny of America contained in the first Puritan who reached its shores, like the whole human race in the first man.

Among the fortunate circumstances that also have favored the establishment and assure the maintenance of the democratic republic in the United States, the first in importance is the choice of the country itself that the Americans inhabit. Their fathers gave them the love of equality and liberty, but it is God who, by giving them an unlimited continent, granted them the means to remain equal and free for a long time.[k]

k. To the side: "≠When a king finds himself troubled by his neighbors, he goes to war; when the people are discontent with their position, they make a revolution.≠"

General well-being favors the stability of all governments, but particularly of democratic government, which rests upon the dispositions of the greatest number, and principally on the dispositions of those who are the most exposed to needs. When the people govern, they must be happy so that they do not overturn the State. Misery produces among them what ambition does among kings. Now, causes that are material and independent of the laws and that can lead to well-being are more numerous in America than they have been in any country in the world, in any period of history. [In Europe the culmination of good laws is to produce well-being; in America all the work of bad laws would scarcely succeed in preventing well-being from being produced.]

In the United States, it is not only legislation that is democratic; nature itself works for the people.

Where to find, in the memory of man, anything resembling what is happening before our eyes in North America?

The famous societies of antiquity were all founded in the midst of enemy peoples who had to be conquered for those societies to be established in their place. Modern peoples have found in several parts of South America vast countries inhabited by peoples who were less enlightened than they, but who had already appropriated the soil by cultivating it. To establish their new States, they had to destroy or subjugate large populations, and they made civilization ashamed of their triumphs.

But North America was inhabited only by wandering tribes who did not think of using the natural riches of the soil. North America was still, properly speaking, a vacant continent, a deserted land, that awaited inhabitants.

Everything is extraordinary among the Americans, their social state as well as their laws; but what is still more extraordinary is the land that holds them.

When the earth was given to men by the Creator, it was young and inexhaustible,[m] but they were weak and ignorant; and when they had learned to take advantage of the treasures that it held in its bosom, they already

m. In the manuscript: "When God created the globe He at once gave part of it over to the efforts of its inhabitants. Providence held the rest in reserve, destined for happier generations.
"The land that thus became the first inheritance of man was young . . ."

covered the face of the land, and soon they had to fight to gain the right to have a refuge and to dwell in liberty.

That is when North America comes into sight, as if God had held it in reserve and it had only just emerged from the waters of the flood.

It presents, as at the first days of creation, rivers whose sources do not run dry, green and moist wildernesses, limitless fields not yet broken by the farmer's plow. In this state, it is no longer offered to the isolated, ignorant and barbaric man of the earliest ages, but to the man already master of the most important secrets of nature, united with his fellows, and educated by an experience of fifty centuries.

At the moment I speak, thirteen million civilized Europeans are spreading tranquilly across fertile wilderness areas whose resources or extent they do not yet exactly know. Three or four thousand soldiers push before them the wandering race of natives; behind the armed men, woodsmen advance who pierce the forests, drive away the wild game, explore the course of rivers and prepare the triumphant march of civilization across the wilderness.

Often, in the course of this work, I have alluded to the material well-being that the Americans enjoy; I have pointed it out as one of the great causes for the success of their laws. This reason had already been given by a thousand others before me: it is the only one that, falling in a way within the awareness of the Europeans, has become popular among us. So I will not expand upon a subject so often treated and so well understood; I will only add several new facts.[n]

It is generally imagined that the wilderness of America is populated with the help of European emigrants who arrive each year on the shores of the New World, while the American population increases and multiplies on the soil that their fathers occupied: that is a great error. The European who reaches the United States arrives there without friends and often without resources; to live, he is forced to hire out his services, and it is rare to see him go beyond the large industrial zone that extends along the ocean. You

---

n. In the margin: "≠The Americans are so fortunate that everything, even including their *vices,* is useful to them."

cannot clear the wilderness without capital or credit;[*] before risking your-self in the middle of the forest, the body must become accustomed to the rigors of a new climate. So it is the Americans who, daily abandoning the place of their birth, go to create for themselves vast domains far away. Thus the European leaves his cottage to go to inhabit the transatlantic shores, and the American, who is born on these very shores, disappears in turn into the emptiness of the central part of America. This double movement of emigration never stops: it begins in the heart of Europe, it continues across the great ocean, it keeps on across the solitude of the New World. Millions of men march at the same time toward the same point of the horizon: their language, their religion, their mores differ, their goal is shared. They have been told that fortune is found somewhere toward the West, and they go in haste to find it.[o] [What are they going to do, in what precise place must they stop? They themselves do not know, but they march forward guided by the hand of God.]

Nothing can be compared with this continual displacement of the hu-man species, except perhaps what happened at the fall of the Roman Em-pire. Then, as today, you saw men rush all in a throng toward the same point and meet turbulently in the same places; but the designs of Provi-dence were different. [Then God wanted to destroy; today He wants to create.] Each new arrival brought in his train destruction and death; today each of them carries with him a seed of prosperity and life.

The distant consequences of this migration of the Americans toward the West is still hidden from us by the future, but the immediate results are easy to recognize: because one part of the former inhabitants moves each year away from the states where they were born, these states, as they grow older, are becoming populated only very slowly; thus in Connecticut, which still numbers only fifty-nine inhabitants per square mile, the population has only grown by a quarter during the past forty years, while in England it has increased by a third during the same period. So the emigrant from Europe always arrives in a country half-full where industry needs hands; he

[*]. A note of explanation and details.
o. Cf. note h for p. 1313 of volume II.

becomes a worker who is well-off; his son goes to find his fortune in an empty country and becomes a wealthy landowner. The first amasses the capital that the second turns to good account, and there is no poverty either among the foreigners or among the natives.

Legislation, in the United States, favors as much as possible the division of property; but a cause more powerful than legislation prevents property from dividing too much.[2] You can see it clearly in the states that are finally beginning to fill up. Massachusetts is the most populated country in the Union; the inhabitants number eighty per square mile, which is infinitely fewer than in France, where there are one hundred sixty-two gathered in the same space.

In Massachusetts, however, it is quite rare that small estates are divided: the eldest generally takes the land; the younger go to find their fortune in the wilderness.

The law abolished the right of primogeniture; but you can say that Providence reestablished it without anyone having to complain, and this time at least it does not offend justice.

You will judge by a single fact the prodigious number of individuals who leave New England in this way to go to move their homes into the wilderness. We are assured that in 1830, among the members of Congress, there were thirty-six who were born in the small state of Connecticut. So the population of Connecticut, which forms only one forty-third of that of the United States, provides one-eighth of the representatives.[p]

The state of Connecticut itself, however, sends only five representatives to Congress: the thirty-one others appear there as representatives of the new states of the West. If these thirty-one individuals had remained in Connecticut, it is probable that instead of being rich landowners, they would have remained small farmers and lived in obscurity without being able to open a political career, and that, far from becoming useful legislators, they would have been dangerous citizens

---

2. *In New England, the land is divided into small estates, but it is no longer being divided.*

p. Tocqueville got this information from Judge Dens of Hartford (non-alphabetic notebooks 2 and 3, YTC, BIIa, and *Voyage, OC,* V, 1, p. 102).

These considerations do not escape the mind of the Americans any more than ours.

Chancellor Kent writes in his *Commentaries on American Law* (vol. IV, p. 380):

> It cannot be doubted that the division of property will produce great evils when it is carried to the extreme; to the extent that each portion of land can no longer provide for the support of a family; but these disadvantages have never been felt in the United States, and many generations will pass before they are felt. The immense area of our uninhabited territory, the abundance of adjacent lands and the continual flow of emigration that, departing from the shores of the Atlantic, goes constantly into the interior of the country, are sufficient and will be sufficient to prevent the breaking up of inherited lands for a long time yet to come.

It would be difficult to portray the greediness with which the American throws himself on this immense prize that fortune offers him. To pursue it he fearlessly defies the Indian's arrow and the diseases of the wilderness; the silence of the woods holds nothing that astonishes him, the approach of ferocious beasts does not rouse him; a stronger passion than love of life constantly spurs him on. Before him extends a continent nearly without limits, and you would say that, already afraid of having no room there, he hurries for fear of arriving too late. I spoke about the emigration from the old states, but what will I say about that from the new? Not fifty years ago Ohio was founded; most of its inhabitants were not born there; its capital has not existed thirty years, and an immense expanse of uninhabited country still covers its territory; the population of Ohio, however, has already started to march again toward the West; most of those who come into the fertile prairies of Illinois are inhabitants of Ohio. These men have left their first home to be comfortable; they leave the second to be still better off: nearly everywhere, they find fortune, but not happiness. Among them, the desire for well-being has become a restless and ardent passion that grows as it is being satisfied. Formerly they broke the ties that bound them to their birthplace; they have formed no other ties since. For them, emigration began as a need; today, it has become in their eyes a kind of game of chance, which they love for the emotions as much as for the gain.

Sometimes man moves so quickly that the wilderness reappears behind him. The forest has only bent under his feet; the moment he passes, it rises up again. It is not unusual, while traveling through the new states of the West, to encounter abandoned dwellings in the middle of the woods; often you find the ruins of a cabin in the deepest solitude, and you are amazed while crossing rough-hewn clearings that attest simultaneously to human power and inconstancy. Among these abandoned fields, over these day old ruins, the ancient forest does not delay growing new shoots; the animals retake possession of their realm; nature comes happily to cover the vestiges of man with green branches and flowers and hastens to make the ephemeral trace of man disappear.

I remember that while crossing⁹ one of the uninhabited districts that still cover the state of New York, I reached the shores of a lake entirely surrounded by forests as at the beginning of the world. A small island arose in the middle of the water. The woods that covered it, spreading their foliage, entirely hid its banks. On the shores of the lake, nothing announced the presence of man; you noticed only a column of smoke on the horizon that, going straight up into the clouds above the top of the trees, seemed to hang from rather than rise into the sky.

An Indian canoe was pulled onto the sand. I took advantage of it to go to visit the island that had first attracted my attention and soon after I reached its shore. The entire island formed one of those delightful uninhabited places of the New World that almost make civilized men feel nostalgia for savage life. A vigorous vegetation proclaimed by its wonders the incomparable fertility of the soil. As in all the wildernesses of North America, a profound silence reigned that was interrupted only by the monotonous cooing of the woodpigeons or by the blows that the woodpecker struck on the bark of the trees. I was very far from believing that this place had formerly been inhabited, nature there seemed so left to itself; but upon reaching the center of the island, I suddenly thought that I had found vestiges of man. Then I carefully examined all the objects in the area, and soon

q. The manuscript adds "by chance." It is not at all by chance that Tocqueville found himself in this sparsely inhabited region of the state of New York. He was there expressly to visit the island that he describes here (see appendix I, *Voyage to Lake Oneida*).

I no longer doubted that a European had come to find a refuge in this place. But how his work had changed appearance! The woods that, long ago, he had hastily cut down to make himself a shelter had since grown shoots; his fence had become living hedges, and his cabin had been transformed into a grove. In the middle of these bushes you still saw a few stones blackened by fire, scattered around a small pile of ashes; undoubtedly this was the place of the hearth: the chimney, collapsing, had covered it with debris. For some time I admired in silence the resources of nature and the weakness of man; and when finally I had to leave these enchanted places, I again repeated with sadness: What! Ruins already![r]

In Europe we are used to regarding as a great social danger restlessness of spirit, immoderate desire for wealth, extreme love of independence. These are precisely all the things that guarantee a long and peaceful future to the American republic. Without these restless passions, the population would concentrate around certain places and, as among us, would soon experience needs difficult to satisfy. How fortunate a country is the New World, where the vices of man are nearly as useful to society as his virtues!

This exercises a great influence on the way in which human actions are judged in the two hemispheres. Often the Americans call praiseworthy industry what we name love of gain, and they see a certain cowardice of heart in what we consider moderation of desires.

In France, simplicity of tastes, tranquillity of mores, spirit of family and love of birthplace are regarded as great guarantees of tranquillity and happiness for the State; but in America, nothing seems more prejudicial to society than such virtues. The French of Canada, who have faithfully preserved the traditions of the old mores, already find it difficult to live in their territory, and this small group of people just born will soon be prey to the miseries of old nations. In Canada, the men who have the most enlightenment, patriotism and humanity, make extraordinary efforts to give the

r. Hervé de Tocqueville: "I believe that in this place Alexis should add a note that would say a few words about the story of the emigrant" (YTC, CIIIb, 1, p. 57).

people a distaste for the simple happiness that is still enough for them. These men celebrate the advantages of wealth, just as among us they would perhaps praise the charms of honest mediocrity, and they take more care to incite human passions than is taken elsewhere to calm such passions. Nothing in their eyes merits more praises than to exchange the pure and tranquil pleasures presented by the native country to the poor man for the sterile enjoyments provided by well-being under a foreign sky; to flee the paternal hearth and the fields where his ancestors rest; to abandon the living and the dead in order to run after fortune.

In our time, America offers men resources always greater than the industry that develops those resources can be.

So in America, you cannot provide enough enlightenment; for all enlightenment, at the same time that it can be useful to whoever possesses it, still turns to the profit of those who do not. New needs are not to be feared there, because all needs are satisfied without difficulty. You do not have to fear giving birth to too many passions, because all passions find an easy and salutary means of satisfaction. You cannot make men too free, because they are almost never tempted to make bad use of liberty.

The American republics of today are like companies of merchants formed to exploit in common the uninhabited lands of the New World and occupied with a prospering commerce.

The passions that most profoundly agitate the Americans are commercial passions and not political passions, or rather they carry into politics the habits of business. They love order, without which business cannot prosper, and they particularly prize regularity of mores, which lays the foundation of good business establishments; they prefer good sense, which creates great fortunes, to genius, which often dissipates them; general ideas frighten their minds, accustomed to positive calculations, and among the Americans, practice is more honored than theory.

You must go to America to understand what power material well-being[s] exercises over political actions and even over opinions themselves, which should be subject only to reason. It is among foreigners that you principally

s. See chapter X of the second part of the second volume.

discover the truth of this. Most of the emigrants from Europe bring to the
New World the wild love of independence and change that is so often born
out of the midst of our miseries. I sometimes met in the United States
some of those Europeans who formerly had been forced to flee their country because of their political opinions. All astonished me by their speeches;
but I was struck by one of them more than any other. As I crossed one of
the most distant districts of Pennsylvania, night surprised me, and I went
to ask for shelter at the door of a wealthy planter: he was a Frenchman. He
made me sit down beside his hearth, and we began to talk freely, as happens
to men who find themselves in the depths of the forest two thousand
leagues from the country where they were born. I was not unaware that
forty years ago my host had been a great leveler and an ardent demagogue.
His name was known to history.[t]

So I was strangely surprised to hear him discuss the right of property as
an economist, I was almost going to say a landholder, would be able to do;
he spoke of the necessary hierarchy that fortune establishes among men,
of obedience to established law, of the influence of good mores in republics,
of the aid that religious ideas lend to order and to liberty: he even cited as
if by accident, in support of one of his political opinions, the authority of
Jesus Christ.

While listening to him, I wondered at the weakness of human reason.
Something is either true or false; how to find out amid the uncertainties of
knowledge and the diverse lessons of experience? A new fact arises that
relieves all my doubts. I was poor, now I am rich; if at least well-being,
while acting upon my conduct, left my judgment free! But no, my opinions
have indeed changed with my fortune, and in the happy outcome from
which I profit, I have really discovered the decisive reason that I had lacked
until then.

Well-being exercises an influence still more freely over the Americans
than over foreigners. The American has always seen before his eyes order
and public prosperity linked together and marching in step, he does not
imagine that they can live separately; so he has nothing to forget, and, unlike

t. This person has not been identified.

so many Europeans, does not need to lose what he retains from his first education.

[Political society, however, is constantly agitated in the United States. But the movement is slow and measured. It influences the details and not the whole of public fortune. It bears more upon men than upon principles. You want to improve constantly, but are afraid of upsetting things; and while desiring the best, you are even more afraid of the worst.

What could I add to succeed in making my thought understood? What occurred to so many of the French republicans under the Empire and to some of the liberals of today happens to the *majority* of men in America. They find in the end that society does well, or nearly so, because they are doing well.]

Of the Influence of Laws on Maintaining the Democratic Republic in the United States

Three principal causes for maintaining the democratic republic.—Federal form.—Town institutions.— Judicial power.

[≠The second general cause that I pointed out as serving to maintain the political institutions of the Americans is found in the very goodness of these institutions, that is to say in their conformity to the social state and physical position.≠]

The principal goal of this book was to make the laws of the United States known; if this goal has been reached, the reader has already been able to judge for himself which ones, among these laws, tend really to maintain the democratic republic and which ones put it in danger. If I have not succeeded in the whole course of this book, I will succeed even less in this chapter.

So I do not want to pursue the course that I have already covered, and a few lines must suffice for me to summarize.

Three causes seem to contribute more than all the others to maintaining the democratic republic in the New World:

The first is the federal form that the Americans adopted, and that allows the Union to enjoy the power of a large republic and the security of a small one.

I find the second in the town institutions that, by moderating[u] the despotism of the majority, give the people at the same time the taste for liberty and the art of being free.

The third is found in the constitution of the judicial power. I have shown how much the courts serve to correct the errors of democracy and how, without ever being able to stop the movements of the majority, they succeed in slowing and directing them.

Of the Influence of Mores on Maintaining the Democratic Republic in the United States

I said above that I considered the mores as one of the great general causes to which maintaining the democratic republic in the United States can be attributed.

I understand the expression *mores* here in the sense that the ancients attached to the word *mores;* I apply it not only to mores strictly speaking, which could be called habits of the heart, but to the different notions that men possess, to the diverse opinions that are current among them, and to the ensemble of ideas from which the habits of the mind are formed.[v]

So by this word I understand the whole moral and intellectual state of

u. The manuscript says "by preventing."

v. "I understand by *mores* the whole of the dispositions that man brings to the government of society. Mores strictly speaking, enlightenment, habits, knowledge . . ." (YTC, CVh, 3, p. 58).

Melvin Richter ("The Uses of Theory: Tocqueville's Adaptation of Montesquieu," in *Essays in Theory and History,* Cambridge: Harvard University Press, 1970, pp. 90–91) remarks that Tocqueville, by the term *mores,* designates all that Montesquieu understood by *general spirit:* precedents, mores, habits, economy, style of thought, etc.—with the exception of laws, which he considers apart. But the explanation, which ascribes such a meaning to Tocqueville's bad memory and imprecision of method, is difficult to accept. The distinction between laws and mores seems more understandable if you refer to Rousseau, who defines and understands mores in a fashion quite similar to that of Tocqueville. On this point as on others, Tocqueville read Montesquieu through Rousseau. See *Du contrat social,* book II, chapter XII, *Œuvres complètes,* Paris: Pléiade, 1964, III, pp. 393–94.

a people. My goal is not to draw a picture of American mores; I limit myself at this moment to trying to find out what among them is favorable for maintaining the political institutions.

Of Religion Considered as a Political Institution, How It Serves Powerfully to Maintain the Democratic Republic among the Americans[*]

North America populated by men who professed a democratic and republican Christianity.—Arrival of Catholics.—Why today Catholics form the most democratic and the most republican class.

Alongside each religion is found a political opinion that is joined to it by affinity.[w]

Allow the human spirit to follow its tendency, and it will regulate in a uniform way political society and the holy city; it will seek, if I dare say so, to *harmonize* earth with heaven.[x]

Most of English America was populated by men who, after escaping from the authority of the Pope, submitted to no religious supremacy; so they brought to the New World a Christianity that I cannot portray better than by calling it democratic and republican: this will singularly favor the establishment of the republic and of democracy in public affairs. From the onset, politics and religion found themselves in accord, and they have not ceased to be so since.

[*]. ≠I will examine in the second volume the state of religion in the United States, the sects, the religious mores. Here I am considering it only from the political point of view.≠

w. "Who could deny the fortunate influence of religion on mores and the influence of mores on the government of society?/

"The people see in religion the safeguard and the divine origin of liberty; the rich, the guarantee of their fortune and their life; the statesmen, the safeguard of society; the pioneer, something like his companion in the wilderness" (YTC, CVh, 3, p. 57).

x. In the margin in the first version: "≠Despotism can do without religion, but not liberty.

"Unanimity of statesmen on the utility of religion.≠"

About fifty years ago Ireland began to pour a Catholic population into the United States. For its part, American Catholicism made converts.[y] Today in the Union you find more than a million Christians who profess the truths of the Roman Church.

These Catholics show a great fidelity to the observances of their religion, and are full of ardor and zeal for their beliefs; however, they form the most republican and most democratic class that exists in the United States. This fact is a surprise at first glance, but reflection easily discloses the hidden causes.

[Christianity, even when it demands passive obedience in matters of dogma, is still of all religious doctrines the one most favorable to liberty, because it appeals only to the mind and heart of those whom it wants to bring into subjection.[z] No religion has so disdained the use of physical force as the religion of J[esus (ed.)]. C[hrist (ed.)]. Now, wherever physical force is not honored, tyranny cannot endure. Therefore you see that despotism has never been able to be established among Christians.[a] It has always lived there from day to day and in a state of alarm. When we say that a Christian nation is enslaved, it is in comparison to a Christian people that we judge. If we compare it to an infidel people, the Christian nation would seem free to us.

y. In the manuscript: "American Catholicism spread for its part by numerous conversions."

z. In a first version of the drafts, this sentence is also found: ". . . wants to bring into subjection. If it loves to rule despotically over the will of man, it is after the will has by itself bent to its yoke. No religion . . ." (YTC, CVh, 3, p. 49).

a. Hervé de Tocqueville:

Édouard's advice is to delete this piece up to the words *among the different Christian doctrines.*

I share his opinion concerning only the first paragraph. It is not useful and besides many claims can be challenged. The author says: *no religion has so disdained the use of physical force as much as the religion of Jesus Christ.* Someone will put forward the Albigensians, the Inquisition, the massacre of the Cévennes, etc. Later *despotism has never been able to be established among Christians* is found. Someone will reply by citing Spain since Philip II.

The paragraph on equality, which goes straight to the point and serves as a transition, must be kept here (YTC, CIIIb, 1, pp. 50–51).

I will say something analogous concerning equality.

Of all religious doctrines, Christianity, whatever interpretation you give it, is also the one most favorable to equality. Only the religion of J[esus (ed.)]. C[hrist (ed.)]. has placed the sole grandeur of man in the accomplishment of duties, where each person can attain it; and has been pleased to consecrate poverty and hardship, as something nearly divine.

I will add that among the different Christian doctrines, Catholicism seems to me one of the least contrary to the leveling of conditions.]

I think that it is wrong to regard the Catholic religion as a natural enemy of democracy. Among the different Christian doctrines, Catholicism seems to me on the contrary one of the most favorable to equality of conditions. Among Catholics, religious society is composed of only two elements: priest and people. The priest alone rises above the faithful; everything is equal below him.[b]

In matters of dogma, Catholicism places all minds on the same level; it subjects to the details of the same beliefs the learned as well as the ignorant, the man of genius as well as the common man; it imposes the same observances on the rich as on the poor, inflicts the same austerities on the powerful as on the weak; it compromises with no mortal, and by applying the same measure to each human being, it loves to mix all classes of society together at the foot of the same altar, as they are mixed together in the eyes of God.

So, if Catholicism disposes the faithful to obedience, it does not prepare them for inequality. I will say the opposite about Protestantism,[c] which, in general, carries men much less toward equality than toward independence.[d]

b. In the margin: "≠Catholicism favors the spirit of equality in the manner of absolute power. It places one man beyond all rank and leaves all the others mingled together in the crowd.≠"

c. "Protestantism is the government of the middle classes applied to the religious world" (YTC, CVh, 2, p. 85).

d. Hervé de Tocqueville: "I would delete this sentence for three reasons: 1. It implies a sort of contradiction with the beginning of the chapter where the author attributes to Protestantism the calm and regular establishment of democracy. 2. The thought is little developed. 3. The sentence is not useful here" (YTC, CIIIb, 1, pp. 51–52).

Catholicism is like an absolute monarchy. Remove the prince, and conditions there are more equal than in republics.[e]

The Catholic priest has often come out of the sanctuary to enter into society as a power, and he has come to take a seat amid the social hierarchy; sometimes he then used his religious influence to assure the lasting existence of a political order of which he is part. Then you could see Catholics as partisans of aristocracy by spirit of religion.

But once priests are excluded or withdraw from government, as they are in the United States, there are no men who, by their beliefs, are more disposed than Catholics to carry the idea of equality of conditions into the political world.

So if Catholics in the United States are not strongly led by the nature of their beliefs toward democratic and republican opinions, at least they are not naturally against them, and their social position, as well as their small number, makes it a rule for them to embrace those opinions.[f]

Most Catholics are poor, and they need all citizens to govern in order to reach the government themselves. Catholics are in the minority, and they need all rights to be respected in order to be assured of the free exercise of theirs. These two causes push them, even without their knowledge, toward

---

e. ≠I do not doubt that Protestantism, which places all religious authority in the universality of the faithful acting by themselves, is very favorable to the establishment of [v: indirectly supports the political dogma of the sovereignty of the people and thus serves] republican government. And Catholicism, subject to the intellectual authority of the Pope and Councils, seems to me to have more natural affinity with limited monarchy than with any other government≠ (YTC, CVh, 4, p. 71).

f. Hervé de Tocqueville:

This paragraph is badly written. I would put it this way: *If, moreover, Catholics in the United States were not led by the nature of their belief toward democratic and republican opinions, their social position as well as their small number would make it a rule for them to embrace those opinions.* Delete all the rest. This turn of phrase seems to me to present ideas in a more logical way and to serve as a natural transition to the true reason why Catholics in the United States love the republic. For at bottom you cannot close your eyes to the fact that the ecclesiastical hierarchy of Catholics is much more an image of monarchical government than of republican institutions. Not a word of the prayer must be omitted (YTC, CIIIb, 1, pp. 52–53).

political doctrines that they would perhaps adopt with less ardor if they were rich and predominant.

The Catholic clergy in the United States have not tried to struggle against this political tendency; they seek instead to justify it. Catholic priests in America have divided the intellectual world into two parts: in one, they left revealed dogmas, and there they submit without discussion; in the other, they put political truth, and there they think that God abandoned political truth to the free search of men. Thus, Catholics in the United States are simultaneously the most submissive faithful and the most independent citizens [that there are in the world].

So you can say that in the United States not a single religious doctrine shows itself hostile to democratic and republican institutions. All the clergy there use the same language; [≠and while American publicists make all the miseries of society flow from despotism and inequality of conditions, priests represent despotism and inequality of conditions as the most fertile sources of moral evil≠] opinions there are in agreement with laws, and only one current so to speak rules the human mind.

I was living for a short while in one of the largest cities of the Union when I was invited to attend a political meeting the goal of which was to come to the aid of the Poles, and to send them arms and money.

I found two or three thousand persons gathered in a vast room that had been prepared to receive them. Soon after, a priest, dressed in his ecclesiastical robes, came forward to the edge of the platform intended for the speakers. Those attending, after removing their hats, stood in silence, and he spoke in these terms:

> God all-powerful! God of armies! Thou who sustained the hearts and guided the arms of our fathers when they upheld the sacred rights of their national independence; Thou who made them triumph over an odious oppression, and who granted to our people the benefits of peace and liberty; oh Lord! turn a favorable eye toward the other hemisphere; look with pity upon a heroic people who today struggle as we once did and for the defense of the same rights! Lord, who created all men on the same model, do not allow despotism to come to distort Thy work and to maintain inequality on earth. God all-powerful! watch over the destiny of the Poles, make them worthy to be free; may Thy wisdom rule in their councils, may

Thy strength be in their arms; spread terror among their enemies, divide the powers that plot their ruin, and do not allow the injustice that the world witnessed fifty years ago to be consummated today. Lord, who holds in Thy powerful hand the hearts of peoples as well as those of men, raise up allies for the sacred cause of right; make the French nation arise finally and, emerging from the sleep in which its leaders hold it, come to fight once again for the liberty of the world.

O Lord! never turn Thy face from us; allow us always to be the most religious people, as well as the most free.

God all-powerful, grant our prayer today; save the Poles. We ask Thee in the name of Thy beloved Son, Our Lord Jesus Christ, who died on the cross for the salvation of all men. *Amen.*

The entire assembly repeated *Amen* with reverence.

Indirect Influence Exercised by Religious Beliefs on Political Society in the United States

Morality of Christianity which is found in all sects.—Influence of religion on the mores of Americans.—Respect for the marriage bond.—How religion encloses the imagination of the Americans within certain limits and moderates among them the passion to innovate.—Opinion of Americans on the political utility of religion.—Their efforts to extend and assure its dominion.

I have just shown what the direct action of religion on politics was in the United States. Its indirect action seems even more powerful to me, and it is when religion is not speaking about liberty that it best teaches the Americans the art of being free.[g]

There is an innumerable multitude of sects in the United States. All differ in the worship that must be given to the Creator, but all agree on the

g. To the side: "≠Patriotic affection of the Americans for religion.
"I am not sure that the Americans are convinced of the truth of religion, but I am sure that they are convinced of its utility.≠"

duties of men toward one another. So each sect worships God in its way, but all sects preach the same morality in the name of God. If it is very useful to a man as an individual that his religion be true, it is not the same for society. Society has nothing either to fear or to hope concerning the other life; and what is most important for society is not so much that all citizens profess the true religion but that they profess a religion. All the sects in the United States are, moreover, within the great Christian unity, and the morality of Christianity is the same everywhere. [{In America there are Catholics and Protestants, but Americans profess the Christian religion.}]

You are free to think that a certain number of Americans, in the worship they give to God, follow their habits more than their convictions. In the United States, moreover, the sovereign is religious, and consequently hypocrisy must be common; but America is still the place in the world where the Christian religion has most retained true power over souls; and nothing shows better how useful and natural religion is to man, since the country where today it exercises the most dominion is at the same time the most enlightened and most free.

I said that American priests come down in a general way in favor of civil liberty, without excepting even those who do not allow religious liberty; you do not see them lend their support, however, to any political system in particular. They take care to keep out of public affairs and do not get mixed up in the schemes of the parties. So you cannot say that in the United States religion exercises an influence on laws or on the detail of political opinions, but it directs mores, and it is by regulating the family that it works to regulate the State.

I do not doubt for an instant that the great severity of mores that is noticed in the United States has its primary source in beliefs. Religion there is often powerless to restrain the man amid the innumerable temptations presented by fortune. It cannot moderate in him the ardor to grow rich that comes to goad everyone, but it rules with sovereign power over the soul of the woman, and it is the woman who shapes the mores.[h] America is assuredly the country in the world in which the marriage bond is most respected,

h. See chapter IX of the third part of the second volume.

and in which the highest and most sound idea of conjugal happiness has been conceived.

In Europe, nearly all of the disorders of society are born around the domestic hearth and not far from the marital bed. That is where men conceive scorn for natural bonds and permitted pleasures, taste for disorder, restlessness of heart, instability of desires. Agitated by the tumultuous passions that have often troubled his own dwelling, the European submits only with difficulty to the legislative powers of the State. When, coming from the agitation of the political world, the American returns to the bosom of his family, he immediately encounters the image of order and peace. There, all his pleasures are simple and natural, his joys innocent and tranquil; and as he achieves happiness by the regularity of life, he easily gets used to regulating his opinions as well as his tastes.j

While the European seeks to escape his domestic sorrows by troubling society, the American draws from his home the love of order that he then carries into the affairs of the State.

In the United States, religion regulates not only mores; it extends its dominion even to the mind.

Among the Anglo-Americans, some profess Christian dogmas because they believe them; others, because they fear not appearing to believe them. So Christianity rules without obstacles, with the consent of all; as a result, as I have already said elsewhere, everything is certain and fixed in the moral world, while the political world seems abandoned to discussion and to the experiments of men. Thus the human mind never sees a limitless field before it; whatever its audacity, it feels from time to time that it must stop before insurmountable barriers. Before innovating, it is forced to accept certain primary givens, and to subject its boldest conceptions to certain forms that retard and stop it.

So the imagination of the Americans, in its greatest departures, has only a circumspect and uncertain movement; its ways are hampered and its

j. Basil Hall finds that Tocqueville exaggerated the domestic happiness of Americans (cf. the letter of Tocqueville to Basil Hall reproduced in note d for pp. 819–21 of the second volume).

works incomplete. These habits of restraint are found in political society and singularly favor the tranquillity of the people, as well as the continued existence of the institutions that the people have given themselves. Nature and circumstances had made out of the inhabitant of the United States an audacious man; it is easy to judge so when you see how he pursues fortune. If the mind of the Americans were free of all hindrances, you would soon find among them the boldest innovators and the most implacable logicians in the world. But the revolutionaries of America are obliged to profess publicly a certain respect for Christian morality and equity that does not allow them to violate laws easily when the laws are opposed to the execution of their designs; and if they could rise above their scruples, they would still feel checked by the scruples of their partisans. Until now no one has been found in the United States who has dared to advance this maxim: that everything is allowed in the interest of society. Impious maxim, that seems to have been invented in a century of liberty in order to legitimate all the tyrants to come. [<In France a [illegible word] {man} seeks to justify this enormity by principles and facts, and he goes to take a seat in the councils of the prince.>]

Therefore, at the same time that the law allows the American people to do everything, religion prevents them from conceiving of everything and forbids them to dare everything.[k]

So religion, which among the Americans never directly takes part in the government of society, must be considered as the first of their political institutions; for if it does not give them the taste for liberty, it singularly facilitates their use of it.

It is also from this point of view that the inhabitants of the United States themselves consider religious beliefs. I do not know if all Americans have faith in their religion, for who can read the recesses of the heart? But I am sure that they believe it necessary for maintaining republican institutions. This opinion does not belong to one class of citizens or to one party, but to the whole nation; you find it among all ranks.

In the United States, when a politician attacks a sect, it is not a reason

---

k. In the margin: "≠American liberty was born in the bosom of religion and is still sustained in its arms.≠"

for even the partisans of that sect not to support him; but if he attacks all sects together, each one flees from him, and he remains alone.

While I was in America, a witness appeared before the assizes of the county of Chester (State of New York) and declared that he did not believe in the existence of God and in the immortality of the soul. The presiding judge refused to admit his oath, given, he said, that the witness had destroyed in advance any faith that could be given to his words.[3] The newspapers reported the fact without comment.

Americans mix Christianity and liberty so completely in their mind that it is nearly impossible to make them conceive one without the other; and, among them, this is not one of those sterile beliefs that the past bequeaths to the present and that seem more to vegetate deep in the soul than to live.

I have seen Americans join together to send priests into the new states of the West and to found schools and churches there; they are afraid that religion may come to be lost in the middle of the woods, and that the people who are arising there may not be as free as those from whom they came. I met rich inhabitants of New England who abandoned the country of their birth with the goal of going to lay the foundations of Christianity and liberty on the banks of the Missouri or on the prairies of Illinois. This is how religious zeal in the United States constantly warms up at the hearth of patriotism. You think that these men act uniquely in consideration of the other life, but you are mistaken: eternity is only one of their concerns. If you question these missionaries of Christian civilization, you will be very surprised to hear them speak so often about the good things of this world and to find politicians where you thought to see only men of religion. "All the American republics stand together one with the others, they will say to you; if the republics of the West fell into anarchy or submitted to the yoke

3. *Here are the words in which the* New York Spectator *of 23 August 1831 reports the fact:*

> *The court of common pleas of Chester county (New York) a few days since rejected a witness who declared his disbelief in the existence of God. The presiding judge remarked that he had not before been aware that there was a man living who did not believe in the existence of God; that this belief constituted the sanction of all testimony in a court of justice and that he knew of no cause in a Christian country where a witness had been permitted to testify without such a belief.*

of despotism, the republican institutions that flourish on the shores of the Atlantic Ocean would be in great peril; so we have an interest that these new states are religious, in order that they allow us to remain free."m

Such are the opinions of the Americans; but their error is clear. For each day someone proves to me very learnedly that everything is good in America, except precisely this religious spirit that I admire; and I learn that the only thing missing from the liberty and happiness of the human species, on the other side of the Ocean, is to believe with Spinoza[n] in the eternity of the world, and to uphold with Cabanis that the brain secretes thought. To that I have nothing to reply, in truth, if not that those who use this language have not been to America, and have not seen religious peoples any more than free peoples. So I will await their return.

[≠For me, if something could make me despair of the destiny of Europe, it is to see the strange confusion that reigns there in minds. I see pious men who would like to suffocate liberty, as if liberty, this great privilege of man, was not a nearly holy thing. Further along, I see others who think to arrive at being free by attacking all beliefs, but I do not see any who seem to notice the tight and necessary knot that ties [v: the republic] religion to liberty.≠]

There are men in France who consider republican institutions as the temporary instrument of their grandeur. They measure with their eyes the immense gap that separates their vices and their miseries from power and riches, and they would like to pile up ruins[o] in this abyss in order to try to fill it. These men are to liberty what the free companies of the Middle Ages were to kings; they make war on their own behalf even when they wear his colors; the republic will always live long enough to pull them out of their present low position. I am not speaking to them. But there are others who

m. In the margin: "≠We would not give ourselves all these difficulties if a regulating force existed outside of society. But how to govern yourself [v: an entire people] without the existence [v: support] of beliefs and mores?≠"

n. In place of Spinoza, the manuscript cites Voltaire.

o. In the manuscript: ". . . ruins and riches and they would like to throw the republic down like a narrow passageway and flying bridge over the abyss."

see in the republic a permanent and tranquil state, a necessary end toward which ideas and mores lead modern societies each day, and who would sincerely like to prepare men to be free. When these men attack religious beliefs, they follow their passions and not their interests. Despotism can do without faith, but not liberty. Religion is much more necessary in the republic that they advocate than in the monarchy that they attack, and in democratic republics more than in all others. How could society fail to perish if, while the political bond grows loose, the moral bond does not become tighter? And what to do with a people master of itself, if it is not subject to God?

Of the Principal Causes That Make Religion Powerful in America[p]

Care that the Americans have taken to separate Church and State.—Laws, public opinion, the efforts of priests themselves, work toward this result.—To this cause must be attributed the power that religion exercises on souls in the United States.— Why.—What is today the natural state of man in

p. In an initial plan of the work:

Religious society./
 Nomenclature of the various sects.—From Catholicism to the sect that is furthest from it.
 Quakers, Methodists.—Point out what is antisocial in the doctrine of Quakers, Unitarians.
 Relations among the sects.
 Freedom of worship.—Toleration: in the legal respect; with respect to mores. Catholicism.
 Place of religion in the political order and its degree of influence on American society (YTC, CVh, 1, pp. 26–27).

Several ideas of this part are roughed out in a letter from Tocqueville to Chabrol dated 26 October 1831. Tocqueville answers certain questions that Louis Bouchitté had asked him concerning religion in the United States (YTC, BIa2).

 This passage is not without many similarities to "Note on the religious movement in the United States" by Gustave de Beaumont, very particularly to part III, "Relations of religions with the State" (*Marie*, II, pp. 213–25).

*the matter of religion.—What particular and accidental
cause, in certain countries, works against men
conforming to this state.*

The philosophers of the XVIIIth century explained the gradual weakening of beliefs in a very simple way. Religious zeal, they said, must fade as liberty and enlightenment increase. It is unfortunate that facts do not agree with this theory.q

There is such a European population whose disbelief is equaled only by its brutishness and ignorance, while in America you see one of the most free and most enlightened[r] peoples in the world fulfill with ardor all the external duties of religion.

When I arrived in the United States, it was the religious aspect of the country that first struck my eyes.[s] As I prolonged my journey, I noticed the great political consequences that flowed from these new facts.

I had seen among us the spirit of religion and the spirit of liberty march almost always in opposite directions. Here, I found them intimately joined the one to the other: they reigned together over the same soil.

Each day I felt my desire to know the cause of this phenomenon increase.

To find it out, I asked the faithful of all communions; I sought, above all, the company of priests who are the keepers of the different faiths and who have a personal interest in their continued existence. The religion I

q. I have heard it said in Europe that it was very unfortunate that these poor Americans had religion. When you have been in the United States, conviction that religion is more useful in republics than in monarchies, and in democratic republics more than anywhere else. Disastrous misunderstanding in France. Despotic powers of Europe favor religion./

As for these cut-throats, liberty is the greatest gift of God, it is the republicans, I have nothing to say to them . . . but the others . . . may they know that liberty is an almost *holy* thing [v: what distinguishes us from beasts] (YTC, CVh, 3, p. 57).

r. The manuscript says: ". . . you see the most free and most enlightened . . ."
Hervé de Tocqueville: "Isn't the expression a bit exaggerated?" (YTC, CIIIb, 1 p. 44).

s. Several times Tocqueville uses the same expression in the book while referring to other aspects that attracted his attention, for example, the activity that reigns in the United States.

profess brought me particularly close to the Catholic clergy, and I did not delay in striking up a sort of intimacy with several of its members.[t] To each of them I expressed my astonishment and revealed my doubts. I found that all of these men differed among themselves only on the details; but all attributed the peaceful dominion that religion exercises in their country principally to the complete separation of Church and State. I am not afraid to assert that, during my visit in America, I did not meet a single man, priest or laymen, who did not agree on this point.

This led me to examine more attentively than I had done until then the position that American priests occupy in political society. I realized with

[t]. Few questions have provoked more commentary than the religious beliefs of Tocqueville. All commentators nonetheless take as true the confession of faith made to Madame Swetchine in the famous letter of 26 February 1857 (*Correspondance avec Madame Swetchine, OC,* XV, 2, p. 315). There Tocqueville says that he lost his faith when he was sixteen years old, after reading several passages chosen haphazardly from his father's library. His works and his correspondence allow us, however, to guess his assent to several great dogmas of Catholicism. As Luis Díez de Corral (*La mentalidad política de Tocqueville con especial referencia a Pascal,* Madrid: Real Academia de Ciencias Morales y Políticas, 1965, p. 118) notes, Tocqueville is closer to those who, in the words of Pascal, "seek while groaning," eternally plagued by doubt and uncertainty, captives to the "wager." In this regard, the author writes to Francisque de Corcelle:

> If you know a recipe for belief, for God! give it to me. But what power does the will have over the free processes of the mind? If will alone were sufficient for belief, I would have been devout a long time ago; or rather I would always have been devout, for doubt has always seemed to me the most unbearable of the ills of the world; I have constantly judged it to be worse than death and inferior only to illnesses (*Correspondance avec Corcelle, OC,* XV, 2, p. 29).

A little further in this chapter, Tocqueville explains what perhaps best corresponds to his own sentiment in the matter of religious beliefs. The latter, he says, are abandoned

> by coldness rather than by hatred; you do not reject them, they leave you. While ceasing to believe religion true, the unbeliever continues to judge it useful. Considering religious beliefs from a human aspect, he recognizes their dominion over mores, their influence over laws. He understands how they can make men live in peace and gently prepare men for death. So he regrets faith after losing it, and deprived of a good of which he knows the whole value, he is afraid to take it away from those who still possess it (p. 486).

Also see Luis Díez del Corral, *El pensamiento político de Tocqueville,* Madrid: Alianza Universidad, 1989, pp. 227–71.

surprise that they fill no public position.[4] I did not see a single one of them in the administration, and I discovered that they were not even represented within the assemblies.

The law, in several states, had closed a political career to them;[5] opinion, in all the others.

When finally I found out what the mind of the clergy itself was, I noticed that most of its members seemed to remove themselves voluntarily from power, and to take a kind of professional pride in remaining apart from it.

I heard them anathematize ambition and bad faith, whatever the political opinions that ambition and bad faith carefully used to cover themselves. But I learned, by listening to them, that men cannot be blameworthy in the eyes of God because of these very opinions, when the opinions are sincere, and that there is no more sin in being wrong in matters of government than in being mistaken about the way in which your dwelling must be built or your furrow must be plowed.

I saw them separate themselves with care from all parties, and flee contact with all the ardor of personal interest.

These facts succeeded in proving to me that I had been told the truth. Then I wanted to go back from facts to causes. I asked myself how it could happen that by diminishing the apparent strength of a religion, you

---

4. *Unless you give this name to the functions that many among them occupy in schools. Most education is confided to the clergy.*

5. *See the Constitution of New York, art. 7, #4.*

Id. *of North Carolina, art. 31.*

Id. *of Virginia.*

Id. *of South Carolina, art. 1, #23.*

Id. *of Kentucky, art. 2, #26.*

Id. *of Tennessee, art. 8, #1.*

Id. *of Louisiana, art. 2, #22.*

The article of the Constitution of New York is formulated as follows:

And whereas the ministers of the gospel are, by their profession, dedicated to the service of God and the care of souls, and ought not to be diverted from the great duties of their function; therefore, no minister of the gospel, or priest of any denomination whatsoever, shall, at any time hereafter, under any presence or description whatever, be eligible to, or capable of holding, any civil or military office or place within this State.

came to increase its true power, and I believed that it was not impossible to find out.

Never will the short space of sixty years enclose all of the imagination of man; the incomplete joys of this world will never be enough for his heart. Among all beings, man alone shows a natural distaste for existence and an immense desire to exist: he scorns life and fears nothingness. These different instincts constantly push his soul toward the contemplation of another world, and it is religion that leads him there. So religion is only a particular form of hope, and it is as natural to the human heart as hope itself.[u] It is by a type of mental aberration and with the help of a kind of moral violence exercised over their own nature, that men remove themselves from religious beliefs; an irresistible inclination brings them back to beliefs. Unbelief is an accident; faith alone is the permanent state of humanity.

So by considering religion only from a human viewpoint, you can say that all religions draw from man himself an element of strength that they can never lack, because it is due to one of the constituent principles of human nature.

I know that there are times when religion can add to this influence, which is its own, the artificial power of laws and the support of the physical powers that lead society. We have seen religions, intimately united with

---

u. What touches me more than the miracles and the prophecies is the very character of Christianity. There is the greatest sign of its divine origin. Give honor to all the religious codes of the world, you will see that they necessarily apply to a certain country, to certain mores, to a particular social state or people. I do not examine the proofs of these religions, and I say that they are false, because they are not made for all times and for all men. But Christianity seems universal and immortal like the human species./

The influence that religion exercises over mores in the United States must not be exaggerated; it is not sufficient to make a *virtuous* people, but an *orderly* one./

Its action on the women. It is the women who make mores.

I said that democracy was the form of government in which it was most desirable that the people be happy; it is also the one in which it is most desirable that the people be moral and for the same reason.

I would not hesitate to say, because I write in an irreligious century, that in the United States religion is the first of political institutions. And I even add that I am that much less afraid to say so because of this reason (YTC, CVh, 3, p. 58).

the governments of the earth, dominate souls by terror and by faith at the same time; but when a religion contracts such an alliance, I am not afraid to say, it acts as a man could: it sacrifices the future with the present in mind, and by obtaining a power that is not its due, it puts its legitimate power at risk.

When a religion seeks to found its dominion only on the desire for immortality that equally torments the hearts of all men, it can aim for universality; but when it comes to unite with a government, it must adopt maxims that are applicable only to certain peoples. Therefore, by allying itself to a political power, religion increases its power over some and loses the hope of reigning over all.

As long as a religion relies only on the sentiments that console all miseries, it can attract the heart of the human species. Mingled with the bitter passions of this world, religion is sometimes constrained to defend allies that have offered interest rather than love; and it must reject as adversaries men who often still love it, even as they fight those men with whom religion is united. So religion cannot share the material strength of those who govern without burdening itself with a portion of the hatreds caused by those who govern.

The political powers that appear most established have as a guarantee of their continued existence only the opinions of a generation, the interests of a century, often the life of a man. A law can modify the social state that seems most definitive and most firm, and with it everything changes.

The powers of society are all more or less fleeting, just as our years upon the earth; they rapidly follow one another, like the various cares of life; and you have never seen a government that relied on an invariable disposition of the human heart and that was able to base itself on an immortal interest.

As long as a religion finds its strength in the sentiments, the instincts, the passions that are reproduced in the same way in all periods of history, it defies the effort of time, or at least it can be destroyed only by another religion. [Political powers can do nothing against it.] But when religion wants to rely on the interests of this world, it becomes almost as fragile as all the powers of the earth. Alone, religion can hope for immortality; tied to ephemeral powers, it follows their fortune, and often falls with the passions of the day that sustain those powers.

So by uniting with different political powers, religion can only contract an onerous alliance. It does not need their help to live, and by serving them it can die.

The danger that I have just pointed out exists at all times, but it is not always as visible.

There are centuries when governments appear immortal, and others when you would say that the existence of society is more fragile than that of a man.

Certain constitutions keep citizens in a sort of lethargic sleep, and others deliver them to a feverish agitation.

When governments seem so strong and laws so stable, men do not notice the danger that religion can run by uniting with power.

When governments prove to be so weak and laws so changeable, the peril strikes all eyes, but then there is often no more time to escape. So you must learn to see it from afar.

To the extent that a nation assumes a democratic social state and you see societies lean toward the republic,[v] it becomes more and more dangerous to unite religion with authority; for the time is coming when power will pass from hand to hand, when political theories will succeed one another, when men, laws, constitutions themselves will disappear or change each day, and not for a time, but constantly. Agitation and instability stem from the nature of democratic republics, as immobility and sleep form the law of absolute monarchies.

If the Americans, who change the head of State every four years, who every two years choose new legislators, and replace provincial administrators every year; if the Americans, who have delivered the political world to the experiments of innovators, had not placed their religion somewhere outside of the political world, to what could they cling in the ebb and flow

---

v. In the manuscript: ". . . you see governments lean and rush toward the republic."
Hervé de Tocqueville: "The words *and rush,* which are meaningless, must be struck out; you could put *and are carried toward*" (YTC, CIIIb, 1, p. 46).

of human opinions? Amid the struggle of parties, where would the respect be that religion is due? What would become of its immortality when everything perishes around it?

American priests have seen this truth before anyone else, and they model their conduct on it. They have seen that religious influence had to be renounced, if they wanted to acquire a political power, and they preferred to lose the support of power than to share its vicissitudes.

In America, religion is perhaps less powerful than it has been in certain times and among certain peoples, but its influence is more durable. It has reduced itself to its own forces that no one can take away from it; it acts only within a single circle, but it covers it entirely and predominates within it without effort.

In Europe I hear voices that are raised on all sides; people deplore the absence of beliefs and ask how to give religion something of its former power.

It seems to me that we must first try attentively to find out what should be, today, the *natural state* of men in matters of religion. Then, knowing what we are able to hope and what we have to fear, we will see clearly the goal toward which our efforts must tend.

Two great dangers menace the existence of religions: schisms and indifference.

During centuries of fervor, men sometimes happen to abandon their religion, but they escape its yoke only to submit to the yoke of another religion. Faith changes objects; it does not die. The old religion then excites fervent love or implacable hatred in all hearts; some leave it with anger, others follow it with a new ardor: beliefs differ, irreligion is unknown.

But it is not the same when a religious belief is silently undermined by doctrines that I will call negative, because while asserting the falsity of one religion they establish the truth of no other.

Then prodigious revolutions take place in the human spirit, without man seeming to aid the revolutions with his passions and without suspecting them, so to speak. You see men who allow, as if by forgetfulness, the object of their most cherished hopes to escape. Carried along by an imperceptible current against which they do not have the courage to struggle, but to which they yield with regret, they abandon the faith that they love to follow the doubt that leads them to despair.

During the centuries that we have just described, you abandon your beliefs by coldness rather than by hatred; you do not reject them, they leave you. While ceasing to believe religion true, the unbeliever continues to judge it useful. Considering religious beliefs from a human aspect, he recognizes their dominion over mores, their influence over laws. He understands how they can make men live in peace and gently prepare men for death. So he regrets faith after losing it, and deprived of a good of which he knows the whole value, he is afraid to take it away from those who still possess it.

From his side, the one who continues to believe is not afraid to reveal his faith to all eyes. In those who do not share his hopes, he sees unfortunate men rather than adversaries; he knows that he can gain their esteem without following their example; so he is at war with no one; and not considering the society in which he lives as an arena in which religion must struggle constantly against a thousand fierce enemies, he loves his contemporaries at the same time that he condemns their weaknesses and is distressed by their errors.

Those who do not believe, hiding their unbelief, and those who do believe, showing their faith, create a public opinion in favor of religion; it is loved, it is upheld, it is honored, and you must penetrate to the recesses of souls to discover the wounds that it has received.

The mass of men, whom religious sentiment never abandons, then see nothing that separates them from established beliefs. The instinct of another life leads them without difficulty to the foot of altars and delivers their hearts to the precepts and consolations of faith.

Why does this picture not apply to us?

I notice among us men who have ceased to believe in Christianity without adhering to any religion.

I see others who have halted at doubt, and already pretend to believe no more.

Further along, I meet Christians who still believe and dare not say so.

Amid these lukewarm friends and fiery adversaries, I finally discover a small number of the faithful ready to defy all obstacles and to scorn all dangers for their beliefs. The latter have acted contrary to human weakness in order to rise above common opinion. Carried away by this very effort, they no longer know precisely where they should stop. Since they have seen that, in their country, the first use that man made of independence has been to attack religion, they fear their contemporaries and withdraw with terror from the liberty that the former pursue. Since unbelief appears ? to them as something new, they include in the same hatred everything that is new.[w] So they are at war with their century and their country, and in each of the opinions that are professed there they see a necessary enemy of faith.

Such should not be today the natural state of man in matters of religion.

An accidental and particular cause is found among us that prevents the human spirit from following its inclination and pushes it beyond the limits at which it should naturally stop.

I am profoundly persuaded that this particular and accidental cause is the intimate union of politics and religion.[x]

w. Hervé de Tocqueville:

Here are two thoughts that do not seem correct to me. Why would people be carried beyond truth because, to do good, they had the courage to defy prejudice? Then, you will never find faithful people foolish enough to believe that unbelief is something new. This paragraph is to review. The author has not arrived at the true cause of the estrangement of the clergy and of pious persons from free institutions. You must seek it in the memory of the persecutions that religion suffered as soon as the word liberty resounded in France, and in the fear that the persecutions are repeating. The impression was so strong that it is not erased and that pious persons believe that the aegis of an absolute power is necessary in order for priests to be out of danger and for religion to be able to resist philosophical intolerance. The author can link this thought well to earlier ones, for he speaks on page 15 of men without religion who persecute those who believe with all the fervor of proselytism.

Édouard de Tocqueville: "I agree with father. You must absolutely mention the memories of '93 as a powerful cause of the antipathy of the French clergy for liberal ideas" (YTC, CIIIb, 1, pp. 46–48). The sentence "Since they have seen . . . pursue" was added following the comments of the family.

x. As for me, I cannot believe that the evil is as great or as profound as is supposed. Never will the religious instinct perish in man, and what can better satisfy it than the religion of J[esus (ed.)]. C[hrist (ed.)].? Christianity is not defeated, it is only bowed down. Formerly religion [v: Christianity] allowed itself to be mingled with the powers of the earth, and today I see it as though buried very much alive under their debris.

Unbelievers in Europe pursue Christians as political enemies, rather than as religious adversaries; they hate faith as the opinion of a party much more than as a mistaken belief; and in the priest they reject the representative of God less than the friend of power.

In Europe, Christianity allowed itself to be intimately united with the powers of the earth. Today these powers are falling and Christianity is as though buried beneath their debris. It is a living thing that someone wanted to bind to the dead: cut the ties that hold it and it will rise again.

I do not know what must be done to give Christianity in Europe the energy of youth. God alone would be able to do so; but at least it depends on men to leave to faith the use of all of the forces that it still retains.

How the Enlightenment, Habits, and Practical Experience of the Americans Contribute to the Success of Democratic Institutions

What must be understood by the enlightenment of the American people.—The human mind has received a less profound cultivation in the United States than in Europe.—But no one has remained in ignorance.—Why.—Rapidity with which thought circulates in the half-empty states of the West.— How practical experience serves Americans even more than literary knowledge.

In a thousand places in this work I have pointed out to readers what influence the enlightenment and habits of the Americans exercised on main-

---

So let us try to extricate it; it still has enough strength to rise again, but not to lift the weight that overwhelms it. The Christian religion in Europe resembles an old man whose shoulders are loaded down with a heavy burden; he walks painfully across the obstacles in the road. He bends under the weight; his limbs are heavy, his breathing is labored. He walks only with difficulty and at each step you would say he was about to die (YTC, CVh, 4. p. 67; a nearly identical fragment is found in YTC, CVh, 4, pp. 31–32).

taining their political institutions. So now, few new things remain for me to say.

Until now America has had only a very small number of notable writers; it does not have any great historians and does not have one poet. Its inhabitants see literature strictly understood with a kind of disfavor; and a third-rank city in Europe publishes more literary works each year than the twenty-four states of the Union taken together.ʸ

The American mind withdraws from general ideas; it does not turn toward theoretical discoveries. Politics itself and industry cannot lead it there. In the United States, new laws are made constantly; but great writers are still not found to seek out the general principles of laws.

The Americans have experts on the law and legal commentators; they lack writers on public affairs; and in politics, they give the world examples rather than lessons.[*]

It is the same for the mechanical arts.

In America, the inventions of Europe are applied with sagacity, and after perfecting them, they are marvelously adapted to the needs of the country. Men there are industrious, but they do not cultivate the science of industry. You find good workers and few inventors there. Fulton[†] peddled his genius for a long time among foreign peoples before being able to devote it to his country. [So in America you find none of those great intellectual centers from which fire and light burst forth at the same time {as in Europe}. I do not know if perhaps we should thank heaven. America already carries an immense weight in the destinies of the world; and per-

---

y. See chapters XIII and XIV of the first part of the second volume.

[*]. ≠Say a word about Livingston. He is more of a moralist.≠

[†]. ≠He is the one who applied steam to navigation. He offered his secret to Bonaparte who, after an examination, declared the thing absurd and impractical. As we know, one of the weaknesses of Bonaparte {this extraordinary man} was to want to pass judgment at first sight on matters that were foreign to him. Despite his prodigious perspicacity, too frequently he happened to be mistaken.≠

haps it only lacks great writers to overturn violently in a moment all the old societies of Europe.]ᶻ

So whoever wants to judge the state of enlightenment among the Anglo-Americans opens himself to seeing the same subject from two different views. If he pays attention only to the learned, he will be astonished by their small number; and if he counts the ignorant, the American people will seem to him the most enlightened on earth.

The entire population is placed between these two extremes; I have already said it elsewhere.

[In the United States, you find fewer great landowners and infinitely more landowners than anywhere else; less wealth and more comfort. Minds have been subjected to the same law. There scientific and literary genius is as rare as ability is common, and if you do not find great writers, everyone knows how to write. What could be the state of a few minds seems to have been divided equally among all.]

In New England, each citizen receives the elementary notions of human knowledge; furthermore, he learns the doctrines and the proofs of his religion; he is taught the history of his country and the principal features of the Constitution that governs it. In Connecticut and Massachusetts, it is very rare to find a man who only imperfectly knows all these things, and one who is absolutely ignorant of them is in a way a phenomenon.ᵃ

When I compare the Greek and Roman republics to these republics of America, the manuscript libraries of the first and their coarse populace, to the thousand newspapers that crisscross the second and to the enlightened people that inhabit the republics of America; when I then think of all the efforts that are still made to judge the one with the aid of the others and

---

z. In the margin:

≠Knowledge of reading and writing (but less useful than you think).
Knowledge of laws.
Experience.
Practical habit of affairs.
Extensive and homogeneous civilization. Pioneer, an ax and newspapers.

a. To the side: "≠Instruction of the Americans of New England is less advanced than in our colleges but more complete than in our schools. ≠"

to foresee what will happen today by what happened two thousand years ago, I am tempted to burn my books,[b] in order to apply only new ideas to a social state so new.

You must not indiscriminately extend to the whole Union, moreover, what I say about New England. The more you advance toward the West or toward the South, the more the instruction of the people diminishes. In the states neighboring the Gulf of Mexico, a certain number of individuals are found, as among us, to whom the elements of human knowledge are foreign; but in the United States you would seek in vain for a single district that was plunged into ignorance. The reason for it is simple: the peoples of Europe left the shadows and barbarism in order to advance toward civilization and enlightenment. Their progress was unequal; some ran along the course, others in a way only walked; still others stopped and they are still asleep along the road.

It was not the same in the United States.

The Anglo-Americans arrived fully civilized on the soil that their posterity occupies; they did not have to learn, it was enough for them not to forget. Now, it is the sons of these very Americans who, each year, carry into the wilderness, with their dwelling-place, knowledge already acquired and respect for learning. Education made them feel the usefulness of enlightenment and made them capable of transmitting this very enlightenment to their descendents. So in the United States, society has no childhood; it is born in manhood.

The Americans make no use of the word peasant; they do not employ the word, because they do not have the idea; the ignorance of the first ages, the simplicity of the fields, the rusticity of the village, have not been preserved among them, and they imagine neither the virtues, nor the vices, nor the coarse habits, nor the innocent graces of a civilization being born.

At the extreme limits of the confederated states, at the confines of society and wilderness, is a population of hardy adventurers who, in order to flee the poverty ready to strike them under the paternal roof, have not been

b. Hervé de Tocqueville: "I do not like this idea. Why would you burn your books because a thousand newspapers crisscross the territory of the Union?" (YTC, CIIIb, 1, p. 42).

afraid to plunge into the empty areas of America and seek a new country there. Having barely arrived at the place that must serve him as a refuge, the pioneer hastily cuts down a few trees and raises a cabin under the leafy branches. Nothing offers a more miserable sight than these isolated dwellings. The traveler who approaches them toward the evening notices from afar the flame of the hearth shining through the walls; and at night, if the wind comes up, he hears the roof of foliage move noisily amid the trees of the forest. Who would not believe that this poor cottage serves as a refuge for coarseness and ignorance? You must not, however, establish any correlation between the pioneer and the place that serves him as a refuge. Everything is primitive and savage around him, but he is so to speak the result of eighteen centuries of efforts and experience. He wears city clothing, speaks the language of the city, knows the past, is curious about the future, argues about the present; he is a very civilized man who, for a time, submits to living in the woods and who plunges into the wilderness of the New World with the Bible, an ax and some newspapers.[c]

It is difficult to imagine with what incredible rapidity thought circulates in the heart of these wilderness areas.[6]

I do not believe that there is as great an intellectual movement in the most enlightened and most populated districts of France.[7]

c. Hervé de Tocqueville: "Could you not put: *an ax, tea and newspapers?* Tea, being something of a luxury, gives the idea of civilization" (YTC, CIIIb, 1, p. 43). See, in appendix II, volume II, pp. 1315–16, the description of the dwelling of the pioneer.

6. *I traveled over a part of the frontiers of the United States in a type of open carriage that was called a coach. We moved along briskly day and night over roads scarcely cleared amid immense forests of green trees; when the darkness became impenetrable, my driver lighted branches of larch and we continued our route by their light. Here and there we encountered a cabin amid the woods: it was the post office. At the door of this isolated dwelling, the mailman threw an enormous packet of letters, and we resumed our course at a gallop, leaving to each inhabitant in the neighborhood the care of coming to find his part of the treasure.*

7. *In 1832, each inhabitant of Michigan provided 1.22 fr. to the postal tax, and each inhabitant of Florida 1.5 fr. (see* National Calendar, *1833, p. 244 [249 (ed.)]). In the same year, each inhabitant of the* département du Nord *paid the State, for the same purpose, 1.4 fr. (see* Compte général de l'administration des finances, *1833, p. 623). Now, at this time Michigan still had only seven inhabitants per square league, and Florida, five; instruction was less widespread and activity not as great in these two districts as in most of the states of*

You cannot doubt that in the United States the instruction of the people serves powerfully to maintain the democratic republic. It will be so, I think, everywhere that the instruction that enlightens the mind is not separated from the education that regulates mores.

Nonetheless, I do not exaggerate this advantage, and I am still far from believing, as a great number of people in Europe do, that it is sufficient to teach men to read and write to make them citizens immediately. [<≠I do not consider elementary knowledge as the most potent means to educate the people; it facilitates the study of liberty for them, but it does not give them the art of being free.≠>]

True enlightenment arises principally from experience, and if the Americans had not been accustomed little by little to governing themselves, the book learning that they possess would not be a great help today in succeeding to do so.

I have lived a great deal with the people of the United States, and I cannot say how much I have admired their experience and their good sense.[e]

Do not lead the American to speak about Europe; he will ordinarily show a great presumption and a quite foolish pride. He will be content with those general and indefinite ideas that, in all countries, are such a great help to the ignorant. But interrogate him about his country, and you will see the cloud that enveloped his mind suddenly dissipate; his language will become clear, plain and precise, like his thought. He will teach you what his rights are and what means he must use to exercise them; he will know by what practices the political world operates. You will notice that the rules of administration are known to him and that he has made himself familiar with the mechanism of the laws. The inhabitant of the United States has not

---

the Union, while the département du Nord, *which includes 3,400 inhabitants per square league, is one of the most enlightened and most industrial portions of France.*[d]

d. "It is now a matter of comparing this to France, but for that it would be necessary to have the budget and even statistical details that probably are not to be found [in the *National Calendar* (ed.)]. Ask D'Aunay and N. [*sic*] Roger of the French Academy" (YTC, CVh, 1, p. 16). It undoubtedly concerns Félix Le Peletier d'Aunay and Jean-François Roger.

e. To the side: "It is truly from this side that the Americans are [v: the United States prove to be] superior to all the peoples of the world."

drawn this practical knowledge and these positive notions from books; his formal education may have prepared him to receive them, but has not provided him with them.

It is by participating in legislation that the American learns to know the laws; it is by governing that he finds out about the forms of government. The great work of society is carried out each day before his eyes and, so to speak, by his hands.

In the United States, the whole of the education of men is directed toward politics; in Europe, its principal goal is to prepare for private life. The activity of citizens in public affairs is too rare a fact to be anticipated in advance.

As soon as you cast your eyes on the two societies, these differences are revealed even in their external appearance.

In Europe, we often bring the ideas and habits of private existence into public life, and as we happen to pass suddenly from the interior of the family to the government of the State, you often see us discuss the great interests of society in the same way we converse with our friends.

In contrast, the Americans almost always carry the habits of public life into private life. Among them, the idea of the jury is found in school games, and you find parliamentary forms even in the order of a banquet.

That Laws Serve More to Maintain the Democratic Republic in the United States than Physical Causes, and Mores More than Laws

All the peoples of America have a democratic social state.—
Democratic institutions only continue to exist however among the
Anglo-Americans.—The Spanish of South America, as favored
by physical nature as the Anglo-Americans, are not able to
support the democratic republic.—Mexico, which has adopted
the Constitution of the United States, is not able to do it.—The
Anglo-Americans of the West support it with more difficulty than
those of the East.—Reasons for these differences.

I said that maintaining democratic institutions in the United States had to be attributed to circumstances, laws and mores.[8]

Most Europeans know only the first of these three causes, and they give it a preponderant importance that it does not have.

It is true that the Anglo-Americans brought equality of conditions to the New World. Never were either commoners or nobles found among them; prejudices of birth there have always been as unknown as prejudices of profession. Since the social state is therefore democratic, democracy had no difficulty establishing its dominion.

But this fact is not particular to the United States; nearly all the colonies of America were founded by men equal among themselves or who became equal by inhabiting the colonies. There is not a single part of the New World where Europeans were able to create an aristocracy.

Democratic institutions prosper only in the United States, however.

The American Union has no enemies to fight. It is alone in the middle of the wilderness like an island in the heart of the Ocean.

But nature had isolated in the same way the Spanish of [{Mexico, those of Peru}] South America [{the Portuguese of Brazil, the French of the Antilles, the Dutch of Guyana}], and this isolation did not prevent them from maintaining armies. They made war on each other when foreigners were lacking. Only the Anglo-American democracy, until now, has been able to remain at peace.

The territory of the Union presents a limitless field to human activity; it offers an inexhaustible sustenance to industry and to work. So love of wealth takes the place of ambition there, and well-being quells the fervor of parties.

But in what portion of the world do you meet more fertile wildernesses, larger rivers, more untouched and more inexhaustible riches than in South America? Yet South America cannot support democracy. If, for peoples to be happy, it was sufficient to have been placed in a corner of the universe

---

8. *Here I recall to the reader the general sense in which I take the word* mores; *I understand by this word the whole of the intellectual and moral dispositions that man brings to the state of society.*

and to be able to spread at will over uninhabited lands, the Spanish of South America would not have to complain about their lot. And when they would not enjoy the same happiness as the inhabitants of the United States, they would at least make the peoples of Europe envious. There are, however, no nations on the earth more miserable than those of South America.

Therefore, not only can physical causes not lead to analogous results among the Americans of the South and those of the North, but they cannot even produce among the first something that is not inferior to what is seen in Europe, where physical causes act in an opposite direction.

So physical causes do not influence the destiny of nations as much as is supposed.[f]

I met men of New England ready to abandon a country where they would have been able to find ease and comfort, in order to go to seek their fortune in the wilderness. Nearby, I saw the French population of Canada squeeze itself into a space too small for it, when the same wilderness was near; and while the emigrant of the United States acquired a great estate at the cost of a few days of work, the Canadian paid as much for land as if he still lived in France.

Thus nature, while delivering the uninhabited areas of the New World to Europeans, offers them assets that they do not always know how to use.

I notice among other peoples of America the same conditions of prosperity as among the Anglo-Americans, without their laws and their mores; and these peoples are miserable. So the laws and mores of the Anglo-Americans form the special reason for their grandeur and the predominant cause that I am seeking.

I am far from pretending that there is an absolute good in American laws; I do not believe that they are applicable to all democratic peoples; and, among those laws, there are several that, even in the United States, seem dangerous to me.

You cannot deny, however, that the legislation of the Americans, taken

f. In the margin: "≠So the original equality of conditions and the nature of the country do not explain in a sufficient way what is happening in the United States. Because elsewhere these same causes do not produce the same effects.≠"

as a whole, is well adapted to the genius of the people that it must govern and to the nature of the country.g

So American laws are good, and a great part of the success that the government of democracy achieves in America must be attributed to them; but I do not think that they are the principal cause. And if the laws appear to me to have more influence on the social happiness of the Americans than the very nature of the country, from another perspective I see reasons to believe that they exercise less influence than mores.

The federal laws surely form the most important portion of the legislation of the United States.

Mexico, which is as happily situated as the Anglo-American Union, appropriated these same laws, and it is not able to get accustomed to the government of democracy.

So there is a reason independent of physical causes and laws that makes democracy able to govern the United States.h

But here is what proves it even more. Nearly all the men who inhabit the territory of the Union are born of the same blood. They speak the same language, pray to God in the same way, are subject to the same physical causes, obey the same laws.

So what produces the differences that must be observed among them?

Why, in the [{North}] East of the Union, does republican government appear strong and well-ordered, why does it proceed with maturity and deliberation? What cause marks all its acts with a character of wisdom and lasting existence?

Why, in contrast, do the powers of society in the West [{and in the South}] seem to move haphazardly?

---

g. To the side: "And in certain cases, it would be more correct to say that the Americans prosper despite their laws rather than thanks to them."

h. "Mexico is not able to support the republic, however. The republic prospers only within the Anglo-American Union. From so many similar causes, the Union a different one. And this cause of prosperity which is special prevails over all the others together. The people of the Union are not only the most religious and most enlightened in the world, they are also the ones whose political education is the most advanced" (YTC, CVh, 4, p. 45).

Why, in the movement of affairs, does something disorderly, passionate, you could almost say feverish, reign that does not herald a long future?

I am no longer comparing the Anglo-Americans to foreign peoples; now I am contrasting the Anglo-Americans to each other, and I am seeking why they do not resemble each other. Here all arguments drawn from the nature of the country and from the difference of laws are missing at the same time. I must resort to some other cause; and where will I find this cause, if not in mores?

It is in the East [{North}] that the Anglo-Americans have contracted the longest use of the government of democracy, and that they have formed habits and conceived ideas most favorable to maintaining it. [In the North] Democracy there has little by little penetrated customs, opinions, forms; you find it in all the details of social life as in the laws. It is in the East [{North}] that the book learning and the practical education of the people have been most perfected and that religion has best intermingled with liberty. What are all these habits, these opinions, these customs, these beliefs, if not what I called mores?

In the West, in contrast, a part of these same advantages is still lacking. Many Americans of the states of the West are born in the woods, and they mix with the civilization of their fathers the ideas and customs of savage life. Among them, passions are more violent, religious morality less powerful, ideas less settled. Men there exercise no control over each other, for they scarcely know each other.[j] So the nations of the West show, to a certain extent, the inexperience and the unruly habits of emerging peoples. Societies in the West are formed from old elements; but the assembly is new.[k]

j. In a slip of paper inserted in the manuscript: ·

Three centuries ago the English colonies were founded, but only sixty years ago national and centralized governments were established among them. Before this time citizens [v: subjects], dispersed in a vast wilderness two thousand leagues from the sovereign, lived in an almost complete independence. Which really explains why, among the Americans, individuals always appear experienced and [often] the State, inexperienced.

k. In the North the republic is a strong and well-ordered government, which proceeds

So mores, particularly, make the Americans of the United States, alone among all Americans, capable of supporting the dominion of democracy; and mores also make the various Anglo-American democracies more or less well-regulated and prosperous.

Therefore, in Europe, the influence that the geographic position of the country exercises on the continued existence of democratic institutions is exaggerated. Too much importance is attributed to laws, too little to mores. These three great causes undoubtedly serve to regulate and to direct American democracy; but if they had to be classified, I would say that physical causes contribute less than laws, and laws infinitely less than mores.

I am persuaded that the most fortunate situation and the best laws cannot maintain a constitution in spite of mores, while the latter still turn to good account the most unfavorable positions and the worst laws. The importance of mores is a common truth to which study and experience constantly lead. It seems to me that I find it placed in my mind like a central point; I see it at the end of all my ideas.[m]

I have only one more word to say on this subject.

If, in the course of this work, I have not succeeded in making the reader

location → laws → mores

---

with maturity and deliberation, and which marks all its acts with a character of wisdom and lasting existence. In the West and in the South, the powers of society seem in contrast to move haphazardly, and there you observe, in the movement of affairs, something disorderly, passionate and you could almost say feverish that heralds neither strength nor continued existence [nor (ed.)] a long future (YTC, CVh, 4, p. 47).

m. Of the superiority of mores over laws./

After I have reflected carefully about the principles that make governments act, about those that sustain them or ruin them; when I have spent a good deal of time carefully calculating what the influence of laws is, their relative goodness and their tendency, I always arrive at this point that, above and beyond all these considerations, beyond all these laws, I find a power superior to them. It is the *spirit* and the *mores* of the people, their *character*. The best laws are not able to make a constitution work in spite of the mores; mores turn to good account the worst laws. That is a common truth, but one to which my studies bring me back constantly. It is placed in my mind like a central point; I see it at the end of all my ideas.

Laws, however, work toward producing the spirit, the mores and the character of the people. But in what proportion? There is the great problem that we cannot think about too much (YTC, CVe, p. 52; you can find the same fragment with a few differences, in YTC, CVh, 4, pp. 46–47).

feel the importance that I attributed to the practical experience of the Americans, to their habits, to their opinions, in a word, to their mores, in maintaining their laws, I have missed the principal goal that I set for myself by writing it.

Would Laws and Mores Be Sufficient to Maintain Democratic Institutions Elsewhere than in America?

The Anglo-Americans, transported to Europe, would be obliged to modify their laws.—Democratic institutions must be distinguished from American institutions.—You can imagine democratic laws better than or at least different from those that American democracy has given itself.—The example of America proves only that we must not despair of regulating democracy with the aid of laws and mores.

I said[n] that the success of democratic institutions in the United States was due to the laws themselves and to mores more than to the nature of the country.

But does it follow that these same causes alone transported elsewhere have the same power, and if the country cannot take the place of laws and mores, can laws and mores in turn take the place of the country?

Here you will understand without difficulty that the elements of proof are lacking. In the New World you meet peoples other than the Anglo-Americans, and since these peoples are subject to the same physical causes as the latter, I have been able to compare them to each other.

But outside of America there are no nations that, deprived of the same physical advantages as the Anglo-Americans, have still adopted their laws and their mores.

n. In the manuscript: "I proved . . ."
Édouard de Tocqueville (or Louis de Kergorlay?): "I propose to put: *I believe that I proved.* The peremptory tone must be avoided" (YTC, CIIIb, 1, p. 27).

Therefore we do not have a point of comparison in this matter; we can only hazard opinions.

It seems to me first that the institutions of the United States must be carefully distinguished from democratic institutions in general.

When I think of the state of Europe, its great peoples, its populous cities, its formidable armies, the complexities of its politics, I cannot believe that the Anglo-Americans themselves, transported with their ideas, their religion, their mores to our soil, could live there without considerably modifying their laws.

But you can imagine a democratic people organized in a different manner from the American people.

Is it impossible to conceive of a government based on the real will of the majority, but in which the majority, doing violence to its natural instincts of equality, in favor of order and the stability of the State, would consent to vest a family or a man with all the attributions of the executive power? Can you not imagine a democratic society in which national forces would be more centralized than in the United States, in which the people would exercise a less direct and less irresistible dominion over general affairs, and in which, nonetheless, each citizen, vested with certain rights, would, within his sphere, take part in the working of the government?⁰

What I saw among the Anglo-Americans leads me to believe that democratic institutions of this nature, introduced prudently into so-

o. Hervé de Tocqueville:

Here royalty or the monarchy, and if possible the hereditary monarchy, must find a place. It is indispensable that the author establish that the monarchical State is not incompatible with democratic institutions.

Alexis must pay the greatest attention to avoid a pitfall in which he would be destroyed, that of allowing the belief that he has written a book in favor of the republic. Beyond the fact that reason, enlightened by experience, rejects the possibility of establishing republics strictly speaking among the great European nations, the idea and even the word republic are antipathetic to the very great majority of the French. So if Alexis left the slightest doubt about his dispositions on this subject, he would be blamed by the very greatest number and applauded only by a few scatterbrains and a few muddleheads (YTC, CVh, 3, p. 15).

ciety,P which would mix little by little with the habits and would gradually merge with the very opinions of the people, would be able to subsist elsewhere than in America.q

If the laws of the United States were the only democratic laws that could be imagined or the most perfect that it is possible to find, I understand that you could conclude that the success of the laws of the United States proves nothing for the success of democratic laws in general, in a country less favored by nature.

But if the laws of the Americans seem to me defective in many points, and it is easy for me to imagine others, the special nature of the country does not prove to me that democratic institutions cannot succeed among a people where, physical circumstances being less favorable, the laws would be better.

If men showed themselves to be different in America from what they are elsewhere; if their social state gave birth among them to habits and opinions contrary to those that are born in Europe from this same social state, what happens in the American democracies would teach nothing about what should happen in other democracies.

If the Americans showed the same tendencies as all the other democratic peoples, and their legislators resorted to the nature of the country and to the favor of circumstances in order to keep these tendencies within just

p. In the margin: "I can imagine a democratic nation in which, because political life was more active and more threatened, the executive power was stronger and more active than it has been until now in the New World."

q. Édouard de Tocqueville or Louis de Kergorlay:

Here you seem to formulate a desire, and that seems to me to move away from the goal of your work, beyond other disadvantages that it can have in my view.

Your book can only aspire to a great and general influence if you are very careful not to make yourself into a party man. Now, if you show yourself or if some see you as a republican, you will be considered as a party man.

Take care that this ending does not appear as a plea on behalf of the republic. I tell you this from my soul and conscience, that ending has the appearance of being so and will be regarded as such; now this is what you have always told me you wanted to avoid.

To show, to demonstrate that free institutions can be established in a lasting way only sheltered by morality and religious spirit is a superb thought. It is your whole book. Try not to compromise it (YTC, CIIIb, 1, pp. 27–28).

limits, the prosperity of the United States, having to be attributed to purely physical causes, would prove nothing in favor of peoples who would like to follow their example without having their natural advantages.[r]

But neither the one nor the other of these suppositions is justified by the facts.

I encountered in America passions analogous to those we see in Europe. Some were due to the very nature of the human heart; others, to the democratic state of society.

Thus I found in the United States the restlessness of heart that is natural to man when, all conditions being more or less equal, each one sees the same chances to rise. There I encountered the democratic sentiment of envy expressed in a thousand different ways. I observed that the people often showed, in the conduct of affairs, a great blend of presumption and ignorance, and I concluded that in America, as among us, men were subject to the same imperfections and exposed to the same miseries.

But when I came to examine attentively the state of society, I discovered without difficulty that the Americans had made great and happy efforts to combat these weaknesses of the human heart and to correct these natural defects of democracy.

Their various municipal laws appeared to me as so many barriers that held within a narrow sphere the restless ambition of citizens, and turned to the profit of the town the same democratic passions that could overturn the State. It seemed to me that American legislators had managed to oppose, not without success, the idea of rights to the sentiments of envy; the immobility of religious morality, to the continual movements of the political world; the experience of the people, to their theoretical ignorance; and their habit of affairs, to the hotheadedness of their desires.

So the Americans did not resort to the nature of the country to combat the dangers that arise from their constitution [v: social state] and from their

r. Édouard de Tocqueville or Louis de Kergorlay: "You give, it seems to me, in this paragraph and in a few others of the preceding chapter much too great an influence to the physical nature of a country on the mores and the tendencies of the inhabitants of this country. This influence is not non-existent, but it is far, I believe, from being what you suppose" (YTC, CIIIb, 1, p. 28).

political laws. To the evils that they share with all democratic peoples, they applied remedies that until now only they were aware of; and although they were the first to try them out, they succeeded.

The mores and laws of the Americans are not the only ones that can be suitable for democratic peoples; but the Americans have shown that we must not despair of regulating democracy with the help of laws and mores.

If other peoples, borrowing from America this general and fruitful idea, and without wishing to imitate the inhabitants of America in the particular application that they have made of this idea, attempted to adapt themselves to the social state that Providence imposes on men today, and thus sought to escape the despotism or the anarchy that threatens them, what reasons do we have to believe that they must fail in their efforts?[s]

The organization and the establishment of democracy among Christians is the great political problem of our time. The Americans undoubtedly do not solve this problem, but they provide useful lessons to those who want to solve it.

s. In the manuscript:

If other democratic nations less fortunately situated than the American people, but instructed by experience, succeeded in making use of its discoveries while rejecting its errors, what reason do we have to believe that they must fail in their efforts? So if the example of the United States does not prove in a sufficient way that all countries can adapt themselves to democratic institutions, you can infer even less from it that democratic institutions suit only the United States.

Importance of What Precedes
in Relation to Europe[t]

You easily discover why I have engaged in the research that precedes.[u] The question that I have raised interests not only the United States, but the entire world; not one nation, but all men.

If peoples whose social state is democratic could remain free only when they lived in the wilderness, we would have to despair of the future fate of the human species; for men are marching rapidly toward democracy, and wildernesses are filling.

If it were true that laws and mores were insufficient for maintaining democratic institutions, what other refuge would remain for nations, if not the despotism of one man?[v]

I know that today there are many honest men hardly frightened by this future, who, fatigued by liberty, would love finally to rest far from its storms.[w]

---

t. Hervé de Tocqueville:

I begin my remarks with a general observation which is suggested to me by the very title of this chapter. The author speaks about all of Europe; but he draws his arguments only from the current social state of France, a social state which that of several other great nations of Europe will not resemble for many years to come. All his descriptions portray what is happening in France and not elsewhere. All his predictions relate to France; but he is addressing himself to the whole of Europe. Isn't it to be feared that a strict and exact reader might make this remark with a sort of blame?" (YTC, CIIIb, 1, p. 36).

u. "When I searched for the causes that serve most powerfully to maintain democratic institutions, I did not abandon myself to a vain curiosity. While looking at America, I still saw Europe; and while thinking about American liberty, I thought of that of all men" (YTC, CVh, 4, p. 68).

v. In the manuscript: "if not {monarchy} {absolute power} slavery?"

Édouard de Tocqueville (?): "You must be careful not to use these expressions unstintingly: *slavery, servitude,* which perhaps smack a bit of the orator, as if there were not a thousand degrees between absolute liberty and complete enslavement!" (YTC, CIIIb, 1, pp. 29–30).

w. In the margin:

≠Today.
Liberty with its storms.

But the latter know very badly the port toward which they are heading. Preoccupied by their memories, they judge absolute power by what it was formerly, and not by what it could be today. [There are differences even in despotism, as in liberty.]

If absolute power came to be established once again among the democratic peoples of Europe, I do not doubt that it would take a new form and would show itself with features unknown to our fathers.

There was a time in Europe when the law, as well as the consent of the people, had vested kings with a power almost without limits. But they hardly ever happened to use it.

[They had the right rather than the practice of omnipotence.]

I will not talk about the prerogatives of the nobility, about the authority of the sovereign courts, about the right of corporations, about provincial privileges, which, while softening the blows of authority, maintained a spirit of resistance in the nation.

These political institutions, though often contrary to the liberty of individuals, nonetheless served to foster the love of liberty in souls, and in this respect their utility is easily conceived. Apart from these institutions, opinions and mores raised less known, but no less powerful barriers around royal power.

Religion, love of subjects, the goodness of the prince, honor, family spirit, provincial prejudices, custom and public opinion limited the power of kings and enclosed their authority within an invisible circle.

Despotism with its rigors.

Nothing intermediate between.

Something like the Roman empire.

So there is only one path to salvation, which is to seek to regulate liberty. To moralize democracy.

As for me, I believe that the enterprise is possible.

I am not saying that we must do as America; I am not saying that the Americans have done the best.

(Is there only one type of republic, only one type of royalty?) in the same way there is more than one way to make democracy rule. ≠

Then the constitution of peoples was despotic and their mores, free. Princes had the right, but neither the faculty nor the desire to do everything.

Of the barriers that formerly stopped tyranny, what remains to us today?

Since religion has lost its dominion over souls, the most visible limit that divided good and bad is overturned; all seems doubtful and uncertain in the moral realm; kings and people move there haphazardly, and no one can say where the natural limits of despotism and the bounds of license are.

Long revolutions have forever destroyed the respect that surrounded heads of State. Released from the weight of public esteem, princes can henceforth abandon themselves without fear to being drunk with power.[x]

When kings see, coming before them, the heart of peoples, they are lenient because they feel strong; and they treat the love of their subjects carefully, because the love of subjects is the support of the throne. Then, between the prince and the people, an exchange of sentiments is established whose gentleness recalls within society the interior of the family. Subjects, while murmuring against the sovereign, are still distressed to displease him, and the sovereign strikes his subjects with a light hand, as a father chastises his children.

But once the prestige of royalty has vanished amid the tumult of revolutions; when kings, following each other upon the throne, have one by one exposed to the view of the people the weakness of *right* and the harsh-

x. Hervé de Tocqueville:

Released from the weight of public esteem, etc. First, I observe that this paragraph and the two following are badly placed; they are inserted in a series of ideas that they interrupt. As for the sentence of which I have quoted the first words, it is turned in a picturesque and energetic way, but it lacks clarity; the author wants to say that kings will more easily do ill because they will no longer have to fear the loss of public esteem. There is the sense; but one searches for it. Is the idea, moreover, very correct? Although the prestige of royalty is partially destroyed, a good king who is an honest man will always garner public esteem and this esteem will be a barrier to his passions (YTC, CIIIb, 1, pp. 37–38).

ness of *fact*,[y] no one any longer sees in the sovereign the father of the State, and each one sees a master there. If he is weak, he is scorned; he is hated if he is strong. He is himself full of rage and fear; he sees himself as a stranger in his country and treats his subjects as the vanquished.

When provinces and cities were so many different nations in the middle of the common native land, each one of them had a particular spirit that opposed the general spirit of servitude; but today when, after losing their franchises, their customs, their prejudices and even their memories and their names, all parts of the same empire have become accustomed to obeying the same laws, it is no more difficult to oppress all of them together than to oppress one separately from the rest.

While the nobility enjoyed its power, and still long after it had lost it, aristocratic honor gave an extraordinary strength to individual resistance.

Then you saw men who, despite their impotence, still maintained a high idea of their individual value, and dared to resist in isolation the exertion of public power. [<For honor is a religion; it cannot be conquered by force.>][z]

But today, when all classes are merging together, when the individual disappears more and more in the crowd and is easily lost amid the common obscurity; today, when nothing any longer sustains man above himself, be-

y. Hervé de Tocqueville:

You must put *the weakness of right and the harshness of fact*. It is essential that Alexis be very careful not to strike the fallen Restoration and the deposed and unhappy sovereigns. It would perhaps even be appropriate enough that he not strike Louis-Philippe too hard. Alexis is beginning his career; it would be disagreeable for him to have all the government newspapers against him. This is undoubtedly a very secondary consideration, but it will be good to consider it (YTC, CIIIb, 1, pp. 38–39).

z. Édouard de Tocqueville (?):

All that is good in thought and style. Nothing easier than to keep it while indicating precisely how far we are by our mores from the mores of the Americans. A truth that is good to put in relief, because if we succeed in changing our mores, we will perhaps be worthy of the pure democratic state that is perhaps in fact the best. But how far we are from that! And for how long a time still would a similar attempt be fatal! (YTC, CIIIb, 1, p. 30).

cause monarchical honor has nearly lost its dominion without being replaced by virtue,[a] who can say where the exigencies of [absolute] power and
the indulgences of weakness would stop?

As long as family spirit lasted, the man who struggled against tyranny
was never alone; he found around him clients, hereditary friends, close relatives. And if this support were missing, he still felt sustained by his ancestors
and roused by his descendants. But when patrimonies are dividing, and
when in so few years races are merging, where to locate family spirit?

[≠Within a restless crowd a man surrounded by soldiers will come to
take a place. No one will see in him the father of the State. Each one will

---

a. Of virtue in republics./

The Americans are not a virtuous people and yet they are free. This does not absolutely prove that virtue, as Montesquieu thought, is not essential to the existence
of republics. The idea of Montesquieu must not be taken in a narrow sense. What
this g[reat (ed.)]. m[an (ed.)]. meant is that republics could subsist only by the action
of society over itself. What he means by virtue is the moral power that each individual
exercises over himself and that prevents him from violating the right of others.

When this triumph of man over temptation is the result of the weakness of the
temptation or of a calculation of personal interest, it does not constitute virtue in
the eyes of the moralist; but it is included in the idea of Montesquieu who spoke of
the effect much more than of the cause. In America it is not virtue that is great, it is
temptation that is small, which comes to the same thing. It is not disinterestedness
that is great, it is interest that is well understood, which again comes back to almost
the same thing. So Montesquieu was right although he spoke about ancient virtue,
and what he says of the Greeks and Romans is still applicable to the Americans (YTC,
CVe, pp. 66–67).

During his journey, however, Tocqueville had noted:

The principle of the ancient republics was the sacrifice of particular interest to the
general good. In this sense, you can say that they were *virtuous*. The principle of this
one appears to me to be to make particular interest part of the general interest. A
kind of refined and intelligent egoism seems the pivot on which the whole machine
turns. These people do not trouble themselves to find out if public virtue is good,
but they claim to prove that it is useful. If this last point is true, as I think it is in
part, this society can pass for enlightened, but not virtuous. But to what degree can
the two principles of individual good and general good in fact be merged? To what
point will a conscience that you could call a conscience of reflection and calculation
be able to control the political passions that have not yet arisen, but which will not
fail to arise? That is what the future alone will show us. Sing-Sing, 29 May, 1831 (alphabetic notebook A, YTC, BIIa, and *Voyage, OC,* V, 1, pp. 234–35).

see a master. He will no longer be respected; he will be feared; and love will be replaced by fear.

He himself will be agitated and restless. He will feel that he rules only by force and not by right, by fear and not by love. His subjects will be strangers in his eyes; he himself will be a stranger in theirs. ≠]

What strength remains to customs among a people who have changed entirely and who change constantly, where all the acts of tyranny already have a precedent, where all crimes can rest on an example, where you can find nothing so old that you are afraid to destroy it, nor anything so new that you cannot dare to do it?

What resistance is offered by mores that have already given way so many times?

What can public opinion itself do, when not *twenty*[b] persons are gathered together by a common bond; when there is neither a man, nor a family, nor a body, nor a class, nor a free association that can represent and get this opinion to act?

When each citizen equally impotent, equally poor, equally isolated can oppose only his individual weakness to the organized strength of the government?

In order to imagine something analogous to what would then happen among us,[c] you must resort not to our historical annals. You must perhaps search the memorials of antiquity[d] and refer to those horrible centuries of Roman tyranny, when mores were corrupt, memories obliterated, habits destroyed, [religions shaken], opinions wavering; liberty, chased from the laws, no longer knew where to take refuge in order to find a shelter. Then nothing protected citizens any longer, and citizens no longer protected

---

b. Allusion to the French law of association that demanded prior permission for all meetings of more than twenty persons.

c. In the manuscript: ". . . among the nations of Europe."

d. Édouard de Tocqueville (?): "I contest this idea. Antiquity is so far away, so different from our current social state, that you cannot, I believe, draw from it any point of comparison to what exists today. And I think that amid the general divergence of opinions, the only incontestable point is that what is happening in our time is without precedents" (YTC, CIIIb, pp. 30–31).

themselves; you saw men mock human nature and princes exhaust the mercy of heaven rather than the patience of their subjects.[e]

Those who think to rediscover the monarchy of Henry IV or Louis XIV seem very blind to me. As for me, when I consider the state which several European nations have already reached and toward which all the others are tending, I feel myself led to believe that among them there will soon no longer be a place except for democratic liberty[f] or for the tyranny of the Caesars.[g]

Doesn't this merit reflection? If men must in fact reach the point where they must all be made free or all slaves, all equal in rights or all deprived of rights; if those who govern societies were reduced to the alternative of gradually raising the crowd up to their level or allowing all citizens to fall below

e. "Characteristics of Roman society./

No more {love of country} patriotism.

No more fear of God.

Individual egoism" (YTC, CVh, 4, p. 57). See note a for p. 18.

f. "If peoples saw a stopping point between absolute power and democratic government, they would do well to settle there. But this point does not exist, and they must keep moving" (YTC, CVh, 4, pp. 53–54).

g. Hervé de Tocqueville:

The two paragraphs of these two pages are very beautiful in style, written with great force, but the colors are too dark. The horrible state of Rome under the Caesars is not to be feared for many years, neither for France nor for Europe. For that to happen civilization would have to regress and the Christian religion would have to be destroyed.

Alexis must be careful that he is not accused of having presented a dismal phantasm in order to win acceptance for his democratic ideas. The expression of an orator who wants to move his listeners powerfully can be energetic beyond bounds. That of a writer must always be wise and measured. In all, I would like Alexis to launch out more into the future and apply these last portraits less to the present state.

What Alexis says is true in this sense, that the sovereign of France, like that of Rome, combined in his person a plenitude of powers and authority. He abused them undoubtedly, but not in the same way as the Caesars, nor with the same bloody and ignoble violence. The author could perhaps revise in this sense (YTC, CIIIb, 1, pp. 39–40).

Cf. note e for p. 1249 of the second volume.

the level of humanity, wouldn't this be enough to overcome many doubts, reassure many consciences, and prepare each person to make great sacrifices easily?

Shouldn't the gradual development of democratic institutions and mores then be considered, not as the best, but as the sole means that remains for us to be free; and without loving the government of democracy, wouldn't we be disposed to adopt it as the most applicable and most decent remedy that may be opposed to the present ills of society?[h]

It is difficult to make the people participate in government; it is still more difficult to provide them with the experience and give them the sentiments that they lack to govern well.[j]

The will of democracy is changeable; its agents, crude; its laws, imperfect; I grant it. But if it were true that soon no intermediary must exist between the dominion of democracy and the yoke of one man, shouldn't we tend toward the one rather than subject ourselves voluntarily to the other? And if it were necessary finally to arrive at a complete equality, wouldn't it be better to allow ourselves to be leveled by liberty than by a despot?

Those who, after reading this book, would judge that by writing it I wanted to propose the Anglo-American laws and mores for the imitation of all peoples who have a democratic social state would have made a great error; they would be attached to the form, abandoning the very substance of my thought.[k] My goal has been to show, by the example of America,

h. "If the establishment of liberty [v: democracy] was the sole means available to preserve human independence, shouldn't it be followed with order even by those who do not judge it the most desirable?" (YTC, CVh, 4, p. 9).

j. "I would like the upper classes and the middle classes of all of Europe to be as persuaded as I am myself that henceforth it is no longer a matter of knowing if the people will come to share power, but in what way they will use their power. That alone is where the great problem of the future is located" (YTC, CVh, 3, p. 32).

k. Importance of this fact for Europe.

Irresistible march of democracy.

To regulate it, to instruct it, great problem of the present.

Misfortunes that would result for the human species from not doing so, intolerable despotism, without safeguard. . . . What is happening in America does not show that it can be done, although it does not prove that it must be done in the same way.

that laws and above all mores could allow a democratic people to remain free. I am, moreover, very far from believing that we must follow the example that American democracy has given and imitate the means that it used to attain the goal of its efforts;[m] for I am not unaware of the influence exercised by the nature of the country and antecedent facts on political constitutions, and I would regard it as a great misfortune for humankind if liberty, in all places, had to occur with the same features.[n]

But I think that if we do not manage little by little to introduce and finally to establish democratic institutions among us, and if we abandon giving all citizens the ideas and sentiments that first prepare them for liberty and then allow them the practice of those ideas and sentiments, there will be independence for no one, neither for the bourgeois, nor for the noble,

----

It is the thought, always present, of this future, *irresistible* that (illegible word) was always present to the author of this book.

I proved well that the physical situation of the Americans without their laws and their mores would not suffice, but I did not prove that their laws and their mores are sufficient without their physical situation (YTC, CVh, 2, p. 110).

m. "What I wanted to say . . . that *mores* and *laws* had more power than the *country*. If that is true, why would we not hope to succeed? Why would we despair of making something stable and lasting?

"I am not saying that we must do as the Americans, but we can arrive at the same result by another path, and their example can provide useful light" (YTC, CVh, 4, p. 11).

n. The paragraph is written this way in the manuscript:

The institutions of the United States are not the only ones that must assure the liberty of men. I am certainly far from believing so. I will admit without difficulty that a nation can remain free without having precisely the same habits and the same ideas as the American people. While retracing the laws and portraying the mores of the American democracy, I have not claimed that all democratic peoples can imitate the first and adopt the second, for I am not unaware of the influence exercised by the nature of the country on its political constitution and I would regard it as a great misfortune for humankind if liberty could only occur under a single form. So I am far from believing that in everything we must imitate the government that American democracy has given itself.

nor for the poor, nor for the rich, but an equal tyranny for all; and I foresee that if we do not succeed over time in establishing among us the peaceful dominion of the greatest number, we will arrive sooner or later at the *unlimited* power of one man.°

o. The question of knowing the name of the one who reigns, even the questions of royalty or republic, capital questions in ordinary times, have only a secondary interest, however, in the extraordinary century in which we live, unless they are attached to another still more vast. The great, the capital interest of the century is the organization and education of democracy.

[In the margin: We must not forget, today it is very much more a matter of the very existence of society than of one form of government rather than another, but it is of civilization as much as of laws [v: to know if we will be free or slave], of human dignity as much as of the prosperity of some, of the fate of three or four hundred million men and not of the destiny of a nation. It is much more about the very history of society . . .]

But that is what we scarcely consider. Placed in the middle of a rapid river, we obstinately fix our eyes on some debris that we still see on the bank, while the torrent carries us away and pushes us backward toward the abyss.

I spoke above about men who were present at the ruin of the Roman empire. Let us fear that the same fate (illegible word) us. This time the barbarians will come not out of the frozen North; they are rising from the heart of our fields and from the very midst of our cities (YTC, CVh, 3, p. 31).

CHAPTER 10

Some Considerations on the Present State and Probable Future of the Three Races That Inhabit the Territory of the United States[a]

The principal task that I had set for myself has now been fulfilled; I have succeeded, at least as much as I could, in showing what the laws of the American democracy were; I have made its mores known. I could stop here, but the reader would perhaps find that I have not satisfied his expectation.

You encounter in America something more than an immense and complete democracy; the peoples who inhabit the New World can be seen from more than one point of view.

In the course of this work, my subject often led me to speak about In-

---

a. Added at the last moment, this chapter could not be the object of the critical readings by the family, Kergorlay, or Beaumont. It is not easy to date its composition in a precise way, but many indications lead to the idea that it was written during the spring or summer of 1834. On the 15th of August of that year, his manuscript under his arm, Tocqueville arrived at the chateau de Gallarande, in the Sarthe, invited by Madame Eugénie de Sarce, sister of Gustave de Beaumont. He remained with the Beaumonts until the middle of September. In July, Tocqueville had written to Beaumont to confide in him that he did not believe that Gosselin had read the manuscript and to ask his help on the titles of chapters, which indicates that the manuscript sent to Gosselin did not then constitute the definitive text.

In this chapter, the similarity to the ideas of Beaumont on the Indians and Blacks is clear. It consists not only of the consideration of identical questions; it even touches on sources and citations. Did Beaumont persuade Tocqueville to treat a question that, in the beginning, belonged to *Marie?* Does Tocqueville's decision have something to do with the racial problems that broke out on the East coast of the United States during the summer of 1834? Did Tocqueville review and correct this chapter while with the Beaumont family at the end of the summer? The manuscript of the chapter does not present great differences from the published version and the number of drafts, appreciably less than that for other chapters, attests to a rapid composition.

dians and Negroes, but I never had the time to stop to show what position these two races occupy in the midst of the democratic people that I was busy portraying; I said according to what spirit, with the aid of what laws, the Anglo-American confederation had been formed; I could only indicate in passing, and in a very incomplete way, the dangers that menace this confederation, and it was impossible for me to explain in detail what its chances of enduring were, apart from laws and mores. While speaking about the united republics, I hazarded no conjecture about the permanence of republican forms in the New World, and although alluding frequently to the commercial activity that reigns in the Union, I was not able to deal with the future of the Americans as a commercial people.

These topics touch on my subject, but do not enter into it; they are American without being democratic, and above all I wanted to portray democracy. So I had to put them aside at first; but I must return to them as I finish.[b]

The territory occupied today, or claimed by the American Union, extends from the Atlantic Ocean to the shores of the Pacific Ocean. So in the east or in the west, its limits are those of the continent itself; the territory advances in the south to the edge of the Tropics and then goes back up to the middle of the frozen areas of the North.

The men spread throughout this space do not form, as in Europe, so many offshoots of the same family. You discover among them, from the outset, three naturally distinct and, I could almost say, enemy races. Education, laws, origins and even the external form of their features, have raised an almost insurmountable barrier between them; fortune gathered them together on the same soil, but it mixed them together without being able to blend them, and each one pursues its destiny apart.

Among such diverse men, the first who attracts attention, the first in enlightenment, in power, in happiness, is the white man, the European, man *par excellence;*[c] below him appear the Negro and the Indian.

b. In a draft the paragraph continues in this way: "I am still going to talk about America, but no more about democracy" (YTC, CVh, 3, p. 33).

c. In another version: "{To him belongs the most beautiful portion of the future. Why this unequal sharing of the good things of this world? Who can say?}"

These two unfortunate races have neither birth, nor facial features, nor language, nor mores in common; their misfortunes alone are similar. Both occupy an equally inferior position in the country that they inhabit; both suffer the effects of tyranny; and if their miseries are different, they can blame the same authors for them.

Wouldn't you say, seeing what is happening in the world, that the European is to the men of other races what man himself is to the animals? He makes them serve his purposes, and when he cannot make them bend, he destroys them.[d]

Oppression deprived the descendants of the Africans at a stroke of nearly all the privileges of humanity. The Negro of the United States has lost even the memory of his country; he no longer hears the language spoken by his fathers; he has renounced their religion and forgotten their mores. While thus ceasing to belong to Africa, however, he has acquired no right to the good things of Europe; but he has stopped between the two societies; he has remained isolated between the two peoples; sold by the one and repudiated by the other; finding in the whole world only the home of his master to offer him the incomplete picture of a native land.

The Negro has no family; he cannot see in a woman anything other than the temporary companion of his pleasures and, at birth, his sons are his equals.

Shall I call it a benefit of God or a final curse of His anger, this disposition of the soul that makes man insensible to extreme miseries and often even gives him a kind of depraved taste for the cause of his misfortunes?

Plunged into this abyss of evils, the Negro scarcely feels his misfortune; violence had placed him in slavery; the practice of servitude has given him the thoughts and ambition of a slave; he admires his tyrants even more than he hates them, and finds his joy and his pride in servile imitation of those who oppress him.

His intelligence has fallen to the level of his soul.

The Negro enters into servitude and into life at the same time. What

---

d. To the side of a first version: "≠Why of these three races, is one born to perish, the other to rule and the last to serve?≠"

am I saying? Often he is purchased right from the womb of his mother, and so to speak he starts to be a slave before being born.

Without need as without pleasure, useless to himself, he understands, by the first notions that he receives of existence, that he is the property of another, whose interest is to watch over his days; he sees that the care for his own fate has not devolved upon him. The very use of thought seems to him a useless gift from Providence, and he peacefully enjoys all the privileges of his servility.

If he becomes free, independence often then seems to him to be a heavier chain than slavery itself; for in the course of his existence, he has learned to submit to everything, except to reason; and when reason becomes his sole guide, he cannot recognize its voice. A thousand new needs besiege him, and he lacks the knowledge and the energy necessary to resist them. Needs are masters that must be fought, and he has only learned to submit and to obey. So he has reached this depth of misery in which servitude brutalizes him and liberty destroys him.

Oppression has exercised no less influence over the Indian races, but its effects are different.

[≠Europeans have introduced some new needs and some unknown vices among the savages of North America; but they have not been able entirely to modify the character of these savage bands. Europeans have been able to make their tribes disappear, to invade [v: to take the land away from them] their native land, but they have never submitted to the Europeans. Some have evaded servitude by flight, others by death.≠]

Before the arrival of whites in the New World, the men who inhabited North America lived tranquilly in the woods. Given over to the ordinary vicissitudes of savage life, they exhibited the vices and virtues of uncivilized peoples.[*] Europeans, after scattering the Indian tribes far into the wilderness, condemned them to a wandering and restless life, full of inexpressible miseries.

---

[*]. See on the history, the mores of the natives of America before the arrival of the Europeans and on the philosophy of their languages the very curious research of R. Heckewelder, Duponceau . . . , contained in the first volume of the transactions of the American Philosophical Society, Philadelphia, 1819. Say what [two illegible words] Cooper drew from him.

Savage nations are governed only by opinions and mores.

By weakening the sentiment of native land among the Indians of North America, by scattering their families, by obscuring their traditions, by interrupting the chain of memory, by changing all their habits, and by increasing their needs inordinately, European tyranny has made them more disorderly and less civilized than they already were. The moral condition and physical state of these peoples did not cease to deteriorate at the same time, and they became more barbaric as they became more unhappy. Nonetheless, Europeans have not been able entirely to modify the character of the Indians, and with the power to destroy them, they have never had that of civilizing and subjugating them.

The Negro is placed at the furthest limits of servitude; the Indian, at the extreme limits of liberty. The effects of slavery on the first are scarcely more harmful than the effects of independence on the second.

The Negro has lost even ownership of his person, and he cannot dispose of his own existence without committing a kind of larceny.

The savage is left to himself as soon as he can act. He has hardly known the authority of family; he has never bent his will to that of his fellows; no one has taught him to distinguish a voluntary obedience from a shameful subjection, and he is unaware of even the name of law. For him, to be free is to escape nearly all the bonds of society. He delights in this barbarous independence, and he would prefer to perish rather than to sacrifice the smallest part of it. Civilization has little hold over such a man.

The Negro makes a thousand hapless efforts in order to enter into a society that pushes him away; he bows to the tastes of his oppressors, adopts their opinions, and aspires, by imitating them, to be mingled with them. He has been told since birth that his race is naturally inferior to that of the whites and he is not far from believing it; so he is ashamed of himself. In each one of his features he finds a mark of slavery and, if he could, he would joyfully consent to repudiate himself completely.

The Indian, in contrast, has an imagination entirely filled with the alleged nobility of his origin. He lives and dies amid these dreams of his pride.[e] Far

---

e. In the margin: "≠He perishes by the exaggeration of the sentiments that the first one lacks.≠"

from wanting to bend his mores to ours, he is attached to barbarism as a distinctive sign of his race, and he rejects civilization perhaps still less out of hatred for it than out of fear of resembling the Europeans.[1]

To the perfection of our arts, he wants to oppose only the resources of the wilderness; to our tactics, only his undisciplined courage; to the depth of our plans, only the spontaneous instincts of his savage nature. He succumbs in this unequal struggle.[g]

The Negro would like to mingle with the European, and he cannot do so. The Indian could, to a certain point, succeed in doing so, but he disdains to try. The servility of the one delivers him to slavery, and the pride of the other, to death.

I remember that traveling through the forests that still cover the state of

1. *The native of North America keeps his opinions and even the smallest detail of his habits with an inflexibility that is without example in history. During the more than two hundred years that the wandering tribes of North America have had daily connections with the white race, they have borrowed so to speak neither an idea nor a custom. The men of Europe have, however, exercised a very great influence over the savages. They have made the Indian character more disordered, but they have not made it more European. Finding myself in the summer of 1831 beyond Lake Michigan, in the place named Green-Bay, which serves as the extreme frontier of the United States with the Indians of the Northwest, I met an American officer, Major H., who, one day, after talking to me a great deal about the inflexibility of the Indian character, told me about the following event:*

*"I once knew," he says to me, "a young Indian who had been raised in a college in New England. He had been very successful there, and had taken the full external appearance of a civilized man. When war broke out between us and the English in 1810,[f] I saw this young man again; he was then serving in our army, at the head of some warriors of his tribe. The Americans had allowed Indians in their ranks only on the condition that they abstained from the horrible custom of scalping the defeated. The evening of the battle of ***, C... came to sit down close to the fire of our bivouac; I asked him what had happened to him during the day; he told me, and gradually growing excited with the memory of his exploits, he ended by half-opening his jacket while saying:—'Don't betray me, but see!' In fact I saw," added Major H., "between his body and his shirt, the scalp of an Englishman still dripping with blood."*

f. It certainly concerns the War of 1812. The person Tocqueville was speaking to was Major Lamard (non-alphabetic notebook 1, YTC, BIIa, and *Voyage, OC,* V, 1, pp. 75–78).

g. To the side: "≠The Negro by being a slave loses the taste for and the possibility of being free; the Indian by being free becomes incapable of becoming civilized. The one cannot learn to be free; the other, to put limits on his liberty.≠"

African Americans are told they are inferior, taught to submit. All they know is to serve. Indians fear submission. Their pride does not allow them to be tamed.

Alabama, I arrived one day next to the cabin of a pioneer. I did not want to enter the dwelling of the American, but I went to rest for a few moments at the edge of a spring not far from there in the woods. While I was in this place, an Indian woman came (we then were near the territory occupied by the Creek nation); she held the hand of a small girl five or six years old, belonging to the white race, whom I supposed to be the daughter of the pioneer. A Negro woman followed them. A kind of barbaric luxury distinguished the costume of the Indian woman: metal rings were suspended from her nostrils and ears; her hair, mixed with glass beads, fell freely over her shoulders, and I saw that she wasn't married, for she still wore the shell necklace that virgins customarily put down on the nuptial bed. The Negro woman was dressed in European clothes almost in tatters.

All three came to sit down beside the spring, and the young savage, taking the child in her arms, lavished on her caresses that you could have believed were dictated by a mother's heart; on her side, the Negro woman sought by a thousand innocent tricks to attract the attention of the small Creole. The latter showed in her slightest movements a sentiment of superiority that contrasted strangely with her weakness and her age; you would have said that she received the attentions of her companions with a kind of condescension.

Squatting in front of her mistress, watching closely for each of her desires, the Negro woman seemed equally divided between an almost maternal attachment and a servile fear; while a free, proud, and almost fierce air distinguished even the savage woman's effusion of tenderness.

I approached and contemplated this spectacle in silence; my curiosity undoubtedly displeased the Indian woman, for she suddenly arose, pushed the child far away from her with a kind of roughness, and, after giving me an irritated look, plunged into the woods.

I had often happened to see gathered in the same places individuals belonging to the three human races that people North America. I had already recognized by a thousand various effects the preponderance exercised by the whites. But, in the scene that I have just described, there was something particularly touching: a bond of affection united the oppressed to the oppressors here, and nature, by trying hard to bring them together, made still more striking the immense space put between them by prejudice and laws.

Present State and Probable Future of the Indian Tribes That Inhabit the Territory Possessed by the Union[h]

Gradual disappearance of the native races.—How it is taking place.—Miseries that accompany the forced migrations of the Indians.—The savages of North America had only two means to escape destruction: war or civilization.—They can no longer wage war.—Why they do not want to become civilized when they could do so, and, when they reach the point of wanting to do so, they no longer can.—Example of the Creeks and the Cherokees.—Policy of the particular states toward these Indians.—Policy of the federal government.

All the Indian tribes that formerly inhabited the territory of New England, the Narragansetts, the Mohicans, the Pequots no longer live except in the

---

h. Detached note in the manuscript:

Plan of the chapter.
    1. Destruction of the Indians, *a fact.*
    2. How it is taking place.
You make the wild game flee. You buy the land. (Here introduce commercial mores.)
    3. Inevitable destruction.
    1. War or civilization.
War, they can no longer wage it.
    2. Civilization remains.
Difficulty that hunting peoples have in becoming civilized. It would be necessary to have [in advance (?) (ed.)] to become a farmer.
    Idleness and *pride* that prevent them from wanting to do so.
    When they want to do so, they are not longer able (here I placed the *half-breeds,* perhaps elsewhere). Effects of an incomplete civilization in contact with a complete one.
    What precedes is an imperceptible and so to speak involuntary action of one race on another, but often the positive and voluntary action of governments is joined with it. Cherokees, Creeks, way of acting toward them of the state and federal governments.

The appendix devoted to the Indians in the second volume of *Marie* ("Note on the past state and the present condition of the Indian tribes of North America") gives interesting details on their way of life and their habits that do not appear in Tocqueville's work.
See Harry Liebersohn, *Aristocratic Encounters* (Cambridge: Cambridge University Press, 1998), pp. 92–112.

memory of men; the Lenapes [Delawares] who received Penn, one hundred and fifty years ago, on the banks of the Delaware, have disappeared today.j I met the last of the Iroquois; they were begging. All the nations that I have just named formerly extended as far as the shores of the sea; now you must go more than one hundred leagues into the interior of the continent to meet an Indian. These savages have not only withdrawn, they are destroyed.[2] As the natives move away and die, an immense people comes and increases continuously in their place. Neither a development so prodigious nor a destruction so rapid has ever been seen among nations.

It is easy to indicate the manner in which this destruction is taking place.

When the Indians lived alone in the wilderness from which they are exiled today, their needs were few [and the means to provide for them very numerous]; they made their own arms; river water was their only drink; and they had as clothing the hide of the animals whose flesh served to nourish them.

Europeans introduced to the natives of North America firearms, iron and brandy; they taught them to replace with our fabrics the barbarian clothing that contented Indian simplicity until then. While contracting new tastes, the Indians have not learned the art of satisfying them, and they have had to resort to the industry of whites. In return for these goods, which he himself did not know how to create, the savage could offer nothing, other than the rich furs that his woods still contained. From this moment, the hunt had to provide not only for his needs, but also for the frivolous passions of Europe. He no longer pursued the beasts of the forest only to

j. On a loose slip of paper in the manuscript: "Present state of the relations of the United States with all the Indians who surround their territory. See report of the Secretary of War, L. Cass, 29 November 1833. *National Intelligencer* of 10 December 1833." Beaumont had subscribed to the *National Intelligencer* in 1833. Tocqueville drew from this newspaper many details for writing this chapter.

2. *In the thirteen original states, only 6,273 Indians remain. (See Legislative Documents, 20th Congress, n. 117, p. 90).*

nourish himself, but to obtain the only objects of exchange that he could give us.[3]

While the needs of the natives grew in this way, their resources did not cease to diminish.

From the day when a European settlement forms in the neighborhood of the territory occupied by the Indians, the wild game becomes alarmed.[4] Thousands of savages, wandering in the forests, without fixed abodes, do not frighten the game; but the instant the continuous noises of European industry are heard in some place, the game begins to flee and to withdraw toward the west, where its instinct teaches it that still limitless wildernesses will be found. "But the buffalo is constantly receding," say Messrs. Cass and Clark in their report to Congress, 4 February 1829. "A few years since,

3. *Messrs. Clark and Cass, in their report to Congress, 4 February 1829, p. 23, said:*

The time is already long past when the Indians could supply themselves with the things necessary for their food and clothing without resorting to the industry of civilized men. Beyond the Mississippi, in a country where immense herds of buffalo are still found, live Indian tribes that follow the migrations of these wild animals; the Indians that we are speaking about still find the means to live by following all the customs of their fathers; but the buffalo are constantly withdrawing. Now you can no longer get, except with rifles or traps, the smaller type of wild animals, such as bear, deer, beaver, muskrat, that particularly provide the Indians with what is necessary to sustain life.

It is principally in the northwest that the Indians are forced to expend excessive effort to nourish their families. Often the hunter devotes several days in a row to pursuing game without success; during this time, his family must eat bark and roots or perish; consequently many of them die of hunger every winter.[k]

The Indians do not want to live like the Europeans; they cannot do without the Europeans, however, nor live entirely as their fathers did. You will judge so by this sole fact, the knowledge of which I draw as well from an official source. Some men belonging to an Indian tribe on the shores of Lake Superior had killed a European; the American government forbid trading with the tribe of which the guilty parties were part, until they had been surrendered: which took place.

k. This citation is also found in *Marie*, II, pp. 291–92.

4. *"Five years ago," says Volney in his* Tableau des Etats-Unis, *p. 370, "while going from Vincennes to Kaskaskia, territory included today in the state of Illinois, then entirely wild (1797), you did not cross the prairies without seeing herds of four to five hundred buffaloes; today none of them remain; they crossed the Mississippi by swimming, bothered by hunters and above all by the bells of American cows."*

they approached the base of the Alleghany, and a few years hence they may even be rare upon the immense plains which extend to the base of the Rocky Mountains." I was assured that this effect of the approach of whites [{Europeans}] often makes itself felt two hundred leagues from their frontier. Their influence is exercised therefore on tribes whose name they hardly know and who suffer the evils of usurpation long before knowing the authors of it.[5]

Soon hardy adventurers penetrate the Indian countries; they advance fifteen or twenty leagues beyond the extreme frontier of the whites and go to build the dwelling of civilized man in the very midst of barbarism. It is easy for them to do so: the limits of the territory of a hunting people are poorly fixed. This territory belongs, moreover, to the entire nation and is not precisely the property of anyone; so individual interest defends no part of it.[m]

A few European families, occupying widely separated points, then succeed in chasing forever the wild animals from all the intermediate space that stretches between them. The Indians, who had lived until then in a sort of abundance, find it difficult to survive, still more difficult to obtain the objects of exchange that they need. By making their game flee, it is as if you made the fields of our farmers sterile. Soon they almost entirely lack the means of existence. You then meet these unfortunate people prowling about like famished wolves amid their deserted woods. Instinctive love of native land attaches them to the soil where they were born,[6] and they no

---

5. *You can be persuaded of the truth of what I am advancing here by consulting the general portrait of the Indian tribes contained within the limits claimed by the United States* (Legislative Documents, *20th Congress, n. 117, pp. 90–105). You will see that the tribes in the center of America are rapidly decreasing, although the Europeans are still very far from them.*

m. An identical sentence can be found in *Marie* (II, p. 233).

6. *The Indians, say Messrs. Clark and Cass in their report to Congress, p. 15, are attached to their country by the same sentiment of affection that ties us to ours; and furthermore, to the idea of alienating the lands that the Great Spirit gave to their ancestors, they attach certain superstitious ideas that exercise a great power over the tribes that have still not given anything up or who have given up only a small portion of their territory to Europeans. "We do not sell the place where the remains of our fathers rest," such is the first response that they always make to whoever proposes to buy their lands.*

longer find anything there except misery and death. They finally make up their minds; they leave, and following at a distance the flight of the elk, the buffalo and the beaver, they leave to these wild animals the care of choosing a new homeland for them. So it is not, strictly speaking, the Europeans[n] who chase the natives of America away, it is famine; happy distinction that had escaped the old casuists and that modern [{Protestant}] doctors have discovered.

You cannot imagine the dreadful evils that accompany these forced emigrations. At the moment when the Indians left their paternal lands, they were already exhausted and reduced. The country where they are going to settle is occupied by wandering tribes who see the new arrivals only with jealousy. Behind them is hunger, ahead of them is war, everywhere there is misery. In order to escape so many enemies, they divide up. Each one of them tries to isolate himself in order to find furtively the means to sustain his existence, and lives in the immensity of the wilderness like the outlaw in the bosom of civilized societies. The social bond, long weakened, then breaks. For them, there already was no longer a native land. Soon there will no longer be a people; families will scarcely remain; the common name is being lost, language forgotten, the traces of origin disappear. The nation has ceased to exist. It scarcely lives in the memory of American antiquarians and is known only to a few European scholars.

I would not want the reader to be able to believe that I am exaggerating my descriptions here.[o] I have seen with my own eyes several of the miseries that I have just described; I have gazed upon evils that would be impossible for me to recount.

At the end of the year 1831, I found myself on the left bank of the Mississippi, at a place named Memphis by the Europeans. While I was in this place, a numerous troop of Choctaws (the French of Louisiana call them *Chactas*) came; these savages left their country and tried to pass to the right bank of the Mississippi where they flattered themselves about finding a refuge that the American government had promised them. It was then the

n. If the word *European* is kept here, in most cases it has been crossed out and *Anglo-Americans* substituted.

o. In the manuscript: "that I am inventing [v: creating] descriptions at will here."

heart of winter, and the cold gripped that year with unaccustomed intensity; snow had hardened on the ground, and the river swept along enormous chunks of ice. The Indians led their families with them; they dragged along behind them the wounded, the sick, the newborn children, the elderly about to die. They had neither tents nor wagons, but only a few provisions and weapons. I saw them embark to cross the great river, and this solemn spectacle will never leave my memory. You heard among this assembled crowd neither sobs nor complaints; they kept quiet. Their misfortunes were old and seemed to them without remedy. All the Indians had already entered the vessel that was to carry them; their dogs still remained on the bank; when these animals saw finally that their masters were going away forever, they let out dreadful howls, and throwing themselves at the same time into the icy waters of the Mississippi, they swam after their masters.

The dispossession of the Indians often takes place today in a regular and, so to speak, entirely legal manner.

When the European population begins to approach the wilderness occupied by a savage nation, the government of the United States commonly sends to the latter a solemn embassy. The whites assemble the Indians in a great field and, after eating and drinking with them, say to them:

> What are you doing in the land of your fathers? Soon you will have to dig up their bones to live there. How is the country where you live better than another? Are there woods, marshes and prairies only here where you are, and can you live only under your sun? Beyond these mountains that you see on the horizon, beyond the lake that borders your territory on the west, you find vast countries where wild game is still found in abundance; sell us your lands and go to live happily in those places.

After giving this speech, firearms, woolen clothing, casks of brandy, glass necklaces, tin bracelets, earrings and mirrors are spread out before the eyes of the Indians.[7] If, at the sight of all these riches, they still hesitate, it is

---

7. *See in the* Legislative Documents of Congress, *doc. 117, the account of what happens in these circumstances. This curious piece is found in the report already cited, made*

insinuated that they cannot refuse the consent demanded of them, and that soon the government itself will be unable to guarantee to them the enjoyment of their rights.[*] What to do? Half persuaded, half forced, the Indians move away; they go to inhabit new wildernesses where whites will not leave them in peace for even ten years. In this way the Americans acquire at a very low price entire provinces that the richest sovereigns of Europe could not afford.[8]

---

by Messrs. Clark and Lewis Cass, to Congress, 4 February 1829. Today Mr. Cass is the Secretary of War.

> *The Indians, as has been stated, say* Messrs. Clark and Cass, *reach the treaty ground poor, and almost naked. Large quantities of goods are taken there by the traders, and are seen and examined by the Indians. The women and children become importunate to have their wants supplied, and their influence is soon exerted to induce a sale. Their improvidence is habitual and unconquerable. The gratification of his immediate wants and desires is the ruling passion of an Indian. The expectation of future advantages seldom produces much effect. The experience of the past is lost, and the prospects of the future disregarded. This is one of the most striking traits in their character, and is well known to all who have had much intercourse with them. It would be utterly hopeless to demand a cession of land, unless the means were at hand of gratifying their immediate wants; and when their condition and circumstances are fairly considered, it ought not to surprise us that they are so anxious to relieve themselves.*

[*]. See the treaty with the Osages. Everett, p. 16. *Long's Expedition*, vol. II, p. 245.

8. *On 19 May 1830, Mr. Ed. Everett asserted before the House of Representatives that the Americans had already acquired by* treaty, *east and west of the Mississippi, 230,000,000 acres.*

In 1808, the Osages gave up 48,000,000 acres for an income of 1,000 dollars.

In 1818, the Quapaws gave up 29,000,000 acres for 4,000 dollars; they reserved a territory of 1,000,000 acres for hunting. It had been solemnly sworn that it would be respected; it was not long before it was invaded like the rest.

> *In order to appropriate the uninhabited lands to which the Indians claim ownership, said Mr. Bell, secretary of the Indian affairs committee of Congress, 24 February 1830, we have adopted the practice of paying the Indian tribes the value of their hunting ground after the game has fled or has been destroyed. It is more advantageous and certainly more in conformity with the principles of justice and more humane to act in this way than to take the territory of the savages by force of arms.*
>
> *The practice of buying from the Indians their title of ownership is therefore nothing more than a new mode of acquisition that humanity and expediency have substituted for violence, and that will equally make us masters of the lands that we claim by virtue of*

I have just recounted great evils, I add that they seem irremediable to me. I believe that the Indian race of North America is condemned to perish, and I cannot prevent myself from thinking that the day the Europeans settle on the shores of the Pacific Ocean, that race will have ceased to exist.[9]

The Indians of North America had only two paths to salvation: war or civilization; in other words, they had to destroy the Europeans or become their equal.

At the birth of the colonies, it would have been possible for them, by uniting their forces, to rid themselves of the small number of foreigners who had just arrived at the shores of the continent.[10] More than once, they attempted to do it and saw themselves on the verge of success. Today the disproportion of resources is too great for them to be able to consider such an undertaking.[P] But men of genius still arise among the Indian nations, who foresee the final fate reserved for the savage populations and who seek to bring together all the tribes in a common hatred of Europeans [{and to silence individual animosities in order to deal only with this objective [v:

---

discovery, and that moreover assures us the right of civilized nations to settle the territory occupied by savage tribes.

Until now, several causes have constantly diminished in the eyes of the Indians the value of the soil that they occupy, and then the same causes have led them to sell it to us without difficulty. The practice of buying from the savages their right of occupancy *has therefore never been able, to any perceptible degree, to slow the prosperity of the United States.*

(Legislative Documents, *21st Congress, n. 227, p. 6*).

9. *This opinion seemed to us, moreover, that of nearly all the American statesmen.*

"Judging of the future by the past," said Mr. Cass to Congress, "we cannot err in antici-pating a progressive diminution of their numbers, and their eventual extinction, unless our border should become stationary, and they be removed beyond it, or unless some radical change should take place in [the principles of (ed.)] *our intercourse with them, which it is easier to hope for than to expect."*

10. *See among others the war undertaken by the Wampanoags and the other confederated tribes, under the leadership of Metacom* [King Philip (ed.)], *in 1675, against the colonists of New England, and the war that the English had to withstand in 1622 in Virginia.*

p. According to Beaumont, the only possibility rested on an alliance of Indians with the Black population. Nonetheless, in his novel, this alliance and the revolt that follows lead to a sharp defeat.

to consider all saving themselves}];[*] but their efforts are ineffectual. The tribes that are near the whites are already too weak to offer effective resistance; the others, abandoning themselves to this childish lack of concern about tomorrow that characterizes savage nature, wait for the danger to appear before giving it their attention. The first cannot act, the others do not want to act.

[≠If at the same time that the Indians gave up hope of chasing the Europeans away from American soil, they had succeeded in becoming civilized, they would still be able to avoid the destruction that threatens them, for it is nearly impossible to dispossess a farming people completely.≠]

It is easy to foresee that the Indians will never want to become civilized, or that they will try too late, when they reach the point of wanting to do so.

Civilization is the result of a long work of society that proceeds in the same place and that the different successive generations bequeath to one another. It is among hunting peoples that civilization has the greatest difficulty managing to establish its dominion. Tribes of herders change places, but they always follow a regular order in their migrations and constantly retrace their steps; the dwelling-place of hunters varies like that of the very animals they pursue.

Several times the attempt has been made to bring enlightenment to the Indians while leaving them with the mores of wandering peoples; the Jesuits had tried to do it in Canada, the Puritans in New England.[11] Both accomplished nothing lasting. Civilization was born within the hut and went to die in the woods. The great failing of these legislators of the Indians was not to understand that, to succeed in civilizing a people, it is necessary

[*]. Red Jacket.q Cite and translate the speech of Oconostata in Everett, p. 44. Insert afterward the note from the work.

q. John C. Spencer, on the occasion of a long conversation, provided Tocqueville with information on Red Jacket (alphabetic notebook A, YTC, BIIIa, and *Voyage, OC,* V, 1, pp. 221–23). Edward Everett, for his part, had sent Beaumont several documents on the Indians, including his speech of 1830 to the House of Representatives. Cf. two letters from Beaumont to Edward Everett dated 18 February and 1 May 1832, YTC, BIc.

11. *See the different historians of New England. Also see* Histoire de la Nouvelle-France *by Charlevoix and* Lettres édifiantes. *[See report of the Commission of Indian Affairs, 21st Congress, n. 217, p. 25.]*

above all to get them to settle down, and they can only do so by cultivating the soil; so it was first a matter of making the Indians farmers.

Not only do the Indians not possess this indispensable preliminary of civilization, but also it is very difficult for them to acquire.

Men who have once given themselves over to the idle and adventurous life of hunters feel an almost insurmountable distaste for the constant and regular work required by farming. You can see it even within our societies; but it is even much more visible among peoples for whom hunting habits have become the national customs.

Apart from this general cause, a cause no less powerful is found only among the Indians. I have already pointed it out; I believe I must return to it.

The natives of North America consider work not only as an evil, but also as a dishonor, and their pride struggles against civilization almost as obstinately as their idleness.[12]

There is no Indian so miserable who, in his bark hut, does not maintain a proud idea of his individual value; he considers the cares of industry as degrading occupations; he compares the farmer to the ox that traces the furrow, and in each of our arts he sees only the work of slaves. It is not that he has not conceived a very high idea of the power of whites and of the grandeur of their intelligence; but, if he admires the result of our efforts, he scorns the means that we have used to obtain them, and, even while under our influence, he still believes himself superior to us. Hunting and war seem to him the only cares worthy of a man.[13] So the Indian, deep

12. *"In all the tribes," says Volney in his* Tableau des Etats-Unis, *p. 423,' "there still exists a generation of old warriors who, seeing the hoe handled, do not cease to shout about the degradation of ancient mores and who claim that the savages owe their decline only to these innovations, and that, to recover their glory and their power, it would be sufficient for them to return to their primitive mores."*

13. *In an official document the following portrait is found:*

Until a young man has been engaged with an enemy, and can boast of his prowess, he is held in no estimation, and is considered little better than a woman.

At their great war dances, all the warriors in succession strike the post, as it is called, and recount the feats they have done. The auditory, upon these occasions, is composed of the relations, the friends, and the companions of the narrator, and the intensity of their

within the misery of his woods, nurtures the same ideas, the same opinions as the noble[*] of the Middle Ages in his fortress, and to resemble him fully he only needs to become a conqueror. How strange! It is in the forests of the New World, and not among the Europeans who populate its shores, that the ancient prejudices of Europe are found today.

I have tried more than once, in the course of this work, to make understood the prodigious influence that the social state seemed to me to exercise on the laws and mores of men. Allow me to add a single word to the subject.

When I notice the similarity that exists between the political institutions of our fathers, the Teutons, and those of the wandering tribes of North America, between the customs recounted by Tacitus and those that I was sometimes able to witness, I cannot prevent myself from thinking that the same cause has produced, in the two hemispheres, the same results, and that amid the apparent diversity of human affairs, it is not impossible to find a small number of generative facts from which all the others derive. So in all that we call Teutonic institutions, I am tempted to see only the habits of barbarians, and the opinions of savages in what we call feudal ideas.[r]

---

feelings is manifested by the deep silence with which they listen to his tale, and by the loud shouts with which he is hailed at the termination. Unfortunate is the young man who has no deeds of valor to recount at these assemblages; and instances are not wanting, where young warriors, in the excitement of their feelings, have departed alone from these dances, in search of trophies to exhibit, and of adventures to relate.

[*]. See the piece from Cass and Clark, p. 29, on the need for military glory that makes itself universally felt among them.

r. In the second lecture of his *History of Civilization in Europe*, Guizot asserted that the savage life of the American Indians had some similarity to the mores of the ancient Teutons. He added that the idea of individual independence, that of modern personal liberty, had appeared in Europe on the occasion of the great Teutonic invasions. The same ideas are found, more developed, in the seventh lecture of the course on civilization in France. Montesquieu, Saint-Simon and Boulainvilliers, before Guizot, had shown a great admiration for Teutonic institutions.

Whatever the vices and prejudices that prevent the Indians of North America from becoming farmers and civilized, necessity sometimes forces them to do so.

Several considerable nations of the South, among others those of the Cherokees and the Creeks,[14] found themselves as though encircled by Europeans who, landing on the shores of the Ocean, going down the Ohio and coming back up the Mississippi, surrounded them all at once. They were not chased from place to place, as the tribes of the North were, but were squeezed little by little into limits that were too narrow, as hunters first make an enclosure around a thicket before entering simultaneously into the interior. The Indians, placed then between civilization and death, saw themselves reduced to living shamefully by their work like whites; so they became farmers, and without entirely abandoning either their habits or their mores, they sacrificed what was absolutely necessary for their existence.

The Cherokees went further; they created a written language, established a fairly stable form of government; and, as everything moves with a hurried step in the New World, they had a newspaper[15] before all had clothes.

What singularly favored the rapid development of European habits among these Indians was the presence of half-breeds.[16] Sharing the enlightenment of his father without necessarily abandoning the savage customs

---

14. *These nations today are encompassed in the states of Georgia, Tennessee, Alabama and Mississippi.*

There were formerly in the south (you see the remnants of them) four great nations: the Choctaws, Chickasaws, Creeks and Cherokees.

The remnants of these four nations still had about 75,000 individuals in 1830. There is at present, in the territory occupied or claimed by the Anglo-American Union, a count of about 300,000 Indians. (See Proceedings of the Indian Board in the City of New York.*) Official documents provided to Congress bring the number to 313,130. The reader curious to know the name and strength of all the tribes that inhabit the Anglo-American territory should consult the documents that I have just indicated. (*Legislative Documents, 20th Congress, n. 117, pp. 90–105.*)

15. *I brought back to France one or two copies of this singular publication. [Cite the statistical details that are found in the speech of Everett, p. 26. See* id., *p. 29.]*

16. *See in the report of the committee of Indian affairs, 21st Congress, n. 227, p. 23, what makes the half-breeds multiply among the Cherokees; the principal cause goes back to the War of Independence. Many Anglo-Americans from Georgia, having taken England's side, were forced to withdraw among the Indians and married there.*

of his maternal race, the half-breed forms the natural link between civilization and barbarism. Wherever half-breeds have multiplied, savages are seen to modify little by little their social state and change their mores.[17]

So the success of the Cherokees proves that the Indians have the ability to become civilized, but it in no way proves that they can succeed in doing so.[s]

This difficulty that the Indians find in submitting to civilization arises from a general cause that is nearly impossible for them to elude.

17. *Unfortunately half-breeds have been fewer and have exercised a smaller influence in North America than anywhere else.*

Two great nations of Europe peopled this portion of the American continent: the French and the English.

The first did not take long to enter into unions with the young native women; but misfortune decreed that a secret affinity be found between the Indian character and theirs. Instead of giving to the barbarians the taste and habits of civilized life, it was they who often became passionately attached to savage life; they became the most dangerous inhabitants of the wilderness, and won the friendship of the Indian by exaggerating his vices and his virtues. M. de Sénonville [Denonville (ed.)], Governor of Canada, wrote to Louis XIV, in 1685: "For a long time we believed it necessary to move the savages near us to make them more French; we all have good grounds to recognize that we were wrong. Those who moved near us did not become French, and the French who haunted them became savage. They pretend to dress like them, to live like them" (Histoire de la Nouvelle-France, *by Charlevoix, vol. II, p. 345).*

The Englishman, in contrast, living stubbornly attached to the opinions, the customs and to the slightest habits of his fathers, remained in the middle of the American wilderness what he was within the cities of Europe; so he wanted to establish no contact with the savages that he despised, and carefully avoided mingling his blood with that of the barbarians.

Thus, while the Frenchman exercised no salutary influence on the Indians, the Englishman was always a stranger to them.

s. Note on a small sheet of paper separate from the manuscript, but which, according to Tocqueville's indications, should have been placed here:

> I recall having been very surprised in the middle of the woods by hearing savages shout to me: *bonjour* with an air of friendship. This attachment of the Indians to the [lacking: *French* (ed.)] is due in part to very honorable causes: "If we pay attention," say Messrs. Clark and Cass in their report to Congress, doc. n. 117, p. 11, "to the influence acquired and exercised by the French on the Indians, influence whose visible traces you still see today after two generations have passed, you will be led to conclude that the French used their power with honor and impartiality."

The attraction of savage life for Europeans and the scorn of savage populations for civilization appear in the *Discours sur l'origine de l'inégalité* of Rousseau (*Oeuvres complètes,* Paris: Pléiade, 1964, III, note XVI, pp. 220–21).

If you cast an attentive eye on history, you discover that in general barbaric peoples have risen little by little by themselves, and by their own efforts, toward civilization.

When it happened that they went to draw enlightenment from a foreign nation, they did so with the rank of conquerors, and not the position of the vanquished.

When the conquered people are enlightened and the conquering people half-savage, as in the invasion of the Roman Empire by the nations of the North, or in that of China by the Mongols, the power that victory assures to the barbarian is enough to keep him at the level of the civilized man and allow him to move as his equal, until he becomes his equal; the one has strength in his favor, the other, intelligence; the first admires the arts and sciences of the vanquished, the second envies the power of the conquerors. The barbarians end by introducing the civilized man into their palaces, and the civilized man in turn opens his schools to them. But when the one who possesses physical force enjoys intellectual preponderance at the same time, it is rare for the vanquished to become civilized; he withdraws or is destroyed.

Therefore you can say in a general way that savages are going to seek enlightenment with weapons in hand, but that they do not receive it.[t]

If the Indian tribes who now inhabit the center of the continent could find in themselves enough energy to undertake becoming civilized, they would perhaps succeed. Superior then to the barbarian nations that surround them, they would little by little gain strength and experience, and, when the Europeans finally appeared on their frontiers, they would be in a state, if not to maintain their independence, at least to make their rights to the soil recognized and to become integrated with the conquerors. But the misfortune of the Indians is to enter into contact with the most civi-

---

t. In the margin, in a first version:

≠It is sufficient to see the natives of North America to be persuaded that their race is in no way inferior to ours. The social state has so to [speak (ed.)] drawn around the mind of the Indians a narrow circle, but in this circle, they show themselves the most intelligent of all men. There is without doubt in what the Cherokees have done more [v: as much] natural genius than in the greatest efforts of civilized peoples.≠

lized, and I will add the most greedy people of the globe, while they are themselves still half barbarian; to find in their teachers, masters, and to receive oppression and enlightenment at the same time.[u]

Living within the liberty of the woods, the Indian of North America was miserable, but he felt inferior to no one; from the moment he wants to enter into the social hierarchy of the whites, he can occupy only the last rank; for he enters ignorant and poor into a society where knowledge and wealth reign. After leading an agitated life, full of evils and dangers, but filled at the same time with emotions and grandeur,[18] he must submit to a

u. In his "Report on the proposed law concerning the extraordinary credits asked for Algeria" (*Moniteur universel,* 1 June 1847, pp. 1379–84, reproduced in *OC,* III, 1, pp. 309–89), Tocqueville suggests taking into account the errors of the conquest of America and preventing the destruction of the Arabs by Western civilization (pp. 327–30).

18. *There is in the adventurous life of hunting peoples some irresistible attraction that catches hold of the heart of man and carries him away despite his reason and experience. You can be persuaded of this truth by reading the* Mémoires de Tanner.

Tanner is a European who was carried off at the age of six by the Indians and who remained for thirty years in the woods with them. It is impossible to see anything more dreadful than the miseries he describes. He shows us tribes without chiefs, families without nations, isolated men, mutilated remnants of powerful tribes, wandering haphazardly amid the ice and among the desolate wilderness areas of Canada. Hunger and cold pursue them; each day life seems ready to escape from them. Among them, mores have lost their sway, traditions are without power. Men become more and more barbaric. Tanner shares all these evils; he knows his European origin, he is not forcibly kept far from whites; he goes, on the contrary, each year to trade with them, to wander through their dwelling-places, to see their comfort; he knows that the day he wants to reenter civilized life he will easily be able to succeed in doing so, and he remains thirty years in the wilderness. When he finally returns to civilized society, he confesses that the existence whose miseries he has described has secret charms for him that he cannot define; he returns there constantly after having left and pulls himself away from so many evils only with a thousand regrets; and when he has finally settled among the whites, several of his children refuse to come to share with him his tranquillity and his comfort.

I met Tanner myself at the entry to Lake Superior. He appeared to me still to resemble a savage much more than a civilized man.

You do not find in the work of Tanner either order or taste; but the author draws, even unknowingly, a lively picture of the prejudices, passions, vices and above all the miseries of those among whom he lived.

Viscount Ernest de Blosseville, author of an excellent work on the penal colonies of England, has translated the Mémoires de Tanner.[v] *The Viscount de Blosseville added to his*

---

translation notes of great interest that will allow the reader to compare the facts recounted by Tanner with those already related by a great number of ancient and modern observers.

All those who desire to know the present state and to foresee the future destiny of the Indian races of North America should consult the work of the Viscount de Blosseville.

v. In the first edition: *"of Tanner* and will publish them in the course of the year about to begin."

George W. Pierson (*Tocqueville and Beaumont in America,* p. 235) indicates that the travelers met Tanner on the steamboat *Ohio,* on the way to Detroit, 19 July 1831, and that the latter offered them his book. Beaumont gives the following account of a conversation with Tanner, that he places on the Mississippi:

> The Choctaws were being escorted by an agent of the American government charged with implementing their removal. This man, who did not know the language of the Indians, had an interpreter close to them, an inhabitant of the United States named Tanner, who is famous in America for having spent more than thirty years among the savage tribes of the north. I congratulated myself all the more about meeting him because I had often desired to do so; this circumstance, joined with the interest that the misfortune of the Indians inspired in me, suggested to me the thought of crossing the Mississippi with them and accompanying them to their new territory. ≠I shared this idea with my traveling companion who very much approved it.≠ As soon as I had resolved to do so, I felt a burst of joy and enthusiasm thinking that I was going to see the beautiful forests dreamed of in my imagination, the vast prairies described by Cooper, and the profound solitudes unknown in the Old World.
>
> The signal for the departure was given and Tanner, with whom I soon began to converse, assured me that in less than a day we would reach the mouth of the Arkansas and that one day more would be enough for us to move up the river a distance of more than 150 miles.
>
> While we descended the Mississippi, I did not cease questioning Tanner about the mores of the Indians and about the causes for their misfortune. He gave me notions full of interest about them that I would like one day to be able to make known in all their scope.—"You, who sympathize with their misfortunes," he says to me, "hurry to know them!, for soon they will have disappeared from the earth. The forests of Arkansas are *given forever* to them! These are, it is true, the terms of the treaty! But what mockery! The lands that they occupied in Georgia had also been given to them, thirty years ago, *forever!* They will be left in this new country that is abandoned to them as long as their lands are not needed. But as soon as the American population finds itself too squeezed together on the left bank of the Mississippi, it will sweep into the fertile countries of the other bank and the Indian will again undergo the fate that was reserved for him, that of retreating before European civilization. Note," Tanner also said to me, "that it is, to a certain point, in the interest of the Indian to act in this way at the approach of whites; in fact he lives almost exclusively on game, and the game itself moves away as soon as civilized society approaches it. It is enough to put a large road through a country to chase away all the wild buffaloes. The Indian who goes closely along with them is only following his means of existence, but by

monotonous, obscure and degraded existence. To earn by hard work and amid shame the bread that must nourish him, such in his eyes is the sole result of this civilization that is praised to him.

And he is not always sure to obtain even this result.

When the Indians undertake to imitate the Europeans their neighbors, and like them to cultivate the land, they soon find themselves exposed to the effects of a very destructive competition. The white is master of the secrets of agriculture. The Indian starts out crudely in an art that he does not know. The one easily makes great harvests grow, the other extracts the fruits of the earth only with a thousand efforts.

The European is placed amid a population that he knows and whose needs he shares.

The savage is isolated in the middle of an enemy people whose mores, language and laws he knows incompletely, but without whom he cannot manage. Only by exchanging his products for those of the whites can he become well-off, for his compatriots are nothing more than a feeble help to him.

Therefore, when the Indian wants to sell the fruits of his work, he does not always find the buyer that the European farmer easily finds, and he can produce only at great cost what the other delivers for a small price.

So the Indian has escaped from the evils to which barbarian nations are exposed only to subject himself to the greatest miseries of civilized peoples, and he finds almost as much difficulty living amid our abundance as within his forests.

---

constantly advancing toward the west, he will meet the Pacific Ocean.—This will be the end of his journey and of his life. How many years will pass before his ruin? You could not say. Each vessel from Europe that brings to America new inhabitants accelerates the destruction of the Indians. After halting in Arkansas, the Choctaws will be pushed back beyond the Rocky Mountains; this will be their second stage; and when the wave of the American population arrives, they will not be able either to remain or to go beyond. Their destiny will be fulfilled."

While Tanner thus spoke to me, I felt penetrated by a profound sadness.

This conversation belongs to the notes and drafts of *Marie* (YTC, Beaumont, CIX). The details that precede and follow this conversation appear in *Marie*, II, pp. 48–55 and 292–93.

At home, however, the habits of the wandering life are still not destroyed. Traditions have not lost their dominion; the taste for hunting has not been extinguished. The savage joys that he formerly experienced deep within the woods are then represented by the most vivid colors in his troubled imagination; the privations that he endured there seem to him less dreadful in contrast, the perils that he encountered less great. The independence that he enjoyed among his equals contrasts with the servile position that he occupies in civilized society.

From another perspective, the solitude where, for so long, he lived free is still near him; a few hours of walking can restore it to him. For the half-cleared field from which he draws hardly enough to feed himself, the whites, his neighbors, offer him a price that to him seems high. Perhaps this money that the Europeans present to him would allow him to live happily and tranquilly far from them. He leaves his plow, picks up his weapons, and goes into the wilderness again forever.[19]

19. *This destructive influence that very civilized peoples exercise on those who are less so is noticeable among the Europeans themselves. [{See what Volney says in his* Tableau du climat et du sol des Etats-Unis, *p. 360.}]*

Some French had founded, nearly a century ago, in the middle of the wilderness, the city of Vincennes on the Wabash. They lived there in great abundance until the arrival of the American emigrants. The latter soon began to ruin the old inhabitants by competition; then they bought their lands from them for a small sum. At the moment when Volney, from whom I borrow this detail, came upon Vincennes, the number of French was reduced to a hundred individuals, most of whom were prepared to move to Louisiana or Canada. These French were honest men, but without enlightenment and without industry; they had contracted part of the savage habits. The Americans, who were perhaps inferior to them from the moral point of view, had an immense intellectual superiority over them; they were industrious, educated, rich, and used to governing themselves.

I myself saw in Canada, where the intellectual difference between the two races is much less pronounced, the Englishman, master of commerce and industry in the country of the Canadian, stretch out on all sides and squeeze the Frenchman into limits too narrow.

In the same way, in Louisiana, nearly all the commercial and industrial activity is concentrated in the hands of the Anglo-Americans.

Something still more striking is happening in the province of Texas; the state of Texas is, as you know, part of Mexico and serves as the frontier with the United States. For several years, Anglo-Americans have entered individually into this province still poorly populated, bought lands, taken hold of industry, and rapidly taken the place of the original population. You can foresee that if Mexico does not hasten to stop this movement, Texas will not take long to escape from it.

You can judge the truth of this sad portrait by what is happening among the Creeks and the Cherokees, whom I cited.

These Indians, in the little that they have done, have surely shown as much natural genius as the peoples of Europe in their wider undertakings; but nations, like men, need time to learn, whatever their intelligence and their efforts.[w]

While these savages worked to become civilized, the Europeans continued to envelop them from all sides and to squeeze them in more and more. Today, the two races have finally met; they touch each other. The Indian has already become superior to his father, the savage, but he is still very inferior to the white, his neighbor. With the aid of their resources and their enlightenment, the Europeans did not take long to appropriate most of the advantages that possession of the soil could provide to the natives; the Europeans settled among them, seized the land or bought it at a low price, and ruined the Indians by a competition that the latter could in no way sustain. Isolated in their own country, the Indians no longer formed anything except a small colony of inconvenient foreigners in the middle of a numerous and dominating people.[20]

If a few differences comparatively not very perceptible in European civilization lead to such results, it is easy to understand what must happen when the most perfected civilization of Europe enters into contact with Indian barbarism.

w. On a detached sheet: "Put the piece from Jefferson on Logan to prove capacity of the Indians. See *Notes On Virginia*, p. 153."

20. *See, in the* Legislative Documents, *21st Congress, n. 89, the excesses of all kinds committed by the white population on the territory of the Indians. Sometimes the Anglo-Americans settle on one part of the territory, as if land was lacking elsewhere, and troops from Congress must come to expel them; sometimes they carry away the livestock, burn the houses, cut down the fruit of the natives or use violence against their persons.*

All these documents provide evidence that each day the natives are victims of abuse by force. Normally the Union maintains an agent among the Indians charged with representing it; the report of the agent for the Cherokees is found among the documents that I am citing; the language of this official is nearly always favorable to the savages. "The intrusion of whites into the territory of the Cherokees," he says, p. 12, "will cause the ruin of those who live there leading a poor and inoffensive existence." Further along you see that the state of Georgia, wanting to narrow the limits of the Cherokees, proceeds to a boundary marking; the federal agent remarks that, having been made only by the whites and without full hearings, the boundary marking has no value.

Washington said, in one of his messages to Congress: "We are more enlightened and more powerful than the Indian nations; it is to our honor to treat them with kindness and even with generosity."

This noble and virtuous policy has not been followed.

The greediness of the colonists usually joins with the tyranny of the government. Although the Cherokees and the Creeks were settled on the soil they inhabited before the arrival of the Europeans, although the Americans often negotiated with them as with foreign nations, the states within which they find themselves did not want to recognize them as independent peoples, and undertook to subject these men, barely out of the forests, to their magistrates, to their customs and to their laws.[21] Misery had pushed these unfortunate Indians toward civilization, oppression drives them today back toward barbarism. Many of them, leaving their half-cleared fields, resume the habit of savage life.

If you pay attention to the tyrannical measures adopted by the legislatures of the states of the South, to the conduct of their governors and the actions of their courts, you will easily be convinced that the complete expulsion of the Indians is the final goal toward which all their efforts simultaneously tend. The Americans of this part of the Union enviously regard the lands that the natives possess;[22] they feel that the latter have not yet completely lost the traditions of savage life, and before civilization has firmly attached them to the soil, they want to reduce them to despair and force them to move away.

Oppressed by the particular states, the Creeks and Cherokees addressed

21. *In 1829, the state of Alabama divides the territory of the Creeks into counties and submits the Indian population to European magistrates.*

In 1830, the state of Mississippi classes the Choctaws and the Chickasaws with the whites and declares that those among them who take the title of chief will be punished with a fine of 1,000 dollars and a year in prison.

When the state of Mississippi thus extended its laws over the Choctaw Indians who lived within its limits, the latter assembled together; their chief showed them what the claim of the whites was and read to them some of the laws to which the whites wanted to subject them. The savages declared with one voice that it would be better to plunge again into the wilderness. (Mississippi Papers.)

22. *The Georgians, who find themselves so bothered by the nearby presence of the Indians, occupy a territory that still does not number more than seven inhabitants per square mile. In France, there are one hundred sixty-two individuals in the same space.*

the central government. The latter is not insensitive to their misfortunes; that government would sincerely like to save the remnants of the natives and assure them the free possession of the territory that it guaranteed to them.[23] But when it seeks to execute this plan, the particular states put up a formidable resistance, and then the central government resolves without difficulty to let a few savage tribes, already half destroyed, perish in order not to put the American Union in danger.[x]

Powerless to protect the Indians, the federal government would at least like to ease their lot; to this end, it has undertaken to transport them at its expense to other places.[*]

23. *In 1818, Congress ordered that the territory of Arkansas would be visited by American commissioners, accompanied by a deputation of Creeks, Choctaws and Chickasaws. This expedition was commanded by Messrs. Kennerly, McCoy, Wash Hood and John Bell. See the different reports of the commissioners and their journal in the papers of Congress, n. 87, House of Representatives.*

x. Note not included in the chapter, but which appears in the manuscript in this place:

> Extract from a speech given before a town meeting of Philadelphia, 11 January 1830:
> Can a government founded on the celebrated statement of the rights of man that accompanies our Declaration of Independence consent shamelessly to violate among others those very rights for which it then fought? If *dependent* nations have been able to declare themselves *independent*, how can we refuse to allow nations that are already independent to remain so? Is the people that abuses its power in order to exercise tyranny externally a sincere friend of liberty? And would it not be tyrannical to drive a nation from its partially cultivated lands and from its homes and to send it to create a new settlement in the wilderness, where greed will not long allow it to remain in peace, if we are to judge the future by the past? Amid the discouragement that they must feel, will the Indians even have the energy to undertake what we expect of them?
> The expulsion of the Moors from Spain is universally considered an act of tyranny. The Moors, however, were the sons of the former conquerors and the former enemies of the religion and mores of Spain. The Cherokees are in no way the enemies of the people of the United States.

This note is found with others in a copy that is not in Tocqueville's hand. A note on the jacket of the section on the Indians explains the origin of the copies: "To dictate or copy before thinking about correcting." The copies remaining in this jacket consist of unpublished fragments and notes.

[*]. See the instructions of the Secretary of War to Generals Cannall [Carroll (ed.)] and Goffre [Coffee (ed.)], dated 30 May 1830.

There are 75,000 Indians to transport.

Between the latitudes of 33rd and 37th degrees north, extends a vast country that has taken the name Arkansas, from the principal river that waters it. It borders on one side the frontier of Mexico, on the other, the banks of the Mississippi. A multitude of small streams and rivers cut across it from all sides; the climate is mild and the soil fertile. Only a few wandering hordes of savages are found there.[*] It is to a section of this country, which is closest to Mexico and at a great distance from American settlements, that the government of the Union wants to transport the remnants of the native populations of the South.

At the end of the year 1831, we were assured that 10,000 Indians had already gone to the banks of the Arkansas; others arrived every day. But Congress has not been able to create as well a unanimous will among those whose fate it wanted to determine. Some consent with joy to move away from the home of tyranny; the most enlightened refuse to abandon their growing crops and new dwellings; they think that if the work of civilization is interrupted, it will not be resumed again; they fear that sedentary habits, barely contracted, will be permanently lost in the middle of still savage countries where nothing is prepared for the subsistence of a farming people; they know that in this new wilderness they will find enemy hordes and, to resist them, they no longer have the energy of barbarism and have not yet acquired the strength of civilization. The Indians easily discover, moreover, all that is provisional in the settlement that is proposed to them. Who will assure them that they will finally be able to rest in peace in their new refuge? The United States promises to maintain them there; but the territory that they now occupy had formerly been guaranteed to them by the most solemn oaths.[24] Today the American government does not, it is true, take their

---

[*]. See *Journey of Long,* vol. II.

24. *You find, in the treaty made with the Creeks in 1790, this clause: "The United States solemnly guarantee to the Creek Nation, all their lands within the limits of the United States to the westward and southward of the boundary described in the preceding article."*

The treaty concluded in July 1791 with the Cherokees contains what follows: "The United States solemnly guarantee to the Cherokee nation, all their lands not hereby ceded. If any citizen of the United States, or other person not being an Indian, shall settle on any of the Cherokees' lands, such person shall forfeit the protection of the United States, and the Cherokees may punish him or not, as they please." Art. [7 and (ed.)] *8.*

lands from them, but it allows their lands to be invaded. In a few years, undoubtedly, the same white population that now presses around them will again be at their heels in the solitude of Arkansas; they will then find the same evils again without the same remedies; and sooner or later without land, they will still have to resign themselves to dying.

There is less cupidity and violence in the way the Union acts toward the Indians than in the policy followed by the states; but the two governments equally lack good faith.

The states, while extending what they call the benefit of their laws to the Indians,[y] count on the fact that the latter will prefer to move away than to submit; and the central government, while promising these unfortunate people a permanent refuge in the West, is not unaware that it is not able to guarantee it to them.[25]

Therefore, the states, by their tyranny, force the savages to flee; the Union, by its promises and with the aid of its resources, makes the flight easy. These are different measures that aim at the same end.[26]

y. Note of Tocqueville on a small sheet of paper not part of the manuscript: "It is admitted by all, says Mr. Everett in his speech, that the Indians are not able to live under the laws of the states. The Indians say it; the government says it. The states do not deny it. Clearly the laws of whites have not been made for the Indians; we and they are in agreement on this point."

25. *That does not prevent promising it to them in the most formal manner. See the letter of the President addressed to the Creeks, 23 March 1829* (Proceedings of the Indian Board in the City of New York, *p. 5): "Beyond the great river Mississippi,* [. . . (ed.) . . .]*—your father has provided a country large enough for all of you* [. . . (ed.) . . .]*. There your white brothers will not trouble you; they will have no claim to the land, and you can live upon it, you and all your children, as long as the grass grows or the water runs, in peace and plenty. It will be yours for ever."*

In a letter written to the Cherokees by the Secretary of the War Department, 18 April 1829, this official declares to them that they must not deceive themselves about retaining the enjoyment of the territory that they occupy at the moment, but he gives them this same positive assurance for the time when they will be on the other side of the Mississippi (same work, p. 6). As if the power that he now lacked would not be lacking in the same way then!

26. *To have an exact idea of the policy followed by the particular states and by the Union vis-à-vis the Indians, you must consult: 1. the laws of the particular states relating to the Indians (this collection is found in the legislative documents, 21st Congress, n. 319); 2. the laws of the Union relating to the same subject, and in particular that of 30 March 1802 (these laws are found in the work of Mr. Story entitled:* Laws of the United States *); 3. finally, to know*

"By the will of our Father in Heaven, the Governor of the whole world," said the Cherokees in their petition to Congress,[27] "the red man of America has become small, and the white man great and renowned."

When the ancestors of the people of these United States first came to the shores of America, they found the red man strong—though he was ignorant and savage, yet he received them kindly, and gave them dry land to rest their weary feet. They met in peace, and shook hands in token of friendship.

Whatever the white man wanted and asked of the Indian, the latter willingly gave. At that time the Indian was the lord, and the white man the suppliant. But now the scene has changed. The strength of the red man has become weakness. As his neighbors increased in numbers, his power became less and less, and now, of the many and powerful tribes who once covered these United States, only a few are to be seen—a few whom a sweeping pestilence has left. The Northern tribes, who were once so numerous and powerful, are now nearly extinct. Thus it has happened to the red man of America.

Shall we, who are remnants, share the same fate? [. . . (ed.) . . .]

The land on which we stand we have received as an inheritance from our fathers, who possessed it from time immemorial, as a gift from our common Father in Heaven. [. . . (ed.) . . .] They bequeathed it to us as their children, and we have sacredly kept it, as containing the remains of our beloved men. This right of inheritance we have never ceded nor ever forfeited. Permit us to ask what better right can the people have to a country than the right of inheritance and immemorial peaceable possession? We know it is said of late by the State of Georgia, and by the Executive of the United States, that we have forfeited this right—but we think this is said gratuitously. At what time have we made the forfeit? What great crime have we committed, whereby we must forever be divested of our country?[z] Was it when we were hostile to the United States, and took part with the King of Great Britain, during the struggle for independence? If so, why was not this forfeiture declared in the first treaty of peace between

---

what the current state is of the relations of the Union with all of the Indian tribes, see the report made by Mr. Cass, Secretary of War, 29 November 1823.

27. *19 November 1829. This piece is translated word for word.*

z. In the manuscript: ". . . of our country and rights?"

the United States and our beloved men? Why was not such an article as the following inserted in the treaty: "The United States give peace to the Cherokees, but, for the part they took in the late war, declare them to be but tenants at will, to be removed when the convenience of the States, within whose chartered limits they live, shall require it"? That was the proper time to assume such a possession. But it was not thought of, nor would our forefathers have agreed to any treaty whose tendency was to deprive them of their rights and their country.

Such is the language of the Indians; what they say is true; what they foresee seems inevitable to me.

From whatever side you envisage the destiny of the natives of North America, you see only irremediable evils. If they remain savage, they are pushed ahead and kept on the move; if they want to become civilized, contact with men more civilized than they delivers them to oppression and misery. If they continue to wander from wilderness to wilderness, they perish; if they undertake to settle down, they still perish. They can become enlightened only with the aid of Europeans, and the approach of Europeans depraves them and pushes them back toward barbarism. As long as you leave them in their empty wilderness, they refuse to change their mores, and when they are finally forced to want to change them, there is no more time to do so.

The Spanish unleash their dogs on the Indians as on wild beasts; they pillage the New World like a city taken by assault, without discrimination and without pity; but you cannot destroy everything, fury has an end. The rest of the Indian populations that escaped the massacres ended up mingling with their conquerors and adopting their religion and their mores [{the Indians today share the rights of those who conquered them and one day perhaps will rule over them}].[28]

The conduct of the Americans of the United States toward the natives radiates, in contrast, the purest love of forms and of legality. Provided that the Indians remain in the savage state, the Americans do not in any way

28. *But the Spanish must not be honored for this result. If the Indian tribes had not already been settled on the soil by agriculture at the moment of the arrival of the Europeans, they would have undoubtedly been destroyed in South America as in North America.*

get involved in their affairs and they treat them as independent peoples; they do not allow themselves to occupy their lands without having duly acquired them by means of a contract; and if by chance an Indian nation is no longer able to live in its territory, the Americans take it fraternally by the hand and lead it themselves to die outside of the country of its fathers.

The Spanish, with the help of monstrous crimes without precedents, while covering themselves with an indelible shame [{that will live as long as their name}], were not able to succeed in exterminating the Indian race, nor even in preventing it from sharing their rights;[a] the Americans of the United States have achieved this double result with a marvelous ease, calmly, legally, philanthropically, without shedding blood, without violating a single one of the great principles of morality[29] in the eyes of the world. You cannot destroy men while better respecting the laws of humanity.

[{This world is, it must be admitted, a sad and ridiculous theater.}]

a. Several of these ideas already appear in a letter from Tocqueville to his mother, dated 25 December 1831, from Mississippi (YTC, BIa1, reproduced in *OCB*, VII, pp. 99–106). In a travel note after this letter, and dated 3 January 1832, Tocqueville remarks:

Why of all the European races of the New World is the English race the one that has most preserved the purity of its blood and has least mingled with the native races? Apart from powerful reasons drawn from national character, from temperament, a particular cause of difference exists. Spanish America was peopled by adventurers attracted by thirst for gold, and who, transplanted alone on the other side of the Atlantic, found themselves forced in a way to contract unions with the women of the countries they inhabited. The English colonies were peopled by men who fled their country out of religious passion, or whose goal, by coming to the New World, was to live there by cultivating the land. They came with women and children and were able at once to form a complete society (pocket notebook 3, YTC, BIIa, and *Voyage*, *OC*, V, 1, p. 192).

29. *See among others the report made by Mr. Bell in the name of the Committee of Indian Affairs, 24 February 1830, in which it is established, p. 5, by very logical reasons, and where it is proved very learnedly that: "The fundamental principle, that the Indians had no right by virtue of their ancient possession either of soil, or sovereignty, has never been abandoned expressly or by implication." That is to say that* the Indians, by virtue of their ancient possession, have acquired no right of either property or sovereignty, fundamental principle that has never been abandoned, either expressly or tacitly.

While reading this report, written moreover by a skillful hand, you are astonished by the facility and ease with which, from the first words, the author gets rid of arguments founded on natural right and reason, that he calls abstract and theoretical principles. The more I

Position That the Black Race Occupies in
the United States;[30] Dangers to Which
Its Presence Exposes the Whites[c]

---

*consider it, the more I think that the only difference that exists between the civilized man and
the one who is not, in relation to justice, is this: the one contests in the judicial system the rights
that the other is content to violate.*

30. *Before treating this matter, I owe the reader a warning. In a book that I spoke about
already at the beginning of this work, and that is now on the verge of appearing, M. Gustave
de Beaumont, my traveling companion, had as his principal object to make the position of
Negroes amid the white population of the United States known in France. M. de Beaumont
has thoroughly treated a question that my subject has only allowed me to touch upon. His
book, whose notes contain a very great number of very precious and entirely unknown legislative and historical documents, also presents scenes whose energy can be equaled only by the
truth. The work of M. de Beaumont should be read by those who want to understand to what
excesses of tyranny men are pushed little by little once they have begun to go beyond nature
and humanity.*[b]

b. This note does not exist in the manuscript.

c. To ask about Blacks.

1. Black population, slave and emancipated in the United States (illegible word).

2. Is it true that the laws of the Carolinas and Georgia forbid teaching slaves to
read and write? Gazette of December.

(1) How do these laws set about to prohibit the (illegible word)?

(2) What does the President want for [the (ed.)] bank, to destroy it or to replace
it?

(3) What did he do against the federal courts. (YTC, CVh, 2, p. 86).

The Quaker Collection of the library of Haverford College in Pennsylvania preserves
three pages of questions in English concerning the "colored population." A note from
the last page attributes these questions to Tocqueville, but the writing is that of Gustave
de Beaumont. The questions bear upon the separation of Blacks and whites in the
schools, hospitals, churches and other public places, on the intellectual equality of the
two races, on the possibility of a gradual abolition, and on the danger of a race war.
Beaumont is concerned as well about the differences between the law and its execution:
"In a government founded upon the will of the people, *the public opinion* secures the
impartial execution of the law?—How is it possible that the law is *impartially* executed
in reference to black people when the public opinion concerning such people is not
impartial itself?" It has not been possible to identify the person to whom this inquiry is
addressed. It probably concerns one of the persons that Tocqueville and Beaumont met
in Pennsylvania (see George W. Pierson, *Tocqueville and Beaumont in America,* pp. 782–
86). With the kind permission of Haverford College, Pennsylvania (Quaker Collection,
E. W. Smith, no. 95).

Why it is more difficult to abolish slavery and to make its mark disappear among modern peoples than among ancient peoples.— In the United States, prejudice of whites against Blacks seems to become stronger as slavery is destroyed.—Situation of Negroes in the states of the North and the South.—Why the Americans abolish slavery.—Servitude, which brutalizes the slave, impoverishes the master.—Differences that you notice between the right bank and the left bank of the Ohio.—To what they must be attributed.—The Black race moves back toward the South as slavery does.—How this is explained.—Difficulties that the states of the South have in abolishing slavery.—Dangers for the future.—Preoccupation of minds.—Founding of a Black colony in Africa.—Why the Americans of the South increase the rigors of slavery, at the same time that they are growing disgusted with it.

The Indians will die in isolation as they lived; but the destiny of the Negroes is in a way intertwined with that of the Europeans. Although the two races are bound to each other, they do not blend together. It is as difficult for them to separate completely as to unite.

The most formidable of all the evils that threaten the future of the United States arises from the presence of Blacks on their soil. When you seek the cause of the present troubles and future dangers of the Union, you almost always end up at this first fact, from no matter where you start.

Men generally need to make great and constant efforts to create lasting evils; but there is one evil that enters into the world furtively. At first, you barely notice it amid the usual abuses of power; it begins with an individual whose name is not preserved by history; it is deposited like an accursed seed at some point in the soil; it then feeds on itself, spreads effortlessly, and grows naturally with the society that received it. This evil is slavery.

Christianity had destroyed servitude; the Christians of the sixteenth century reestablished it; but they never allowed it in their social system other than as an exception, and they took care to restrict it to a single one of the human races. They therefore gave humanity a wound not as extensive, but infinitely more difficult to heal.[d]

Two things must be carefully distinguished: slavery in itself and its consequences.

The immediate evils produced by slavery were nearly the same among ancient peoples as they are among modern peoples, but the consequences of these evils were different. Among the ancients the slave belonged to the same race as his master, and often he was superior to him in education and in enlightenment.[31] Liberty alone separated them; once liberty was granted, they easily blended.

So the ancients had a very simple means to rid themselves of slavery and its consequences; this means was emancipation, and as soon as they used it in a general way, they succeeded.[f]

---

d. "Europeans by destroying millions of Indians in the New World inflicted a horrible, but temporary evil on humanity. Slavery [v: the presence of Blacks] is an evil that feeds on itself [v: perpetuates itself with the generations], that is constantly reborn, and that can only cease by evils greater than itself" (YTC, CVh, 2, p. 93).

31. *We know that several of the most celebrated authors of antiquity were or had been slaves: Aesop and Terence are among this number. Slaves were not always taken from among barbarian nations; war put very civilized men into servitude.*[e]

e. In the work of Thomas Clarkson *An Essay on the Slavery and Commerce of the Human Species* (London: J. Phillips, 1788, pp. 13–16), you find reflections very similar to those of Tocqueville on the difference between modern and ancient slavery; the author likewise cites Aesop and Terence as examples of civilized slaves. Beaumont possessed a French edition of this book in his library (Cf. *Marie*, I, pp. 296–301), as well as the following works on slavery: Brissot de Warville, *Examen critique des "Voyages dans l'Amérique septentrionale" de M. le marquis de Chastellux;* Marquis de Condorcet, *Réflexions sur l'esclavage des Noirs;* Thomas Clarkson, *Essai sur les désavantages de la traite;* Benjamin S. Frossard, *La cause des esclaves nègres et des habitants de la Guinée, portée au tribunal de la justice, de la religion, de la politique;* Daniel Lescallier, *Réflexions sur le sort des noirs dans nos colonies;* Théophile Mandar, *Discours sur le commerce et l'esclavage des nègres* (this information is contained in the thesis of Alvis Lee Tinnin, *Gustave de Beaumont, Prophet of the American Dilemma,* New Haven, Yale University, 1961).

f. When it is said that slavery is disappearing, it has disappeared in effect. Nothing like that. Prejudices that remain. Law of New England. As slavery withdraws, whites fear blending more, become scornful. Small number of mulattos. School, church and industry [separate(?) (ed.)]. The laws less harsh, hatreds more so. Slavery was cruel. You can make slavery end, but not the prejudices that it gave birth to; you can make the Negro cease to be a slave, but not make him become the equal of the white (YTC, CVh, 2, pp. 95–96).

Not that the marks of servitude in antiquity did not still continue to exist for some time after servitude was destroyed. [{Real inequality was followed by social inequality.}]

There is a natural prejudice that leads man to scorn the one who has been his inferior, long after he has become his equal; real inequality produced by fortune or law is always followed by an imaginary inequality that has its roots in mores; but among the ancients this secondary effect of slavery came to an end. The emancipated man so strongly resembled the men who were born free that it soon became impossible to distinguish him from them.

What was more difficult among the ancients was to change the law; what is more difficult among modern peoples is to change mores, and for us the real difficulty begins where in antiquity it ended.

This happens because among modern peoples the non-material and transitory fact of slavery is combined in the most fatal way with the material and permanent fact of the difference of race. The memory of slavery dishonors the race, and race perpetuates the memory of slavery.

There is not an African who came freely to the shores of the New World; from that it follows that all those who are found there today are slaves or emancipated. Thus the Negro, together with life, transmits to all of his descendants the external sign of his shame. Law can destroy servitude; but only God alone can make its mark disappear.g

The modern slave differs from the master not only in liberty, but also in origin. You can make the Negro free, but he remains in the position of a stranger vis-à-vis the European.

That is still not all. In this man who is born in lowliness, in this stranger that slavery introduced among us, we scarcely acknowledge the general features of humanity. His face appears hideous to us, his intelligence seems limited to us, his tastes are base; we very nearly take him for an intermediate being between brute and man.[32]

---

g. "When you see the difficulty of destroying the inequality in the laws, you understand what is impracticable about destroying the one in nature" (YTC, CVh, 2, p. 90).

32. *For whites to abandon the opinion that they have conceived of the intellectual and moral inferiority of their former slaves, it would be necessary for Negroes to change, and they cannot change as long as this opinion persists.*

So after abolishing slavery, modern peoples still have to destroy three prejudices much more elusive and more tenacious than slavery: the prejudice of the master, the prejudice of race, and finally the prejudice of the white.

It is very difficult for us, who have had the good fortune to be born among men whom nature made our fellows and the law our equals; it is very difficult for us, I say, to understand what insurmountable distance separates the Negro of America from the European. But we can have a remote idea of it by reasoning by analogy.[h]

We formerly saw among us great inequalities whose principles were only in legislation. What more fictitious than a purely legal inequality! What more contrary to the instinct of man than permanent differences established among men clearly similar! These differences have continued to exist for centuries however; they still continue to exist in a thousand places; everywhere they have left imaginary marks that time can scarcely erase. If the inequality created solely by laws is so difficult to uproot, how to destroy the one that seems to have its immutable foundations in nature itself?[m]

As for me, when I consider what difficulty aristocratic bodies of whatever nature have merging with the mass of the people, and the extreme care that they take to preserve for centuries the imaginary barriers that separate them, I despair of seeing an aristocracy founded on visible and imperishable signs disappear.[n]

h. In the margin: "≠I regard the mixing of races as the greatest misfortune of humanity.≠"

m. "Among the Americans slavery seemed contrary neither to religion nor to the interest of the State; what was more difficult was to establish it in the laws" (YTC, CVh, 3, pp. 2–3).

n. In the margin:

≠Thus in America prejudice seems to grow stronger as slavery withdraws. The difference becomes marked in the mores as it fades away in the laws. In several countries of Europe different peoples found themselves together. They took centuries to blend; but they were similar on all points. The Moors who hardly differed from the Spanish could not manage to mingle with them. If the various offshoots of the same human family have so much difficulty mingling and blending, how to admit that two radically different races will ever manage to do so? If a slight difference in the nature of features was found to be a nearly insurmountable obstacle, what will it be when you find a difference so great that what appears beautiful to one seems the height of ugliness to the other?≠

So those who hope that one day the Europeans will blend with the Negroes seem to me to entertain a chimera. My reason does not lead me to believe it, and I see nothing in the facts that indicate it.

Until now, wherever whites have been the most powerful, they have held Negroes in degradation or in slavery. Wherever Negroes have been the strongest, they have destroyed whites; it is the only accounting that might ever be possible between the two races.

If I consider the United States of our day, I see clearly that in a certain part of the country the legal barrier that separates the two races is tending to fall, but not that of mores. I see slavery receding; the prejudice to which it gave birth is immovable.

In the part of the Union where Negroes are no longer slaves, have they drawn nearer to whites? Every man who has lived in the United States will have noted that an opposite effect has been produced. [{In no part of the Union are the two races as separated as in New [England (ed.)] [v: the North].}]

Racial prejudice seems to me stronger in the states that have abolished slavery than in those where slavery still exists, and nowhere does it appear as intolerant as in the states where servitude has always been unknown.[f] o

---

o. These alphabetical notes appear in the manuscript, but not the text of the notes, which is found, however, in one of the drafts:

(a) Among the states where slavery is abolished, Massachusetts is the only one I know that has prohibited the legitimate union of the two races. See *Laws of Massachusetts,* vol. I, p. [blank (ed.)].

(b) Among the states that have abolished slavery or did not allow it, the states of Delaware, Ohio, Indiana and Illinois are the only ones I know that have excluded Negroes from electoral rights. In the others the law is silent about it and consequently allows it. In the constitution of the state of New York, amended in 1821, Negroes can vote, but particular property qualifications are required of them, which makes the permission of the law illusory.

(c) In most of the states where slavery is abolished, the law does not make any color distinction while establishing the qualification for the jury. But as it leaves an arbitrary power to the officials charged with drawing up the list, care is taken never to put the name of a Black on it.

(d) While I was in New York a French (illegible word) [Creole (?) (ed.)] from the Antilles, coming to the theater, {was taken for a mulatto and refused} was resisted in

It is true that in the North of the Union the law allows Negroes and whites to contract legitimate unions;[a] but opinion declares vile the white who joins in marriage with a Negro woman; and it would be difficult to cite an example of such a deed.

In nearly all the states where slavery is abolished, the Negro has been given electoral rights;[b] but if he presents himself to vote, he risks his life.P Oppressed, he can make a complaint, but he finds only whites among his judges. The law opens the juror's seat to him,[c] but prejudice pushes him away from it. His son is excluded from the school where the descendant of the European goes to be instructed. In the theaters he cannot, even at the price of gold, buy the right to sit next to the one who was his master;[d] in the hospitals he lies apart. The Black is allowed to beseech the same God as the whites, but not to pray to him at the same altar. He has his priests

---

his entry to the boxes of the dress circle for which he had purchased the right at the door. He did not understand English; a violent quarrel ensued that nearly had unfortunate consequences; with his swarthy tint it was assumed that he could indeed be a mulatto.

(e) It is right to note that in general Negroes are mingled with whites in Catholic churches. Protestantism establishes in the religious order the government of the middle classes, and the haughtiness of the middle classes toward the people is known.

(f) Not only does Ohio not allow slavery, but it prohibits the entry into its territory of free Negroes and forbids them to acquire anything there.

(g) The gradual abolition of slavery was declared in Pennsylvania in 1780. In Massachusetts this abolition goes back to the very period of the constitution in 1779; Connecticut began to abolish slavery in 1784. The state of New York in 1799. *Kent's Commentaries,* vol. II, p. 201 (YTC, CVh, 2, pp. 76–77).

Note g belongs to the following paragraph, in the margin in the manuscript: "Slavery today is abolished in {two-thirds} of the Union (here a note on the precise number of states where slavery does not exist. I believe that the number does not exceed twelve, but these are the most important). There are portions of the territory where it has been destroyed for nearly a half century,g others that never allowed it in their midst."

Beaumont described the incident of the Creole twice, with many details (*Marie,* I, p. v, note and pp. 193–97).

p. Draft, under a paper pasted into place: ". . . life. The law made them the equals of whites. In public places they can take a place next to whites, but if they try to do so, people flee their approach. The same hospitals are open to them, but they occupy separate places. Even in the prisons care is taken not to mingle the two races ≠and it seems to be believed that to force a murderer to breathe the same air as a Negro is to degrade him more. His sons . . .≠"

and his churches.[e] The gates of heaven are not closed to him: but inequality scarcely stops at the edge of the other world. When the Negro is no more, his bones are thrown aside, and the difference in conditions is found again even in the equality of death.

Thus the Negro is free, but he is not able to share either the rights or the pleasures or the labors or the pains or even the tomb of the one whose equal he has been declared to be; he cannot meet him anywhere, either in life or in death.

[{What miserable mockery this is.}]

In the South where slavery still exists, Negroes are less carefully kept aside; they sometimes share the labors of whites and their pleasures; to a certain point they are permitted to mix with them. Legislation is more harsh in their regard; habits are more tolerant and milder.

In the South the master is not afraid to raise his slave up to his level, because he knows that if he wishes he will always be able to throw him back into the dust. In the North the white no longer distinctly sees the barrier that should separate him from a degraded race, and he withdraws with all the more care from the Negro because he fears that someday he will merge with him.

With the American of the South, nature sometimes reasserts its rights and for a moment reestablishes equality between Blacks and whites. In the North pride silences even the most imperious passion of man. The American of the North would perhaps consent to make the Negro woman the temporary companion of his pleasures if the legislators had declared that she must not aspire to share his bed; but she is able to become his wife, and he withdraws from her with a kind of horror.

This is how in the United States the prejudice that pushes Negroes away seems to increase proportionately as Negroes cease to be slaves, and how inequality becomes imprinted in the mores as it fades in the laws.

But if the relative position of the two races that inhabit the United States is as I have just shown, why have the Americans abolished slavery in the north of the Union, why do they keep it in the south, and what causes them to aggravate its rigors there?

It is easy to answer. Slavery is being destroyed in the United States not in the interest of the Negroes, but in that of the whites.

[≠America has given great truths to the world, but it has as well provided the world with the demonstration of an admirable truth. Christianity had condemned slavery as *odious,* the experience of the United States proves it *deadly.*≠]

The first Negroes were imported into Virginia about the year 1621.[33] So in America, as in all the rest of the world, servitude was born in the South. From there it gained ground step by step; but as slavery moved up toward the North the number of slaves kept decreasing;[34] there were always very few slaves in New England.[q]

The colonies were founded; a century had already passed, and an extraordinary fact began to strike everyone's attention. The provinces that possessed no slaves so to speak grew in population, in wealth, and in well-being more rapidly than those that had them.

In the first, however, the inhabitant was forced to cultivate the soil himself or to hire the services of another man; in the second, he found at his disposal workers whose efforts were not paid. So there was work and expense on one side, leisure and economy on the other. But the advantage remained with the first.

This result seemed all the more difficult to explain because the emigrants, all belonging to the same European race, had the same habits, the

---

33. *See* History of Virginia *by Beverley. See also, in the* Mémoires de Jefferson, *curious details about the introduction of Negroes into Virginia and about the first act that prohibited their importation in 1778.*

34. *The number of slaves was smaller in the North, but the advantages resulting from slavery were not disputed more there than in the South. In 1740, the legislature of the state of New York declares that the direct importation of slaves must be encouraged as much as possible, and that smuggling must be severely punished as tending to discourage the honest merchant* (Kent's Commentaries, *vol. II, p. 206). You find in the historical Collection of* Massachusetts, *vol. IV, p. 193, the curious research of Belknap on slavery in New England. The result is that, as early as 1630, Negroes were introduced, but that from that moment legislation and mores showed themselves opposed to slavery.*

Also see in this place the way in which public opinion, then the law, managed to destroy servitude.

q. "Slavery which begins in the south and spreads to the north, abolition of slavery which begins in the north and spreads to the south" (YTC, CVh, 2, p. 51).

same civilization, the same laws, and differed only in slightly perceptible nuances.

Time continued to march. Leaving the shores of the Atlantic Ocean, the Anglo-Americans [{Europeans}] plunged every day further into the uninhabited areas of the West; there they encountered new terrains and climates; they had to conquer obstacles of different kinds; their races mingled, men of the South went toward the North, men of the North descended toward the South. Among all these causes, the same fact was reproduced at each step; and in general the colony in which there were no slaves became more populated and more prosperous than the one in which slavery was in force.

So as things advanced you began to see that slavery, so cruel to the slave, was deadly to the master.

But this truth was conclusively proved on the banks of the Ohio.

The river that the Indians had named the Ohio, or the Beautiful River par excellence, waters one of the most magnificent valleys that man has ever made his dwelling-place. Rolling terrain extends on the two banks of the Ohio where the soil offers inexhaustible treasures to the plowman every day; on the two banks the air is equally healthy and the climate temperate; each one of them forms the extreme boundary of a vast state. On the left the state that follows the thousand curves made by the Ohio in its course is called Kentucky; the other borrowed the name of the river itself. The two states differ only on one single point: Kentucky allowed slaves, the state of Ohio cast all of them out.[35]

So the traveler who, placed in the middle of the Ohio, allows himself to be carried along by the current until the river flows into the Mississippi navigates, so to speak, between liberty and servitude; and he has only to glance around him to judge in an instant which one is most favorable to humanity.

On the left bank of the river, the population is scattered; from time to time you see a gang of slaves with a carefree air crossing fields half deserted; the primeval forest constantly reappears; you would say that society

35. *Ohio not only does not allow slavery, but it prohibits the entry of free Negroes into its territory and forbids them to acquire anything there. See the statutes of Ohio.*

is asleep; man seems idle; it is nature that offers the image of activity and life.

From the right bank arises, in contrast, a confused murmur that proclaims from afar the presence of industry; rich crops cover the fields; elegant dwellings announce the taste and the attentions of the plowman; on all sides comfort is revealed; man seems rich and content: he is working.[36]

The state of Kentucky was founded in 1775; the state of Ohio was founded only twelve years later:[r] twelve years in America is more than a half-century in Europe. Today the population of Ohio already exceeds that of Kentucky by 250,000 inhabitants.[37]

These diverse effects of slavery and of liberty are easily understood; they are sufficient to explain clearly the differences that are found between ancient civilization and that of today.

On the left bank of the Ohio work merges with the idea of slavery; on the right bank, with that of well-being and progress; there it is debased, here it is honored. On the left bank of the river you cannot find workers belonging to the white race; they would be afraid of resembling slaves; you must rely on the efforts of Negroes. On the right bank you would look in vain for someone idle; the white extends his activity and his intelligence to all undertakings.

Thus the men who in Kentucky are charged with exploiting the natural riches of the soil have neither enthusiasm nor enlightenment; while those who could have these two things do nothing or go into Ohio in order to make use of their industry and to be able to exercise it without shame.

It is true that in Kentucky masters make slaves work without being

---

36. *It is not only the individual man who is active in Ohio; the state itself undertakes immense enterprises; between Lake Erie and the Ohio the state of Ohio has established a canal by means of which the Mississippi Valley communicates with the River of the North. Thanks to this canal the merchandise of Europe that arrives in New York can descend by water as far as New Orleans, across more than five hundred leagues of the continent.*

r. In the margin: "Ohio began to be inhabited 1787. Kentucky 1775. Daniel Boone." Notebook E contains several notes on Ohio and Kentucky (YTC, BIIa, and *Voyage, OC,* V, 1).

37. *Exact figure according to the census of 1830:*

> Kentucky,   *688, 844.*
> Ohio,   *937, 679.*

obliged to pay them, but they gain little benefit from their efforts, while the money that they would have given to free laborers would have been repaid with great interest by the value of their work.[s]

The free worker is paid, but he works faster than the slave, and rapidity of execution is one of the great elements of economy. The white sells his help, but you buy it only when it is useful; the Black has nothing to claim as the price for his services, but you are obliged to feed him all the time; he must be sustained in his old age as in his mature years, in his unproductive childhood as during the fruitful years of his youth, during illness as in health. It is therefore only by paying that you obtain the work of these two men: the free worker receives a salary; the slave, an education, food, care, clothing. The money that the master spends for the maintenance of the slave melts away little by little and on small particulars; you hardly notice it. The salary that you give to the worker is given all at once, and it seems to enrich only the one who receives it; but in reality the slave has cost more than the free man, and his efforts have been less productive.[38]

The influence of slavery extends still further; it penetrates even into the very soul of the master, and gives his ideas and his tastes a particular direction.

On the two banks of the Ohio nature has given man an enterprising and energetic character; but on each side of the river he makes a different use of this common quality.

s. The paragraph that follows is not in the manuscript.

38. *Apart from these causes, which make the labor of free workers, wherever they abound, more productive and more economical than that of slaves, another one must be pointed out that is particular to the United States. Over the whole surface of the Union the way to cultivate sugar cane successfully has not yet been found except on the banks of the Mississippi, near the mouth of this river, on the Gulf of Mexico. In Louisiana the cultivation of sugar cane is extremely advantageous; nowhere does the farmer gain such a great value from his efforts; and since a certain relationship is always established between the costs of production and the products, the price of slaves is very high in Louisiana. Now since Louisiana is one of the confederated states, slaves can be transported there from all parts of the Union; so the price given for a slave in New Orleans raises the price of slaves in all the other markets. The result of this is that, in countries where the land returns little, the cost of cultivation by slaves continues to be very considerable, which gives a great advantage to the competition of free workers.*

The white of the right bank, obliged to live by his own efforts, made material well-being the principal goal of his existence; and since the country that he inhabits presents inexhaustible resources to his industry, and offers constantly recurring lures to his activity, his ardor to acquire has surpassed the ordinary limits of human cupidity. You see him, tormented by the desire for wealth, go boldly down all the paths that fortune opens to him; he becomes indiscriminately seaman, pioneer, manufacturer, farmer, bearing with an equal constancy the work or the dangers attached to these different professions. There is something marvelous in the resources of his genius, and a sort of heroism in his greediness for gain.

The American of the left bank scorns not only work, but all the enterprises that work brings to success; living in idle comfort, he has the tastes of idle men; money has lost a part of its value in his eyes; he pursues fortune less than excitement and pleasure, and he expends to these ends the energy that his neighbor deploys elsewhere; he passionately loves the hunt and war; he takes pleasure in the most violent exercises of the body; the use of arms is familiar to him, and from his childhood he has learned to risk his life in single combat. So slavery not only prevents whites from making a fortune, it turns them away from wanting to do so.

The same causes, operating continuously for two centuries in opposite directions in the English colonies of North America, have ended by creating a prodigious difference between the commercial capacity of the Southerner and that of the Northerner. Today only the North has ships, factories, railroads and canals.

This difference is noticeable not only in comparing the North and the South, but in comparing the inhabitants of the South among themselves. Nearly all the men in the southernmost states of the Union who devote themselves to commercial enterprises and seek to utilize slavery have come from the North; each day the men of the North spread into this part of the American territory where there is less competition for them to fear; there they discover resources that the inhabitants did not notice, and submitting to a system that they disapprove of, they succeed in turning it to better account than those who, having established the system, still uphold it.

If I wanted to push the parallel further, I would easily prove that nearly all the differences that are noticeable between the character of the Americans in the South and the North are born out of slavery; but this would go beyond my subject. I am trying at this moment to find out not what all the effects of servitude are, but what effects servitude produces on the material prosperity of those who have accepted it.

[≠What I limit myself to saying at this moment is this. The Americans are, of all modern peoples, those who have pushed equality and inequality furthest among men. They have combined universal suffrage and servitude. They seem to have wanted to prove in this way the advantages of equality by opposite arguments. It is claimed that the Americans, by establishing universal suffrage and the dogma of sovereignty [of the people], have made clear to the world the advantages of equality. As for me, I think that they have above all proved this by establishing servitude, and I find that they establish the advantages of equality much less by democracy than by slavery.≠]

This influence of slavery on the production of wealth could only be very imperfectly known by antiquity. Servitude existed then in all the civilized world, and the peoples who did not know it were barbarians.

So Christianity destroyed slavery only by asserting the rights of slaves; today you can attack it in the name of the master. On this point interest and morality are in agreement.[t]

t. Tocqueville bases the greatest part of his argument against slavery on considerations of an economic type. Beaumont does as much in *Marie* (I, pp. 133–35, 303–304). Certain critics have not failed to blame Tocqueville for having nearly abandoned philosophical and religious arguments. The reason for this omission seems to be a tactical choice rather than lack of awareness. Not only had Tocqueville heard it asserted right from the mouths of several Americans that slavery would disappear because it was not profitable, but he was also aware that the discussion on slavery had henceforth left the religious and moral realm to take place principally on economic grounds. Even a partisan of slavery like Achille Murat had not hesitated to write that slavery would disappear "when free labor is cheaper than the labor of slaves" (Achille Murat, *Esquisse morale et politique des États-Unis,* Paris: Crochard Libraire, 1832, p. 110). It is not impossible that Tocqueville had read this book. Alphabetic notebook A (small notebook A, YTC, BIIa) contains the following note (omitted in *Voyage, OC,* V, 1): "Authors who have written on the United States. Letters on the United States by Achille Murat, son of the ex-king of Naples, Bossage, 1830." The partisans of abolition used arguments of an economic type as well.

As these truths manifested themselves in the United States, you saw slavery retreat little by little before the light of experience.

Servitude had begun in the South and afterward spread toward the North; today it is withdrawing. Liberty, starting in the North, is moving without stopping toward the South. Among the large states Pennsylvania today forms the extreme limit of slavery to the North, but even within these limits it is shaken; Maryland, which is immediately below Pennsylvania, is preparing daily to do without it, and Virginia, which comes after Maryland, is already debating its utility and its dangers.[39]

You can cite in particular, based on Beaumont's library, one of the first modern antislavery works, the book of Benjamin S. Frossard, *La cause des esclaves nègres et des habitants de la Guinée portée au tribunal de la justice, de la religion, de la politique . . .* (Lyon: Aimé de la Roche, 1789, 2 vol.), and Thomas Hamilton (*Men and Manners in America,* Philadelphia: Carey, Lea and Blanchard, 1833, pp. 317–22), which Beaumont cites in his book, and who also uses arguments of this type.

The French Society for the Abolition of Slavery, to which Beaumont and Tocqueville belonged, proclaimed in 1837: "Abolition of slavery can no longer in any civilized country give rise to a discussion of principles: the only question with which enlightened minds have to be concerned today is that of the means by which this abolition could be realized without disruption in the colonies." *Revue des deux mondes,* X, 4th series, 1837, p. 418 (see the speech of Tocqueville on the English experience, reproduced on page 422).

See on this subject Sally Gersham, "Alexis de Tocqueville and Slavery," *French Historical Studies* 9, no. 3 (1976): 467–83; Richard Resh, "Alexis de Tocqueville and the Negro. Democracy in America Reconsidered," *Journal of Negro History* 48, no. 4 (1963): 251–60; Gerald M. Bonetto, "Tocqueville and American Slavery," *Canadian Review of American Studies* 15, no. 2 (1984): 129–39; Harvey Mitchell, *America After Tocqueville* (Cambridge: Cambridge University Press, 2002); and August H. Nimitz, Jr., *Marx, Tocqueville and Race in America* (Lanham, Md.: Lexington Books, 2003), pp. 1–39.

39. *There is a particular reason that is finally detaching the two last states that I have just named from the cause of slavery.*

The former wealth of this part of the Union was founded principally on the cultivation of tobacco. Slaves were particularly appropriate to this cultivation. Now, it happens that for quite a few years tobacco has been losing its market value; the value of the slaves, however, remains always the same. Thus the relationship between the costs of production and the products is changed. So the inhabitants of Maryland and of Virginia feel more disposed than they were thirty years ago either to do without slaves in the cultivation of tobacco, or to abandon the cultivation of tobacco and slavery at the same time.

No great change in human institutions takes place without discovering, among the causes of this change, the inheritance law.

When unequal division ruled in the South, each family was represented by a rich man who did not feel the need any more than he had the taste for work; the members of his family that the law had excluded from the common inheritance lived around him in the same manner, as so many parasitic plants; you then saw in all the families of the South what you still see today in the noble families of certain countries of Europe, where the younger sons, without having the same wealth as the eldest son, remain as idle as he. This similar effect was produced in America and in Europe by entirely analogous causes. In the South of the United States the entire race of whites formed an aristocratic body at the head of which stood a certain number of privileged individuals whose wealth was permanent and whose leisure was inherited.[u] These leaders of the American nobility perpetuated the traditional prejudices of the white race in the body that they represented, and maintained the honorable character of idleness. Within this aristocracy you could find poor men, but not workers; poverty there seemed preferable to industry; so Black workers and slaves encountered no competitors, and whatever opinion you might have about the utility of their efforts you very much had to use them, since they were the only ones available.

From the moment when the law of inheritance was abolished all fortunes began to diminish simultaneously, all families moved in the same way closer to the state in which work becomes necessary to existence; many among them entirely disappeared; all foresaw the moment when it would be necessary for each man to provide for his needs by himself. Today you still see the rich, but they no longer form a compact and hereditary body; they were

u. Many of Tocqueville's ideas on the South of the United States come from conversations that he had during the months of September and October 1831 with Brown, John Quincy Adams and Latrobe (non-alphabetic notebooks 2 and 3, YTC, BIIa, and *Voyage, OC,* V, 1, pp. 87–152). At the beginning of November Tocqueville was so convinced of the existence of an aristocratic spirit in the South that, when he met Charles Carroll, he immediately saw in his manners and his way of life the proof of the existence of the southern aristocracy that he had been told had already nearly disappeared.

not able to adopt a spirit, to persevere there, and to make it penetrate into all ranks. So the prejudice that condemned work began to be abandoned by common accord; there were more poor, and the poor were able without being ashamed to concern themselves with the means of gaining their livelihood. Thus one of the most immediate effects of equal division was to create a class of free workers. From the moment when the free worker entered into competition with the slave, the inferiority of the latter made itself felt, and slavery was attacked in its very essence, which is the interest of the master.

As slavery retreats, the Black race follows it in its backward march, and returns with it toward the tropics from where it originally came.

This can seem extraordinary at first glance; we will soon understand it. By abolishing the principle of servitude, the Americans do not free the slaves.

Perhaps what is about to follow would be difficult to understand if I did not cite an example. I will choose that of the state of New York. In 1788, the state of New York prohibits the sale of slaves within it. This was a roundabout way of prohibiting importation. From that moment the number of Negroes no longer grows except by the natural increase of the Black population. Eight years later a more decisive measure is taken, and it is declared that from July 4, 1799 onward, all children born of slave parents will be free. All means of increase are then closed; there are still slaves, but you can say that servitude no longer exists.

From the period when a state of the North also prohibits the importation of slaves, Blacks are no longer removed from the South to be transported to that state.

From the moment when a state of the North forbids the sale of Negroes, the slave, no longer able to leave the hands of the one who owns him, becomes a burdensome property, and there is an interest in transporting him to the South.

The day when a state of the North declares that the son of a slave will be born free, the slave loses a great part of his market value; for his posterity can no longer be part of the market, and again there is a great interest in transporting him to the South.

Thus the same law prevents slaves from the South from coming to the North and pushes those of the North toward the South.

But here is another cause more powerful than all those that I have just discussed.

As the number of slaves diminishes in a state, the need for free workers makes itself felt. As free workers take over industry, since the work of the slave is less productive, the slave becomes a second-rate or useless property, and again there is a great interest in exporting him to the South where competition is not to be feared.

So the abolition of slavery does not bring the slave to liberty; it only makes him change masters. From the north he passes to the south.

As for the emancipated Negroes and those who are born after slavery has been abolished, they do not leave the North to go to the South, but they find themselves vis-à-vis the Europeans in a position analogous to that of the natives; they remain half civilized and deprived of rights amid a population that is infinitely superior to them in wealth and enlightenment; they are exposed to the tyranny of laws[40] and to the intolerance of mores.[v] More unfortunate from a certain perspective than the Indians, they have against them the memories of slavery, and they cannot claim possession of a single piece of land; many succumb to their misery;[41] others concentrate in the cities where, undertaking the roughest work, they lead a precarious and miserable existence.

Since the number of whites is increasing at twice the rate after the abolition of slavery, Blacks would soon be as if swallowed up amid the waves of a foreign population, even if the number of Negroes continued to grow in the same way as in the period when they were not yet free.

---

40. *The states where slavery is abolished ordinarily attempt to make it quite difficult for free Negroes to stay in their territory; and since a sort of emulation among the different states is established on this point, the unfortunate Negroes can only choose among evils.*

v. Cf. Beaumont, *Marie*, I, pp. 161–65, 333–38.

41. *There is a great difference between the mortality of whites and that of Blacks in the states where slavery is abolished: from 1820 to 1831, in Philadelphia only one white died out of forty-two individuals belonging to the white race, while one Negro died there out of twenty-one individuals belonging to the Black race. Mortality is not so great by far among Negro slaves.* (*See* Emmerson's [Emerson's (ed.)] Medical Statistics, *p. 28.)*

A land cultivated by slaves is in general less populated than one cultivated by free men; America is, moreover, a new country; so at the moment when a state abolishes slavery, it is still only half full. Scarcely is servitude destroyed there and the need for free workers felt, than you see a crowd of hardy adventurers rushing in from all parts of the country; they come to profit from the new resources which are going to open to human industry. The land is divided among them; on each portion a family of whites settles and takes possession of it. It is also toward the free states that European emigration heads. What would the poor man of Europe do, coming to find comfort and happiness in the New World, if he went to inhabit a country where work was stained with shame?

Thus the white population grows by its natural movement and at the same time by an immense emigration, while the Black population does not receive emigrants and becomes weaker. Soon the proportion that existed between the two races is reversed. The Negroes form nothing more than unfortunate remnants, a small, poor and wandering tribe lost in the middle of an immense people, master of the land; and nothing more is noticed of their presence except the injustices and the rigors to which they are subjected.

In many of the states of the West the Negro race has never appeared; in all the states of the North it is disappearing. So the great question of the future is shrinking within a narrow circle; it thus becomes less formidable, but no easier to resolve.

The further south you go, the more difficult it is to abolish slavery usefully. This results from several material causes that must be developed.

This first is climate: it is certain that as Europeans approach the tropics work becomes proportionately more difficult for them; many Americans even claim that below a certain latitude it ends up becoming fatal to them, while the Negro submits to it without dangers;[42] but I do not think that

---

42. *This is true in the places where rice is cultivated. Rice plantations, which are unhealthy in all countries, are particularly dangerous in those that are struck by the burning sun of the tropics. Europeans would have a great deal of difficulty cultivating the land in this part of the New World, if they wanted to insist on making it produce rice. But can't one do without rice plantations?*

this idea, so favorable to the laziness of the man of the South, is based on experience. It is not hotter in the South of the Union than in the south of Spain or of Italy.[43] Why would the European not be able to accomplish the same work there? And if slavery was abolished in Italy and in Spain without having the masters perish, why wouldn't the same thing happen in the Union? So I do not believe that nature has forbidden the European of Georgia or of Florida, under pain of death, to draw their subsistence from the land themselves; but this work would assuredly be more painful and less productive for them than for the inhabitants of New England.[44] With the free worker in the South losing in this way a part of his superiority over the slave, it is less useful to abolish slavery.

All the plants of Europe grow in the North of the Union; the South has special products.

It has been noted that slavery is an expensive means to cultivate cereal crops. Whoever grows wheat in a country where servitude is unknown normally keeps in his service only a small number of workers; at harvest time and during planting he brings together many others, it is true; but the latter live at his place only temporarily.

To fill his warehouses or to sow his fields, the farmer who lives in a slave state is obliged to maintain throughout the entire year a great number of servants, whom he needs only during a few days; for, unlike free workers, slaves cannot, while working for themselves, wait for the moment when you must come to hire their labor. You must buy them in order to use them.

So slavery, apart from its general disadvantages, is naturally less applicable to countries where cereal crops are cultivated than to those where other products are harvested.

The cultivation of tobacco, cotton and, above all, sugar cane requires,

---

43. *These states are closer to the Equator than Italy and Spain, but the continent of America is infinitely colder than that of Europe.*

44. *Spain formerly had transported a certain number of peasants from the Azores into a district of Louisiana called Attakapas. Slavery was not introduced among them; it was an experiment. Today these men still cultivate the land without slaves; but their industry is so listless that it scarcely provides for their needs.*

on the contrary, constant attention. There you can employ women and children that you could not use in the cultivation of wheat. Thus slavery is naturally more appropriate to the country where the products that I have just named are grown.

Tobacco, cotton, sugar cane grow only in the South; there they form the principal sources of the wealth of the country. By destroying slavery the men of the South would find themselves with these alternatives: either they would be forced to change their system of cultivation, and then they would enter into competition with the men of the North, more active and more experienced than they; or they would cultivate the same products without slaves, and then they would have to bear the competition of the other states of the South that would have retained slaves.

Thus the South has particular reasons for keeping slavery that the North does not have.ʷ

But here is another motive more powerful than all the others. The South would indeed be able, if really necessary, to abolish slavery; but how would the South rid itself of Blacks? In the North slavery and slaves are chased away at the same time. In the South you cannot hope to attain this double result at the same time.

While proving that servitude was more natural and more advantageous in the South than in the North, I showed sufficiently that the number of slaves must be much greater there. The first Africans were brought into the South; that is where they have always arrived in greater number. As you go further south, the prejudice that holds idleness in honor gains power. In the states that are closest to the tropics there is not one white man who works. So Negroes are naturally more numerous in the South than in the North. Each day, as I said above, they become more numerous; for, in proportion as slavery is destroyed at one end of the Union, Negroes accumulate in the other. Thus the number of Blacks is increasing in the South, not only by the natural movement of the population, but also by the forced

---

w. "Cultivation by slaves is infinitely less advantageous to the north than it was formerly for two reasons.

"The first that certain very costly products such as tobacco have fallen [in price].

"The second that the price of slaves has always remained very high because of New Orleans where they are very expensive" (YTC, CVh, 2, p. 86).

emigration of the Negroes of the North. The African race, to grow in this part of the Union, has reasons analogous to those that make the European race increase so quickly in the North.

In the state of Maine there is one Negro for every three hundred inhabitants; in Massachusetts one for every one hundred; in the state of New York two for every one hundred; in Pennsylvania three; in Maryland thirty-four; forty-two in Virginia, and fifty-five finally in South Carolina.[45] Such was the proportion of Blacks in relation to whites in the year 1830. But this proportion changes constantly: every day it becomes smaller in the North and greater in the South.

It is clear that in the southernmost states of the Union you cannot abolish slavery as you have in the states of the North without running very great dangers that the latter did not have to fear.

We have seen how the states of the North carefully handled the transition between slavery and liberty. They keep the present generation in irons and free future races; in this way Negroes are introduced into society only little by little, and while the man who could make bad use of his independence is retained in servitude, the one who can still learn the art of being free, before becoming master of himself, is liberated.

It is difficult to apply this method to the South. When you declare that beginning at a certain time the son of the Negro will be free, you introduce the principle and the idea of liberty into the very heart of servitude; the Blacks who are kept in slavery by the legislator and who see their sons emerge from it are astonished by this unequal division that destiny makes between them; they become restless and angry. From that moment slavery has in their view lost the type of moral power that time and custom gave

---

45. *In the American work entitled* Letters on the Colonization Society, *by Carey, 1833, you read the following:* "In South Carolina, for forty years, the Black race has been increasing faster than the white race. By combining the population of the five states of the South that first had slavery, Maryland, Virginia, North Carolina, South Carolina, and Georgia, you discover," *Mr. Carey says again,* "that from 1790 to 1830, whites have increased in the proportion of 80 per 100 in these states, and Blacks in the proportion of 112 per 100."

In the United States, in 1830, the men belonging to the two races were distributed in the following manner: states where slavery is abolished, 6,565,434 whites, 120,520 Negroes. States where slavery still exists, 3,960,814 whites, 2,208,102 Negroes.

it; it is reduced to being nothing more than a visible abuse of force. [Thus the law that sets the son at liberty makes it more difficult to keep the father a slave.] The North had nothing to fear from this contrast, because in the North Blacks were small in number and whites very numerous. But if this first dawn of liberty came to break upon two million men at the same time, the oppressors would have to tremble.[x]

After emancipating the sons of their slaves, the Europeans of the South would soon be compelled to extend the same benefit to the entire Black race.

In the North, as I said above, from the moment when slavery is abolished, and even from the moment when it becomes probable that the time of its abolition is approaching, a double movement takes place. Slaves leave the country to be transported more to the South; whites of the northern states and the emigrants from Europe rush to take their place.

These two causes cannot work in the same way in the last states of the South. On the one hand, the mass of slaves is too great there to be able to

---

x. Tocqueville will study in detail the systems of emancipation in his parliamentary report on slavery (*Rapport fait au nom de la commission chargée d'examiner la proposition de M. de Tracy relative aux esclaves des colonies,* Paris: A. Henry, 1839, reproduced in *OC,* III, 1, pp. 41–78). The committee recommends that, after the immediate abolition of slavery in the French colonies, the State become the tutor of Blacks during a transition period by educating them and selling their work at a low price. The revenue will serve to amortize the indemnities to the former owners. Each of the emancipated will receive a minimal salary and a parcel of land from the State.

Tocqueville will defend the conclusions of the committee in a series of articles on abolition published in the *Siècle,* 22 and 28 October, 8 and 21 November, 6 and 14 December 1843 (reproduced in *Écrits et discours politiques, OC,* III, 1, pp. 79–111). A few critics have noted that in his reflections on slavery Tocqueville allowed his nationalist ideas to prevail over his antislavery principles. See on this subject Seymour Drescher, *Dilemmas of Democracy: Tocqueville and Modernization,* Pittsburgh: University of Pittsburgh Press, 1968; Melvin Richter, "Tocqueville on Algeria," *Review of Politics* 25, no. 3 (1963): 363–98; Irving M. Zeitlin, *Liberty, Equality and Revolution in Alexis de Tocqueville,* Boston: Little, Brown and Company, 1971.

In his novel Beaumont discusses in a little more detail the process of emancipation. Gradual emancipation seems to him too costly, and he is of the opinion that Jefferson's idea of giving a portion of the territory to emancipated Negroes is dangerous. The confrontation of the two races seems as inevitable to him as to Tocqueville. (Cf. *Marie,* I, pp. 314–38.)

hope to make them leave the country;[y] on the other hand, the Europeans and the Anglo-Americans of the North dread coming to live in a country where work has still not been rehabilitated. Moreover, they rightly regard the states where the proportion of Negroes surpasses or equals that of whites as threatened by great misfortunes, and they refrain from bringing their industry there.

Thus by abolishing slavery, the men of the South would not succeed, like their brethren of the North, in making Negroes arrive gradually at liberty; they would not appreciably diminish the number of Blacks, and to hold them in check they would be alone. So in the course of a few years you would see a great people of free Negroes placed in the middle of a more or less equal nation of whites.

The same abuses[z] of power that maintain slavery today would then become the source of the greatest dangers that whites in the South would have to fear. Today the descendant of Europeans alone possesses the land; he is the absolute master of industry; he alone is rich, enlightened, armed. The Black possesses none of these advantages; but he can do without them, he is a slave. Once free, charged with watching over his own fate, can he remain deprived of all these things without dying? So what made the strength of the white, when slavery existed, exposes him to a thousand perils after slavery is abolished.

Left in servitude, the Negro can be held in a state near that of the brute; free, he cannot be prevented from becoming educated enough to appreciate the extent of his ills and to catch sight of the remedy to them. There is, moreover, a singular principle of relative justice that is found very deeply buried in the human heart. Men are struck much more by the inequality that exists within the interior of the same class than by the inequalities that are noticed among different classes. Slavery is understood; but how to imag-

y. "In the South the mass of slaves is too considerable for anyone ever to hope of diminishing the number of them very noticeably by exportation. You must wait until death, by making them disappear little by little, removes them along with the just terrors to which they give rise.

Here is one side of the subject, let us envisage another [text interrupted (ed.)]" (YTC, CVh, 2, p. 102).

z. The manuscript says: "The same causes."

ine the existence of several million citizens eternally bent down by infamy and given over to hereditary miseries? In the North a population of emancipated Negroes experiences these evils and feels these injustices; but it is weak and reduced; in the South it would be numerous and strong.

From the moment that you allow whites and emancipated Negroes to be placed on the same soil as peoples who are strangers to each other, you will understand without difficulty that there are only two possibilities in the future: Negroes and whites must either blend entirely or separate.

I have already expressed my conviction about the first means.[46] I do not think that the white race and the Black race will come to live on an equal footing anywhere.

But I believe that the difficulty will be even greater in the United States than anywhere else.[a] If a man happens to stand outside of the prejudices of religion, of country, of race, and this man is king, he can work surprising revolutions in society. An entire people cannot so to speak rise above itself in this way.

A despot coming to join the Americans and their former slaves under the same yoke would perhaps succeed in mixing them together; as long as the American democracy remains at the head of affairs, no one will dare to attempt such an undertaking, and you can anticipate that, the more the whites of the United States are free, the more they will seek to separate themselves.[47]

I said elsewhere that the true link between the European and the Indian was the half-breed; in the same way, the true transition between the white

46. *This opinion, moreover, is based on authorities much more weighty than I. In the* Mémoires de Jefferson, *among others, you read: "Nothing is more clearly written in the book of destiny than the emancipation of the Blacks, and it is just as certain that the two races equally free will not be able to live under the same government. Nature, habit and opinion have established insurmountable barriers between them." (See* Extrait des Mémoires de Jefferson, *by M. Conseil.)*

a. In the margin: "≠Of all governments those that have the least power over mores are free governments.≠"

47. *If the English of the Antilles had governed themselves, you can count on the fact that they would not have granted the act of emancipation that the mother country has just imposed.*

and the Negro is the mulatto. Wherever there is a very great number of mulattos, the fusion between the two races is not impossible.

There are parts of America where the European and the Negro have so crossed that it is difficult to meet a man who is completely white or completely Black. Having reached this point, the two races can really be said to have mingled; or rather, in their place, a third has appeared that takes after the two without being precisely either the one or the other.

Of all Europeans the English are the ones who have least mingled their blood with that of the Negroes. You see more mulattos in the South of the Union than in the North, but infinitely fewer than in any other European colony. Mulattos are very few in the United States; they have no strength by themselves, and in the quarrels between the races they ordinarily make common cause with the whites. This is how in Europe you often see the lackeys of great lords put on nobility with the people.

This pride of origin, natural to the English, has been singularly increased further among the Americans by the individual pride given birth by democratic liberty. The white man of the United States is proud of his race and proud of himself.

Besides, since whites and Negroes do not come to mingle in the North of the Union, how would they mingle in the South? Can you suppose for one moment that the American of the South, placed as he will always be between the white man in all his physical and moral superiority and the Negro, can ever think of mixing with the latter? The American of the South has two energetic passions that will always lead him to separate himself: he will be afraid of resembling the Negro, his former slave, and of descending below the white, his neighbor.

If it were absolutely necessary to foretell the future, I would say that in the probable course of things the abolition of slavery in the South will make the repugnance that the white population feels there for the Blacks grow. I base this opinion on what I have already noted analogously in the North. I said that the white men of the North withdraw from Negroes all the more carefully as the legislator blurs the legal separation that should exist between them. Why would it not be the same in the South? In the North when whites are afraid of ending by blending with Blacks, they fear an imaginary danger. In the South where the danger would be real, I cannot believe that the fear would be less.[b]

If, on the one hand, you recognize (and the fact is not doubtful) that in the extreme South Blacks are constantly accumulating and growing faster than whites; if, on the other hand, you concede that it is impossible to foresee the time when Blacks and whites will come to mingle and to draw the same advantages from the state of society, must you not conclude that in the states of the South Blacks and whites will sooner or later end by getting into a struggle?

What will the final result of this struggle be?

You will easily understand that on this point you must confine yourself to vague conjectures. With difficulty the human mind manages in a way to draw a great circle around the future; but within this circle chance, which escapes all efforts, is in constant motion. In the portrait of the future chance always forms the obscure point where the sight of intelligence cannot penetrate. What you can say is this: in the Antilles it is the white race that seems destined to succumb; on the continent, the Black race.

In the Antilles whites are isolated in the middle of an immense population of Blacks;[c] on the continent Blacks are placed between the sea and an innumerable people who already extend above them as a compact mass, from the frozen areas of Canada to the borders of Virginia, from the banks

b. These notes in the manuscript seem instead to be the plan for the rest of this section:

≠If he does not mingle, what? Examine the various possibilities. Here nothing dogmatic, no fear for the white race of America, on the contrary for the Black race. Perhaps they will separate? Perhaps they will wage a war of extermination? This is probable as long as the Union lasts because the South leans on the North.

Finally reason to preserve *slavery* and all its *rigors* for the good of the two races.

If the two races cannot blend together in the southernmost states of the Union, what then will be their fate? You easily understand that on this point you must necessarily confine yourself to vague conjectures. In all human events there is an immense portion abandoned to chance or to secondary causes that escapes entirely from forecasts and calculations.≠

c. "We have already seen the *whites destroyed* in the Antilles. Our sons will see the *Blacks destroyed* in most of the United States, this at the end of the successive retreat of Negroes toward the South" (YTC, CVh, 2, p. 95).

of the Mississippi to the shores of the Atlantic Ocean. If the whites of North America remain united, it is difficult to believe that Negroes can escape the destruction that threatens them; they will succumb by sword or misery. But the Black populations accumulated along the Gulf of Mexico have chances for salvation if the struggle between the two races comes about when the American confederation has dissolved. Once the federal link is broken, the men of the South would be wrong to count on lasting support from their brothers of the North. The latter know that the danger can never reach them; if a positive duty does not compel them to march to the aid of the South, you can foresee that the sympathies of race will be powerless.

Whatever the period of the struggle may be, the whites of the South left to themselves will moreover present themselves in the contest with an immense superiority of enlightenment and means; but the Blacks will have for them numbers and the energy of despair. Those are great resources when you have weapons in hand. Perhaps what happened to the Moors of Spain will then happen to the white race of the South [(something not very probable, it is true)]. After occupying the country for centuries, it will finally withdraw little by little toward the country from which its ancestors came in the past, abandoning to the Negroes the possession of a country that Providence seems to intend for the latter, since they live there without difficulty and work more easily there than whites.

The danger, more or less remote but inevitable, of a struggle between the Blacks and whites who populate the South of the Union presents itself constantly as a painful dream to the imagination of the Americans. The inhabitants of the North talk daily about these dangers, although they have nothing directly to fear from them. They seek in vain to find a means to ward off the misfortunes that they foresee.

In the states of the South the inhabitants are silent. They do not speak about the future with strangers; they avoid talking about it with friends; each person hides it so to speak from himself. The silence of the South has something more frightening about it than the noisy fears of the North.

This general preoccupation of minds has given birth to an almost unknown enterprise that can change the fate of one part of the human race.

Fearing the dangers that I have just described, a certain number of American citizens gather as a society with the goal of exporting at their expense to the coasts of Guinea the free Negroes who would like to escape the tyranny that weighs upon them.[48]

In 1820, the society that I am speaking about succeeded in founding in Africa, at 7 degrees of north latitude, a settlement to which it gave the name *Liberia*.[d] The latest news announced that two thousand five hundred Negroes were already gathered at this place. Transported to their former country, the Blacks have introduced American institutions there. Liberia has a representative system, Negro jurors, Negro magistrates, Negro priests; you see churches and newspapers there, and by a singular turn of the vicissitudes of this world whites are forbidden to settle within its walls.[49]

There certainly is a strange twist of fortune! Two centuries have passed since the day when the inhabitant of Europe undertook to carry Negroes from their family and their country to transport them to the shores of

---

48. *This society took the name Colonization Society of Blacks.*

See its annual reports, and notably the fifteenth. Also see the brochure already indicated entitled: Letters on the Colonization Society and On Its Probable Results, *by M. Carey, Philadelphia, April 1833.*

d. "You read in the *National Intelligencer* of 14 January 1834, a curious article on Liberia, from which it follows that at this period the colony had a newspaper entitled *Liberia Herald* which contained pieces on history and on ethics and a page of advertisements.

"See the letter addressed by Mr. Voorhead [*sic* (ed.)] captain of the ship *John Adams* to the Secretary of the Navy, published in the *National Intelligencer* of January 1834" (YTC, CVh, 2, p. 75).

This is the letter of P. F. Voorhees in which he describes his visit to Monrovia. This letter was published on 13 February 1834 in the review cited. Tocqueville also seems to have found in the same newspaper information about the Bank and the division of federal territories.

A note from his pocket notebook 1 also shows that he thought about visiting the colony established by Negroes in Wilberforce, Canada: "Colony that the *colored men* are establishing at Wilberforce in upper Canada. It can be interesting to visit" (YTC, BIIa, and *Voyage, OC,* V, 1, p. 153). The project was not accomplished.

49. *This last regulation has been penned by the founders of the settlement themselves. They were afraid that something analogous to what is happening on the frontiers of the United States would happen in Africa, and that the Negroes, like the Indians, entering into contact with a race more enlightened than theirs, would be destroyed before being able to become civilized.*

North America. Today you meet the European busy again carting the descendants of these very Negroes across the Atlantic Ocean in order to take them back to the land from which he had once uprooted their fathers. Barbarians have drawn the enlightenment of civilization from within servitude and have learned in slavery the art of being free.[e]

Until today Africa was closed to the arts and sciences of whites. The enlightenment of Europe, imported by Africans, will perhaps penetrate there. So there is a beautiful and great idea in the founding of Liberia; but the idea, which can become so fruitful for the Old World, is sterile for the New.

In twelve years the Society for the colonization of Blacks has transported to Africa two thousand five hundred Negroes. During the same time period, about seven hundred thousand of them were born in the United States.

If the colony of Liberia were in the position to receive each year thousands of new inhabitants, and the latter in a condition to be brought there usefully; if the Union took the place of the Society, and if annually it used its riches[50] and its ships to export Negroes to Africa, it still would not be able to balance just the natural increase of the population among the Blacks; and by not removing each year as many men as those born, it would not even manage to suspend the development of the evil that is growing each day in its bosom.[51]

The Negro race will no longer leave the shores of the American continent, where the passions and the vices of Europe made it come; it will disappear from the New World only by ceasing to exist. The inhabitants

---

e. Note in the manuscript: "{To civilization by stultification.}"

50. *Many other difficulties as well would be met in such an enterprise. If the Union, in order to transport Negroes from America to Africa, undertook to buy Blacks from those whose slaves they were, the price of Negroes increasing in proportion to their rarity would soon rise to enormous amounts, and it is inconceivable that the states of the North would consent to make such an expenditure, whose benefits they would not receive. If the Union removed the slaves of the South by force or acquired them at a low price set by the Union, it would create an insurmountable resistance among the states located in this part of the Union. From the two sides you end up at the impossible.*

51. *In 1830, there were in the United States 2,010,527 slaves, and 319,467 emancipated; in all 2,329,994 Negroes; which formed a little more than one fifth of the total population of the United States in the same period.*

of the United States can postpone the misfortunes that they fear, but they cannot today destroy the cause of them.

I am obliged to admit that I do not consider the abolition of slavery as a means to delay in the states of the South the struggle of the two races.[f]

The Negroes can remain slaves for a long time without complaining; but once among the number of free men, they will soon become indignant about being deprived of nearly all the rights of citizens; and not able to become the equals of whites, they will not take long to prove to be their enemies.

In the North emancipating the slaves was all profit; you rid yourself in this way of slavery, without having anything to fear from free Negroes. The latter were too few ever to claim their rights. It is not the same in the South.

The question of slavery was for the masters in the North a commercial and manufacturing question; in the South it is a question of life or death. So you must not confuse slavery in the North and in the South.

God keep me from trying, like certain American authors, to justify the principle of the servitude of Negroes; I am only saying that all those who have allowed this painful principle in the past are not equally free to abandon it today.

I confess that when I consider the state of the South, I discover for the white race that inhabits these countries only two ways to act: to free the Negroes and combine with them; to remain separated from them and hold them in slavery as long as possible.[g] The middle terms seem to me to lead shortly to the most horrible of all civil wars, and perhaps to the ruin of one of the two races.

The Americans of the South envisage the question from this point of view, and they act accordingly. Not wanting to blend together with the Negroes, they do not want to set them free.

f. "I admit that if I had the misfortune to live in a country where slavery had been introduced and I had the liberty of the Negroes in my hand, I would keep myself from opening it" (YTC, CVh, 2, p. 86).

g. Beaumont reached the same conclusion in *Marie,* I, pp. 294–301.

It is not that all the inhabitants of the South regard slavery as necessary to the wealth of the master; on this point many among them agree with the men of the North, and readily admit with the latter that servitude is an evil; but they think that this evil must be maintained in order to live.

Enlightenment, by increasing in the South, made the inhabitants of this part of the territory see that slavery is harmful to the master, and this same enlightenment shows them, more clearly than they had seen until then, the near impossibility of destroying it. A singular contrast results. Slavery becomes established more and more in the laws, as its usefulness is more disputed; and while its principle is gradually abolished in the North, in the South more and more rigorous consequences are drawn from this very principle.

Today the legislation of the states of the South relative to slaves presents a kind of unheard of atrocity, and by itself alone it reveals some profound disturbance in the laws of humanity. It is enough to read the legislation of the states of the South to judge the desperate position of the two races that inhabit them.

It is not that the Americans of this part of the Union have exactly increased the rigors of servitude; they have, on the contrary, made the physical lot of the slaves milder. The ancients knew only chains and death to maintain slavery; the Americans of the South of the Union have found more intellectual guarantees for the continuance of their power. They have, if I many express myself in this way, spiritualized despotism and violence. In antiquity they tried to prevent the slave from breaking his chains; today we have undertaken to remove his desire to do so.

The ancients chained the body of the slave, but they left his mind free and allowed him to become enlightened. In that they were consistent with themselves; then slavery had a natural way out: from one day to another the slave could become free and equal to his master.

The Americans of the South, who do not think that at any time the Negroes can blend with them, have forbidden, under severe penalties, teaching them to read and write.[h] Not wanting to raise them to their level, they hold them as close as possible to the brute.[j]

In all times the hope for liberty had been placed within slavery in order to soften its rigors.

The Americans of the South have understood that emancipation always presented dangers when the emancipated person could not one day come to be assimilated with the master. To give a man liberty and leave him in misery and disgrace, that is to do what, if not to provide a future leader of a slave revolt? It had already been noted for a long time, moreover, that the presence of the free Negro cast a vague restlessness deep within the soul of those who were not free, and made the idea of their rights penetrate their soul like an uncertain glimmer. The Americans of the South have in most cases removed from the masters the ability to emancipate.[52]

I met in the South[k] of the Union an old man who formerly had lived in an illegitimate union with one of his Negro women. He had had several children with her, who coming into the world became slaves of their father. Several times the latter had thought to bequeath them at least liberty, but years had gone by before he was able to overcome the obstacles raised to emancipation by the legislator. During this time old age came, and he was about to die. He then imagined his sons led from market to market and passing from paternal authority to the rod of a stranger. These horrible images threw his dying imagination into delirium. I saw him prey to the agonies of despair, and I then understood how nature knew how to avenge the wounds done to it by laws.

These evils are awful, without doubt; but are they not the foreseeable and necessary consequence of the very principle of servitude among modern peoples?

---

h. To the side, with a note: "≠ (Verify this). See *National Intelligencer,* December 1833. South Carolina. ≠" Possible reference to a speech by O'Connell, delivered on the occasion of an antislavery meeting, and reproduced in the number for 5 December 1833 of this review. See note c of p. 548.

j. "Blacks are a foreign nation that you have conquered and to whom you give a nationality and the means of resistance by emancipating them or even by enlightening them" (YTC, CVh, 2, p. 98).

52. *Emancipation is not forbidden, but subjected to formalities that make it difficult.*

k. In a variant, he specifies that the story took place in North Carolina.

From the moment when Europeans took their slaves from within a race of men different from their own, that many among them considered as inferior to other human races, and with which all envisaged with horror the idea of ever assimilating, they supposed slavery to be eternal; for, between the extreme inequality that servitude creates and the complete equality that independence naturally produces among men, there is no intermediate lasting state. The Europeans vaguely sensed this truth, but without admitting it. Every time it concerned Negroes, you saw the Europeans obey sometimes their interest or their pride, sometimes their pity. Toward the Black they violated all the rights of humanity, and then they instructed him in the value and inviolability of these rights. They opened their ranks to their slaves, and when the latter attempted to enter, they chased them away in disgrace. Wanting servitude, the Europeans allowed themselves to be led despite themselves or without their knowing toward liberty, without having the courage of being either completely iniquitous or entirely just.

If it is impossible to foresee a period when the Americans of the South will mix their blood with that of the Negroes, can they, without exposing themselves to perishing, allow the latter to attain liberty? And if, in order to save their own race, they are obliged to want to keep them in chains, must you not excuse them for taking the most effective means to succeed in doing so?

What is happening in the South of the Union seems to me at the very same time the most horrible and the most natural consequence of slavery. When I see the order of nature overturned, when I hear humanity cry out and struggle in vain under the laws, I admit that I do not find the indignation to condemn the men of today, authors of these outrages; but I summon up all of my hatred against those who after more than a thousand years of equality introduced servitude again into the world.

Whatever the efforts of the Americans of the South to keep slavery, moreover, they will not succeed forever. Slavery, squeezed into a single point of the globe, attacked by Christianity as unjust, by political economy as fatal; slavery, amid the democratic liberty and the enlightenment of our age, is not an institution that can endure. It will end by the deed of the slave or by that of the master. In both cases, great misfortunes must be expected.

If you refuse liberty to the Negroes of the South, they will end by seizing it violently themselves; if you grant it to them, they will not take long to abuse it.

What Are the Chances for the American Union to Last? What Dangers Threaten It?[m]

What makes preponderant strength reside in the states rather than in the Union.—The confederation will last only as long as all the states that make it up want to be part of it.—Causes that should lead them to remain united.—Utility of being united in order to resist foreigners and in order not to have foreigners in America.—Providence has not raised natural barriers between the different states.—There are no material interests that divide them.—Interest that the North has in the prosperity and union of the South and of the West; the South with those of the North and of the West; the West with those of the other two.—Nonmaterial interests that unite the Americans.—Uniformity of opinions.—Dangers to the confederation arise from the difference in the characters of the men who compose it and in their passions.—Characters of the men of the South and of the North.—Rapid growth is one of the greatest perils of the Union.—March of the population toward the northwest.— Gravitation of power in this direction.—Passions to which these rapid movements of fortune give birth.—The Union subsisting, does its government tend to gain strength or to become weaker?— Various signs of weakening.—Internal improvements.— Uninhabited lands.—Indians.—Affair of the Bank.— Affair of the tariff.—General Jackson.

The maintenance of what exists in each one of the states that compose the Union depends in part on the existence of the Union. So it is necessary to

---

m. Original title: FUTURE OF THE EUROPEANS WHO INHABIT THE UNITED STATES.

examine first what the probable fate of the Union is. But first of all it is good to settle on one point; if the current confederation came to break up, it seems to me incontestable that the states that are part of it would not return to their original individuality. In place of one Union, several of them would form. I do not intend to try to find out on what bases these new Unions would come to be established; what I want to show are the causes that can lead to the dismemberment of the current confederation.

To succeed I am going to be obliged to go over again some of the roads that I have previously traveled. I will have to review several subjects that are already known. I know that by acting in this way I am exposing myself to the reproaches of the reader; but the importance of the matter that remains for me to treat is my excuse. I prefer to repeat myself sometimes than not to be understood, and I prefer to harm the author rather than the subject.

The law-makers who drew up the Constitution of 1789 tried hard to give the federal power a separate existence and a preponderant strength.

But they were limited by the very conditions of the problem that they had to resolve. They had not been charged with constituting the government of a single people, but with regulating the association of several peoples; and whatever their desires, they always had to end up dividing the exercise of sovereignty.

[≠In this division the law-makers of the Union found themselves still enclosed in a circle out of which they were not free to go.

The conditions of the division were fixed in advance and by the very nature of things. To the Union reverted the direction of all general interests, to the states the government of all special [v: provincial] interests.

The portion of the Union in this division of sovereignty seems at first view greater than that of the states; and in actual fact it is the smallest.

The general interests of the country touch its inhabitants only from time to time. The interests of locality, every day. The government of the Union has more power than that of the states, but you rarely feel it act. The provincial government does smaller things, but it never rests. The one assures the independence and the greatness of the country, something that does not immediately touch upon individual well-being; the other regulates liberty, fortune, life, the entire future of each citizen.

So true political life is found in the state and not in the Union. Americans are attached to the Union by principle, to their state by sentiment and by instinct. They must in a way rise above themselves in order to sustain federal sovereignty against that of the states. ≠]ⁿ

In order to understand well what the consequences of the division were, it is necessary to make a short distinction between the acts of sovereignty.

There are matters that are national by their nature, that is to say that are related only to the nation taken as a body, and can be confided only to the men or to the assembly that represents most completely the entire nation. I will put in this number war and diplomacy.

There are others that are provincial by their nature, that is to say that are related to certain localities and can be appropriately treated only in the locality itself. Such is the budget of towns.

Finally, matters are found that have a mixed nature: they are national in that they interest all of the individuals who make up the nation; they are provincial in that there is no necessity that the nation itself provides for it. These are, for example, the rights that regulate the civil and political state of the citizens. There is no social state without civil and political rights. So these rights interest all citizens equally; but it is not always necessary to the existence and to the prosperity of the nation that these rights be uniform, and consequently that they be regulated by the central power.

So among the matters that sovereignty deals with,° there are two nec-

n. In the margin: "≠The nationality of the Union is an opinion, the nationality of the states, a sentiment.

"The real strength of society is in the state not in the Union.≠"

In another place on the same page: "≠Thus interests, habits, sentiments combine to concentrate true political life in the states.≠"

o. What must be understood by the word *sovereignty* and the words *right of sovereignty.*/

The sovereign power, always a *single* being.

The sovereign power.—The *people.*

Acts of sovereignty.—*All acts whatever of the public authority.*

Authors of these acts.—*The sovereign power delegates the power to do these acts either to one single individual or to several. It puts these acts in whatever categories it pleases.*

essary categories; you find them again in all well-constituted societies, whatever the base, moreover, on which the social pact has been established.

Between these two extreme points are placed, like a floating mass, general but non-national matters that I have called mixed. Since these matters are neither exclusively national nor entirely provincial, the care of providing for them can be attributed to the national government or to the provincial government, following the conventions of those who are becoming associated, without missing the purpose of the association.

Most often simple individuals unite in order to form the sovereign power and their combination makes up a people. Above the general government they have given themselves you then find only individual strengths or collective powers, each of which represents a very minimal fraction of the sovereign power. Then as well it is the general government that is most naturally called to regulate not only matters national by their essence, but the greatest portion of the mixed matters that I already mentioned. The localities are reduced to the portion of sovereignty that is indispensable to their well-being.

Sometimes, by a fact prior to the association, the sovereign power is composed of already organized political bodies; then it happens that the provincial government takes charge of providing not only for the matters exclusively provincial by their nature, but also for all or part of the mixed

---

Theoretical division of acts.—*Principal acts, lesser acts* depending on whether they interest directly the whole or the parts of the sovereign power when, by an order of things prior to the association, the sovereign power is composed of *individuals* and is consequently represented by a single people.

Practical consequence.—When the sovereign power delegates the exercise of all the principal acts to the same person (man or assembly), tendency that this man or assembly gathers all the others.

When it delegates the exercise of principal acts to several, contrary tendency.

Another consequence. When the sovereign power is composed of *individuals,* tendency to gather the exercise of all the principal acts into the same hands, into what others?

When composed of nations, contrary tendency.

Single people goes to despotism, confederation to anarchy.

Fears of the French of dismemberment, absurd.

Id. of the Americans of consolidation.

After the theory, make this perceptible in practice (YTC, CVh, 1, pp. 75–77).

matters of which it was just a question. This is because the confederated nations, which were themselves sovereign powers before their union, and which, although they are united, continue to represent a very considerable fraction of the sovereign power, intended to cede to the general government only the exercise of the rights indispensable to the union.P

When the national government, apart from the prerogatives inherent in its nature, finds itself vested with the right to regulate the mixed matters of sovereignty, it possesses a preponderant strength. Not only does it have many rights, but all the rights that it does not have are at its mercy, and it is to be feared that it will go so far as to take away from the provincial governments their natural and necessary prerogatives.[*]

When it is, on the contrary, the provincial government that finds itself vested with the right to regulate the mixed matters, an opposite tendency reigns in society. Preponderant strength then resides in the province, not

p. Each isolated individual has an absolute right over himself, right that has no limit in the material world except his strength, in the moral world except justice and reason.

A people, which is a collection of individuals, possesses a right of the same nature.

This right then takes the name of sovereignty.

≠The people, taking this term in the sense not of a class but of all the classes of citizens, the people.≠

Every time an independent people acts and in whatever manner it acts, it does an act of sovereignty. ≠So you would try in vain to establish a distinction among the acts of public authority between those that are due essentially to the right of sovereignty and those that are not inherent to it. What you can do is to distinguish between the most and the least important of the habitual actions of the sovereign power.≠

The sovereign power delegates a part or the totality of the exercise of its power either to a man or to several.

But all the acts of the public authority, whatever they may be, derive from the expressed or presumed will of the sovereign power. Sovereignty can have a multitude of agents, but there is always only one sovereign power.

[In the margin] A people, an association of peoples, always represents a unique individual. Sovereignty can have a multitude of agents, but there is always only one sovereign power, just as in one man there is always only one will applied to different objects and served by different organs (YTC, CVh, 1, pp. 82–84).

[*]. The central government of France possesses the right to act in everything in the name of the nation and the right to regulate all matters of internal administration that have a general character. These are immense prerogatives but it [they (ed.)] are not enough for it and it uses the strength that they give to it to direct the use of communal funds and to interfere in [interrupted text (ed.)].

in the nation; and you must fear that the national government will end up being stripped of privileges necessary to its existence.^q

So single peoples are naturally led toward centralization, and confederations toward dismemberment.^r

It only remains to apply these general ideas to the American Union.

To the particular states reverted inevitably the right to regulate purely provincial matters.

In addition these same states retained that of fixing the civil and political capacity of citizens, of regulating the relationships of men with each other, and of administering justice to them; rights that are general in their nature, but that do not necessarily belong to the national government.

We have seen that to the government of the Union was delegated the power to command in the name of the entire nation in cases where the nation would have to act as one and the same individual. It represented the nation vis-à-vis foreigners; it led the common forces against the common enemy. In a word it was concerned with matters that I have called exclusively national.

In this division of the rights of sovereignty the part of the Union still seems at first glance greater than that of the states; a slightly more thorough examination demonstrates that in fact it is less.

q. I cannot prevent myself from thinking that the men in America who fear the encroachments of the central government confuse two essentially distinct things: complete and incomplete sovereignty.

In countries where sovereignty is not divided, and where the provinces administer themselves and do not govern themselves, town [v: provincial] liberties are always in danger. The natural tendency of society is to concentrate strength at the center and it is only by a constant effort that provincial liberties are maintained.

But in a State [v: country] where sovereignty is divided, the greatest strength finding itself placed in the extremities not at the center, the tendency of the society is to split up and it is only with effort that it remains united. Consequently you have seen nearly all the States where (illegible word) sovereignty was undivided finish [by (ed.)] arriving at administrative despotism and the confederations at anarchy (YTC, CVh, 2, pp. 48–49).

r. "The natural tendency of a people, if you do not oppose it, is to concentrate social forces indefinitely until you arrive at pure administrative despotism. The natural tendency of confederations is to divide these forces indefinitely until you arrive at dismemberment" (YTC, CVh, 1, p. 78).

[≠The Union is an almost imaginary being that is not easily apparent to the senses≠.]

The government of the Union executes more vast enterprises, but you rarely feel it act. The provincial government does smaller things, but it never rests and reveals its existence at each instant.

The government of the Union watches over the general interests of the country; but the general interests of a people have only a debatable influence on individual happiness.

The affairs of the province, in contrast, visibly influence the well-being of those who inhabit it.

The Union assures the independence and the greatness of the nation, things that do not immediately touch individuals. The state maintains the liberty, regulates the rights, guarantees the fortune, assures the life, the entire future of each citizen.

The federal government is placed at a great distance from its subjects; the provincial government is within reach of all. It is enough to raise your voice in order to be heard by it. The central government has for it the passions of a few superior men who aspire to lead it; on the side of the provincial government is found the interest of second-rate men who only hope to obtain power in their state; and it is these who, placed near the people, exercise the most power over them.

So the Americans have much more to expect and to fear from the state than from the Union; and following the natural march of the human heart, they must be attached much more intensely to the first than to the second.

[≠But men, whatever you say, are not led only by interests; they obey habits and sentiments.≠

{True patriotism remained with the state and did not pass to the Union. The state has an ancient existence, the Union is comparatively a new thing.}]

In this habits and sentiments are in agreement with interests.

When a compact nation divides its sovereignty and reaches the state of confederation, memories, customs, habits struggle for a long time against the laws and give the central government a strength that the latter deny it. When confederated peoples unite in a single sovereignty, the same causes act in the opposite direction. I do not doubt that if France became a confederated republic like that of the United States, the government would at first show itself to be more energetic than that of the Union; and if the Union constituted itself as a monarchy like France, I think that the American government would remain for some time weaker than ours. At the moment when national life was created among the Anglo-Americans, provincial existence was already old, necessary relationships were established between the towns and individuals of the same states; you were accustomed there to considering certain matters from a common point of view, and to dealing exclusively with certain enterprises as representing a special interest.[s]

The Union is an immense body that offers to patriotism a vague object to embrace. The state has settled forms and circumscribed limits; it represents a certain number of things known and dear to those who inhabit it. It blends with the very image of the land, is identified with property, with family, with memories of the past, with the work of the present, with dreams of the future. So patriotism, which most often is only an extension of individual egoism, has remained with the state and has not so to speak passed to the Union.

Thus interests, habits, and sentiments unite to concentrate true political life in the state, and not in the Union.

You can easily judge the difference in the strength of the two governments by seeing each of them move within the circle of its power.

Every time that a state government addresses itself to a man or to an

---

s. Among the causes that can hasten the dismemberment of the Union in the first rank is found the state of weakness and inertia into which the federal government would fall, if the central power came to this degree of feebleness that it could no longer serve as arbiter among the different provincial interests and could not effectively defend the confederation against foreigners; its usefulness would become doubtful, and the Union would no longer exist except on paper; and each state would tend to separate itself from it in order to find its strength in itself.

So it is very important, granting the fact of the Union, to try to find out if the federal government tends to gain or to lose power.

The question of the strength and of the weakness of the federal government, important moreover in itself and separate from the question of the duration of the Union, would still be important; for the strength or the weakness of the federal government, even if it had no influence on the duration of the Union, would necessarily have an influence on prosperity and its progress (YTC, CVh, 1, pp. 80–81).

association of men its language is clear and imperative; it is the same with the federal government when it is speaking to individuals; but as soon as it finds itself facing a state, it begins to talk at length: it explains its motives and justifies its conduct; it argues, advises, hardly ever commands. If doubts arise about the limits of the constitutional powers of each government, the provincial government claims its right with boldness and takes prompt and energetic measures to sustain it. During this time the government of the Union reasons; it appeals to the good sense of the nation, to its interests, to its glory; it temporizes, negotiates; only when reduced to the last extremity does it finally determine to act. At first view you could believe that it is the provincial government that is armed with the strength of the whole nation and that Congress represents a state.

So the federal government, despite the efforts of those who constituted it, is, as I have already said elsewhere, by its very nature a weak government that more than any other needs the free support of the governed in order to subsist.

It is easy to see that its object is to realize with ease the will that the states have to remain united. This first condition fulfilled, it is wise, strong and agile. It has been organized in such a way as usually to encounter only individuals before it and to overcome easily the resistance that some would like to oppose to the common will; but the federal government has not been established with the expectation that the states or several among them would cease to want to be united.

If the sovereignty of the Union today entered into a struggle with that of the states, you can easily foresee that it would succumb; I doubt even that the battle would ever be engaged in a serious way.[t] Every time that an obstinate resistance is put up against the federal government, you will see

---

t. What singularly favors the *Union* is that all the confederated states have reached more or less the same *degree* of civilization and the same *type* of civilization. They are thus *naturally* more suited for working together than a single nation whose parts would not be perfectly homogeneous on this point.

The lack of homogeneity on this point, which hinders the government of a single nation, is particularly contrary to a confederation because there the differences between the ideas and the mores of diverse populations find a *legal* expression and strength.

it yield. Experience has proven until now that when a state stubbornly wanted something and demanded it resolutely, the state never failed to obtain it; and that when it clearly refused to act,[53] it was left free to do so.

If the government of the Union had a force of its own, the physical situation of the country would make the use of it very difficult.[54]

The United States covers an immense territory; long distances separate the states; the population is spread over a country still half wilderness. If the Union undertook by arms to hold the confederated states to their duty,

---

What will perhaps always prevent Switzerland from forming a very really united country, is that the differences between the civilization of the *cantons* is striking. The difference between the *canton* of Vaud and that of Appenzell is like that between the XIXth century and the XVth.

The central government in confederations is always by its nature weaker than the governments of States (for many reasons), but that is above all true when it is not an active sovereignty that is being carved up, but several sovereignties that are merging. In this case the memories, habits, interests struggle for a long time in the *opposite direction* against the laws. The central government would for a long time remain very much stronger in France than in the United States, even if France would become a federated republic. The central government of the United States will for a long time remain weaker than the current government of France, even if the Union would become a monarchy. When national life was created among the Anglo-Americans.

Federal government.

Union requires in order to subsist rare simplicity of mores or of needs, or very advanced civilization.

Weakness of the Union proven by facts.

1. All the *amendments* to the Constitution have been made in order to restrict federal power. The federal government abandoned in practice certain of its prerogatives and took no new ones. Every time that the state resolutely stood up to the Union, it more or less gained what it wanted.

1. Georgia in 1793 refusing to obey the decision of the Supreme Court. See Kent, volume 1, p. 278.

2. Rebellion in Pennsylvania against the whiskey tax (YTC, CVh, 2, pp. 79–80).

53. *See the conduct of the states of the North in the War of 1812. "During this war," Jefferson says in a letter of 17 [14 (ed.)] March 1817 to General Lafayette, "four of the eastern states were no longer tied to the Union except as dead bodies to living men"* (Correspondance de Jefferson, *published by Conseil) [vol. II, pp. 296–97 (ed.)].*

54. *The state of peace in which the Union finds itself gives it no pretext for having a permanent army. Without a permanent army, a government has nothing prepared in advance in order to take advantage of the favorable moment, to overcome resistance, and to take sovereign power by surprise.*

its position would be analogous to that of England at the time of the War of Independence.

Moreover, a government, were it strong, could only with difficulty escape the consequences of a principle, once it accepted that principle itself as the foundation of the public law that is to govern it. The confederation has been formed by the free will of the states; the latter by uniting did not lose their nationality and did not merge into one and the same people. If today one of these very states wanted to withdraw its name from the contract, it would be quite difficult to prove that it could not do so. The federal government, in order to combat it, would not rely in a clear way on either force or law.

For the federal government to triumph easily over the resistance that a few of its subjects might put up, it would be necessary for the particular interest of one or of several of them to be intimately linked to the existence of the Union, as has often been seen in the history of confederations.

I suppose that, among these states that the federal bond gathers together, there are some that alone enjoy the principal advantages of union, or whose prosperity depends entirely on the fact of union; it is clear that the central power will find in them a very great support for maintaining the others in obedience. But then it will no longer draw its strength from itself, it will draw it from a principle that is contrary to its nature. Peoples confederate only to gain equal advantages from union, and in the case cited above the federal government is strong because inequality reigns among the united nations.

I suppose again that one of the confederated states has gained a preponderance great enough to take hold of the central power by itself alone; it will consider the other states as its subjects and, in the alleged sovereignty of the Union, will make its own sovereignty respected. Then great things will be done in the name of the federal government, but truly speaking this government will no longer exist.[55]

In these two cases the power that acts in the name of the confederation

---

55. *In this way, the province of Holland in the republic of the Netherlands and the emperor in the German Confederation sometimes put themselves in the place of the Union, and exploited the federal power in their particular interest.*

becomes that much stronger the more you move away from the natural state and the acknowledged principle of confederations.

In America the present union is useful to all the states, but it is essential to none. If several states broke the federal bond, the fate of the others would not be compromised, even though the sum of their happiness would be less. Just as there is no state whose existence or prosperity is entirely[u] linked to the present union, neither is there one that is disposed to make very great personal sacrifices to preserve it.

From another perspective, no state is seen for now to have, out of ambition, a great interest in maintaining the confederation as we see it today. All undoubtedly do not exercise the same influence in federal councils, but there is not one of them that should flatter itself about dominating them and that can treat the other confederated states as inferiors or subjects.

So it seems to me certain that if one portion of the Union wanted seriously to separate from the other, not only would you not be able to prevent it from doing so, but you would not even be tempted to try. So the present Union will last only as long as all the states that compose it continue to want to be part of it.

This point settled, we are now more at ease: it is no longer a matter of trying to find out if the states currently confederated will be able to separate, but if they will want to remain united.

Among all the reasons that make the present union useful to the Americans, you find two principal ones whose evidence easily strikes everyone.

Although the Americans are so to speak alone on their continent, commerce gives them as neighbors all the peoples with whom they traffic. So despite their apparent isolation, the Americans need to be strong, and they can only be strong by remaining united.

The states by dividing would not only diminish their strength vis-à-vis foreigners, they would create foreigners on their own soil. From that moment they would enter into a system of internal customs; they would divide valleys by imaginary lines; they would imprison the course of rivers and

u. The published text says "entirely," while the manuscript says "intimately," a word that seems to work better.

hinder in all ways the exploitation of the immense continent that God granted them as their domain.

Today they have no invasion to fear, consequently no army to maintain, no taxes to levy [no military despotism to fear]; if the Union came to break apart, the need for all these things would perhaps not take long to make itself felt.

So the Americans have an immense interest in remaining united.

From another perspective it is nearly impossible to discover what type of material interest one portion of the Union would have, for now, to separate from the others.

When you cast your eyes over a map of the United States and you see the chain of the Allegheny Mountains running from the Northeast to the Southwest and covering the country over an expanse of 400 leagues, you are tempted to believe that the purpose of Providence was to raise between the Mississippi basin and the coasts of the Atlantic Ocean one of those natural barriers that, opposing the permanent relationships of men with each other, form like necessary limits to different peoples.

But the average height of the Allegheny Mountains does not surpass 800 meters.[56] Their rounded summits and the spacious valleys that they enclose within their contours present easy access in a thousand places. There is more. The principal rivers that come to empty their waters into the Atlantic Ocean, the Hudson, the Susquehanna, the Potomac, have their sources beyond the Allegheny Mountains on the open plateau that borders the Mississippi basin. Leaving this region[57] they come out through the rampart that seemed as though it should throw them back toward the west and, once within the mountains, trace natural routes always open to men.

So no barrier is raised between the different parts of the country occupied today by the Anglo-Americans. The Allegheny Mountains are far from serving as limits to peoples; they do not even mark the boundaries of states.

---

56. *Average height of the Allegheny Mountains according to Volney* (Tableau des États-Unis, *p. 33), 700 to 800 meters; 5,000 to 6,000 feet, according to Darby; the greatest height of the Vosges is 1,400 meters above sea level.*

57. *See* View of the United States, *by Darby, pp. 64 and 79.*

New York, Pennsylvania and Virginia enclose them within their precincts and extend as far to the west as to the east of these mountains.[58]

The territory occupied today by the twenty-four states of the Union and the three great districts that are not yet placed among the number of states, although they already have inhabitants, covers an area of 131,144 square leagues,[59] that is to say that it already presents a surface almost equal to five times that of France.[*] In these limits are found a varied soil, different temperatures, and very diverse products.

This great expanse of territory occupied by the Anglo-American republics has given birth to doubts about the maintenance of their union. Here distinctions must be made: conflicting interests are sometimes created in the different provinces of a vast empire and end up coming into conflict; then it happens that the great size of the State is what most compromises its duration. But if the men who cover this vast territory do not have conflicting interests among themselves, its very expanse must be useful to their prosperity, for the unity of government singularly favors the exchange that can be made with the different products of the soil, and by making their flow easier, it increases their value.

Now, I clearly see different interests in the different parts of the Union, but I do not find any that conflict with each other.

The states of the South are nearly exclusively agricultural; the states of the North are particularly manufacturing and commercial; the states of the West are at the same time manufacturing and agricultural. In the South tobacco, rice, cotton and sugar are harvested; in the North and in the West, corn and wheat. These are the diverse sources of wealth. But in order to draw upon these sources, there is a means common and equally favorable to all; it is the Union.[w]

---

58. *The chain of the Allegheny Mountains is not higher than that of the Vosges and does not offer as many obstacles as the latter to the efforts of human industry. So the countries situated on the eastern slope of the Allegheny Mountains are as naturally linked to the Valley of the Mississippi as Franche-Comté, upper Burgundy and Alsace are to France.*

59. *1,002,600 square miles. See* View of the United States, *by Darby, p. 435.*

[*]. France, according to Malte-Brun, volume VIII, p. 178, has an area of 26,739 square leagues.

w. These ideas appear in two letters of Carey published in the *National Intelligencer* of 28 and 31 December 1833. Tocqueville more than likely became aware of them.

The North, which carries the riches of the Anglo-Americans to all parts of the world and the riches of the world into the Union, has a clear interest in having the confederation continue to exist as it is today, so that the number of American producers and consumers that it is called to serve remains the greatest possible. The North is the most natural middleman between the south and the west of the Union, on the one hand, and the rest of the world, on the other; so the North should want the South and the West to remain united and prosperous so that they provide raw materials for its manufacturing and cargo for its ships.

The South and the West have on their side a still more direct interest in the preservation of the Union and the prosperity of the North. The products of the South are in large part exported overseas; so the South and the West need the commercial resources of the North. They should want the Union to have a great maritime power in order to be able to protect them effectively. The South and the West should contribute willingly to the costs of a navy, although they do not have ships; for if the fleets of Europe came to blockade the ports of the South and the Mississippi delta, what would become of the rice of the Carolinas, the tobacco of Virginia, the sugar and cotton that grow in the valleys of the Mississippi? So there is not a portion of the federal budget that does not apply to the preservation of a material interest common to all the confederated states.

[To clarify this subject even more I want to make a comparison drawn from France.

Provence gathers oil and Flanders harvests wheat; Burgundy produces wine and Normandy raises livestock. Do these different provinces find in the diversity of products reasons to hate each other? Isn't [it (ed.)] on the contrary the diversity of these products that gives them a common interest in remaining united in order to exchange them more freely?

Georgia seems to me to have the same reasons to remain united with Massachusetts as Provence with Flanders, and Ohio appears to me as naturally linked to the state of New York as Burgundy to Normandy.][x]

---

x. In a first version:

≠It is not in the interests but in the passions[1] of the Americans that you must seek the causes of ruin that threaten the American Union.

Apart from this commercial utility, the South and the West of the Union find a great political advantage in remaining united with each other and with the North.

The South encloses in its bosom an immense population of slaves, a population threatening at present, still more threatening in the future.

The states of the West occupy the bottom of a single valley. The rivers that water the territory of these states, originating from the Rocky or the Allegheny Mountains, all come to mingle their waters with that of the Mississippi and flow with it toward the Gulf of Mexico. The states of the West are entirely isolated by their position from the traditions of Europe and the civilization of the Old World.

So the inhabitants of the South should desire to preserve the Union in order not to live alone in the face of the Blacks, and the inhabitants of the West, in order not to find themselves enclosed within the central part of America without free communication with the world.

The North for its part should want the Union not to divide, in order to remain as the link that joins this great body to the rest of the world.

So there exists a tight bond among the material interests of all parts of the Union.

I will say as much for the opinions and the sentiments that you could call the non-material interests of man.

The inhabitants of the United States speak a great deal about their love

---

What most compromises the fate of the Union is its very prosperity, is the rapid growth of some parts.≠

The states that adhere to . . .

1. ≠This is clearly seen. The south, which has the greatest need to remain united, gives signs of impatience. The north and the west, which could by themselves alone form an immense republic, most want the union.

If interests alone were sufficient to maintain the Americans in the Union, there would be no portion of the United States where the federal Constitution had warmer adherents than in the south.

The south needs the north not only to guarantee the importation of its products, but also to defend it from the Negroes who live in its bosom.

The Americans of the south are, however, the only ones who threaten to break the federal bond.

So you must seek reasons other than those taken from interests properly speaking.≠

of country; I admit that I do not trust this considered patriotism that is based upon interest and that interest, by changing object, can destroy.

Nor do I attach a very great importance to the language of the Americans, when each day they express the intention of preserving the federal system that their fathers adopted.

What maintains a large number of citizens under the same government is much less the reasoned will to remain united than the instinctive and in a way involuntary accord that results from similarity of sentiments and resemblance of opinions.

I will never admit that men form a society by the sole fact that they acknowledge the same leader and obey the same laws; there is a society only when men consider a great number of objects in the same way; when they have the same opinions on a great number of subjects; when, finally, the same facts give rise among them to the same impressions and the same thoughts.[y]

Whoever, considering the question from this point of view, would study what is happening to the United States, would discover without difficulty that their inhabitants, divided as they are into twenty-four distinct sovereignties, constitute nonetheless a single people; and perhaps he would even come to think that the state of society more truly exists within the Anglo-American Union than among certain nations of Europe that have nevertheless only a single legislation and are subject to one man alone.[z]

---

y. "What truly constitutes a society is not having the same government, the same laws, the same language, it is having on a great number of points the same *ideas* and the same *opinions*. The first things are all material. They are the means by which ideas and opinions reign. Note well that for the despotic form itself (the one that has least need for a *society*) to be lasting, it must rely on this base" (YTC, CVh, 2, p.77).

z. Bond of American society./

Research what the ideas common to the Americans are. Ideas about the future. Faith in human perfectibility, faith in civilization that is judged favorably in every respect. Faith in liberty! This is universal.

Faith in the good sense and *definitive* reason of the people. This is general but not universal.

You can do on that a very interesting (illegible word).

The true bond of the Americans is this much more than love of country and nationality. These two things are more apparent than real, but the others differentiate

Although the Anglo-Americans have several religions, they all have the same way of envisaging religion.[a]

They do not always agree on the means to take in order to govern well and vary on some of the forms that are appropriate to give to the government, but they agree on the general principles that should govern human societies. From Maine to Florida, from the Missouri to the Atlantic Ocean, they believe that the origin of all legitimate powers is in the people. They conceive the same ideas on liberty and on equality; they profess the same opinions on the press, the right of association, the jury, the responsibility of the agents of power.

If we pass from political and religious ideas to the philosophical and moral opinions that regulate the daily actions of life and guide conduct as a whole, we will note the same agreement.

---

the Americans from all other peoples. What makes their common bond is what separates them from the others.

[To the side: Many men in France believe that American society is lacking [a (ed.)] bond. False idea. It has more of a true bond than ours.]

Shared ideas. *Philosophical and general ideas.*

That interest well understood is sufficient to lead men to do good.

That each man has the ability to govern himself.

That good is relative and that there it [makes (ed.)] continual progress in society; that nothing there is or should be finished forever.

More special ideas, advantages of equality (YTC. CVh, 2, p. 78).

This note already contains the seeds of many ideas of the first part of the second volume.

a. Tocqueville had copied into one of his travel notebooks the following fragment, an extract from a letter that he had written 8 July 1831 to Louis de Kergorlay:

It is clear that there still remains here a greater core of the Christian religion than in any country in the world, to my knowledge, and I do not doubt that this disposition of minds still influences the political regime. It gives a moral and well-ordered turn to ideas; it stops the lapses of the spirit of innovation; above all it makes very rare the disposition of the soul, so common among us, that makes you rush forward against all obstacles *per fas et nefas* [by all possible paths] toward the goal that you have chosen. It is certain that a party, whatever desire it had to gain a result, would still believe itself obliged to march toward it only by means that would have an appearance of morality and would not openly shock religious beliefs, always more or less moral even when they are false (alphabetic notebook A, YTC, BIIa, and *Correspondance avec Kergorlay, OC,* XIII, 1, p. 231; this fragment is not published in *Voyage, OC,* V, 1).

The Anglo-Americans[60] place moral authority in universal reason, as they do political power in the universality of citizens, and they consider that you must rely on the sense of all in order to discern what is permitted or forbidden, what is true or false. Most of them think that knowledge of his interest well understood is sufficient to lead a man toward the just and the honest. They believe that each person by birth has received the ability to govern himself, and that no one has the right to force his fellow to be happy. All have an intense faith in human perfectibility; they judge that the diffusion of knowledge must necessarily produce useful results, ignorance must lead to harmful effects; all consider society as a body in progress; humanity as a changing scene, where nothing is or should be fixed forever, and they admit that what seems good to them today can be replaced tomorrow by something better that is still hidden.[b]

I do not say that all these opinions are correct, but they are American.

At the same time that the Anglo-Americans are thus united with each other by these shared ideas, they are separated from all other peoples by a sentiment, pride.

For fifty years it has not ceased to be repeated to the inhabitants of the United States that they form the only religious, enlightened and free people. They see that among them until now democratic institutions have pros-

---

60. *I think I do not need to say that by this expression:* the Anglo-Americans, *I mean only to speak about the great majority of them. A few isolated individuals always stand outside of this majority.*

b. At the same time that the Americans are thus united with each other by opinions, what separates them from others, *pride.*

They are separated from all other peoples.

Religion, by a sentiment of pride.

Politics, they believe [themselves (ed.)] alone democratic.

Philosophy, are in a state to be free.

Economy, (illegible word) are wise.

If we pass from political and religious ideas to philosophical opinions, properly speaking, to those that regulate the daily actions of life and direct conduct as a whole, I will note the same agreement.

Most Americans accept that the knowledge of interest well understood is sufficient to lead men to honesty (YTC, CVh, 2, p. 103).

pered, while they fail in the rest of the world; so they have an immense opinion of themselves, and they are not far from believing that they form a species apart in the human race.

Thus the dangers that menace the American Union do not arise from diversity of opinions any more than from that of interests. They must be sought in the variety of characters and in the passions of the Americans.

The men who inhabit the immense territory of the United States have nearly all come from a shared stock; but over time climate and above all slavery have introduced marked differences between the character of the English of the South and the character of the English of the North.

It is generally believed among us that slavery gives to one portion of the Union interests contrary to those of the others. I have not noted that this was the case. Slavery has not created interests in the South contrary to those of the North; but it has modified the character of the inhabitants of the South, and has given them different habits.

I have shown elsewhere what influence servitude had exercised on the commercial capacity of the Americans of the South; this same influence extends equally to their mores.

The slave is a servant who does not argue and who submits to everything without a murmur. Sometimes he murders his master, but he never resists him. In the South there are no families so poor that they do not have slaves. The American of the South from his birth finds himself invested with a kind of domestic dictatorship; the first notions that he receives of life make him know that he is born to command, and the first habit that he contracts is that of dominating without difficulty. So education tends powerfully to make the American of the South a man haughty, quick, irascible, violent, ardent in his desires, impatient with obstacles; but easy to discourage if he cannot triumph with the first blow.

The American of the North does not see slaves rush up around his cradle. He does not even find free servants, for most often he is limited to providing for his needs by himself. Soon after he is born, his mind is presented with the idea of necessity from all directions. So he learns early to know on his own the exact natural limit of his power; he does not expect to bend by force wills that are opposed to his, and he knows that to gain the support of his fellows it is above all necessary to win their favor. So he is patient, thoughtful, tolerant,[c] slow to act, and persevering in his designs.

In the southern states the most pressing needs of man are always satisfied. Thus the American of the South is not preoccupied by the material needs of life; someone else takes care of thinking about them for him. Free on this point, his imagination is directed toward other greater and less precisely defined matters. [<So the whites in the south form an aristocratic body {kind of aristocracy}. Consequently a certain feudal tendency reigns in their thoughts and in their tastes.>] The American of the South loves grandeur, luxury, glory, fame, pleasures, idleness above all; nothing forces him to make efforts in order to live, and as he has no necessary work, he falls asleep and does not undertake even useful work.

Because equality of fortunes reigns in the North, and slavery no longer exists there, man there is absorbed, as it were, by these very material concerns that the white scorns in the South. From his birth he is busy fighting poverty, and he learns to place material comfort above all the enjoyments of the mind and heart. His imagination, concentrated on the small details of life, fades, his ideas are fewer and less general, but they become more practical, clearer and more precise. Since he directs all the efforts of his intelligence only toward the study of well-being, he does not take long to excel there; he knows admirably how to make the most of nature and of men in order to produce wealth; he understands marvelously the art of making society work toward the prosperity of each one of its members, and of extracting from individual egoism the happiness of all.

The man of the North has not only experience, but also learning; but he does not prize knowledge as a pleasure. He values it as a means, and he avidly takes hold only of its useful applications.

The American [{man}] of the South is more spontaneous, more witty, more open, more generous, more intellectual and more brilliant.

The American [{man}] of the North is more active, more reasonable, more enlightened and more skillful.

---

c. In the margin: "≠ *Tolerant* indicates a virtue. A word would be needed that indicates the interested and necessary toleration of a man who needs others. ≠"

The one has the tastes, prejudices, weaknesses and the grandeur of all aristocracies.

The other, the qualities and failings that characterize the middle class.

Bring two men together in society, give to these two men the same interests and in part the same opinions; if their character, their enlightenment and their civilization differ, there is a great chance that they will not get along. The same remark is applicable to a society of nations.[*]

So slavery does not attack the American confederation directly by interests, but indirectly by mores.

The states that joined the federal pact in 1790 numbered thirteen; the confederation counts twenty-four of them today. The population that amounted to nearly four million in 1790 had quadrupled in the space of forty years; in 1830 it rose to nearly thirteen million.[61]

Such changes cannot take place without danger.

For a society of nations as for a society of individuals, there are three principal ways to last: the wisdom of the members, their individual weakness, and their small number.

The Americans who withdraw from the shores of the Atlantic Ocean in order to plunge into the West are adventurers impatient with any kind of yoke, greedy for wealth, often cast out by the states where they were born. They arrive in the middle of the wilderness without knowing each other. There they find to control them neither traditions nor family support, nor examples. Among them the rule of laws is weak, and that of mores is weaker still. So the men who daily populate the valleys of the Mississippi are inferior in all ways to the Americans who inhabit the old limits of the Union. They already exercise, however, a great influence in its councils, and they

---

[*]. It is to this diversity of characters that you must resort in order to explain how every time there is a division of opinion among the Anglo-Americans, you have seen the North on one side and the South on the other, often without being able to see the same division found in their interests. {See from the time of Washington the question of the tax on distilled liquors. Marshall, vol. 5, p. 185.}

61. *Census of 1790*   *3,929,328*
    Census of 1830   *12,856,165.*

arrive at the government of common affairs before having learned to manage themselves.[62]

The weaker the members are individually, the greater the society's chances to last, for they then have security only by remaining united. When, in 1790, the most populated of the American republics did not have 500,000 inhabitants,[63] each one of them felt its insignificance as an independent people, and this thought made obedience to a federal authority easier. But when one of the confederated states numbers 2,000,000 inhabitants, as does the state of New York, and covers a territory whose area is equal to one-quarter of that of France,[64] it feels strong by itself, and if it continues to desire the union as useful to its well-being, it no longer regards it as necessary to its existence; it can do without it; and agreeing to remain there, it does not take long to want to be preponderant in it.

The mere multiplication of members of the Union would already tend powerfully to break the federal bond. All men placed at the same point of view do not look at the same objects in the same way. This is so with all the more reason when the point of view is different. So as the number of American republics increases, you see the chance to gather the assent of all to the same laws diminish.

Today the interests of the different parts of the Union are not in conflict with each other; but who could foresee the various changes that the near future will bring about in a country where each day creates cities and every five years nations?

Since the founding of the English colonies the number of inhabitants doubles every twenty-two years or so; I do not see any causes that should for the next century stop this progressive movement of the Anglo-American population. Before one hundred years have passed I think that the territory

62. *This, it is true, is only a temporary peril. I do not doubt that with time society will become settled and orderly in the west, as it has already become on the shores of the Atlantic Ocean.*

63. *Pennsylvania had 431,373 inhabitants in 1790.*

64. *Area of the state of New York, 6,213 square leagues (46,500 square miles). See* View of the United States, *by Darby, p. 435.*

occupied or claimed by the United States will be covered by more than one hundred million inhabitants and divided into forty states.[65]

I admit that these one hundred million men do not have different interests; I grant them all, on the contrary, an equal advantage in remaining united, and I say that, by the very fact that they are one hundred million, forming forty distinct and unequally powerful nations, the maintenance of the federal government is nothing more than a happy accident.

I would like to believe in human perfectibility; but until men have changed in nature and are completely transformed, I will refuse to believe in the duration of a government whose task is to hold together forty diverse peoples spread over a surface equal to half of Europe,[66] to avoid rivalries, ambition, and struggles among them, and to bring the action of their independent wills together toward the accomplishment of the same projects.

But the greatest risk that the Union runs by growing comes from the continual displacement of forces that takes place within it.

From the shores of Lake Superior to the Gulf of Mexico, you count as the crow flies about four hundred French leagues. Along this immense line winds the frontier of the United States; sometimes it stays within these limits, most often it penetrates well beyond into the wilderness. It has been calculated that along this entire vast front whites advanced each year on average seven leagues.[67] From time to time an obstacle presents itself: it is an unproductive district, a lake, an Indian nation that is met unexpectedly

---

65. *If the population continues to double in twenty-two years, for another century, as it has done for two hundred years, in 1852 you will number in the United States twenty-four million inhabitants, forty-eight in 1874, and ninety-six in 1896. It will be so even if you encountered on the western slope of the Rocky Mountains terrain that was unsuitable for agriculture. The lands already occupied can very easily hold this number of inhabitants. One hundred million men spread over the soil occupied at this moment by the twenty-four states and the three territories that compose the Union would only give 762 individuals per square league, which would still be very far from the average population of France, which is 1,006; from that of England, which is 1,457; and which would remain even below the population of Switzerland. Switzerland, despite its lakes and mountains, numbers 783 inhabitants per square league. See Malte-Brun, vol. VI, p. 92.*

66. *The territory of the United States has an area of 295,000 square leagues; that of Europe, according to Malte-Brun, vol. VI, p. 4, is 500,000.*

67. *See* Legislative Documents, *20th Congress, n. 117, p. 105.*

in its path. The column then stops an instant; its two extremities bend toward each other and, after they have rejoined, the advance begins again. There is in this gradual and continuous march of the European race towards the Rocky Mountains something providential; it is like a flood of men that rises unceasingly and that swells each day by the hand of God.

Within this first line of conquerors cities are built and vast states are founded. In 1790, scarcely a few thousand pioneers were found spread across the valleys of the Mississippi; today these same valleys hold as many men as the entire nation contained in 1790. The population there reaches nearly four million inhabitants.[68] The city of Washington was founded in 1800, at the very center of the American confederation; now this city finds itself at one of its extremities. The representatives of the last states of the West,[69] in order to take their seats in Congress, are already obliged to make a journey as long as that of the traveler who goes from Vienna to Paris.

All the states of the Union are carried along at the same time towards wealth; but all cannot grow and prosper in the same proportion.

In the north of the Union detached branches of the Allegheny Mountain chain, advancing to the Atlantic Ocean, form spacious harbors and ports always open to the largest ships. From the Potomac, in contrast, and following the coast of America to the mouth of the Mississippi, you find nothing more than a flat and sandy terrain. In this part of the Union the mouths of nearly all the rivers are obstructed, and the ports that are open here and there in the middle of lagoons do not present to ships the same depth and offer to commerce much smaller facilities than those of the North.

To this first inferiority which arises from nature another is joined that comes from laws.

We have seen that slavery, which is abolished in the North, still exists in the South, and I have shown the fatal influence that it exercises on the well-being of the master himself.

68. *3,672,317, census of 1830.*

69. *From Jefferson, capital of the state of Missouri, to Washington, you count 1,019 miles, or 420 postal leagues* (American Almanac, *1831, p. 43 [44 (ed.)]*).

So the North must be more commercial[70] and more industrious than the South. It is natural that population and wealth concentrate there more rapidly.

The states situated on the shore of the Atlantic Ocean are already half populated. Most of the lands have an owner; so those states cannot receive the same number of emigrants as the states of the West that still offer an unlimited field to industry. The basin of the Mississippi is infinitely more fertile than the coast of the Atlantic Ocean. This reason added to all the others vigorously pushes the Europeans toward the West. This is rigorously demonstrated by figures.

If you work with the whole of the United States, you find that in forty years the number of inhabitants there has more or less tripled. But if you envisage only the basin of the Mississippi, you discover that in the same period of time the population[71] there has become thirty-one times greater.[72]

Each day the center of federal power is displaced. Forty years ago the

70. *In order to judge the difference that exists between the commercial movement of the South and that of the North, it is enough to glance at the following picture:*

In 1829, the ships of large and small commerce belonging to Virginia, the two Carolinas and Georgia (the four large states of the South) had a tonnage of only 5,243.

In the same year, the vessels of the state of Massachusetts alone had a tonnage of 17,322 (Legislative Documents, *21st Congress, 2nd session, n. 140, p. 244).*

Thus the state of Massachusetts alone had three times more ships than the above-named four states.

The state of Massachusetts, however, has only 959 square leagues of area (7,335 square miles) and 610,014 inhabitants, while the four states that I am speaking about have 27,204 square leagues (210,000 miles) and 3,047,767 inhabitants. Thus the area of the state of Massachusetts forms only one thirtieth of the area of the four states, and its population is five times smaller than theirs (View of the United States, *by Darby). Slavery harms in several ways the commercial prosperity of the South: it diminishes the spirit of enterprise among whites, and it prevents them from finding at their disposal the sailors that they need. The navy recruits in general only from the lowest class of the population. Now it is slaves who in the South form this class, and it is difficult to use them at sea; their service would be inferior to that of whites, and you would always have to be afraid that they might revolt in the middle of the ocean, or might take flight when reaching foreign shores.*

71. View of the United States, *by Darby, p. 444.*

72. *Note that, when I speak about the basin of the Mississippi, I am not including the portion of the states of New York, Pennsylvania and Virginia, placed west of the Allegheny Mountains, and that should, however, be considered as also part of it.*

majority of the citizens of the Union were on the shores of the sea in the vicinity of the place where Washington is rising today; now it is deeper into the land and more to the North; you can be sure that within twenty years it will be on the other side of the Allegheny Mountains. Assuming that the Union continues to exist, the basin of the Mississippi, because of its fertility and its extent, is necessarily called to become the permanent center of federal power. In thirty or forty years the basin of the Mississippi will have taken its natural rank. It is easy to calculate that then its population, compared to that of the states placed on the shores of the Atlantic, will be in proportion of about 40 to 11. So in a few more years the leadership of the Union will escape completely from the states that formed it, and the population of the valleys of the Mississippi will predominate in federal councils.

This continuous gravitation of strength and federal influence toward the Northwest is revealed every ten years, when, after doing a federal census of the population, the number of representatives that each state must send to Congress is fixed once again.[73]

In 1790, Virginia had nineteen representatives in Congress. This number continued to grow until 1813, when we saw it attain the figure of twenty-three. From this time it began to decrease. In 1833 it was no more than twenty-one.[74] During this same period the state of New York followed an

73. *You notice then that during the ten years that have just passed one state increased its population in the proportion of 5 to 100, as Delaware; another was in the proportion of 250 to 100, as the territory of Michigan. Virginia finds that, during the same period, it increased the number of its population in the relationship of 13 to 100, while the adjacent state of Ohio increased the number of its population in the proportion of 61 to 100. See the general table contained in the* National Calendar;[d] *you will be struck by the inequality in the fortune of the different states.*

d. It concerns the *American Almanac for 1832*, p. 162. The *National Calendar* also contains figures on the census, but the percentages given by Tocqueville belong to the *American Almanac*.

74. *You are going to see further along that during the last period the population of Virginia grew in the proportion of 13 to 100. It is necessary to explain how the number of the representatives of a state can decrease when the population of the state, far from decreasing itself, is advancing. I take as point of comparison Virginia, which I have already cited. The number of representatives of Virginia, in 1823, was in proportion to the total number of representatives of the Union; the number of representatives of Virginia in 1833 is equally in proportion to the total number of representatives of the Union in 1833, and in proportion in relation to its population, which increased during these ten years. So the relation of the new number of*

opposite progression: in 1790, it had in Congress ten representatives; in 1813, twenty-seven; in 1823, thirty-four; in 1833, forty. Ohio did not have a single representative in 1803; in 1833 it had nineteen.

It is difficult to conceive of a lasting union between two peoples one of whom is poor and weak, the other rich and strong, even if it would be proved that the strength and wealth of one is not the cause of the weakness and poverty of the other. Union is still more difficult to maintain in a time when one is losing strength and when the other is in the process of gaining it.

This rapid and disproportionate increase of certain states threatens the independence of the others. If New York, with its two million inhabitants and its forty representatives, wanted to pass a law in Congress, it would perhaps succeed. But even if the most powerful states did not seek to oppress the least powerful, the danger would still exist, for it is in the possibility of the deed almost as much as in the deed itself.

The weak rarely have confidence in the justice and reason of the strong. So the states that are growing less quickly than the others cast a look of distrust and envy on those that fortune favors. From that comes this profound malaise and this vague uneasiness that you notice in one part of the Union, and that contrast with the well-being and confidence that reign in the other. I think that the hostile attitude taken by the South has no other causes.

The men of the South are of all Americans those who should most hold on to the Union, for they are the ones who above all would suffer from being abandoned to themselves; but they are the only ones who threaten to break the bond of the confederation. What causes that? It is easy to say: the South, which provided four Presidents to the confederation;[75] which knows today that federal power is escaping from it; which each year sees

---

representatives from Virginia to the old will be proportional, on the one hand, in relation to the new total number of representatives to the old, and, on the other, in relation to the proportions of increase for Virginia and for the entire Union. Thus in order for the number of representatives from Virginia to remain stationary, it is sufficient that the relation of the proportion of increase of the small country to that of the large be the inverse of the relation of the new total number of representatives to the old; if this proportion of increase of the Virginia population is in a weaker relation to the proportion of increase of the entire Union, as the new number of representatives of the Union with the old, the number of representatives of Virginia will be decreased.

75. *Washington, Jefferson, Madison and Monroe.*

the number of its representatives to Congress decrease and those of the North and of the West increase; the South, populated by ardent and irascible men, is getting angry and is becoming uneasy. It looks at itself with distress; examining the past, it wonders each day if it is not oppressed. If it comes to find that a law of the Union is not clearly favorable to it, it cries out that it is being abused by force; it complains ardently, and if its voice is not heard, it becomes indignant and threatens to withdraw from a society whose costs it bears, without getting any profits.

"The tariff laws," said the inhabitants of Carolina in 1832, "enrich the North and ruin the South, for, otherwise, how could you imagine that the North, with its inhospitable climate and arid soil, would constantly increase its wealth and power, while the South, which is the garden of America, is falling rapidly into decline?"[76]

If the changes that I have talked about took place gradually, so that each generation at least had the time to pass by along with the order of things that it had witnessed, the danger would be less; but there is something precipitous, I could almost say revolutionary, in the progress that society makes in America. The same citizen has been able to see his state march at the head of the Union and then become powerless in federal councils. There is one such Anglo-American republic that grew up as quickly as a man, and that was born, grew and reached maturity in thirty years.

It must not be imagined, however, that the states that lose power are becoming depopulated or are declining; their prosperity is not stopping; they are growing even more quickly than any kingdom of Europe.[77] But it

76. *See the report made by its committee to the Convention that proclaimed nullification in South Carolina.*

77. *The population of a country assuredly forms the first element of its wealth. During this same period of 1820 to 1832, when Virginia lost two representatives to Congress, its population increased in the proportion of 13.7 to 100;[e] that of the Carolinas in the relation of 15 to 100, and that of Georgia in the proportion of 51.5 to 100. (See* American Almanac, *1832, p. 162.) Now Russia, which is the European country where the population grows most quickly, only increases in ten years the number of its inhabitants in the proportion of 9.5 to 100; France in that of 7 to 100, and Europe as a whole in that of 4.7 to 100 (see Malte-Brun, vol. VI, p. 95).*

e. Draft of the note in the manuscript: "The population grew by 145,000 inhabitants or 13.7 percent in ten years. See fifth census. It seems to me that by following this progression the population of Virginia would take about 75 years to double."

seems to them that they are becoming poor because they are not becoming rich as quickly as their neighbor, and they believe they are losing their power because they suddenly come in contact with a power greater than theirs.[78] So it is their sentiments and their passions that are wounded more than their interests. But isn't this enough for the confederation to be at risk? If since the beginning of the world peoples and kings had in view only their true utility, you would hardly know what war was among men.

Thus the greatest danger that threatens the United States arises from their very prosperity; it tends to create among several of the confederated states the intoxication that accompanies the rapid augmentation of wealth, and, among others, the envy, distrust and the regrets that most often follow its loss.

The Americans rejoice when contemplating this extraordinary movement; they should, it seems to me, consider it with regret and with fear. Whatever they do, the Americans of the United States will become one of the greatest peoples of the world; they will cover nearly all of North America with their offspring; the continent that they inhabit is their domain, it cannot escape them. So what presses them to take possession of it today? Wealth, power and glory cannot fail to be theirs, and they rush toward this immense fortune as if only a moment remained for them to grasp it.

I believe I have demonstrated that the existence of the present confederation depends entirely on the agreement of all the confederated states to want to remain united; and from this given I tried to find out what the causes are that could lead the different states to want to separate. But there are two ways for the Union to perish. One of the confederated states can want to withdraw from the contract and thus break the common bond violently; most of the remarks that I have made before apply to this case. The federal government can progressively lose its power by a simultaneous tendency of the united republics to take back the use of their independence. The central power, deprived successively of all of its prerogatives, reduced

---

78. *It must be admitted, however, that the depreciation that has taken place in the value of tobacco for fifty years has notably diminished the comfort of the farmers of the South; but this fact is independent of the will of the men of the North as it is of theirs.*

by a tacit agreement to powerlessness, would become incapable of fulfilling its object, and the second Union would perish like the first, by a sort of senile weakness.

The gradual weakening of the federal bond, which leads finally to the annulment of the Union, is moreover in itself a distinct fact that can lead to many other less extreme results before producing that final result. The confederation would still exist, though the weakness of its government could already have reduced the nation to powerlessness, and caused internal anarchy and the slowing of the general prosperity of the country.

So after trying to find out what is leading^f the Anglo-Americans to become disunited, it is important to examine whether, given the Union's continued existence, their government is enlarging the sphere of its action or is narrowing it, whether it is becoming more energetic or weaker.

The Americans are clearly preoccupied by a great fear. They notice that among most peoples of the world the exercise of the rights of sovereignty tend to become concentrated in a few hands, and they are afraid of the idea that it will end up by being so among them. The statesmen themselves experience these terrors, or at least pretend to experience them; for in America centralization is not popular, and you cannot more skillfully court the majority than by rising against the alleged encroachments of the central power. The Americans refuse to see that in countries where this centralizing tendency that frightens them manifests itself, you find only a single people, while the Union is a confederation of different peoples; a fact that is sufficient to disrupt all of the expectations based on the analogy.

I admit that I consider these fears of a great number^g of Americans as entirely imaginary. Far from fearing like them the consolidation of sovereignty in the hands of the Union, I believe that the federal government is becoming weaker in a visible way.

To prove what I am advancing on this point I will not resort to old

f. In the manuscript: "what could lead . . ."
g. The manuscript says: "of some Americans."

facts, but to those that I was able to witness or that have taken place in our time.[h]

When you examine attentively what is happening in the United States, you discover without difficulty the existence of two contrary tendencies; they are like two currents that travel over the same bed in opposite directions.

During the forty-five years that the Union has existed time has dealt with a host of provincial prejudices that at first militated against it. The patriotic sentiment that attached each of the Americans to his state has become less exclusive. By getting to know each other better the various parts of the Union have drawn closer. The mail, that great link between minds, today penetrates into the heart of the wilderness;[79] steamboats make all points of the coast communicate with each other daily. Commerce descends and goes back up the rivers of the interior with an unparalleled rapidity.[80] To these opportunities created by nature and art are joined instability of desires, restlessness of spirit, and love of riches that, constantly pushing the American out of his house, put him in communication with a great number of his fellow citizens. He travels his country in all directions; he visits all the populations that inhabit it. You do not find a province of France whose inhabitants know each other as perfectly as the 13 million men who cover the surface of the United States.

---

h. In the margin: "≠So the existence of the Union [v: the will to remain united], a matter of chance. Its *dismemberment,* something always possible, something inevitable with time.

"The weakening of the federal government as government apart from *dismemberment,* another question.≠" The first intention of Tocqueville had been to acknowledge in the introduction of the second part his error as to the danger of the dissolution of the United States (see note b for p. 690 of the second volume and James T. Schleifer, *The Making of Tocqueville's "Democracy in America,"* pp. 102–11.

79. *In 1832, the district of Michigan, which has only 31,639 inhabitants and still forms only a wilderness scarcely cleared, showed the development of 940 miles of post roads. The nearly entirely wild territory of Arkansas was already crossed by 1,938 miles of post roads. See* The Report of the Postmaster General, *30 November 1833. Carrying newspapers alone throughout the Union brings in 254,796 dollars per year. [These documents are found in* National Calendar, *1833, p. 244. See "Report of the Postmaster General,"* National Intelligencer, *12 December 1833.]*

80. *In the course of ten years, from 1821 to 1831, 271 steamboats were launched just on the rivers that water the valley of the Mississippi [*National Almanac, *1832, p. 255]. In 1829, there were 256 steamboats in the United States. See* Legislative Documents, *n. 140, p. 274.*

At the same time that the Americans mingle, they assimilate; the differences that climate, origin and institutions have placed between them diminish. They all get closer and closer to a common type. Each year thousands of men who have left the North spread throughout all parts of the Union: they bring with them their beliefs, their opinions, their mores, and as their enlightenment is superior to that of the men among whom they are going to live, they do not take long to take hold of affairs and to modify society to their profit. This continual emigration of the North toward the South singularly favors the fusion of all the provincial characters into one single national character.ʲ So the civilization of the North seems destined to become the common measure against which all the rest must model themselves one day.ᵏ

As the industry of the Americans makes progress, you see the commercial bonds that unite all the confederated states tighten, and the union moves from opinions into habits. The passage of time finally makes a host of fantastic terrors that tormented the imagination of the men of 1789 disappear. The federal power has not become oppressive; it has not destroyed the independence of the states; it does not lead the confederated states to monarchy; with the Union the small states have not fallen into dependence on the large. The confederation has continued to grow constantly in population, in wealth, in power.

So I am persuaded that in our times the Americans have fewer natural difficulties living united than they found in 1789; the Union has fewer enemies than then.ᵐ

j. Beaumont had written during his journey: "American uniformity./

"One of the principal causes of the uniformity of mores among the Americans, which is always going to increase, comes from the spirit of emigration of the inhabitants of New England, who bring everywhere their enterprising, industrious and mercantile spirit. (Baltimore, 31 October 1831)" (YTC, CIX).

k. At the time of his conversation with Tocqueville and Beaumont, John Latrobe, a lawyer from Baltimore, had insisted a great deal on the differences between the south and the north of the United States and had not hesitated to assert: "I believe that all the American continent must model itself one day on New England" (non-alphabetic notebooks 2 and 3, YTC, BIIa, and *Voyage, OC*, V, 1, p. 111).

m. "All superior men for the Union, all secondary men against" (YTC, CVh, 2, p. 50).

And yet, if you want to study carefully the history of the United States over forty-five years, you will easily be persuaded that the federal power is declining.

It is not difficult to point out the causes of this phenomenon.

At the moment when the Constitution of 1789 was promulgated, everything was perishing in anarchy; the Union that followed this disorder excited much fear and hatred; but it had ardent friends because it was the expression of a great need. So although more attacked then than it is today, the federal power rapidly reached its maximum power, as usually happens to a government that triumphs after inflaming its forces in the struggle. In this period the interpretation of the Constitution seemed to expand rather than narrow federal sovereignty, and the Union presented in several respects the spectacle of one and the same people led, within as without, by a single government.[n]

But in order to reach this point the people in a way surpassed itself.

The Constitution had not destroyed the individuality of the states, and all bodies, whatever they may be, have a secret instinct that carries them toward independence. This instinct is still more pronounced in a country like America, where each village forms a kind of republic accustomed to governing itself.

So there was an effort made by the states that submitted to federal preponderance. And every effort, even if crowned with a great success, cannot fail to weaken with the cause that gave it birth.

As the federal government consolidated its power, America resumed its rank among nations, peace reappeared on its borders, public credit recovered; confusion was succeeded by a settled and [well-regulated] order that allowed individual industry to follow its natural path and develop in liberty.

This very prosperity began to make the Americans lose sight of the cause

n. In the margin: "≠It was the temporary effect of the will of the sovereigns, and not the permanent effect of the fusion of all sovereignty into a single one. If that had been the case, the power of the Union instead of diminishing would have increased constantly.≠"

that had produced it; the danger having passed, they no longer found in themselves the energy and patriotism that had helped to avert it. Delivered from the fears that preoccupied them, they lapsed easily into the course of their habits and abandoned themselves without resistance to the ordinary tendency of their inclinations. From the moment when a strong government no longer seemed necessary, some began again to think that it was a nuisance. Everything prospered with the Union, and no one separated from the Union; but they hardly wanted to feel the action of the power that represented it. In general they desired to remain united, and in each particular fact they tended to become independent again. The principle of confederation was each day more easily accepted and less applied; thus the federal government itself, by creating order and peace, brought about its decline.

As soon as this disposition of minds began to show itself outwardly, party men who live on the passions of the people began to exploit it to their profit.

From that moment the federal government found itself in a very critical situation; its enemies had popular favor, and by promising to weaken it, they gained the right to lead it.[o]

From that period onward every time the government of the Union entered into a contest with that of the states, it has almost never ceased to retreat. When there has been an occasion to interpret the terms of the federal Constitution, the interpretation has most often been against the Union and favorable to the states.

The Constitution gave the federal government the care of providing for the national interests. It had been thought that it was up to the federal government to do or to encourage in the interior the great undertakings (*internal improvements*) that were of a nature to increase the prosperity of the entire Union, such as, for example, canals.

The states became frightened by the idea of seeing an authority other than their own thus dispose of a portion of their territory. They feared that the central power, acquiring a formidable patronage in this way within their

---

o. In the margin: "≠I believe, but it is to be verified, that the entry of the republicans {federalists} to power was the first step, step indirect but real along this path.≠"

own area, would come to exercise an influence there that they wanted to reserve entirely to their agents alone.P

The democratic party that was always opposed to all developments of the federal power then raised its voice; Congress was accused of usurpation; the head of State, of ambition. The central government intimidated by this uproar ended by recognizing its error itself, and by withdrawing strictly into the sphere that was drawn for it.

The Constitution gives the Union the privilege of dealing with foreign peoples. The Union had in general considered the Indian tribes that border the frontiers of its territory from this point of view. As long as these savages agreed to flee before civilization, the federal right was not contested; but from the day when an Indian tribe undertook to settle on a piece of land, the surrounding states claimed a right of possession over these lands and a right of sovereignty over the men within them. The central government hastened to recognize both, and after dealing with the Indians as with independent peoples, it delivered them as subjects to the legislative tyranny of the states.[81]

Among the states that were formed along the Atlantic shore, several extended indefinitely to the West into the wilderness where Europeans had not yet penetrated. Those whose limits were irrevocably fixed jealously saw the immense future open to their neighbors. The former, in a spirit of conciliation and in order to facilitate the act of Union, agreed to draw limits for themselves and abandoned to the confederation all the territory that could be found beyond those limits.[82]

Since this period the federal government has become the proprietor of

---

p. In the margin: "≠Examine here the succession of messages of the various Presidents who have followed each other for forty years. But wait to see if I cannot find an agent for this research.≠" See note a for p. 84.

81. *See in the Legislative Documents that I have already cited in the chapter on the Indians the letter of the President of the United States to the Cherokees, his correspondence on this subject with his agents, and his messages to Congress.*

82. *The first act of cession took place on the part of the state of New York in 1780; Virginia, Massachusetts, Connecticut, South Carolina, North Carolina followed this example at different periods. Georgia was the last; its act of cession dates only from 1802.*

all the unsettled land[TN6] found outside of the thirteen states originally confederated. It is the federal government that undertakes to divide and to sell
that land, and the money that is brought in is put exclusively into the treasury of the Union. With the aid of this revenue the federal government
buys the Indians' lands from them, opens roads in new districts, and
facilitates with all its power the rapid development of society there.

Now, it has happened that in these very wilderness areas, formerly ceded
by the inhabitants on the shores of the Atlantic, new states have formed
over time. Congress has continued to sell, to the profit of the entire nation,
the unsettled lands that these states still enclose within them. But today
those states claim that once constituted they should have the exclusive right
to apply the proceeds of these sales to their own use. Since complaints had
become more and more threatening, Congress believed it necessary to take
away from the Union a part of the privileges that it had enjoyed until then,
and at the end of 1832, it passed a law that, without ceding to the new
republics of the West the ownership of their unsettled lands, nonetheless
applied the greatest part of the revenue that was drawn from it to their profit
alone.[83]

It is sufficient to travel across the United States to appreciate the advantages that the country derives from the bank.[r] These advantages are of several kinds; but there is one above all that strikes the foreigner; the notes of

TRANSLATOR'S NOTE 6: American historians usually refer to the matter Tocqueville is discussing here as the controversy over public lands. Given the context, to translate
terrain inculte or *terres incultes* as *uncultivated land(s)* would miss the point; I have therefore used the term *unsettled land(s)*, that is, public land not yet settled.

83. *The President refused, it is true, to assent to this law, but he completely accepted its
principle. See* Message *of 8 December 1833.*[q]

q. A note in another place of the chapter points out: "On all that see the language
of the President in 1833, *National Calendar*, p. 27."

r. The discussion on the Bank of the United States and the question of the tariff
formed in the beginning two distinct sections under the titles: AFFAIR OF THE BANK
OF THE UNITED STATES and NULLIFICATION AFFAIR. The first section began in this
place with this sentence: "The attacks directed at this moment against the Bank of the
United States can be considered as new proofs of the weakening of the federal principle."
The details cited by Tocqueville could he been found in the congressional debates
published in the *National Intelligencer* at the end of 1833 and in the first months of 1834.

the Bank of the United States are accepted at the same value on the wilderness frontier as in Philadelphia, the seat of its operations.[84]

The Bank of the United States, however, is the object of great hatred. Its directors have declared themselves against the President, and they are accused not improbably of having abused their influence in order to hinder his election. So the President, with all the fervor of a personal enmity, attacks the institution that the former represent. What has encouraged the President to pursue his vengeance in this way is that he feels supported by the secret instincts of the majority.

The Bank forms the great monetary link of the Union as the Congress is its great legislative link, and the same passions that tend to make the states independent of the central power tend toward the destruction of the Bank.

The Bank of the United States always holds in its hands a great number of the notes belonging to the provincial banks; every day it can oblige the latter to redeem their notes in specie. For the Bank, in contrast, such a danger is not to be feared; the greatness of its available resources allows it to meet all expenses. Their existence thus threatened, the provincial banks are forced to exercise restraint and to put into circulation only a number of notes proportionate to their capital. Only with impatience do the provincial banks endure this salutary control. So the newspapers that are their creatures and the President, made by his interest into their organ, attack the Bank with a kind of fury. Against it they stir up local passions and the blind democratic instinct of the country. According to them the directors of the Bank form an aristocratic and permanent body whose influence cannot fail to make itself felt in the government, and must sooner or later alter the principles of equality on which American society rests.

The struggle of the Bank against its enemies is only one incident in the great battle that the provinces wage in America against the central power;

84. *The current Bank of the United States was created in 1816, with a capital of 35,000,000 dollars (185,500,000 fr.); its charter expires in 1836. Last year Congress passed a law to renew it, but the President refused his assent. Today the struggle is engaged by both sides with an extreme violence, and it is easy to predict the coming fall of the Bank.*

the spirit of independence and democracy, against the spirit of hierarchy and subordination. I am not claiming that the enemies of the Bank of the United States are precisely the same individuals who on other points attack the federal government; but I am saying that the attacks against the Bank of the United States are the result of the same instincts that militate against the federal government, and that the large number of the enemies of the first is an unfortunate symptom of the weakening of the second.

But the Union[s] has never shown itself more feeble than in the famous tariff affair.[85]

The wars of the French Revolution and that of 1812, by preventing free communication between America and Europe, had created factories in the north of the Union. When peace had reopened the road to the New World to European products, the Americans believed they had to establish a system of tariffs that could at the very same time protect their emerging industry and pay off the amount of debts that the wars had made them contract.

The states of the South,[t] which have no manufacturing to encourage and which are only agricultural, did not take long to complain about this measure.

I am not claiming to examine here what could be imaginary or real in their complaints, I am telling the facts.

From 1820 onward, South Carolina declared in a petition to Congress that the tariff law was *unconstitutional, oppressive* and *unjust.* After that Georgia, Virginia, North Carolina, the state of Alabama and that of Mississippi, made more or less energetic complaints along the same lines.

---

s. Here the section on the Bank of the United States ended and the one on nullification began, which finished with the words: "no use would be made of it" [p. 624].

85. *For details of this affair, see principally* Legislative Documents, *22nd Congress, 2nd session, n. 30.*

t. Some weeks before leaving America the author admitted to his brother, Édouard: "I have only a superficial idea of the *South* of the Union, but in order to know it as well as the North, it would be necessary to have stayed there six months" (letter of 20 January 1832, YTC, BIa2). Various complications, including a very severe winter, a shipwreck, and the illness of Tocqueville, considerably reduced the time that the two friends had decided to spend in the South. Their stay in New Orleans lasted scarcely two days.

Far from taking these murmurings into account, Congress, in the years 1824 and 1828, again raised the tariff duties and again sanctioned the principle.

Then was produced or rather was recalled in the South a celebrated doctrine that took the name of *nullification.*[u]

I have shown in its place that the purpose of the federal Constitution was not to establish a league, but to create a national government. The Americans of the United States, in all cases foreseen by their Constitution, form only one and the same people. On all those points the national will expresses itself, as among all constitutional peoples, with the aid of a majority. Once the majority has spoken, the duty of the minority is to submit.

Such is the legal doctrine, the only one that is in agreement with the text of the Constitution and the known intention of those who established it.

The *nullifiers* of the South claim on the contrary that the Americans, by uniting, did not intend to blend into one and the same people, but that they only wanted to form a league of independent peoples; it follows that each state, having preserved its complete sovereignty if not in action at least in principle, has the right to interpret the laws of Congress, and to suspend within its borders the execution of those that to it seem opposed to the Constitution or to justice.

The entire doctrine of nullification is found in summary in a sentence pronounced in 1833 before the Senate of the United States by Mr. Calhoun, avowed head of the nullifiers of the South:

"The Constitution is a compact, to which the states are parties in their sovereign capacity; and that, as in all other cases of compact between parties having no common umpire, each has a right to judge for itself [the extent of its reserved powers]."[v]

---

u. "Nullifiers. See art. of the Revue" (YTC, CVh, 2, p. 43). Was it the *Revue des deux mondes?*

v. These ideas appear in the speech of 26 February 1833 (reply to Webster), reproduced in the *National Intelligencer* of 26 March 1833. Tocqueville had as well obtained first-hand information on this subject during his visit to Philadelphia in October 1831.

Tocqueville writes to his father on 7 October 1831:

We are in a great hurry to arrive in this last city. A remarkable event is happening there at this moment; all the partisans of free trade have sent deputies who form what

It is clear that such a doctrine destroys the federal bond in principle and in fact brings back the anarchy from which the Constitution of 1789 had delivered the Americans.

When South Carolina saw that Congress showed itself deaf to its complaints, it threatened to apply to the federal tariff law the doctrine of the nullifiers. Congress persisted in its system; finally the storm broke.

In the course of 1832, the people of South Carolina[86] called a national [state] convention to decide on the extraordinary means that remained to be taken; and on November 24 of the same year this convention published, under the name of an ordinance, a law that nullified the federal tariff law, and forbade levying the duties that were set forth there, and forbade accepting appeals that could be made to the federal courts.[87] This ordinance was supposed to be put in force only in the following month of February,

---

the Americans call a *convention;* it is a great assembly that, outside of the powers of the State, discusses one of the questions most likely to agitate political passions in this country, raises all the constitutional questions, and under the pretext of drafting a petition to Congress, really plays the role of Congress. We are very curious to see how things go within this convention. We will see there one of the most extreme consequences of the dogma of the sovereignty of the people (YTC, BIa2).

In a note of 14 October of the same year, Tocqueville summarizes in this way his ideas on the convention: "Of all that I have seen in America, it is the convention that most struck me as the dangerous and impractical consequence among us of the sovereignty of the people" (alphabetic notebook B, YTC, BIIa, and *Voyage, OC,* V, 1, p. 238). Memories of the revolution were too intense for Tocqueville to be able to accept the arguments of Sparks and Gilpin who, in 1833, wrote to him to assure him that the resolution of the tariff problem had contributed more to strengthening than to weakening the Union (Jared Sparks to Tocqueville, 30 August 1833; H. D. Gilpin to Tocqueville, 24 September 1833, in YTC, CId). Tocqueville got the opposite argument from the very mouth of a former President of the United States, John Quincy Adams (non-alphabetic notebooks 2 and 3, YTC, BIIa, and *Voyage, OC,* V, 1, p. 97). James T. Schleifer (*The Making of Tocqueville's "Democracy in America,"* pp. 110–111) notes the little attention given by critics to the interpretations of Sparks and Gilpin.

86. *That is to say a majority of the people; for the opposing party, called Union Party, always numbered a very strong and very active minority in its favor. Carolina can have about 47,000 voters; 30,000 were favorable to nullification, and 17,000 opposed.*

87. *This ordinance was preceded by a report of a committee charged with preparing the draft; this report contains the exposition and the purpose of the law. You read there, p. 34:*

and it was pointed out that if Congress modified the tariff before this time, South Carolina would agree not to follow up on its threats with other measures. Later, but in a vague and unspecified way, the desire to submit the question to an extraordinary assembly of all the confederated states was expressed.

While waiting, South Carolina armed its militia and prepared for war.

What did Congress do? Congress, which had not listened to its entreating subjects, lent its ear to their complaints as soon as it saw them with weapons in hand.[88] It passed a law[89] according to which the duties set in the tariff were to be progressively reduced over ten years, until they had reached the point of not exceeding the needs of the government. Thus Congress completely abandoned the tariff principle. For a duty that protected industry, Congress substituted a purely fiscal measure.[90] In order to hide its defeat, the government of the Union took recourse in an expedient that is much used by weak governments: while yielding on the facts, it showed itself inflexible on the principles. At the same time that Congress changed the tariff legislation, it passed another law by virtue of which the

---

When the rights reserved to the several States are deliberately invaded, it is their right and their duty to "interpose for the purpose of arresting the progress of the evil of usurpation, and to maintain, within their respective limits, the authorities and privileges belonging to them as independent sovereignties" [Virginia Resolutions of 1798. (ed.)]. *If the several States do not possess this right, it is in vain that they claim to be sovereign. [. . . (ed.) . . .] South Carolina claims to be a sovereign State. She recognizes no tribunal upon earth as above her authority. It is true, she has entered into a solemn compact of Union with other sovereign States, but she claims, and will exercise the right to determine the extent of her obligations under that compact, nor will she consent that any other power shall exercise the right of judgment for her. And when that compact is violated by her co-States, or by the Government which they have created, she asserts her unquestionable right "to judge of the infractions as well as of the mode and measure of redress"* [Kentucky Resolutions of 1798 (ed.)].

88. *What really decided Congress on this measure was a demonstration by the powerful state of Virginia, whose legislature offered to serve as arbiter between the Union and South Carolina. Until then, the latter had seemed entirely abandoned, even by the states that had protested with it.*

89. *Law of 2 March 1833.*

90. *This law was suggested by Mr. Clay and passed in four days in both houses of Congress by an immense majority.*

President was vested with an extraordinary power to overcome by force the resistance that then was no longer to be feared.

South Carolina did not even agree to leave to the Union these weak appearances of victory; the same national [state] convention that had nullified the tariff law, having assembled again, accepted the concession that had been offered to it; but at the same time it declared that it would only persist more forcefully in the doctrine of the nullifiers, and to prove it, it annulled the law that conferred extraordinary powers on the President, even though it was very certain that no use would be made of it.

Nearly all the actions that I have just spoken about took place during the Presidency of General Jackson. You cannot deny that in the tariff affair the latter upheld the rights of the Union with skill and vigor. I believe, however, that, among the number of dangers that the federal power runs today, you must include the very conduct of the one who represents it.

Some persons in Europe have formed an opinion concerning the influence that General Jackson can exercise in the affairs of his country that seems very extravagant to those who have seen things up close.

You have heard it said that General Jackson had won battles, that he was an energetic man, led by character and habit to the use of force, avid for power and a despot by taste. All that is perhaps true, but the consequences that have been drawn from these truths are great mistakes.

It has been imagined that General Jackson wanted to establish a dictatorship in the United States, that he was going to make the military spirit reign there, and extend the central power to the point of endangering provincial liberties. In America the time for such undertakings and the century of such men has not yet arrived. If General Jackson had wanted to dominate in this way, he would assuredly have lost his political position and compromised his life; so he has not been so imprudent as to attempt it.

Far from wanting to extend federal power, the current President represents, on the contrary, the party that wants to restrict this power to the clearest and most precise terms of the Constitution, and that does not accept any interpretation that can ever be favorable to the government of the Union; far from presenting himself as the champion of centralization, General Jackson is the agent of provincial jealousies; it is the *decentralizing* passions (if I can express myself in this way) that brought him to sovereign power. He remains and prospers there by flattering these passions each day. General Jackson is the slave of the majority; he follows it in its will, in its desires, in its half-discovered instincts, or rather he divines it and runs to put himself at its head.

Each time that the government of the states struggles with that of the Union it is rare that the President is not the first to doubt his right; he is almost always ahead of the legislative power; when there is room for interpretation on the extent of federal power, he lines up in a way against himself; he belittles himself, he hides, he stands aside.[*] It is not that he is naturally weak or an enemy of the union; when the majority declared itself against the pretensions of the nullifiers of the South, you saw him put himself at its head, formulate with clarity and energy the doctrine that the majority professed and be the first to call for the use of force. General Jackson, to use a comparison borrowed from the vocabulary of American parties, seems to me *federal* by taste and *republican* by calculation.[w]

After thus demeaning himself before the majority in order to win its favor, General Jackson rises again; he then marches toward the objects that the majority itself pursues, or toward those that it does not see with jealousy, overturning every obstacle before him. Strong due to a support that his predecessors did not have, he tramples underfoot his personal enemies wherever he finds them, with an ease that no President has found; on his own responsibility he takes measures that none before him would ever have dared to take; it even happens that he treats the national representation with a sort of almost insulting disdain; he refuses to approve the laws passed by Congress, and often neglects to respond to this great body. He is like a favorite who sometimes treats his master rudely. So the power of General Jackson is constantly increasing; but that of the President is decreasing. In

---

[*]. See message of 1832, *in fine* [at the end]. *National Calendar,* p. 31.

w. The remarks on Jackson and the American Presidency earned Tocqueville severe criticisms from Thomas H. Benton (*Thirty Years' View; or, a History of the Working of the American Government for Thirty Years, from 1820 to 1850,* New York: Appleton and Company, 1854, I, pp. 111–14). For an introduction to the ideas of Tocqueville on the Presidency, see Hugh Brogan, "Tocqueville and the American Presidency," *Journal of American Studies* 15, no. 3 (1981): 357–75. See as well note f for p. 372.

his hands the federal government is strong; it will pass enervated to his successor.

Either I am strangely mistaken, or the federal government tends each day to become weaker; it is withdrawing successively from affairs, it is narrowing more and more the circle of its action. Naturally weak, it is abandoning even the appearance of strength. From another perspective I thought I saw in the United States that the sentiment of independence was becoming more and more intense in the states, the love of provincial government more and more pronounced.

The Union is desired; but reduced to a shadow. They want it strong in certain cases and weak in all the others; they pretend that in time of war it can gather in its hand the national forces and all thē resources of the country, and that in time of peace it does not so to speak exist; as if this alternation between debility and vigor was natural.

I see nothing that can for now stop this general movement of minds; the causes that have given it birth do not cease to operate in the same direction. So it will continue, and it can be predicted that, unless some extraordinary circumstance arises, the government of the Union will grow weaker each day.

I believe however that we are still far from the time when the federal power, incapable of protecting its own existence and bringing peace to the country, will fade away in a sense by itself. The Union is in the mores, it is desired; its results are clear, its benefits visible. When it is noticed that the weakness of the federal government compromises the existence of the Union, I do not doubt that we will see the birth of a movement of reaction in favor of strength.

The government of the United States is, of all the federal governments that have been established until now, the one that is most naturally destined to act; as long as you do not attack it in an indirect manner by the interpretation of its laws, as long as you do not profoundly alter its substance, a change of opinion, an internal crisis, a war, could suddenly restore the vigor that it needs.

What I wanted to note is only this: many men among us think that in the United States there is a movement of minds that favors centralization of power in the hands of the President and Congress. I claim that an opposite movement is clearly observed. As the federal government grows older, far from gaining strength and threatening the sovereignty of the states, I say that it tends to become weaker each day, and that the sovereignty of the Union alone is in danger. That is what the present reveals. What will be the final result of this tendency, what events can stop, slow or hasten the movement that I have described? The future hides them, and I do not claim to be able to lift its veil.

Of Republican Institutions in the United States, What Are Their Chances of Lasting?

The Union is only an accident.—Republican institutions have more of a future.—The republic is, for now, the natural state of the Anglo-Americans.—Why.—In order to destroy it, it would be necessary to change all the laws at the same time and modify all the mores.—Difficulties that the Americans have in creating an aristocracy.

The dismemberment of the Union, by introducing war within the states confederated today and with it permanent armies, dictatorship and taxes, could in the long run compromise the fate of republican institutions there.

But you must not confuse the future of the republic with that of the Union.[x]

The Union is an accident that will only last as long as circumstances favor it, but the republic seems to me the natural state of the Americans, and only the continuous action of contrary causes acting always in the same way could replace it with monarchy.[y]

---

x. *"Division of the American empire./*

"When I spoke to Mr. Schermerhorn about the possible division that could take place among the united provinces, he seemed to me not to believe that the thing was to be feared in the least in the near future, but thinks that it could happen someday *by and by.*

"April 1831" (YTC, BIIb, unpublished travel note).

y. In the margin: "≠The republic in the United States does not arise only from the laws, but from the nature of the country, from habits, from mores.≠"

The Union exists principally in the law that created it. A single revolution, a change in public opinion can shatter it forever. The republic has deeper roots.ᶻ

z. Of the different ways that you can imagine the republic./

What is understood by republic in the United States is an ordered State actually based on the enlightened will of the people. It is a government where [v: liberty of discussion and thought reigns from which] resolutions mature over a long time, are debated slowly and are executed with maturity. What is called the republic in the United States is the tranquil rule of the majority. The majority, after it has had the time to recognize itself and to take note of its existence, is the source of all powers. But the majority itself is not omnipotent; above it in the moral world are found humanity and reason, in the material world, vested rights. The majority in its omnipotence recognizes these two barriers, and if it has sometimes happened to overturn them, it felt itself carried away by its passions beyond its rights, just as man constantly happens to do evil, while entirely recognizing the existence and the sanctity of virtue. That is what is understood by republic in the United States.

[In the margin: I cannot believe that the Roman republic could have begun at the time of Catilina./

It is this government that must leave to each man the largest part of his independence and liberty and that is the farthest removed from despotism.]

[To the side: In all the countries where this republic would be practical, I would be a republican.]

But we have made strange discoveries in Europe and we are much more advanced than that.

The republic according to certain men in Europe is not the rule of the majority as has been believed until now; it is the rule of those who speak in the name of the majority. It is not the people who act in these kinds of governments, it is those who want the greatest good for the people. Republican government is, moreover, the only one in which the right to do everything must be recognized and that must not keep strictly to any divine or human law in order to reach the end that it proposes, which is nothing other than the greatest happiness of humanity. This end in itself alone justifies all the rest.

[In the margin: Happy distinction that allows acting in the name of nations without consulting them.]

Republican liberty does not try to persuade but to break; it proceeds only by sudden movements and always has the ax or the hammer in hand in order to make its way in the world.

[In the margin: Republican liberty is the power to dare anything (illegible word, crossed out), it is scorn for all the rules, [v: holy laws] from those of morality to those of common sense.

You believed that the cause of aristocracy was lost. But here are (illegible word). I tell you that those men are the only partisans of aristocracy, at least not still the aristocracy of the rich and the nobles in truth. They are the aristocracy of cut-th[roats (ed.)]

[≠ Dispersed over an immense and half empty [a] territory, the Americans have found themselves from the beginning divided into a great number of small distinct societies that were not naturally attached to a common center.

When I see one of these alleged republicans, it seems to me that I always hear him say [v: see the executioner in his official outfit standing on the scaffold crying out]: Peoples of the earth (for it is always the entire earth that he addresses from their [*sic*] rooftop) come to us, for except for your fathers there has never been anything more foolish than you, and if you do not put your destiny in our hands, you will never be able to prosper, unless we get involved in your destiny.

You imagined, fellow citizens, that the republic was by its nature a mild and prosperous government, and you thought that the trial that had formerly been made of it among us must not be imputed to the system itself, but to those who put it into practice and to the extraordinary circumstances in which the (illegible word) was found; know that the republic that we are proposing is very exactly the one that you have seen in the past, and that it can be established as such only with the aid of a profound and radical revolution in property and in ranks. Some have told you that the men made so famous by the misfortunes of a generation were madmen, miserable men intoxicated with power and blood by an unexpected success, and that you must not charge liberty with the evils that they did in its name. Beware of listening to such language, fellow citizens; the men that you hear about did only what they had to do. What are called their crimes are actions as beautiful as they are immortal. They sacrificed themselves for you, ungrateful men, even while slitting your throats. You would perhaps be tempted to believe that we, their successors, adopt their love for the good while deploring their errors; do not be mistaken, fellow citizens; we think that in our time as in theirs dictatorship alone can save the country and that liberty can be established only after punishing writers [v: all our adversaries] by death, and that respect for rights can arise only after trampling all rights under foot. [v: We admire on all points these great men and we burn to walk in their steps; while waiting, we kiss the sacred dust where they left their footprint. And even their costumes, holy relic, we would like to make reappear in order to begin from now on to resemble them in a few ways.]

So come to us dear fellow citizens, come so we can share your fortunes among ourselves [v: so we can trample your beliefs underfoot] and so we can cut your throat following the principles that we received from our fathers and that we will leave to our children. How to resist such language? Aren't these agreeable speeches and pleasant missionaries?

[To the side: As long as those who sincerely want the establishment of the republic do not push far away from their ranks such miserable men, the kings of Europe can still rest easy on their thrones] (YTC, CVh, 2, pp. 68–74).

This fragment, of complicated transcription, contains various other variants and versions.

a. While preparing the plan for this chapter, Tocqueville had noted: "The republic is in a way the natural state of *small, enlightened* States" (YTC, CVh, 2, p. 43).

So it was necessary that each one of these small societies took care of its own affairs, since nowhere did you see a central authority that could naturally provide for them. Town and provincial liberty were introduced to America by the English, but they arose there all by themselves by the very nature of things. Now, town and provincial liberty are the basis of [v: the only lasting foundation that you can give to] republican institutions and as long as they exist in the United States, the United States will remain republican.≠]

What is understood by republic in the United States is the slow and tranquil action of society on itself. It is an ordered state actually based on the enlightened will of the people. It is a conciliatory government, where resolutions mature over a long time, are debated slowly and are executed with maturity.

Republicans in the United States value mores, respect beliefs, recognize rights. They profess this opinion, that a people must be moral, religious and moderate, in proportion as it is free. What is called a republic in the United States is the tranquil rule of the majority. The majority, after it has had the time to recognize itself and to take note of its existence, is the common source of powers. But the majority itself is not omnipotent. Above it in the moral world are found humanity, justice and reason; in the political world, vested rights. The majority recognizes these two barriers, and if it happens to cross them, it is because the majority has passions, like every man; and like him, it can do evil while perceiving good. [{For me, I will have no difficulty in saying, in all countries where the republic is practical, I will be republican.}]

But we have made strange discoveries in Europe.

According to some among us, the republic is not the rule of the majority, as we have believed until now; it is the rule of those who answer for the majority. It is not the people who lead these sorts of governments, but those who know the greatest good of the people: happy distinction, that allows acting in the name of nations without consulting them, and claiming their gratitude while trampling them underfoot.[b] Republican government is,

b. "≠Royalty has had its valets and its spies, why would the republic not have its cut-throats?

moreover, the only one in which the right to do everything must be recognized, and that can despise what men until now have respected, from the highest laws of morality to the ordinary rules of common sense.

Until our time it had been thought that despotism was odious, whatever its forms. But it has been discovered in our day that there are legitimate tyrannies and holy injustices in the world, provided that they are exercised in the name of the people.

[≠That is not a vague theory; they are maxims that are professed while basing them on facts. These doctrines have found ardent missionaries. I believe that I hear them saying to us:

You imagined, they say to us, that the republic was by its nature a free and tolerant government, and you thought perhaps that the trial that had formerly been made of it among us must not be imputed to the system itself, but to those who put it into practice and to the extraordinary circumstances in which this country found itself.≠]c

The ideas that the Americans have formed about the republic singularly facilitate its use for them and ensure that it will last.d Among them, if the practice of republican government is often bad, at least the theory is good, and the people always finish by conforming their acts to it.

It was impossible in the beginning and it would still be very difficult in America to establish a centralized administration. Men are spread over too large a space and are separated by too many natural obstacles for one man to be able to undertake to direct the details of their existence. So America is par excellence the country of provincial and town government.

"An aristocracy of wolves, worse.

"Great capitals annul the representative system≠" (YTC, CVj, 2, p. 22).

c. In the margin: "≠Some limit themselves to praising the disinterestedness of Robespierre and the greatness of soul of Danton. Others go still further.≠"

d. Tocqueville wrote to Ernest de Chabrol, 9 June 1831:

Here we are very far from the ancient republics, it must be admitted, and yet this people is republican and I do not doubt that it will be for a long time still. And the republic is for it the best of governments.

I explain this phenomenon to myself only by thinking that America finds itself for now in a physical situation so happy that particular interest is never contrary to general interest, which is certainly not the case in Europe (YTC, BIa2).

To this cause, whose action made itself equally felt on all the Europeans of the New World, the Anglo-Americans added several others that are particular to them.

When the colonies of North America were established, municipal liberty had already penetrated English laws as well as mores, and the English emigrants adopted it not only as something necessary, but also as a good whose value they knew.

[We have seen furthermore that in this matter the influence exercised by the country has been greater or lesser depending on the circumstances that accompanied colonization and the previously contracted habits of the colonists.

The French carried to America the tradition of absolute monarchy; the English came there with the customs of a free people.

≠When the French arrived in Canada they first founded a city that they called Québec. From this city the population spread little by little by degrees, like a tree that spreads it roots in a circle. Québec has remained the central point, and the French of Canada are still today only one and the same people, submitted in most cases to one and the same government.≠

{It was not this way in the United States, above all in the part of the country that was called New England.}] We have seen, furthermore, how the colonies were founded. Each province and each district so to speak was populated separately by men strangers to one another, or associated for different ends.

So the English of the United States found themselves from the beginning divided into a great number of small distinct societies that were attached to no common center, and it was necessary for each one of these small societies to take care of its own affairs, since nowhere did you see a central authority that naturally had to and easily could provide for them.

Thus the nature of the country, the very manner in which the English colonies were founded, the habits of the first emigrants, all united to develop town and provincial liberties there to an extraordinary degree.

In the United States the institutions of the country are therefore as a whole essentially republican; to destroy in a lasting way the laws that established the republic, it would be necessary in a way to abolish all the laws all at once.

If today a party undertook to establish a monarchy in the United States, it would be in a still more difficult position than whoever would want at the present moment to proclaim the republic in France. Royalty would not find legislation prepared for it in advance, and then in actual fact you would see a monarchy surrounded by republican institutions.[e]

The monarchical principle would penetrate with as much difficulty into the mores of the Americans.

In the United States, the dogma of the sovereignty of the people is not an isolated doctrine that is attached neither to the habits nor to the ensemble of dominant ideas; you can on the contrary envisage it as the last link in a chain of opinions that envelops the entire Anglo-American world. Providence has given to each individual, what ever he is, the degree of reason necessary for him to be able to direct himself in the things that interest him exclusively. Such is the great maxim on which in the United States civil and political society rests: the father of the family applies it to his children, the master to his servants, the town to those it administers, the province to the town, the state to the provinces, the Union to the states. Extended to the whole of the nation, it becomes the dogma of the sovereignty of the people.

[≠So the republican principle of the sovereignty of the people is not only a political principle, but also a civil principle.≠]

Thus in the United States the generative principle of the republic is the same one that regulates most human actions. So the republic, if I can express myself in this way, penetrates the ideas, the opinions and all the habits of the Americans at the same time that it is established in their laws; and in order to succeed in changing the laws, they would have to be changed wholesale as it were. In the United States the religion of the greatest number itself is republican; it subjects the truths of the other world to individual reason, as politics relinquishes to the good sense of all the responsibility for the interests of this one; and it agrees that each man should freely take the

e. "25 October 1831.—The people are always right, that is the dogma of the republic the same as the king can do no wrong is the religion of monarchical States. It is a great question to know if one is more false than the other; but what is very certain is that neither the one nor the other is true" (pocket notebook 3, YTC, BIIa, and *Voyage, OC,* V, 1, p. 184).

path that will lead him to heaven, in the same way that the law recognizes the right of each citizen to choose his government.

Clearly only a long series of facts, all having the same tendency, can substitute for this ensemble of laws, opinions and mores an ensemble of the opposite mores, opinions and laws.

If the republican principles must perish in America, they will succumb only after a long social effort, frequently interrupted, often resumed; several times they will seem to arise again, and will disappear never to return only when an entirely new people will have taken the place of those who exist today. Now, nothing can portend such a revolution, no sign announces it.

What strikes you the most on your arrival in the United States is the type of tumultuous movement in which political society is immersed. The laws change constantly, and at first view it seems impossible that a people so little sure of its will does not soon substitute for the present form of its government an entirely new form. These fears are premature. There are as regards political institutions two types of instability that must not be confused. The one is attached to secondary laws; that one can reign for a long time within a well-settled society. The other constantly shakes the very foundations of the constitution, and attacks the generative principles of the laws; this one is always followed by troubles and revolutions; the nation that suffers it is in a violent and transitory state. Experience demonstrates that these two types of legislative instability do not have a necessary link between them, for we have seen them exist conjoined or separately depending on times and places. The first is found in the United States, but not the second. The Americans frequently change the laws, but the foundation of the Constitution is respected.

Today the republican principle reigns in America as the monarchical principle dominated in France under Louis XIV. The French of that time were not only friends of monarchy, but also they did not imagine that you could put anything in its place; they acknowledged it as you acknowledge the course of the sun and the vicissitudes of the seasons. Among them royal power had no more advocates than adversaries.

This is how the republic exists in America, without struggle, without opposition, without proof, by a tacit agreement, a sort of *consensus universalis.*

Nonetheless, I think that by changing their administrative procedures as often as they do, the inhabitants of the United States compromise the future of republican government.

Hampered constantly in their projects by the continual changeability of legislation, it is to be feared that men will end up considering the republic as an inconvenient way to live in society; the evil resulting from the instability of secondary laws would then put into question the existence of the fundamental laws, and would lead indirectly to a revolution. But this time is still very far from us.

What you can foresee from now on is that by leaving the republic the Americans would pass rapidly to despotism, without stopping for a very long time at monarchy. Montesquieu said that there was nothing more absolute than the authority of a prince who followed a republic since the undefined powers that had been given without fear to an elective magistrate are then put into the hands of a hereditary leader.[f] This is generally true but particularly applicable to a democratic republic. In the United States the magistrates are not elected by a particular class of citizens, but by the majority of the nation; they represent immediately the passions of the multitude, and depend entirely on its will; so they inspire neither hate nor fear. Also I have noted the little care that has been taken to limit their powers by tracing limits to its action, and what an immense share has been left to their arbitrariness. This order of things has created habits that would survive it. The American magistrate would keep his undefined power while ceasing to be responsible, and it is impossible to say where tyranny would then stop.

[≠If Napoleon had followed Louis XIV, {he would have found royal power strong but surrounded by impediments that would have imposed limits on his spirit of domination} he would have shown himself more stable but not as absolute as he was. Napoleon following a representative of the people could do anything.≠]

There are men among us who are waiting to see aristocracy arise in Amer-

---

f. Montesquieu, *Considérations sur les causes et la grandeur des Romains et de leur décadence,* chapter XV, in *Œuvres complètes* (Paris: Pléiade, 1951), I, p. 150.

ica and who already foresee with exactitude the period when it must grasp power.

I have already said, and I repeat, that the current movement of American society seems to me more and more democratic.

I do not claim, however, that one day the Americans will not end by restricting among themselves the circle of political rights, or by confiscating these very rights for the profit of one man; but I cannot believe that they will ever grant the exclusive use of those rights to a particular class of citizens or, in other words, that they will establish an aristocracy.

An aristocratic body is composed of a certain number of citizens who, without being placed very far from the crowd, raise themselves nonetheless in a permanent manner above it; you touch and cannot strike them; you mix with them each day, and cannot merge with them.

It is impossible to imagine anything more contrary to the nature and to the secret instincts of the human heart than a subjugation of this type; left to themselves men will always prefer the arbitrary power of a king to the regular administration of nobles.

In order to last an aristocracy needs to establish inequality in principle, to legalize it in advance, and to introduce it into the family at the same time that it spreads it throughout the society; all things that repulse natural equity so strongly that only by coercion can you obtain them from men.

Since human societies have existed I do not believe that you can cite the example of a single people that, left to itself and by its own efforts, has created an aristocracy within itself; all the aristocracies of the Middle Ages are daughters of conquest. The conqueror was the noble, the conquered the serf. Force then imposed inequality, which once entered into the mores lasted by itself and passed naturally into the laws.

You have seen societies that, because of events prior to their existence, are so to speak born aristocratic, and that are then led by each century back toward democracy. Such was the fate of the Romans, and that of the barbarians who came after them. But a people who, starting from civilization and democracy, would come closer by degrees to inequality of conditions, and would finish by establishing within itself inviolable privileges and exclusive categories, there is something that would be new in the world.

Nothing indicates that America is destined to be the first to give such a spectacle.

[≠I do not know if the Americans, like all peoples who have run the course before them, will end by submitting to one master, but I cannot believe that they will ever have a true aristocracy./

A party that undertook to establish monarchy in America today would find itself in as difficult a position as the one that wanted to proclaim the republic in France. In France you would implant the republican principle in the middle of secondary institutions that are still eminently monarchical. In America you would establish a king who would find in his hands only republican institutions.≠]

Some Considerations on the Causes of the Commercial Greatness of the United States

The Americans are called by nature to be a great maritime people.—Extent of their shores.—Depth of the ports.—Greatness of the rivers.—It is however much less to physical causes than to intellectual and moral causes that you must attribute the commercial superiority of the Anglo-Americans.—Reason for this opinion.—Future of the Anglo-Americans as commercial people.—The ruin of the Union would not stop the maritime development of the peoples who compose it.—Why.—The Anglo-Americans are naturally called to serve the needs of the inhabitants of South America.—They will become, like the English, the carriers of a large part of the world.

From the Bay of Fundy to the Sabine River in the Gulf of Mexico, the coast of the United States extends the length of about nine hundred leagues.

These coasts form a single unbroken line; they are all placed under the same rule.

No people in the world can offer to commerce deeper, more vast and more secure ports than the Americans.

The inhabitants of the United States form a great civilized nation that fortune has placed in the middle of the wilderness, twelve hundred leagues from the principal center of civilization. So America has daily need of Europe. With time the Americans will undoubtedly manage to produce or to manufacture at home most of the objects that they need, but the two continents will never be able to live entirely independent of each other; too many natural bonds exist between their needs, their ideas, their habits and their mores.

[≠Europe has no less need of the United States than the latter of Europe.≠]

The Union has products that have become necessary to us, and that our soil totally refuses to provide, or can do so only at great cost. The Americans consume only a very small part of these products; they sell us the rest.

So Europe is the market of America, as America is the market of Europe; and maritime commerce is as necessary to the inhabitants of the United States in order to bring their raw materials to our ports as to transport our manufactured goods to them.

So the United States would have to provide great resources to the industry of maritime peoples, if they gave up commerce themselves, as the Spanish of Mexico have done until now; or they would have to become one of the premier maritime powers of the globe. This alternative was inevitable.

The Anglo-Americans have at all times shown a decided taste for the sea. Independence, by breaking the commercial ties that united them to England, gave their maritime genius a new and powerful development. Since this period the number of ships of the Union has increased in a progression almost as rapid as the number of inhabitants. Today it is the Americans themselves who carry to their shores nine-tenths of the products of Europe.[91] It is also

---

91. *The total value of imports for the year ending 30 September 1832 was 101,029,266 dollars. Imports brought on foreign ships represented only a sum total of 10,731,037 dollars, about one tenth.*[g]

g. Tocqueville obtained this information from the *American Almanac* for 1834, pp. 141–42.

the Americans who carry to European consumers three-quarters of the exports of the New World.[92]

The ships of the United States fill the port of Le Havre and that of Liverpool. You see only a small number of English or French vessels in the port of New York.[93]

Thus not only does the American merchant stand up to the competition on his own soil, but he also fights foreigners with advantage on theirs.

This is easily explained. Of all the vessels of the world it is the ships of the United States that cross the seas most cheaply. As long as the merchant marine of the United States keeps this advantage over the others, not only will it keep what it has conquered, but each day it will increase its conquests.

To know why the Americans sail at lower cost than other men is a difficult problem to solve. You are tempted at first to attribute this superiority to some material advantages that nature would have put within their reach alone; but it is not that.

American ships cost almost as much to build as ours;[94] they are not better constructed, and in general do not last as long.

The salary of the American sailor is higher than that of the sailor of

92. *The total value of exports during the same year was 87,176,943 dollars; the value exported on foreign vessels was 21,036,183 dollars, or about one quarter (*William's Register, *1833, p. 398).*

93. *During the years 1829, 1830, 1831, ships with a total tonnage of 3,307,719 entered the ports of the Union. Foreign ships provided a tonnage of only 544,591 of the total. So they were in the proportion of about 16 to 100 (*National Calendar, *1833, p. 304 [305 (ed.)]).*

*During the years 1820, 1826 and 1831, English vessels that entered the ports of London, Liverpool and Hull had a tonnage of 443,800. Foreign vessels that entered the same ports during the same years had a tonnage of 159,431. So the relationship between them was about as 36 to 100 (*Companion to the Almanac, *1834, p. 169).*

In the year 1832, the relationship of foreign ships and English ships that entered the ports of Great Britain was as 20 to 100.

94. *Raw materials in general cost less in America than in Europe, but the price of labor is very much higher there.*

Europe; what proves it is the large number of Europeans that you find in the merchant marine of the United States.[h]

So how do the Americans sail more cheaply than we?

I think that you would look in vain for the causes of this superiority in material advantages; it is due to purely intellectual and moral qualities.

Here is a comparison that will make my thought clear.

During the wars of the Revolution the French introduced into military art a new tactic that troubled the oldest generals and all but destroyed the oldest monarchies of Europe. They undertook for the first time to do without a host of things that until then had been judged indispensable to war; they required from their soldiers new efforts that civilized nations had never demanded from theirs; you saw them do everything on the run, and without hesitating risk the life of men in view of the result to be gained.

The French were less numerous and less rich than their enemies; they possessed infinitely fewer resources; they were constantly victorious, however, until the latter decided to imitate them.

The Americans introduced something analogous to commerce. What the French did for victory, they do for economy.[j]

The European navigator ventures only with prudence onto the sea; he leaves only when the weather is inviting; if an unforeseen accident happens to him, he returns to port; at night he furls part of his sails, and when he

---

h. *Commerce.*

Mr. *Schermerhorn* claimed that the construction of vessels, the pay of sailors and the different expenses of navigation cost more for the Americans than for the French; he attributed the superiority of the first only to their extreme activity, constantly stimulated by the passion to make a fortune, and the almost total absence of restriction. *It is an established opinion in France that the Americans are the merchants of the world who sail at least expense.*

    April 1831 (unpublished travel note, YTC, BIIa).

j. "The Americans apply to commerce the same principles and the same manner that Bonaparte applied to war" (YTC, CVj, 2, p. 18).

sees the Ocean turn white as land nears, he slows his course and checks the sun.

The American neglects these precautions and defies these dangers. He leaves while the storm is still raging; night and day he spreads all of his sails to the wind; while in route, he repairs his ship strained by the storm; and when he finally approaches the end of his journey, he continues to sail toward the shore as if he already saw port. [≠He often perishes, but even more often he reaches port before his competitors.≠]

The American is often shipwrecked;[k] but no navigator crosses the sea as rapidly as he. [≠Of all men the American seems to me to be the one who has conceived the greatest and the most accurate idea of the value of time. There is no portion so small of day or night that does not have a value . . . in his eyes. He saves hours as the Dutch merchant saved capital. That is the secret of his success.≠] Doing the same things that someone else does in less time, he can do them at less cost.

Before coming to the end of a long voyage, the European navigator believes that he must touch land several times on his way. He loses precious time looking for a port of call or awaiting the opportunity to leave one, and each day he pays the duty to remain there.

The American navigator leaves from Boston to go to buy tea in China. He arrives in Canton, remains there a few days and comes back. He has covered in less than two years the entire circumference of the globe, and he has seen land only once. During a crossing of eight or ten months he has drunk brackish water and lived on salted meat; he has fought constantly against the sea, against disease, against boredom; but upon his return he can sell a pound of tea for one penny less than the English merchant. The goal is reached.

I cannot express my thought better than by saying that the Americans put a kind of heroism in their way of doing commerce.

k. Francis Grund (*The Americans, in Their Moral, Social and Political Relations,* Boston: Marsh, Capen and Lyon, 1837, pp. 293–94) denies this assertion. In his opinion the number of accidents was not proportionately higher in the American navy, because the number of miles covered by American ships was superior to that covered by European ships. Grund is inspired otherwise on many occasions by the *Democracy,* without ever ceasing to criticize Tocqueville.

[≠Heroism that is not only calculation, but also suggested by nature.

Natural heroism that must give them not only the trade of America but make them carriers to nations.≠]

It will always be very difficult for the merchant of Europe to follow the same course as his competitor from America. The American, while acting in the way I described above, is following not only a calculation; he is above all obeying his nature.

The inhabitant of the United States experiences all the needs and all the desires to which an advanced civilization gives rise, and he does not find around him as in Europe a society skillfully organized to satisfy them; so he is often obliged to obtain by himself the various objects that his education and his habits have made necessary for him. In America it sometimes happens that the same man plows his field, builds his house, fashions his tools, makes his shoes and weaves by hand the crude fabric that has to cover him. This harms the perfection of industry, but serves powerfully to develop the intelligence of the worker. There is nothing that tends more to materialize man and remove from his work even the trace of soul than the great division of labor. [<With the division of labor you do better and more economically what you already did, but you do not innovate. The division of labor is an element of wealth more than of progress.

The art of dividing labor is the art of confiscating the intelligence of the greatest number for the profit of a few.>]^m In a country like America where

m. *Intelligence of the people in America.*/

It has been noted in Europe that division of labor made man infinitely more suitable for taking care of the detail to which he was applying himself, but reduced his *general capacity.* The worker thus classed becomes past master in his specialty, brute in all the rest. Example of England. Frightening state of the working classes in this country.

What makes the American of the people so intelligent a man is that the division of labor does not exist so to speak in America. Each man does a little of everything. He does each thing not as well as the European who takes care of it exclusively, but his general capacity is one hundred times greater. Great cause of superiority in the habitual matters of life and in the government of society (YTC, CVe, p. 53).

J. B. Say had criticized the effects of the division of labor in chapter VIII of the first volume of his *Traité d'économie politique.* Tocqueville and Beaumont read Say aboard the *Havre* during their Atlantic crossing. We do not know if it was the *Traité* or the six volumes of *Cours d'économie politique.* In 1834 when he prepared his memoir on pauperism, following his visit to England the preceding year, Tocqueville also read the work

specialized men are so rare, you cannot require a long apprenticeship of each one of those who take up a profession. So the Americans find it very easy to change profession, and they make the most of it, depending on the needs of the moment. You meet some of them who have been successively lawyers, farmers, merchants, evangelical ministers, doctors. If the American is less skillful than the European in each trade, there are hardly any of them that are entirely unknown to him. His ability is more general, the circle of his intelligence is wider. So the inhabitant of the United States is never stopped by any axiom of trade; he escapes all prejudices of profession; he is no more attached to one system of operation than to another; he does not feel more tied to an old method than to a new one; he has created no habit for himself, and he easily escapes from the sway that foreign habits could exercise over his mind, for he knows that his country resembles no other, and that its situation is new in the world [so he always follows his reason and never practice].

The American inhabits a land of wonders, around him everything is constantly stirring, and each movement seems to be an improvement. So the idea of the new is intimately linked in his mind to the idea of the better. Nowhere does he see the limit that nature might have put on the efforts of man; in his eyes what is not is what has not yet been attempted.[n]

This universal movement that reigns in the United States, these frequent reversals of fortune, this unexpected displacement of public and private wealth, all join together to keep the soul in a sort of feverish agitation that admirably disposes it to all efforts, and maintains it so to speak above [itself and] the common level of humanity. For an American all of life happens like a game of chance, a time of revolution, a day of battle.

These same causes, operating at the same time on all individuals, finish

---

of Viscount Alban de Villeneuve-Bargemont (*Economie politique chrétienne, ou recherches sur la nature et les causes du paupérisme* . . . , Paris: Paulin, 1834, 3 vols.), in which England is the constant example of the evils produced by the excesses of industry.

n. "≠For the American the past is in a way like the future: it does not exist. He sees nowhere the natural limit that nature has put on the efforts of man; according to him what is not, is what has not yet been tried≠" (YTC, CVh, 2, p. 47).

by stamping an irresistible impulse on the national character. So an American taken at random must be a man ardent in his desires, enterprising, adventurous, above all an innovator. This spirit is found in fact in all his works; he introduces it into his political laws, into his religious doctrines, into his theories of social economy, into his private industry; he carries it everywhere with him, deep in the woods, as well as within the cities. It is this same spirit applied to maritime commerce that makes the American sail more quickly and more cheaply than all the merchants of the world.

As long as the sailors of the United States keep these intellectual advantages and the practical superiority that derives from them, not only will they continue to provide for the needs of the producers and consumers of their country, but also they will tend more and more to become, like the English,[95] the carriers of other peoples.

This is beginning to be achieved before our eyes. Already we are seeing American sailors introduce themselves as middlemen in the commerce of several of the nations of Europe;[96] America offers them an even greater future.

The Spanish and the Portuguese founded in South America great colonies that have since become empires. Civil war and despotism today desolate these vast countries. The population movement is stopping, and the small number of men who live there, absorbed by the concern of defending themselves, scarcely feel the need to improve their lot.

But it cannot always be so. Europe left to itself managed by its own efforts to pierce the shadows of the Middle Ages; South America is Christian like us; it has our laws, our customs; it contains all the seeds of civilization that have developed within European nations and their offshoots; beyond what we had, South America has our example: why would it remain forever barbarous?

95. *It must not be believed that English vessels are uniquely occupied in transporting foreign goods to England or in transporting English products to foreigners; today the merchant marine of England is like a great enterprise of public carts, ready to serve all producers of the world and to connect all peoples. The maritime genius of the Americans leads them to raise an enterprise rivaling that of the English [and often they will manage to serve the same producers more cheaply].*

96. *One part of the commerce of the Mediterranean is already done on American vessels.*

It is clearly only a question of time here. A more or less distant period will undoubtedly come when the South Americans will form flourishing and enlightened nations.

But when the Spanish and the Portuguese of South America begin to experience the needs of civilized peoples, they will still be far from able to satisfy them themselves; newly born to civilization, they will be subject to the superiority already acquired by their elders. They will be farmers for a long time before becoming manufacturers and merchants, and they will need the intervention of foreigners in order to go and sell their products overseas and to obtain in exchange the objects whose necessity will now make itself felt.

You cannot doubt that the Americans of North America are called one day to provide for the needs of the Americans of South America. Nature placed the first near the second. It thus provided the North Americans with great opportunities to know and estimate the needs of the South Americans, to strike up permanent relations with these peoples, and gradually to take possession of their market. The merchant of the United States could lose these natural advantages only if he was very inferior to the merchant of Europe; and he is, on the contrary, superior to him on several points. The Americans of the United States already exercise a great moral influence over all the peoples of the New World. From them comes enlightenment. All the nations that inhabit the same continent are already accustomed to considering them as the most enlightened, most powerful and wealthiest offshoots of the great American family. So they turn their view constantly toward the Union and they assimilate themselves, as much as it is within their power, to the peoples that compose it. Each day they come to draw political doctrines from the United States and borrow laws from them.

The Americans of the United States are vis-à-vis the peoples of South America precisely in the same situation as their fathers, the English, vis-à-vis the Italians, the Spanish, the Portuguese and all those peoples of Europe who, being less advanced in civilization and industry, receive from their hands most of the objects of consumption.

England is today the natural center of commerce of nearly all the nations that are near it; the American Union is called to fulfill the same role in the other hemisphere. So every people that arises or that grows up in the New

World arises and grows up there in a way to the profit of the Anglo-American.

If the Union came to break up, the commerce of the states that formed it would undoubtedly be slowed for some time in its development, but less than is thought. It is clear that whatever happens the commercial states will remain united. They all touch each other; among them there is a perfect identity of opinion, interests and mores, and alone they can make up a very great maritime power. Thus even if the South of the Union became independent of the North, the result would not be that it could do without the North. I said that the South is not commercial; nothing yet indicates that it must become so.[*] So the Americans of the South of the United States will be obliged for a long time to resort to foreigners in order to export their products and to bring to them the objects that are necessary for their needs. Now of all the middlemen that they can take their neighbors of the North are surely those who can serve them more cheaply. So they will serve them, for the lowest price is the supreme law of commerce. There is no sovereign will or national prejudices that can struggle for long against the lowest price. You cannot see more venomous hatred than that which exists between the Americans of the United States and the English. In spite of these hostile sentiments, however, the English provide to the Americans most manufactured goods, for the sole reason that the English sell them for less than other peoples. The growing prosperity of America thus turns, despite the desire of the Americans, to the profit of the manufacturing industry of England.

---

[*]. ≠This is due to the combination of several natural causes whose influence it is very difficult to combat. The South, if you thus call all the country situated south of the Potomac, possesses very few good mercantile ports and has no military port except Norfolk in Virginia.

As long as slavery exists in [the (ed.)] South you will not be able to recruit sailors there. The population that provides sailors in the North does not exist in the South; it is replaced there by slaves who cannot be used to do commerce.[1] We have seen moreover that slavery takes away from the Americans of the South some of the qualities most appropriate for succeeding on the seas.≠

1. ≠They would not serve as well as white sailors and would desert in foreign countries.≠

Reason shows and experience proves that no commercial greatness is lasting if it cannot be combined as needed with military power.

This truth is as well understood in the United States as anywhere else. The Americans are already in the position of making their flag respected; soon they will be able to make it feared.

I am persuaded that the dismemberment of the Union, far from diminishing the naval forces of the Americans, would tend strongly to increase them. Today the commercial states are linked to those that are not commercial, and the latter often go along only reluctantly with increasing a maritime power from which they profit only indirectly.

If, on the contrary, all the commercial states of the Union formed only one and the same people, trade would become for them a national interest of the first order, so they would be disposed to make very great sacrifices to protect their ships, and nothing would prevent them from following their desires on this point.

[In the present condition in which the affairs of the commercial world find themselves, there is no policy more naturally indicated than that of France.

France is called to be always one of the great maritime powers, but she can never become the first except by chance. Since France cannot hope to dominate the sea in a lasting way, her visible interest is to prevent another from dominating there [v: to rise up against the domination of the sea] and to make the most liberal maxims as regards commerce prevail in the whole world.

Even if the principle of the independence of neutral nations were not based on the right of nations, France should therefore still uphold it with all her strength. The independence of neutral nations is a guarantee against maritime tyranny, and France is the necessary champion of freedom of the seas.

It is from this point of view that France is the natural enemy of England. She will always be so whatever you do, as long as England is able to impose its laws on the ocean.

America is at present in a position analogous to that of France. It is powerful without being able to dominate; it is liberal because it cannot oppress.

So America is the natural ally of France, in the same way that England is its enemy.° Everything that is done to the profit of the naval greatness of the United States is done in a way to the profit of France; for the maritime power of the Americans, by increasing, divides the dominion of the sea and gives to the French the liberty that they need.

If maritime forces come to reach a balance between England and America, which will happen I think in a period that is not far away, the role of France will be, by going alternately to the side of the weaker, to prevent either one of them from entirely dominating the sea and thus to maintain liberty there.

But this balance itself will not be settled.]

I think that nations, like men, almost always show from their youth the principal features of their destiny. When I see in what spirit the Anglo-Americans manage commerce, the opportunities that they find for doing it, the successes that they achieve, I cannot keep myself from believing that one day they will become the premier maritime power of the globe. They are pushed to take possession of the seas, as the Romans to conquer the world.

o. Tocqueville expressed himself in similar terms in a letter to John C. Spencer of 10 November 1841 (Virginia Historical Society, reproduced in *Correspondance étrangère, OC,* VII, pp. 84–86). Two years later he explains to Niles: "I have let the chain of my relationships with the United States break a bit. I regret it. I would like to renew it. I place there an interest of heart and also of patriotism, for one of the foundations of my politics is that in spite of prejudices and quarrels over details, France and the United States are allies so natural and so necessary to one another that they must never for a moment lose sight of one another" (Letter of 15 June 1843, YTC, DIIa). Tocqueville's brief time at the ministry of foreign affairs coincided paradoxically with a moment of great tension between the two countries.

Conclusion[a]

Here I am approaching the end. Until now, while speaking of the future destiny of the United States, I forced myself to divide my subject into various parts in order to study each one of them with more care.

Now I would like to bring all of them together in a single point of view. What I will say will be less detailed, but more sure. I will see each object less distinctly; I will take up general facts with more certitude. I will be like a traveler who, while coming outside the walls of a vast city, climbs up the adjacent hill. As he moves away, the men that he has just left disappear from his view; their houses blend together; he no longer sees the public squares; he makes out the path of the streets with difficulty; but his eyes follow more easily the contours of the city, and for the first time he grasps its form. It seems to me that I too discover before me the whole future of the English race in the New World. The details of this immense tableau have remained in shadow; but my eyes take in the entire view, and I conceive a clear idea of the whole.

The territory occupied or possessed today by the United States of America forms about one-twentieth of inhabited lands.[b]

However extensive these limits are, you would be wrong to believe that the Anglo-American race will stay within them forever; it is already spreading very far beyond.

There was a time when we too were able to create in the American wil-

---

a. In the manuscript, the conclusion is found in a jacket with the title: ≠FUTURE OF THE REPUBLICAN PRINCIPLE IN THE UNITED STATES.≠

b. In an earlier draft, the conclusion began here with this paragraph: "≠The American confederation occupies or possesses a territory whose surface is estimated at 2,257,374[1] square miles. Thus the United States alone has under its domination about one-twentieth of inhabited lands.≠

"1. ≠ *View of the United States,* by Darby, p. 57.≠"

derness a great French nation and balance the destinies of the New World with the English. France formerly possessed in North America a territory nearly as vast as the whole of Europe. The three greatest[c] rivers of the continent then flowed entirely under our laws. The Indian nations that live from the mouth of the Saint Lawrence to the Mississippi delta heard only our language spoken; all the European settlements spread over this immense space recalled the memory of the homeland; they were Louisbourg, Montmorency, Duquesne, Saint-Louis, Vincennes, La Nouvelle Orléans, all names dear to France and familiar to our ears.

But a combination of circumstances that would be too long to enumerate[1] deprived us of this magnificent heritage. Everyplace where the French were too few and not well established, they disappeared. What was left gathered into a small space and passed under other laws. The four hundred thousand French of Lower Canada today form like the remnant of an ancient people lost amid the waves of a new nation.[d] Around them the foreign population grows constantly; it is spreading in all directions; it even penetrates the ranks of the former masters of the soil, dominates in their cities, and distorts their

---

c. The manuscript says: "The two greatest . . ."

1. *In first place this one: free peoples accustomed to the municipal regime succeed much more easily than others in creating flourishing colonies. The habit of thinking for yourself and governing yourself is indispensable in a new country, where success necessarily depends in large part on the individual efforts of the colonists.*

d. In a small fragment belonging to one of the appendices of the *Penitentiary System*, Tocqueville explains why according to him the French do not have good colonies (repeated in *Écrits et discours politiques, OC*, III, 1, pp. 35–40). Among the reasons advanced he cites the continental character of France, the love of the Frenchman for his country, the legal habits and bad political education that accustom citizens to the existence of a tutelary power ready to help in the slightest difficulty. In the same way Tocqueville explains how Canada, even better than France, allows the damaging effects of administrative centralization to be studied (*L'Ancien Régime et la Révolution, OC*, II, 1, pp. 286–87). See in this regard: Jean-Michel Leclerq, "Alexis de Tocqueville in Canada (24 August to 2 September 1831)," *Revue d'histoire de l'Amérique française* 22, no. 3 (1968): 356–64; Edgar McInnis, "A Letter from Alexis de Tocqueville on the Canadian Rebellion of 1837," *Canadian Historical Review* 19, no. 4 (1938): 394–97; and Gérard Bergeron, *Quand Tocqueville et Siegfried nous observaient . . .* (Quebec: Presses de l'Université du Québec, 1990).

language. This population is identical to that of the United States. So I am right to say that the English race does not stop at the limits of the Union, but is advancing very far beyond toward the northeast.

In the northwest you find only a few unimportant Russian settlements; but in the southwest Mexico arises before the steps of the Anglo-American like a barrier.

Thus there are truly speaking only two rival races that share the New World today, the Spanish and the English.

The limits that are to separate these two races have been fixed by a treaty. But however favorable this treaty may be to the Anglo-Americans, I do not doubt that they are soon going to break it.

Beyond the frontiers of the Union, next to Mexico, extend vast provinces that still lack inhabitants. The men of the United States will penetrate these uninhabited areas even before those who have the right to occupy them. They will appropriate the soil, they will establish a society, and when the rightful owner finally appears, he will find the wilderness made fertile and foreigners calmly settled on his inheritance.

The land of the New World belongs to the first occupant, and empire is the prize for the race.

Countries already populated will have difficulty protecting themselves from invasion.

I have already spoken before about what is happening in the province of Texas. Each day the inhabitants of the United States enter little by little into Texas; they acquire lands there, and even while submitting to the laws of the country, they are establishing the dominion of their language and their mores. The province of Texas is still under the rule of Mexico; but soon you will no longer find any Mexicans there so to speak. Something similar is happening everywhere the Anglo-Americans enter into contact with populations of another origin.

You cannot conceal the fact that the English race has acquired an immense preponderance over all the other European races of the New World. It is very superior to them in civilization, in industry and in power. As long as it has before it only uninhabited or sparsely inhabited countries, as long as it does not find in its path aggregated populations, through which it will be impossible for it to clear a passage, you will see it spread without ceasing. It will not stop at lines drawn in treaties, but will overflow these imaginary dikes from all directions.

[{The Constitution of the United States has been credited with the progress that the population makes each year.}]

What also marvelously facilitates this rapid development of the English race in the New World is the geographic position that it occupies there.

When you go up toward the north above its northern frontiers, you find polar ice, and when you descend a few degrees below its southern limits, you get into the heat of the equator. So the English of America are located in the most temperate zone and the most habitable part of the continent.

You imagine that the prodigious movement that is noted in the increase of the population of the United States dates only from independence. That is an error. The population grew as quickly under the colonial system as today; it doubled the same in about twenty-two years. But then it applied to thousands of inhabitants; now it applies to millions. The same fact that passed unnoticed a century ago strikes all minds today.[e]

The English of Canada, who obey a king, increase in number and spread almost as quickly as the English of the United States, who live under a republican government.

During the eight years that the War of Independence lasted, the population did not cease to increase following the proportion previously indicated.

Although there then existed on the frontiers of the West great Indian nations allied with the English, the movement of emigration toward the West never, so to speak, relented. While the enemy ravaged the coasts

e. In the margin: "≠Nothing can slow it,
neither political event,
nor civil discords,
nor bad laws, nor wars.≠"

of the Atlantic, Kentucky, the western districts of Pennsylvania, the state of Vermont and that of Maine filled up with inhabitants. Nor did the disorder that followed the war prevent the population from growing and stop its progressive march into the wilderness. Thus the difference in laws, the state of peace or the state of war, order or anarchy, influenced only in an imperceptible way the successive development of the Anglo-Americans.

This is easily understood. No causes exist that are general enough to make themselves felt at the same time at all the points of a territory so immense. Thus there is always a large portion of the country where you are sure to find a shelter from the calamities that strike another, and however great the evils may be, the remedy offered is always greater still.

So it must not be believed that it is possible to stop the expansion of the English race of the New World. The dismemberment of the Union, by leading to war on the continent, the abolition of the republic, by introducing tyranny there, can retard its development, but not prevent it from attaining the necessary complement of its destiny. There is no power on earth that can close to the steps of the emigrants this fertile wilderness that is open in all areas to industry and that presents a refuge from all miseries. Future events, whatever they may be, will not take away from the Americans either their climate, or their interior seas, or their great rivers, or the fertility of their soil. Bad laws, revolution and anarchy, cannot destroy among them the taste for well-being and the spirit of enterprise that seems the distinctive character of their race, or completely extinguish the knowledge that enlightens them.

[≠It would be as easy to stop the waves of the sea as to prevent the waves of Anglo-American emigration from reaching the shores of the Pacific Ocean.≠]

Thus amid the uncertainty of the future there is at least one event that is certain. At some period that we can call near at hand, since it concerns the life of peoples, the Anglo-Americans will cover alone all the immense space included between the areas of polar ice and the tropics; they will spread from the strands of the Atlantic Ocean to the shores of the Pacific.

I think that the territory over which the Anglo-American race must someday spread equals three-quarters of Europe.[2] The climate of the Union is, everything considered, preferable to that of Europe; its natural advantages are as great; it is clear that its population cannot fail one day to be proportionate to ours.

Europe, divided among so many diverse peoples; Europe, through constantly recurring wars and the barbarism of the Middle Ages, succeeded in having four hundred ten inhabitants[3] per square league. What cause so powerful could prevent the United States from having as many one day?

Many centuries will pass before the various offshoots of the English race of America cease showing a common physiognomy. You cannot foresee the period when man will be able to establish permanent inequality of conditions in the New World.

So whatever differences are made one day in the destiny of the various offshoots of the great Anglo-American family by peace or war, liberty or tyranny, prosperity or poverty, they will all at least preserve an analogous social state and will have in common customs and ideas that derive from the social state.

The bond of religion alone was sufficient in the Middle Ages to bring the diverse races that peopled Europe together in the same civilization. The English of the New World have a thousand other bonds with each other, and they live in a century when everything is trying to become equal among men.

The Middle Ages was a period of division. Each people, each province, each city, each family then tended strongly to become more individual.[f] Today an opposite movement makes itself felt; peoples seem to march toward unity. Intellectual links unite the most distant parts of the earth, and men cannot remain strangers to one another for a single day, or ignorant of what is happening in no matter what corner of the universe. Conse-

---

2. *The United States alone already covers a space equal to half of Europe. The surface of Europe is 500,000 square leagues; its population 205,000,000 inhabitants. Malte-Brun, vol. VI, book CXIV, p. 4.*

3. *See Malte-Brun, vol. VI, book CXVI, p. 92.*

f. Tocqueville will for the first time use the term "individualism" in chapter II of the second part of the second volume.

quently you notice today less difference between Europeans and their descendants of the New World, despite the Ocean that divides them, than between certain cities of the XIIIth century that were separated only by a river.

If this movement of assimilation brings foreign peoples together, it is opposed with greater reason to the offshoots of the same people becoming strangers to each other.

So a time will come when you will be able to see in North America one hundred and fifty million[g] men[4] equal to one another, who will all belong to the same family, who will have the same point of departure, the same civilization, the same language, the same religion, the same habits, the same mores, and among whom thought will circulate with the same form and will be painted with the same colors. All the rest is doubtful, but this is certain. Now here is a fact entirely new in the world, and imagination itself cannot grasp its import.

Today there are two great peoples on earth who, starting from different points, seem to advance toward the same goal: these are the Russians and the Anglo-Americans.

Both grew up in obscurity; and while the attention of men was occupied elsewhere, they suddenly took their place in the first rank of nations, and the world learned of their birth and their greatness nearly at the same time.

All other peoples seem to have almost reached the limits drawn by nature, and have nothing more to do except maintain themselves; but these two are growing.[5] All the others have stopped or move ahead only with a thousand efforts; these two alone walk with an easy and rapid stride along a path whose limit cannot yet be seen.

The American struggles against obstacles that nature opposes to him; the Russian is grappling with men. The one combats the wilderness and bar-

g. The figure is missing in the manuscript.

4. *It is the population proportionate to that of Europe, by taking the average of 410 men per square league.*

5. *Russia is of all the nations of the Old World the one whose population is increasing most rapidly, keeping the proportion. [See Malte-Brun, vol. VI, p. 95.]*

barism; the other, civilization clothed in all its arms. Consequently the conquests of the American are made with the farmer's plow, those of the Russian with the soldier's sword.

To reach his goal the first relies on personal interest, and, without directing them, allows the strength and reason of individuals to operate.

The second in a way concentrates all the power of society in one man.

The one has as principal means of action liberty; the other, servitude.

Their point of departure is different, their paths are varied; nonetheless, each one of them seems called by a secret design of Providence to hold in its hands one day the destinies of half the world.[h]

h. This passage is one of the best known of the *Democracy,* and probably one of the most cited of the entire book. It gained Tocqueville a reputation as a prophet that has not failed to harm the overall interpretation of his work. If several critics have noted that a similar idea is found among authors as diverse as Edmund Dana, Alexander Hill Everett, the Abbé de Pradt, Madame de Staël, Edward Everett (in two reviews of Pradt), John Bristed, Stendhal, and Michel Chevalier, it must nonetheless be noted that the theories of Tocqueville sometimes differ perceptibly from those of these authors. M. de Pradt (*Du système permanent de l'Europe à l'égard de la Russie et des affaires de l'Orient,* Paris: Pichon and Didier, 1828), for example, does oppose two powers, but they are England as maritime force and Russia as land force. He only incidentally mentions that America could avenge Europe (p. 5). Alexander Everett (*America: Or a General Survey of the Political Situation of the Several Powers of the Western Continent . . . ,* Philadelphia: H. C. Carey and I. Lee, 1827), for his part, conceives three great powers: Russia, England, and the United States.

You cannot understand why Tocqueville terminates his considerations with this affirmation if you forget that his interest in the United States is nearly equal to the one he had for Russia. This is clear not only in his correspondence with the Circourts, Greg, Madame Phillimore, Everett, or Corcelle, but also in long conversations that he was able to have with Theodore Sedgwick in 1834 or with Grandmaison twenty years later. The latter notes that in 1854, Tocqueville continued to think that the Slavic race and the Anglo-Saxon race would one day share the world. His interest in Russia had led him to read the work of Baron de Haxthausen (*Études sur la situation intérieure, la vie nationale et les institutions rurales de la Russie,* Hanover, 1847–1853, 3 vols.). Grandmaison reports that Tocqueville asserted: "a young and intelligent man, courageous enough to learn Russian and to spend some years in Russia, would find there the subject of a very curious study and of a book of high interest that would come to be a counterpart to his own work on America." And he adds: "This idea preoccupied him a great deal; you felt with him the regret of not being able to execute it, and I believe he would have willingly pushed me into this undertaking, if I had given him the slightest opening from my side" ("Séjour d'Alexis de Tocqueville en Touraine, préparation du livre sur l'Ancien Régime,"

Correspondant, 114, 1879, pp. 926–49; cf. p. 943). Beaumont, perhaps persuaded by the author, will do for the *Revue des deux mondes* a review of the book of Haxthausen ("La Russie et les Etats-Unis sous le rapport économique," *Revue des deux mondes,* 2nd series, 5, 1854, pp. 1163–83). See note y for p. 158. Also see on this subject: René Rémond, *Les États-Unis devant l'opinion française, 1815–1852,* Paris: Armand Colin, 1962, I, pp. 378–79 note; Theodore Draper, "The Idea of the 'Cold War' and Its Prophets. On Tocqueville and Others," *Encounter,* 52, 1979, pp. 34–45 (Draper insists on the fact that Tocqueville never considered a possible confrontation between the two countries); Bernard Fabian, Alexis de Tocqueville *Amerikabild: Genetische Untersuchungen über Zusammenhänge mit der Zeitgenössischen, Insbesondere der Englischen Amerika-Interpretation,* Heidelberg: C. Winter, 1957; and Philip Merlan, "A Precursor of Tocqueville," *Pacific Historical Review* 35, no. 4 (1966): 467–68.

Notes

First Part

(A) Page 36

See, concerning the lands of the west that Europeans have not yet penetrated, the two voyages undertaken by Major Long, at the expense of
Congress.

Concerning the great American desert, Mr. Long says notably that a line
must be drawn about parallel to the 20th degree of longitude (meridian of
Washington),[1] beginning at the Red River and ending at the Platte River.
Extending from this imaginary line to the Rocky Mountains, which border
the Mississippi Valley in the west, are immense plains, generally covered
with sand which is unsuitable for agriculture, or strewn with granite stones.
They are deprived of water in the summer. There only great herds of buffalo
and wild horses are found. Some Indian hordes are seen as well, but only
a small number.

Major Long has heard it said that, ascending the Platte River, in the same
direction, this same desert would always be found on the left; but he was
not able personally to verify the accuracy of this report. *Long's Expedition*,
vol. II, p. 361.

Whatever confidence Major Long's account merits, it must not be forgotten, however, that he only crossed the country that he is speaking about,
without making any great zigzags outside the line that he followed.

---

1. *The 20th degree of longitude, following the meridian of Washington, is approximately
the equivalent of the 99th degree following the meridian of Paris.*

(B) Page 38

South America, in the region between the tropics, produces an incredible profusion of climbing plants known by the generic name of creepers. The flora of the Antilles alone offers more than forty different species.

Among the most graceful of these bushes is the grenadilla. Descourtiz,[a] in his description of the plant kingdom of the Antilles, says that this lovely plant attaches itself to trees by means of its tendrils, and forms moving arcades and colonnades, made rich and elegant by the beauty of the crimson flowers, variegated with blue, that decorate them and that delight the sense of smell with the scent they give off; vol. I, p. 265.

The acacia with large pods is a very thick creeper that grows rapidly and, going from tree to tree, sometimes covers more than a half-league; vol. III, p. 227.

(C) Page 40
On the American Languages

The languages spoken by the Indians of America, from the Arctic Pole to Cape Horn, are all formed, it is said, on the same model, and subject to the same grammatical rules; from that it can be concluded that, in all likelihood, all the Indian nations came from the same stock.

Each tribal band of the American continent speaks a different dialect; but the languages strictly speaking are very few in number, which would tend as well to prove that the nations of the New World do not have a very ancient origin.

Finally the languages of America are extremely regular, so it is probable that the peoples who use them have not yet been subjected to great revolutions and have not mixed with foreign nations by necessity or voluntarily;

---

a. M. E. Descourtiz, *Voyages d'un naturaliste et ses observations,* Dufart Père, 1809, 3 vols.

for it is in general the union of several languages into a single one that produces irregularities of grammar.

Not long ago the American languages, and in particular, the languages of North America, attracted the serious attention of philologists. It was discovered then, for the first time, that this idiom of a barbarous people was the product of a system of very complicated ideas and of very clever combinations. It was noticed that these languages were very rich and that, when forming them, great care had been taken to show consideration for the sensitivity of the ear.

The grammatical system of the Americans differs from all others on several points, but principally in this one.

Some peoples of Europe, among others the Germans, have the ability to combine different expressions as needed, and thus to give a complex meaning to certain words. The Indians have extended this ability in the most surprising way, and have succeeded in fixing so to speak at a single point a very large number of ideas. This will be easily understood with the help of an example cited by Mr. Duponceau, in the *Memoirs of the American Philosophical Society.*

When, he says, a Delaware woman plays with a cat or with a dog, you sometimes hear her pronounce the word *kuligatschis.* The word is composed in this way: *K* is the sign of the second person and means you or your; *uli,* which is pronounced *ouli,* is a fragment of the word *wulit,* which means *beautiful, pretty; gat* is another fragment of the word *wichgat,* which means *paw;* finally *schis,* which is pronounced *chise,* is the diminutive ending which carries with it the idea of smallness. Thus, in a single word, the Indian woman has said: Your pretty little paw.

Here is another example that shows with what felicity the savages of America know how to compose their words.

A young man in the Delaware language is called *pilapé.* This word is formed from *pilsit,* chaste, innocent; and from *lénapé,* man: that is to say man in his purity and his innocence.

This ability to combine words is noticeable above all in a very strange way of forming verbs. The most complicated action is often rendered by a single verb; nearly all the nuances of the idea bear upon the verb and modify it.

Those who would like to examine in more detail this subject that I myself have only touched on very superficially, should read:

1. The Correspondence of Mr. Duponceau with the Reverend Hecwelder [Heckewelder (ed.)], relating to the Indian languages. This correspondence is found in the first volume of the *Memoirs of the American Philosophical Society*, published in Philadelphia, in 1819, Abraham Small, pp. 356–464.

2. The grammar of the Delaware or Lenape language by Geiberger,[b] and the preface of Mr. Duponceau, which is added. The whole thing is found in the same collections, vol. III.

3. A very well done summary of these works, contained at the end of volume VI of the *Encyclopedia Americana*.

(D) Page 42

We find in Charlevoix, volume I, p. 235, the history of the first war that the French of Canada had to sustain, in 1610, against the Iroquois. The latter, although armed with bows and arrows, offered a desperate resistance to the French and their allies. Charlevoix, who is not good at doing portraits, shows very well in this piece the contrast that the mores of the Europeans presented to those of the savages, as well as the different ways in which these two races understood honor.

"The French," he says, "grabbed the beaver skins that covered the Iroquois, whom they saw spread out over the ground; the Hurons, their allies, were scandalized by this spectacle. The latter, on their side, began to exercise their ordinary cruelties on the prisoners, and devoured one of those who had been killed, which horrified the French. "Thus," adds Charlevoix, "these barbarians gloried in a disinterestedness that they were surprised not to find in our nation, and did not understand that there was much less evil in stripping the dead than in eating their flesh like wild beasts."

b. David Zeisberger, "A Grammar of the Language of the Lenni Lanâpé," translated by P. S. Duponceau, *Transactions of the American Philosophical Society*, III, 1827, pp. 65–250.

The same Charlevoix, in another place, vol. I, p. 230 [–231 (ed.)], depicts in this way the first torture that Champlain witnessed, and the return of the Hurons to their village.

"After having done eight leagues," he says, "our allies stopped, and, taking one of their captives, they reproached him for all the cruelties that he had exercised on the warriors of their nation who had fallen into his hands, and they declared to him that he must expect to be treated in the same manner, adding that, if he had courage, he would display it by singing. He soon started to sing his song [of death, then his song (ed.)] of war, and all those that he knew, but with a very sad tone, says Champlain, who had not yet had the time to know that all of the music of the savages is somewhat lugubrious. His torture, accompanied by all the horrors that we will speak of later, frightened the French who in vain did their utmost to put an end to it.[c] The following night, because a Huron dreamed that they were being pursued, the retreat changed into a veritable flight, and the savages did not stop anywhere again until they were out of any danger.

"From the moment that they saw the huts of their village, they cut long sticks to which they attached their share of the scalps and carried them triumphantly. At this sight the women ran, jumped in swimming, and, reaching the canoes took these bloody scalps from the hands of their husbands, and hung them around their necks.

"These warriors offered one of these horrible trophies to Champlain, and also made him a present of some bows and some arrows, the only spoils of the Iroquois that they had wanted to take, begging him to show them to the king of France."

Champlain lived alone all one winter amid these barbarians, without his person or his property being compromised for one instant.

(E) Page 64

Although the Puritan rigor that prevailed at the birth of the English colonies of America has already become much weaker, you still find extraordinary traces of it in the habits and in the laws.

---

c. Tocqueville omits here the details of the dismemberment and death of the Indian.

In 1792, at the very period when the anti-Christian republic of France began its ephemeral existence, the legislative body of Massachusetts promulgated the law that you are about to read, in order to force citizens to observe Sunday. Here are the preamble and the principal provisions of this law, which deserves to attract all the reader's attention:

Whereas, says the legislator, Sunday observance is in the public interest; that it produces a useful suspension of work; that it leads men to reflect upon the duties of life and the errors to which humanity is so prone; that it allows us in private and in public to honor God, creator and governor of the universe, and allows us to devote ourselves to those acts of charity that are the adornment and the relief of Christian societies;

Whereas some irreligious or thoughtless persons, forgetting the duties imposed by Sunday and the benefits that society gains from them, profane the Holy Day in pursuit of their pleasures or their work; that this behavior is contrary to their own interests as Christians; that, in addition, it is of a nature to disturb those who do not follow their example, and brings real harm to the entire society by introducing the taste for dissipation and dissolute habits;

The Senate and the House of Representatives order the following:

1. No one will be able, on Sunday, to keep his shop or workshop open. No one will be able, on that day, to be active in any work or business whatsoever, attend any concert, ball or show of any sort, nor pursue any kind of hunt, game, recreation, under penalty of a fine. The fine will not be less than 10 shillings, and will not exceed 20 shillings for each offense.

2. No traveler, driver, carter, except in case of necessity, will be able to travel on Sunday, under penalty of the same fine.

3. Hotelkeepers, retailers, innkeepers, will prevent any person living in their town from visiting them on Sunday, in order to pass the time in pleasure or business. In case of offense, the innkeeper and his guest will pay the fine. Moreover, the innkeeper will lose his license.

4. Whoever, being in good health and without having a sufficient reason, fails for three months to attend public worship will be condemned to a 10 shilling fine.

5. Whoever, within the confines of a church, displays inappropriate behavior will pay a fine of 5 to 40 shillings.

6. The tythingmen of the towns[2] are charged with responsibility for enforcing this law. They have the right to visit on Sunday all the rooms of hotels or public places. The innkeeper who refuses their entry into his establishment will be condemned for this fact alone to a fine of 40 shillings.

The tythingmen must stop travelers and inquire after the reason that has forced them to be on the road on Sunday. Whoever refuses to answer will be condemned to a fine that could be 5 pounds sterling.

If the reason given by the traveler does not seem sufficient to the tythingman, he will bring the said traveler before the justice of the peace of the district (*Law of 8 March 1792. General Laws of Massachusetts,* vol. I, p. 410).

On 11 March 1797, a new law increased the level of fines, half of which was to belong to the one who brought proceedings against the offender. *Same collection,* vol. I, p. 535.

On 16 February, 1816, a new law confirmed these same measures. *Same collection,* vol. II, p. 405.

Analogous provisions exist in the laws of the state of New York, revised in 1827 and 1828. (See *Revised Statutes,* 1st part, ch. XX, p. 675). It is said there that on Sunday no one will be able to hunt, fish, gamble or frequent establishments where drink is served. No one will be able to travel, if it is not out of necessity.

This is not the only trace left in the laws by the religious spirit and the austere mores of the first emigrants.

You read in the revised statutes of the state of New York, vol. I, p. 662 [–663 (ed.)], the following article:

Every person who shall win or lose at play, or by betting at any time, the sum or value of twenty-five dollars or upwards, within the space of twenty-four hours, shall be deemed guilty of a misdemeanor, and on conviction shall be fined not less than five times the value or sum so lost or won; which [. . . (ed.) . . .] shall be paid to the overseers of the poor of the town. [. . . (ed.) . . .]

---

2. *These are officials elected each year who, by their functions, are at the very same time close to the rural guard and to the officer of the criminal investigation department.*

Every person who shall [. . . (ed.) . . .] lose at any time or sitting the sum or value of twenty-five dollars or upwards[. . . (Ed) . . .] may [. . . (ed.) . . .] sue for and recover the money. [. . . (ed.) . . .] The overseers of the poor of the town where the offense was committed may sue for and recover the sum or value so lost and paid, together with treble the said sum or value, from the winner thereof for the benefit of the poor.

The laws that we have just cited are very recent; but who could comprehend them without going back to the very origin of the colonies? I do not doubt that today the penal portion of this legislation is only very rarely applied; the laws retain their inflexibility when the mores have already bent before the movement of the times. Sunday observance in America, however, is still what most strikes the foreigner.[d]

There is notably a large American city in which, beginning Saturday evening, social movement is as if suspended. You cross it at the hour that seems to invite those of mature years to business and youth to pleasure, and you find yourself in a profound solitude. Not only is no one working, but also no one appears to be alive. You hear neither the movement of industry nor the accents of joy, nor even the confused murmurings that arise constantly within a large city. Chains are hung in the vicinity of the churches; the half-closed shutters of the houses only reluctantly allow a ray of sunlight to penetrate the dwelling of the citizens. Scarcely here and there do you see an isolated man who is passing noiselessly through deserted crossroads and along abandoned streets.

The next morning at the beginning of day, the rattle of carriages, the noise of hammers, the cries of the population begin again to make themselves heard; the city awakens; a restless crowd rushes toward the centers of commerce and industry; everyone stirs, everyone becomes agitated, everyone hurries around you. A sort of lethargic drowsiness is followed by a feverish activity; you would say that each person has only a single day at his disposal in order to gain wealth and to enjoy it.

d. See the appendix SECTS IN AMERICA.

(F) Page 70

It is needless to say that, in the chapter that you have just read, I did not intend to do a history of America. My only goal was to enable the reader to appreciate the influence that the opinions and mores of the first emigrants exercised on the fate of the different colonies and on that of the Union in general. So I had to limit myself to citing a few unconnected fragments.

I do not know if I am wrong, but it seems to me that by following the path that I am only pointing out here, someone could present some portraits of the first years of the American republic that would be worthy of the attention of the public, and that would undoubtedly provide material for statesmen to consider. Not able to devote myself to this work, I wanted at least to facilitate it for others. So I believed that I should present here a short list and an abridged analysis of the works that seemed to me most useful to draw upon.

In the number of general documents that could fruitfully be consulted, I will place first the work entitled: *Historical Collection of State Papers and other authentic documents, intended as materials for an history of the United States of America,* by Ebenezer Hazard.

The first volume of this compilation, which was printed in Philadelphia in 1792, contains the exact text of all the charters granted by the crown of England to the emigrants, as well as the principal acts of the colonial governments during the first years of their existence. You find there, among others, a great number of authentic documents on the affairs of New England and Virginia during this period.

The second volume is dedicated almost entirely to the acts of the confederation of 1643. This federal pact, which took place among the colonies of New England, with the goal of resisting the Indians, was the first example of union given by the Anglo-Americans. There were also several other confederations of the same nature, until that of 1776, which led to the independence of the colonies.

The historical collection of Philadelphia is found in the Royal Library.

Each colony has as well its historical memorials, several of which are very precious. I begin my study with Virginia, which is the state populated earliest.

The first of all the historians of Virginia is its founder Captain John Smith. Captain Smith left us a volume in quarto, entitled: *The General History of Virginia and New-England, by Captain John Smith, some time governor in those countryes and admiral of New-England,* printed in London in 1627. (This volume is found at the Royal Library.) The work of Smith is embellished with very interesting maps and plates, which date from the time when it was printed. The account of the historian extends from the year 1584 to 1626. Smith's book is esteemed and deserves to be so. The author is one of the most famous adventurers who appeared in the century full of adventurers; he lived at the end of that century. The book itself breathes this fervor of discoveries, this spirit of enterprise that characterized the men of that time; there you find those chivalrous mores that were mixed with business and were made to serve the acquisition of wealth.

But what is remarkable above all in Captain Smith is that he mixed, with the virtues of his contemporaries, qualities that remained foreign to most of them; his style is simple and clear, all of his accounts have the stamp of truth, his descriptions are not ornate.

This author throws precious light on the state of the Indians at the period of the discovery of North America.

The second historian to consult is Beverley. The work of Beverley, which forms a volume in duodecimo, was translated into French and printed in Amsterdam in 1707. The author begins his accounts in the year 1585 and ends them in the year 1700. The first part of his book contains historical documents, properly so called, relative to the early years of the colony. The second contains a curious portrait of the state of the Indians at that distant period. The third gives very clear ideas about the mores, social state, laws and political habits of the Virginians at the time of the author.

Beverly was of Virginian origin, which made him say at the beginning "that he begs readers not to examine his work with too strict a critical eye, seeing that since he was born in the Indies, he does not aspire to purity of language." Despite this modesty of the colonist, the author shows throughout his book that he bears the supremacy of the mother country with impatience. You find as well in the work of Beverley numerous traces of this spirit of civil liberty that has, since that time, animated the English colonies of America. You also find the trace of the divisions that have existed for such a long time among them, and that delayed their independence. Beverley detests his Catholic neighbors of Maryland still more than the English government. The style of this author is simple; his accounts are often full of interest and inspire confidence. The French translation of Beverley's history is found in the Royal Library.

I saw in America, but I was not able to find again in France, a work that also merits consultation; it is entitled: *History of Virginia,* by William Stith. This book offers interesting details, but it seemed long and diffuse to me.

The oldest and best document that you can consult on the history of the Carolinas is a small book in quarto, entitled: *The History of Carolina,* by John Lawson, printed in London in 1718.

The work of Lawson contains first a voyage of discovery in the west of Carolina. This voyage is written as a journal; the accounts of the author are confused; his observations are very superficial; you only find a quite striking portrait of the ravages caused by smallpox and brandy among the savages of this period, and an interesting portrait of the corruption of mores that reigned among them, and that the presence of the Europeans favored.

The second part of the work of Lawson is dedicated to retracing the physical state of Carolina and to making its products known.

In the third part, the author does an interesting description of the mores, customs and government of the Indians of this period.

There is often spirit and originality in this portion of the book.

The history by Lawson ends with the charter granted to Carolina at the time of Charles II.

The general tone of this work is light, often licentious, and forms a perfect contrast with the profoundly grave style of the works published at this same time in New England.

The history by Lawson is an extremely rare document in America that cannot be obtained in Europe. There is, however, a copy of it in the Royal Library.

From the southern extremity of the United States, I pass immediately to the northern extremity. The intermediate space was populated only later.

I must first point out a very curious compilation entitled: *Collection of the Massachusetts Historical Society,* printed for the first time in Boston in 1792, reprinted in 1806. This work is not in the Royal Library, nor, I believe, in any other.

The collection (which continues) contains a host of very precious documents relating to the history of the different states of New England. There you find unpublished correspondence and authentic pieces that were hidden away in the provincial archives. The complete work of Gookin relating to the Indians has been inserted there.

Several times, in the course of the chapter to which this note belongs, I pointed out the work of Nathaniel Morton entitled: *New England's Memorial.* What I said about this work is enough to prove that it is worthy to draw the attention of those who would like to know the history of New England. The book by Nathaniel Morton forms a volume in octavo, reprinted in Boston in 1826. It is not in the Royal Library.

The most respected and most important document that we possess on the history of New England is the work of the Reverend Cotton Mather, entitled: *Magnalia Christi Americana, or the ecclesiastical history of New England,* 1620–1698, 2 vol. in octavo, reprinted in Hartford in 1820. I do not believe that it is found in the Royal Library.

The author divided his work into seven books.

The first presents the history of what prepared and led to the founding of New England.

The second contains the life of the first governors and principal magistrates who administered this country.

The third is consecrated to the life and works of the evangelical ministers who, during this same period, led souls there.

In the fourth, the author describes the founding and development of the university of Cambridge (Massachusetts).

In the fifth, he explains the principles and discipline of the Church of New England.

The sixth is consecrated to retracing certain facts that denote, according to Mather, the salutary action of Providence on the inhabitants of New England.

In the seventh, finally, the author teaches us the heresies and troubles to which the Church of New England has been exposed.

Cotton Mather was an evangelical minister who, born in Boston, spent his life there.

All the ardor and all the religious passions that led to the founding of New England animate and give life to his accounts. You frequently find traces of bad taste in his way of writing; but he captivates, because he is full of enthusiasm that ends by communicating itself to the reader. He is often intolerant, more often gullible; but you never see in him the desire to deceive; sometimes his work even presents beautiful passages and true and profound ideas such as these:

> Before the arrival of the Puritans, he says, vol. I, ch. IV, p. 61, the English had tried several times to settle the country that we live in; but since they did not aim higher than the success of their material interests, they were soon defeated by obstacles; this wasn't the case with the men who arrived in America, pushed and sustained by a noble religious idea. Although the latter found more enemies than perhaps the founders of any other colony ever had, they persisted in their plan, and the settlement that they established still exists today.

Mather sometimes mixes, with the austerity of these portraits, images full of sweetness and tenderness. After speaking about an English lady whose religious fervor had brought her to America with her husband, and who soon succumbed to the hardships and miseries of exile, he adds:

"As for her virtuous spouse, Isaac Johnson, Esq., He try'd to live without her, lik'd it not, and dy'd" (V. I, p. 71.)

Mather's book admirably reveals the time and country that he is trying to describe.

If he wants to teach us what motives led the Puritans to seek a refuge beyond the seas, he says:

> The God of Heaven served as it were, a summons upon the spirits of his people in the English nation; stirring up the spirits of thousands which

never saw the faces of each other, with a most unanimous inclination to leave all the pleasant accommodations of their native country; and go over a terrible ocean, into a more terrible desart [*sic*], for the pure enjoyment of all his ordinances.

It is now reasonable that before we pass any further [he adds] the reasons of this undertaking should be more exactly made known unto the posterity of those that were the undertakers, lest they come at length to forget and neglect the true interest of New-England. Wherefore I shall now transcribe some of them from a manuscript, wherein they were then tendered unto consideration.

[. . . (ed.) . . .]

First, It will be a service unto the Church of great consequence, to carry the Gospel into those parts of the world, and raise a bulwark against the kingdom of antichrist, which the Jesuites [*sic*] labour to rear up in all parts of the world.

Secondly, All other Churches of Europe have been brought under desolations; and it may be feared that the like judgments are coming upon us; and who knows but God hath provided this place to be a refuge for many, whom he means to save out of the General Destruction.

Thirdly, The land grows weary of her inhabitants, insomuch that man, which is the most precious of all creatures, is here more vile and base than the earth he treads upon: children, neighbors, and friends, especially the poor, are counted the greatest burdens, which if things were right would be the chiefest earthly blessings.

Fourthly, We are grown to that intemperance in all excess of riot, as no mean estate almost will suffice a man to keep sail with his equals, and he that fails in it, must live in scorn and contempt: hence it comes to pass, that all arts and trades are carried in that deceitful manner, and unrighteous course, as it is almost impossible for a good upright man to maintain his constant charge, and live comfortably in them.

Fifthly, The schools of learning and religion are so corrupted, as [. . . (ed.) . . .] most children, even the best, wittiest, and of the fairest hopes, are perverted, corrupted, and utterly overthrown, by the multitude of evil examples and licentious behaviours in these seminaries.

Sixthly, The whole earth is the Lord's garden, and he hath given it to the sons of Adam, to be tilled and improved by them: why then should we stand starving here for places of habitation and in the mean time suffer whole countries, as profitable for the use of man, to lye [*sic*] waste without any improvement?

Seventhly, What can be a better or nobler work, and more worthy of a christian, than to erect and support a reformed particular Church in its infancy, and unite our forces with such a company of faithful people, as by a timely assistance may grow stronger and prosper; but for want of it, may be put to great hazard, if not be wholly ruined.

Eighthly, If any such as are known to be godly, and live in wealth and prosperity here, shall forsake all this to join with this reformed church, and with it run the hazard of an hard and mean condition, it will be an example of great use, both for the removing of scandal and to give more life unto the faith of God's people in their prayers for the plantation, and also to encourage others to join the more willingly in it.

Later, explaining the principles of the Church of New England on moral matters, Mather rises up violently against the custom of drinking toasts at dinner, which he calls a pagan and abominable habit.

He proscribes with the same rigor all ornaments that women can put in their hair, and condemns without pity the fashion of showing the neck and arms that, he says, is becoming established among them.

In another part of the work, he recounts at great length several instances of witchcraft that frightened New England. You see that the visible action of the devil in the affairs of this world seems to him an incontestable and proven truth.

In a great number of places in this same book a spirit of civil liberty and political independence is revealed that characterized the contemporaries of the author. Their principles in matters of government appear at each step. Thus, for example, you see the inhabitants of Massachusetts, from the year 1630 [1636 (ed.)], ten years after the founding of Plymouth, devote 400 pounds sterling to the establishment of the university of Cambridge.

If I pass from general documents relating to the history of New England to those that relate to the various states included in its limits, I will first have to point out the work entitled: *The History of the Colony of Massachusetts, by Hutchinson, Lieutenant-Governor of the Massachusetts province,* 2 vols. in octavo. A copy of this book is found in the Royal Library; it is a second edition printed in London in 1765.

The history of Hutchinson, which I cited several times in the chapter to which this note relates, begins in the year 1628 and finishes in 1750. A great air of truthfulness reigns in the whole book; the style is simple and unaffected. This history is very detailed.

The best document to consult, for Connecticut, is the history of Benjamin Trumbull, entitled: *A Complete History of Connecticut, Civil and Ecclesiastical, 1630–1764,* 2 vols. in octavo, printed in 1818 at New Haven. I do not believe that Trumbull's work is found in the Royal Library.

This history contains a clear and cold exposition of all the events that took place in Connecticut during the period indicated by the title. The author drew upon the best sources, and his accounts retain the stamp of truth. All that he says about the early years of Connecticut is extremely interesting. See notably in his work the Constitution of 1639, vol. I, ch. VI, p. 100 [–103 (ed.)]; and also the Penal Laws of Connecticut, vol. I, ch. VII, p. 123.

The work of Jeremy Belknap entitled: *History of New Hampshire,* 2 vols. in octavo, printed in Boston in 1792, is rightly well regarded. See particularly, in Belknap's work, ch. III of the first volume. In this chapter, the author gives extremely valuable details about the political and religious principles of the Puritans, about the causes of their emigration, and about their laws. There you find this interesting quotation from a sermon delivered in 1663:

> New England must constantly recall that it was founded for a religious purpose and not for a commercial purpose. It is written on its forehead that it professed purity in matters of doctrine and discipline. May merchants and all those who are busy piling up money remember, therefore, that it is religion, and not gain, that was the object of the founding of these colonies. If there is someone among us who, in his estimation of the world and of religion, looks upon the first as 13 and takes the second

only as 12, he is not prompted by the sentiments of a true son of New England.

Readers will find in Belknap more general ideas and more power of thought than that presented until now by the other American historians.

I do not know if this book is found in the Royal Library.

Among the states of the center that are already old, and that merit our interest, the states of New York and Pennsylvania stand out above all. The best history that we have of the state of New York is entitled: *History of New York,* by William Smith, printed in London in 1757. A French translation exists, also printed in London in 1757, 1 vol. in duodecimo. Smith provides us with useful details on the wars of the French and English in America. He is, of all the American historians, the one who best shows the famous confederation of the Iroquois.

As for Pennsylvania, I cannot do better than to point to the work of Proud entitled: *The History of Pennsylvania, From the Original Institution and Settlement of That Province, under the First Proprietor and Governor William Penn, in 1681 till after the Year 1742,* by Robert Proud, 2 vols. in octavo, printed in Philadelphia in 1797.

This work particularly deserves the attention of the reader; it contains a host of very interesting documents on Penn, the doctrine of the Quakers, the character, mores, customs of the first inhabitants of Pennsylvania. As far as I know, it is not in the Royal Library.

I do not need to add that among the most important documents relative to Pennsylvania are the works of Penn himself and those of Franklin. These works are known by a great number of readers.

Most of the books that I have just cited had already been consulted by me during my stay in America. The Royal Library has kindly entrusted me with some of them; others have been loaned to me by Mr. Warden, former consul general of the United States to Paris, author of an excellent book on America. I do not want to conclude this note without extending to Mr. Warden the expression of my gratitude.

(G) Page 84

You find what follows in the *Mémoires de Jefferson:*

> In the first years of the English settlement in Virginia, when land was obtained for little, or even for nothing, several far-seeing individuals acquired great land concessions, and desiring to maintain the splendor of their families, they entailed their wealth to their descendants. The transmission of these properties from generation to generation, to men who carried the same name, had finally produced a distinct class of families that, with the legal privilege of perpetuating their wealth, thus formed a kind of patrician order distinguished by the grandeur and the luxury of their holdings. It was from among this group that the king usually chose the members of his council (*Jefferson's Memoirs*).

In the United States, the principal provisions of English law relating to inheritance were universally rejected.

> The first rule of inheritance is, says Mr. Kent, that if a person owning real estate, dies seized, or as owner, without devising the same, the estate shall descend to his lawful descendants in the direct line of lineal descent; and if there be but one person, then to him or her alone, and if more than one person, and all of equal degree of consanguinity to the ancestor, then the inheritance shall descend to the several persons as tenants in common in equal parts [. . . (ed.) . . .] without distinction of sex.

This rule was prescribed for the first time in the state of New York by a statute of 23 February 1786 (see *Revised Statutes,* vol. III; *Appendix,* p. 48); it has been adopted since in the revised statutes of the same state. It prevails now throughout the United States, the sole exception being that, in the state of Vermont, the male heir has a double share. *Kent's Commentaries,* vol. IV, p. 370.

Mr. Kent, in the same work, vol. IV, pp. 1–22, reviews American legislation relative to *entail.* The outcome is that before the American Revolution the English laws on *entail* formed the common law in the colonies. Entail strictly speaking (*Estates' tail*) was abolished in Virginia in 1776 (this abolition took place on the motion of Jefferson; see *Jefferson's Memoirs*), in the state of New York in 1786. The same abolition has taken place since in North Carolina, Kentucky, Tennessee, Georgia, Missouri. In Vermont, the states of Indiana, Illinois, South Carolina and Louisiana, entail has always been unusual. The states that believed they had to keep English legislation relative to entail modified it in a way to remove its principal aristocratic characteristics. "Our general principles in matters of government," says Mr. Kent, "tend to favor the free circulation of property."[e]

What singularly strikes the French reader who studies American legislation relative to inheritance is that our laws on the same matter are still infinitely more democratic than theirs.

American laws divide the wealth of the father equally, but only in the case where his will is not known: "for every man, says the law, in the State of New York (*Revised Statutes,* vol. III; *Appendix,* p. 51), has full liberty, power and authority, to dispose of his goods by a will, to bequeath, divide, in favor of whatever person it may be, provided that he does not make out his will in favor of a political body or an organized company."

French law makes equal or nearly equal division the rule of the testator.

Most of the American republics still allow entail and limit themselves to restricting the effects.

French law allows entail in no case.[f]

If the social state of Americans is still more democratic than ours, our laws are thus more democratic than theirs. This is explained better than you think: in France democracy is still busy demolishing; in America it reigns tranquilly over the ruins.

e. The quoted text reads: "The general policy of this country does not encourage restraints upon the power of alienation of land." *Kent's Commentaries,* volume IV, p. 17.

f. Hervé de Tocqueville: "I read that with surprise. The law authorizes the father testator to favor one of his children. In collateral line it leaves a very much greater latitude" (YTC, CIIIb, 2, p. 99).

(H) Page 97
Summary of Electoral Conditions in the United States

All the states grant the enjoyment of electoral rights at age twenty-one. In all the states, you have to have resided a certain time in the district where you vote. This time varies from three months to two years.

As for the property qualification: in the state of Massachusetts, to be a voter, you have to have 3 pounds sterling of income, or 60 of capital.

In Rhode Island, you have to own property valued at 133 dollars (704 francs).

In Connecticut, you have to have a property with an income of 17 dollars (about 90 francs). A year of service in the militia gives the right to vote as well.

In New Jersey, the voter must have wealth of 50 pounds sterling.

In South Carolina and Maryland, the voter must own 50 acres of land.

In Tennessee, you must own some property.

In the states of Mississippi, Ohio, Georgia, Virginia, Pennsylvania, Delaware, New York, it is sufficient, to be a voter, to pay taxes: in most of these states, service in the militia is the equivalent of paying taxes.

In Maine and in New Hampshire, it is sufficient not to be included on the list of the poor.

Finally in the states of Missouri, Alabama, Illinois, Louisiana, Indiana, Kentucky, Vermont, no condition is required having to do with the wealth of the voter.

Only North Carolina, I think, imposes on the voter for the Senate conditions other than those imposed on voters for the House of Representatives. The first must own property of 50 acres of land. It is sufficient, in order to be able to elect representatives, to pay a tax.

(I) Page 161

A prohibitive system exists in the United States. The small number of customs officials and the great extent of coastline make smuggling very easy;

it is done infinitely less there than elsewhere, however, because each person works to repress it.

Since there is no preventive surveillance in the United States, you see more fires there than in Europe; but in general they are extinguished sooner, because the surrounding population does not fail to go quickly to the place of danger.

(K) Page 165

It is not correct to say that centralization was born out of the French Revolution; the French Revolution perfected it, but did not create it. The taste for centralization and the mania for regulation go back in France to the period when the jurists entered into the government; which takes us back to the time of Philippe le Bel [the Fair]. Since that time, these two things have never ceased to increase. Here is what M. de Malesherbes, speaking in the name of the *Cour des aides,* said to King Louis XVI in 1775:[3]

> There remained to each body, to each community of citizens the right to administer its own affairs; a right that we do not say was part of the original constitution of the kingdom, for it goes back much further: it is natural law, it is the law of reason. But it has been taken away from your subjects, Sire, and we will not be afraid to say that the administration has fallen in this respect into excesses that can be called childish.
>
> Since powerful ministers made it a political principle not to allow the national assembly to be convoked, we have gone step by step to the point of declaring null and void deliberations of the inhabitants of a village when they are not authorized by an *intendant;* so that, if this community has an expenditure to make, the assent of the subdelegate of the *intendant* must be gained, consequently the plan that he adopted must be followed, the workers that he favors must be used, they must be paid as he sees fit; and if the community has a court case to sustain, it must also be authorized to do so by the *intendant;* the case must be argued before this first tribunal before being brought before the courts. And if the opinion of the *inten-*

3. *See* Mémoires pour servir à l'histoire du droit public de la France en matière d'impôts, *p. 654, printed in Brussels in 1779.*

dant is against the inhabitants, or if their adversary has the ear of the *intendant,* the community is deprived of the ability to defend its rights. Here, Sire, are the means by which some have worked to smother in France all municipal spirit, to extinguish, if it could be done, even the sentiments of citizens; the entire nation has been so to speak *prohibited* and it has been given guardians.g

What could you say better today, now that the French Revolution has made what are called its *conquests* in the matter of centralization?

In 1789, Jefferson wrote from Paris to one of his friends: "Never was there a country where the mania for governing too much had taken deeper roots and done more mischief than in France." Letter to Madison, 28 August 1789.

The truth is that in France, for several centuries, the central power has always done all that it could to extend administrative centralization; in this course it has never had any other limit than its strength.

The central power born from the French Revolution went further in this than any of its predecessors, because it was stronger and more clever than any of them. Louis XIV submitted the details of communal existence to the wishes of the *intendant;* Napoleon submitted them to those of the minister. It is always the same principle, extended to consequences more or less remote.

(L) Page 170

This immutability of the constitution in France is a necessary consequence of our laws.

And, to speak first about the most important of all the laws, that which regulates the order of succession to the throne, what is more immutable in its principle than a political order based on the natural order of succession

g. Count de Boissy d'Anglas, *Essais sur la vie, les écrits et les opinions de M. de Malesherbes* (Paris: Treuttel and Würtz, 1819), I, pp. 305–6 (quoted in YTC, CVh, 5, p. 3). We know that this idea that the process of centralization predates the Revolution is the principal thesis of the *Old Regime and the Revolution.*

Also see Luis Díez del Corral, *El pensamiento político de Tocqueville* (Madrid: Alianza Universidad, 1989), pp. 137–80.

from father to son? In 1814, Louis XVIII had this perpetuity of the law of political succession acknowledged in favor of his family. Those who settled the results of the revolution of 1830 followed his example; only they established the perpetuity of the law to the profit of another family; in this they imitated chancellor Maupeou, who, while instituting the new *parlement* on the ruins of the old, took care to declare in the same ordinance that the new magistrates would be irremovable as their predecessors were.

The laws of 1830 do not, any more than those of 1814, indicate any means to change the constitution. Now, it is clear that the ordinary means of legislation cannot be sufficient for that.

From what does the king derive his powers? From the constitution. From what the peers? From the constitution. From what the deputies? From the constitution. How then would the king, the peers and the deputies be able, by uniting, to change something in a law by the sole virtue of which they govern? Outside the constitution they are nothing; so on what ground would they stand in order to change the constitution? One of two things: either their efforts are powerless against the charter, which continues to exist in spite of them, and then they continue to rule in its name; or they succeed in changing the charter, and then, since the law by which they exist no longer exists, they are no longer anything themselves. By destroying the charter, they are destroyed.

That is still much more obvious in the laws of 1830 than in those of 1814. In 1814, the royal power put itself, in a way, outside and above the constitution; but in 1830, by its own admission, it is created by the constitution and is absolutely nothing without it.

Thus a part of our constitution is immutable, because it has been joined with the destiny of a family; and the whole of the constitution is equally immutable, because no legal means are seen to change it.

All this is not applicable to England. Since England has no written constitution, who can say that its constitution is being changed?

(M) Page 171

The most respected authors who have written about the English constitution establish, as though trying to out do each other, this omnipotence of Parliament.

Delolme says [book I (ed.)], ch. x, p. 77: *It is a fundamental principle with the English lawyers, that parliament can do everything, except making a woman a man or a man a woman.*

Blackstone expresses himself still more categorically, if not more energetically, than Delolme; in these terms [book V, ch. II]:

"The power and jurisdiction of Parliament," says sir Edward Coke (4 Inst. 36), "is so transcendent and absolute, that it cannot be confined, either for causes or persons, within any bounds. And of this high court," he adds, "it may be truly said, *Si antiquitatem spectes, est vetustissima; si dignitatem, est honoratissima; si jurisdictionem, est capacissima.* It hath sovereign and uncontrollable authority in making, confirming, enlarging, restraining, abrogating, repealing, reviving, and expounding of laws concerning matters of all possible denominations, ecclesiastical, or temporal, civil, military, maritime, or criminal: this being the place where that absolute despotice [*sic*] power, which must in all governments reside somewhere, is entrusted by the constitution of these kingdoms. All mischief and grievances, operations and remedies, that transcend the ordinary course of laws are within the reach of this extraordinary tribunal. It can regulate or new model the succession to the crown; as was done in the reign of Henry VIII and William III. It can alter the established religion of the land; as was done in a variety of instances, in the reigns of king Henry VIII. and his three children. It can *change and create afresh even the constitution of the kingdom* and of parliaments themselves; as was done by the act of union and the several statutes for triennial and septennial elections. It can, in short, do everything that is not naturally impossible; and therefore some have not scrupled to call it's [*sic*] power, by a figure rather too bold, the *omnipotence* of parliament."

(N) Page 185

There is no subject on which the American constitutions agree more than on political jurisdiction.

All the constitutions that deal with this subject give the house of representatives the exclusive right to accuse, except only the Constitution of North Carolina, which grants the same right to the grand juries (article 23).

Nearly all the constitutions give to the senate, or to the assembly that takes its place, the exclusive right to judge.

The only penalties that the political courts can pronounce are: dismissal or banning from public offices in the future. Only the Constitution of Virginia allows pronouncing all types of penalties.

Crimes that can lead to political jurisdiction are: in the federal Constitution (sect. IV, art. I) [Article II, Section 4 (ed.)], in that of Indiana (art. 3, pp. 23 and 24), of New York (art. 5), of Delaware (art. 5), high treason, corruption and other high crimes or misdemeanors;

In the Constitution of Massachusetts (ch. I, sect. II), of North Carolina (art. 23), and of Virginia (p. 252), bad conduct and bad administration;

In the Constitution of New Hampshire (p. 105), corruption, reprehensible schemes, and bad administration;

In Vermont (ch. II, art. 24), bad administration;

In South Carolina (art. 5), Kentucky (art. 5), Tennessee (art. 4), Ohio (art. 1, #23, 24), Louisiana (art. 5), Mississippi (art. 5), Alabama (art. 6), Pennsylvania (art. 4), crimes committed in office.

In the states of Illinois, Georgia, Maine and Connecticut, no crime is specified.

(O) Page 276

It is true that the powers of Europe can wage great maritime wars against the Union; but it is always easier and less dangerous to sustain a maritime war than a continental war. Maritime war requires only a single kind of effort. A commercial people that consents to give its government the money needed is always sure to have fleets. Now, sacrifices of money can be concealed from nations much more easily than sacrifices of men and personal efforts. Defeats at sea, moreover, rarely compromise the existence or the independence of the people who experience them.

As for continental wars, it is clear that the peoples of Europe cannot wage dangerous wars against the American Union.

It is very difficult to transport to and to maintain in America more than 25,000 soldiers; this represents a nation of about 2,000,000 people. The greatest European nation fighting against the Union in this way is in the same position as a nation of 2,000,000 inhabitants would be in a war against one of 12,000,000. Add to this that the American has all of his resources at hand and the European is 1,500 leagues from his, and that the immensity of the territory of the United States alone would present an insurmountable obstacle to conquest.

Second Part

(A) Page 298

In April 1704 the first American newspaper appeared. It was published in Boston. See *Collection of the Historical Society of Massachusetts,* vol. VI, p. 66.

You would be wrong to believe that the periodical press has always been entirely free in America; attempts were made there to establish something analogous to prior censorship and to the surety bond.

Here is what you find in the legislative documents of Massachusetts, for the date of 14 January 1722.

The committee named by the general assembly (the legislative body of the province) to study the affair relating to the newspaper entitled: *New England Courant*[h]

---

h. In the first edition: "*Courant* (which was written by the celebrated Franklin) . . ." The error was corrected in the following editions.

thinks that the tendency of the said newspaper is to ridicule religion and make it sink into contempt; that the holy authors are treated in a profane and irreverent manner; that the conduct of the ministers of the Gospel is interpreted with malice; that the government of His Majesty is insulted, and that the peace and tranquillity of this province are disturbed by the said newspaper; consequently, the committee is of the opinion that, in the future, James Franklin, printer and editor, be forbidden to print or publish the said newspaper or any other writing, without having submitted them in advance to the Secretary of the province. The justices of the peace of the town of Suffolk will be charged with obtaining from Mr. Franklin a bond that will be a pledge for his good conduct during the coming year.

The proposal of the committee was accepted and became law, but the effect was null. The newspaper eluded the interdiction by putting the name of *Benjamin* Franklin in place of *James* Franklin beneath its columns, and opinion finally put an end to the measure.

(B) Page 445

In order to be county voters (those who represent landed property) before the reform bill passed in 1832, it was necessary to have by sole ownership or by lifetime lease capital in land bringing in 40 shillings in net income. This law was made under Henry VI, about 1450. It has been calculated that 40 shillings at the time of Henry VI would be equivalent to 30 pounds sterling today. This amount adopted in the XVth century was allowed to remain, however, until 1832, which proves how much the English constitution became democratic over time, even while appearing immobile. See *Delolme,* book I, ch. IV; also see *Blackstone,* book I, ch. IV.

English jurors are chosen by the county sheriff (*Delolme,* vol. I, ch XII [XIII (ed.)]. The sheriff is in general a prominent man of the county; he fulfills judicial and administrative functions; he represents the King, and is named by him every year (*Blackstone,* book I, ch. IX). His position puts him above suspicion of corruption on the part of the parties; if, moreover, his impartiality is put in doubt, the jury that he has named can be recused en masse, and then another officer is charged with choosing new jurors. See *Blackstone,* book III, ch. XXIII.

To have the right to be a juror, it is necessary to own capital in land, with a value of at least 10 shillings in income. (*Blackstone,* book III, ch. XXIII). You will note that this condition was imposed during the reign of William and Mary, that is toward 1700, a period when the value of money was infinitely higher than today. You see that the English based their jury system, not on capacity but on landed property, like all their other political institutions.

In the end farmers were admitted to the jury, but it was required that their leases be very long, and that they have a net income of 20 shillings, apart from the rent. (*Blackstone,* idem.)

(C) Page 445

The federal constitution introduced the jury into the courts of the Union in the same way that the states had introduced it into their particular courts; in addition, the federal constitution did not establish its own rules about the choice of jurors. Federal courts draw from the ordinary list of jurors that each state has drawn up for its use. So it is the laws of the states that must be examined to know the theory of the composition of the jury in America. See Story's *Commentaries on the Constitution,* book III, ch. XXXVIII, pp. 654–59; Sergeant's *Constitutional Law,* p. 165. Also see the federal laws of 1789, 1800 and 1820 on the subject.

To show clearly the principles of the Americans regarding the composition of the jury, I have drawn upon the laws of states far from each other. Here are the general ideas that can be derived from this examination.

In America, all citizens who are voters have the right to be jurors. The large state of New York has, however, established a slight difference between those two capacities; but it is in the direction opposite to our laws, that is to say, there are fewer jurors than voters in the state of New York. In general, you can say that in the United States the right to be part of a jury, like the right to elect representatives, extends to everyone; but the exercise of this right is not put indiscriminately into all hands.

Each year a body of municipal or district magistrates, called *selectmen* in New England, *supervisors* in the state of New York, *trustees* in Ohio, parish *sheriffs* in Louisiana, choose for each district a certain number of citizens having the right to be jurors, and among whom they assume the capacity to be so. These magistrates, being elected themselves, do not excite distrust; their powers are very extensive and very arbitrary, like those of republican magistrates in general, and it is said that they often use those powers, above all in New England, in order to remove unworthy or incompetent jurors.

The names of the jurors thus chosen are sent on to the county court, and from the totality of these names, the jury that must deliver the verdict in each affair is drawn by lot.

The Americans have, moreover, tried by all possible means to put the jury within reach of the people, and to make it as little burdensome as possible. Since the jurors are very numerous, each person's turn comes scarcely every three years. The sessions are held in the chief seat of each county; the county corresponds more or less to our *arrondissement.* Thus, the court comes to be located near the jury, instead of drawing the jury close to it, as in France; finally the jurors are paid, either by the state, or by the parties. They receive, in general, one dollar (5.42 fr.) per day, apart from travel expenses. In America the jury is still regarded as a burden, but it is a burden easy to bear, and one you submit to without difficulty.

See Brevard's *Digest of the Public Statute Law of South Carolina,* 2nd vol., p. 338; *id.,* vol. I, pp. 454 and 456; *id.,* vol. II, p. 218.

See *The General Laws of Massachusetts revised and published by authority of the legislature,* vol. II, pp. 331, 187 [141].

See *The Revised Statutes of the State of New York,* vol. II, pp. 720, 411, 717, 643.

See *The Statute Law of the State of Tennessee,* vol. I, p. 209.

See *Acts of the State of Ohio,* pp. 95 and 210.

See *Digeste général des actes de la législature de la Louisiane,* vol. II, p. 55.

(D) Page 449

When you closely examine the constitution of the civil jury among the English, you easily discover that the jurors never escape the control of the judge.

It is true that the verdict of the jury, civil as well as criminal, generally includes fact and law in a simple statement. Example: A house is claimed by Peter as one he bought, here is the fact. His adversary raises the objection of the incompetence of the seller, here is the law. The jury limits itself to saying that the house will be put back in Peter's hands; thus it decides fact and law. When introducing the jury in civil matters, the English did not keep the infallibility of the opinion of the jurors that they granted in criminal matters, when the verdict is favorable.

If the judge thinks that the verdict has made a false application of the law, he can refuse to receive it, and send the jurors back to deliberate.

If the judge allows the verdict without comment, the proceedings are still not entirely settled: there are several paths of recourse open against the decision. The principal one consists of asking the courts to void the verdict and to assemble a new jury. It is true to say that such a demand is rarely granted and never more than two times. Nonetheless, I saw the case happen before my eyes. See *Blackstone,* book III, ch. XXIV; *id.,* book III, ch. XXV.